Lecture Notes in Computer Science

Vol. 192: Automata on Infinite Words. Proceedings, 1984. Edited by M. Nivat and D. Perrin. V, 216 pages.1985.

Vol. 193: Logics of Programs. Proceedings, 1985. Edited by R. Parikh. VI, 424 pages. 1985.

Vol. 194: Automata, Languages and Programming. Proceedings, 1985. Edited by W. Brauer. IX, 520 pages. 1985.

Vol. 195: H. J. Stüttgen, A Hierarchical Associative Processing System. XII, 273 pages. 1985.

Vol. 196: Advances in Cryptology. Proceedings of CRYPTO '84. Edited by G. R. Blakley and D. Chaum. IX, 491 pages. 1985.

Vol. 197: Seminar on Concurrency. Proceedings, 1984. Edited by S. D. Brookes, A. W. Roscoe and G. Winskel. X, 523 pages. 1985.

Vol. 198: A. Businger, PORTAL Language Description. VIII, 186 pages. 1985.

Vol. 199: Fundamentals of Computation Theory. Proceedings, 1985. Edited by L. Budach. XII, 533 pages. 1985.

Vol. 200: J. L. A. van de Snepscheut, Trace Theory and VLSI Design. VI, 0–140 pages. 1985.

Vol. 201: Functional Programming Languages and Computer Architecture. Proceedings, 1985. Edited by J.-P. Jouannaud. VI, 413 pages. 1985.

Vol. 202: Rewriting Techniques and Applications. Edited by J.-P. Jouannaud. VI, 441 pages. 1985.

Vol. 203: EUROCAL '85. Proceedings Vol. 1, 1985. Edited by B. Buchberger. V, 233 pages. 1985.

Vol. 204: EUROCAL '85. Proceedings Vol. 2, 1985. Edited by B. F. Caviness. XVI, 650 pages. 1985.

Vol. 205: P. Klint, A Study in String Processing Languages. VIII, 165 pages. 1985.

Vol. 206: Foundations of Software Technology and Theoretical Computer Science. Proceedings, 1985. Edited by S. N. Maheshwari. IX, 522 pages. 1985.

Vol. 207: The Analysis of Concurrent Systems. Proceedings, 1983. Edited by B. T. Denvir, W. T. Harwood, M. I. Jackson and M. J. Wray. VII, 398 pages. 1985.

Vol. 208: Computation Theory. Proceedings, 1984. Edited by A. Skowron. VII, 397 pages. 1985.

Vol. 209: Advances in Cryptology. Proceedings of EUROCRYPT '84. Edited by T. Beth, N. Cot and I. Ingemarsson. VII, 491 pages. 1985.

Vol. 210: STACS 86. Proceedings, 1986. Edited by B. Monien and G. Vidal-Naquet. IX, 368 pages. 1986.

Vol. 211: U. Schöning, Complexity and Structure. V, 99 pages. 1986.

Vol. 212: Interval Mathematics 1985. Proceedings, 1985. Edited by K. Nickel. VI, 227 pages. 1986.

Vol. 213: ESOP 86. Proceedings, 1986. Edited by B. Robinet and R. Wilhelm. VI, 374 pages. 1986.

Vol. 214: CAAP '86. 11th Colloquium on Trees in Algebra and Programming. Proceedings, 1986. Edited by P. Franchi-Zannettacci. VI, 306 pages. 1986.

Vol. 215: Mathematical Methods of Specification and Synthesis of Software Systems '85. Proceedings, 1985. Edited by W. Bibel and K. P. Jantke. 245 pages. 1986.

Vol. 216: Ch. Fernstrom, I. Kruzela, B. Svensson, LUCAS Associative Array Processor: Design, Programming and Application Studies. XII, 323 pages. 1986.

Vol. 217: Programs as Data Objects. Proceedings, 1985. Edited by H. Ganzinger and N. D. Jones. X, 324 pages. 1986.

Vol. 218: Advances in Cryptology – CRYPTO '85. Proceedings, 1985. Edited by H. C. Williams. X, 548 pages. 1986.

Vol. 219: Advances in Cryptology – EUROCRYPT '85. Proceedings, 1985. Edited by F. Pichler. IX, 281 pages. 1986.

Vol. 220: RIMS Symposia on Software Science and Engineering II. Proceedings, 1983 and 1984. Edited by E. Goto, K. Araki and T. Yuasa. XI, 323 pages. 1986.

Vol. 221: Logic Programming '85. Proceedings, 1985. Edited by E. Wada. IX, 311 pages. 1986.

Vol. 222: Advances in Petri Nets 1985. Edited by G. Rozenberg. VI, 498 pages. 1986.

Vol. 223: Structure in Complexity Theory. Proceedings, 1986. Edited by A. L. Selman. VI, 401 pages. 1986.

Vol. 224: Current Trends in Concurrency. Overviews and Tutorials. Edited by J. W. de Bakker, W.-P. de Roever and G. Rozenberg. XII, 716 pages. 1986.

Vol. 225: Third International Conference on Logic Programming. Proceedings, 1986. Edited by E. Shapiro. IX, 720 pages. 1986.

Vol. 226: Automata, Languages and Programming. Proceedings, 1986. Edited by L. Kott. IX, 474 pages. 1986.

Vol. 227: VLSI Algorithms and Architectures – AWOC 86. Proceedings, 1986. Edited by F. Makedon, K. Mehlhorn, T. Papatheodorou and P. Spirakis. VIII, 328 pages. 1986.

Vol. 228: Applied Algebra, Algorithmics and Error-Correcting Codes. AAECC-2. Proceedings, 1984. Edited by A. Poli. VI, 265 pages. 1986.

Vol. 229: Algebraic Algorithms and Error-Correcting Codes. AAECC-3. Proceedings, 1985. Edited by J. Calmet. VII, 416 pages. 1986.

Vol. 230: 8th International Conference on Automated Deduction. Proceedings, 1986. Edited by J. H. Siekmann. X, 708 pages. 1986.

Vol. 231: R. Hausser, NEWCAT: Parsing Natural Language Using Left-Associative Grammar. II, 540 pages. 1986.

Vol. 232: Fundamentals of Artificial Intelligence. Edited by W. Bibel and Ph. Jorrand. VII, 313 pages. 1986.

Vol. 233: Mathematical Foundations of Computer Science 1986. Proceedings, 1986. Edited by J. Gruska, B. Rovan and J. Wiedermann. IX, 650 pages. 1986.

Vol. 234: Concepts in User Interfaces: A Reference Model for Command and Response Languages. By Members of IFIP Working Group 2.7. Edited by D. Beech. X, 116 pages. 1986.

Vol. 235: Accurate Scientific Computations. Proceedings, 1985. Edited by W. L. Miranker and R. A. Toupin. XIII, 205 pages. 1986.

Vol. 236: TEX for Scientific Documentation. Proceedings, 1986. Edited by J. Désarménien. VI, 204 pages. 1986.

Vol. 237: CONPAR 86. Proceedings, 1986. Edited by W. Händler, D. Haupt, R. Jeltsch, W. Juling and O. Lange. X, 418 pages. 1986.

Vol. 238: L. Naish, Negation and Control in Prolog. IX, 119 pages. 1986.

Vol. 239: Mathematical Foundations of Programming Semantics. Proceedings, 1985. Edited by A. Melton. VI, 395 pages. 1986.

Vol. 240: Category Theory and Computer Programming. Proceedings, 1985. Edited by D. Pitt, S. Abramsky, A. Poigné and D. Rydeheard. VII, 519 pages. 1986.

Vol. 241: Foundations of Software Technology and Theoretical Computer Science. Proceedings, 1986. Edited by K.V. Nori. XII, 519 pages. 1986.

Vol. 242: Combinators and Functional Programming Languages. Proceedings, 1985. Edited by G. Cousineau, P.-L. Curien and B. Robinet. V, 208 pages. 1986.

Vol. 243: ICDT '86. Proceedings, 1986. Edited by G. Ausiello and P. Atzeni. VI, 444 pages. 1986.

Vol. 244: Advanced Programming Environments. Proceedings, 1986. Edited by R. Conradi, T.M. Didriksen and D.H. Wanvik. VII, 604 pages. 1986

Lecture Notes in Computer Science

Edited by G. Goos and J. Hartmanis

287

Kesav V. Nori (Ed.)

FST and TCS 7

Foundations of Software Technology and Theoretical Computer Science

Seventh Conference, Pune, India
December 17–19, 1987
Proceedings

Springer-Verlag
Berlin Heidelberg New York London Paris Tokyo

Editor

Kesav V. Nori
Tata Research Development and Design Centre
1, Mangaldas Road, Pune 411 001, India

CR Subject Classification (1987): C.2, D.1–3, F, H.1–2, I.1, I.2.3–4

ISBN 3-540-18625-5 Springer-Verlag Berlin Heidelberg New York
ISBN 0-387-18625-5 Springer-Verlag New York Berlin Heidelberg

Printed in Germany

Printing and binding: Druckhaus Beltz, Hemsbach/Bergstr.
2145/3140-543210

PREFACE

The FST&TCS conferences have provided an annual occasion for interaction between active research communities in India and abroad. This year, there were 105 submissions, from 14 countries, of which 31 were selected. The quality of papers received was such that we have expanded the conference to three days. This year, the venue of the conference makes it possible to have a large number of the participants stay together, and continue their interaction beyond conference hours. We hope that this adds to the value of the conference for its participants.

The Journal of Theoretical Computer Science has a tradition of bringing out a special issue every year containing papers whose first versions were in the Proceedings of an FST&TCS Conference. This has been a stimulus to authors to submit papers in this area to FST&TCS conferences. This year, the Journal of Logic Programming has evinced a similar interest. We hope that this tradition spreads to other areas of the conference.

Considering the improving quality of submissions, as well as increasing numbers of submissions, the present conference calendar is very tight with respect to the reviewing process. This year, we could not consider some papers because of inadequate review. We hope that the new calendar will help us overcome this problem, and avoid disappointment to authors whose papers have suffered from it.

Acknowledgements

On behalf of the Technical Programme Committee, I would like to place on record our appreciation to

- the Invited Speakers for their valuable participation;
- the authors of submitted papers for their interest in FST&TCS;
- the reviewers, whose judgement helped us maintain quality;
- Departments of Electronics and Science & Technology of the Government of India for their financial support;
- Dr. E. Bhagiratharao, Director, IAT, for providing us with a wonderful venue for the conference, for accommodating a large number of the participants in their residential campus, and extending us much organisational help;
- V. Buzruk, L. D'Netto, C. Duvedi, D. Felfeli, S. S. Girimaji, R. V. Godbole, S. M. Joshi, M. Pavan Kumar, P. Lobo, D. S. Prasad, G. S. Reddy, S. Singhani, M. Subramaniam for extensive organisational and secretarial support;
- Dr. Sanjeev Kumar for invaluable assistance throughout.

Pune, September 1987 — Kesav V. Nori

Conference Advisory Committee

D Bjorner (Denmark)
A Chandra (IBM Res.)
B Chandrasekaran (Ohio State)
S Crespi Reghizzi (Milan)
Z Galil (Columbia)
D Gries (Cornell)
M Joseph (Warwick)
A Joshi (Pennsylvania)
U Montanari (Pisa)
A Nakamura (Hiroshima)
R Narasimhan (TIFR)
M Nivat (Paris)
R Parikh (New York)
S Rao Kosaraju (John Hopkins)
S Sahni (Minnesota)
W A Wulf (Tartan Labs.)

Programme Committee

A Bagchi (IIM, Calcutta)
C R Muthukrishnan (IIT, Madras)
K V Nori (TRDDC, PUNE)
L M Patnaik (IISc, Bangalore)
H V Sahasrabuddhe (Poona University)
R Sangal (IIT, Kanpur)
R Siromoney (Madras Christian College)
C E Veni Madhavan (IISc, Bangalore)

List of Reviewers

S A Andreasson, Goteborg, Sweden
V Arvind, IIT, Kanpur
A Bagchi, IIM, Calcutta
C Bajaj, Purdue
G Barua, IIT, Kanpur
F Bellick, Lund, Sweden
V P Bhatkar, TRDDC, Pune
G P Bhattacharjee, IIT, Kharagpur
B B Bhattacharya, Nebraska
S Biswas, IIT, Kanpur
F J Brandenburg, Passau, FRG
S D Brooks, Carnegie-Mellon
U Buy, Amherst
J W Carr III, Florida
D Carvar, Louisiana
R Chandrasekharan, NCST
J Cheriyan, IIT, Delhi
H A Choi, Michigan
B Courcelle, Bordeaux, France
U Dayal, CCA, Cambridge
N Deo, Central Florida
P Dublish, IIT, Delhi
N Francez, MCC, Texas
R K Ghosh, IIT, Kanpur
M S Gopalakrishnan, Pune
A K Goswani, Warwick
V R Govindarajan, Amherst
P Gupta, IIT, Kanpur
L Hans, Eotvos Lovand, Budapest
H Heller, Munchen, FRG
M Hennessy, Sussex, UK
M Hofri, Technion, Haifa
S Holmstroum, Goteborg, Sweden
S Homer, Boston
R Kannan, Carnegie-Mellon
D Kapur, General Electric
S Kapur, IIT, Delhi
H Karnick, IIT, Kanpur
P L Kilpatrick, Belfast
S C Kothari, Iowa State
H J Kreowski, Bremen, FRG
M S Krishnamurthy, RPI, Troy
S Kumar, TRDDC, Pune
S A Kumar, TIFR, Bombay
V Kumar, Austin
V S Lakshmanan, IISc, Bangalore
J L Lassez, IBM
Y J Lin, Austin
K Lodaya, TIFR
M Maher, IBM
S N Maheshwari, IIT, Delhi
V M Malhotra, IIT, Kanpur
A D McGettrick, Strathclyde, UK
R McNaughton, General Electric
S L Mehndiratta, IIT, Bombay
J Misra, Austin
A K Mittal, IIT, Kanpur
H Mohanty, ECIL, Hyderabad
S P Mudur, NCST
A Mukhopadhyay, IIT, Kanpur
B S N Murthy, IIT, Delhi
C R Muthukrishnan, IIT, Madras
P Narendran, General Electric
S Navathe, Florida
K V Nori, TRDDC, Pune
J T Oden, Austin
A K Pal, IIM, Calcutta
P Pandya, TIFR, Bombay
L M Patnaik, IISc, Bangalore
K V S Prasad, Goteborg, Sweden
S V Rajopadhye, Oregon
I V Ramakrishna, Stony Brook
M V Ramakrishna, Michigan
K Ramamritham, Amherst
S Ramani, NCST, Bombay
A G Rao, TCS, Bombay
D S Rosenblum, Stanford
H V Sahasrabuddhe, Pune
R Sangal, IIT, Kanpur
A Sanyal, IIT, Kanpur
S K Sen, IISc, Bangalore
R K Shyamsunder, Pennsylvania
R Siromoney, MCC, Madras
N Soundarajan, Ohio State
P K Srimani, Southern Illinois
R Stansifer, Purdue
D Stemple, Amherst
D K Subramaniam, IISc, Bangalore
P Subramaniam, TIFR, Bombay
V V Vazirani, Bell Labs
C E Veni Madhavan, IISc, Bangalore
M Wand, Boston
M R Wang, Texas
W A Wulf, Tartan Labs

TABLE OF CONTENTS

ALGEBRAIC OPERATIONAL SEMANTICS

Yuri Gurevich
Electrical Engineering and Computer Science
University of Michigan
Ann Arbor, MI 48109-2122, USA

Ask around what a relational data base is and you may hear that it is essentially a bunch of relations. But a relational data base is more than a bunch of relations. It is generally a dynamic object and may be updated. In some cases, it may even drop a relation or acquire a new one.

Here is a similar question. What is a Pascal (or whatever imperative programming language you prefer) machine? When you write a Pascal program, you address some agent, the executor of your program. You may write "While ... do ...", and the agent is supposed to understand and obey. Who or what is that agent? The agent can be your specific computer equipped with a specific compiler. But suppose you want to write a portable program able to run on many different machines with different compilers. Then the agent is an abstract Pascal machine. There is no precise description of such machine in Pascal texts however.

Apparently, there is a difficulty in describing formally dynamic objects of Computer Science. Even in the very simple case of Turing machines, the standard definition of a machine as a tuple (say, (Q, Σ, f, s) where Q and Σ are nonempty finite sets, f: $Q \times \Sigma \dashrightarrow Q$, and s belongs to Q) is not very satisfactory. It is usually accompanied with an informal description of Turing machines where one learns in particular about the tape and whether the tape is bounded from one side. The tuple is merely a code for a Turing machine within the given class of Turing machines. The situation is different from that in mathematics where for example the definition of a graph as a pair (V, E) such that V is a nonempty set and E is a symmetric binary relation on V is an honest definition.

We believe that the source of the difficulty is the lack of mathematical structures naturally suited to model dynamic objects of computer science. To this end, we have introduced the notion of evolving (or dynamic) algebras (or structures) [1] In particular, evolving algebras have been used to model programming language Modula-2; a family of Modula-2 machines with bounded resources is described in [2].

In the talk, we will define evolving algebras and demonstrate their use as abstract machines. In addition, we will pose different problems related to evolving algebras.

References:

1 Yuri Gurevich, Logic and the Challenge of Computer Science, in Current Trends in Computer Science, ed. Egon Börger, Computer Science Press, 1987, 1-57.

2 Yuri Gurevich and James M. Morris, Algebraic Operational Semantics for Modula-2, Technical Report CRL-TR-10-87, University of Michigan, July 1987.

K.G.Subramanian,
Do Long Van
and
Rani Siromoney
Department of Mathematics,
Madras Christian College,
Tambaram, Madras 600 059.

Abstract

A DTOL system is unambiguous if no two different sequences of morphisms yield the same word from an axiom. A subfamily of DTOL systems with decidable ambiguity problem is exhibited. Four different sufficient conditions for a DTOL system to be unambiguous are formulated. These DTOL systems are very much suitable for the construction of public key cryptosystems based on L systems. We also prove that for DOL systems over a binary alphabet, the ambiguity problem is effectively decidable. This result has useful applications in the construction of public key cryptosystems which encrypt plain-texts over a binary alphabet using a TOL system obtained from an underlying unambiguous DOL system.

1. Introduction

Ambiguity of grammars and languages has been one of the basic topics of study. Ambiguity related to context-free grammars has been widely studied [5,8] and the notion of ambiguity in OL systems [7] is examined in [6].

Recently, based on the theory of L systems, a public-key cryptosystem (PKC) is constructed in [9] to ensure secrecy of data, with the encryption key involving a TOL system [7] obtained from an underlying 'unambiguous' DTOL system. This requirement of unambiguity of a DTOL system is shown to be undecidable in [2].

In this paper, motivated by the criterion of unambiguity of a DTOL system in the construction of a PKC, we examine DTOL systems with regard to the notion of ambiguity. We exhibit a class of DTOL systems for which the ambiguity of the system is effectively decidable. Indeed, the problem of deciding ambiguity of this class of DTOL systems reduces to testing whether a certain set of words is a code or not, which can be done by Sardinas-Patterson algorithm [1,3,4]. We also establish different sufficient conditions based on codes, for a DTOL system to be unambiguous and obtain thereby four incomparable families of unambiguous DTOL systems. These families are thus suitable for construction of PKC's of the kind considered in [9].

We then examine ambiguity of DOL systems. We prove that, for DOL systems over a binary alphabet, the ambiguity problem is effectively decidable. This result has useful applications in the construction of public key cryptosystems of the kind considered in [10], when plaintexts over a binary alphabet are encrypted using a TOL system obtained from an underlying unambiguous DOL system.

2. A family of DTOL systems with decidable unambiguity problem

We assume familiarity with L systems [7].

Given a DTOL system $S = (\Sigma,\{h_o,\dots,h_n\},w)$, we denote by $L(S)$, the language generated by S and by I, the set $\{0,1,\dots,n\}$.

We say that S is unambiguous [2], if

$h_{i_1}h_{i_2}\dots h_{i_r}(w)=h_{j_1}h_{j_2}\dots h_{j_s}(w)$ implies $i_1i_2\dots i_r=j_1j_2\dots j_s$,

where $i_1i_2\dots i_r$ and $j_1j_2\dots j_s$ are words in I^*.

Definition 2.1 We denote by F, the family of DTOL systems $S = (\Sigma, \{h_o,h_1,\dots,h_n\},w)$ satisfying the following conditions:

i) for each $i\in I$, there is an $x_i\in \Sigma^*$, such that $h_i(w) = wx_i$, and ii) for each such x_i and each $j \in I$, $h_j(x_i) = x_i$.

Example 2.1 The DTOL system $S = (\{a,b,c\}, \{h_o,h_1\}, c)$ where h_o,h_1 are given by $h_o(a) = ab$, $h_o(b) = \lambda$, $h_o(c) = cabab$, $h_1(a) = \lambda$, $h_1(b) = ab$, $h_1(c) = cababab$, where λ denotes the empty word, satisfies the conditions of Definition 2.1 and thus $S\in F$.

Proposition 2.1 Let $S = (\Sigma,\{h_o,\dots,h_n\},w)$ be a DTOL system in F. Let $h_i(w) = wx_i$ $(i=0,\dots,n)$ be such that $x_i \neq x_j$ if $i \neq j$ $(i,j \in I)$. Then S is unambiguous iff the set $X = \{x_o,x_1,\dots,x_n\}$ is a code over Σ.

Proof: For any $i_1i_2\dots i_r\in \Sigma^*$, we have, by definition

$h_{i_1}h_{i_2}\dots h_{i_r}(w) = wx_{i_1}x_{i_2}\dots x_{i_r}$. Suppose S is unambiguous. If X were not a code, then there would exist $x_{i_1},\dots,x_{i_r},x_{j_1},\dots,x_{j_s}$ in X such that $x_{i_1}\dots x_{i_r} = x_{j_1}\dots x_{j_s}$ with $x_{i_1} \neq x_{j_1}$. This implies

$h_{i_1}\dots h_{i_r}(w) = h_{j_1}\dots h_{j_s}(w)$ with $i_1 \neq j_1$. This contradicts the hypothesis. Thus X must be a code.

Conversely, we assume that X is a code. Then, since $x_i\neq\lambda(i=0,\dots,n)$

we have $|h_i(y)| > |y|$, for all $y \in L(S)$, $(i=0,\dots,n)$. Let now

$$h_{i_1}h_{i_2}\dots h_{i_r}(w) = h_{j_1}\dots h_{j_s}(w).$$

Then clearly, $i_1\dots i_r = \lambda$ iff $j_1\dots j_s = \lambda$. Assume that both $i_1\dots i_r$ and $j_1\dots j_s$ are $\neq \lambda$. Then we have $wx_{i_1}\dots x_{i_r} = wx_{j_1}\dots x_{j_s}$ and therefore

$$x_{i_1}\dots x_{i_r} = x_{j_1}\dots x_{j_s}.$$

Since X is a code, this implies $r = s$ and $x_{i_k} = x_{j_k}$ $(k=1,\dots,r)$ and consequently $i_1\dots i_r = j_1\dots j_s$. Thus S is unambiguous.

Theorem 2.1 There exists an algorithm to decide whether or not a DTOL system S in F is unambiguous.

Proof: To decide whether or not S is unambiguous, we have the following algorithm:

1) Check whether there exist i,j with $i \neq j$ $(i,j \in I)$ such that $x_i = x_j$. If yes, S is ambiguous. If not, we move on to the next step.

2) Check whether or not the set $X = \{x_o,\dots,x_n\}$ is a code. The existence of an algorithm for such a verification is guaranteed by Sardinas-Patterson theorem [1,3,4]. By Proposition 2.1, S is unambiguous iff X is a code.

Example 2.2 The DTOL system $S = (\{a,b,c\}, \{h_o,h_1\}, c)$ where h_o, h_1 are defined by

$$h_o(a) = h_1(a) = a,\ h_o(c) = ca$$

$$h_o(b) = h_1(b) = b,\ h_1(c) = cb$$

is in F and is unambiguous as $a \neq b$ and $\{a,b\}$ is a code.

Example 2.3 The DTOL system S in example 2.1 is ambiguous for abab≠ababab but {abab,ababab} is not a code. Indeed, we have, for example,

$$h_oh_1(c) = h_1h_o(c) = \text{cababababab}.$$

3. Codes and unambiguity of DTOL systems

We now formulate sufficient conditions based on codes [1] for a DTOL system to be unambiguous.

Definition 3.1 We denote by F_1, the family of DTOL systems $S = (\Sigma, \{h_o,\dots,h_n\}, w)$ for which there exists a code X over Σ such that

i) h_i is injective on Σ, $i = 0,\dots,n$,

ii) $h_i(\Sigma) \subsetneq X$ $(i = 0,\dots,n)$ and $h_i(\Sigma) \cap h_j(\Sigma) = \emptyset$ if $i \neq j$, for $i,j \in I$.

iii) alph $(w) \subsetneq$ Alph $(h_i(w))$, $(i = 0,\dots,n)$, where Alph (y) denotes the set of letters occuring in y.

iv) For every i, $(i = 0,\dots,n)$, there exists $a_i \in$ Alph (w) such that

$|h_i(a_i)| > 1$.

Proposition 3.1 Every DTOL system S in F_1 is unambiguous.

Proof: Let $S = (\Sigma, \{h_o, h_1, \ldots, h_n\}, w)$. Every element y of L(S) is of the form $y = h_{i_1} h_{i_2} \ldots h_{i_k}(w)$

We now verify by induction on k that $Alph(w) \subseteq Alph(y)$, for all $y \in L(S)$. Indeed, for k=0, the assertion is trivial. Suppose $k > 0$ and the assertion is true for k-1. We have

$$y = h_{i_1}[h_{i_2} \ldots h_{i_k}(w)].$$

By the induction assumption $Alph(w) \subseteq Alph(h_{i_2} \ldots h_{i_k}(w))$. Thus,

$$Alph(h_{i_1}(w)) \subseteq Alph(h_{i_1}[h_{i_2} \ldots h_{i_k}(w)]) = Alph(y).$$

From (iii) in definition 3.1, it follows that $Alph(w) \subseteq Alph(y)$. Then by (iv) of definition 3.1, we have $|h_i(y)| > |y|$, for all $y \in L(S)$. Therefore, if $h_{i_1} h_{i_2} \ldots h_{i_r}(w) = h_{j_1} h_{j_2} \ldots h_{j_s}(w)$, then $i_1 \ldots i_r = \lambda$ iff $j_1 \ldots j_s = \lambda$.

We now verify by induction on k=r+s, that if both $i_1 i_2 \ldots i_r$ and $j_1 j_2 \ldots j_s$ are $\neq \lambda$, then we also have $i_1 i_2 \ldots i_r = j_1 j_2 \ldots j_s$. Indeed, for k=2, we have $h_{i_1}(w) = h_{j_1}(w)$. By the fact that X is a code and by (ii) of definition 3.1, it follows that $i_1 = j_1$. Assume that the assertion is true for all $k' < k$ and $k > 2$. By the same argument as above, we have $i_1 = j_1$. Then, by (i) of definition 3.1, it follows that $h_{i_2} \ldots h_{i_r}(w) = h_{j_2} \ldots h_{j_s}(w)$. Since $k > 2$, we have $i_2 \ldots i_r,\ j_2 \ldots j_s \neq \lambda$. By the induction assumption, it follows that $i_2 \ldots i_r = j_2 \ldots j_s$ and therefore $i_1 i_2 \ldots i_r = j_1 j_2 \ldots j_s$. Thus S is unambiguous.

Example 3.1 The DTOL system $S_1 = (\{a,b\}, \{h_o, h_1\}, ab)$ where h_o, h_1 are given by $h_o(a) = ba$, $h_o(b) = ab$, $h_1(a) = bb$, $h_1(b) = aab$, satisfies all the conditions of definition 3.1, as $X = \{ba, ab, bb, aab\}$ is a code and thus S is unambiguous.

A code X is called uniform if all the elements of X are of the same length.

Definition 3.2 We say that a DTOL system $S = (\Sigma, \{h_o, \ldots h_n\}, w)$ belongs to the family F_2, if there exists an uniform code X over Σ, such that

i) h_i is injective on Σ, $(i = 0, \ldots, n)$

and ii) $h_i(\Sigma) \subsetneq X$ and $h_i(\Sigma) \cap h_j(\Sigma) = \emptyset$ if $i \neq j$ for $i, j \in I$.

Proposition 3.2 Every DTOL system S in F_2 is unambiguous.

Proof: It is easy to see that the conditions of definition 3.2 imply $|h_i(a)| > 1$, for all $a \in \Sigma$, $i = 0, \ldots, n$. Thus $|h_i(y)| > |y|$, for all $y \in L(S)$, $i = 0, \ldots, n$. The rest of the proof is similar to that of proposition 3.1 and is therefore omitted.

Example 3.2 The DTOL system $S_2 = (\{a,b\}, \{h_o,h_1\}, ab)$ where h_o,h_1 are defined by $h_o(a) = aa$, $h_o(b) = ab$, $h_1(a) = ba$, $h_1(b) = bb$ satisfies the conditions of definition 3.2, as $X = \{aa,ab,ba,bb\}$ is an uniform code and thus S_2 is unambiguous.

Definition 3.3 We denote by F_3, the family of DTOL systems $S = (\Sigma, \{h_o,\dots,h_n\}, w)$ for which there is an (n+1)-element code $X=\{x_o,\dots,x_n\}$ such that

i) $h_i(w) = wx_i$ $(i = 0,\dots,n)$

ii) $h_i(x_j) \in X^*$ (for all $i,j \in I$)

iii) h_i is injective on Σ and $h_i(\Sigma)$ is a code $(i = 0,\dots,n)$.

iv) $|h_i(a)| > 1$, for $a \in \Sigma$ $(i = 0,\dots,n)$.

Proposition 3.3 Every DTOL system in F_3 is unambiguous.

Proof: By conditions (i) and (ii) of definition 3.3, every element of L(S) has the form wu for some $u \in X^*$. Then, by (i) and (iv), we have $|h_i(y)| > |y|$, for all $y \in L(S)$. Let $h_{i_1}\dots h_{i_r}(w) = h_{j_1}\dots h_{j_s}(w)$. Then, clearly $i_1\dots i_r = \lambda$ iff $j_1\dots j_s = \lambda$. We now verify by induction on $k = r+s$, that if both $i_1\dots i_r$ and $j_1\dots j_s \neq \lambda$, then we also have $i_1\dots i_r = j_1\dots j_s$. Indeed, for $k = 2$, we have $h_{i_1}(w) = h_{j_1}(w)$ which implies $x_{i_1} = x_{j_1}$ and therefore $i_1 = j_1$. Assume $k > 2$ and the assertion is true for all $k' < k$. Let $h_{i_2}\dots h_{i_r}(w) = wu$, $h_{j_2}\dots k_{j_s}(w) = wv$, where $u,v \in X^*$. We have then $h_{i_1}(wu) = h_{j_1}(wv)$ i.e. $wx_{i_1}h_{i_1}(u) = wx_{j_1}h_{j_1}(v)$ and therefore, $x_{i_1}h_{i_1}(u) = x_{j_1}h_{j_1}(v)$ where $h_{i_1}(u)$ and $h_{j_1}(v)$ are in X^* by (ii) of definition 3.3. If $i_1 \neq j_1$, then $x_{i_1} \neq x_{j_1}$ and so the last equality contradicts the fact that X is a code. Thus $i_1 = j_1$ and we have by (iii) of definition 3.3,

$$h_{i_2}\dots h_{i_r}(w) = h_{j_2}\dots h_{j_s}(w).$$

Since $k > 2$, we have $i_2\dots i_r, j_2\dots j_s \neq \lambda$. By the induction hypothesis it follows that $i_2\dots i_r = j_2\dots j_s$ and consequently, we have $i_1\dots i_r = j_1\dots j_s$. Hence S is unambiguous.

Example 3.3 The DTOL system $S_3 = (\{a,b\}, \{h_o,h_1\}, a)$ where h_o,h_1 are given by $h_o(a) = aa$, $h_o(b) = b$, $h_1(a) = aab$, $h_1(b) = ab$ satisfies all the conditions of definition 3.3 as $X = \{a,ab\}$ is a 2-element code and thus S_3 is unambiguous.

A code X is called a prefix code, if no element of X is a proper left factor of an element of X.

Definition 3.4 We denote by F_4, the family of DTOL systems $S = (\Sigma, \{h_o,\dots,h_n\}, w)$ for which there is a (n+1)-element prefix code $X = \{x_o, x_1,\dots,x_n\}$ such that

i) $h_i(w) = wx_iy_i$, y_i Σ^* and $|h_i(a)| > 1$, $a \in \Sigma$ $(i=0,\ldots,n)$

ii) h_i is injective on Σ and $h_i(\Sigma)$ is a code $(i=0,\ldots,n)$

Proposition 3.4 Every DTOL system S in F_4 is unambiguous.

Proof: By definition 3.4, we have $|h_i(y)| > |y|$ for all $y \in L(S)$. Suppose $h_{i_1}h_{i_2}\ldots h_{i_r}(w) = h_{j_1}h_{j_2}\ldots h_{j_s}(w)$. Then clearly, $i_1\ldots i_r = \lambda$ iff $j_1\ldots j_s = \lambda$. We now prove by induction on $k = r+s$ that if both $i_1i_2\ldots i_r$ and $j_1j_2\ldots j_s \neq \lambda$ then we have $i_1i_2\ldots i_r = j_1j_2\ldots j_s$. Indeed, for k=2, we have $h_{i_1}(w) = h_{j_1}(w)$ i.e., $wx_{i_1}y_{i_1} = wx_{j_1}y_{j_1}$ and consequently, $x_{i_1}y_{i_1} = x_{j_1}y_{j_1}$. Since X is a prefix code this implies $x_{i_1} = x_{j_1}$ and therefore $i_1 = j_1$. Suppose now $k > 2$ and the assertion is true for all $k' < k$. Let $h_{i_2}\ldots h_{i_r}(w) = wu$, $h_{j_2}\ldots h_{j_s}(w) = wv$ for some $u, v \in \Sigma^*$. We have $h_{i_1}(wu) = h_{j_1}(wv)$. i.e., $wx_{i_1}y_{i_1}h_{i_1}(u) = wx_{j_1}y_{j_1}h_{j_1}(v)$ and therefore $x_{i_1}y_{i_1}h_{i_1}(u) = x_{j_1}y_{j_1}h_{j_1}(v)$. Since X is a prefix code, this implies $x_{i_1} = x_{j_1}$ and consequently $i_1 = j_1$. By (ii) of definition 3.4, h_{i_1} is injective. So we have $h_{i_2}\ldots h_{i_r}(w) = h_{j_2}\ldots h_{j_s}(w)$, which, by the induction assumption, implies $i_2\ldots i_r = j_2\ldots j_s$ and consequently $i_1\ldots i_r = j_1\ldots j_s$. We thus have proved that S is unambiguous.

Example 3.4 The DTOL system $S_4 = (\{a,b\}, \{h_o,h_1\}, a)$ where h_o, h_1 are given by $h_o(a) = aab$, $h_o(b) = b$, $h_1(a) = aba$, $h_1(b) = bb$ satisfies the condition of definition 3.4, as $X = \{x_1,x_2\}$ with $x_1=a$, $x_2=ba$ is a prefix code and we can take $y_1=b$, $y_2=\lambda$. Thus S_4 is unambiguous.

Remark: It is easy to see that

$$S \in F_i - \bigcup_{\substack{j\neq i \\ 1\leq j\leq 4}} F_j \quad (i=1,\ldots,4).$$

This implies that the four families considered are pairwise incomparable and also show that the sufficient conditions formulated are not necessary conditions.

4. On the public-key cryptosystems of [9]

In [9], a public-key cryptosystem is constructed using a DTOL system. It is of interest to note that the illustration in [9] uses the DTOL system $S = (\{a,b\}, \{h_o,h_1\}, ab)$ where h_o, h_1 are given by

$h_o(a) = ab$, $h_o(b) = b$,

$h_1(a) = a$, $h_1(b) = ba$

and this system belongs to $F_3 \cap F_4$.

The families considered here provide DTOL systems very much suitable for public-key cryptosystems of the kind considered in [9]. We illustrate with an example, which is of interest in the sense that the increase in the length of words during encryption is slow and the decryption is very easy and quick.

Consider $S_5 = (\Sigma, \{h_o, h_1\}, w)$, where $\Sigma = \{a,b,c\}$, $w = c$ and h_o, h_1 are given by

$h_o(a) = h_1(a) = a$, $h_o(c) = ca$,

$h_o(b) = h_1(b) = b$, $h_1(c) = cb$.

It is easy to se that $S_5 \in F \cap F_3 \cap F_4$.

Let $\Delta = \{c_1, c_2, \ldots, c_8\}$. Define the morphism $g : \Delta^* \to \Sigma^*$ by

$g(c_4) = g(c_7) = a$, $g(c_1) = g(c_8) = b$,

$g(c_2) = g(c_6) = c$, $g(c_3) = g(c_5) = \lambda$.

Define the substitutions σ_o and σ_1 over Δ^* by

$\sigma_o : c_1 \to c_8c_3$, $c_2 \to c_5c_2c_7$, $c_2 \to c_6c_3c_4$,
$c_3 \to c_3c_5$, $c_4 \to c_4c_3$, $c_4 \to c_3c_7$,
$c_5 \to c_5c_5$, $c_6 \to c_2c_5c_7$, $c_6 \to c_2c_3c_4$,
$c_7 \to c_5c_7$, $c_8 \to c_1c_3$.

$\sigma_1 : c_1 \to c_5c_8$, $c_2 \to c_6c_3c_1$, $c_2 \to c_2c_5c_8$,
$c_3 \to c_5c_3$, $c_4 \to c_5c_7c_3$, $c_5 \to c_3c_3$,
$c_6 \to c_6c_5c_8$, $c_6 \to c_2c_3c_1$, $c_7 \to c_4c_3$,
$c_8 \to c_8c_5$.

Choose $u = c_3c_2c_5$.

The quadruple $(\Delta, \sigma_o, \sigma_1, u)$ can now be publicised as the encryption key.

Consider the plaintext 010. The encryption must start from u and use σ_o, σ_1 and σ_o. One possible derivation goes as follows:

$$u = c_3c_2c_5 \underset{\sigma_o}{\Rightarrow} c_3c_5c_6c_3c_4c_5c_5$$
$$\underset{\sigma_1}{\Rightarrow} c_5c_3c_3c_3c_6c_5c_8c_5c_3c_5c_7c_3c_3c_3c_3c_3$$
$$\underset{\sigma_o}{\Rightarrow} c_5c_5c_3c_5c_3c_5c_3c_5c_2c_5c_7c_5c_5c_1c_3c_5c_5c_3c_5c_5c_5c_5c_7c_3c_5c_3c_5c_3c_5 c_3c_5 = x.$$

Thus the word x constitutes an encryption of the plaintext 010. We now use the secret decryption key (Σ, h_o, h_1, w, g) to recover the original plaintext. We have

$g(x) = caba = h_0h_1h_0(c)$.

Thus the plaintext desired is 010.

Instead of S_5 we can also use the system

$S_6 = (\Sigma, \{h_0, h_1\}, w)$ belonging to $F_3 \cap F_4$, where $\Sigma = \{a,b\}$, $w = a$, h_0 and h_1 are defined by

$h_0(a) = aa$, $h_0(b) = b$

$h_1(a) = ab$, $h_1(b) = b$.

5. A class of DOL systems with decibable ambiguity problem

Definition 5.1 A DOL system $S = (\Sigma, h, w)$ is called unambiguous, if, for any $n, m \geq 0$, the equality

$$h^n(w) = h^m(w) \tag{5.1}$$

implies $n = m$. Otherwise, we say that S is ambiguous.

We denote by F', the family of all DOL systems $S = (\Sigma, h, w)$ with $|\Sigma| \leq 2$.

Theorem 5.1 The ambiguity problem is decidable for the family F' of DOL systems. In other words, there exists an algorithm for deciding whether or not a given DOL system S in F' is unambiguous.

The proof of the theorem is based on certain lemmas, which we establish first.

Lemma 5.1 Let $S = (\Sigma, h, w)$ be a DOL system. If for all $u \in L(S)$, the language generated by S, $|h(u)| > |u|$ (5.2)
then S is unambiguous.

Proof: Assume equation (5.1) with $n \neq m$. We can assume, by symmetry, $n > m$. Then by (5.2) we have $|h^n(w)| = |h(h^{n-1}(w))| > |h^{n-1}(w)| = |h(h^{n-2}(w))| > |h^{n-2}(w)| = \ldots > |h(h^m(w))| > |h^m(w)|$, which contradicts (5.1). Thus $n = m$, i.e., S is unambiguous.

Lemma 5.2 Let $S = (\Sigma, h, w)$ be a DOL system with $|\Sigma| = 1$, say, $\Sigma = \{a\}$. Then S is unambiguous iff $|h(a)| \geq 2$.

Proof: Suppose $|h(a)| \geq 2$. Then for all $u \in \Sigma^*$, $|h(u)| > |u|$. By Lemma 5.1, S is unambiguous.

Conversely, suppose S is unambiguous. If $|h(a)| = 0$, that is, $h(a) = \lambda$, then for all $n \geq 1$, $h^n(w) = \lambda$, which contradicts the hypothesis. If $|h(a)| = 1$, that is, $h(a) = a$, then for all $n \geq 0$,

$h^n(w) = w$, which is also a contradiction. Thus $|h(a)| \geqslant 2$.

Lemma 5.3 If $S = (\Sigma, h, w)$ is a DOL system such that
i) for all $a \in \Sigma$, $h(a) \neq \lambda$,
ii) $Alph(w) \subsetneq Alph(h(w))$ and
iii) there exists $a \in Alph(w)$ such that $|h(a)| \geqslant 2$, then S is unambiguous.

Proof: Clearly, every element of L(S) has the form $h^n(w)$, for some $n \geqslant 0$. By induction on n, we can prove that for all $u \in L(S)$, $|h(u)| > |u|$. By Lemma 5.1, S is unambiguous.

Lemma 5.4 If $S = (\Sigma, h, w)$, with $\Sigma = \{a,b\}$, is a DOL system such that $h(a), h(b) \neq \lambda$, then we can effectively find whether S is unambiguous or not.

Proof: We consider various cases.

Case (i): $|Alph(w)| = 1$. i.e., $Alph(w) = \{a\}$. The following subcases arise.

1) $Alph(h(a)) = \{a,b\}$. Then $|h(a)| \geqslant 2$ and S satisfies all the conditions of Lemma 5.3 and so S is unambiguous.

2) $Alph(h(a)) = \{a\}$. Then $h(a) = a^k$, $k \geqslant 1$. If $k = 1$, then for all $n \geqslant 0$, $h^n(w) = w$ and so S is unambiguous. If $k > 1$, then S satisfies conditions of Lemma 5.3 and so S is unambiguous.

3) $Alph(h(a)) = \{b\}$. Then $h(a) = b^k$, $k \geqslant 1$, and $h(w) \in b^+$. Let $w' = h(w)$ and consider $S' = (\Sigma, h, w')$. The following situations are possible.

a) $Alph(h(b)) = \{a,b\}$. Then S' satisfies the conditions of Lemma 5.3 and so S' is unambiguous. Now assume (5.1). Then either $n = m = 0$ or $n,m \geqslant 1$. The latter implies $h^{n-1}(w') = h^{m-1}(w')$ which in turn implies $n = m$, as S' is unambiguous. Thus S is unambiguous.

b) $Alph(h(b)) = \{b\}$. Then $h(a) = b^r$, $r \geqslant 1$. Consider $S' = (\{b\}, h, w')$ where $w' = h(w)$. By Lemma 3.2, S' is unambiguous iff $r \geqslant 2$. Since $Alph(w) = \{a\}$ and $Alph(h^n(w)) = \{b\}$, for all $n \geqslant 1$, either $n = m = 0$ or $n,m \geqslant 1$. The latter implies $h^{n-1}(w') = h^{m-1}(w')$, which implies $n = m$, if S' is unambiguous. This means that S is unambiguous iff S' is so. Thus S is unambiguous iff $n \geqslant 2$.

c) $Alph(h(b)) = \{a\}$. Then $h(b) = a^t$, $t \geqslant 1$. If $k = t = 1$, then for all $n \geqslant 0$, $h^{2n}(w) = w$ and so S is unambiguous. If $k > 1$ or $t > 1$, we consider $S' = (\{a\}, g, w)$ where $g = h^2$. We have $g(a) = h(h(a)) = h(b^k) = a^{tk}$, $tk \geqslant 2$. By Lemma 5.1, S' is unambiguous.

Assume now (5.1). Since $\mathrm{Alph}(w) = \{a\}$, $\mathrm{Alph}(h^{2n+1}(w)) = \{b\}$ and $|h^{2n}(w)| > |w|$, either $n=m=0$, or $n,m \geqslant 1$. If $n,m \geqslant 1$, then n,m are both either odd or even. If $n=2r$, $m=2s$, then by (5.1), we have $g^r(w) = g^s(w)$ By unambiguity of S', $r = s$ and therefore $n = m$. If $n = 2r+1$, $m = 2s+1$, consider $S'' = (\{b\}, g, w)$, where $g = h^2$, $w' = h(w)$. Since

$$g(b) = h^2(b) = h(a^t) = a^{kt},\ kt \geqslant 2,$$

S'' is unambiguous. From (5.1), we have

$$h^{2r+1}(w) = h^{2s+1}(w)$$

implies $h^{2r}(w') = h^{2s}(w')$. i.e. $g^r(w') = g^s(w')$. By unambiguity of S'', we obtain $r = s$ and therefore, $n = m$. Thus we have proved that S is unambiguous.

Case (ii) $\mathrm{Alph}(w) = \{a,b\}$.

We consider the following subcases.

1) $\mathrm{Alph}\ h(w) = \{a,b\}$

a) Either $|h(a)| > 1$ or $|h(b)| > 1$, then S satisfies the conditions of Lemma 5.3 and therefore S is unambiguous.

b) $|h(a)| = |h(b)| = 1$. Then, if $h(a) = a$, $h(b) = b$, then for all $n \geqslant 0$, $h^n(w) = w$. Thus S is ambiguous. If $h(a) = b$, $h(b) = a$, then for all $n \geqslant 0$, $h^{2n}(w) = w$. Thus S is ambiguous.

2) $|\mathrm{Alph}(w)| = 1$, say $\mathrm{Alph}\ h(w) = \{a\}$. Consider $S = (\{a\}, h, w'=h(w))$. By lemma 5.2, S' is unambiguous iff $|h(a)| \geqslant 2$. Now assume (5.1). Since $\mathrm{Alph}\ h^k(w) = a$, for all $k \geqslant 1$, either $n=m=0$ or $n,m \geqslant 1$. If $n,m \geqslant 1$, the $h^{n-1}(w') = h^{m-1}(w')$, which implies $n = m$ if S' is unambiguous. So S is unambiguous iff S' is so. Thus S is unambiguous iff $|h(a)| \geqslant 2$.

Lemma 5.5 If $S = (\Sigma, h, w)$ where $\Sigma = \{a,b\}$, such that $h(a) \neq \lambda$, $h(b) = \lambda$, then we can effectively find whether S is unambiguous or not.

Proof: Case (i) $\mathrm{Alph}\ h(a) = \{a\}$, $h(a) = a^k$, $k > 1$.

1) $\mathrm{Alph}\ (w) = \{a,b\}$ or $\{a\}$ and $k \geqslant 1$ (5.3)

Consider $S' = (\{a\}, h, w')$ where $w' = h(w)$. By Lemma 5.2, S is unambiguous iff $|h(a)| \geqslant 2$. We prove now S is unambiguous iff S' is so. The 'only if' part is trivial. We prove the 'if' part. Assume now (5.1). By (5.3) either $n = m = 0$, or $n,m \geqslant 1$. If $n,m \geqslant 1$, then (5.1) implies $h^{n-1}(w') = h^{m-1}(w')$, which in turn implies $n = m$, by unambiguity of S'. Thus S is unambiguous iff $|h(a)| \geqslant 2$.

2) $\mathrm{Alph}\ (w) = \{b\}$. Then S is unambiguous, since, for all $n \geqslant 1$, $h^n(w) = \lambda$.

3) $\mathrm{Alph}\ (w) = \{a\}$ and $k = 1$. Then S is ambiguous, since for all $n \geqslant 0$, $h^n(w) = w$.

Case (ii) Alph $h(a) = \{b\}$. Then S is ambiguous, since, for all $n \geqslant 2$, $h^n(w) = \lambda$.

Case (iii) Alph $h(a) = \{a,b\}$.

1) Alph $(w) = \{b\}$. Then S is ambiguous, since, for all $n \geqslant 1$, $h^n(w)=\lambda$.

2) Alph $(w) = \{a,b\}$.

a) $|h(a)| = 1$. Then S is ambiguous since for all $n \geqslant 2$, $h^n(w) = h^2(w)$.

b) $|h(a)|_a > 1$. Then it is easy to see that for all $u \in L(S)$, $|h(u)|_a > |u|_a$.

Thus S is unambiguous.

Lemma 5.6 If $S = (\Sigma, h, w)$ is a DOL system such that $h(a) = \lambda$, for all $a \in \Sigma$, then S is ambiguous.

Proof: This lemma is obvious, since for all $n \geqslant 1$, $h^n(w) = \lambda$.

Proof of Theorem 5.1: The algorithm deciding the ambiguity problem of the family F' can be easily constructed from lemmas 5.1 to 5.6.

Remark In [10], a public key cryptosystem based on L systems is constructed. The encryption of a plaintext is done using a TOL system obtained from an underlying DOL system. The DOL systen is to be unambiguous for the decryption to be possible.

If the alphabet is binary, Theorem 5.1 provides an algorithm for deciding whether a DOL system is unambiguous or not and thus has useful applications in the choise of a DOL system as required in [10].

References

[1] J.Berstel and D.Perrin (1985), 'Theory of Codes', Academic Press, New York.

[2] J.Dassow (1984), A note on DTOL systems, Bull. EATCS, 22, 11-14.

[3] Do Long Van (1982), Codes avec des mots infinis, RAIRO informatique Theorique 16, 371-386.

[4] Do Long Van (1985), Ensembles code-compatibles et une generalisation du theoreme de Sardinas-Patterson, Theo. Comp. Sci. 38,123-132.

[5] S.Ginsburg (1966), 'The Mathematical Theory of Context-free languages', McGraw Hill, New York.

[6] A.Reedy and W.J.Savitch (1974), Ambiguity in developmental systems, Proc. of the 1974 Conf. on Biologically Motivated Automata Theory, 97-105.

[7] G.Rozenberg and A.Salomaa (1980), 'The Mathematical Theory of L systems', Academic Press, New York.

[8] A.Salomaa (1973), 'Formal Languages', Academic Press, New York.

[9] A.Salomaa (1985), 'Computation and Automata', Encyclopaedia of Mathematics and its Applications, 25, Cambridge University Press, New York.

[10] K.G.Subramanian, R.Siromoney and Abisha Jeyanthi (1987), A DOL-TOL public-key cryptosystem, To appear in Inform. Proc. Lett.

The equivalence problem for n-tape finite automata with simple cycles *

Karel Culik II

Department of Computer Science

University of South Carolina

Columbia, S. C. 29208, U. S. A.

and Matti Linna

Department of Mathematics

University of Turku

Turku, Finland.

Abstract

The equivalence problem for 2-tape deterministic finite automata was shown decidable by Bird in 1973, for n-tapes the problem is still open. We show that it is decidable for the restricted class of simple automata. An n-tape deterministic finite automaton is simple if at most one cycle goes through each of its states.

1 Introduction

The notion of an n-tape finite automaton was introduced by Rabin and Scott [6]. In [2] the inclusion problem for deterministic (one-way) n-tape automata was shown undecidable and the equivalence problem stated as open. For two tapes the equivalence problem was shown decidable by Bird [1] in 1973, however, for $n > 2$ it remains open. The decidability of the special case of one-letter alphabet (on all tapes) follows from [4]. For nondeterministic automata the equivalence problem is undecidable even for two tapes one of them with one-letter alphabet [5].

In this paper we introduce a restricted class of n-tape deterministic finite automata with simple cycles (at most one cycle goes through each state) and show that the equivalence problem for this class is decidable. We also show some general results related to the equivalence problem.

In Section 2, after basic definitions, we illustrate by some examples how some quite different but equivalent automata can be constructed systematically. These techniques are then formalized in later sections.

In Section 3 we first define a general normal form, so-called no-merge normal form, for deterministic n-tape automata and then using the concept of 'unrolling of cycles', we show that certain operations preserve the determinism as well as the normal form. These operations, one of them being the left quotient with respect to a given n-tuple of words, are crucial in Section 4, where an algorithm for solving the equivalence for automata with simple cycles is presented.

*This research was supported by the Natural Sciences and Engineering Research Council of Canada Grant. No. A-7403

2 Preliminaries

For n-tuples $u = (u_1, u_2, \ldots, u_n)$ and $v = (v_1, v_2, \ldots, v_n)$ of words over a finite alphabet Σ, the *concatenation* of u and v is defined as

$$uv = (u_1v_1, u_2v_2, \ldots, u_nv_n).$$

The *length* of u, denoted by $|u|$, is the sum of the lengths of the words u_i $(i = 1, \ldots, n)$. The notation $u \leq v$ (resp., $u < v$) for n-tuples u and v means that there exists an n-tuple w with $|w| \geq 0$ (resp., $|w| > 0$) such that $uw = v$.

In the literature *finite (deterministic) n-tape automata* are defined in many different ways. The definition used in this paper is similar to that given by Bird [1]. The only difference is in defining the acceptance of n-tuples which in our case is more general. However, as far as the equivalence problem is considered the definitions are equivalent.

A *finite deterministic n-tape automaton* (with an endmarker) is a 6-tuple $A = (Q, \Sigma \cup \{\#\}, \delta, q_0, F, k)$, where

(i) Q and Σ are finite sets called the *set of states* and the *input alphabet*, respectively;

(ii) $\# \notin \Sigma$ is the *endmarker*;

(iii) δ is a (partial) function : $Q \times (\Sigma \cup \{\#\}) \to Q$, called the *transition function*;

(iv) $q_0 \in Q$ is the *initial state*;

(v) $F \subseteq Q$ is the *set of final states*; and

(vi) k is a function $Q \to \{1, 2, \ldots, n\}$, called the *tape selector function.*

We say that an n-tuple $(u_1, u_2, \ldots, u_n)$ of words over $\Sigma \cup \{\#\}$ *takes* this automaton to the state q if, for some $m \geq 0$, there exists a sequence of states $q_1, q_2, \ldots, q_m$ together with a word $a_1a_2 \ldots a_m$ over $\Sigma \cup \{\#\}$ such that

(i) $\delta(q_{i-1}, a_i) = q_i$, $(i = 1, 2, \ldots, m)$;

(ii) $q_m = q$; and

(iii) for $j = 1, 2, \ldots, n$, u_j is the word obtained by selecting, in order, all letters a_i from $a_1a_2 \ldots a_m$ such that $k(q_{i-1}) = j$.

An n-tuple $(u_1, u_2, \ldots, u_n)$ of words over Σ is *accepted* by the automaton A if the n-tuple $(u_1\#, u_2\#, \ldots, u_n\#)$ takes A to some final state. The set of all n-tuples accepted by A is denoted by $R(A)$. Two automata A_1 and A_2 are said to be *equivalent* if $R(A_1) = R(A_2)$.

Remark. The automata defined above are deterministic in the following sense. Firstly, the transition function δ is defined as in the case of usual finite automata and, secondly, the tape selection function k uniquely determines the tape to be read next. This implies that for each n-tuple of words there is at most one computation in A.

Perhaps the most natural way to represent n-tape automata is to use diagrams as in the case of usual finite automata. The values of the tape selector are shown as states labels, see the following examples. The initial state is distinguished by an arrow entering it and the states with double circles are the final states. Since in our examples the final states do not have any outgoing edges, they are not labeled.

Example 1. The 2-tape deterministic automata A, B shown in Figure 1 are equivalent and accept all pairs of words over $\Sigma = \{a\}$.

Intuitively speaking, we can say that the aa-cycle of automaton B is unnecessary in the sense that after reading an equal number of a's from both tapes it is still possible to read more a's from the first tape or from the second tape. We can also say that the automaton A is obtained from automaton B by breaking this aa-cycle.

Example 2. Both of the automata in Figure 2 accept the set

$$R = \{(a^i, a^j) \mid i - j \equiv 1 \pmod 3\}$$

Also in this case we can say that the aa-cycle of the smaller automaton is broken into the aaa-cycle (where each a comes from the first tape).

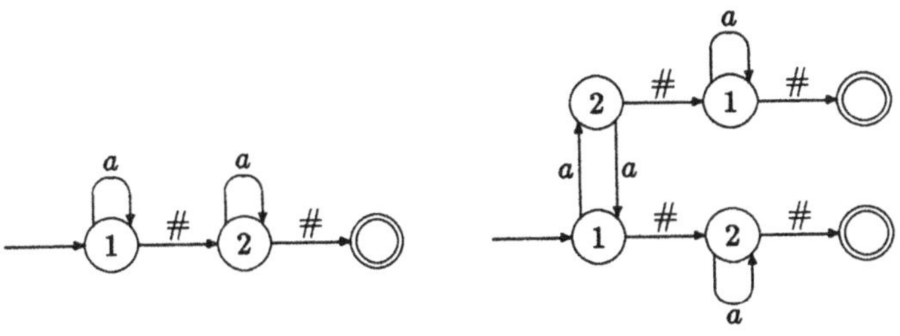

Figure 1: Equivalent 2-tape automata

Example 3. Another way to obtain equivalent automata is to reorder some labels of the edges or reorder even more complex structures, for instance cycles, as it is done in the following example. Obviously, both of the automata in Figure 3 accept the set

$$R = \{(a^i, a^j, a^k) \mid j = i + k\}$$

of 3-tuples.

Equivalent automata can also be constructed by unrolling or rolling cycles. This operation,

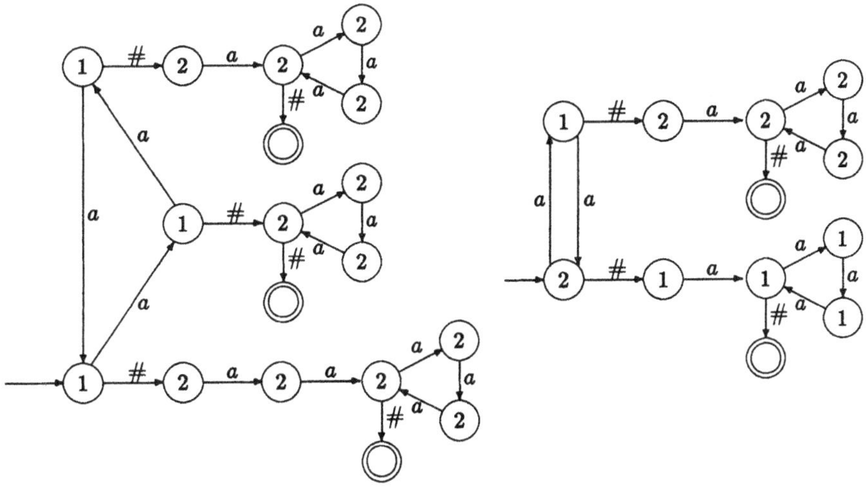

Figure 2: Equivalent 2-tape automata

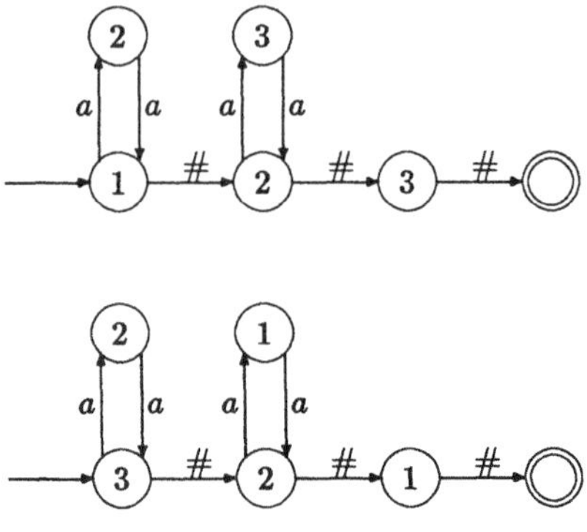

Figure 3: Equivalent 3-tape automata

crucial for some of our results, will be defined precisely in the next chapter.

Finally, in this section we recall some of the known results related to the equivalence problem for n-tape automata. For 2-tape deterministic automata the equivalence was shown to be decidable by Bird [1]. The proof is complicated but the algorithm is nice; it is based on four simple operations on automata. For $n \geq 3$ the problem is still open. Moreover, it can be shown that a natural generalization of the Bird's algorithm fails already in the case of Example 3.

Another approach is to consider the cardinality of the alphabet Σ. The equivalence is decidable for one-letter alphabet. In this case the set of accepted n-tuples can be represented by semilinear vector sets. For these sets even the inclusion problem is decidable (see e.g. Ginsburg [3]). Ibarra [4] has shown that also in the case of reversal-bounded multicounter machines the accepted set of n-tuples is always a semilinear set.

It is known that the inclusion problem is undecidable for deterministic n-tape automata [2]. In the nondeterministic case Ibarra [5] has obtained a sharp result, the equivalence is undecidable even in 2-tape case if at least one of the tapes is over a one-letter alphabet.

3 Unrolling of cycles

In this section we will first define a normal form, so called "no-merge" normal form, for n-tape automata and then use the concept of unrolling of cycles to prove some general results needed later on.

We say that a given n-tape automaton A is in *no-merge normal form* if, for each state q, there is exactly one path without repetitions of states from the initial state q_0 to the state q, i.e. a path of the form $q_0, q_1, \ldots, q_m$, where $q_m = q$ and $q_i \neq q_j$ for all $i \neq j$.

Lemma 1 *For a given n-tape automaton an equivalent n-tape automaton in no-merge normal form can be effectively constructed.*

Proof. Let $A = (Q, \Sigma \cup \{\#\}, \delta, q_0, F, k)$ be a given automaton. A normal form automaton $A_1 = (Q_1, \Sigma \cup \{\#\}, \delta_1, q_0, F_1, k_1)$ is constructed as follows. Consider first all the transitions from q_0 in A. If $\delta(q_0, a) = q_0$ for $a \in \Sigma$ then define $\delta_1(q_0, a) = q_0$. If $\delta(q_0, a) = q$ for some $a \in \Sigma$ and $q \neq q_0$ and $\delta(q_0, b) \neq q$ for all $b \neq a$ then let $\delta_1(q_0, a) = q$. If in A there are $m, m \geq 2$, different transitions from q_0 to some state, say q $(q \neq q_0)$, then for each such transition, say b-transition, add a copy, say q_b, of the state q to the set Q_1 and define $\delta_1(q_0, b) = q_b$. Then the following procedure is repeated recursively for each state q_1 of A_1.

Let q_1 be a copy of some state q of A. For each $a \in \Sigma$ such that a copy of the state $\delta(q,a)$ does not occur in the unique path without repetitions from q_0 to q_1 in A_1, create a copy, say q_2, of the state $\delta(q,a)$ and define $\delta_1(q_1,a) = q_2$. If the state $\delta(q,a)$ has a copy, say q_2, in the unique path from q_0 to q_1, then let $\delta_1(q_1,a) = q_2$.

It is easy to see that this recursive procedure ends after a finite number of steps. Namely, the length of the longest path in A_1 without repetitions of states is at most the number of the states in A. Finally, F_1 is defined to be the set of all copies of the states in F and k_1 is defined so that the values assigned to a state of A and to its copy in A_1 are equal. □

Next we will define the concept of *unrolling of cycles* in a given automaton. Let $A = (Q, \Sigma \cup \{\#\}, \delta, q_0, F, k)$ be an n-tape automaton in no-merge normal form. Consider a cycle

$$q_1, q_2, \ldots, q_{m+1},$$

where $m \geq 1$, $q_1 = q_{m+1}$, and $q_i \neq q_j$ $(i,j = 1, \ldots, m)$, of A together with a word $a_1a_2 \ldots a_m$ such that

$$\delta(q_i, a_i) = q_{i+1} \quad (i = 1, 2, \ldots, m).$$

Without lost of generality we may assume that q_1 is the (unique) state of this cycle reached first from the initial state q_0.

We say that the cycle $q_1, q_2, \ldots, q_{m+1}$ labeled by $a_1a_2 \ldots a_m$ is *unrolled once* if the automaton A is replaced by the automaton A_2 constructed in two steps below. First let

$$A_1 = (Q \cup \{q'_1, \ldots, q'_m\}, \Sigma \cup \{\#\}, \delta_1, q_0, F, k_1),$$

where $q'_1, \ldots, q'_m$ are new states and δ_1 is defined for each $a \in \Sigma \cup \{\#\}$ as follows:

$\delta_1(q,a) = q'_1$ if $\delta(q,a) = q_1$ and q is the predecessor of q_1 in the spanning tree of A;
$\delta_1(q,a) = \delta(q,a)$ for all $q \in Q$ such that q is not the predecessor of q_1;
$\delta_1(q'_m, a_m) = q_1$;
$\delta_1(q'_i, a) = \delta(q_i, a)$ if $\delta(q_i, a)$ is in the spanning tree of A before q_1; and
$\delta_1(q'_i, a) = q'_j$ if $\delta(q_i, a) = q_j, 1 \leq i, j \leq m-1$.
Moreover,

$$k_1(q) = k(q) \text{ for all } q \in Q;$$
$$k_1(q'_i) = k(q_i) \text{ for all } i = 1, 2, \ldots, m.$$

Finally, the automaton A_2 is obtained from A_1 so that for each $q_i (i = 1, \ldots, m)$ having one or more exits from the cycle, these exits and the transitions following them (together with the states) them are copied so that they start from q'_i $(i = 1, \ldots, m)$ and every transition back to some state q_j is replaced by the corresponding transition to the state q_j. Moreover, every transition back to a state before q_1 in the spanning tree of A is copied as such.

After unrolling the aa-cycle of automaton A in Figure 4 we get the automaton A_2 shown in Figure 5.

By the definition of unrolling, the set of n-tuples accepted remains unchanged. Moreover, the automaton obtained is also in no-merge normal form.

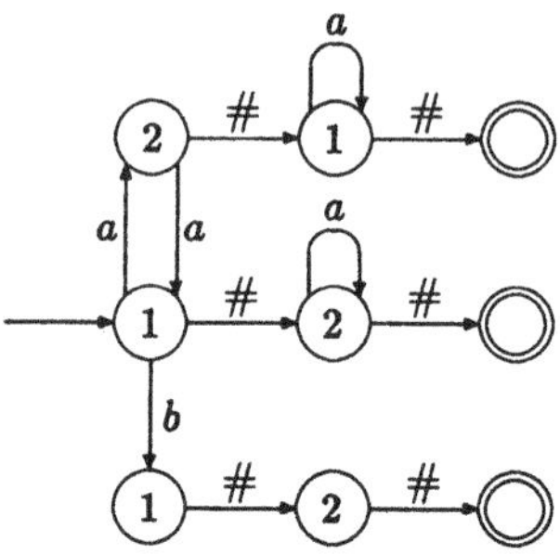

Figure 4: Automaton A

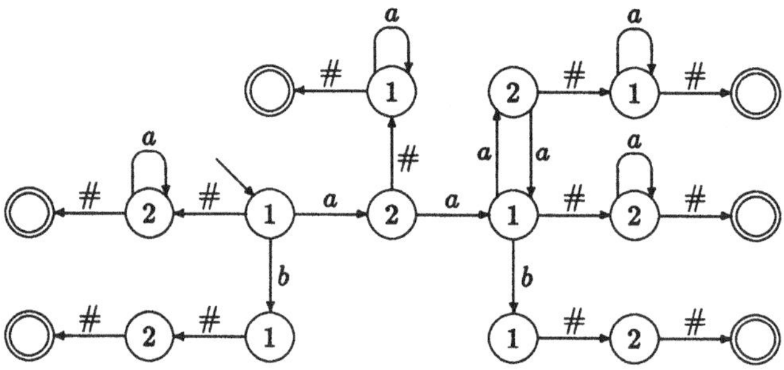

Figure 5: Automaton A_2

Let $R = R(A)$, where $A = (Q, \Sigma \cup \{\#\}, \delta, q_0, F, k)$ is a deterministic n-tape automaton, and let u be an n-tuple of words over Σ. Denote

$$\begin{aligned} R_u &= \{w \in R \mid w = uw' \text{ for some } n\text{-tuple } w'\} \\ R_{\neg u} &= R \setminus R_u \quad \text{(the \textit{complement} of } R_u \text{ with respect to } R) \\ u \setminus R &= \{w \mid uw \in R\} \quad \text{(the left \textit{quotient} of } R) \end{aligned}$$

The following lemma, needed in Section 4, shows that each of the three sets of n-tuples can be accepted by a deterministic n-tape automaton.

Lemma 2 *For a given deterministic n-tape automaton A and a given n-tuple u of words over Σ one can effectively construct deterministic n-tape automata A_1, A_2 and A_3 such that $R(A_1) = R_u, R(A_2) = R_{\neg u}$ and*
$R(A_3) = u \setminus R$.

Proof. We may assume that A is in no-merge normal form. The proof is based on unrolling of cycles. Consider first the case $|u| = 1$. Without loss of generality we may assume that u is of the form $u = (a, \varepsilon, \ldots, \varepsilon)$, where $a \in \Sigma$ and ε is the empty word. Let A' be the deterministic n-tape automaton obtained from A by unrolling the cycles of A in the following order:

(i) every cycle is unrolled before its subcycles;

(ii) if a cycle begins before another cycle and they are not subcycles of each other, the former cycle is unrolled first; and

(iii) if two or more cycles have the same beginning state but they are not subcycles of each other, the unrolling is done in the alphabetical order (or in some other fixed order).

An application of the step (i) (respectively (ii) or (iii)) usually produces many copies of subcycles (respectively, copies of other cycles). The unrolling procedure is then applied to all these copies at the same time and every cycle and its copies are unrolled only once. This guarantees that the unrolling procedure stops after a finite number of steps. It is also clear that each a-transition, where a is the first letter read from the first tape, is in the spanning tree. We recall that $u = (a, \varepsilon, \ldots, \varepsilon)$.

Now the automaton A_2 accepting $R_{\neg u}$ is obtained from A' simply by removing from the spanning tree of A' all a-transitions (as well as the whole subautomata after them), where a is the first letter read from the first tape.

The automaton A_1 consists of all those paths (together with the corresponding cycles) of A' from the initial state to some final state which contain an a-transition in a proper place.

The automaton A_3 is obtained as follows. If $\delta(q, a) = q'$ is an a-transition in A' in a proper place and

$$\delta(q, a_i) = q_1 \quad (i = 1, \ldots, r)$$

are all other transitions from q, then the label a is removed, the states q and q' are merged together and all a_i-transitions (together with the corresponding subautomata) are removed.

Finally, if $|u| = m$ with $m \geq 2$, then in the first and second case the unrolling procedure is repeated m times and the automata A_1 and A_2 are constructed using the spanning tree as before. In the case of the left quotient the proof is by a straightforward induction on the length of u. □

4 Equivalence test for simple automata

In this section we will prove the decidability of the equivalence problem for a restricted class of deterministic n-tape automata. The result obtained is a generalization of the one-letter case.

Definition 1 *We say that a deterministic n-tape automaton is simple if no two of its cycles have a common state.*

Lemma 3 *For every simple automaton A there effectively exists an equivalent simple automaton B in no-merge form.*

Proof. The conversion to no-merge normal form described in the proof of Lemma 1 preserves the property of being simple. □

Note that all the automata in our previous examples are simple. Also both 4-tape automata shown in Figure 6 are simple. They are equivalent, each accepts the relation

$$R = \{(a^i, a^j, a^k, a^l) \mid i = j \text{ or } k = l\}.$$

Lemma 4 *For every deterministic n-tape automaton A over a one-letter alphabet an equivalent simple automaton in no-merge normal form can be effectively constructed.*

Proof. By Lemma 1, we may assume that A is already in no-merge normal form. Without loss of generality we may assume that A does not read from a tape after it has seen an endmarker on that tape.

Now, if there are two cycles going through some common state, there is also a state q and two letters, say a and b, such that $\delta(q,a) \neq \delta(q,b)$ and a is a label in one cycle and b in the other. Since Σ contains only one letter, either a or b is the endmarker. This means that after the endmarker it is still possible to read letters from the same tape, a contradiction. $\square$

The algorithm of testing the equivalence for our restricted class of automata is based on the following concept.

Let A be a given simple n-tape automaton in no-merge form. The *depth of a path* from the initial state to some final state in A is the number of cycles in that path. The *depth of the automaton* A, denoted by $d(A)$, is the maximum of the depths of its paths.

For instance, both the automata in Figure 6 are of depth three.

The following lemma is an immediate consequence of the definitions.

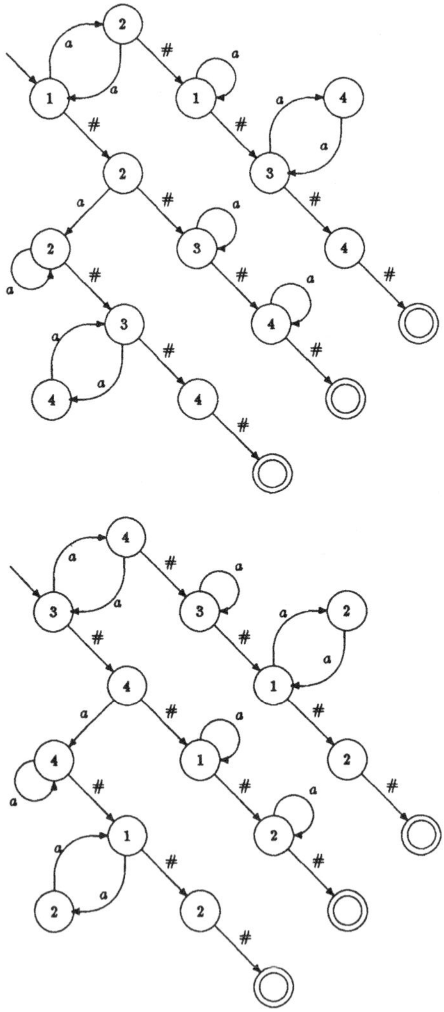

Figure 6: Equivalent 4-tape automata

Lemma 5 *The unrolling of cycles preserves the properties of being simple and in no-merge normal form. Moreover, the depth of an automaton remains unchanged.*

Theorem 1 *The equivalence problem is decidable for simple deterministic n-tape automata.*

Proof. Let A_1 and A_2 be two simple deterministic n-tape automata. By Lemma 3 we may assume that they are in no-merge normal form. Denote $R_1 = R(A_1)$ and $R_2 = R(A_2)$ and assume that $d(A_1) \geq d(A_2)$. The proof is by induction on the sum $d = d(A_1) + d(A_2)$ of the depths of A_1 and A_2.

If $d = 0$ then R_1 and R_2 are finite and the equivalence is clearly decidable.

Assume now that the equivalence is decidable for $d \leq d_0$ and let $d = d_0 + 1$. We have two cases to be considered.

Assume first that the initial state of A_1 begins a cycle labeled by an n-tuple u. This implies that

$$R_1 = u^* R_1$$

and more precisely

$$R_1 = u^*(R_1)_{\neg u}.$$

Here the set $(R_1)_{\neg u}$ is accepted by the automaton, say A_1', obtained from A_1 by removing the last transition, i.e. the transition back to the initial state, of the u-cycle. This follows from the fact that every exit-transition from the u-cycle has a label different from the corresponding label in the cycle.

If now

$$u^* R_2 \neq R_2$$

then

$$R_1 \neq R_2.$$

If

$$u^* R_2 = R_2 \tag{1}$$

then obviously

$$R_1 = R_2$$

if and only if

$$(R_1)_{\neg u} = (R_2)_{\neg u}. \tag{2}$$

So it is sufficient to test both of the equalities (1) and (2). This is done as follows.

Obviously,

$$u^* R_2 = R_2$$

if and only if

$$(R_2)_{\neg u} = ((R_2)_{u^i})_{\neg u^{i+1}} \tag{3}$$

for all $i \geq 0$. Now, since we consider automata with simple cycles, there is an effective upper bound, denoted by k, such that if (3) holds true for $i \leq k$, then it is valid for all $i \geq 0$. Namely, if we consider all the state sets of A_2 reached after reading the last symbol corresponding to the relations $u, u^2, \ldots$, then there are integers j and k, $j < k$, such that the state sets corresponding to u^j and u^k are equal. This k can then be taken as an upper bound. This implies that to test the equation (1) and (2) it is sufficient to test whether

$$(R_1)_{\neg u} = ((R_2)_{u^i})_{\neg u^{i+1}} \text{ for } i = 0, 1, \ldots, k. \tag{4}$$

But now the lefthand side is accepted by A_1' with $d(A_1') = d(A_1) - 1$, and each set in the righthand side by an automaton with depth smaller than or equal to $d(A_2)$ by Lemma 5. So (4) can be tested by induction.

Assume secondly that the initial state of A_1 does not begin a cycle. Let $\Sigma' \subseteq \Sigma$ be the set of all the labels of the edges beginning from the initial state of A_1. For each $a \in \Sigma'$ construct an automaton A_2^a such that

$$R(A_2^a) = a \setminus R_2.$$

Now

$$R_1 = R_2$$

if and only if

$$a \setminus R_1 = a \setminus R_2 \quad \text{for} \quad a \in \Sigma' \tag{5}$$

and

$$a \setminus R_2 = \emptyset \quad \text{for} \quad a \in \Sigma \setminus \Sigma'. \tag{6}$$

The equalities (6) can be easily tested. If the answer is positive, consider separately the equalities (5). Now an automaton accepting the set $a \setminus R_1$ for some $a \in \Sigma'$ is obtained simply by removing the a-transition from the beginning. Then we can repeat either the first or the second procedure depending on whether the automaton has a cycle in the beginning. □

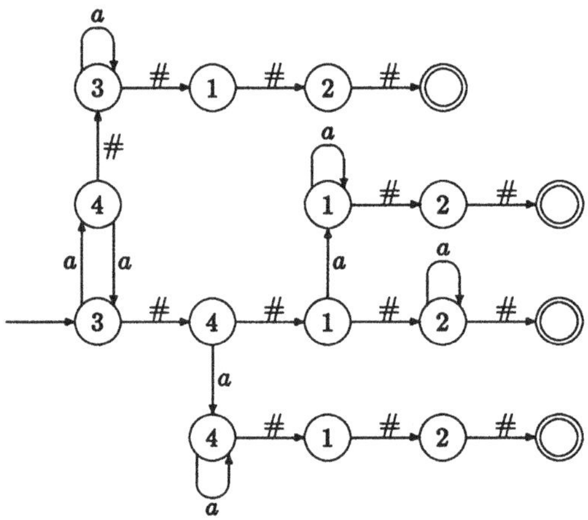

Figure 7: Automaton B

Example 4. If we apply the algorithm of the preceding proof to the automata A_1 and A_2 in Figure 6, then $u = (a, a, \varepsilon, \varepsilon)$ and the automaton A_1' is obtained simply by removing from A_1 the a-edge entering the initial state. An automaton B accepting the set $(R_2)_{\neg u}$ is shown in Figure 7 and it is obtained by the method of Lemma 2.

References

[1] M. Bird, The Equivalence Problem for Deterministic Two-Tape automata, *Journal of Computer and System Sciences* **7** (1973), 218-236.

[2] P.C. Fischer and A.L. Rosenberg, Multitape One-Way Nonwriting Automata, *Journal of Computer and System Sciences* **2** (1968), 88-101.

[3] S. Ginsburg, The Mathematical Theory of Context-Free Languages, McGraw-Hill, New York (1966).

[4] O.H. Ibarra, Reversal-Bounded Multicounter Machines and Their Decision Problems, *Journal ACM* **25** (1978), 116-133.

[5] O.H. Ibarra, The Unsolvability of the Equivalence Problem for ε-free NGSM's with Unary Input (Output) Alphabet and Applications, *SIAM J. Comput.* **7** (1978), 524-532.

[6] M.O. Rabin and D. Scott, Finite Automata and Their Decision Problems, *IBM J. Res. Develop.* **3** (1959), 114-125.

Relating the Degree of Ambiguity of Finite Automata to the Succinctness of their Representation

Oscar H. Ibarra and Bala Ravikumar

Department of Computer Science
University of Minnesota
Minneapolis, Minnesota 55455

Abstract

We consider the problem of how the size of a nondeterministic finite automaton (nfa) representing a regular language depends on the degree of ambiguity of the nfa. We obtain results for the unary and bounded inputs, and partial results for the unrestricted inputs. One of the main results of this paper shows that for unrestricted inputs, deterministic, unambiguous and nondeterministic machines form a hierarchy with respect to the number of states, solving an open problem of Stearns and Hunt. We also propose a new approach to the study of the succinctness of representation through regularity preserving closure properties and obtain some results in this direction.

1. Introduction

Ever since Rabin and Scott [RABI58] introduced the concept of a nondeterministic finite automaton (nfa), the problems concerning the representation or size complexity of regular languages have been studied extensively. Since regular languages have a plethora of different representations, the study of concise representations of regular languages seems to provide an endless stream of problems. In light of some recent developments relating the degree of randomness of strings to the size complexity of machines accepting them (this is the idea of Kolmogorov complexity, see e.g., [PAUL79].), there is a renewed interest in the study of succinct representations of regular languages. We begin with a brief summary of some earlier results in this area.

Meyer and Fischer [MEYE71] considered the blow-up in the number of states when converting an nfa to a deterministic finite automaton (dfa) and showed that, in the worst-case, the number of states in a minimum dfa equivalent to an nfa of n states is 2^n. The same problem has also been considered when the underlying alphabet is unary. In this case, the blow-up, although smaller than 2^n, is still exponential. To obtain an exact expression for the blow-up seems to be difficult. Moore [MOOR71], Mandl [MAND73], and recently Denes et al. [DENE85] have obtained a near-optimal bound of $\Theta\ (e^{(n \log n)^{1/2}})$ for this problem. Schmidt [SCHM78] compared the relative succinctness offered by several pairs of devices, which included, apart from finite-state devices, pushdown machines. Kintala and Wotschke [KINT86] defined the amount of nondeterminism as the minimum number of nondeterministic moves on any accepted input and established a hierarchy of succinctness based on the amount of nondeterminism. The same authors [KINT86] also introduced the concept of concurrent conciseness and compared the concurrent conciseness of degree automata, probabilistic automata and nfa's. Ehrenfeucht and Zeiger [EHRE76] obtained several results comparing the relative succinctness of finite automata and regular expressions. Stearns and Hunt [STEA85] studied the degree of ambiguity in an nfa defined as follows. An nfa is said to be k-ambiguous if, for each string accepted, there are at most k accepting computations. An nfa is said to be finitely ambiguous if it is k-ambiguous for some k. Chan and Ibarra [CHAN83] proved that it is decidable to test if a given nfa is finitely ambiguous. Ibarra and Ravikumar [IBAR86] further classified the nfa's (that are not finitely ambiguous) to polynomially ambiguous and exponentially ambiguous nfa's. An nfa is said to be polynomially ambiguous if there is a polynomial p(.) such that the number of accepting computations for any string of length n is at most p(n). We call an arbitrary nfa as exponentially ambiguous since the number of derivations of a string of length n is at most exponential in n. It was shown in [IBAR86] that the above classification is recursive. The present work was motivated by the following question regarding the above classification: How is the succinctness of representation related to the degree of ambiguity?

In this work, we compare the following families of devices: a) DFA (deterministic finite automata), b) UNA (unambiguous nfa, i.e., 1-ambiguous nfa's), c) FNA (finitely ambiguous nfa's), d) PNA (polynomially ambiguous nfa's), and e) ENA (exponentially ambiguous nfa's). For a collection X of devices (such as X = UFA, etc.), let X(b) denote the subset of X with the property that each device in this subset accepts a bounded language (i.e., a language whose strings are of the form $a_1^{i_1} a_2^{i_2} \cdots a_k^{i_k}$). Also, for two classes of devices A and B, let (A, B) denote the fact that B can be exponentially more succinct than A, and A = B denote the fact that each device in A can be converted to an *equivalent* device in B with a polynomial blow-up and vice-versa. We present results comparing UNA(b), FNA(b), PNA(b) and ENA(b). Specifically, We show that (UNA(b) , FNA(b)), FNA(b) = PNA(b), and PNA(b) = ENA(b) hold. For unrestricted inputs, we conjecture that (FNA , PNA) and (PNA , ENA), and offer candidates for proving the claim. We also provide an evidence for the later conjecture by proving a special case of it.

Concurrent conciseness of a family A of devices over two families B and C was defined in [KINT86] as a simultaneous succinctness of A over B and C. By 'simultaneous', we mean that the same language family bears witness to the succinctness of A over B, and also of B over C. Concurrent conciseness is an important generalization of the concept of conciseness, and it was an open problem stated in Stearns and Hunt [STEA85] whether DFA, UNA and ENA form a hierarchy with respect to concurrent conciseness. We show that DFA, UNA and PNA form a concurrently concise hierarchy, thus resolving the open problem of Stearns and Hunt in the affirmative.

We also propose a new approach to the succinctness problem through 'closure properties'. We define the closure (with respect to an operation •) for a class A of finite-state devices (not for a class of languages) as follows. Let • be a regularity preserving operation, and let M_1, $M_2 \in$ A. Then $L(M_1) \bullet L(M_2)$ is regular, and assuming that A is universal in the sense that it can accept the class of all regular languages, there is an M ∈ A such that $L(M) = L(M_1) \bullet L(M_2)$. The question is: "What is the size of the smallest such M, as a function f of the numbers of states of M_1 and M_2?" If f is bounded by a polynomial, then we say that A is closed under • Closure properties show interesting contrast between various subclasses of nfa's. For example, we show that the class DFA is not closed under concatenation or Kleene star, but ENA is closed under these operations. Apart from the fact that many results regarding succinctness can be sharpened through the closure properties, we feel that this study is of interest in its own right. We prove several closure and nonclosure properties for the various classes of devices mentioned above.

The main results are presented in Sections 3, 4 and 5, following some preliminaries in Section 2.

2. Preliminaries

We begin with some basic definitions and notations. Define a dfa M to be a 5-tuple $M = <Q, \Sigma, \delta, q_0, F>$, where Q is a finite set of states, Σ is a finite alphabet, $q_0 \in Q$ is the start state, $F \subseteq Q$ is the set of accepting states and δ is defined as $\delta : Q \times \Sigma \to Q$. An nfa is defined as a 5-tuple $<Q, \Sigma, \delta, q_0, F>$, where all the components are exactly as above except δ, which is defined as a map $\delta : Q \times \Sigma \to 2^Q$. We do not allow ϵ-moves in an nfa. We further assume that the fa's are reduced, i.e., they do not have useless states (thus, all the states are reachable from the start state on some input and from each state, an accepting state can be reached on some input). $|M|$ denotes the number of states in M. This will be used as the size complexity of a machine. The ambiguity function $a_M(n)$ of an nfa M was defined in [IBAR86] as the maximum number of *accepting* computations for any string w such that $|w| = n$ and $w \in L(M) =$ the language accepted by M. An nfa is said to be k-ambiguous (for a fixed k) if $a_M(n) \leq k$, for all n. 1-ambiguous nfa's are called unambiguous. An nfa is polynomially ambiguous if there exists a polynomial p(.) such that $a_M(n) \leq p(n)$ for all n. The unrestricted nfa is called exponentially ambiguous since the number of derivations for a string of length n is bounded by c^n for some c (which depends on the number of states in the machine).

Let Γ be a countably infinite collection of symbols. We use DFA to denote the collection of dfa's whose input alphabet is a finite subset of Σ. In the same way, the collections of unambiguous, finitely, polynomially and exponentially ambiguous nfa's are denoted by UNA, FNA, PNA and ENA respectively. Clearly DFA $\subseteq$ UNA $\subseteq$ FNA $\subseteq$ PNA $\subseteq$ ENA. To make a more definite reference to the type of ambiguity of a nfa, we use the following definition. An nfa of a given type X (in the above sequence of inclusions) is said to be *strictly* of type X if it is of type X, but not of any *preceding* type. For example, a polynomially ambiguous nfa is strictly polynomially ambiguous if it is not finitely ambiguous. We will also be interested in the following subsets of these class of collections. When the input of any fixed device in any of these collections is restricted to a unary alphabet, we obtain the families DFA(u), UNA(u), etc. It should be clear that there can be two devices M_1 and M_2 in DFA(u), for example, such that M_1 has $\{a_1\}$ as its alphabet while M_2 has $\{a_2\}$ as its alphabet. When the underlying languages accepted by these collections are bounded (i.e., languages of the form $a_1^* a_2^* \cdots a_r^*$, where $a_i \in \Sigma$), we obtain the collections DFA(b), UNA(b), etc. We denote the collections of two-way dfa's (whose head can move on either directions on the input tape) by 2-DFA and those of sweeping dfa (which are restricted 2-dfa whose head can reverse only on the endmarkers) by SDFA. Their restrictions to unary and bounded languages will be denoted by 2-DFA(u), 2-DFA(b), etc. The name of a collection of devices in l letters (such as dfa, una, etc.) will denote an arbitrary individual device of a particular type.

The following definition of f-conciseness is essentially due to [KINT86]:

Definition. A class of automata C_1 is f-concise over another class C_2 if and only if there is an infinite sequence of languages $\{L_n\}$ such that

(i) for all n, there exists a n-state automaton M_n in C_1 accepting L_n.

(ii) for infinitely many n, every M in C_2 accepting L_n must have at least f(n) states.

We write A-f(n)→B to denote the fact that A is f-concise over B. Since we are mainly interested in contrasting polynomial growths with exponential growths, we also need the following *coarser* definition. We denote by (A , B) the fact that A is f-concise over B for some f that cannot be bounded by a polynomial. If (A , B) is not true, then we write $B \leq A$. Thus, if $B \leq A$, then any M $\in$ B can be converted to an equivalent M' in A with at most a polynomial increase in the number of states. We write $A = B$ to denote the fact that $A \leq B$ *and* $B \leq A$. If $B \leq A$ and if it is not true that $A \leq B$, then we write $B < A$. Observe that it is possible that (A , B) and (B , A) are both true. In this case, we write $A <> B$. (A and B are *incomparable*.)

3. Succinctness Problem for Unary and Bounded Languages

In this section, we compare the representation powers of the classes UNA(b), FNA(b), PNA(b) and ENA(b). We first prove that (UNA(u) , FNA(u)) and that FNA(u) = PNA(u) = ENA(u). We then extend these results to the case of bounded languages. We also present some results comparing 2-DFA(u) with some of the classes stated above. These results are in contrast with the results of Sakoda and Sipser [SAKO78] and Sipser [SIPS79]. At present, the relationship between DFA(u) and UNA(u) is not known. We conjecture that DFA(u) = UNA(u). Finally we also make some remarks comparing PNA and ENA.

We need the following preliminary results.

Our first lemma is from [SCHM78].

Lemma 1. Let $M = <Q, \Sigma, \delta, q_0, F>$ be an unambiguous nfa with m states. The shortest word not accepted by M is no longer than m+1.

Proof. See Lemma 4.5 of [SCHM78]. □

Our next result is from [IBAR86] (see also [WEBE86]). This result provides a characterization of polynomial and exponential ambiguities of nfa's. Before we state the result, we need the following notation. In an nfa $M = <Q, \Sigma, \delta, q_0, F>$, for p, q $\in$ Q and w $\in \Sigma^*$, define N(p,w,q) to be the number of ways in which w can be derived starting from p, ending in q.

Lemma 2. Let $M = <Q, \Sigma, \delta, q_0, F>$ be an nfa.

(i) A necessary and sufficient condition for M to be strictly exponentially ambiguous is that there exists a $q \in Q$ and a string $w \neq \epsilon$ such that $N(q,w,q) \geq 2$.

(ii) A necessary and sufficient condition for M to be strictly polynomially ambiguous is that M is not exponentially ambiguous and there exist states p, q and a word $w \neq \epsilon$ such that $p \in \delta(p, w)$, $q \in \delta(p, w)$ and $q \in \delta(q, w)$.

Figures 1 and 2 show examples of polynomially and exponentially ambiguous nfa's.

Our next lemma is from [MAND73].

Lemma 3. If M is an nfa over a unary alphabet, $|M| = n$, in which the start state q_0 is in a loop (i.e., there is a $w \neq \epsilon$ such that $q_0 \in \delta(q_0 , w)$), then there exists a dfa M′ such that $|M'| < n^2$ and $L(M') = L(M)$.

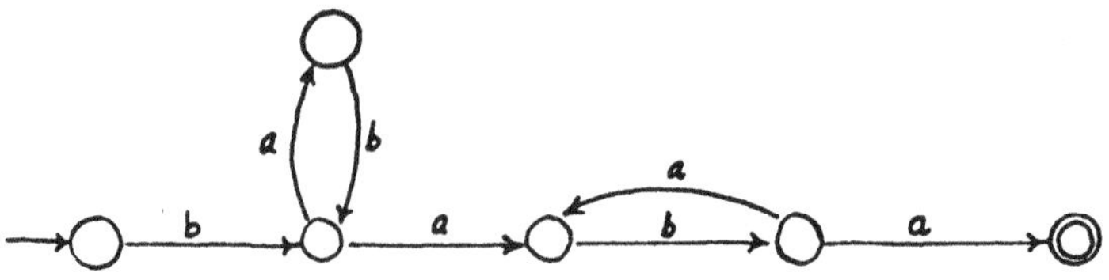

Figure 1. Example of a polynomially ambiguous nfa.

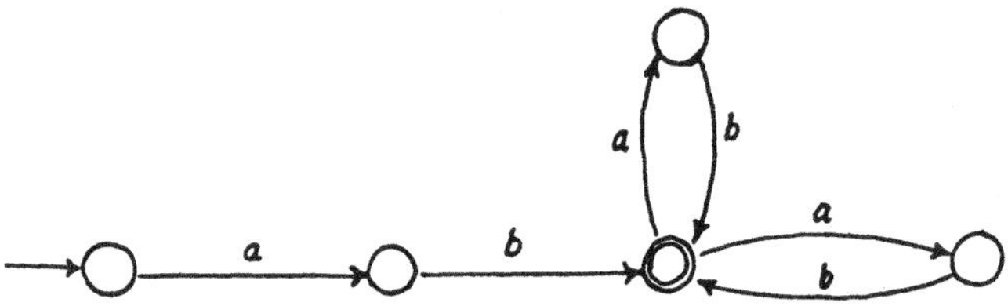

Figure 2. Example of an exponentially ambiguous nfa.

The above result has been observed to be true [MAND73] even when M has more than one start state, with the modified hypothesis that all the start states are in a loop. We now prove the result comparing UNA(u), FNA(u), PNA(u) and ENA(u).

Theorem 1. UNA(u) < FNA(u) and FNA(u) = PNA(u) = ENA(u).

Proof. We first show that UNA(u) < FNA(u). Since UNA(u) $\leq$ FNA(u), it is enough to show that (UNA(u) , FNA(u)). Define a collection of languages as follows. Let p_i denote the ith prime number and L_k be defined as:

$L_k = \{ a^n \mid n \not\equiv 0 \pmod{p_j} \text{ for some } j \leq k \}$.

It is easy to see that L_k can be accepted by an fna with $\sum_{i=1}^{k} p_i$ states. Such an fna for k = 3 is shown in Figure 3.

By the prime number theorem [KRAN85], $p_i = O(i \log i)$, so $\sum_{i=1}^{k} p_i = O(\sum_{i=1}^{k} i \log i) = O(k^3)$.

We next show that any una accepting L_k requires at least $\prod_{i=1}^{k} p_i - 1$ states. To show this, let M be any una accepting L_k. We see that the shortest string not accepted by L_k is $a^{p_1 p_2 \cdots p_k}$. Thus, by Lemma 1, the size of M must be at least $\prod_{i=1}^{k} p_i - 1 \geq 2^k - 1$. This proves that (UNA(u) , FNA(u)). Using the f-conciseness notation of [KINT86] (see Section 2), the above result can be stated in a sharper form as FNA(u)-$(2^{n^{1/3}}-1)$→UNA(u).

We next show that FNA(u) = PNA(u) = ENA(u).

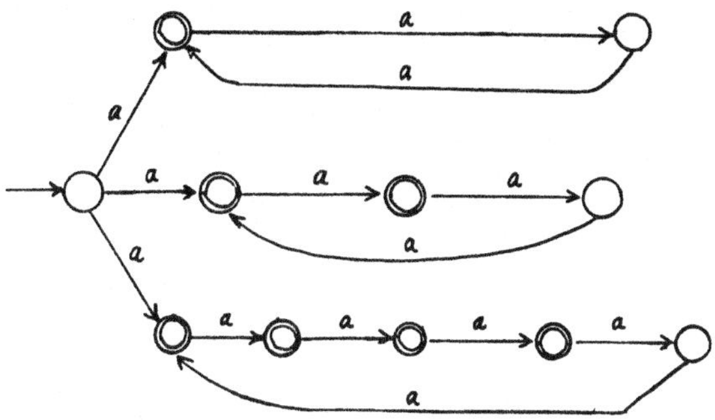

Figure 3. An fna accepting L_3.

The proof makes use of Lemma 3. Let M be an exponentially (or polynomially) ambiguous nfa with $|M| = n$. We consider the *condensation graph* of M (introduced by [KUIC70]). Let Q be the set of states of M. We consider the graph associated with M. We define a relation $R \subseteq Q \times Q$ as follows: $(q_i, q_j) \in R$ if and only if q_i and q_j are reachable from each other. It is easy to see that R is an equivalence relation. Let $V = \{Q_1, \ldots, Q_m\}$ be the partition of Q induced by R. Define C(M), the condensation graph of M as $C(M) = <V, E>$ where $E = \{<Q_i, Q_j> \mid$ there exists p in Q_i and q in Q_j such that there is a (directed) path from p to q$\}$. Note that C(M) is acyclic. Let Q_0 be such that q_0 is in Q_0. To convert M to an fna M′, we proceed as follows:

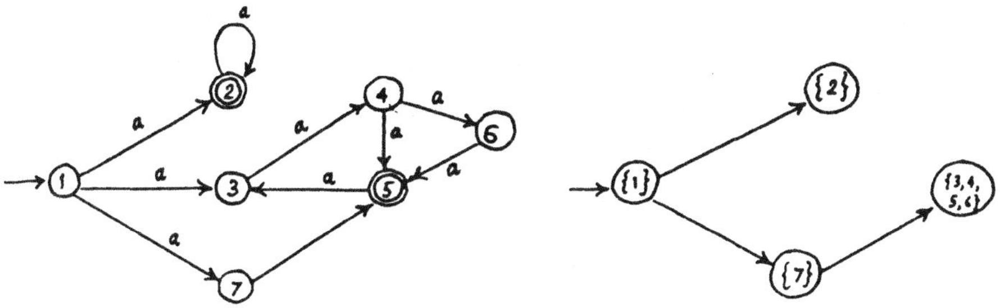

Figure 4. A machine M and its condensation graph C(M).

First define a subset T of V recursively as follows: Q is in T if and only if (i) $|Q| > 1$, and (ii) for any predecessor Q' of Q, $|Q'| = 1$.

For each Q in T, we define two associated regular languages $A_1(Q)$ and $A_2(Q)$ as follows. $A_1(Q)$ denotes the regular language accepted by an nfa whose states are the states of M that are reachable from the states of Q and whose start states are the states in Q that have arcs entering from some predecessor of Q in C(M). $A_2(Q)$ is a finite subset of a* defined by: $A_2(Q) = \{ a^i \mid$ there exists a path of length i from Q_0 to Q in C(M) }. The following example shows $A_1(Q)$ and $A_2(Q)$ for the machine M of Figure 4. For Q = {3,4,5,6}, $A_1(Q)$ is accepted by the machine in Figure 5, and $A_2(Q) = \{a, a^2\}$.

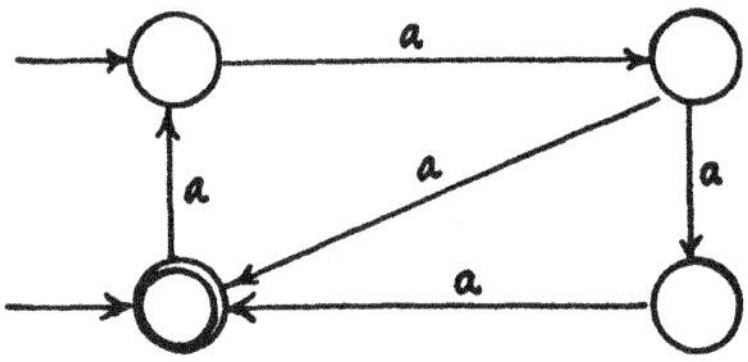

Figure 5. A machine accepting $A_1(Q)$ (with multiple start states).

We observe that $L(M) = \bigcup_{Q \in V} A_1(Q).A_2(Q)$. To construct M′ , we first construct dfa's (of size at most $O(n^2)$ as seen from Lemma 2) to accept $A_1(Q)$, for all Q. Then we construct M′ by adding n more states and providing additional arcs to generate the strings in $A_2(Q)$. We avoid formal construction and illustrate it in Figure 6 by showing M′ corresponding to M of Figure 4.

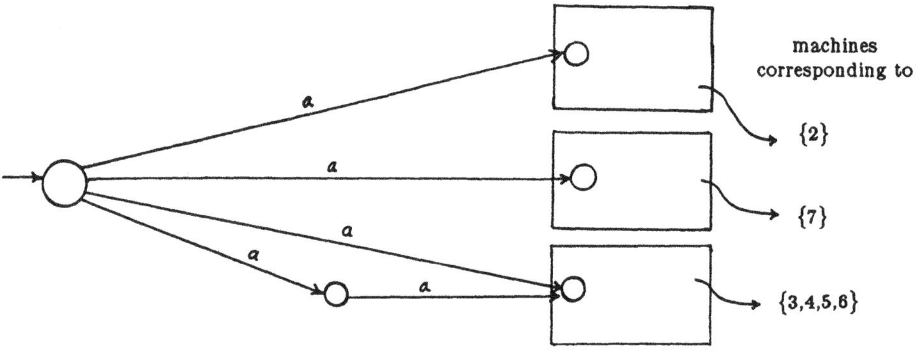

Figure 6. M′ corresponding to M of Figure 4.

It can be seen that the resulting fna satisfies our requirements. □

As a corollary to Theorem 1, we have:

Corollary 1. Let M be a finitely ambiguous nfa over unary alphabet, $|M| = n$. We can find a finite collection $\{M_i\}$, i=1,2,... of ufa's, $|M_i| \leq n$, such that $L(M) = \bigcup_i M_i$.

The above corollary addresses to a finite-state analog of a problem of Eilenberg [EILE74] as to whether every finitely ambiguous cfl can be expressed as a finite union of unambiguous cfl's. The above corollary may not hold for nfa's over larger alphabets. We next show how to extend Theorem 1 to bounded languages.

Theorem 2. (UFA(b) , FNA(b)) and FNA(b) = PNA(b) = ENA(b)

Proof. The fact that (UFA(b) , FNA(b)) follows from Theorem 1. In the rest of the proof, we show that FNA(b) = PNA(b) = ENA(b). For simplicity, we consider bounded languages L such that $L \subseteq a^*b^*$. The proof can be extended to arbitrary bounded languages in an obvious way. Let $L \subseteq a^*b^*$

be regular and let M be an ena accepting L and let $|M| = n$. We show that L can be accepted by a fna with at most p(n) states for some polynomial p(.). The intuitive idea behind the proof is simple, and we illustrate it with an example. Intuitively, any states of an nfa accepting $L \subseteq a^* b^*$ can be partitioned in to two sets A and B as follows: for some state q, if all the arcs incident into q are labeled a, then q is in A, else it is in B. For the nfa given in Figure 7, the partition is as shown in Figure 8.

Clearly if p,q are in A (in B) and if $q \in \delta(p, t)$, then t=a (t=b). As a next step, we introduce additional states in A and B so that in the resulting machine, there are only ϵ-arcs from A to B. See Figure 9. Then using Theorem 1, we can convert the nfa's induced by the states of A and of B to fna's. Finally, the removal of ϵ-arcs (which does not increase the number of states nor the degree of ambiguity) yields a fna. □

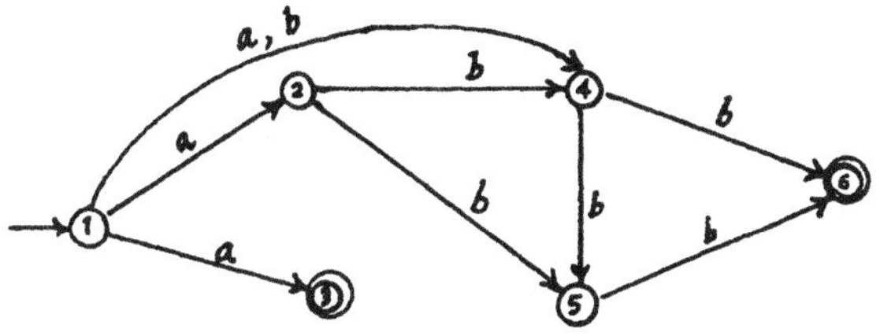

Figure 7. An nfa.

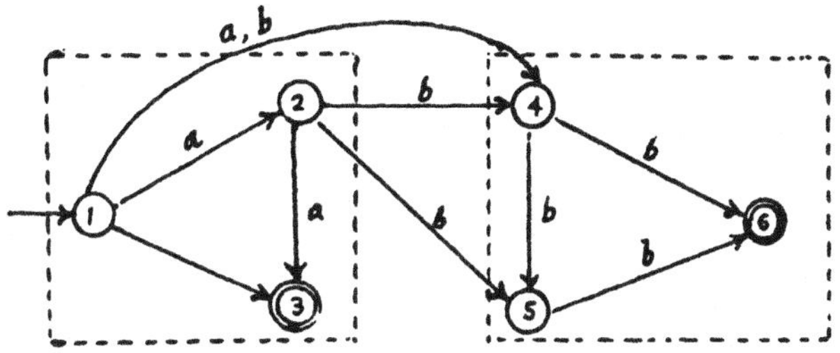

Figure 8. Partition of states in the nfa of Figure 7.

We conclude this section with a brief discussion of the relative conciseness of the collections 2-DFA(u) and NFA(u). The problem of 2-DFA vs. NFA was considered in [SAKO78] and [SIPS79]. [SAKO78] showed that (ENA , 2-DFA) and conjectured that ENA <> 2-DFA, but this claim is (to the best of our knowledge) still open. [SIPS79] proved that (SDFA , ENA), a weaker claim. Berman [BERM79] and Seiferas [SIPS79] showed that (SDFA , 2-DFA). In contrast to the above claims, we prove the following result.

Theorem 3. (ENA(u) , DFA(u)), ENA(u) < 2-DFA(u) and 2-DFA(u) = SDFA(u).

Proof.

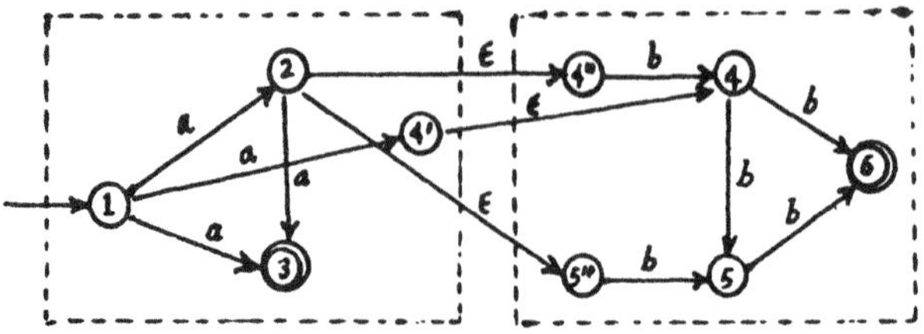

Figure 9. An nfa with ε-moves corresponding to the nfa of Figure 7.

(i) Using the collection of languages $\{L_k\}$, $k=1,2,\ldots$, (of Theorem 1), it is easy to show that (ENA(u) , 2-DFA(u)).

(ii) To prove the desired claim, we have to show two results, viz., ENA(u) $\leq$ 2-DFA(u) and (ENA(u) , 2-DFA(u)). We first outline a proof of the former result. We have to show that any given nfa M over a unary alphabet can be converted to a 2-dfa with a polynomial blow-up in the number of states. Using Theorem 1, we first convert M to a fna M′ as shown in Figure 6. Now it is easy to construct a 2-dfa that simulates this fna by choosing the various computational paths during different sweeps. We next prove that (ENA(u) , 2-DFA(u)). Consider the collection F_k of languages defined as: $F_k = \{a^n \mid n \text{ is divisible by } p_j \text{ for } \textit{all } j \leq k\}$. It is easy to show that F_k can be accepted by a $\sum_{j=1}^{k} p_j$ state 2-dfa, and any nfa accepting F_k requires at least $\prod_{j=1}^{k} p_j$ states. This completes the proof of (ii).

(iii) The proof is easy and left to the reader. □

We conclude this section with some remarks regarding the succinctness problem for unrestricted inputs. The result (DFA , UNA) was proved by Meyer and Fischer [MEYE71] using the following candidate: $L_m = L(r_m)$ be defined by the regular expression $r_m = (0+1+\epsilon)^m\, 1\, (0+1)^{m-1}$. L_m has the property that it can be accepted by a ufa with 2m+1 states and that any dfa that accepts L_m requires at least 2^m states. The result (UNA , FNA) immediately follows from Theorem 1 since it holds even for languages over unary alphabet. We conjecture that (FNA , PNA) and (PNA , ENA) hold and offer the following candidate languages.

For (FNA , PNA): Let $L_k = L(r_k)$ where $r_k = (0+1)^*1(0+1)^k1(0+1)^*$. Figure 10 shows a pna with k+3 states accepting L_k:

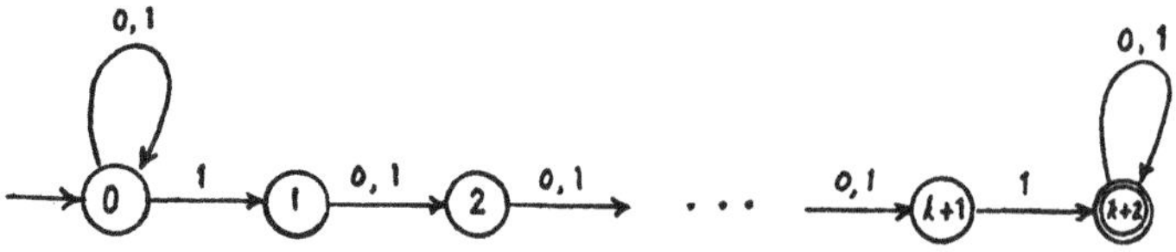

Figure 10. A pna for L_k.

We conjecture that any fna accepting L_k requires $\Omega(2^k)$ states.

For (PNA , ENA): Let $L_k = \{\, a^n \mid n \not\equiv 0 \pmod{p_j} \text{ for some } j \leq k \,\}$, where p_j is the j-th prime number. (Recall that this collection of languages was used in Theorem 1.) Now let $A_k = (\#L_k\#)^*$. It is easy to see that there exists an ena of size $O(\sum_{i=1}^{k} p_i) = O(k^3)$ states accepting A_k.

We conjecture that the number of states in any pna accepting A_k is not bounded by a polynomial in k. Although we do not have a proof of this result, we provide some evidence for this result by showing that among a restricted class of pna's, none with fewer than $2^{k/2}$ states can accept A_k. The restricted machines M can be defined as follows: There is only one state q in Q, the set of states of M, such that for any q', q'' in Q, if $q'' \in \delta(q', \#)$, then $q'' = q$. Informally it means that there is only one state in M with arcs labeled "#" entering in to it. We now prove the following claim regarding restricted pna's:

Claim. Let M be a restricted pna accepting A_k. Then $|M| \geq 2^{k/2}$.

Proof. Let $M = <Q, \Sigma, \delta, q_0, \{f\}>$. Clearly f is the only state such that for some $q \in Q$, $f \in \delta(q,\#)$. Define $Q_1 = \{q \mid f \in \delta(q,\#)\}$ and $Q_2 = \{q \mid q \in \delta(f,\#)\}$. For any $p \in Q_2$ and $q \in Q_1$, define $M_{p,q}'$ as: $M_{p,q}' = <Q, \Sigma, \delta, p, \{q\}>$. Next define $M_{p,q}$ from $M_{p,q}'$ as follows: (i) Remove all the edges labeled # from $M_{p,q}'$ and (ii) reduce the resulting nfa.

First observe that $Q_1 \cap Q_2 = \emptyset$, for if $q \in Q_1 \cap Q_2$, then for some string $w \in A_k$, $f \in \delta(q_0, w)$ and hence, $f \in \delta(q_0, w\#\#)$, which implies that $w\#\# \in A_k$, a contradiction. We claim that $M_{p,q}$ is a ufa for all $p \in Q_1$ and $q \in Q_2$, as seen from the following argument. For, if $M_{p,q}$ is ambiguous, then there is a word $w \neq \epsilon$ such that $N(p,w,q) \geq 2$. In this case, for the original machine M, $N(f,\#w\#,f) \geq 2$. Thus, by Lemma 2, M is exponentially ambiguous, a contradiction. Further, using the same argument, we observe that $L(M_{p,q}) \cap L(M_{r,s}) \neq \emptyset$ for p,q,r and s such that $(p,q) \neq (r,s)$. Now it is easy to construct a ufa M' with the following properties: (i) $|M'| \leq \sum_{p,q} |M_{p,q}| + 1$ and (ii) $L(M') = A_k$. The construction of M' is by simply introducing a new start state and having ϵ-transitions to the start states of all $M_{p,q}$'s and then removing the ϵ-transitions. We now show that $L(M) = A_k$. Since it is obvious that $L(M') \subseteq A_k$, we need only to show that $A_k \subseteq L(M')$. Let $\#w\# \in A_k$. Then, $\#w\#\#w\#$ is also in A_k. Since M is a restricted machine, any computation (i.e., any sequence of states) on the input $\#w\#$ will terminate in f, and hence $f \in \delta(f, \#w\#)$. Thus $w \in L(M_{p,q})$ for some p,q and so $w \in L(M')$. This completes the proof that $A_k = L(M')$. The bound on the number of states in M' is obvious. Thus, if $|M| = t$, then $|M'| \leq t^2$. From Lemma 1, we see that $t^2 \geq |M'| \geq \prod_i p_i$ and thus $t \geq 2^{k/2}$. This proves the desired claim. □

Table 1 summarizes the results on succinctness for unary and bounded languages.

4. Concurrent Conciseness of Representations

Concurrent conciseness was introduced in [KINT86] as an important generalization of 'usual' conciseness for the following reasons:

> 'Assume that we have three classes of automata C_1, C_2 and C_3. One is often able to prove the conciseness of C_2 over C_1 using a sequence of languages $\{A_n\}$, and the conciseness of C_3 over C_2 using another sequence of languages $\{B_n\}$. The problem is that $\{A_n\}$ and $\{B_n\}$ have often very little in common since $\{A_n\}$ exploits the advantages of C_2 over C_1 and $\{B_n\}$ exploits the advantages of C_3 over C_2. Concurrent conciseness addresses the question whether there is *one* sequence of languages which concurrently establishes the conciseness of

	UNA	FNA	PNA	ENA	2-DFA
DFA	?	<	<	<	<
UNA		<	<	<	<
FNA			=	=	<
PNA				=	<
ENA					<

Table 1. Succinctness results for unary and bounded inputs.

C_2 over C_1 and that of C_3 over C_2.'

Following [KINT86], we quantify the concurrent conciseness as follows.

Definition. Say that C_1 is f,g-*concurrently concise* over C_2 and C_3 denoted by C_1-f(n)→C_2-g(n)→C_3 for some f(n) and g(n) if C_1 is f-concise over C_2 and C_2 is g-concise over C_3 for the same sequence of languages.

Since our primary concern in this paper has been to contrast the polynomial growth and the superpolynomial growth, we need the following coarser definition. We write (A, B, C) to denote the fact that A-f(n)→B-g(n)→C, where f and g are both super-polynomials. Thus (A, B, C) means that, in a strong sense, A, B and C form a hierarchy with respect to concise representations. Our next result is to show that (DFA, UNA, PNA). This result settles an open problem mentioned by Stearns and Hunt [STEA85].

Theorem 4. DFA-$2^{\sqrt{n}/4}$→UNA-$(n/16)^{\log n-4}$→PNA

Proof. Consider the collection $\{J_k\}$ of languages defined as:

$J_k = \{ x\ 1\ y \mid x, y \in \{0,1\}^*, |y| = k^2$ and x has a substring of the form 1z1 where $|z| = k \}$. We show the following:

Claim 1. J_k can be accepted by a $O(k^2)$-state pna.

Proof. We describe informally a pna accepting J_k. M_k uses O(k) states to verify the existence of the substring 1z1, and counts k^2 characters following a 1 to accept strings in J_k. It is easy to see that M_k satisfies our requirements. (end of claim 1)

Claim 2. Any dfa accepting J_k requires at least 2^{k^2} states.

Proof. It is easy to prove this claim. We briefly outline the idea behind the proof. Let M_k be a dfa accepting J_k. During its computation, M_k should 'remember' the last k^2 characters in finite control, otherwise M_k can be 'fooled'. (end of claim 2)

Claim 3. There exists a $(2^{k+3} + k^2 + 1)$-state ufa accepting J_k.

Proof. We first construct a dfa M_k' with 2^{k+3} states to accept the language $\{ x1y1z \mid x, y, z \in \{0,1\}^*, |y| = k \}$. M_k' has as its states q_σ where σ in $\{0,1\}^*$ with $|\sigma| \leq k+2$. q_λ is the start state. The δ-function of M_k' is constructed in such a way that $\delta(q_\lambda, w) = q_w$ if $|w| = k+2$, else $\delta(q_\lambda, w) = q_{w'}$ where w' is a suffix of w of length k+2. The accepting states of M_k' are $F = \{q_w \mid w = 1w'1$ for some w' of length $k\}$. We modify M_k' to M_k as follows:

A. Introduce new states $p_0, p_1, \ldots, p_{k^2}$, and introduce the following transitions:

$\delta(p_i, 0) = \delta(p_i, 1) = \{p_{i+1}\}$ if $i < k^2$,

B. Remove the transitions from all the states of F in M_k' and add the following transitions:

$\delta(p, 0) = \{p\}$, $\delta(p, 1) = \{p, p_0\}$ for all p in F.

C. The only accepting state of M_k is the state p_{k^2}.

Figure 11 shows the construction of M_k from M_k' :

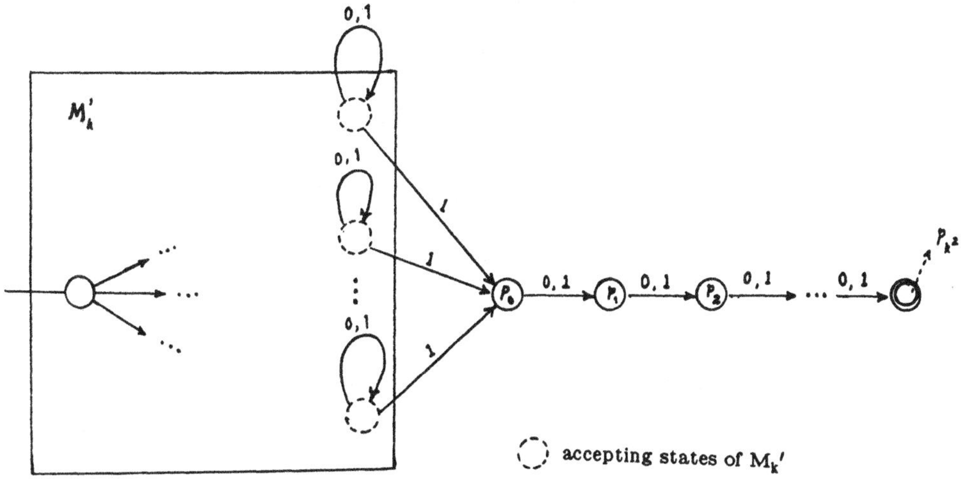

Figure 11. M_k constructed from M_k' .

Clearly M_k is an ufa such that $L(M_k) = J_k$. (end of claim 3)

The final step in the proof is the following claim:

Claim 4. Any ufa accepting the language J_k has at least $2^{k/4}$ states.

Proof. The basic machinery used in this proof is a vector-space argument which was originally proposed by Schmidt [SCHM78] (Theorem 3.9). This technique has also been used by Sipser in [SIPS79].

Let M be a ufa accepting J_k. We want to show that $|M| \geq 2^{k/4}$. In the rest of the proof, we follow the notation used in Theorem 3.9 of [SCHM78].

Let $x \in \{0,1\}^{k+1}$, and assume that $K_x = \{q_1, q_2, \ldots, q_{f(x)}\}$ is the set of states reachable from q_0 via x. Define for each i, $(1 \leq i \leq f(x))$, the set $A_i^x = \{ y$ in $\{0,1\}^{k+1} \mid$ there exists a $q \in F \cap \delta(q_i, y10^{k^2}) \}$. Thus A_x^i is the set of words of length k+1 which lead from the state q_i (in K_x) to acceptance. Define $A = \{ \{A_x^i\}, i = 1,2,\ldots,f(x)\}, x \in \{0,1\}^{k+1}$, the collection of sets $\{A_x^i\}$. Let $B_1, B_2, \ldots, B_m$ be a listing of the members of A without repetitions. Let $K = \{ q \mid q \in \delta(q_0, x)$ for some x in

$\{0,1\}^{k+1}$ }. For any $q \in K$, associate the set $B_j = \{ y$ in $\{0,1\}^{k+1} \mid$ there exists a q in $F \cap \delta(q, y10^{k^2})$ }. Since this mapping is on-to, $m \leq |K|$. Also since $|K| \leq |M|$, we have $m \leq |M|$. We complete the proof of claim 4 by showing that $m \geq 2^{k/4}$.

To do this, we interpret the subsets of $\{0,1\}^{k+1}$ as elements of the 2^n-dimensional vector-space over the field Z_2. Let x_i, $i \leq 2^{k+1}-1$, be the binary representation of i with a padding of 0's (at the left) to make $|x_i| = k+1$. With each $C \subseteq \{0,1\}^{k+1}$, we associate the vector $\overline{C} = (c_{2^{k+1}-1}, c_{2^{k+1}-2}, \ldots, c_1, c_o)$, where $c_j = 1$ if and only if $x_j \in C$. For simplicity, assume that k is odd. The proof can be easily modified to handle the case when k is even.

Now let $T \subseteq \{0,1\}^{k+1}$ be defined as: $T = \{ w \mid$ number of 0's in w is $(k+1)/2 \}$. For any $x \in T$, consider the set $A_x = \bigcup_{i=1}^{f(x)} A_x^i$ defined as above. A_x thus consists of y's such that $x\ y\ 1\ 0^{k^2} \in J_k$. Since M is unambiguous, the sets $A_x^1, \ldots, A_x^{f(x)}$ are mutually disjoint and further, all the A_x^i's occur among the B_i's, the vector $\overline{A_x}$ can be written as a linear combination of vectors $\{\overline{B_i}\}$, i=1,2,...,m, i.e., there exist $t_1, t_2, \ldots, t_m$ such that:

$$\overline{A_x} = \sum_{j=1}^{m} t_j \overline{B_j} \qquad (1)$$

Consider the set of vectors $V = \{ \overline{A_y} \mid y \in T \}$. We shall show that V is linearly independent, as follows. Let $y_1, y_2, \ldots, y_r$ ($r = \binom{k}{k/2}$) be an arbitrary but fixed ordering of T. We define a boolean matrix U of order $r \times 2^k$ as follows:

$$U = \begin{bmatrix} \overline{A_{y_1}} \\ \overline{A_{y_2}} \\ \overline{A_{y_3}} \\ \cdots \\ \overline{A_{y_r}} \end{bmatrix}$$

Thus the rows of U are the vectors $\overline{A_{y_1}}, \overline{A_{y_2}}, \ldots, \overline{A_{y_r}}$. Proving that V is linearly independent is equivalent to proving that the rank of U is r. We prove the latter by showing that there exists a sub-matrix $\overline{U}$ of U of order $r \times r$ such that the columns of $\overline{U}$ are permutations of the complement of the identity matrix, $\overline{I_n}$ given by

$$\overline{I_n} = \begin{bmatrix} 011 \cdots 1 \\ 101 \cdots 1 \\ \cdots\cdots \\ 111 \cdots 0 \end{bmatrix}$$

For any i, $1 \leq i \leq r$, define g(i) as the integer obtained by complementing the bits in the string y_i. Now the submatrix is defined by the set of columns $\{g(i)\}$, i=1,2,...r. We claim that, in the column g(i) of U, the only 0 entry is $U_{i,g(i)}$. For a string x, let $\overline{x}$ denote the string obtained by interchanging the 0's and 1's in x. Clearly, the string $y_i\ \overline{y_i}10^{k^2}$ notin J_k since for any pair of positions $(t,\overline{t})$ separated by k in $y_i\ \overline{y_i}$, the t-th and $\overline{t}$-th letters are complementary. Thus, $U_{i,g(i)} = 0$. Next we observe that $U_{j,g(i)} = 1$ for any $j \neq i$. This follows from the fact that $y_j\overline{y_i}10^{k^2}$ is in J_k as seen from the following argument. Since $y_j \neq y_i$, it follows that there exists a t, $1 \leq t \leq k$, such that the t-th letter of y_j is the same as the t-th letter of $\overline{y_i}$. Thus, $y_j\overline{y_i}10k^2 \in J_k$. Thus the dimension of the submatrix $\{g(i)\}$, i=1,2,...,r is r = the dimension of the vector space $V = \binom{k}{k/2}$. Thus from (1) it follows that the number of B_i's must also be at least $\binom{k}{k/2}$. Thus, $m \geq \binom{k}{k/2} \geq 2^{k/4}$. (end of claim 4)

The claim made in Theorem 5 follows from the proofs of claims 1 - 4. □

Since both $2^{\sqrt{n}/4}$ and $(n/16)^{\log n-4}$ are superpolynomial, we obtain the following Corollary.

Corollary 2. (DFA , UNA , PNA)

This corollary settles the open problem of [STEA85] of whether it is possible to have a simultaneous non-polynomial blow-ups among the three collections, DFA, UNA and ENA. In fact, our result shows a stronger result.

It appears that the same candidate languages $\{J_k\}$ can be used to prove (DFA , FNA , PNA). This can be done by showing a claim stronger than Claim 4 of Theorem 5, namely: Any fna accepting J_k requires f(k) states for some superpolynomial f(). Also open is the following concurrent conciseness claim: (FNA , PNA , ENA). Of course, this is harder than the open problem (FNA , PNA) mentioned in Section 4.

5. Closure Properties of Classes of Finite-state Devices

In this section, we consider the closure properties of various classes of finite-state devices. We ask the question: "If L_1 and L_2 are accepted by *small* machines of type A, is it true that $L_1 \bullet L_2$ can also accepted by a *small* machine of type A?", where • is a regularity preserving operation. If the answer is "yes", then we say that A is closed under •, otherwise not. Many of the succinctness claims made earlier can be sharpened by this study. This study is also motivated by the following consideration. It is well-known that the conversion of an nfa to a dfa blows-up the number of states exponentially. But it is not clear if such a blow-up occurs only in 'pathological cases'. Now suppose we have two dfa's A and B and suppose we want to construct a machine to accept L(A).L(B). It is easy to obtain an nfa C from A and B. This nfa is 'natural' (not pathological since it occurs as a consequence of a natural operation), and it is interesting to know if the blow-up is exponential even when converting such natural nfa's. Unfortunately, the answer is yes. Thus we feel that this study is of interest in its own right. The following definition is essentially due to Sakoda and Sipser [SAKO78].

Definition. Let A be a collection of devices, and • be a regularity preserving operation. We say that A is closed under • if there exists a polynomial p(.) such that the following holds: For any $M_1, M_2 \in A$, there is an $M \in A$ such that $L(M) = L(M_1) \bullet L(M_2)$ and $|M| \leq p(\max\{|M_1|, |M_2|\})$.

We study the closure of the collections DFA, UFA, FNA, PNA, ENA and 2-DFA under the following fundamental regularity preserving operations: union, intersection, complementation, concatenation, Kleene Star and reversal. The following table contains a summary of results. A Y denotes that the closure property holds and an N denotes that it does not. ? indicates that the problem is open. A number by the side of a Y or N mark denotes the location of a proof in the next theorem. (Proofs of obvious closure properties are omitted.)

Theorem 5. The closure properties as indicated in the table hold.

Proof.

(1) Let L_1 and $L_2 \subseteq \{0,1\}^*$ be defined by the following regular expressions $r_1 = (0+1)^*$ and $r_2 = 1(0+1)^{n-1}$. There exist dfa with 2 and n states respectively, accepting L_1 and L_2. It is also easy to see (using the Myhill-Nerode theorem [HOPC79]) that $L_1.L_2$ cannot be accepted by a dfa with p(n)

	DFA	UNA	FNA	PNA	ENA	2-DFA
union	Y	Y	Y	Y	Y	Y
intersection	Y	Y	Y	Y	Y	Y
complement	Y(7)	?	N(7)	N(7)	N(7)	Y(3)
reversal	N(4)	Y(4)	Y(4)	Y(4)	Y(4)	Y(4)
concatenation	N(1)	N(5)	?	Y	Y	?
Kleene star	N(2)	N(6)	?	?	Y	?

Table 2. Closure properties.

states for any polynomial p(.).

(2) To prove this result, we first define a large alphabet, similar to the alphabet used in [SAKO78] to obtain a "hardest language" for the problem of conversion from 1-nfa to 2-dfa.

Let B_n be the set of bipartite graphs with 2n vertices, whose vertex partition has n vertices each. Pictorially, the graphs are represented as in Figure 12, with the vertices occuring in two columns (left and right). The directed edges are from left to right and each vertex has outdegree at most 1. Figure 12 shows two members of the alphabet B_4.

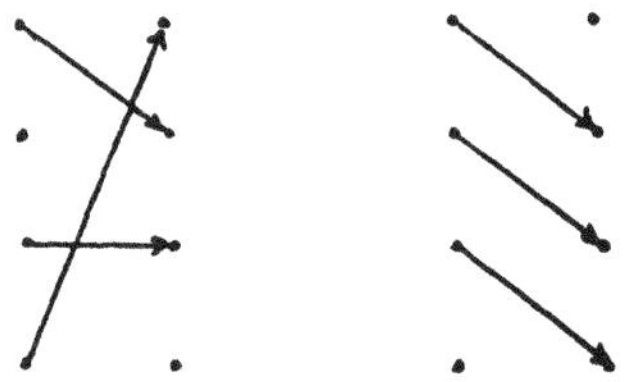

Figure 12. Two members of B_4.

For two graphs G_1 and G_2, the product $G_1 \otimes G_2$ is defined as a graph obtained by superposing the right boundary of G_1 with the left boundary of G_2. Figure 13 shows the graph $G_1 \otimes G_2$ for G_1 and G_2 of Figure 12.

The notion of product can be extended in an obvious way to several graphs. In a product graph, the start vertex is the vertex in the first column of the leftmost boundary and the terminal vertex is the last column of the rightmost boundary (u and v respectively in the above figure.)

Now we define a collection of languages L_k as follows: $L_k = \{ G_1 \cdots G_r \mid G_i \in B_k$ for all i, and $G_1 \otimes G_2 \otimes \ldots \otimes G_r$ has a directed path from start to terminal vertex $\}$. It is easy to see that L_k can

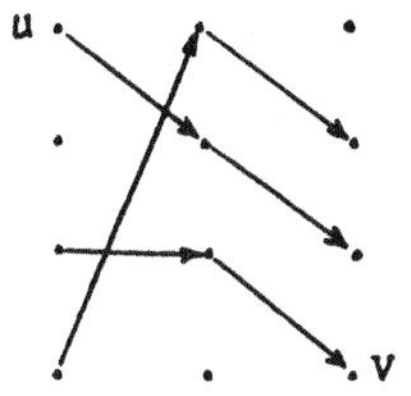

Figure 13. The graph of $G_1 \otimes G_2$.

be recognized by a dfa with k states. We show that any dfa recognizing L_k^* has at least 2^k states. The proof is based on Myhill-Nerode theorem [HOPC79]. For any string $G_1 \cdots G_r$, define $\sigma(G_1 \cdots G_r) \subseteq \{1,2,...,k\}$ as follows. In the product graph $G_1 \otimes ... \otimes G_r$, add new edges from the last row to the first row on all columns except the first and last columns. An integer i, $1 \leq i \leq k$, is in $\sigma(G_1 \cdots G_r)$ if in the resulting graph, there is a path from the start vertex to the vertex on the ith row of the last column. Let M be a dfa that accepts L_k^*, and let δ be its transition function. It is easy to see that if $\delta(q_0, G_1 \cdots G_m) = q_i$, and $\delta(q_0, G_1' \cdots G_n') = q_j$, and if $\sigma(G_1 \cdots G_m) \neq \sigma(G_1' \cdots G_n')$, then q_i and q_j are not equivalent. Thus, there are at least 2^k equivalence classes and the claim follows from Myhill-Nerode theorem. Finally, we observe that the large alphabet B_k can be mapped to $\{0,1\}$ and the lower bound claim still holds.

(3) This result was proved by Sipser [SIPS80] as an application of a general result that any deterministic off-line TM using bounded space can be made halting.

(4) For DFA, the nonclosure immediately follows from the collection of languages due to Meyer and Fischer [MEYE71] presented in the proof of Theorem 4. The closure for the other families follow from the fact that if M is an nfa and F the set of accepting states in M, then M′ accepting $L(M') = (L(M)^r$ can be accepted as follows: (i) introduce a new start state q, and add the transitions q' $\delta(q, \epsilon)$ for all q' $\in$ F, and (ii) reverse the directions of all the edges in M. Clearly M′ preserves the type of ambiguity of M as seen from Lemma 2, and $|M'| \leq |M| + 1$.

(5) To prove that ufa's are not closed under concatenation, we need a result of [SCHM78]: Let $C_k = \{ x \# y \mid |x| = |y| = k, \text{ and } x \neq y \}$. It was shown in [SCHM78] that any ufa accepting C_k requires at least 2^k states. We define the languages

$L_1 = \{ x \mid |x| \leq k \}$,

$L_2 = \{ ay \# x_1 b x_2 \mid a, b \in \{0,1\}, a \neq b, |y| \leq k-1, |y| = |x_2|, |x_1| + |x_2| = k-1 \}$.

$L_3 = \{ x \# y \mid |x| = |y| = k \}$.

It is easy to see that L_1, L_2 and L_3 can all be accepted by ufa's with O(k) states and that $L_1 \cdot L_2 \cap L_3 = C_k$. Since ufa's are closed under intersection, the desired claim follows from Schmidt's result.

(6) The nonclosure of ufa's under Kleene star follows from the fact that $C_k = (L_1 \cup L_2)^* \cap L_3$.

(7) It is easy to see that the results on complement hold even over unary alphabet. □

6. Concluding Remarks

In this paper, we compared the relative succinctness of nondeterministic finite automata of various degrees of ambiguities and established that the machines with greater degrees of ambiguity tend to be more succinct. These results are refinements and improvements of earlier results of similar kind such as presented in [MEYE71], [SCHM78] etc. We presented a result on the concurrent conciseness of NFA over UFA and DFA, solving an open problem due to Stearns and Hunt. We also studied the succinctness of various classes of finite state- devices through regularity preserving transformations.

Among the problems that remain open, we mention the following:

(1) Prove that DFA(u) = UNA(u). Schmidt [SCHM87] has suggested that Lemma 4.5 in [SCHM78] may be useful in proving this.

(2) Prove that (FNA , PNA) and (PNA , ENA).

(3) Prove that FNA is not closed under concatenation.

It appears that the the candidate language $D_k \subseteq \{0,1\}^*$ is suitable for both problems (2) and (3). The collection D_k is: $D_k = \{ w \mid w = x\,1\,y\,1\,z,\ x, y, z \text{ in } \{0,1\}^*, |y| = k \}$. It is easy to see that D_k can be accepted by a pna with O(k) states. It remains to be shown that any fna accepting D_k requires at least $\Omega(r^k)$ for some $r > 0$. In addition to solving open problems (2) and (3), this claim would also settle an open problem stated in Section 5, namely to prove that (DFA , FNA , PNA).

Acknowledgement

This work was supported in part by NSF grants DCR-8420935 and DCR-86040603.

References

[BERM79] Berman, P., A note on sweeping automata, *ICALP* 1979, pp. 91–97.

[CHAN83] Chan, T. and O. Ibarra, On the finite-valuedness problem for sequential machines, *Theoretical Computer Science*, 1983, pp. 95–101.

[DENE85] Denes, J., K.H. Kim and F.W. Rouch, Automata on one symbol, *Studies in Pure Mathematics* 1985, pp. 127–134.

[EHRE76] Ehrenfeucht, A. and P. Zeiger, Complexity measures for regular expressions, *Journal of Computer and System Sciences*, 12, 1976, pp. 134–146.

[EILE74] Eilenberg, S., *Automata, Languages and machines*, Vol. A, Academic Press, NY 1974.

[HOPC79] Hopcroft J. and J. Ullman, *Introduction to Automata Theory, Formal Languages and Computation,* Addison-Wesley, 1979.

[IBAR86] Ibarra, O. and B. Ravikumar, On sparseness, ambiguity and other decision problems for acceptors and transducers, *Third Annual Symposium on Theoretical Aspects of Computer Science,* Orsay, France, 1986, pp. 171–179.

[KINT80] Kintala C. and D. Wotschke, Amounts of nondeterminism in finite automata, *Acta Informatica,* 1980, pp. 199–204.

[KINT86] Kintala C. and D. Wotschke, Concurrent conciseness of degree, probabilistic, nondeterministic and deterministic finite automata, *Fourth Symposium on Theoretical Aspects of Computer Science*, 1986, pp. 291–305.

[KRAN85] Kranakis, E., *Primality and Cryptography*, Yale University Technical Report, 1985.

[KUIC70] Kuich, W., On the entropy of context-free languages, *Information and Control*, 1970, pp. 173–200.

[MAND73] Mandl, R., Precise bounds associated with the subset construction on various classes of nondeterministic finite automata, *Seventh Princeton Conference on Information and System Science*, 1973, pp. 263–267.

[MEYE71] Meyer, A. and M. Fischer, Economy of description by automata, grammars, and formal Systems, *Proc. of Twelfth IEEE Symposium on Switching and Automata Theory*, 1971, pp. 188–191.

[MOOR71] Moore, F., On the bounds for state-set size in the proofs of equivalence between nondeterministic and two-way automata, *IEEE Transactions on Computers*, 20, 1971, pp. 1211–1214.

[PAUL79] Paul, W., Kolmogorov complexity and lower bounds, *2nd International Conference on Fundamentals of Computation Theory*, 1979.

[RABI59] Rabin, M. and D. Scott, Finite automata and their decision problems, *IBM Journal of Research and Development*, 3, 1959, pp. 114–125.

[SAKO78] Sakoda, W. and M. Sipser, Nondeterminism and the size of two-way finite automata, *Proceedings of Tenth Annual ACM Symposium on Theory of Computing*, 1978, pp. 275–286.

[SCHM78] Schmidt, E., Succinctness of descriptions of context-free, regular and finite languages, Ph. D. Thesis, *Cornell University*, 1978.

[SCHM87] Schmidt, E., (private communication).

[SIPS79] Sipser, M., Lower bounds on the size of sweeping automata, *Proc. of Eleventh Annual ACM Symposium on Theory of Computing*, 1979, pp. 360–364.

[SIPS80] Sipser, M., Halting space-bounded computations, *Theoretical Computer Science*, 1980, pp. 335–338.

[STEA85] Stearns, R. and H. Hunt, On the equivalence and containment problems for unambiguous regular expressions, regular grammars and finite automata, *SIAM Journal of Computing*, 14, 1985, pp. 598–611.

[WEBE86] Weber, A. and H. Seidl, On the degree of ambiguity of finite automata, *Proc. of Math. Foundations of Comp. Science*, 1986, pp. 620–629.

AUTOMATA, GAMES, AND POSITIVE MONADIC THEORIES OF TREES [1]

Michel PARIGOT
Equipe de Logique, CNRS UA 753
Université Paris 7, UFR de Mathématiques,
2 place Jussieu, 75251 PARIS Cedex 05

Abstract: The present paper uses a game theoretic approach to make a fine study of the monadic theory of the infinite binary tree. We characterize some natural classes of monadic formulas in terms of alternating automata; in particular we give a hierarchy of automata corresponding to the hierarchy of alternation of quantifiers for weak monadic formulas. These characterizations lead to efficient decision procedures.

Introduction:

The connection between the monadic theory of the infinite binary tree (called S2S) and automata is now well understood. The story begins in 1969, when Rabin [9] introduced automata working on infinite trees and proved in this way the decidability of S2S. But the proof remained for a long time mysterious, being a succession of cumbersome constructions.

It was Büchi [1] and [2] who brought the mathematical principles to the light, reducing the complementation to a kind of determinancy result. But this is really with the paper of Gurevich and Harrington [3] that the subject becomes transparent. They consider certain games between two players, where the existence of a "special" winning strategy is equivalent to the existence of an accepting run of the automaton; the complementation problem appears, in this way, as a "special" determinancy result.

The games we define in this paper are slightly different from those of [3], in that they use alternating automata instead of nondeterministic ones. Alternating automata have been introduced by Muller and Schupp [6] as an alternative approach to S2S where the complementation is easy, being reducible to a classical determinancy result. In our perspective, alternating automata become games: an accepting run of the alternating automaton is nothing else but a winning strategy in a certain game, and complementation is just classical determinancy of this game.

[1] This work was supported by the PRC "Mathématiques et Informatique". A first version has been presented at the meeting of this PRC held at Paris in April 1986.

Certainly, "special" winning strategies are again needed, this time for projection. Gurevich-Harrington's result fully applies here, and for the full theory S2S it makes no difference whether one uses alternating or nondeterministic automata. The situation changes when we investigate subtheories of S2S and in that case alternating automata turns out to be better, as the results of this paper will show (for instance the characterization of the Σ_n hierarchy of weak monadic formulas in terms of alternating automata – theorem 4 – has no counterpart in terms of non-deterministic automata).

The main advantage of this game theoretic approach is the simplicity of the constructions involved: they are in a certain sense optimum and, for that reason, allow a fine study of monadic theories of trees, giving precise definability results and efficient decision procedures. The new results we obtain in that way are:

Theorem 2 *Let L be a tree language. The following are equivalent:*
(1) L is defined by a positive monadic formula.
(2) L is recognized by an alternating automaton with Büchi acceptance.
(3) L is recognized by a non-deterministic automaton with Büchi acceptance

This characterization of positive monadic formulas fill in the gap between the two results of Rabin for weak monadic formulas [10] and for monadic formulas [9]. The way we associate alternating automata to formulas in the proof of theorem 2 leads to a decision procedure for positive monadic formulas with n alternations of quantifiers, whose complexity in time is exactly n exponentials.

Theorem 4 *Let L be a tree language. The following are equivalent:*
(1) L is defined by a weak monadic formula having n alternations of quantifiers
(2) L is recognized by an alternating automaton with Büchi acceptance having n alternations of accepting and refusing states

Theorem 4 states an exact correspondance betweeen alternation of quantifiers of the classical Σ_n hierarchy of weak monadic formulas (which has been shown to be strict by Thomas [11], using the hierarchy of recursively enumerable degrees) and alternation of accepting and refusing states for automata. This is the first result of that kind for monadic theories of trees, and we can hope to use it for a model-theoretic study of this theories.

Together with the results of Rabin [9], [10], and of Muller, Schupp and Saoudi [7], this two theorems give a almost complete panorama of the correspondance between monadic formulas and automata in the context of monadic theories of trees. In [8] we use them to investigate temporal logic.

Our paper is self-contained with one exception, the uniform determinancy of G_δ games, which is proved in [3]. We thank Dan Drai and Paul Schupp for helpfull discussions. Our interest in alternating automata grew from conversations with Paul Schupp.

1. BASIC DEFINITIONS.

Trees. Let X be a finite set. The set X^* of finite sequences of elements of X is partially ordered as follows: $s \leq t$ if and only if $t = su$ for some $u \in X^*$. The empty sequence is denoted by Λ, and the last element of a sequence s by $e(s)$. If $s,t \in X^*$, $x \in X$ and $t = sx$, then t is called a *successor* of s.

A *tree* is a subset A of X^* (for a certain finite set X) such that: if $uv \in A$ and $u \neq \Lambda$, then $u \in A$. An element of a tree is often called a *node*; a *terminal node* is a node without successor; a *root* is a node which is not the successor of another node. A *branch* of a tree A is a maximal linearly ordered subset of A. A *frontier* of a tree A is a subset C of A such that for each branch Π of A, $\Pi \cap C$ contains a unique node; since each node of A has a finite number of successors, C is a finite set. If A is a finite tree, the set of terminal nodes of A is a frontier of A, called *the frontier* of A and denoted by $Fr(A)$.

Let A be a tree and s a node of A; the tree A_s is the set of all t satisfying $st \in A$. If B is a tree, the result of substituting B for A_s in A is the tree defined by $C = \{t \in A;\ s \not\leq t\} \cup \{su;\ u \in B\}$.

In this paper D and Σ will be arbitrary but fixed finite sets whose elements are called respectively *directions* and *letters*. A *Σ-tree* is a pair (T,α) where T is the tree D^* and α: $T \longrightarrow \Sigma$ a labelling.

Automata. An *alternating automaton* is a tuple $M = (Q,\Sigma,\delta,I,W)$,where Q is a finite set of states, Σ is a finite set of letters, $I \in \mathcal{P}(\mathcal{P}(Q))$ is the initial configuration, δ: $Q\times\Sigma \longrightarrow \mathcal{P}(\mathcal{P}(Q\times D))$ is the transition function, and $W \subseteq Q^\omega$ is the accepting set. A *determinisation* of the transition function δ is a function f: $Q\times\Sigma \longrightarrow \mathcal{P}(Q\times D)$ satisfying $f(q,\sigma) \in \delta(q,\sigma)$. The set of all determinisations of δ is denoted by $det(\delta)$. If $d \in D$ and $f \in det(\delta)$, then f_d denotes the function from $Q\times\Sigma$ to $\mathcal{P}(Q)$ defined by $f_d(q,\sigma) = \{p;\ (p,d) \in f(q,\sigma)\}$. A *nondeterministic automaton* is a particular alternating automaton where the transition function is a map from $Q\times\Sigma$ to $\mathcal{P}(Q^D)$, and the initial configuration is a set of singletons.

The intuition behind alternating automata is the following: an element $\delta(q,\sigma)$ of $\mathcal{P}(\mathcal{P}(Q\times D)$ has to be interpreted as a disjunction of conjunctions; the automaton being at state q and reading a letter σ choose <u>one</u> element X of $\delta(q,\sigma)$ and make at the same time <u>all</u> the transitions indicated in X (X consists of pairs (q,d) indicating "move in direction d and enter in state q"). The difference with the non-deterministic case is that an alternating automaton can make more than one computation at each node of the tree.

The power of an automaton depends on the topological complexity of its accepting set. In order to obtain the power of arbitrary monadic formulas one needs accepting sets which are boolean combinations of G_δ sets (G_δ sets are countable intersections of open sets). We will see that for positive monadic formulas, it suffices to consider automata with G_δ accepting sets: precisely, we say that an alternating automaton (Q,Σ,δ,I,W) is ***positive*** (resp. ***negative***) if there exists $F \subseteq Q$ such that $\nu \in W$ if and only if the set of all states that appear infinitely often in ν meets F (resp. does not meets F). For weak monadic formulas, the corresponding alternating automata have boolean combinations of open sets as accepting sets: we say that an alternating automaton is ***weak*** if there exist $\mathcal{F} \in \mathcal{P}(\mathcal{P}(Q))$ such that $\nu \in W$ if and only the set of states which appear in ν belongs to $\mathcal{F}$. We will often write the accepting condition (F or $\mathcal{F}$) instead of the accepting set W, and use (M,q) to denote the automaton M with {{q}} as new initial configuration.

Games. The precise working of an alternating automaton is the best explained as a game. Given a Σ-tree (T,α) and an alternating automaton $M = (Q,\Sigma,\delta,I,W)$ we consider the following game $J(M,\alpha)$ between two players I and II playing respectively subsets and elements of $Q\times D$. The game $J(M,\alpha)$ is the set of (finite or infinite) sequences (called ***plays***) $\xi = X_0c_0X_1c_1\ldots X_nc_n\ldots$ satisfying $X_0 = X\times\{\Lambda\}$ with $X \in I$ and for each $i\geq 0$, $c_i = (q_i,d_i) \in X_i$ and $X_{i+1} \in \delta(q_i,\alpha(d_1\ldots d_i))$. The sequence $c_1c_2\ldots c_n\ldots$ is the ***computation*** associated to α (computations will be considered both as elements of $(Q\times D)^{\leq\omega}$ and elements of $Q^{\leq\omega}\times D^{\leq\omega}$).

A ***strategy*** for player I (resp. II) in the game $J(M,\alpha)$ is a function F assigning to each finite play ξ of even (resp. odd) length a subset (resp. element) $F(\xi)$ of $Q\times D$ in such a way that $\xi F(\xi)$ is a play. A play ***in accordance with*** the strategy F for I (resp. II) is a play $X_0c_0\ldots X_nc_n\ldots$ such that for all $i\geq 0$, $X_i = F(X_0c_0\ldots X_{i-1}c_{i-1})$ (resp. $c_i = F(X_1c_1\ldots X_i)$). A computation ***in accordance with*** F is a computation associated to a play in accordance with F.

An infinite computation ν is ***accepting*** if $\nu \in W\times D^\omega$, and ***refusing*** in the other case. A strategy F for I (resp. II) in $J(M,\alpha)$ is ***winning*** if all the infinite computations in accordance with F are accepting (resp. refusing). An automaton M ***accepts*** a Σ-tree (T,α) if I has a winning strategy in $J(M,\alpha)$; the set of Σ-trees accepted by M is called the ***language recognized*** by M.

The main mathematical result we will use in this paper is the determinancy of certain games: if the accepting set of M is Borel, then the game $J(M,\alpha)$ is determined, i.e. one of the players has a winning strategy. Determinancy of Borel games is a very difficult result due to Martin [4], but we just need here a simple and well known version (already proved in 1954 by Wolfe) for G_δ games.

Fact 1. Let M be a positive alternating automaton. Then one of the players has a winning strategy in the game $J(M,\alpha)$.

Computation trees. A strategy F for I in the game $J(M,\alpha)$ can be considered as a ***computation tree*** R of the automaton M on the tree (T,α): R is the tree of all finite computations in accordance with F. A computation tree R can be defined directly as a tree satisfying

(i) the set of roots of R is $X \times \{\Lambda\}$ for a certain $X \in I$.

(ii) the set of successors of an element (u,s) of R is $\{(uq,sd)\ ;\ (q,d) \in X\}$, for a certain $X \in \delta(e(u),\alpha(s))$.

A computation tree can also be considered as a *run* of the automaton M on the tree (T,α), i.e. a function $r: T \longrightarrow \mathcal{P}(Q^*)$ assigning to each node s of T the set of $u \in Q^*$ such that $(u,s) \in R$ (in the case of a nondeterministic automaton r(s) is a singleton and will be identified with its unique element). A computation tree will be denoted by an uppercase letter and the run by the corresponding lowercase letter. An element u of r(s) is called an *s-computation* and e(u) is called the *result* of the s-computation.

Uniform computation trees. A computation tree R of M on (T,α) is called *n-uniform* if for all $s \in D^n$, s-computations with the same result have the same extensions, i.e. for all $(u,s),(v,s) \in R$, if $e(u) = e(v)$ then $R_{(u,s)} = R_{(v,s)}$. A computation tree is *uniform* if it is n-uniform for each n. Uniform computation trees correspond to functions from T to $Det(\delta)$.

Note that it is immediate to transform a winning computation tree R in a winning n-uniform computation tree - independently of the accepting set of the automaton. The same result is true (but not immediate) with uniform in the place of n-uniform for positive automata:

Fact 2 (Gurevich-Harrington, theorem 4 of [3]). Let M be a positive alternating automaton. If there exists a winning computation tree of M on (T,α), then there exists a winning uniform computation tree of M on (T,α).

From a mathematical point of view, the main difference between the cases of weak monadic formulas and positive monadic formulas, precisely is that the proof of the equivalence with alternating automata requires the existence of winning uniform computation trees in the latter case.

Monadic formulas. We consider a Σ-tree (T,α) as monadic second order structure of domain T with the following primitives

- the ordinary inclusion $\subseteq$ between sets of nodes
- for each direction d, a binary relation S_d between sets of nodes defined by $X\ S_d\ Y$ if and only if $Y = \{sd;\ s \in X\}$
- for each letter $\sigma \in \Sigma$, a constant P_σ of set of nodes defined by $P_\sigma = \{s;\ \alpha(s)=\sigma\}$

Monadic formulas are built upon these primitives using propositional connectives, existential quantification over finite and arbitrary sets, and universal quantifi-ation over finite and arbitrary sets. Variables ranging over finite sets are denoted by X,Y,..., and variables ranging over arbitrary sets by U,V,...Note that first order quantification is interpretable in such a monadic language.

2. BASIC CONSTRUCTIONS.

Complementation. For alternating automata there is a very nice solution to the complementation problem due to Muller and Schupp [6], which becomes transparent in terms of games. Let $M = (Q,\Sigma,\delta,I,W)$ be an alternating automaton where W is a Borel accepting set. By determinancy of games, M does not accepts a tree (T,α) if and only if II has a winning strategy in $J(M,\alpha)$. It is easy to see that a winning strategy for II in $J(M,\alpha)$ is equivalent to a winning strategy for I in $J(\tilde{M},\alpha)$ where $\tilde{M} = (Q,\Sigma,\tilde{\delta},\tilde{I},\tilde{W})$ is the ***complement*** of M defined as follows

$\tilde{\delta}(q,\sigma)$ is the set of all $X \subseteq Q{\times}D$ such that for all $Y \in \delta(q,\sigma), |Y \cap X| = 1$

$\tilde{I}$ is the set of all $X \subseteq Q{\times}D$ such that for all $Y \in I$, $|Y \cap X| = 1$

$\tilde{W} = Q^{\omega}-W$

The existence of a construction of the complement which does not increase the number of states is the main property of alternating automata.

The remaining constructions are variations on well known themes.

Union. Let $M_1 = (Q_1,\Sigma,\delta_1,I_1,W_1)$ and $M_2 = (Q_2,\Sigma,\delta_2,I_2,W_2)$ be alternating automata. The ***union*** of M_1 and M_2 is the automaton $M_1 \vee M_2 = (Q,\Sigma,\delta,I,W)$ where $Q = Q_1 \cup Q_2$, $\delta = \delta_1 \cup \delta_2$, $I = I_1 \cup I_2$, and $W = W_1 \cup W_2$. Note that the computation trees of $M_1 \vee M_2$ are the computation trees of M_1 and M_2. Therefore $M_1 \vee M_2$ accepts (T,α) iff M_1 or M_2 accepts (T,α).

The intersection $M_1 \wedge M_2$ of M_1 and M_2 is obtained by a similar construction.

Existentialisation. Let $M = (Q,\Sigma,\delta,I,F)$ be a positive alternating automaton. We call ***existentialisation*** of M the nondeterministic automaton $M' = (\mathcal{P}(Q),\Sigma,\gamma,I,\mathcal{P}(F))$ where the transition fonction $\gamma: \mathcal{P}(Q){\times}\Sigma \longrightarrow \mathcal{P}(\mathcal{P}(Q)^D)$ is defined as follows:

$\gamma(X,\sigma)$ is the set of all $\{(\cup\{f_d(q,\sigma);q{\in}X\},d);\ d{\in}D\}$ for $f \in \det(\delta)$.

The existentialisation of M indicates at each node s of T the set of results of s-computations of an uniform run of M. To be more precise, call ***trace*** of a uniform run r of M on (T,α) the function r': $T \longrightarrow \mathcal{P}(Q)^*$ defined by $e(r'(s)) = \{e(u);\ u{\in}r(s)\}$; it is readily seen that the runs of the existentialisation of M are exactly the traces of uniform runs of M. In particular, the existentialisation M' of an alternating automaton M is equivalent to M on finite trees.

Composition. Let $M_1 = (Q_1,\Sigma,\delta_1,I_1,F_1)$ and $M_2 = (Q_2,\Sigma,\delta_2,I_2,F_2)$ be alternating automata and let f be a function from Q_1 to $\mathcal{P}(Q_2)$. The ***composition*** of M_1 and M_2 by f is the automaton $M = (Q,\Sigma,\delta,I,F)$ defined by $Q = Q_1 \cup Q_2$, $I = I_1$, $F = F_2$, and

$$\delta(q,\sigma) = \begin{cases} \delta_1(q,\sigma) \cup \{\{(z,d);\ z\in f(q),\ (q,d)\in X\};\ X\in\delta_1(q,\sigma)\} & \text{if } q \in Q_1 \\ \delta_2(q,\sigma) & \text{if } q \in Q_2 \end{cases}$$

The automaton M begins like M_1 and ,at each step, has the choice of changing to M_2 via f in the following way: instead of going in a certain state $q_1 \in Q_1$, it goes in the states $q \in f(q_1)$ and then runs like M_2. To be more precise, M accepts (T,α) iff there exists a finite subtree R_0 of a computation tree of M_1 on (T,α) and for each $(u,s) \in Fr(R_0)$ and each $q \in f(e(u))$ a winning computation tree of (M_2,q) on (T_s,α_s).

Finitary projection. Let $M = (Q,\Sigma\times\Delta,\delta,I,F)$ be a positive alternating automaton. Let N_1 be the projection on Σ of the existentialisation of M, and N_2 the restriction of M to Σ. The ***finitary projection*** of M is the composition N of N_1 and N_2 by the identity function of $\mathcal{P}(Q)$. We will show that N precisely recognizes the finitary projection of the language recognized by M.

As composition of N_1 and N_2, N accepts (T,α) if and only if there exists a finite subtree T_0 of T such that

(1) there exists a computation tree R_0 of N_1 on $(T_0,\alpha|T_0)$ and, for each $(u,s) \in Fr(R_0)$ and $q \in e(u)$, a winning computation tree $R_{s,q}$ of (N_2,q) on (T_s,α_s).

By the choice of N_1 and N_2, (1) is equivalent to the existence of an extension β of α to $\Sigma\times\Delta$ such that $\beta(s) = \alpha(s)0...0$ for $s \notin T_0$, and satisfying

(2) there exists a computation tree R_0 of the existentialisation of M on $(T_0,\beta|T_0)$ and, for each $(u,s) \in Fr(R_0)$ and $q \in e(u)$, a winning computation tree $R_{s,q}$ of (M,q) on (T_s,β_s)

By the definition of the existentialisation, (2) is equivalent to

(3) there exists a uniform computation tree R_1 of M on $(T_0,\beta|T_0)$ and, for each $(u,s) \in Fr(R_1)$, a winning computation tree $R_{s,e(u)}$ of $(M,e(u))$ on (T_s,β_s).

The latter condition is equivalent to the existence of a winning computation tree (T,β).

3. FROM ALTERNATING TO NONDETERMINISTIC AUTOMATA.

A simulation of stable alternating automata by non deterministic one which increase the number of states of one exponential is given in [7]. The same result holds for positive alternating automata.

Theorem 1. Let M be a positive alternating automaton with n states. There exists a positive nondeterministic automaton M' with 2^{2n} states which accepts exactly the same trees as M.

Proof. Let M = (Q,Σ,δ,I,F) be a positive alternating automaton. For each run r of M on a Σ-tree (T,α), we define a function ξ_r from R to {0,1} as follows:

- if x is a root then $\xi_r(x) = 0$
- if $x = (uq,sd)$, then $\xi_r(x) = 0$ if and only if either for all $v \in r(s)$, $\xi_r(v,s) = 1$, or $\xi_r(u,s) = 0$ and $e(u) \notin F$

Lemma: r is winning if and only if (*) each branch Π of T contains infinitely many nodes s such that for all $u \in r(s)$, $\xi_r(u,s) = 1$.

Proof of the lemma: If (*) holds, then r is clearly winning. We prove the converse. Let Π be a branch of T and $S = \cup\{r(s);\ s \in \Pi\}$ the tree of s-computations. Consider $s \in \Pi$ and $u \in r(s)$ such that $\xi_r(u,s) = 0$; the set of all $v \in S_u$ that do not meet F is a finite-branching tree without infinite branch (because r is winning); thus this tree is finite and there exists $t \geq s$ such that for all $uv \in r(t)$, v meets F. Therefore, if s is a node of Π such that for all $u \in r(s)$, $\xi_r(u,s) = 0$, then there exists $t \geq s$ such that for all $v \in r(t)$, $\xi_r(v,t) = 1$. Condition (*) follows by induction.

Now the required positive nondeterministic automaton M' is just an automaton which computes at each node s of the tree T the set of all pairs $(e(u),\xi_r(u,s))$ coming from s-computations u of an uniform run r of M on (T,α). More precisely, let $M' = (Q',\Sigma,\delta',I',F')$ where $Q' = \mathcal{P}(Q\times\{0,1\})$, $F' = \mathcal{P}(Q\times\{1\})$, $I' = \{X\times\{0\};\ X\in I\}$, and δ' is a function from $Q'\times\Sigma$ to $\mathcal{P}(Q'^D)$ defined as follows

- if $Z \subseteq Q\times\{1\}$, then $\delta'(Z,\sigma)$ is the set of all functions

  $d \mapsto \cup\{f_d(q,\sigma)\times\{0\};\ (q,1)\in Z\}$ for $f \in Det(\delta)$

- if $Z \not\subseteq Q\times\{1\}$, then $\delta'(Z,\sigma)$ is the set of all functions

  $d \mapsto \cup\{f_d(q,\sigma)\times\{1\};\ (q,1)\in Z \text{ or } ((q,0)\in Z \text{ and } q\in F)\}\cup$

  $\cup\{f_d(q,\sigma)\times\{0\};\ (q,0)\in Z \text{ and } q\notin F\}$ for $f \in Det(\delta)$

We can associate to each uniform run r of M a run r' of M' defined by $e(r'(s)) = \{(e(u),\xi(u,s));\ u\in r(s)\}$. Using the above lemma we see that ' is a function from the set of winning uniform runs of M on (T,α) onto the set of winning runs of M' on (T,α). Therefore M and M' accept the same trees.

Remark: The simulation of an alternating automaton by non deterministic one is relatively easy, but in order to prove that it works, the existence of winning uniform runs is needed (this is also true for stable alternating automata).

4. POSITIVE MONADIC FORMULAS.

A *positive monadic formula* is an element of the closure of the set of all quantifier-free formulas by conjunction, disjunction, universal quantification over finite sets, existential quantification over finite sets and arbitrary sets. Roughly speaking, a positive monadic formula is a monadic formula without universal quantification over arbitrary sets.

Theorem 2. Let L be a tree language. The following are equivalent:

(1) L is defined by a positive monadic formula.

(2) L is recognized by a positive alternating automaton.

(3) L is recognized by a positive nondeterministic automaton.

Proof. (1) $\Rightarrow$ (2) We associate to each positive monadic formula an equivalent positive alternating automaton. We proceed by induction, beginning with automata equivalent to quantifier-free formulas. For disjunction, conjunction and existential quantification over finite sets, just take union, intersection and finitary projection; the automata obtained in this way remain positive. Consider a formula $\forall\bar{X}\varphi$; the induction hypothesis gives a positive alternating automaton M equivalent to φ and thus a negative alternating automaton $\tilde{M}$ equivalent to $\neg\varphi$; the finitary projection N of $\tilde{M}$ is a negative alternating automaton equivalent to $\exists\bar{X}\neg\varphi$; the complement of N is a positive alternating automaton equivalent to $\forall\bar{X}\varphi$. Consider now a formula $\exists\bar{U}\varphi$; the induction hypothesis gives a positive alternating automaton equivalent to φ; by theorem 1, there exists a positive nondeterministic automaton N equivalent to M; the projection of N is a positive nondeterministic automaton equivalent to $\exists\bar{U}\varphi$.

(2) $\Rightarrow$ (3) is just theorem 1. (here is the place where we need uniform runs)

(3) $\Rightarrow$ (1) Let $M = (Q,\Sigma,\delta,I,F)$ be a positive nondeterministic automaton. Then M accepts (T,α) if and only if

(*) there exists a partition $(U_q)_{q\in Q}$ of T in accordance with α, δ and I such that, for all $s \in T$, there exists a frontier S of T_s such that each element of S belongs to a U_q with $q\in F$.

The condition (*) is clearly expressible by a positive monadic formula.

Remark: Let φ be a positive monadic formula of lenght n written in prenex form with k alternations of quantifiers and beginning with $\exists$. The nondeterministic automaton equivalent to φ given by the above proof has $\leq 2_k(cn)$ states, for a certain constant c. Using this we can give a decision procedure for positive monadic formulas of the class $\exists_k$ (i.e. with k alternations of quantifiers and beginning with $\exists$) whose complexity in time is k-exponential (ie exponential iterated k times). A detailed proof will be given in an other paper.

5. WEAK MONADIC FORMULAS.

A ***weak monadic formula*** is a monadic formula where quantification is restricted to finite sets (note that weak monadic formulas are particular positive monadic formulas). A ***stable alternating automaton*** is a positive alternating automaton $M = (Q,\Sigma,\delta,I,F)$ such that no cycle of the transition diagram meets both F and $\tilde{F}$; this means that the computations become stabilized after a finite number of steps. An ***alternate chain*** of M is a sequence $q_0 \ldots q_n$ of states such that for all $i<n$, (i) q_{i+1} is accessible from q_i in the transition diagram, (ii) $q_{i+1} \in F$ if and only if $q_i \in \tilde{F}$. Note that there is a bound on the lenght of alternate chains of a stable alternating automaton.

The following theorem has been proved by Muller, Saoudi and Schupp [7] using in an essential way one direction of Rabin's result [10] and , implicitly, uniform runs . We present here a simpler direct proof which do not require uniform runs.

Theorem 3. Let L be a tree language. The following are equivalent:

(1) L is defined by a weak monadic formula.

(2) L is recognized by a weak alternating automaton.

(3) L is recognized by a stable alternating automaton.

Proof. (2) $\Longleftrightarrow$ (3) Let $M = (Q,\Sigma,\delta,I,\mathcal{F})$ be a weak alternating automaton. We change M into a stable alternating automaton $M' = (\mathcal{P}(Q)\times Q,\Sigma,\delta',I',F')$ in the following way:

- $\delta'(((X,q),\sigma)$ is obtained from $\delta(q,\sigma)$ by replacing each (q',d) with $((X\cup\{q'\},q'),d)$
- I' is obtained from I by replacing each q with $\{q\}$
- $F' = \{(X,q);\ X \in \mathcal{F}\}$

Conversely, in order to change a stable alternating automaton $M = (Q,\Sigma,\delta,I,F)$ into a weak alternating automaton, it suffices to replace F by by the set $\mathcal{F}$ of all $X \subseteq Q$ such that there exists a computation $(\bar{q},s)$ of M with $e(\bar{q}) \in F$ and $\bar{q}$ an enumeration of X. The stability of M ensures the equivalence of the two acceptance conditions.

(1) $\Longrightarrow$ (3) The proof is similar to that of theorem 2. Just remark that complement, finitary projection, and union of stable automata are stable.

(3) $\Longrightarrow$ (1) We associate with each stable alternating automaton $M = (Q,\Sigma,\delta,I,F)$ a weak monadic formula $\varphi(x,\bar{U})$ such that : M accepts (T_t,α_t) if and only if $\varphi(x,\bar{U})$ is satisfied by t in (T,α) (the transformation of $\varphi(x,\bar{U})$ in a formula $\varphi(\bar{U})$ equivalent to M is immediate)

We proceed by induction on the maximal length of alternate chains in M. We can suppose that M has a unique initial state, since if $\varphi_q(x,\bar{U})$ is the formula associated with (M,q), then the formula associated with M is

$$\bigvee_{X\in I} \bigwedge_{q\in X} \varphi_q(x,\bar{U}).$$

If all the alternate chains have length 1, then either the initial state is in F and the formula is $x = x$, or the initial state is in $\tilde{F}$ and the formula is $x \neq x$. Assume now that all the alternate chains of M have length $\leq$ n+1. We can also suppose that the initial state of M is not in F (by replacing ,if necessary, M by its complement). In this situation, M accepts (T_t,α_t) if and only if there exists a subtree T_0 of T_t and a uniform computation tree R_0 of M on T_0 such that for all $(u,s) \in Fr(R_0)$

(a) there exists $(v,s') \in R_0$ such that $(v,s') \leq (u,s)$ and $e(v) \in F$

(b) there exists an winning computation tree of $(M,e(u))$ on T_s.

By (a), for each $(u,s) \in Fr(R_0)$, the automaton $(M,e(u))$ is equivalent to a stable alternating automaton $(M',e(u))$ whose chains are all of length $\leq$n (it suffices to remove the states of M which are not accessible from $e(u)$). Thus, by induction hypothesis, there exists a weak monadic formula $\varphi_{e(u)}(x,\bar{U})$ such that: $(M,e(u))$ accepts (T_s,α_s) if and only if s satisfy $\varphi_{e(u)}(x,\bar{U})$ in (T_t,α_t).

Therefore M accepts (T_t,α_t) if and only if

(*) there exists a finite subtree T_0 of T_t, there exists a partition $(P_f)_{f\in det(\delta)}$ of T_0, for each branch X of T_0, for each partition $(X_q)_{q\in Q}$ of X in accordance with (P_f), there exists $q \in F$ such that $X \cap X_q \neq \emptyset$, and for all $s \in Fr(T_0) \cap X_q$, s satisfy $\varphi_q(x,\bar{U})$.

The condition (*) is clearly expressible by a weak monadic formula.

Remark. Using both theorem 1 and one direction of Rabin's result [10], we find an other equivalent condition:

(4) L is both recognized by a positive and a negative alternating automaton.

6. THE Σ_n HIERARCHY OF WEAK MONADIC FORMULAS.

Bounded quantifications are quantifications of the form $\exists x\in Y$ and $\exists X\subseteq Y$; as usual $(\exists X\subseteq Y)\varphi$ is defined as $\exists X(X\subseteq Y \wedge \varphi)$. A formula φ is ***bounded by*** $\bar{Y}$ if the only quantifications which appear in φ are bounded quantifications $\exists X\subseteq Y$ with Y in $\bar{Y}$.

The Σ_n hierarchy of weak monadic formulas is defined as follows:

- a Σ_1 ***formula*** is a formula of the form $\exists\bar{X}\varphi$ where φ is bounded by $\bar{X}$

- a Σ_{n+1} ***formula*** is a formula of the form $\exists\bar{X}\varphi$ where φ is a boolean combination of Σ_n formulas and formulas bounded by $\bar{X}$

Remark: The Σ_n hierarchy and the $\exists_n$ hierarchy are both hierarchies of alternations of quantifications, but there is an important difference between them: the Σ_n

hierarchy begins with bounded formulas and the $\exists_n$ hierarchy by atomic formulas. In our context, the Σ_n hierarchy is relevant for definability results, and the $\exists_n$ hierarchy for complexity results.

A ***Σ_n chain*** (resp. Π_n chain) of an alternating automaton $M = (Q,\Sigma,\delta,I,F)$ is an alternate chain $q_0 \ldots q_n$ of M with $q_0 \in \tilde{F}$ (resp. $q_0 \in F$) . A ***Σ_n automaton*** (resp. Π_n automaton) is a stable alternating automaton without Π_n chains (resp. Σ_n chain).

<u>Theorem 4</u>. Let L be a tree language. The following are equivalent:

(1) L is defined by a Σ_n formula.

(2) L is recognized by a Σ_n automaton.

<u>Proof</u>. (1) $\Rightarrow$ (2) We prove by induction on n that each Σ_n formula is equivalent to a Σ_n automaton.

Let $\varphi(\bar{U})$ be a Σ_1 formula. We first note that $(T,\alpha) \models \varphi(\bar{U})$ if and only if there exists a finite subtree T_0 of T such that $(T_0,\alpha|T_0) \models \varphi(\bar{U})$. Let $M = (Q,\Sigma,\delta,q_0,F)$ be a nondeterministic automaton which recognize the set of all finite trees which satisfy $\varphi(\bar{U})$. We transform M into a Σ_1 automaton $M' = (Q\cup\{f\},\Sigma,\delta',q_0,\{f\})$ where

$\delta'(q,\sigma) = \delta(q,\sigma)$ if $q \in Q-F$

$\delta'(q,\sigma) = \delta(q,\sigma) \cup \{\{f\}\times D\}$ if $q \in F$

$\delta'(f,\sigma) = \{\{f\}\times D\}$

Clearly, M' accepts (T,α) if and only if there exists a finite subtree T_0 of T such that M accepts $(T_0,\alpha|T_0)$. Therefore M' is equivalent to $\varphi(\bar{U})$.

Consider now a Σ_{n+1} formula $\exists\bar{Y}(\varphi_1(\bar{U},\bar{Y})\wedge\varphi_2(\bar{U},\bar{Y}))$ where $\varphi_1(\bar{U},\bar{V})$ is a Π_n formula and $\varphi_2(\bar{U},\bar{Y})$ a formula bounded by $\bar{Y}$. Suppose that Σ and Δ are the alphabets corresponding to $\bar{U}$ and $\bar{V}$. Let M_1 be a Σ_n automaton equivalent to $\varphi_1(\bar{U},\bar{V})$, and M_2 be a nondeterministic automaton equivalent to $\varphi_2(\bar{U},\bar{V})$ on finite Σ-trees. Let N_1 be the projection on Σ of the existentialisation of $M_1 \wedge M_2$, and N_2 be the restriction to Σ of $M_1 \wedge Id(Q_2)$ - where $Id(Q_2)$ is an automaton which may start in anyone of the states of Q_2 and then stays for ever in this state. Finally, consider the composition N of N_1 and N_2 by the identity function of $\mathcal{P}(Q_1 \cup Q_2)$.

The automaton N accepts the Σ-tree (T,α) if and only if there exists a finite subtree T_0 of T such that

(a) there exists a computation tree R of N_1 on $(T_0,\alpha|T_0)$ and, for each $(s,u) \in Fr(R)$ and $q \in e(u)$, a winning computation tree $R_{s,q}$ of (N_2,q) on (T_s,α_s).

The condition (a) is equivalent to the existence of an extension β of α to $\Sigma\times\Delta$ such that $\beta(s) = \alpha(s)0\ldots0$ if $s \notin T_0$ and satisfying

(b) there exists an uniform computation tree R' of $M_1 \wedge M_2$ on $(T_0,\beta|T_0)$, and, for each $(s,u) \in Fr(R')$, a winning computation tree $R'_{s,e(u)}$ of $(M_1 \wedge Id(Q_2),e(u))$ on (T_s,β_s).

Since a computation tree of $M_1 \wedge M_2$ is the union of a computation tree of M_1 and a computation tree of M_2, and since a winning computation tree of $(M_1 \wedge Id(Q_2),q)$ is either a winning computation tree of M_1 or $(\{q\}\times D)^*$ (depending on whether $q \in Q_1$ or $q \in Q_2$), the condition (b) is equivalent to

(c) there exists a winning computation tree of M_1 on (T,β) and a winning computation tree of M_2 on $(T_0,\beta|T_0)$.

Thus N is equivalent to the formula $\exists\bar{Y}(\varphi_1(\bar{U},\bar{Y})\wedge\varphi_2(\bar{U},\bar{Y}))$.

(2) $\Longrightarrow$ (1) We prove by induction on n that, for each Σ_n automaton, there exists a Σ_n formula $\varphi(x,\bar{U})$ such that: M accepts (T_t,α_t) if and only if $\varphi(x,\bar{U})$ is satisfied by t in (T,α).

First let $M = (Q,\Sigma,\delta,I,F)$ be a Σ_1 automaton. Since M has no Π_1 chain, M accepts (T_t,α_t) if and only if there exists a computation tree R of M on (T_t,α_t) and a frontier S of R such that for all $(u,s) \in S$, $e(u) \in F$; this means that there exists a finite subtree T_0 of T_t and a uniform computation tree R_0 of M on $(T_0,\alpha|T_0)$ such that for all $(u,s) \in Fr(R_0)$, $e(u) \in F$. Thus M accepts (T_t,α_t) if and only if there exists a finite subtree T_0 of T_t such that:

(d) there exists a partition $(P_f)_{f\in det(\delta)}$ of T_0 such that for each branch X of T_0 and each partition $(X_q)_{q\in Q}$ of X in accordance with the labelling α_t and the partition (P_f), if $x \in X \cap Fr(T_0)$ then $x \in X_q$ for a certain $q \in F$.

Condition (d) is expressible by a formula bounded by T_0, and thus the existence of a winning run of M on (T_t,α_t) is expressible by a Σ_1 formula.

Now, let $M = (Q,\Sigma,\delta,I,F)$ be a Σ_{n+1} automaton. Then M accepts (T_t,α_t) if and only if there exists a subtree T_0 of T_t and an uniform computation tree R_0 of M on T_0 such that for all $(u,s) \in Fr(R_0)$

(α) there exists $(v,s') \in R_0$ such that $(v,s') \leq (u,s)$ and $e(v) \in F$

(β) there exists a winning computation tree of $(M,e(u))$ on T_s.

It follows from (α) that, for each $(u,s) \in Fr(R_0)$, the automaton $(M,e(u))$ is equivalent to a Π_n automaton $(M',e(u))$. Thus, by the induction hypothesis, there exists a Π_n formula $\varphi_{e(u)}(x,\bar{U})$ such that: $(M,e(u))$ accepts (T_s,α_s) if and only if s satisfies $\varphi_{e(u)}(x,\bar{U})$ in (T_t,α_t). Therefore M accepts (T_t,α_t) if and only if

(e) there exists a finite subtree T_0 of T_t, there exists a partition $(P_f)_{f\in det(\delta)}$ of T_0, for each branch X de T_0, for each partition $(X_q)_{q\in Q}$ of X in accordance with α_t and (P_f), there exists $q \in F$ such that $X \cap X_q \neq \emptyset$, and for all $s \in Fr(T_0) \cap X_q$, s satisfy $\varphi_q(x,\bar{U})$.

It is easy to verify that (e) is expressible by a Σ_{n+1} formula.

REFERENCES

[1] J.R. BUCHI, *Using determinancy of games to eliminate quantifiers*, **Lecture Notes in Computer Science**, vol. 56, Springer, 1977, pp. 367-378.

[2] J.R. BUCHI, *State-strategies for games in* $F_{\sigma\delta} \cap G_{\delta\sigma}$, **Journal of Symbolic Logic**, vol. 48 (1983), pp. 1171-1198.

[3] Y. GUREVICH and L. HARRINGTON, *Trees, automata and games*, **14th Symposium on Theory of Computing** (1982), pp. 60-65.

[4] D.A. MARTIN, *Borel determinancy*, **Annals of Mathematics**, vol. 102 (1975), pp. 363-371.

[5] Y.N. MOSCHOVAKIS, *Descriptive set theory*, North-Holland, 1980.

[6] D.E. MULLER and P.E.SCHUPP, *Alternating automata on infinite objects, determinacy and Rabin's theorem*, **Lecture Notes in Computer Science**, vol. 192, Springer, 1985, pp. 100-107.

[7] D.E. MULLER, A. SAOUDI, and P.E. SCHUPP, *Alternating automata, the weak monadic theory of the tree, and its complexity*, **Proceedings ICALP 1986**.

[8] M. PARIGOT, *Automata as modal operators*, preprint.

[9] M.O. RABIN, *Decidability of second order theories and automata on infinite trees*, **Transations A.M.S.**, vol. 141 (1969), pp. 1-35.

[10] M.O. RABIN, *Weakly definable relations and special automata*, **Mathematical Logic and Foundations of Set Theory**, North Holland, 1970, pp. 1-23.

[11] W. THOMAS, *A hierarchy of sets of infinite trees*,

AN ALGORITHM FOR COLOURING PERFECT PLANAR GRAPHS

Iain A. Stewart
Computing Laboratory, University of Newcastle Upon Tyne,
Claremont Tower, Claremont Road,
Newcastle Upon Tyne, NE1 7RU, England.

Abstract : We present an algorithm to properly colour a perfect, planar graph G using $\gamma(G)$ colours. This algorithm has time complexity $O(n^{3/2})$ and is recursive, based on the Lipton-Tarjan Separator Algorithm.

1. Introduction

The problem of colouring certain graphs has been extensively researched over the years, with perhaps the most famous result being the well-known Four Colour Theorem which states that any planar graph can be coloured with at most 4 colours. Once we have discovered existence results, such as the one above, we often turn our attention to actually producing a colouring of a given graph, using a prescribed number of colours, as efficiently as possible.

Take, for example, the case of planar graphs. Obviously, in order to produce a colouring of a planar graph G using the least number of colours possible, that is $\gamma(G)$ colours where, by the above, $\gamma(G)$ is at most 4, we must first of all discover $\gamma(G)$. However, even the problem of testing for 3-colourability in a planar graph with vertices of degree at most 4 is NP-complete [**5**] and so clearly the problem of discovering $\gamma(G)$ for an arbitrary planar graph G is also NP-complete. Hence any algorithm to produce a colouring of such a graph G, using $\gamma(G)$ colours, will be NP-complete. This suggests that it might be wise to look at certain classes of planar graphs separately.

One such class of graphs are the perfect, planar graphs. Arbitrary perfect graphs are of major theoretical interest and have applications in scheduling problems [**10**], the optimization of computer storage, the analysis of genetic structure and the synchronization of parallel processes [**3**]. A more theoretical property of the class of perfect, planar graphs is that an important open conjecture relating to the theory of arbitrary perfect graphs has been shown to be true for this restricted class. This conjecture, first proposed by Berge [**1**], is called the Strong Perfect Graph Conjecture and asserts that a graph G is perfect if and only if G contains no hole nor antihole, where a hole is a chordless odd-length cycle of length greater than 3, and an antihole is the complement of a hole. As mentioned above, the Strong

Perfect Graph Conjecture has been verified for planar graphs [11], as well as for the classes of toroidal graphs [4], 3-chromatic (K_4-free) graphs [12] and $K_{1\text{-}3}$-free graphs [9]. We shall use the fact that a perfect, planar graph contains no hole extensively throughout the rest of this paper.

In this paper we present an algorithm to properly colour a perfect, planar graph G with n vertices, using $\gamma(G)$ colours, that has time complexity $O(n^{3/2})$. This time complexity compares favourably with the best-known (to us, at least) such algorithm due to Tucker and Wilson [13] which takes $O(n^2)$ time. With regard to colouring the other classes of perfect graphs, mentioned above, for which the Strong Perfect Graph Conjecture holds, Hsu [6] obtained an $O(n^{5/2})$ algorithm for properly colouring a perfect, $K_{1\text{-}3}$-free graph G, using $\gamma(G)$ colours.

2. Definitions

A *graph* $G=(V, E)$ consists of a finite set of vertices V together with a set of edges E joining some pairs of vertices, where there is at most one edge joining any two vertices and no edge joins a vertex to itself (our definition of a graph corresponds to what most people refer to as a simple graph). An *induced subgraph* $G'=(V', E')$ of G has a set of vertices $V' \subseteq V$ and a set of edges $E' \subseteq E$ such that E' is the retriction of E to the vertices V'. The *complement* $C(G)=(V, C(E))$ of a graph $G=(V, E)$ is a graph with the same vertex set as G, with two vertices joined in C(G) if and only if they are not joined in G. The graph G is *planar* if it is possible to represent the graph on a plane in which the vertices are distinct points, the edges are simple curves and no two edges cross each other.

A *proper colouring* of a graph G (often abbreviated to a *colouring*) is a colouring of the vertices of G such that if two vertices are joined by an edge then they are of different colours. The least number of colours needed to colour a graph G, $\gamma(G)$, is called the *chromatic number* of G and G is said to be *k-chromatic* if it can be properly coloured by at most k colours. A *clique* K_m is a set of m vertices of G, each of which is joined to all the others in the set. The number of vertices in the largest clique of G, $\omega(G)$, is called the *clique number* of G. A graph G is *perfect* if $\gamma(G')=\omega(G')$ for all induced subgraphs G' of G, including G itself.

Given a vertex v in a graph $G=(V, E)$, we call the number of edges of E with v as an end-vertex the *degree* of v. A *path* P in a graph $G=(V, E)$, of length k-1, is a sequence $(v_1, v_2, ..., v_k)$ of distinct vertices in G, for some k not less then 1, such that (v_i, v_{i+1}) is an edge of E for $i=1, ..., k-1$. If the path P, as above, is such that (v_1, v_k) is an edge of E then we call P a *cycle* of length k. The path or cycle P is *chordless* if the subgraph of G induced by the vertices $\{v_1, v_2, ..., v_k\}$ has no other edges different from those in P, except perhaps the edge (v_k, v_1) if P is not a cycle.

Two vertices of a graph $G=(V, E)$ are *connected* if there is a path joining them. Clearly we can separate the vertices of G into disjoint sets where the union of these sets is V and two vertices are in the same set if and only if they are connected. The subgraphs of G induced by each of these sets are the *connected components* of G. Suppose the graph G is properly coloured where the colours are given by the integers 1, 2, ..., m. An *i-j component* is a connected component of the subgraph of G induced by the vertices of colours i and j. An *i-j interchange* at v is an exchange of all the colours of the vertices in the i-j component containing v. Notice that an i-j interchange maintains a proper colouring.

3. The Algorithm

We present a recursive procedure for colouring a perfect, planar graph G using $\gamma(G)$ colours. This method differs from the usual inductive technique for colouring planar graphs, where the fact that a planar graph always has a vertex of degree at most 5 is often used.

We make use of the Lipton-Tarjan Separator Algorithm [7]. A set of vertices C is called a *separator* of a graph G if the n vertices of G can be partitioned into sets A, B and C such that no edge of G joins a vertex of A with a vertex of B, and further neither A nor B contains more than 2n/3 vertices. The Lipton-Tarjan Separator Algorithm can be stated as follows.

Theorem [7] : *Every planar graph G has a separator C of size* $(8n)^{1/2}$ *which can be discovered in O(n) time.*

Similar results regarding separators of planar graphs have been obtained, notably those of Miller [8], where the planar graph is assumed to be 2-connected (that is, any two distinct vertices can be connected by two vertex-disjoint paths) and the vertices of the separator can then form a cycle, and Djidjev [2], where the separator has a smaller size to that above and in fact has size at most $(6n)^{1/2}$.

Our algorithm works by considering the two subgraphs, G_a and G_b, of G, induced by the sets of vertices $A \cup C$ and $B \cup C$ respectively. Having recursively coloured G_a and G_b separately, we modify the two colourings so that the vertices of C are identically coloured in both G_a and G_b. This clearly gives a colouring of G.

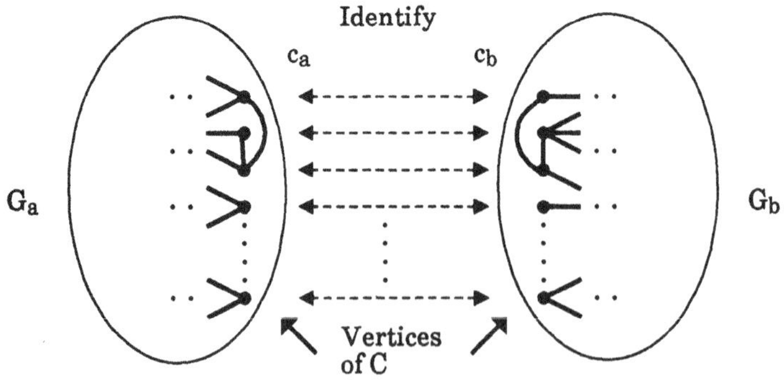

FIGURE 1 : The initial graph H

Consider the graph H consisting of a copy of the (coloured) graph G_a disjoint from a copy of the (coloured) graph G_b, as shown in Fig. 1. Notice that for each vertex $c \in C$, where C is considered as a subset of the vertices of G, there are two vertices c_a and c_b of H, where c_a (resp. c_b) is the vertex in the copy of G_a (resp. G_b) corresponding to c. Henceforth we shall refer to this copy of G_a (resp. G_b) simply as G_a (resp. G_b).

Choose any vertex $c \in C$. Clearly we may arrange the colourings of G_a and G_b so that c_a and c_b have the same colour. Form a new graph, which we still call H, by identifying each pair of vertices d_a and d_b, for some $d \in C$, that have identical colours, renaming such a vertex simply as d_{ab}. Notice that H is still properly coloured and at least one pair of vertices are identified, namely c_a and c_b.

Choose any pair of vertices c_a and c_b of H, corresponding to some $c \in C$, that still remain in H and so consequently are of different colours. Without loss of generality, suppose that c_a is coloured 1 and c_b is coloured 2. Consider the 1-2 component of H containing c_a. If c_b is not in this 1-2 component then we can perform a 1-2 interchange at c_a and identify c_a and c_b, together with any other identically coloured pairs of vertices corresponding to some vertices of C, as above (the situation after some identifications is shown in Fig. 2).

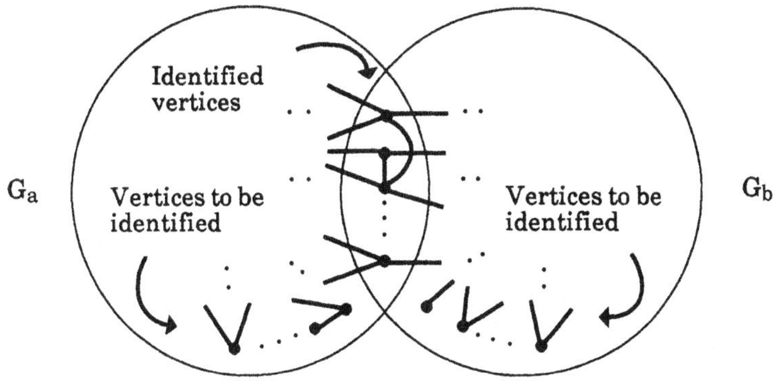

FIGURE 2 : The graph H after some identifications

Conversely, suppose that c_b is in the 1-2 component of H containing c_a. Then there is a 1-2 path P from c_a to c_b, which we may clearly assume is chordless. Hence there is a subpath P' of P between a pair of vertices d_a and d_b, corresponding to some $d \in C$, such that no other pair of vertices e_a and e_b, corresponding to some other $e \in C$, lie on P' (clearly P' might be P with $d_a = c_a$ and $d_b = c_b$). The pair of vertices are again necessarily of different colours. Without loss of generality assume that d_a is coloured 1 and d_b is coloured 2. As there are no pair of vertices e_a and e_b, as above, on P' then clearly the chordless path P' of H corresponds to a chordless cycle Q of G where P' and Q have the same length. As P' is a 1-2 path then it has odd length and so Q has odd length. But G is perfect and by the fact, mentioned earlier, that the Strong Perfect Graph Conjecture is true for planar graphs, G can have no chordless odd-length cycles of length greater than 3. Hence P' and Q both must have length 3. Because of the structure of H either d_a or d_b must be joined to a vertex f_{ab} that came from an identification of f_a and f_b, corresponding to some vertex $f \in C$. But since the subgraph of G induced by the vertices of C is a subgraph of both G_a and G_b then clearly if d_a (resp. d_b) is joined to f_{ab} in H then d_b (resp.d_a) is joined to f_{ab} in H. Hence whatever the case P' is not chordless which yields a contradiction. Thus c_b is not in the 1-2 component of H containing c_a, and so after a 1-2 interchange at c_a, as above, we are always able to identify c_a and c_b.

Clearly by proceeding in this manner we shall eventually identify all pairs of vertices corresponding to vertices of C and our final graph H will in fact yield a proper colouring of G.

A more formal "pidgin language" description of our algorithm is as follows.

apply the planar separator algorithm to G and obtain the sets of vertices A, B and C;
form the subgraphs G_a and G_b of G;
colour G_a and G_b recursively, making sure c_a and c_b have the same colour in G_a and G_b respectively, for some $c \in C$;
form the graph H;
identify all vertices d_a and d_b, in G_a and G_b respectively, that are of the same colour;
WHILE *there exists vertices d_a and d_b, for some vertex $d \in C$,* DO
    BEGIN
    perform a col(d_a)-col(d_b) interchange at d_a;
    identify d_a and d_b, together with any other identically coloured such pairs of vertices;
    END

(Here, col(d), for some vertex d, denotes the colour of that vertex).

4. The Implementation

Suppose we are given a perfect, planar graph G with n vertices and wish to colour it with $\gamma(G)$ colours using the algorithm described above. Let f(n) be the time taken to so colour such an n-vertex graph. Firstly, we apply the Lipton-Tarjan Separator Algorithm to obtain our sets of vertices A, B and C as described earlier. This takes O(n) time. Next we recursively colour the subgraphs of G induced by the sets of vertices $A \cup C$ and $B \cup C$. This takes time at most $f(an+(8n)^{1/2}) + f((1-a)n+(8n)^{1/2})$ for some constant a where $\frac{1}{3} \leqq a \leqq \frac{2}{3}$. Finally we modify the colourings as described earlier to obtain our colouring of G. Suppose this modification can be acheived in $O(n^{3/2})$ time. Then the total time f(n) taken to colour G is such that

$$f(n) \leqq f(an+(8n)^{1/2}) + f((1-a)n+(8n)^{1/2}) + cn^{3/2}$$

for some constant c. Suppose, by induction, that $f(m) \leqq km^{3/2}$ for all $m<n$. Then by simple mathematical analysis of the above inequality concerning f(n) we can easily show that $f(n)=O(n^{3/2})$. Hence to complete the proof that our algorithm is of $O(n^{3/2})$ time complexity

we must show that the modification of the colouring given earlier can be done in $O(n^{3/2})$ time.

We begin by remarking that all graphs will be stored as a series of adjacency lists, one for each vertex. The sets of vertices A, B, C and so on, are stored via arrays indexed by the vertices with a 1 in the ith array cell if vertex i is in a given set and a 0 otherwise. As can be seen, we use only the usual data structures.

We first of all need to form the initial version of the graph H, as described earlier. Clearly we can do this in O(n) time by taking a copy H_a of the subgraph of G induced by the vertices of $A \cup C$, together with a copy H_b of the subgraph of G induced by the vertices of $B \cup C$, being careful to distinguish copies of vertices in C that are in $A \cup C$ from copies of the same vertices that are in $B \cup C$. We do, however, wish to retain a correspondance between two copies of the same vertex of C in the sense that if we are given an adjacency list of one of the copies we can immediately (that is, without any searching) locate the adjacency list of the other copy. We assume that the colours of the vertices of H_a and H_b are stored in two separate arrays, both of size O(n).

As we see from the description of the algorithm, there are two main operations done throughout. The first is the operation of finding the i-j component of H containing a given vertex, of colour i or j, and the second is the operation of identifying two vertices c_a and c_b, for some $c \in C$. To find the i-j component of H containing some given vertex we can clearly use a modified depth-first search which takes O(n) time as it is a well-known fact that a planar graph on n vertices has O(n) edges. To identify two vertices is just as straightforward. Suppose c_a and c_b, for some $c \in C$, are the two vertices to be identified. We simply take all vertices adjacent to c_a in H and, as long as they do not correspond to vertices of C that have already been identified (that is, they do not appear already on the adjacency list of c_b), we add them to the adjacency list of c_b. This process clearly takes O(n) time.

Given that the two major operations described above can both be done in O(n) time, it is easy to see that the modification can be completed in $O(n^{3/2})$ time. We simply note that the number of i-j interchanges done, for some colours i and j, and the number of identifications made are both at most $|C|$. As $|C|$ is $O(n^{\frac{1}{2}})$ then clearly the modification of the colouring can be done in $O(n^{3/2})$ time.

5. Final Remarks

If the two colourings above can be modified in O(n) time then by proceeding exactly as before we can show that the time complexity is O(nlog n). This is clearly the best that we can hope for using the Lipton-Tarjan Planar Separator Algorithm.

References

1 C. BERGE, Sur une conjecture relative au problème des codes optimaux, *Comm. 13ieme Assemblee Gen. URSI*, Tokyo, 1962.

2 H. N. DJIDJEV, On the problem of partitioning planar graphs, *SIAM J. Algebraic Discrete Methods* **3** (1982), 229-240.

3 M. GOLUMBIC, "Algorithmic Graph Theory and Perfect Graphs", Academic Press, New York, 1980.

4 C. GRINSTEAD, "Toroidal Graphs and the Strong Perfect Graph Conjecture", Ph.D Thesis, UCLA, 1978.

5 M. GAREY, D. JOHNSON AND L. STOCKMEYER, Some simplified NP-complete graph problems, *Theoretical Computer Science* **1** (1976), 237-267.

6 W. HSU, "How to Colour Claw-Free Perfect Graphs", Tech. Report #435, Cornell School of Operations Reseach and Industrial Eng., 1979.

7 R. LIPTON AND R. E. TARJAN, A separator theorem for planar graphs, *SIAM J. Appl. Math.* **36** (1979), 177-189.

8 G. L. MILLER, Finding small simple cycle separators for 2-connected planar graphs, *Sixteenth Symp. Theory of Comp.* 1984, 376-382.

9 K. PARTHASARATHY AND G. RAVINDRA, The strong perfect graph conjecture is true for $K_{1\text{-}3}$-free graphs, *J. Combinatorial Theory Ser. B* **21** (1976), 212-223.

10 A. TUCKER, Perfect graphs and an application to optimizing municipal services, *SIAM Rev.* **15** (1973), 585-590.

11 A. TUCKER, The strong perfect graph conjecture for planar graphs, *Canad. J. Math.* **25** (1973), 103-114.

12 A. TUCKER, Critical perfect graphs and perfect 3-chromatic graphs, *J. Combinatorial Theory Ser. B* **23** (1977), 143-149.

13 A. TUCKER AND D. WILSON, An $O(N^2)$ algorithm for colouring perfect planar graphs, *Journal of Algorithms* **5** (1984), 60-68.

Efficient Algorithms for Domination and Hamilton Circuit Problems on Permutation Graphs

P.Shanthi Sastry, N.Jayakumar, and C.E. Veni Madhavan
Dept. of Computer Science and Automation
Indian Institute of Science
Bangalore 560 012, INDIA

Abstract

The domination and Hamilton circuit problems are of interest both in algorithm design and complexity theory. The domination problem has applications in facility location and the Hamilton circuit problem has applications in routing problems in communications and operations research.

The problem of deciding if G has a dominating set of cardinality at most k, and the problem of determining if G has a Hamilton circuit are NP-Complete. Polynomial time algorithms are, however, available for a large number of restricted classes. A motivation for the study of these algorithms is that they not only give insight into the characterization of these classes but also require a variety of algorithmic techniques and data structures. So the search for efficient algorithms, for these problems in many classes still continues.

A class of perfect graphs which is practically important and mathematically interesting is the class of permutation graphs. The domination problem is polynomial time solvable on permutation graphs. Algorithms that are already available are of time complexity $O(n^2)$ or more, and space complexity $O(n^2)$ on these graphs. The Hamilton circuit problem is open for this class.

We present a simple $O(n)$ time and $O(n)$ space algorithm for the domination problem on permutation graphs. Unlike the existing algorithms, we use the concept of geometric representation of permutation graphs. Further, exploiting this geometric notion, we develop an $O(n^2)$ time and $O(n)$ space algorithm for the Hamilton circuit problem.

1. Introduction

Given a graph $G=(V,E)$, where V is a finite set of vertices and E is the set of edges, a set of vertices $D \subseteq V$ is a dominating set if every vertex in V-D is adjacent to some vertex in D. The domination problem or the problem of finding a minimum cardinality dominating set is of interest both in algorithm design and complexity theory. It has applications in facility location [6]. Interesting applications of the concept of domination in coding theory and combinatorial optimization are given in Cockayne and Hedetniemi [2]. Another interesting problem with applications in routing in communications and operations research, is the problem of finding a Hamilton circuit. A Hamilton circuit is a circuit that includes all the vertices of a graph, a circuit being a closed walk that traverses every vertex once, except the starting vertex. A graph is Hamiltonian if it has a Hamilton circuit.

It is well known that the problem of deciding if G has a dominating set of cardinality at most k, and the problem of determining if G has a Hamilton circuit are NP-Complete, Garey and Johnson [4]. Polynomial-time algorithms are, however, available for a large number of restricted classes of graphs. A motivation for the study of these algorithms is that they not only give insight into the characterization of these classes but also require a variety of algorithmic techniques and data structures. So the search for efficient algorithms, for these problems in many classes still continues.

A class of perfect graphs which is practically important and mathematically interesting is the class of permutation graphs. Applications for these graphs arise in air-traffic scheduling and memory-resource management in a multiprogramming computer [5].

The domination problem is polynomial-time solvable on permutation graphs. Algorithms that are already available are of time complexity $O(n^2)$ or more on these graphs. Further, these algorithms are of space complexity $O(n^2)$ in the worst case. The Hamilton circuit problem is open for this class [7].

We present a simple $O(n)$ time and $O(n)$ space algorithm for the domination problem on permutation graphs. Unlike the existing algorithms, we use the concept of geometric representation of permutation graphs, introduced by Supowit [8]. Further, exploiting this geometric notion, we develop an $O(n^2)$ time and $O(n)$ space algorithm for the Hamilton circuit problem.

Definition. Let $= (\pi_1, \ldots, \pi_n)$ be a permutation of the set $\{1, \ldots, n\}$. Let $G=(V,E)$ be the graph, $V=\{1, \ldots, n\}$, $E=\{(i,j) : (i-j)(\pi_i^{-1} - \pi_j^{-1}) < 0\}$. Here, π^{-1} denotes the ith element of the inverse permutation π^{-1} of π. A graph G is called a permutation graph if G is isomorphic to $G[\pi]$ for some permutation π.

A simple consequence of the definition of permutation graphs, is that if π^{-1} is the inverse permutation of π then $G[\pi^{-1}]$ is isomorphic to $G[\pi]$.

2. The Geometric Representation

Supowit [8] uses the partial order $\leq$, on a set of points on the plane, where for any two points (r_1, s_1) and (r_2, s_2) $(r_1, s_1) \leq (r_2, s_2)$ if $r_1 \leq r_2$ and $s_1 \leq s_2$ and gives a geometric characterization of permutation graphs as follows. Consider this partial order on the set of points $P = \{(i, \pi_i^{-1}), i=1, \ldots, n\}$. Then, clearly, two vertices are adjacent in G if and only if they are comparable under this order. The independent sets of $G[\pi]$ thus correspond to chains and the cliques correspond to antichains of this partially ordered set P. Permutation graphs are then represented geometrically by plotting the points of P in the plane with i values along the x-axis and the π_i^{-1} values along the y-axis. Since each point in this representation corresponds uniquely to a vertex of V, we use 'points' and 'vertices' interchangeably when discussing the algorithms.

Given the geometric representation, we define two rectilinear paths Max(P) and Min(P). The points on Max(P) are given by the right-to-left minima of the permutation π and the points of Min(P) are given by the left-to-right maxima of π (Fig.2.1). If we draw the axes at any point v in this representation, the vertices that are adjacent to v lie in two regions - the second quadrant and the fourth quadrant. For points of Max(P) and Min(P) all the adjacent vertices lie only in one region - the fourth and the second quadrant respectively. We denote the two rectilinear paths by T and B respectively. Let $t_p, \ldots, t_1$ be the right-to-left minima of π and $b_1, \ldots, b_q$ be the left-to-right maxima of π. $Max(V) = \{r_i : 1 \leq i \leq p, r_i = (t_i, \pi^{-1}_{t_i})\}$ and $Min(V) = \{s_i : 1 \leq i \leq q, s_i = (b_i, \pi^{-1}_{b_i})\}$.

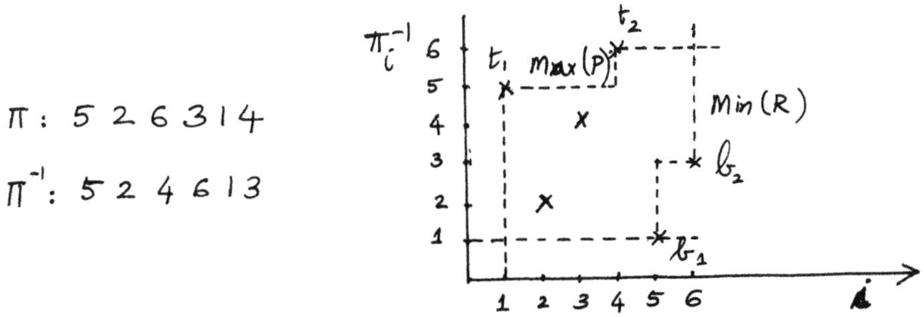

Fig. 2.1 Geometric Representation

3. The Domination Algorithm

The 'geometric' property of permutation graphs has not been used before for the design of domination algorithms. We exploit this property and present a simple O(n) time, O(n) space algorithm for the domination problem. Unlike the algorithms of Farber and Keil [3] and Brandstadt and Kratsch [1], our algorithm does not require any additional data structures other than that required for the representation of the input.

From the geometric representation it is clear that Max(V) and Min(V) are dominating sets of $G = G[\pi]$. But they are not of minimum cardinality (Fig. 3.1). So we try and select points from both the paths to get the minimum cardinality dominating set.

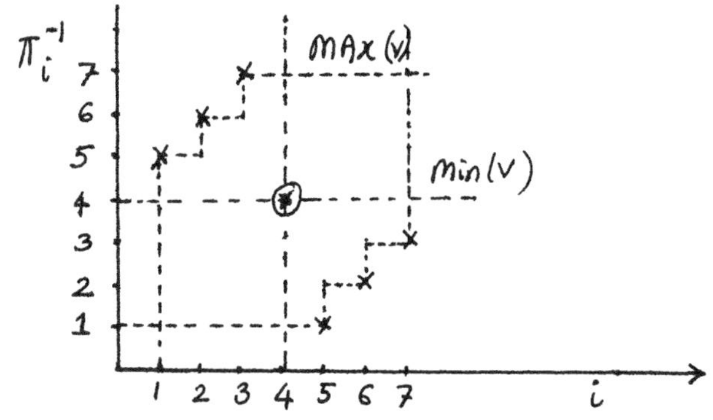

Fig. 3.1 Non-minimality of Max(V) and Min(V)

We first give an informal explanation of the algorithm.

We start with the point s_1 and draw the vertical line at b_1. Let this vertical meet the Max path between the points t_i and t_{i+1}. The points to the left of b_1 are all dominated by b_1. If there are points between b_1 and t_{i+1} then we have to include one of t_i or b_2. If there are no points between b_1 and t_{i+1} then we include one of t_{i+1} or b_2.

To select one of t_i and b_2, we check whether there is only one t_i less than b_2 or if b_2 is the only point with y-value less than y-value of t_i. In the first case we include t_i in the dominating set, otherwise we include b_2. Similarly, to select one of t_{i+1} or b_2 we check if there is only one b with y-value less than the y-value of t_{i+1} and x-value greater than t_{i+1} or if t_{i+1} is the only point less than b_2. In the first case, we include b_2, otherwise we include t_{i+1}.

We proceed in this manner till such time as one of the paths is exhausted. We then include the last point of the path that is exhausted.

When we include a point t_k and a point b_m such that t_k and b_m are adjacent to each other, it may happen that a single point is sufficient to dominate all the points dominated by t_k and b_m (Fig. 3.1). Such a point is both a left-to-right minimum and a right-to-left maximum of π in this segment. Thus we ensure that there is no such point in the procedure Reduce before we include points in the dominating set.

The entire procedure is repeated by starting with r_1, r_p and s_q in turn. Clearly for r_p and s_q we work in a top down fashion and make small modifications in order to perform the scan. The minimum cardinality set of the four sets thus obtained constitutes a minimum cardinality dominating set of G.

We give below the algorithm to perform the scan starting with b_1. It can be used for the scan starting with t_1 and with modifications for the scans starting with r_p and s_q. It works on connected permutation graphs. The connected components of a permutation graph can be constructed in O(n) time.

Algorithm 1

Input : The defining permutation π of a permutation graph G.
Output : A minimum cardinality dominating set D of G.

Step 1. Find

i. the inverse permutation π^{-1} of π.

ii. the right-to-left minima t_p, ..., t_1 and the left-to-right maxima b_1, ..., b_q of π^{-1}

i:=1; k:=1

if Scan 1 then D:=b_1 else D:=t_1

Step 2. If a point t in T has been included in D then go to Step 3;
While t_k <b_i and k<> p do k:=k+1;
If k<> p then
begin
    t_1 := t_{k-1} ; t_r := t_k;
    if there are points between b_i and t_r then

```
begin
    t_1 := t_{k-1} ; t_r := t_k;
    if there are points between b_i and t_r then
    begin
       m:=i+1;
       while π^{-1}_{b_m} < π^{-1}_{t_1} do m:=m+1;
       if the number of increments in m > 1 then
       begin
         D:=D∪{t_1} ; i:=m; k:=1;
  **     if the previous point included in D is b∈B and if
         t_1 is adjacent to b then reduce
       end
       else
        D:=D∪{b_{i+1}} ; i:=i+1;
    end
    else
    begin
       m:=i+1;
       while π^{-1}_{b_m} < π^{-1}_{t_r} do m:=m+1;
       if the number of increments in m > 1 then
       begin
          D:= D∪{t_r} ; i:=m; k:=r; repeat **
       end
       else
         D:=D∪{b_{i+1}} ; i:=i+1;
  end
else
   D:=D∪{t_p} ;
Step 3. if a point b ∈ B has been included in D then go to
Step2;
while π^{-1}_{b_i} < π^{-1}_{t_k} and i <> q do i:=i+1;
if i<>q then
  begin
    b_1 := b_{i-1} ; b_h := b_i;
    if there are points with y-values between π^{-1}_{t_k} and π^{-1}_{b_h}
    then
    begin
      m:=k+1;
      while t_m < b_1 do m:=m+1;
```

```
      if the number of increments in m > 1 then
      begin
        D:=D∪ {b_1} ; i:=1; k:=m;
      end
      else
       D:= D∪ {t_{k+1}} ; k:=k+1;
    end
    else
    begin
       m:=k+1;
       while t_m < b_r do m:=m+1;
       if the number of increments in m > 1 then
       begin
          D:=D∪ {b_h} ; i:=h; k:=m;
       end
       else
         D:=D∪ {t_{k+1}} ; k:=k+1;
    end
   else
      D:=D∪ {b} ;
   goto Step 2.
Proc
   reduce
   begin
   min:= π_b ; max:= π_{t_m} ;
   for j:=1 to b-t_m -1 do
   begin
     if π_{t+j} <min then min:= π_{t+j}; lrmin (t_m+j) := 'true';
     if π_{b-j}  max then max:= π_{b-j}; rlmax (b-j):= 'true';
   end
   for j:=1 to b-t_m-1 do
     if lrmin(j) and rlmax(j) then D:=D- {t_m ,b} ∪ {j} ; exit
   end
```

Correctness and Complexity

The correctness of the algorithm is given by the following.

Step 1 determines the points of Max(V) and Min(V). In step 2 we find, at each stage, all the vertices dominated by b_i. We then find the largest right-to-left minimum less than b_i and the smallest right-to-left minimum greater than b_i. In the matching diagram, selecting one of the points t_l, t_r, or b_{i+1} corresponds to selecting the line that goes as far right as possible. Similarly for the t_i's we always select the line that goes as far right as possible (Fig. 3.2).

Clearly the algorithm is of time complexity O(n), since each vertex is visited only once.

Matching Diagram. The matching diagram is obtained by writing 1, ...,n in a line and writing π_1, ..., π_n in a parallel line below this and drawing line segments L_i joining i in the first row and i in the second row. Two vertices i and j are adjacent if the line segments L_i and L_j intersect.

π = 5,1,4,2,9,3,7,8,10,12,13,6,15,11,14

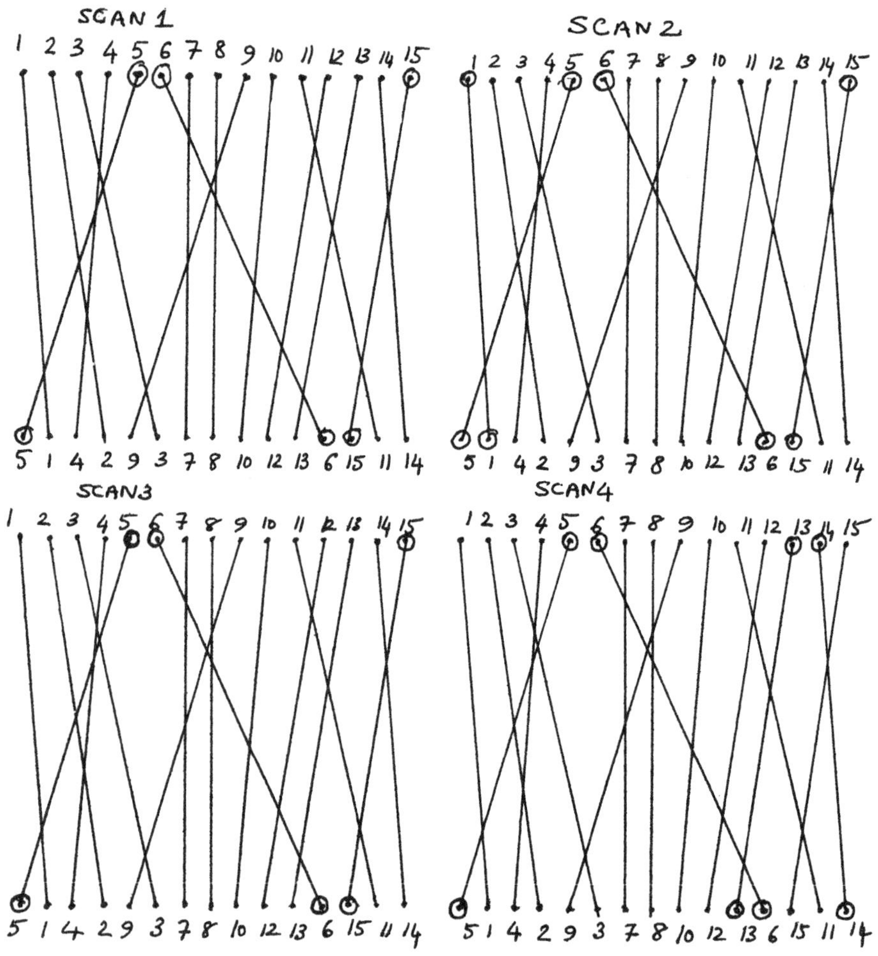

Fig.3.2 Working of the Algorithm 1

4. The Hamilton Circuit Algorithm

There is no known polynomial time algorithm for the Hamilton circuit problem on permutation graphs. Motivated by the domination algorithm using the geometric representation, we develop an $O(n^2)$ time and $O(n)$ space algorithm for the Hamilton circuit problem on these graphs.

In order to get the points that are adjacent to any vertex v, we can draw the axes through v and perform four types of scans: left-to-right traversal (lr-trav), top-down traversal (td-trav), bottom-up traversal (bu-trav) and right-to-left traversal (rl-trav) (Fig.4.1). With v as the origin the fourth quadrant is called the lower dominating region, and the second quadrant is called the upper dominating region.

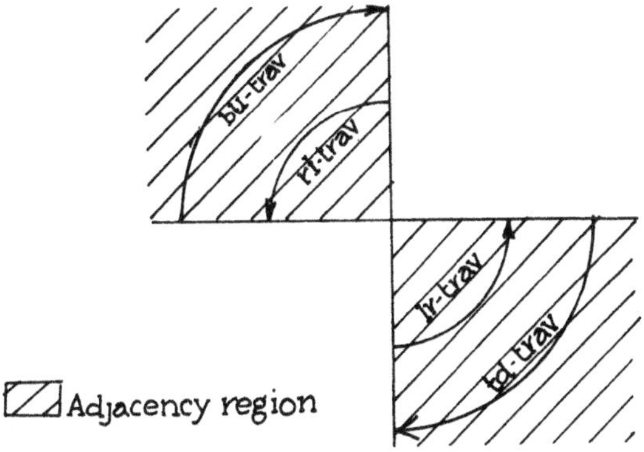

Fig.4.1 The Adjacency region and Traversals

We now give an explanation of the algorithm.

The algorithm consists of two phases. In the first phase, the points are marked in order to direct the circuit which is to be constructed in the second phase.

Initially, t_1 and t_p are marked as 'sentinels', $t_2, \ldots, t_{p-1}$ as R-points and all other points as F-points.

Phase 1. We start with t_1 and perform the td-trav at t_1. We find a point q_1 which has a minimum angle and mark q_1 as an R-point. If q_1 lies in the adjacency region of t_2 then we start with t_2 and repeat the same procedure till we find a point in the adjacency region of t_3 and so on. If q_1 does not lie in the adjacency region of t_2 then we do a td-trav at q_1. This procedure is repeated till we find a point that lies in the adjacency region of t_2. We then continue as before. At any stage, starting from t_i, if we cannot find a q_k by performing the procedure in the adjacency region of t_{i+1} then we declare that the graph is not Hamiltonian. **Phase 1 stops when we reach the sentinel t_p.**

Phase 2. Phase 2 is divided into two stages: forward traversal and reverse traversal.

In the forward traversal we start from the sentinel t_1 and traverse through the F-points till we reach the other sentinel t_p, by performing lr-trav or bu-trav. If there exist any F-points to the right of t_p, then they are marked as R-points. Now we commence the reverse traversal. This is the same as the forward traversal except that we traverse through the R-points till we reach the sentinel t_1. If this procedure is completed successfully then the graph has a Hamilton circuit and the points as given by the order of traversal constitute a Hamilton circuit.

Forward Traversal. t_1 is first included in the Hamilton circuit. With t_1 as origin we perform the lr-trav and find a point, say u, with minimum angle. u is included in the Hamilton circuit. Using u we again perform lr-trav. This procedure is repeated till we find no point in the lower dominating region of the point that is last included in the Hamilton circuit. We then start the bu-trav and select the point with minimum angle and proceed in this manner till we find a point v with no F-point in the upper dominating region. We again start lr-trav at p and continue this process till we reach the sentinel t_p. When we reach a point from which there are no more F-points to be traversed, it must be adjacent to t_p. If it is, then the forward traversal is successful. Otherwise the graph has no Hamilton circuit.

Reverse Traversal. This is almost similar to the forward traversal except that we traverse through the R-points starting from sentinel t_p and perform td-trav and rl-trav. If the reverse traversal is terminated without exhausting all the vertices of G then the graph has no Hamilton circuit. Otherwise a Hamilton circuit has been constructed

Algorithm 2.

Input : The defining permutation π of a permutation graph G.

Output : A Hamilton circuit H of G.

Step 1. Find

i. the inverse permutation π^{-1} of π.

ii. the right-to-left minima $t_p, \ldots, t_1$ and the left-to-right maxima $b_1, \ldots, b_q$ of π^{-1}.

```
     mark t_1 and t_p as sentinels, t_2, ..., t_p as R-points and all
    other points as F-points
    i=1 ; u:=t_1 ; hamilton:='true'
Phase 1 Step 2. while u ≠ t_p do
    begin
       if hamilton do
       begin
         if all the points in the lower dominating region are
         exhausted then hamilton:='false';
         else
         begin
           if t_i = t_p go to Step 3;
           do td-trav at u and find the point q with minimum
           angle;
           mark q as an R-point;
           if q is in the adjacency region of t_{i+1} then
           u:=t_{i+1} ; i:=i+1; else u:=q
         end
       end
    end
    Step 3. if there are points to the right of t_p then mark them
    as R-points;
forward  step 4. H:=H∪ {t_1} ; u:=t_1;
traversal
    while u≠t_p do
    begin
       while there are F-points in the lower dominating region of
       u do
       begin
           do lr-trav and find an F-point v with minimum angle;
           u:=v; H:=H∪ {v} ;
       end
       while there are F-points in the upper dominating region
       of u do
       begin
          do bu-trav and find an F-point v with minimum angle;
          u:=v; H:=H∪ {v} ;
       end
       if there are no more F-points check if t_p is in the adjacency
       region of u;
       if 'yes' goto Step 5 else hamilton :='false'
    end
```

```
reverse
traversal  Step 5. if hamilton do
           begin
              while u≠t1 do
              begin
                while there are R-points in the lower dominating region
                of u do
                begin
                  do td-trav and find an R-point v with minimum angle;
                  u:=v; H:=H∪{v} ;
                end
                while there are R-points in the upper dominating region
                of u do
                begin
                   do rl-trav and find an R-point v with minimum angle;
                   u:=v; H:=H∪{v} ;
                end
                if there are no more R-points check if t1 is in the
                adjacency region of u;
                if 'yes' then print H else hamilton:='false'
             end
           end
```

Correctness and Complexity

There is no edge between t_1 and t_p. If there is a Hamilton circuit there has to be a path between t_1 and t_p. The idea of the algorithm is to construct two paths between the sentinels. The first path is constructed in the forward traversal and the second path is constructed in the reverse traversal. Phase 1 marks the vertices that are to be included in the second path and hence it is essential that for each t_i we find a point q_k which lies in the dominating region of the next vertex in Max(v). During the traversals of the adjacency regions, we choose the points which have minimum angles. This process ensures that the hamilton circuit of the given graph, if one exists, is generated as the boundary of a simple polygon with as few crossing edges as possible. If there is more than one point, at any time with the same angle we select the one that is closer to the current origin. This avoids backtracking.

The complexity of the algorithm is $O(n^2)$ since we perform one traversal at each vertex in the worst case and each traversal encounters atmost O(n) points. The angles can be found in O(n) time.

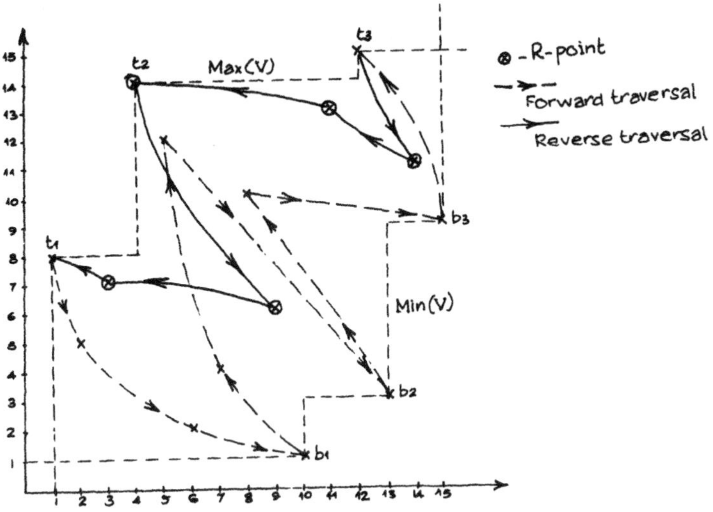

Fig.4.2 Working of the Algorithm 2

π = 10,6,13,7,2,9,3,1,15,8,14,5,11,4,12

Conclusions. Both the algorithms have been implemented and tested on all the 6-permutations and random permutations of larger length. The geometric representation seems to be efficient for many algorithms. It would be interesting to study if this representation will give efficient algorithms for other problems like matching, planarity testing, etc.

References

[1] A. Brandstadt and D. Kratsch, "On the restriction of some NP-complete Graph Problems to Permutation Graphs", Proc. of Foundations of Computation Theory '85, Lecture Notes in Computer Science 199, Springer, Berlin 1985.

[2] E.J. Cockayne and S.T. Hedetniemi, "Towards a Theory of Domination in Graphs", Networks, 7(1977) pp.247-261.

[3] M. Farber and J.M. Keil, "Domination in Permutation Graphs", J. Algorithms, 6(1985) pp.309-321.

[4] M.R. Garey and D.S. Johnson, "Computers and Intractability: A Guide to the Theory of NP-completeness," W.H. Freeman and Co., New York 1977.

[5] M.C. Golumbic, "Algorithmic Graph Theory and Perfect Graphs", Academic Press, New York, 1980.

[6] O.Kariv and S.L. Hakimi, "An Algorithmic approach to Network Location Problems 1. The p-centers", SIAM J. Appl. Math., 37(1979)

[7] D.S. Johnson, "NP-completeness Column: An Ongoing guide", J. Algorithms, 6(1985) pp.434-451.

[8] K.J. Supowit, "Decomposing A set of Points into Chains with an Application to Permutation and Circle Graphs", Info. Proc.Letters, 21(1985) pp. 249-252.

FAST PARALLEL ALGORITHMS FOR THE SUBGRAPH HOMEOMORPHISM AND THE SUBGRAPH ISOMORPHISM PROBLEM FOR CLASSES OF PLANAR GRAPHS

Andrzej Lingas
Department of Computer and Information Science
Linköping University, 581 83 Linköping, Sweden

Andrzej Proskurowski[1]
Department of Computer and Information Science
University of Oregon, Eugene, Oregon 97403, USA

Abstract

We consider the problems of subgraph homeomorphism with fixed pattern graph, recognition, and subgraph isomorphism for some classes of planar graphs. Following the results of Robertson and Seymour on forbidden minor characterization, we show that the problems of fixed subgraph homeomorphism and recognition for any family of planar graphs closed under minor taking are in $\mathcal{NC}$ (*i.e.*, they can be solved by an algorithm running in poly-log time using polynomial number of processors). We also show that the related subgraph isomorphism problem for biconnected outerplanar graphs is in $\mathcal{NC}$. This is the first example of a restriction of subgraph isomorphism to a non-trivial graph family admitting an $\mathcal{NC}$ algorithm.

1. INTRODUCTION

The subgraph homeomorphism problem is to determine whether a graph is homeomorphic to a subgraph of another graph. A graph H is homeomorphic to a graph G if the graph resulting from contracting all maximal paths in G with inner vertices of degree two to single edges is isomorphic to H. Thus, the subgraph homeomorphism problem can be viewed as a generalization of the subgraph isomorphism problem. The latter problem is to determine whether a graph is isomorphic to a subgraph of another graph. For instance, if H is an n-vertex circuit and G is an n-vertex planar graph of valence 3, $n \in N$, then determining whether H is homeomorphic to a subgraph of G is equivalent to determining whether H is isomorphic to a subgraph of G which is in turn equivalent to the $\mathcal{NP}$-complete problem of determining whether a planar graph of valence 3 has a Hamiltonian circuit [GJ]. Thus, the subgraph homeomorphism and isomorphism problems are $\mathcal{NP}$-complete even if G and H range only over connected planar graphs of valence 3. Subgraph isomorphism also remains $\mathcal{NP}$-complete when the first input graph is a forest and the other input graph is a tree [GJ]. Analogous $\mathcal{NP}$-completeness results hold for the directed versions of the two problems [GJ]. However, in this paper we consider only undirected graphs.

If we fix the first graph H as a pattern graph then this fixed subgraph isomorphism problem is trivially solvable in polynomial time while the fixed subgraph homeomorphism problem remains open (in the undirected case) [As, FHW]. On the other hand, there are two known restrictions of the general subgraph isomorphism problem to non-trivial graph families that are solvable in polynomial sequential time. Trees constitute one of these families [Ma, Rey], the other is the class

[1]Research of this author was partially supported by the Office of Naval Research under contract N00014-86-0419

of biconnected outerplanar graphs [Li86]. (A graph is outerplanar if it can be embedded in the plane such that all its vertices lie on the outer face [H, Mi].)

Another view of the subgraph homeomorphism problem is as a generalization of the disjoint connected paths problem, DCP, defined as follows: Given a graph G and a set of vertex pairs $(s_i, t_i), 1 \leq i \leq k$, decide whether there exists a set of pairwise vertex-disjoint paths P_i in G connecting s_i with t_i. Also this problem is $\mathcal{NP}$-complete even if restricted to planar graphs [FHW]. However, if the number k of vertex pairs is bounded the problem seems to become more tractable. For $k = 2$, there are polynomial-time sequential algorithms for DCP (see [GJ,RS85]). Recently, Robertson and Seymour have showed that for an arbitrary fixed k, the DCP problem restricted to planar graphs is solvable in polynomial time [RS85]. Since the fixed subgraph homeomorphism problem is trivially polynomial-time reducible to the DCP problem with appropriately chosen fixed k, the result of Robertson and Seymour yields also a polynomial time solution to the problem of fixed subgraph homeomorphism for planar graphs.

A well known application of the subgraph homeomorphism problem is the recognition problem for classes of graphs that can be characterized by the absence of some forbidden substructures. For instance, the recognition problem for planar graphs can be reduced to two fixed subgraph homeomorphism problems with K_5 and $K_{3,3}$ as the pattern graphs (see, for instance [H]). A similar characterization of planar graphs is provided by the operation of minor taking which can be viewed as a generalization of the path contraction operation used in the definition of subgraph homeomorphism. A graph H is a minor of another graph G if G can be reduced to H by deletion and contraction of edges. A graph is planar if and only if it does not have a minor isomorphic to K_5 or $K_{3,3}$. Many other non-trivial classes of graphs can be also characterized by a finite list of forbidden minors, for instance outerplanar graphs, series-parallel graphs, partial 3-trees, bounded genus graphs [CH,APC,RS86]. For fixed H, the problem of testing whether G has a minor isomorphic to H can be be reduced to a finite number of fixed subgraph homeomorphism problems [RS85]. Thus, the problems of subgraph homeomorphism, DCP, minor containment, and recognition for several classes of graphs are intimately related. Often a solution to one of them yields solutions to the others.

As yet, there are no known efficient parallel algorithms even for the fixed versions of these problems (with the exception of the DCP problem with $k = 1$ [QD]). The situation is similar in the case of restricted subgraph isomorphism problems. It is only known that subgraph isomorphism for trees is solvable by a Las Vegas $\mathcal{NC}$ algorithm [LK].

In this paper, we consider the problems of DCP with fixed k, fixed subgraph homeomorphism, and recognition for any class of planar graphs closed under minor taking, and the subgraph isomorphism problem for biconnected outerplanar graphs. We show that all these problems can be solved in poly-log time using a polynomial number of processors, *i.e.*, they are in the class $\mathcal{NC}$ [C,Ru,P]

Our parallel algorithms for the problems of DCP with fixed k, fixed subgraph homeomorphism, and recognition for any class of planar graphs closed under minor taking rely on the idea of a sequential method of Robertson and Seymour for the so restricted DCP problem [RS85]. In turn, the sequential method is implied by their interesting, bounded separator theorem for the above classes of planar graphs [RS85].

The subgraph isomorphism problem for biconnected outerplanar graphs can be sequentially solved by a recursive reduction to a monotone path finding problem in cubic time [Li86]. (Note that the reduction of PARTITION to this restriction of subgraph isomorphism given in [Sy82] is pseudo-polynomial and does not establish its $\mathcal{NP}$-completeness [Sy85].) Unfortunately, the recursive depth of the sequential algorithm in [Li86] is proportional to the size of the input graphs in the worst case. To obtain a recursive, efficient parallel algorithm, we need decrease the size of the input graphs by a constant factor in each recursive call. A straightforward way of doing it by using a two-vertex '$\frac{1}{3} - \frac{2}{3}$' separator [LT] in the first graph and guessing its image in the second graph can lead to hyper-polynomial number of considered components of the second graph.

We present a parallel algorithm for subgraph isomorphism restricted to biconnected outerplanar graphs, using a two-level, outerplanar graph cutting technique, and show that it can be implemented by uniform circuits of poly-log depth and polynomial size. In this way, we establish the membership of this restriction of the subgraph isomorphism problem in the class $\mathcal{NC}$. No other restriction of the subgraph isomorphism problem to a non-trivial graph family is presently known to be in $\mathcal{NC}$.

We leave a more precise estimation of the parallel complexity of the presented algorithms to the final version. However, even not very sophisticated circuit implementations of our algorithms yield the membership of the considered problems in $\mathcal{NC}^3$. It is worth pointing out that analogous $\mathcal{NC}$ algorithms can be designed for the construction version of the considered decision problems.

The paper is organized as follows: In Section 2 we derive the $\mathcal{NC}$ algorithms for the problems of DCP with fixed k, fixed subgraph homeomorphism, and recognition for any class of planar graphs closed under minor taking. In Section 3 we reduce the subgraph isomorphism problem for biconnected outerplanar graphs to a more restricted problem of polygon imbedding. In Section 4 we present a parallel algorithm for the latter problem which implies the membership of the former problem in $\mathcal{NC}$. In Section 5 we discuss further potential applications of our techniques. In particular, they probably could be used to establish the membership of the subgraph isomorphism problem for three-connected planar graphs of bounded width in $\mathcal{NC}$.

In this paper, we use standard set and graph theoretic notation and definitions (for instance, see [AHU,H]). For the definitions of parallel random access machine, uniform circuit families, the classes $\mathcal{NC}^k, \mathcal{NC}$, and the corresponding notions of reducibility, the reader is referred to [C,P,Rei,Ru].

2. THE RECOGNITION AND SUBGRAPH HOMEOMORPHISM PROBLEMS FOR CLASSES OF PLANAR GRAPHS

To start with we need the following definition.

Definition 2.1 A class of graphs $\mathcal{F}$ is said to be *minor-closed* (closed under minor taking operation) if for every graph $G \in \mathcal{F}$ all its minors are also in $\mathcal{F}$. For a minor-closed class $\mathcal{F}$, a graph $H \notin \mathcal{F}$ is a *minimal forbidden minor* if every minor of H is in $\mathcal{F}$.

Robertson and Seymour [RS86] consider characterization of minor-closed classes of graphs through finite sets of minimal forbidden minors.

Fact 2.1[RS86]: For any minor-closed class of graphs there is a finite set of minimal forbidden minors. ∎

In [RS85], the problem of testing if a given graph G has a minor isomorphic to a fixed graph H is reduced to the problem of subgraph homeomorphism for G with respect to a set of *fixed* graphs. H is a minor of G if and only if G has a subgraph homeomorphic to any graph from a finite list of graphs derived from H.

Fact 2.2[RS85, Thm.4.1]: Let H be a graph. There is a finite list of graphs $H_1, \ldots, H_n$ such that for any graph G the following are equivalent:

(i) G has a minor isomorphic to H.

(ii) G contains a subgraph homeomorphic to one of $H_1, \ldots, H_n$. ∎

By the above fact, it suffices to solve the subgraph homeomorphism problem by an $\mathcal{NC}$ algorithm to show that the minor containment problem is in $\mathcal{NC}$. In their general form, the two problems can be probably solved by parallelization of a sequential algorithm outlined in a recent work of Robertson and Seymour [RS86]. In this paper, however, we consider only the case of planar graphs.

We follow Robertson and Seymour [RS85] in using their bounded separator theorem to 'divide and conquer' the complexity of the problem. A *separation* (V_1, V_2) of G is a pair of subsets of $V(G)$ such that $V_1 \cup V_2 = V(G)$ and no edge of G joins a vertex of $V_1 - V_2$ with a vertex of $V_2 - V_1$.

Fact 2.3[RS85, Thm.4.2]: For any planar graph H there is a number N with the following property. For every graph G with no minor isomorphic to H, and every subset X of $V(G)$, there is a separation (V_1, V_2) of G such that $\#((V_1 - V_2) \cap X), \#((V_2 - V_1) \cap X) \leq \frac{2}{3}\#(X)$ and $\#(V_1 \cap V_2) \leq N$.
■

Below, we specify more formally the problem of disjoint connecting paths to which the subgraph homeomorphism problem easily reduces.

Definition 2.2 Given a graph G and two *terminal vertices* $s, t \in V(G)$, a *path of length* k *connecting* s and t is a sequence of vertices $v_0, v_1, ..., v_k$ such that $v_0 = s$, $v_k = t$, and $(v_{i-1}, v_i) \in E(G)$ for every $i, 1 \leq i \leq k$. Two paths are *disjoint* if they have no common non-terminal vertices. An instance of *disjoint connecting paths* problem is an undirected graph G and a *terminal set* $P = \{(s_1, t_1), ..., (s_n, t_n)\}$ which is a subset $V(G) \times V(G)$. We will denote the set of terminal vertices in P by $V(P)$. A set M of k disjoint paths in G is a *DCP* for P if there is a bijection $b : P \rightarrow M$ such that for $(s,t) \in P$, $b((s,t))$ connects s with t.

In the following, we describe a procedure which for a given planar graph H and the corresponding integer N specified in Fact 2.3, takes as the input a graph G and a terminal set P in G with $\#V(P) \leq k$. The procedure either reports that G has a minor isomorphic to H or reports whether DCP for P in G exists. In the body of the procedure, called *DCP-or-Minor*, the instruction **halt** is interpreted as terminating the execution of the parallel procedure on all recursion levels. *DCP-or-Minor* uses an auxiliary procedure *Divide*. Given a separation (V_1, V_2) of a graph G and a terminal set P in G, *Divide* returns a family of pairs of terminal sets, P_1 and P_2, representing all possible reductions of the original DCP problem for P in G to DCP subproblems for P_1 in $G(V_1)$ and P_2 in $G(V_2)$.

procedure *Divide*(V_1, V_2, P);
begin
Construct the graph $L = (V(L), E(L))$ where $V(L) = L_1 \cup L_2 \cup L_3$ and L_1, L_2, L_3 are defined as follows: $L_1 = (V_1 - V_2) \cap V(P)$, $L_2 = (V_2 - V_1) \cap V(P)$, and $L_3 = V_1 \cap V_2$. $E(L)$ consists of all edges between L_1 and L_3, all edges between L_2 and L_3, and all edges between vertices of L_3;
for every set M of disjoint connecting paths for P in L
do in parallel
begin set Q to the set of edges of the paths in M;
  return $P_1 = (V_1 \times V_1) \cap Q$, and $P_2 = (V_2 \times V_2) \cap Q$
end-do
end(*Divide*);

Since *Divide* is always invoked for constantly bounded $\#V(P)$ and $\#V_1 \cap V_2$, all the sets M can be found by brute force and their number is constantly bounded. *DCP-or-Minor* is now defined as follows.

procedure *DCP-or-Minor*(G, P, H, N);
$G = (V(G), E(G))$ is the input graph;

P is the input terminal set with at most k terminal pairs;
$H = (V(H), E(H))$ is the fixed planar minor;
N is the constant implied for H by Fact 2.3.
{Returns one of the following three answers:
(i) 'minor': G has a minor isomorphic to H. This follows from Fact 2.3
  when no separation satisfying the theorem exists.
(ii) 'DCP exists': there exist disjoint connecting paths for P in G.
(iii) 'no DCP': there is no disjoint connecting paths for P in G }

begin {DCP-or-Minor}
if $\#V < 3N$
  then return the answer through solving the *DCP*
      problem for P in $G(V)$ by brute force
  else begin $\{\#V \geq 3N\}$
  for every subset S of N vertices of $V(G)$ **do in parallel**
    begin (S)
    find the connected components $C_1, ..., C_l$ of $G(V - S)$;
    if there is a separation (V_1, V_2) such that
      $V_1 \cap V_2 = S$, $V_1 \cup V_2 = V(G)$, $\#(V_1 - V_2), \#(V_2 - V_1) \leq \frac{2}{3}\#V(G)$,
      and V_1, V_2 are sums of $C_i \cup S$
     then insert (V_1, V_2) into *separations*
  end-do(S);
  if *separations*$=\emptyset$
    then return 'minor' and **halt**
    else select (V_1, V_2) from *separations*;
  for every pair (P_1, P_2) of terminal sets in *Divide*(V_1, V_2, P)
  do in parallel
  begin(P_1, P_2)
    for $i = 1, 2$ **do in parallel**
    begin(i)
    if $\#V(P_i) \leq \max(5N, 2k)$ {k is the fixed bound on $\#P$}
    then
    begin if *DCP-or-Minor*$(G(V_i), P_i, H, N)$ returns 'DCP exists'
        then $DCP[V_i, P_i] :=$ **true**
    end(then-clause)
    else begin $\{\#V(P_i) > \max(5N, 2k)\}$
    for every subset T of N vertices of V_i **do in parallel**
     begin (T)
     find the connected components $D_1, ..., D_l$ of $G(V_i - T)$;
     if there is a separation (W_1, W_2) such that
       $W_1 \cap W_2 = T$, $W_1 \cup W_2 = V_i$,
       $\#((W_1 - T) \cap V(P_i)), \#((W_2 - T) \cap V(P_i)) \leq \frac{2}{3}\#V(P_i)$,
       and W_1, W_2 are sums of $D_i \cup T$
     then insert (W_1, W_2) into *separations*$[i]$
     end-do(T);
    if *separations*$[i]=\emptyset$
     then return 'minor' and **halt**
     else select (W_1, W_2) from *separations*$[i]$;
    for every pair of terminal sets Q_1, Q_2 in *Divide*(W_1, W_2, P_i)
    do in parallel

begin (Q_1, Q_2)
  for $j = 1, 2$ **do in parallel**
    begin (j)
    set $answer[j]$=DCP-or-$Minor(G(W_j), Q_j, H, N)$
    end-do(j);
  if $answer[1]$ and $answer[2]$ report existence of DCP
    then $DCP[V_i, P_i] :=$ **true**
end-do(Q_1, Q_2);
if $DCP[V_i, P_i] \neq$ **true then** $DCP[V_i, P_i] :=$ **false**
end {else-clause($\#V(P_i) > \max(5N, 2k)$)}
end-do(i);
if $DCP[V_1, P_1] \wedge DCP[V_2, P_2]$ **then** $DCP[V, P] :=$ **true**
end-do(P_1, P_2);
if $DCP[V, P]$ **then** return('DCP exists') **else** return('no DCP')
end(*DCP-or-Minor*)

In the following we develop two lemmas asserting the correctness of the above procedure and the possibility of its efficient parallel implementation.

Lemma 2.1: The procedure *DCP-or-Minor* is correct.

Proof: If the procedure returns 'minor', the correctness of the answer follows immediately from Fact 2.3, since no postulated separation was found, as either *separation* or *separation*$[i]$ was found empty. If the procedure returns 'DCP exists' or 'no DCP' in G for P then the correctness of the answer is implied by the following two claims:

(i) $DCP[V_1, P_1]$ and $DCP[V_2, P_2]$ are correctly evaluated for all pairs (P_1, P_2) of terminal sets produced by *Divide*(V_1, V_2, P).

(ii) For the graph G with $V(G) > 3N$ and a separation (V_1, V_2) fulfilling the conditions of Fact 2.3, there exist DCP in G for P if and only if there is a pair (P_1, P_2) of terminal sets produced by *Divide*(V_1, V_2, P) such that both DCP in $G(V_1)$ for P_1 and DCP in $G(V_2)$ for P_2 exist.

In turn, the correctness of evaluating $DCP[V_i, P_i]$ results from the inductive hypothesis asserting the correctness of *DCP-or-Minor* for smaller graphs and from the following: If $\#V(P_i) > \max(5N, 2k)$, and the required separation (W_1, W_2) of $G(V_i)$ exists then DCP in $G(V_i)$ for P_i exist if and only if there is a pair (Q_1, Q_2) of terminal sets produced by *Divide*(W_1, W_2, P_i) such that for $j = 1, 2$, *DCP-or-Minor*$(G(W_j), Q_j, H, N)$ returns 'DCP exists'.

To complete the proof it remains to show that *DCP-or-Minor* always terminates. The latter follows from the fact that in any recursive call of *DCP-or-Minor* the size of the new input graph is smaller than than that of the original graph. ∎

Lemma 2.2. Let H be a fixed planar graph, N a fixed integer satisfying the thesis of Fact 2.3 for H, and let k be a fixed integer. For any graph G and any terminal set P in G with at most k terminal pairs, the procedure *DCP-or-Minor*(G, P, H, N) can be realized by an $\mathcal{NC}$ algorithm.

Proof: By [SV, Theorem 1] it suffices to show that the procedure will execute in poly-log time when carefully implemented on a parallel random access machine with concurrent read and concurrent write, using polynomial number of processors. The poly-log time performance and the polynomial upper bound on the number of processors rely on the following claims:

(i) We can check whether the required separation of V or V_i exists and if so, construct such a separation in poly-log time using a polynomial number of processors.

(ii) Let $k_0 = \max(5N, 2k)$. The cardinality of the family of terminal set pairs returned by *Divide* is bounded from above by the constant $2^{(k_0+2N)(k_0+2N-1)}$ in any call of *Divide* during the execution of *DCP-or-Minor*(G, P, H, N).

(iii) The procedure *Divide* can be implemented to run in poly-log time on polynomial number of processors.

(iv) The recursion depth of *DCP-or-Minor*(G, P, H, N) is logarithmic.

The claims (i), (iii), and (iv) imply poly-log running time. The claims (ii) and (iv) imply that the recursion tree of *DCP-or-Minor*(G, P, H, N) has a polynomial number of nodes which combined with claims (i) and (iii) ensures a polynomial number of processors.

Let us prove the above four claims. According to the body of *DCP-or-Minor*, to implement (i) in the case of the V-separation, we proceed as follows. For all subsets S of $V(G)$ with at most N vertices, we test whether S induces the required separation by finding the connected components of $G(V - S)$. Note that for a fixed N the number of such subsets S is polynomial and the connected components can be found in poly-log time, using polynomial number of processors [QD]. Knowing the connected components, we can easily find their cardinalities in poly-log time using linear number of processors. Now, we can easily check whether it is possible to sum the connected components, say $C_1, ..., C_l$, and S into appropriate sets V_1 and V_2, and if so construct such a pair (V_1, V_2). This can be done by sorting the cardinalities in decreasing order, computing all their prefix sums in parallel, and applying binary search. By [Ak], these steps can be efficiently performed in parallel. In the case of V_i-separation, we proceed analogously. The only difference is that instead of the cardinalities of the connected components of $G(V_i) - T$, we consider the cardinalities of their intersections with $V(P_i)$.

To prove (ii), we first observe that the cardinality of $V(P)$ (in recursive calls, $P = P_i$ or $P = Q_j$) never exceeds k_0 and the cardinality of $V(P_i)$ is bounded by $k_0 + N$. Clearly, the former implies the latter as $V(P_1 \cup P_2) - V(P)$ consists of at most N vertices. The two statements can be proved by induction on the depth of recursive call of *DCP-or-Minor* in decreasing depth order. Whenever there are more than k_0 vertices in $V(P_i)$, either the procedure halts or a separation (W_1, W_2) is constructed such that $W_1 \cap W_2 = T$, $W_1 \cup W_2 = V_i$, $\#((W_1 - T) \cap V(P_i)), \#((W_2 - T) \cap V(P_i)) \leq \frac{2}{3}\#V(P_i)$. Hence, there are no more than $\frac{2}{3}(k_0 + N) + N$ vertices in $V(Q_j)$ which implies $\#V(Q_j) \leq k_0$ by $k_0 \geq 5N$. This completes the proof of the two statements. It follows now that the family of terminal set pairs returned by *Divide* during the execution of *DCP-or-Minor*(G, P, H, N) never exceeds $(2^{(k_0+2N)(k_0+2N-1)/2})^2$.

To show (iii), it is sufficient to observe that after sorting the vertices in V_1 and V_2 respectively, we can test a vertex in G for membership in V_1 and V_2 in poly-log time. This enables us to construct the graph L efficiently in parallel. Since L has never more than $k_0 + 2N$ vertices by the analysis in (ii), the remaining part of the body of the procedure can be executed in constant time.

To show (iv), it is sufficient to observe that in each recursive call in the body *DCP-or-Minor* the number of vertices of the new input graph is a constant fraction of that of the original graph. ∎

A class of planar graphs is non-trivial if it is non-empty and different from the class of all planar graphs. By using *DCP-or-Minor* and Lemmas 2.1 and 2.2, we can show that the DCP problem with a bounded number of terminal pairs for non-trivial classes of planar graphs is in $\mathcal{NC}$.

Theorem 2.1: Let $\mathcal{F}$ be a non-trivial minor-closed class of planar graphs and let k be a positive integer. The problem of testing for any graph G in $\mathcal{F}$, and any terminal set P in G of at most k pairs whether DCP for P in G exists is in $\mathcal{NC}$.

Proof: Since $\mathcal{F}$ is non-trivial and planarity is preserved under minor taking, $\mathcal{F}$ has at least one planar forbidden minor H by Fact 2.1. Now, it is sufficient to call *DCP-or-Minor*(G, P, H, N) where N is the integer constant specified by Fact 2.3. Since G is assumed to be in $\mathcal{F}$, it cannot have a minor isomorphic to H. Thus, we obtain as the answer either 'DCP exists' or 'no DCP'. Now, Lemmas 2.1 and 2.2 imply the thesis. ∎

Combining Theorem 2.1 with the obvious reduction of the fixed subgraph isomorphism problem to a polynomial number of DCP problems with fixed k, we obtain the following theorem.

Theorem 2.2: Given a minor-closed class $\mathcal{F}$ of planar graphs, and a planar graph H, the subgraph homeomorphism problem for H and any graph G in $\mathcal{F}$ is in $\mathcal{NC}$.

Proof: To begin with, we need the following definition. A terminal set P in G corresponds to H if $(V(P), P)$ is a graph isomorphic to H. It is clear that H is homeomorphic to a subgraph of G if and only if there is a (terminal) subset P of $V(G) \times V(G)$ corresponding to H such that DCP for P in G exists. Note that since the graph H is fixed, the number of all such terminal sets P to test for DCP in G is polynomial in the size of G. Thus, by Theorem 2.1, we can perform all these tests and return the conjuction of their results in poly-log time using a polynomial number of processors. ∎

In turn, by combining Fact 2.1 and Theorem 2.2 with the reduction of the minor containment problem to that of subgraph homeomorphism (given in Fact 2.2), we obtain the following theorem.

Theorem 2.3: Given a minor-closed class $\mathcal{F}$ of planar graphs, the recognition problem for $\mathcal{F}$ is in $\mathcal{NC}$.

Proof: Our efficient parallel algorithm for the recognition problem consists of two major steps. First, we test the input graph for planarity using Miller-Reif's algorithm [MR]. Their algorithm runs on a concurrent read, concurrent write PRAM with $n^{O(1)}$ processors in time $O(\log n)$ ([MR, Theorem 26]). Hence, it can be implemented by $\mathcal{NC}$ circuits [SV, Theorem 1]. In the second step, we assume the input graph G to be planar and test whether it is in $\mathcal{F}$ by checking if it has a minor isomorphic to at least one of minimal forbidden minors defining $\mathcal{F}$ (see Fact 2.1). Since planarity is preserved under minor taking operation it is enough to perform these tests only for such planar minors for $\mathcal{F}$ to know whether G is in $\mathcal{F}$. Our method of performing the test relies on Fact 2.2 and Theorem 2.2. For each planar minimal forbidden minor K for $\mathcal{F}$, we use (by Fact 2.2) the finite list of planar graphs $H_1(K), ..., H_l(K)$ such that G has a minor isomorphic to K if and only if at least one of the graphs on the list is homeomorphic to a subgraph of K. Thus, we test each such a planar graph $H_i(K)$ and G for subgraph homeomorphism using the parallel algorithm described in the proof of Theorem 2.2. By finiteness of the list of minimal forbidden minors K of $\mathcal{F}$ and finiteness of the lists $H_1(K), ..., H_l(K)$, and Theorem 2.2, we obtain the thesis. ∎

3. A REDUCTION OF SUBGRAPH ISOMORPHISM FOR BICONNECTEDD OUTERPLANAR GRAPHS TO POLYGON IMBEDDING

In this and the next sections, we consider the subgraph isomorphism problem for *outerplanar graphs*. An outerplanar graph is a graph which can be embedded in the plane in such a way that all its vertices lie on the exterior face [Mi]. We shall call such an embedding of a graph in the plane, an *outerplanar embedding*. By [MR], we can easily deduce the following lemma:

Lemma 3.1: Given a biconnected outerplanar graph, we can find the cycle bounding the exterior face of its outerplanar embedding using $\mathcal{NC}$ circuits.

Proof sketch: Extend the input graph by a single vertex w adjacent to all original vertices. Note that the resulting graph is still planar. Find a planar embedding of the new graph. It is easy to see that the vertices adjacent to w in the clockwise order around w form the sought cycle. A planar embedding of the new graph can be constructed by a concurrent read, concurrent write PRAM with $n^{O(1)}$ processors in time $O(\log n)$ (Theorem 26 in [MR]). Hence, it can be constructed by $\mathcal{NC}$ circuits by Theorem 1 in [SV], and consequently, the whole procedure can be performed by $\mathcal{NC}$ circuits. ∎

Using the following definitions of planar figures in terms of standard geometric notation (see [PS]), we will be able to specify outerplanar embeddings of biconnected outerplanar graphs more precisely.

Definition 3.1 A *partial triangulation* of a simple polygon is a set of non-intersecting diagonals of the polygon. A *partially triangulated polygon* (PTP for short) Q is a union of a simple polygon and a partial triangulation of the simple polygon. The vertices of the simple polygon are vertices of Q, whereas the edges of the simple polygon and the diagonals from the partial triangulation of the simple polygon are edges of Q. The former edges of Q are called *boundary edges* of Q, the latter edges of Q are called *diagonal edges* of Q.

Mitchell observes in [Mi] that a biconnected outerplanar graph is in fact a partially triangulated polygon. By Lemma 3.1, we have:

Lemma 3.2: Given a biconnected outerplanar graph, we can find its outerplanar embedding in the form of a partially triangulated (convex) polygon using $\mathcal{NC}$ circuits.

It follows that a biconnected outerplanar graph has a unique outerplanar embedding (in the topological sense) up to the mirror image (see also [Sy82]).

Definition 3.2. A partially triangulated polygon with a distinguished boundary edge is called a *rooted, partially triangulated polygon* (RPTP for short). The distinguished edge is called the *root* of the RPTP. Given a RPTP P, the graph induced by P is denoted by $G(P)$. Now, given two RPTP, P and Q, we say that P can be *root-imbedded* into Q if and only if there is an isomorphism between $G(P)$ and a subgraph of $G(Q)$ that maps the root of P on the root of Q, and preserves the clockwise ordering of the vertices on the perimeter of P. Such an isomorphism is called a *root-imbedding* of P into Q.

In the following lemma, we show that the problem of subgraph isomorphism for biconnected outerplanar graphs is efficiently reducible (in parallel) to the problem of testing two RPTP's for root-imbedding.

Lemma 3.3: The problem of subgraph isomorphism for biconnected outerplanar graphs is $\mathcal{NC}$ reducible to the problem of testing whether an RPTP can be root-imbedded in another RPTP.

Proof sketch: Let G and H be biconnected outerplanar graphs. By Lemma 3.2, we can find outerplanar embeddings P and Q of G and H, respectively, in the form of partially triangulated convex polygons, using $\mathcal{NC}$ circuits. Let Q' be the mirror image of Q. Let us root P at its arbitrary boundary edge e. It is clear that G is isomorphic to a subgraph of H if and only if there is a subfigure R of Q (or Q'), and an edge d of Q (Q') such that R is a partially triangulated polygon consisting of all edges of Q (Q') on a given side of d and of the edge d on its boundary, and P can be root-imbedded in the RPTP R rooted at d. Note that there is only a linear number of candidates for such subfigures R. Hence, the reduction can be done by $\mathcal{NC}$ circuits. ∎

To specify and analyze our parallel algorithm for root-imbedding for RPTP in the next section, we need also the following definitions and lemmas.

Definition 3.3. Let P be a RPTP with n vertices. The *diagonal separator* of P is a diagonal or a diagonal edge of P that partitions P into two RPTP, each of no more than $\frac{2}{3}n + 2$ vertices.

For a PTP P, the tree $T(P)$ *dual* to P consists of vertices in one-to-one correspondence to the inner faces of P and of edges connecting vertices corresponding to adjacent faces in P.

Lemma 3.4: Given a RPTP P, we can find a diagonal separator of P using $\mathcal{NC}$ circuits.

Proof sketch: First, we triangulate P to obtain a completely triangulated polygon P'. It can be done by a concurrent read, exclusive write PRAM using a polynomial number of processors in poly-log time [ACGOY], and hence it can be implemented by $\mathcal{NC}$ circuits [SV]. Given P', we can construct the tree $T(P')$ dual to P' in constant time, in parallel. Now, to find a diagonal separator of P, it is sufficient to find a $\frac{1}{3} - \frac{2}{3}$ vertex separator of $T(P')$ with vertex weights appropriately defined (such a separator always exists [LT], see [Li85] for the details). This can be done by communicating the total weight of $T(P')$ to each vertex v of $T(P')$, and finding the total weight of descendants of v for each vertex v of $T(P')$. The latter can be done by using Euler's path techniques by $\mathcal{NC}$ circuits (combine [TV] with [SV]). ∎

Definition 3.4. Let P be a PTP. Given two edges e and d of P, let γ be the path in $T(P)$ between the two closest vertices in $T(P)$ corresponding to the faces adjacent to e and d respectively. Then, the *dual path* between e and d is the sequence of diagonal edges of P that separate the faces in the sequence of faces in P corresponding to γ.

Lemma 3.5: Given two edges e and d of a PTP, we can find the dual path between e and d and its middle element, using $\mathcal{NC}$-circuits.

Proof sketch: As in the proof of Lemma 3.4, we first build the tree T dual to the completely triangulated polygon P'. Next, the dual path can be easily constructed from the corresponding vertex path in T. The latter path can be found by using a standard $O(\log n)$ method on a concurrent read, exclusive write parallel RAM with $O(n^2)$ processors. In the j-th iteration of the method, we find, for each vertex v in the tree, the path from v to its ancestor at distance 2^j by concatenating the path from v to its ancestor at distance 2^{j-1} with the copied path between the two ancestors of v. By [SV], the method can be implemented by (uniform) circuits of unbounded fan-in, $O(\log n)$ depth and polynomial size. Hence, it can be implemented by $\mathcal{NC}^2$ circuits. Given the dual path, we can find its median by finding for each its element the number of preceding and following elements which can be easily implemented by $\mathcal{NC}$ circuits.∎

4. A PARALLEL ALGORITHM FOR IMBEDDING OF PARTIALLY TRIANGULATED POLYGONS

Our parallel algorithm for the problem of root-imbedding for PTP consists of two recursive procedures $RI1$ and $RI2$. The first procedure tests whether the input RPTP P can be root-imbedded in the input RPTP Q. First, it finds a diagonal separator of Q and then it guesses its image in Q by trying all possible pairs of vertices of Q in parallel. To check whether the bottom part of P cut off by the diagonal separator (*i.e.*, the part not containing the root) can be root-imbedded in the corresponding part of Q cut off by the guessed image of the separator, the procedure calls recursively itself. To check whether the upper part of Q (the part containing the root) can be imbedded in the upper part of Q such that the root of P is mapped on the root of Q and the diagonal separator on its guessed image, the procedure $RI1$ calls $RI2$. The latter procedure solves the above problem as follows. First, it finds the dual path from the diagonal separator to the root of P. If the dual path is empty then it cuts off the left and right part of the upper part of P along the diagonals connecting the left and right endpoints of the diagonal separator and the root of P respectively (if for instance, the left endpoints overlap, the left part is empty). Analogously, it cuts off the corresponding left and right part from the upper part of Q. Next, $IR2$ tests whether the left and the right upper part of P can be respectively root-imbedded in those of the upper part of Q by calling the procedure $RI1$, twice in parallel. If both tests are positive, it returns YES. If the

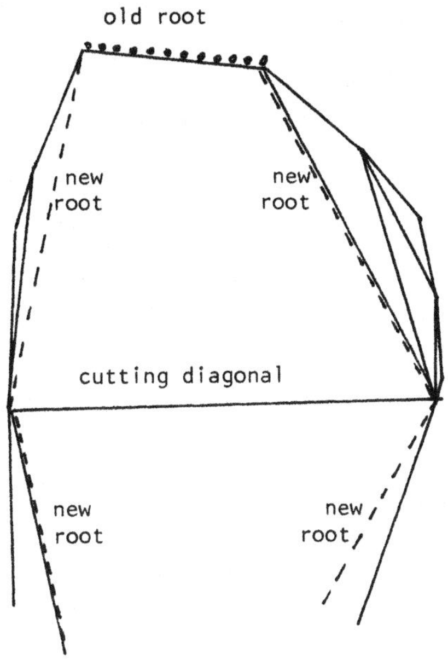

Fig. 4.1.

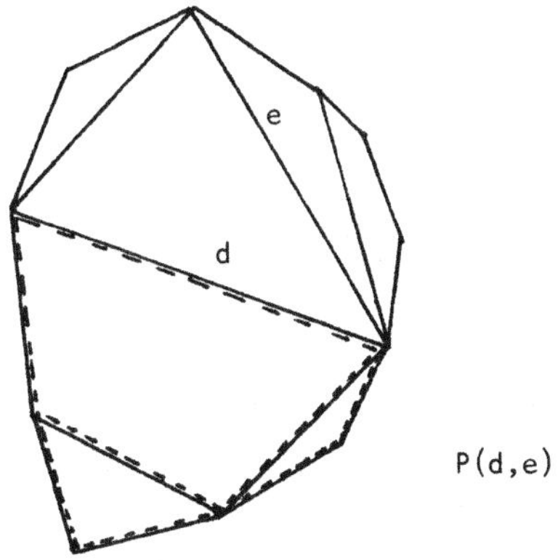

Fig. 42. The PTP P(d,e) is marked with dashed lines.

dual path contains more edges, the procedure *RI*2 finds the median and then guesses an image of the median in the upper part of Q by trying all possible pairs of vertices of the upper part of Q, in parallel. To check whether the upper and bottom part of the upper part of P divided by the median can be respectively imbedded in the corresponding parts of the upper part of Q divided by the guessed image of the median, it calls recursively itself twice in parallel.

The use of the diagonal separator and the path median ensures an $O(\log^2 n)$ recursive depth of the algorithm composed of the two procedures. Since by Lemmas 3.4 and 3.5, the problems of finding the diagonal separator, the dual path, and its median can be solved by $\mathcal{NC}$ circuits, we can conclude that the procedure can be implemented by uniform circuits of poly-log depth. The crux is to observe that the circuits need only a polynomial number of processors. This follows from the fact that each figure occurring as a parameter in the recursive calls of *RI*1 can be obtained from P or Q by cutting along a single diagonal/edge in P or Q, or a straight line segment between two vertices in Q. In the latter case, all edges intersecting this segment are deleted from Q. The above fact holds inductively for the bottom parts. For the upper parts, it is sufficient to observe that neither the root of P or Q nor the 'horizontal' cutting edges (*i.e.*, diagonal separators and the medians) occur in the final RPTP's that are produced by *RI*2 and become parameters of *RI*1 (see Fig. 4.1). It follows that the number of figures that are parameters in the recursive calls of *RI*1 is polynomial. Hence, the number of different figures occurring as parameters in the recursive calls of *RI*2 is also polynomial, since they are obtained from the figures being parameters of *RI*1 by cutting along at most two single diagonals/edges. We conclude that the number of distinct, potential recursive calls of *RI*1 and *RI*2 is polynomial. Therefore, we can implement all these potential recursive calls using a bottom-up method of poly-log depth taking a polynomial number of processors.

Thus, we have the following theorem.

Theorem 4.1: The problem of root-imbedding for RPTP is in $\mathcal{NC}$.

Combining Lemma 3.3 with Theorem 4.1, we obtain the main result of this section.

Theorem 4.2: The problem of subgraph isomorphism for biconnected outerplanar graphs is in $\mathcal{NC}$.

We conclude this section with a more formal description of the procedures *RI*1 and *RI*2. To simplify the notation, we assume that the input RPTP's are convex and no vertical line passes through any pair of their vertices. In the body of the procedure, $X(p)$ denotes the X coordinate of p.

We need also the following definition.

Let R be a PTP. Given a sequence $\alpha = v_1, v_2, ..., v_k$ of vertices of R, and a fragment β of R, we denote by $R(\alpha, \beta)$ the largest PTP such that:

(i) if there is no more than one vertex in α then it is empty;
(ii) it consists of some edges of R and the edges $(v_1, v_2), ..., (v_{k-1}, v_k)$;
(iii) the edges $(v_1, v_2), ..., (v_{k-1}, v_k)$ form a continuous fragment of its perimeter;
(iv) it is disjoint from β.

See Fig. 4.2 for an example.

The two procedures are specified as follows.

```
procedure RI1(P, Q)
begin
if P has three vertices then
  begin
    if Q contains a triangle then return YES else return NO
  end
```

```
else
  begin
    find a diagonal separator (v1, v2) of P where X(v1) < X(v2);
    P1 ← P((v1, v2), {root(P)}) rooted at (v1, v2);
    P2 ← P((v1, v2), P1 − {(v1, v2)});
    for all vertices w1, w2 of Q where (w1, w2) is not the root of Q
    do in parallel
    begin
      if (v1, v2) is an edge of P and (w1, w2) is not an edge of Q
      then return NO and halt;
      Q1 ← Q((w1, w2), {root(Q)}) rooted at (w1, w2);
      Q2 ← Q((w1, w2), Q1 − {(w1, w2)});
      if RI1(P1, Q1) ∧ RI2(P2, Q2, (v1, v2), (w1, w2), root(P), root(Q))
      then return YES else return NO
    end
  end
end
```

```
procedureRI2(P, Q, (v1, v2), (w1, w2), (v'1, v'2), (w'1, w'2))
begin
D ← the dual path from (v1, v2) to (v'1, v'2) in P;
if D = ∅ then
  begin
    if (v1, v'1) is an edge of P and (w1, w'1) is not an edge of Q
    or (v2, v'2) is an edge of P and (w2, w'2) is not an edge of Q
    then return NO and halt;
    PL ← P((v1, v'1), {v2, v'2}) rooted at (v1, v'1);
    QL ← Q((w1, w'1), {w2, w'2}) rooted at (w1, w'1);
    PR ← P((v2, v'2), {v1, v'1}) rooted at (v2, v'2);
    QR ← Q((w2, w'2), {w1, w'1}) rooted at (w1, w'1);
    if RI1(PL, QL) ∧ RI1(PR, QR) then return YES else return NO
  end
else
  begin
    (v3, v4) ← the middle edge in D where X(v3) < X(v4);
    PU ← P((v3, v4), {(v1, v2)});
    PD ← P((v3, v4), {(v'1, v'2)});
    for all vertices w3 and w4 of Q
      where (w3, w4) is different from (w1, w2) and (w'1, w'2)
    do in parallel
    begin
      QU ← Q((w3, w4), {(w1, w2)});
      QD ← Q((w3, w4), {(w'1, w'2)});
      if RI2(PU, QU, (v3, v4), (w3, w4), (v'1, v'2), (w'1, w'2))∧
         RI2(PD, QD, (v1, v2), (w1, w2), (v3, v4), (w3, w4))
      then return YES else return NO
    end
  end
end
```

5. EXTENSIONS

The problem of subgraph isomorphism for biconnected outerplanar graphs can be seen as an abstraction of two following geometric problems for partially triangulated polygons P, Q :

(i) decide whether P is similar to a subfigure of Q;

(ii) decide whether P is congruent to a subfigure of Q.

The two problems can be respectively termed as the problems of sub-similarity and sub-congruency for partially triangulated polygons. Both have potential applications in pattern recognition.

The problems of sub-similarity and sub-congruency for partially triangulated polygons can be solved analogously to the problem of subgraph isomorphism for biconnected outerplanar graphs. First, we reduce both problems to their rooted versions (where the mapping on a distinguished boundary edge is fixed), using $\mathcal{NC}$-circuits. Then, we solve the rooted versions by subsequently modifying the parallel algorithm for root-imbedding for RPTP. In the case of the sub-similarity problem, we appropriately add tests for the congruency of angles formed by the roots and cutting edges of P and Q with the adjacent edges. In the case of the sub-congruency problem, we add also tests for edge length equality for the roots and cutting edges, respectively. The above modifications of the procedures $RI1$ and $RI2$ do not affect their asymptotic, worst-case circuit complexity. Hence, in analogy to Theorem 3.2, we have that the problems of sub-similarity and sub-congruency for partially triangulated polygons are in $\mathcal{NC}$.

It seems also possible to generalize our $\mathcal{NC}$ algorithm for subgraph isomorphism restricted to biconnected outerplanar graphs to include three-connected planar graphs of bounded width. We say that a planar graph G has width $\leq k$ if for any vertex v in any planar embedding of G there is a path composed of at most k edges/diagonals connecting v with the outer face.

The idea of a generalization of our $\mathcal{NC}$ algorithm would rely on the following insights:

(i) Any three-connected planar graph has at most two different embeddings on the sphere. These can be constructed by an $\mathcal{NC}$ algorithm [MR].

(ii) Three-connected planar graphs of width $\leq k$ have a $\frac{1}{3}-\frac{2}{3}$ separator in the form of edge/diagonal path of constantly bounded length. Such a separator can be found using an $\mathcal{NC}$-algorithm.

(iii) The above edge/diagonal paths would be used in the analogous manner to that of diagonal separators, median separators, *etc.*. Note that there is a polynomial number of such paths.

(iv) In order to keep the total length of cuts on the perimeter of each considered subfigure constantly bounded, it would be necessary to use yet another cutting procedure, resembling the V_i-separation from the procedure *DCP-or-Minor* (section 2). This would ensure a polynomial number of subfigures that could ever be considered. Hence, we would again obtain only a polynomial number of potential recursive calls.

As for the methods of Section 2, we suspect that similar methods can be used to design efficient parallel algorithm for the discussed problems restricted to families of not necessarily planar graphs (for instance, partial k-trees [AP]).

6. REFERENCES

[ACGOY] A. Aggarwal, B. Chazelle, L. Guibas, C. O'Dunlaing, and C. Yap, Parallel Computational Geometry, in *Proc. 25th Annual IEEE Symposium on Foundations of Computer Science 1985*, 468-477.

[AHU] A.V. Aho, J.E. Hopcroft and J.D. Ullman, *The Design and Analysis of Computer Algorithms*, (Addison-Wesley, Reading, Massachusetts, 1974).

[AP] S. Arnborg and A. Proskurowski, Characterization and recognition of partial 3-trees, *SIAM Journal of Algebraic and Discrete Methods* 7, 2(1986), 305-314.

[APC] S. Arnborg, A. Proskurowski, and D.G. Corneil, Forbidden minors characterization of partial 3-trees, *UO-CIS-TR-86-07*, University of Oregon (1986);

[Ak] S.G. Akl, *Parallel Sorting Algorithms*, (Academic Press, New York, 1985).

[As] T. Asano, An approach to the subgraph homeomorphism problem, *Theoretical Computer Science*, 38 (1985), 249-267.

[C] S.A. Cook, The Classification of Problems which have Fast Parallel Algorithm, in *Proc. Foundations of Computation Theory, Borgholm, Sweden 1983*, Springer-Verlag LNCS 158.

[CH] G. Chartrand and F. Harary, Planar permutation graphs, *Ann. Inst. Henri Poincaré Sec. B* 3(1967), 433-438.

[FHW] S. Fortune, J. Hopcroft, and J. Wyllie, The directed subgraph homeomorphism problem, *Theoretical Computer Science 10* (1980), 111-121.

[GJ] M.R. Garey, D.S. Johnson, *Computers and Intractability. A Guide to the Theory of NP-completeness* (Freeman, San Francisco, 1979).

[H] F. Harary, *Graph Theory* (Addison-Wesley, Reading Massachusetts, 1969).

[Li85] A. Lingas, On partitioning polygons, in *Proc. of 1st ACM Symposium on Computational Geometry, Baltimore 1985.*

[Li86] A. Lingas, Subgraph Isomorphism for Biconnected Outerplanar Graphs in Cubic Time, in *Proc. 3rd STACS, Orsay 1986*, Springer-Verlag, LNCS 210.

[LK] A. Lingas, M. Karpinski, Subtree isomorphism and bipartite perfect matching are mutually NC reducible, *manuscript* (1986).

[LT] R.J. Lipton and R.E. Tarjan, Applications of a planar separator theorem, *SIAM J. Computing 9*, 3(1980), 513-524.

[Ma] D.W. Matula, Subtree isomorphism in $O(n^{\frac{5}{2}})$, *Annals of Discrete Mathematics 2* (1978), 91-406.

[Mi] S.L. Mitchell, Linear algorithms to recognize outerplanar and maximal outerplanar graphs, *Information Processing Letters 9*, 5(1979), 229-232.

[MR] G. Miller and J.H. Reif, Parallel Tree Contraction and its Applications, in *Proc. 26th Annual IEEE Symposium on Foundations of Computer Science 1985*, 478-489.

[RS85] N. Robertson and P.D. Seymour, Disjoint paths - a survey, *SIAM J. Alg. Disc. Meth.*, Vol. 6 (1985), No. 2, 300-305.

[RS86] N. Robertson and P.D. Seymour, Graph minors - a survey, submitted for publication (1986).

[P] N. Pippenger, On simultaneous resource bounds, in *Proc. 20th Annual IEEE Symposium on Foundations of Computer Science 1979*, 307-311.

[PS] F.P. Preparata and M.I. Shamos, *Computational Geometry, An Introduction*, Texts and Monographs in Computer Science, Springer-Verlag, New York.

[Rei] K.R. Reischuk, Parallel Machines and their Communication Theoretical Limits, in *Proc. 3rd STACS, Orsay 1986*, Springer-Verlag, LNCS 210.

[QD] M.J. Quinn and N. Deo, Parallel Graph Algorithms, *Computing Surveys, Vol. 16, No. 3* (1984), 320-348.

[Rey] S.W. Reyner, An analysis of a good algorithm for the subtree problem, *SIAM J. Computing 6* (1977), 730-732.

[Ru] W.L. Ruzzo, On uniform circuit complexity, *J. Computer and System Science 22* (1981), 365-383.

[SV] L. Stockmeyer and U. Vishkin, Simulation of Parallel Random Access Machines by Circuits, *SIAM J. Computing 13* (1984), 409-422.

[Sy82] M.M. Sysło, The subgraph isomorphism problem for outerplanar graphs, *Theoretical Computer Science 17* (1982), 91-97.

[Sy85] M.M.Sysło, private communication.

[TV] R.E. Tarjan and U. Vishkin, Finding Bi-connected Components and Computing Tree Functions in Logarithmic Parallel Time, in *Proc. 25th Annual IEEE Symposium on Foundations of Computer Science 1984*, 12-20.

IMPROVED BOUNDS FOR COVERING GENERAL POLYGONS WITH RECTANGLES

Christos Levcopoulos
Department of Computer and Information Science
Linköping University, S-581 83 Linköping, Sweden

During the fabrication of masks for integrated circuits, the polygons on the pattern generator must be covered by rectangles preferably of minimum number. The rectangles must lie within the polygons. Let P be an arbitrary input polygon coverable by rectangles, with n vertices, possibly including polygonal holes. Let $\mu(P)$ denote the minimum number of rectangles required to cover P, and lying totally within P. In this paper we show that in the RAM model $O(n \log n + \mu(P))$ time suffices to compute a set of rectangles covering P. This improves the $O(n \times \mu(P))$ bound known before. To prove this bound we solve an open problem concerning the approximation behavior of a proposed simple covering heuristic. Namely, we show that in the worst case it produces $O(n \log n + \mu(P))$ rectangles to cover P. (The previously proved bound was $O(n \times \mu(P))$.) Also, we prove the tightness of this upper bound for almost all pairs of values of n and $\mu(P)$.

INTRODUCTION

A common method for fabricating VLSI chips is the optical method with the automatic block-flasher [He82]. It works by exposing rectangles of any size and any orientation. The rectangles have to cover the polygonal area of each layer of the circuit, without crossing its boundaries. Usually the polygonal areas which have to be covered are isothetic, i.e. the edges are horizontal or vertical. However, in many cases the edges may have arbitrary orientations, e.g. in chips for bubble memory elements [He82]. To minimize the cost of the fabrication, it is desirable to minimize the number of covering rectangles.

Several results have been proved concerning the isothetic version of the problem, i.e. when P is isothetic and the covering rectangles also must have isothetic edges only. Even in this case, if P has holes it is NP-hard to find an optimal rectangular covering [Ma79]. Some results for special cases of this problem were obtained in [CKSS], [YIH] and [FK84],

It appears that the more general, i.e. non-isothetic version of the problem, is much more difficult. It is not even known whether the optimal solution can be computed in exponential time. Using the proof technique in [OR82] (se also [Ch80]), Tarski's decidability results can be applied to prove that the decision version of the problem is computable.

Polygons with acute interior angles cannot be covered with a finite number of rectangles. Therefore, in the literature one assumes that all interior corners of the input polygons are at least of 90 degrees [He82], [LL84].

Hegedüs implemented a program which covers general polygons with rectangles and presented some empirical results concerning its performance [He82].

To present further previous results we need the following notation. By P we denote an arbitrary input polygon (with no acute interior angles), possibly with polygonal holes. We denote by

n the number of vertices of P,

s the shortest distance between every two non-incident edges of P,
l the length of the longest edge of P,
b the diameter of the largest circle lying within P,
$\mu(P)$ the minimum number of rectangles required to cover P,

Refining some preliminary results in [LL84] and in [Le84], a heuristic for covering general polygons, based on Voronoi diagrams, was presented in [Le85]. In the continuation H will denote this heuristic. The heuristic H computes first the faces of the generalized Voronoi diagram of P (polygonal skeleton) [Ki79], and then covers each faces independently in a simple way. Let $H(P)$ denote the number of rectangles produced by H to cover an input polygon P. It was shown in [Le85] that H covers (any polygon) P in time $O(n \log n + H(P))$, and that in worst case $H(P) = \Theta(n \times \log(\frac{\min(l,b)}{s}))$. As the factor $\frac{\min(l,b)}{s}$ can be arbitrarily larger than $\mu(P)$, the approximation behavior of H and its worst-case time performance in terms of the length of the input and of the optimal output (i.e. n and $\mu(P)$ remained an open problem. The only proved property of H concerning this aspect was that $H(P) = O(n \times \mu(P))$ [Le85].

In this paper we solve this open problem. The $O(n \times \mu(P))$ bound on $H(P)$ is improved to $O(n \log n + \mu(P))$. (The latter bound is always better, for large n, because it holds that $\mu(P) = \Omega(\sqrt{n})$.)

We have also to study whether the worst-case upper bound on $H(P)$ is tight. It turns out that it is tight, if $\mu(P) = \Omega(n^{0.5+\epsilon})$ (where ϵ stands for any fixed constant greater than zero). The examples constructed to show this, show also that the lower bound is tight for the approximation behavior of all algorithms which fail to produce rectangles passing through many sharp funnel-like pieces. Also, it is tight for all coverings where each rectangle has some side which is parallel to some edge of the polygon. (Both the heuristic H and the heuristic in [He82] produce only such rectangles.)

DEFINITIONS AND PREVIOUS RESULTS WHICH ARE USED IN THIS PAPER

In [Le85] we introduced the concept of a *funnel*, defined with the help of generalized Voronoi diagrams [Ki79]. Let P be any polygon. A *funnel cell* of P is a trapezoidal piece of a Voronoi face in P, having the following properties. Let A, B, C, D be the vertices of the trapezoid in clockwise order, such that AD is parallel to and shorter than BC (Fig. 1). The segment AB lies on an edge of P, say e, and the segment CD is a Voronoi edge bounding the Voronoi face induced by e in P [Ki79]. In addition, it is required that the maximal rectangle with base AB, lying within P, does not cover the trapezoid.

By this definition of funnel cells, and by the definition of generalized Vononoi diagrams [Ki79], it follows that the mirror image of a funnel cell with respect to the Voronoi edge bounding the cell is also a funnel cell. Such a pair of funnel cells with a Voronoi edge separating them comprises a *funnel* of P.

Let ϕ be any funnel of P. We define the *base (top)* of ϕ to be the two longer (shorter) edges of ϕ which are not on the boundary of P (Fig. 1). The remaining two edges of ϕ are called *arms*. By $\tau(\phi)$ we denote the length of the top of ϕ, and by $\beta(\phi)$ the length of its base. The *sharpness* of ϕ, denoted by $\sigma(\phi)$, is defined to be the ratio $\beta(\phi)/\tau(\phi)$. (Informally, if ϕ is very sharp then its looks as if its arms build an acute angle.) Next, the *characteristic angle* of ϕ, denoted by $\alpha(\phi)$, is defined to be half the smallest angle built by the intersection of the straight extensions of the arms of ϕ. The *funnel ratio* of the funnel, denoted by $\rho(\phi)$, is the expression $1 + \frac{1}{1-tan(\alpha(\phi))}$. Finally, by $\mu'(\phi)$ we denote the minimum number of rectangles not intersecting the arms of ϕ which are required to cover ϕ (i.e., the difference from ordinary covering is here that the rectangles are allowed to intersect the top and the base of ϕ). When it is clear from the context which funnel we refer to, we shall simply write τ, β etc. instead of $\tau(\phi), \beta(\phi)$ etc. In the following, $\mathcal{F}$ will denote the set of all funnels in (the arbitrary input polygon) P.

Recall that H denotes the heuristic in [Le85] and $H(P)$ the number of rectangles produced by that heuristic to cover the input polygon P. We need some previous results stated in the following lemma:

Lemma 1 (from Theorem 1 in [Le85], adapted to our notation here):
(a) It holds that $H(P) = O(n + \sum_{\phi \in \mathcal{F}} \mu'(\phi))$.
(b) The time performance of the heuristic H is $O(n \log n + H(P))$.
(c) There are $O(n)$ funnels in P (i.e. $\#\mathcal{F} = O(n)$).
(d) Let ϕ be any funnel. It holds that $\mu'(\phi) = \Theta(\mu(\phi)) = \Theta(\log_{\rho(\phi)} \sigma(\phi))$.

THE $O(n \log n + \mu(P))$ UPPER BOUND

In this section we prove the following theorem:

Theorem 1. It holds that $H(P) = O(n \log n + \mu(P))$. More precisely, it holds that $H(P) = O(n + f \log f + \mu(P))$, where f is the number of funnels of P. The total running time of the covering algorithm H is also $O(n \log n + \mu(P))$.

By Lemma 1, the bound on the time performance stated in the theorem follows from the bound on $H(P)$. Therefore, we can concentrate on the first part of the theorem. By using Lemma 1 one can show that $H(P) = O(n \log n + \mu(P))$ unless, informally, in the optimal covering of P there are a lot of thin and long rectangles which are shared by many funnels. To prove Theorem 1, we have to study some properties of coverings consisting mainly of such shared rectangles. Therefore, we prove the following lemma:

Lemma 2. Let ϕ be any funnel of P, such that $\mu(\phi) \geq 5$ and let R be an arbitrary set of rectangles within P covering ϕ. Let R_1 be the subset of R consisting of the rectangles in R with some endpoint in ϕ. Then it holds that $\mu(\phi) = O(\log(\#(R - R_1)) + \#R_1)$.

Proof: We refine the idea from the proof of the lower bound on the number of rectangles needed to cover funnels, presented in [Le84].

Let A, B, C, B', A', D be the vertices of ϕ in counter-clockwise order, such that A', D, A are the vertices on the top of ϕ (Fig. 1). We may assume that ϕ is placed so that the vertices A' and A have equal x-coordinates. (By this assumption, D and C have equal y-coordinates.) By α we denote, as usually, the angle (A, A', B') minus 90 degrees, and by ρ we denote the number $1 + \frac{1}{1 - tan(\alpha)}$.

Let R_1' (respectively R_2') be the subset of R consisting of all rectangles in R which overlap with the part of the funnel which lies to the left of BB', and which have no endpoint (respectively have some endpoint) to the left of the vertical line passing through D. Let k_1 and k_2 be the cardinality of R_1' and R_2' respectively. The set R_1' is a subset of R_1, so we have $k_1 \leq \#R_1$. Similarly, it holds that $R_2' \subseteq \{R - R_1\}$, so we have $k_2 \leq \#(R - R_1)$. Since the part of the funnel which lies to the right of BB' can be easily covered with one rectangle, (namely a rectangle whose one side is BB' and whose other side includes the point C), we have $\mu'(\phi) \leq k_1 + k_2 + 1$. So, since it is assumed in the lemma that $\mu'(\phi) \geq 5$, we have $k_1 + k_2 \geq 4$. Therefore, the lemma follows easily if it holds $\mu'(\phi) = O(1)$, or, equivalently by Lemma 1, if $\log_\rho(\sigma(\phi)) = O(1)$. So, we may assume in the following that $\log_\rho(\sigma(\phi)) \geq 6$.

By the above discussion, to prove the lemma it suffices to show that $\log_\rho \sigma = O(\log(k_2) + k_1)$ This relation follows easily from the following proposition:

Proposition 1: If $k_1 = 0$, then $k_2 = \Omega(\sigma/\rho)$. Otherwise, it holds that $k_1 \geq \log_\rho(\frac{\sigma}{2})$, where $k_1 + k_2 \geq 4$ and $log_\rho(\sigma) \geq 6$.

Proof of Proposition 1: Let r be any rectangle in R_1' or in R_2'. The *crossing* of r, denoted by C_r, is defined to be the length of the maximal intersection between r and a vertical segment in ϕ.

Let h be any vertical segment within ϕ and touching the arms of ϕ.

(i) The greatest possible crossing of a rectangle which touches or intersects h is $\leq (\rho - 1) \times |h|$

This crossing can be achieved only if the rectangle is a square whose leftmost corner touches h at its middlepoint, and whose upper and lower corner touch the arms of ϕ (Fig. 1). In this case the crossing is equal to the distance between these two corners, i.e. $\frac{|h|}{1-tan(\alpha)}$).

By these arguments, any rectangle in R_2' has crossing not greater than $(\rho - 1)$ times the length of the maximal vertical segment within ϕ which passes through D. Since α is less than 45 degrees, the length of this segment is $< \sqrt{2} \times \tau(\phi)$. Thus, we obtain the following conclusion:

Statement 1: The sum of the crossings of all rectangles in R_2' is $\leq (\rho - 1) \cdot \sqrt{2} \cdot \tau(\phi) \cdot k_2$.

Since the rectangles in $R_1' \cup R_2'$ cover the part of ϕ to the left of BB', the sum of their crossings must be at least $|BB'|$. Thus, if $k_1 = 0$, that is, this part of ϕ is covered only by rectangles in R_2', then by Statement 1 it holds that $k_2 \geq \frac{|BB'|}{(\rho-1)\times\sqrt{2}\times\tau(\phi)}$. Since the length of BB' is at least $\frac{\beta(\phi)}{\sqrt{2}}$, and $\sigma = \beta(\phi)/\tau(\phi)$, we obtain that $k_2 \geq \frac{\sigma}{2\times(\rho-1)}$. This proves the first part of the proposition.

It remains to consider the case when $k_1 \geq 1$. Let $r_1, r_2, ..., r_{k_1}$ be the rectangles in R_1', ordered from left to right according to their leftmost corners. Let c_i, for $1 \leq i \leq k_1 + 1$ be the sum of crossings of all rectangles in R_2' and, if $i \geq 2$, then also of all rectangles r_j for $1 \leq j < i$. Next, let h_i, $1 \leq i \leq k_1$, denote the maximal vertical segment within ϕ passing through the leftmost corner of the rectangle r_i. By the definitions of R_1' and R_2', it follows that the part of the funnel to the left of h_i (if it is non-empty) is covered only by rectangles in R_2' and, if $i \geq 2$, then also by the rectangles r_j for $1 \leq j < i$. This means that the sum of crossings of all these rectangles must be no less than $|h_i|$, i.e. $c_i \geq |h_i|$. On the other hand, by the relation (i), the crossing of the rectangle r_i is not greater than $(\rho - 1) \times |h_i|$, and therefore not greater than $(\rho - 1) \times c_i$. Therefore, for $1 \leq i \leq k_1$ it holds that $c_{i+1} \leq c_i + (\rho - 1) \times c_i = \rho \times c_1$. Since, by Statement 1, it holds $c_1 \leq (\rho - 1) \times \sqrt{2} \times \tau(\phi)$, we obtain $c_i \leq \rho^i \times \sqrt{2} \times \tau(\phi)$. But, as argued above, the sum of crossings of all rectangles in R_1' and R_2', i.e. c_{k_1}, must be not less than $|BB'|$. Thus, we obtain $k_1 \geq \log_\rho(\frac{|BB'|}{\sqrt{2}\times\tau(\phi)}) \geq \log_\rho(\sigma/2)$. This completes the proof of Proposition 1 and of Lemma 2. ∎

Proof of Theorem 1: According to Lemma 1, to show the theorem it suffices to show that $\sum_{\phi\in\mathcal{F}} \mu(\phi) = O(f \log f + \mu(P))$.

Let R be a minimum set of rectangles covering P, i.e. $\#R = \mu(P)$. For any funnel ϕ in $\mathcal{F}$, let $r(\phi)$ denote the number of rectangles in R which have some endpoint in ϕ. Also, let r' be the maximum number such that some funnel of P overlaps with r' rectangles in R which do not have any endpoint in this funnel. Since any rectangle can have endpoints in at most four funnels, it holds that $\mu(P) \geq \max(r', \frac{1}{4} \times \sum_{\phi\in\mathcal{F}} r(\phi))$. So, it suffices to show that

(*) $\sum_{\phi\in\mathcal{F}} \mu(\phi) = O(f \log f + r' + \sum_{\phi\in\mathcal{F}} r(\phi))$.

Since $f = \#\mathcal{F}$, to prove the above relation it is enough to show that for each funnel ϕ in $\mathcal{F}$, the relation $\mu(\phi) = O(\log f + r'/f + r(\phi))$ holds. By Lemma 2, and by the definitions of r' and $r(\phi)$, for any funnel ϕ in $\mathcal{F}$ we have $\mu(\phi) = O(log(r') + r(\phi))$. So, to prove (*), it suffices to show that $log(r') + r(\phi) = O(\log f + r'/f + r(\phi))$, or to show that for all integers f and r' greater than

1, the inequality $\log(r') \le 2 \times (\log f + r'/f)$ holds. To see that this inequality holds, we observe that if r' is less than f^2, then $\log(r') < 2 \times \log f$. Otherwise, r' is not less than f^2, so we have $\sqrt{r'} \le r'/f$. Since in the latter case r' is not less than 4, we obtain $log(r') \le 2 \times \sqrt{r'} \le 2r'/f$. This completes the proof of the theorem. ∎

THE $\Omega(n \log n + \mu(P))$ LOWER BOUND

In this section we construct examples showing that the $O(n \log n + \mu(P))$ worst-case bound on $H(P)$ proved in the previous section is tight even if $\mu(P)$ is asymptotically smaller than n.

From the method of the proof it follows that any algorithm which achieves an $o(n \log n) + O(\mu(P))$ worst-case bound on the number of rectangles produced uses global information, in order to cover the funnels of the input polygon in a coordinated way. For example, such an algorithm would have to use much more rectangles to cover some funnels, than what is necessary from a local point of view. Also, for some input polygons, many rectangles produced by such an algorithm should have orientations different from the edges of the input polygon.

Theorem 2. For any sufficiently large integer n and any fixed constant ϵ, $\epsilon \ge 0$, there exists a polygon P with n vertices such that $\mu(P) = O(n^{0.5+\epsilon})$, and $H(P) = \Omega(n \log n)$. More generally, any covering algorithm which does not use rectangles passing through a large number of funnels or which uses only rectangles with some side parallel to some edge of P, produces $\Omega(n \log n)$ rectangles to cover P.

Proof: Since the bounds in the statement of the theorem are asymptotic, and ϵ is a fixed independent constant, we may assume without loss of generality that $\epsilon \le 0.4$ and that n is so large that $n^{\frac{\epsilon}{2}}$ is also very large. Let k be the integer $\lfloor n^{\frac{\epsilon}{2}} \rfloor$. We may also assume that k is odd. In this proof we construct a polygon P, such that $\mu(P) = O(\sqrt{n} \times k^2)$, and that any covering of P which does not include rectangles passing through many funnels has $\Omega(n \log k)$ rectangles. This is sufficient because, by the definition of k, we have $\log k \ge \log(n^{\frac{\epsilon}{2}}) - 1 \ge \frac{\log n \times \epsilon}{2} - 1$ and, since ϵ is fixed, $\log k = \Omega(\log n)$.

Let m be equal to the largest integer such that $n \ge 4 + 3 \times m^2$. We construct P as follows. The outer boundary of P is a rectangle with sides parallel to the x or y axis. In addition to the vertices at the corners of the rectangle, there are $n - 3m - 4$ vertices (of 180 degrees) on the boundary of the rectangle. Furthermore, there are m^2 triangular holes in P, arranged regularly in m rows, and m columns (Fig. 2). The upper left corner of the outer rectangle is the origin and the lower right corner has (x, y)-coordinates $(m + 3, -(3 + (m - 1) \times (k - 1)))$.

Each triangular hole consists of one horizontal side above, and two sides below, one with slope -2 and one with slope 2. The length of the horizontal side is $1 - \frac{1}{k}$. By these definitions, to give the exact coordinates of each triangle it suffices to give the coordinates of its lower vertex. The lower vertex of the j-th triangle in the i-th row has coordinates $(0.5 + j, 2 + (i - 1) \times (k - 1))$. This completes the description of P.

In the way P is defined, in each row the triangles in the row are so close to each other that they build $m - 1$ funnels of sharpness k. Thus, in P there are totally $m \times (m - 1)$ or simply $\Theta(n)$ funnels having the same shape. The characteristic angle of each funnel is equal to $arctan(0.5)$, so, by Lemma 1, $\Omega(\log k)$ rectangles are required to cover such a funnel. Hence, in any set of rectangles covering P, where each rectangle overlaps with a constant number of funnels only, there are $\Omega(n \log k)$ rectangles.

On the other hand, let R be any rectangular covering of P consisting only of rectangles having some side parallel to some edge of P. There are only three possible orientations for the rectangles in R. Also, any rectangle in R which overlaps with two or more funnels, has a side of length at most $1/k$. For any funnel ϕ of P, the part of ϕ which can be covered by such rectangles shared by several funnels corresponds to an area coverable by three rectangles only. Thus, for sufficiently large k, at least $\mu'(\phi) - 3 = \Omega(\log k)$ additional rectangles in R overlap only ϕ, and with no other funnel. So, again, we obtain that $\#R = \Omega(n \log k)$.

It remains to show that $\mu(P) = O(\sqrt{n} \times k^2)$. For all integers i and j, $1 \leq i \leq m$ and $1 \leq j \leq m-1$, the (i,j)-th trapezoid is defined to be the symmetrical trapezoid whose left side is the right side of the j-th triangle in the i-th row, and whose right side is the left side of the triangle immediately to the right, i.e. of the $(j+1)$-th triangle. The set of all these trapezoids is denoted by $\mathcal{T}$.

The parts of P except for the trapezoids in $\mathcal{T}$ can be covered by $O(\sqrt{n})$ rectangles as follows. The area between the i-th and the $(i+1)$-th row, for $1 \leq i \leq m-1$, is covered by an isothetic rectangle touching the left and right side of the outer boundary of P, and having horizontal sides touching the triangles in the i-th and $(i+1)$-th row. Similarly the area above the first row and below the m-th row is covered by two rectangles. It remains to cover for each row the area to the left of the first and to the right of the m-th triangle, and it is not difficult to see that $O(\sqrt{n})$ rectangles are enough for this purpose.

For each trapezoid in $\mathcal{T}$, the *top*, respectively the *base* of the trapezoid is defined to be the upper, respecively lower horizontal side of the trapezoid. Observe that the base of each trapezoid has length one, while the top has length $\frac{1}{k}$.

For any integers i, j_1 and j_2, where $1 \leq i \leq m-1$ and j_1, j_2 are in the range $[1..m]$, we say that the trapezoids (i, j_1) and $(i+1, j_2)$ form a *proper pair* iff the lower trapezoid (i.e. in the $(i+1)$-th row) lies in the half-infinite area bounded from above by the lines which are the extensions of the left and right sides of the upper trapezoid. To cover most trapezoids, for each proper pair of trapezoids we insert a maximal rectangle within P which includes the tops of both trapezoids of the pair, deleting all duplications. Let us call R the set of these maximal rectangles. We claim that (a) R contains $O(\sqrt{n} \times k^2)$ rectangles, and that (b) all but $2k-2$ trapezoids are completely covered by the rectangles in R. Finally, we insert $O(k \log k)$ rectangles to cover the $2k+2$ non-covered trapezoids. In this way, the total number of produced rectangles is $O(\sqrt{n} \times k^2)$. It remains to prove the claims (a) and (b) above.

First we need the following definitions. We say that a trapezoid in $\mathcal{T}$ is *frame-placed* iff it is at most the $\frac{k-1}{2}$-th or at least the $(m - \frac{k-1}{2})$-th trapezoid in its row (remember that k is odd). We say that a rectangle in R is *induced* by a trapezoid t in $\mathcal{T}$ iff it is the maximal rectangle including the top of t and the top of another trapezoid which forms a proper pair together with t (a rectangle is often induced by many trapezoids).

To show the claim (a), we establish that (i) any trapezoid induces at most k rectangles in R (exactly k rectangles if it is not frame-placed), and (ii) any rectangle in R is induced by a trapezoid which is either frame-placed or belongs to the first row. Both (i) and (ii) can be easily checked, using the regularity of the polygon. Since the total number of frame-placed trapezoids is $m \times (k-1)$, the claim (a) follows.

To see that the claim (b) holds, we observe by straight-forward geometric arguments that the only trapezoids which are not completely covered by the rectangles in R are the frame-placed trapezoids in the first and in the last low, i.e. $2k-2$ trapezoids in total. ∎

FINAL REMARKS AND FURTHER RESEARCH

In this paper we have shown that the heuristic proposed in [Le85] covers any polygon P with n vertices with rectangles in time $O(n \log n + \mu(P))$. We conjecture that this time performance is optimal in the RAM model, for most pairs of values of n and $\mu(P)$. However, we can do better in the case when the input polygon P is hole-free. If $T(n)$ denotes the time needed to triangulate the hole-free polygon, then $O(T(n)+\mu(P))$ time should suffice to compute a rectangular covering [Le87]. (Due to recent unpublished results by Tarjan and van Wyk, it holds $T(n) = o(n \log n)$.)

Unfortunately, as we show in Theorem 2, by using the heuristic in [Le85] or other similar heuristics which do not use global information to make covering decisions, we cannot obtain a good approximation for $\mu(P)$ when $\mu(P)$ is much smaller than $n \log n$. Again, however, we can do better in the hole-free case. For example, we show that the heuristic H computes a covering consisting of $\Theta(n+\mu(P))$ rectangles. By using recent results about Davenport-Schinzel sequences [W86], we show that this is in worst case $\Theta(\mu(P) \times \alpha(n,n))$, where $\alpha(n,n)$ stands for the inverse of a version of Ackermann's function [Le87].

Another polynomial time covering heuristic whose approximation behavior is of particularly interesting is the greedy one. It inserts at every step a rectangle which covers as large yet uncovered area as possible, until the polygon is completely covered. Although this greedy heuristic is not as efficient as H, we conjecture that it produces only $O(\mu(P) \times \log n)$ rectangles to cover an arbitrary polygon P. For example, for the family of polygons used to show Theorem 2, it produces a number of rectangles which is optimal, within a constant factor.

ACKNOWLEDGMENTS

I would like to thank Andrzej Lingas for reading a version of this paper and providing some helpful comments.

REFERENCES

[Ch80] Chazelle, B.M., "Computational Geometry and Convexity", PhD Dissertation, 1980, pp 140-145.

[CKSS] Chaiken, S., D.J. Kleitman, M. Saks and J. Shearer, "Covering Regions by Rectangles", SIAM J. Alg. Disc. Meth., vol. 2, no. 4, 1981.

[FK84] Franzblau, D., D. Kleitman, "An Algorithm for Constructing Regions with Rectangles", Proc. 16th Annual ACM Symp. on Theory of Comp., 1984.

[He82] Hegedüs, A., "Algorithms for covering polygons by rectangles, Computer Aided Design", vol. 14, no. 5, 1982.

[Ki79] Kirkpatrick, D.G., "Efficient computation of continuous skeletons", 20th Annual IEEE Symp. on Found. of Comp. Sc., 1979.

[Le84] Levcopoulos, C., "On Covering Regions with Minimum Number of Rectangles", Proc. International Workshop on Parallel Computing and VLSI, Amalfi, Italy, 1984 (North Holland).

[Le85] Levcopoulos, C., "A Fast Heuristic for Covering Polygons by Rectangles", Proc. Fundamentals of Comp. Theory, Cottbus, GDR, 1985 (LNCS Springer-Verlag).

[Le87] Levcopoulos, C., "Covering hole-free polygons with rectangles" (preliminary title), in preparation.

[LL84a] Levcopoulos, C., A. Lingas, "Covering Polygons with Minimum Number of Rectangles", STACS'84, Paris (LNCS Springer Verlag).

[Ma79] Masek, W.J., "Some NP-complete set covering problems", manuscript, MIT, August 1979.

[OR82] O'Rourke, J., "The decidability of covering by convex polygons", manuscript, The John Hopkins University, May 1982.

[OS83] O'Rourke, J., and K.J. Supowit, "Some NP-hard Polygon Decomposition Problems", IEEE Trans. on Information Theory, Vol. IT-29, 2, (1983), 181-190.

[PS85] Preparata, F.P., and M.I. Shamos, "Computational Geometry", New York, Springer-Verlag, 1985.

[YIH] Yamashita, M., T. Ibaraki and N. Honda, "The minimum number cover problem of a rectilinear region by rectangles", Toyohashi Univ. of Technology, 1984. (abstract appeared in the Bulletin of EATCS, October 1984).

[W86] Wiernik, A., "Planar Realizations of Nonlinear Davenport-Schinzel Sequences by Segments", in Proc. of the 27th IEEE Symp. on Foundations of Computer Science, October 1986.

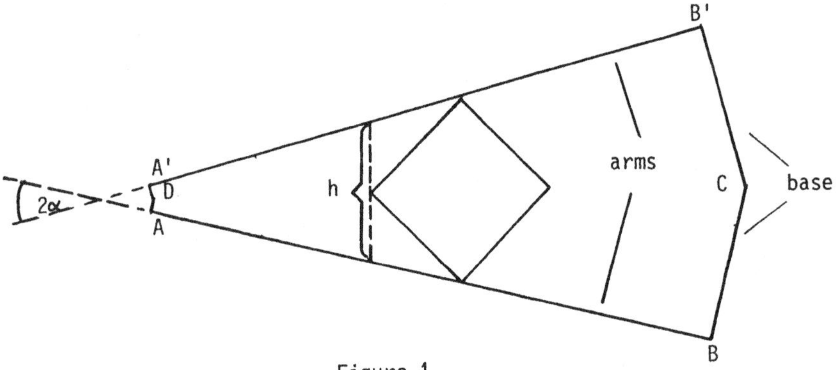

Figure 1.

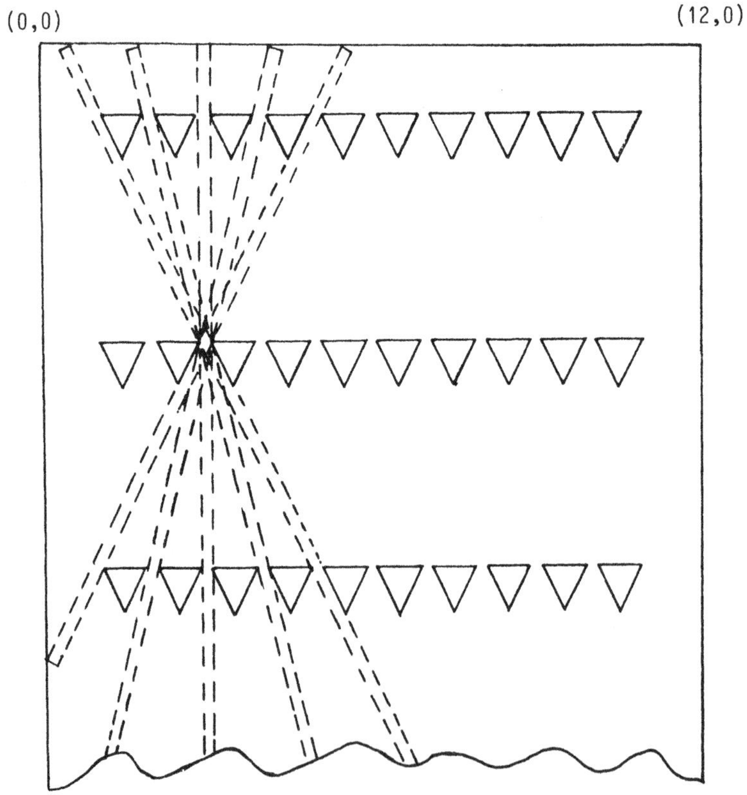

Figure 2: The upper piece of P if $m = 10$ and $k = 5$.
The (pieces of) the rectangles induced by one trapezoid in P
are drawn with broken line segments

Submodule Construction as Equation Solving in CCS

Joachim Parrow*
Laboratory for Foundations of Computer Science
University of Edinburgh

Abstract

A method for solving CCS equations of type $(A|X)\backslash L \approx B$, where X is unknown, is presented. The method is useful in a top-down design methodology: if a system (B) and some of its submodules (A) are specified, solving such an equation amounts to constructing the missing submodules. The method works by successively transforming equations into simpler equations, in parallel with generation of a solution. It has been implemented as a semi-automatic program, which has been applied to the generation of receivers of two alternating-bit protocols.

1 Introduction

One of the most important and difficult fields in computer science is to develop methods for construction of complex systems. Most design methodologies rely on *modularization*: systems are partitioned into sets of submodules, and each submodule is given a specification. These specifications contain sufficient information for combining the modules. Thus, implementation details can be disregarded in most stages of the design.

In this paper, we will consider the particular problem of designing systems composed of several nondeterministic modules executing in parallel. As an example, consider a communication protocol, where the submodules are a sender, a receiver, and a medium. In [MB83], Merlin and Bochmann observe that when all but one of the submodules have been specified, a specification of the remaining module can be derived automatically. For example, when the sender and medium have been specified, the specification of the receiver can be deduced. One limitation in [MB83] is that specifications are expressed in terms of execution sequences. This means that they do not contain enough information to determine some aspects, e.g. deadlock potentials, of the behaviour of the system. Thus, a receiver satisfying the automatically generated specification may cause deadlocks.

Our contribution in this paper is to apply the ideas in [MB83] to a more refined specification method, namely Milner's Calculus of Communicating Systems (CCS, see e.g. [Mil80]). Specifications are in CCS called *agents*, and there is a notion of *observation equivalence*, written $\approx$, between agents. Essentially, two agents are observation equivalent if they can not be distinguished by an external observer. This equivalence is more discriminating than comparing execution sequences; in particular it is sensitive to deadlock potentials. There is also a formal syntax for combining agents: a system composed of agents $A_1, A_2, \ldots, A_n$ executing in parallel and communicating over channels L is written

$$(A_1|A_2|\cdots|A_n)\backslash L$$

In a top-down design methodology, the designer starts with an agent, call it B, representing the behaviour of the whole system to be constructed. He divides the system into n modules,

*On leave from the Swedish Institute of Computer Science, Stockholm, Sweden

communicating over channels L, and proceeds to construct for each module i an agent A_i. The criterion for a correct construction is that

$$(A_1|\cdots|A_n)\backslash L \approx B$$

Now, assume that the designer has actually constructed all modules but one, say A_n. The missing module can then be obtained as a solution for X of the CCS equation (for clarity, put $A = A_1|\cdots|A_{n-1}$):

$$(A|X)\backslash L \approx B \qquad (\dagger)$$

The theory of such equations has to some extent been studied by Shields ([Shi86b]); we defer a discussion on this and other related work to section 8.

Unfortunately, equations of type (†) may in general have several solutions, some of which are unsuitable for implementation. There are several reasons for this. Some solutions, although correct, are unnecessarily complex. For example, consider a communication protocol where the receiver always retransmits each acknowledgment at least a million times. This receiver might be formally correct, but would be highly inefficient. Other solutions are correct only in a formal sense, because of idealizations in the specification. An example of this is presented in section 7. Since we believe it impossible to give general criteria on good solutions, we feel that a semi-automatic procedure, where a designer can guide the generation of agents towards suitable solutions, is appropriate. In this way our method differs from that of Shields.

We have developed such a procedure and implemented it as a program, which accepts equations of type (†) where A and B are finite state agents, and B is deterministic. Having tested the program on nontrivial examples, we conclude that when it runs without user interaction, strange solutions might result. Operated by a designer with some idea of what a good solution will look like, more sensible solutions will be generated. The program helps the designer to find an agent which is guaranteed to be (formally) correct, or convinces him that no such agent exists.

The procedure is based on stepwise transformation of equations into simpler equations. As an example (we here assume the reader to be familiar with the fundamental concepts of CCS), assume that we want to solve

$$a.NIL\,|\,X \;\approx\; a.b.NIL + b.a.NIL$$

Here, the right hand side can do actions a and b. Since $a.NIL$ can only do a, X must supply the b action. Substituting $b.Y$ for X, we get the equation

$$a.NIL\,|\,b.Y \;\approx\; a.b.NIL + b.a.NIL$$

and by applying the expansion theorem on the left hand side we get

$$a.(NIL\,|\,b.Y) + b.(a.NIL\,|\,Y) \;\approx\; a.b.NIL + b.a.NIL$$

but by congruence properties, this is implied by

$$\begin{cases} NIL\,|\,b.Y & \approx\; b.NIL \\ a.NIL\,|\,Y & \approx\; a.NIL \end{cases}$$

We have now transformed the original equation into two simpler equations, and by similar reasoning we will find that $Y = NIL$ solves them both. Hence, $X = b.NIL$ is a solution.

The rest of this paper is structured as follows. In section 2 we define the syntax and semantics of the part of CCS which is related to our work. In section 3 we present the ideas of transforming equations in general, and provide a sufficient requirement for a transformation to be sound. Sections 4 and 5 contain the particular transformations needed for solving equations of type (†), and a proof that these transformations are complete in the sense that if there is a solution, then it can be generated by a sequence of transformations. In section 6 we describe an implementation in the form of a semi-automatic program. This program is applied in section 7 to nontrivial examples: generating the receiver and medium of two versions of the alternating-bit protocol. Section 8 contains ideas for extending this work, and comparisons with similar efforts.

2 Preliminaries

In this section, we establish the notation for the rest of the paper. Although all concepts will be formally defined, the reader is advised to consult some introduction to CCS such as [Mil80] for intuition.

Assume a set **Act** of *actions* where the *inverse* of action a is $\bar{a}$. The unobservable action τ has no inverse. Let **Id** be a set of *identifiers*. The set **Ag** of *agents* is the smallest set that contains **Id** and is closed under the following operators:

$a.$ (called prefixing) for $a \in \mathbf{Act}$; prefix operator.

$+$ (called nondeterministic choice); binary infix operator.

$|$ (called parallel composition); binary infix operator.

$\backslash L$ (called restriction) for $L \subseteq \mathbf{Act} - \{\tau\}$, L finite; postfix operator.

NIL agent constant.

As a shorthand for $(A|B)\backslash L$ we will write $A \parallel_L B$, or even $A \parallel B$ when L is unimportant or understood from the context. As a shorthand for $A_1 + A_2 + \cdots + A_n$ we write

$$\sum_{i=1}^{n} A_i$$

If $n = 1$, the above sum is just A_1, and if $n = 0$ it is NIL.

An *environment* $\mathcal{E}$ is a partial function from **Id** to **Ag**. An identifier is said to be *bound* by $\mathcal{E}$ if it is in the domain of $\mathcal{E}$, otherwise it is *free* in $\mathcal{E}$. The behaviour of an agent (i.e. the transitions that the agent can perform) is always determined with respect to an environment. Thus, we have for each $a \in \mathbf{Act}$ and environment $\mathcal{E}$ the binary transition relation $\xrightarrow{a}_{\mathcal{E}}$ on agents. These relations are defined to be the smallest relations satisfying the following clauses, which can be regarded as the operational semantics of the operators:

$$\frac{}{a.A \xrightarrow{a}_{\mathcal{E}} A} \qquad \frac{A \xrightarrow{a}_{\mathcal{E}} A'}{B + A \xrightarrow{a}_{\mathcal{E}} A'} \qquad \frac{A \xrightarrow{a}_{\mathcal{E}} A'}{A + B \xrightarrow{a}_{\mathcal{E}} A'}$$

$$\frac{A \xrightarrow{a}_{\mathcal{E}} A'}{A|B \xrightarrow{a}_{\mathcal{E}} A'|B} \qquad \frac{A \xrightarrow{a}_{\mathcal{E}} A'}{B|A \xrightarrow{a}_{\mathcal{E}} B|A'} \qquad \frac{A \xrightarrow{a}_{\mathcal{E}} A',\ B \xrightarrow{\bar{a}}_{\mathcal{E}} B'}{A|B \xrightarrow{\tau}_{\mathcal{E}} A'|B'}$$

$$\frac{A \xrightarrow{a}_{\mathcal{E}} A',\ a \notin L,\ \bar{a} \notin L}{A\backslash L \xrightarrow{a}_{\mathcal{E}} A'\backslash L} \qquad \frac{\mathcal{E}(X) \xrightarrow{a}_{\mathcal{E}} A}{X \xrightarrow{a}_{\mathcal{E}} A}$$

An agent B is a *derivative* of A (w.r.t. an environment $\mathcal{E}$) if for some $n \geq 0$ there are actions $a_1, \ldots, a_n$ such that

$$A \xrightarrow{a_1}_{\mathcal{E}} \cdots \xrightarrow{a_n}_{\mathcal{E}} B$$

If $n = 0$, this formula is interpreted as $A = B$.

We define the *experiment* relation $\xRightarrow{\hat{a}}_{\mathcal{E}}$, $a \in \mathbf{Act}$ on agents in the following way:

$$A \xRightarrow{\hat{a}}_{\mathcal{E}} B \text{ iff } \begin{cases} \text{for some } n \geq 0\text{: } A \underbrace{\xrightarrow{\tau}_{\mathcal{E}} \cdots \xrightarrow{\tau}_{\mathcal{E}}}_{n \text{ times}} B & \text{if } a = \tau \\ \text{for some } n, m \geq 0\text{: } A \underbrace{\xrightarrow{\tau}_{\mathcal{E}} \cdots \xrightarrow{\tau}_{\mathcal{E}}}_{n \text{ times}} \xrightarrow{a}_{\mathcal{E}} \underbrace{\xrightarrow{\tau}_{\mathcal{E}} \cdots \xrightarrow{\tau}_{\mathcal{E}}}_{m \text{ times}} B & \text{if } a \neq \tau \end{cases}$$

When the environment is understood from the context we will drop the index $\mathcal{E}$ in $\rightarrow$ and $\Longrightarrow$.

An agent A is *deterministic* iff all its derivatives B satisfy the following:

$$\text{for all } a\text{: } B \stackrel{\hat{a}}{\Longrightarrow} B' \text{ and } B \stackrel{\hat{a}}{\Longrightarrow} B'' \text{ implies } B' = B''$$

Essentially, this means that the agent can never do any τ-actions, and that for each action a there is at most one transition labelled a from any given derivative.

Let $\sqsubseteq$ be the usual order on partial functions, i.e. $f \sqsubseteq g$ iff for all x such that $f(x)$ is defined, $g(x) = f(x)$. Applied on environments, we say that $\mathcal{F}$ *extends* $\mathcal{E}$ if $\mathcal{E} \sqsubseteq \mathcal{F}$.

Let $\mathcal{E}$ be an environment. Extend the notion of (syntactic) subexpressions of agents by including $\mathcal{E}(X)$ as a subexpression of X, for all identifiers X bound by $\mathcal{E}$. A free identifier Y is *guarded* in the agent A, iff all occurrences of Y in subexpressions of A are in subexpressions of type $a.B$. An agent is *well guarded* iff all free identifiers are guarded in it. This means that the initial transitions from the agent are not affected by extending $\mathcal{E}$. An agent is *closed* iff all identifiers in all subexpressions of it are bound. This means that neither transitions from the agent, nor transitions from any derivative, are affected by extending $\mathcal{E}$.

With respect to a particular environment, a binary relation R on closed agents is a *simulation* iff ARB implies:

$$\begin{array}{l}\text{for all } a \text{ and } A' \text{ such that } A \stackrel{\hat{a}}{\Longrightarrow} A' \\ \quad \text{there exists a } B' \text{ such that } B \stackrel{\hat{a}}{\Longrightarrow} B' \text{ and } A'RB'\end{array}$$

If both R and R^{-1} are simulations, R is said to be a *bisimulation*. Two closed agents A and B are *observation equivalent*, written $A \approx B$, iff there exists a bisimulation R such that ARB. Observation equivalence is extended to non-closed agents by $A \approx B$ iff in all extensions where A and B are closed, $A \approx B$.

We will in the following use a, b, ... to denote actions, A, B, ... to denote agents, X, Y, ... to denote identifiers, and $\mathcal{E}$, $\mathcal{F}$, ... to denote environments.

3 Tableaux

As mentioned in the introduction, our aim is to present a procedure for solving equations of type $A \parallel X \approx B$ by successive transformations of equations. We formalise this reasoning by using tableaux. A *tableau* consists of two parts: a *goal* Γ and an environment $\mathcal{E}$. The intuition behind a tableau is that it represents an intermediate stage in producing a solution: the goal says what remains to be done, and the environment records the solution produced so far. A goal is a unary predicate over environments. For example, the goal "$X \approx Y$" is true of the environments assigning observationally equivalent agents to X and Y. As another example, the goal "$X + X \approx X$" is true of all environments.

In order to solve an equation of type $A \parallel X \approx B$ we will start with an initial tableau with goal "$A \parallel X \approx B$" and an environment where A and B are closed and X is free, meaning "it remains to find an environment satisfying $A \parallel X \approx B$." The procedure then works by successively simplifying the equations and extending the environment until a tableau with goal *true* is reached. The environment of that tableau will contain the desired solution.

In the rest of this section we will make these ideas formally rigorous. We use the following goals and satisfaction relation $\models$ between environments and goals:

$$\begin{array}{ll}\mathcal{E} \models \textit{true} & \text{always} \\ \mathcal{E} \models A \approx B & \text{for all } \mathcal{E} \text{ such that } A \approx B \text{ in } \mathcal{E} \\ \mathcal{E} \models \Gamma \wedge \Gamma' & \text{iff } \mathcal{E} \models \Gamma \text{ and } \mathcal{E} \models \Gamma' \\ \mathcal{E} \models \Gamma \supset \Gamma' & \text{iff for all } \mathcal{F} \sqsupseteq \mathcal{E},\ \mathcal{F} \models \Gamma \text{ implies } \mathcal{F} \models \Gamma'\end{array}$$

Note the definition of implication, reminiscent of Kripke-semantics for intuitionistic logic. The idea is that "Γ implies Γ'" is true when any evidence of Γ, i.e. extension of the environment where Γ holds, is also evidence of Γ'. Here, this can be thought of as implicit universal quantification over free identifiers. Actually, $\supset$ will never occur in any of our tableaux, but this notion of logical implication is convenient when formulating results about tableau transformations. In particular, we will use it when formulating the soundness result.

An important property of the satisfaction relation is the *preservation property*: if an environment satisfies a goal, then all extensions of the environment also satisfy the goal.

Proposition 1 (preservation property) *If* $\mathcal{E} \models \Gamma$ *and* $\mathcal{E} \sqsubseteq \mathcal{F}$, *then* $\mathcal{F} \models \Gamma$

Proof: By induction on Γ. It is important that the atomic goals (of type $A \approx B$) possess the preservation property; our definition of observation equivalence on non-closed agents ensures this. □

We will write $\langle \Gamma, \mathcal{E} \rangle$ for a tableau with goal Γ and environment $\mathcal{E}$. A tableau $\langle \Gamma, \mathcal{E} \rangle$ is *satisfiable* if there exists an extension $\mathcal{F}$ of $\mathcal{E}$ that satisfies Γ.

In the following, let $\longrightarrow$ represent a transformation, i.e. a binary relation, on tableaux. We say that such a transformation is *safe* if whenever $\langle \Gamma, \mathcal{E} \rangle \longrightarrow \langle \Gamma', \mathcal{E}' \rangle$, then $\mathcal{E} \sqsubseteq \mathcal{E}'$ and $\mathcal{E}' \models \Gamma' \supset \Gamma$. This means that safe transformations can only add to the environment, and only strengthen the goal. Thus, if the resulting tableau is satisfiable by a particular environment, then the original tableau is also satisfiable by the same environment. Note, however, that a safe transformation might transform a satisfiable tableau into an unsatisfiable one. As an example of a safe transformation, by the expansion theorem in CCS:

$$\langle (a.A \parallel_{\{a\}} X) \approx B,\ \emptyset \rangle \longrightarrow \langle \tau.(A \parallel_{\{a\}} Y) \approx B,\ \langle X \mapsto \bar{a}.Y \rangle \rangle$$

We now prove that safe tableau transformations are indeed sound: if we start with a tableau and successively transform it until we arrive at the goal *true*, then we have derived an extension of the environment which satisfies the original goal.

Proposition 2 (Soundness) *Let* $\longrightarrow^*$ *be the reflexive transitive closure of* $\longrightarrow$. *If* $\longrightarrow$ *is safe, then for all tableaux* $\langle \Gamma, \mathcal{E} \rangle$:

$$\text{If } \langle \Gamma, \mathcal{E} \rangle \longrightarrow^* \langle \mathit{true}, \mathcal{F} \rangle \text{ then } \mathcal{E} \sqsubseteq \mathcal{F} \text{ and } \mathcal{F} \models \Gamma$$

Proof: If $\longrightarrow$ is safe, then $\longrightarrow^*$ is safe. This is proven by induction on the length of the transformation sequence; here the preservation property is crucial. Hence, by the definition of safe transformations we get that

$$\langle \Gamma, \mathcal{E} \rangle \longrightarrow^* \langle \mathit{true}, \mathcal{F} \rangle \text{ implies } \mathcal{E} \sqsubseteq \mathcal{F} \text{ and } \mathcal{F} \models \mathit{true} \supset \Gamma$$

But $\mathcal{F} \models \mathit{true} \supset \Gamma$ is easily seen to be true iff $\mathcal{F} \models \Gamma$ is true. □

The tableau framework is not limited to solving equations of type $A \parallel X \approx B$. Indeed, it can be applied to any equation in CCS, or even to any predicates which have the preservation property.

4 Finite Agents

We will present a tableau method for solving $A \parallel X \approx B$ where A and B are *finite state*, i.e. having only finitely many syntactically different derivatives. Thus, the initial tableau is of type $\langle A \parallel X \approx B,\ \mathcal{E} \rangle$, where $\mathcal{E}$ only contains definitions of identifiers appearing in A and B. The main idea is to guess the initial actions of X, and subsequently split the equation into several, hopefully smaller, equations.

In general, a goal will be a conjunction of equations of type $E \approx C$, where C is closed in the environment. To present the tableau transformation $\longrightarrow$ in a readable way, we first give the transformations which are sufficient when A and B are finite, i.e. do not contain any recursively defined identifiers. There are two types of transformation rules: *instantiations* extend the environment, and *consequences* strengthen the goal.

- *Instantiation*: If $\langle \Gamma, \mathcal{E} \rangle$ is a tableau with $A \parallel X \approx B$ in the goal, and X is free in $\mathcal{E}$, then

$$\left\langle X \mapsto \sum_{i=1}^{n} a_i.X_i \right\rangle$$

  can be added to $\mathcal{E}$. Here, $a_1, \ldots, a_n$ are actions and $X_1, \ldots, X_n$ are fresh (free in $\mathcal{E}$) and distinct identifiers.

- *Consequence*: $\langle \Gamma, \mathcal{E} \rangle \longrightarrow \langle \Gamma', \mathcal{E} \rangle$ if Γ' is obtained from Γ in one of the following ways:

  - *Equivalence*: An equation $E \approx B$, where E and B are observation equivalent (w.r.t. $\mathcal{E}$) can be removed. Here, removing the last conjunct of a goal means to replace the goal with *true*.
  - *Splitting*: If Γ contains an equation $E \approx B$ where E is well guarded, and the transitions from E are $E \xrightarrow{e_j}_{\mathcal{E}} E_j$ for $j \in [1, \ldots, n]$, and there are agents $B_1, \ldots, B_n$ such that:

$$\text{for all } j\text{: } B \overset{\widehat{e_j}}{\Longrightarrow}_{\mathcal{E}} B_j$$

  and also

$$\mathcal{E} \models \left(\sum_{j=1}^{n} e_j.B_j \right) \approx B$$

  then the equation $E \approx B$ can be replaced by the equations

$$\bigwedge_{j=1}^{n} (E_j \approx B_j)$$

The rules deserve some comments. The instantiation transformation amounts to guessing the initial actions $a_1, \ldots, a_n$ of X. In section 6 we will provide heuristics for this. The equivalence transformation will be applied sparingly, since it is computationally expensive to check observation equivalence. If, as in this section, we restrict attention to finite agents, then it is sufficient to apply the equivalence transformation to "$NIL \approx NIL$". Even if arbitrary finite state agents are considered, it suffices to apply the equivalence transformation in the final stage of a transformation sequence (cf. the proof of proposition 7).

The purpose of the splitting rule is to split an equation $E \approx B$ into a set of equations $E_j \approx B_j$, where all E_j are derivatives of E and all B_j are derivatives of B. When B is deterministic, the requirements on B_j can be simplified as demonstrated by the following proposition:

Proposition 3 *Assume the following:*

$$\begin{array}{lcl} \tilde{e} & = & \{e_1, \ldots, e_n\} \text{ a finite set of actions} \\ \tilde{e}_o & = & \tilde{e} - \{\tau\} \\ B & & \text{An agent, deterministic and closed in } \mathcal{E} \\ \tilde{b}_o & = & \{b \neq \tau : \text{for some } B',\, B \xrightarrow{b}_{\mathcal{E}} B'\} \end{array}$$

Then, the premises of the splitting rule

$$\text{for all } j\text{: } B \overset{\widehat{e_j}}{\Longrightarrow}_{\mathcal{E}} B_j \qquad (A1)$$

$$\mathcal{E} \models \left(\sum_{j=1}^{n} e_j.B_j\right) \approx B \tag{A2}$$

are equivalent with

$$\text{for all } j: \begin{cases} B = B_j & \text{if } e_j = \tau \\ B \xrightarrow{e_j}_{\mathcal{E}} B_j & \text{if } e_j \neq \tau \end{cases} \tag{B1}$$

$$\tilde{e}_o \subseteq \tilde{b}_o \text{ and, if } \tau \notin \tilde{e},\ \tilde{e}_o = \tilde{b}_o \tag{B2}$$

Proof:

(A1 ⇒ B1) By A1, for each j there are two cases:

1. $e_j = \tau$. Since $B \stackrel{\hat{\tau}}{\Longrightarrow} B$ is always true for any B, and B is deterministic, it follows $B = B_j$.
2. $e_j \neq \tau$. Then, by A1, $B \xrightarrow{\tau} \cdots \xrightarrow{\tau} B' \xrightarrow{e_j} B'' \xrightarrow{\tau} \cdots \xrightarrow{\tau} B_j$. Since B, and hence B'', are deterministic, it follows $B = B'$ and $B'' = B_j$, i.e. $B \xrightarrow{e_j} B_j$.

(A2 ⇒ B2) Since B is deterministic, it follows that $\tilde{b}_o$ is the set of observable experiments possible from B, i.e. $\tilde{b}_o = \{b \neq \tau : \text{for some } B'\text{: } B \stackrel{\hat{b}}{\Longrightarrow} B'\}$. By A2, this implies $\tilde{e}_o \subseteq \tilde{b}_o$. Also, if $\tau \notin \tilde{e}$, then $\tilde{e} = \tilde{e}_o$ is the set of observable experiments possible from $\sum_j e_j.B_j$, whence by A2, $\tilde{e}_o = \tilde{b}_o$.

(B1 ⇒ A1) Immediate.

(B1 and B2 ⇒ A2) Let I be the identity relation on agents which are closed in $\mathcal{E}$. It is straightforward to verify that under conditions B1 and B2, the relation

$$I \cup \left\langle \sum_{j=1}^{n} e_j.B_j\,,\ B \right\rangle$$

is a bisimulation, whence A2 follows. □

Thus, to perform a splitting of $E \approx B$ when B is deterministic, first compute (by the operational semantics in section 2) the transitions from E and B. Then, if condition B2 holds, condition B1 gives the agents B_j. If B2 does not hold, no splitting transformation is applicable.

A simple example might be illuminating at this point: assume that we want to solve

$$(a.b.NIL|X)\backslash\{b\} \approx a.c.NIL$$

In the following, we write tableaux as boxes with goals to the left and environments to the right. For this particular example, we write $\|$ for $\|_{\{b\}}$. Hence, the original tableau is:

$a.b.NIL \parallel X \approx a.c.NIL$	$\emptyset$

Only an instantiation transformation is applicable here. By the heuristics (to be described in section 6), X should have an initial $\bar{b}$ action to match the potential b transition in $a.b.NIL$. Instantiating X to $\bar{b}.Y$ gives

$a.b.NIL \parallel X \approx a.c.NIL$	$X \mapsto \bar{b}.Y$

The left hand side of the equation is now well guarded. Both sides of the equation can initially do an a transition: for the left hand side the result is "$b.NIL \parallel X$", and for the right hand side the result is "*c.NIL*". The premises of the splitting rule are satisfied, and as a result of the splitting we get

$b.NIL \parallel X \approx c.NIL$	$X \mapsto \bar{b}.Y$

The left hand side is still well guarded, and can now only do a τ transition, resulting in "$NIL \parallel Y$". By another splitting:

$NIL \parallel Y \approx c.NIL$	$X \mapsto \bar{b}.Y$

Of course, it is now easy to see that $Y = c.NIL$ will solve this goal. Following our method strictly, it is time to supply the initial actions of Y. By the heuristics, Y should have an initial c to conform with the initial c transition in the right hand side:

$NIL \parallel Y \approx c.NIL$	$X \mapsto \bar{b}.Y$ $Y \mapsto c.Z$

By a splitting we get

$NIL \parallel Z \approx NIL$	$X \mapsto \bar{b}.Y$ $Y \mapsto c.Z$

After instantiating Z to *NIL*, and applying a final splitting transformation we get

$NIL \approx NIL$	$X \mapsto \bar{b}.Y$ $Y \mapsto c.Z$ $Z \mapsto NIL$

The equivalence transformation removes the last equation; we get the goal *true* and the environment contains the desired solution, which can be written $\bar{b}.c.NIL$.

There seems to be a fair amount of tedium in applying the tableau method even to simple problems. Our point is that this tedium can be automated. Indeed, the program described in section 6 will do the above steps automatically.

To demonstrate the soundness of this tableau method (i.e. that when the goal *true* is reached, the environment will make the original goal true), we prove that $\longrightarrow$ is safe, and appeal to proposition 2.

Proposition 4 $\longrightarrow$ *is safe.*

Proof: For the instantiation and equivalence transformations this is obvious. For the splitting transformation, if $E \xrightarrow{e_j} E_j$ are the transitions from E and E is well guarded, then $E \approx \sum_j e_j.E_j$. Also, by congruence properties of $\approx$,

$$\bigwedge_{j=1}^{n}(E_j \approx B_j) \quad \text{implies} \quad \left(\sum_{j=1}^{n} e_j.E_j\right) \approx \left(\sum_{j=1}^{n} e_j.B_j\right)$$

Thus, from $\bigwedge_j E_j \approx B_j$ and the premises of the splitting rule we infer $E \approx B$, i.e. the goal is made stronger by replacing $E \approx B$ with $\bigwedge_j E_j \approx B_j$. □

For finite agents, $\longrightarrow$ is complete in the following sense: starting with any satisfiable equation $A \parallel X \approx B$ where A and B are finite, the goal *true* can eventually be reached:

Proposition 5 (Completeness) *Let* Γ *be a satisfiable goal* $A \parallel X \approx B$ *where* A *and* B *are finite agents. Then, there exists an environment* $\mathcal{F}$ *such that*

$$\langle \Gamma, \emptyset \rangle \longrightarrow^* \langle true, \mathcal{F} \rangle$$

Proof: See the proof of the related proposition 7. □

5 Finite State Agents

Obviously, with the tableau method in the previous section, it is impossible to generate environments with recursively defined identifiers. The following extension of the instantiation transformation will amend this situation:

- *Instantiation by identification*: If $\langle \Gamma, \mathcal{E} \rangle$ is a tableau with $A \parallel X \approx B$ in the goal, X is free in $\mathcal{E}$, and Y is an identifier bound by $\mathcal{E}$, then

$$\langle X \mapsto Y \rangle$$

can be added to $\mathcal{E}$.

Thus, it is possible to "identify" a free identifier with a bound identifier. Clearly, the extended tableau transformation is still safe. Instead of adding $\langle X \mapsto Y \rangle$ to the environment, we can uniformly substitute X by Y in the tableau — this has the same effect in terms of the $\rightarrow_{\mathcal{E}}$ relations, and hence does not affect observation equivalence w.r.t. $\mathcal{E}$.

A simple example will illustrate how the tableau method is used. Let $A \mapsto a.A$ and $B \mapsto a.B + b.B$ be an environment and assume we want to find an X satisfying $A|X \approx B$. The initial tableau is (for convenience, we do not show $A \mapsto a.A$ and $B \mapsto a.B + b.B$; these are tacitly present in the environment):

$A \vert X \approx B$	$\emptyset$

According to the heuristics, X should have an initial b action to conform with the initial b in B. By instantiating X to $b.Y$ we get

$A \vert X \approx B$	$X \mapsto b.Y$

Now the left hand side is well guarded. Both sides of the equation can do a and b transitions; after a splitting we get

$A \vert X \approx B$ $A \vert Y \approx B$	$X \mapsto b.Y$

The first equation in the goal is identical with the original equation. In the second equation Y is free, and should be instantiated. The heuristics suggest that Y should be identified with X, since they are in the same equations. Identifying Y with X yields:

$A \vert X \approx B$ $A \vert X \approx B$	$X \mapsto b.X$

There are now no free identifiers in the tableau. The goal contains two (identical) equations, these are true in the environment and can be removed. Hence, "$X \mapsto b.X$" is the desired solution.

In the rest of this section we will prove that the tableau transformation is complete. The following lemma is crucial. It says that if an equation is in a form suitable for a splitting transformation, i.e. the left hand side is well guarded, then it can always be subjected to a splitting transformation which preserves satisfiability.

Lemma 6 *Let $\langle \Gamma, \mathcal{E} \rangle$ be a satisfiable tableau, i.e. there exists an extension $\mathcal{F}$ of $\mathcal{E}$ such that $\mathcal{F} \models \Gamma$. If an equation in Γ is $E \approx B$, where E is well guarded and B is closed in $\mathcal{E}$, and the initial transitions from E are $E \xrightarrow{e_j} E_j$ for $j \in [1, \ldots, n]$, then there exist agents $B_1, \ldots, B_n$ such that*

$$\text{for all } j\text{: } B \stackrel{\widehat{e_j}}{\Longrightarrow}_{\mathcal{E}} B_j$$

and

$$\mathcal{E} \models \left(\sum_{j=1}^{n} e_j.B_j\right) \approx B$$

and

$$\mathcal{F} \models \bigwedge_{j=1}^{n} (E_j \approx B_j)$$

Proof: In all extensions of $\mathcal{E}$ we have that $E \stackrel{\widehat{e_j}}{\Longrightarrow} E_j$; in particular this must hold in $\mathcal{F}$. By the premises, $E \approx B$ is true in $\mathcal{F}$. Thus, for all $j = 1, \ldots, n$ the following diagram (where we write $\Updownarrow$ for $\approx$ in environment $\mathcal{F}$)

$$\begin{array}{ccc} E & \stackrel{\widehat{e_j}}{\Longrightarrow}_{\mathcal{F}} & E_j \\ \Updownarrow & & \\ B & & \end{array}$$

can be completed with agents B_j to a commuting diagram

$$\begin{array}{ccc} E & \stackrel{\widehat{e_j}}{\Longrightarrow}_{\mathcal{F}} & E_j \\ \Updownarrow & & \Updownarrow \\ B & \stackrel{\widehat{e_j}}{\Longrightarrow}_{\mathcal{F}} & B_j \end{array}$$

This implies that

$$\mathcal{F} \models \bigwedge_{j=1}^{n} (E_j \approx B_j)$$

Since B is closed in $\mathcal{E}$, $B \stackrel{\widehat{e_j}}{\Longrightarrow}_{\mathcal{F}} B_j$ implies $B \stackrel{\widehat{e_j}}{\Longrightarrow}_{\mathcal{E}} B_j$. By congruence properties of $\approx$ with respect to guarded sum, we get (w.r.t. $\mathcal{F}$):

$$\sum_{j=1}^{n} e_j.B_j \approx \sum_{j=1}^{n} e_j.E_j \approx E \approx B$$

However, since B and all B_j are closed under $\mathcal{E}$, this implies that w.r.t. $\mathcal{E}$:

$$\sum_{j=1}^{n} e_j.B_j \approx B$$

□

For the completeness result we make the following definitions: an agent is in *parallel form* iff it is in the form $A \parallel X$ where X is an identifier. An equation $E \approx B$ is in parallel form iff its left hand side E is in parallel form, and its right hand side B is closed. The completeness result is that if a satisfiable goal consists of a finite number of equations in parallel form, then the goal *true* can be derived:

Proposition 7 (Completeness) *Let $\langle \Gamma, \mathcal{E} \rangle$ be a satisfiable tableau where Γ consists of finitely many equations in parallel form, and all agents in the equations are finite state. Then, there exists an environment $\mathcal{F}$ such that*

$$\langle \Gamma, \mathcal{E} \rangle \longrightarrow^{*} \langle true, \mathcal{F} \rangle$$

Proof: The following proof outlines the algorithm behind our implementation of the tableau method described in section 6.

Since all involved agents are finite state, and the goal is satisfiable, it must be satisfiable by a finite environment[1]. Call this environment $\mathcal{F}$. Such an environment can be defined by a *finite* number, call it n, of applications of the instantiation transformation.

Apply induction on $n =$ the number of necessary applications of the instantiation transformation. For $n = 0$, no instantiations are necessary. Hence, $\mathcal{F} = \mathcal{E}$ and Γ is true of $\mathcal{E}$, whence all equations can be removed by the equivalence transformation.

For the inductive step, $n \geq 1$, i.e. at least one instantiation is necessary. We assume the proposition for $n - 1$, and will prove it for n. Perform the following procedure:

1. Distinguish between marked and unmarked equations in Γ. Originally, all equations are unmarked.

2. For each unmarked equation, such that the identifier to the right of $\|$ is bound by $\mathcal{E}$, do the following steps:

   (a) Apply a splitting transformation to the equation. This is always possible, since if an identifier is bound, it is well guarded (this follows from the form of the instantiation transformations), and hence lemma 6 applies. The result of the splitting will be a finite set of equations in parallel form.

   (b) Mark each resulting equation which has been treated before by this procedure (this requires remembering all equations treated by the procedure).

3. Perform the steps under 2 repeatedly until there are no more unmarked equations with a bound identifier to the right of $\|$. This will eventually happen: since all involved agents are finite state, only a finite number of different equations can be generated with splitting transformations.

The resulting goal still is satisfiable by $\mathcal{F}$, and still consists of a finite number of equations in parallel form. There are now two different cases:

1. There are no unmarked equations left at all. There may still be free identifiers in the goal, but their instantiation will not matter for the truth of Γ, since they will never be exercised when determining possible transitions. Hence, if Γ is true of one extension of $\mathcal{E}$, it is true of all extensions. But Γ is true of $\mathcal{F}$, thus it is true of all extensions, hence also of $\mathcal{E}$. This contradicts the assumption that at least one more instantiation is necessary.

2. There is at least one unmarked equation left. This equation must have a free identifier to the right of $\|$. Thus, it is possible to apply an instantiation transformation to the goal. By choosing the transformation in accordance with $\mathcal{F}$, the goal can now be satisfied by the rest of $\mathcal{F}$, i.e. by $n - 1$ applications of instantiation. By induction, the proposition follows. □

Finally, it can be proven that if $A \parallel X \approx B$ has a solution, then it has a solution bounded in size by the sizes of A and B. Hence, it is decidable whether it has a solution or not.

6 An Implementation

Our program for solving equations with the tableau method works in the following way: first, the user enters the equation $A \parallel_L X \approx B$ that he wants to solve. A and B must be finite state, and B must be deterministic. Also, the expected sort of the solution must be given (alternatively, the program will compute an expected sort). Thereafter, a semi automatic procedure will start

[1] A finite set of recursive equations with guarded sum is sufficient to express any finite state agent; see eg. [Mil84].

as outlined in the proof of proposition 7: by treating all equations with splitting transformations until no new equations are generated.

The program does all splitting transformations automatically. When a free identifier X is to be instantiated, the program permits the user to identify X with a previously bound identifier, or guess the initial actions of X. When the program discovers that the goal is unsatisfiable (e.g. by finding it impossible to perform a splitting transformation) it backtracks to the preceding instantiation.

The practical use of such a program would be small, were it not for the fact that good heuristics for the instantiations can be presented. At each instantiation the user decides whether to follow or disregard the heuristics, and can thus avoid solutions which would not be suitable for implementation. The user can explore different possibilities and backtrack at will. He can even run the program in an automatic mode, where all instantiations are made according to the heuristics.

The most important information presented to the user when a free identifier X is to be instantiated are the sets of *admissible* actions and *useful* actions. An action a is *inadmissible* for X if there is an equation $A \parallel X \approx B$ such that if X were instantiated with an initial action a, then the equation would be unsatisfiable. Inadmissibility is in general hard to check, but it can be approximated by k-inadmissibility as follows: for an agent A, let $Tr_k(A)$ be the set of traces (transition sequences where τ transitions have been deleted) of length $\leq k$. An action a is k-inadmissible for X if $Tr_k(A \parallel a.NIL) \not\subseteq Tr_k(B)$. This means that if X were instantiated with an initial action a, then there would be traces (of length k) of $A \parallel X$ which are not traces of B. For every k, k-inadmissibility implies inadmissibility. When determining which actions are admissible, the program tries each action for k-inadmissibility up to some predetermined maximum value of k. The higher maximum value of k, the more accurate the admissibility test, and the more computation time is spent in determining admissibility. The user can interactively modify this maximum value.

In the equation $A \parallel_L X \approx B$, an action a is *useful* for X, if there is a transition of a derivative of $A \parallel_L X$ which depends on the fact that X can do an initial a transition. The useful actions can be computed as follows: say that a is *covered* by L if $a \in L$ or $\bar{a} \in L$. Then, all actions not covered by the restriction L are useful for X. Furthermore, an action a is useful for X if A can perform a transition sequence, not containing any actions covered by L, but containing $\bar{a}$ — in this case, an initial a in X can result in a synchronisation with this $\bar{a}$ in A.

As an example of these concepts, consider the equation (from section 4)

$$a.b.NIL \parallel_{\{b\}} X \approx a.c.NIL$$

Here, the action $\bar{b}$ is useful for X (it can result in a synchronisation with b). Also, $\bar{b}$ is admissible. The action c is useful, but not admissible — in fact, it is even 1-inadmissible.

Instead of guessing the initial moves of X, the user can decide to identify X with a bound identifier. At each choice, the program supplies the user with a list of adequate bound identifiers. An identifier Y is *adequate* for X if the equations containing X constitute a subset of the equations containing Y, and the admissible and useful actions of X agree with the initial actions of Y. The intuition is that this is a strong indication that X could successfully be identified with Y: a solution for Y will always also be a solution for X.

A simple example will illustrate the program. Assume that we seek an agent X, which in parallel with a buffer of capacity one yields a buffer of capacity two. A buffer of capacity one on channels a and b is defined by

$$A \mapsto a.b.A$$

and a buffer of capacity two on channels a and c is

$$\begin{cases} B \mapsto a.B' \\ B' \mapsto c.B + a.c.B' \end{cases}$$

The user also has to supply the restriction L for solving $A \parallel_L X \approx B$, in this case the restriction is $\{b\}$. The program infers a sort for the solution, in this case it is $\{\bar{b}, c\}$, and the user acknowledges this.

Now the tableau method begins. We will here display the choice points as tableaux: to the left are equations containing the free identifier under consideration (note that the complete tableau contains more equations that are not immediately relevant for this identifier), in the middle is the solution generated so far, and to the right are the recommendations of the program. The first choice point is:

$A \parallel X \approx B$		No adequate bound identifiers Admissible and useful actions: $\{\bar{b}\}$

The user is presented with a menu of various alternatives; in this case he chooses to instantiate X according to the recommendation (the only initial action is $\bar{b}$) The next choice point is:

$A \parallel X_1 \approx B'$	$X \mapsto \bar{b}.X_1$	No adequate bound identifiers Admissible and useful actions: $\{c\}$

Again, following the recommendation leads to the next choice point:

$A \parallel X_2 \approx B$ $b.A \parallel X_2 \approx B'$	$X \mapsto \bar{b}.X_1$ $X_1 \mapsto c.X_2$	Adequate bound identifiers: X Admissible and useful actions: $\{\bar{b}\}$

Now, following the recommendation to identify X_2 with X, the program discovers that there are no more free identifiers, and proceeds to check the environment against the goal[2]. In this case, the environment satisfies the goal, and the program reports the solution to the user:

$$\begin{cases} X \mapsto \bar{b}.X_1 \\ X_1 \mapsto c.X \end{cases}$$

The solution can be written $X \mapsto \bar{b}.c.X$, i.e. it defines as expected a buffer of capacity one.

When run in the automatic mode, the program resolves the instantiations according to the *maximal* strategy:

1. If there is at least one adequate bound identifier, then identify with one of them.

2. If there are no adequate bound identifiers, then instantiate with the set of all admissible and useful actions.

The strategy is called "maximal" because the solutions will in general be agents that have maximal freedom: if more transitions are added, then they would either cause inadmissible behaviour, or would never be exercised. Maximality might, or might not, be a sensible criterion for good solutions. For most small examples, such as those presented in this paper (excepting section 7), the strategy produces the expected solutions automatically. It should be noted that the maximal strategy is not complete for satisfiable goals: it sometimes results in a diverging sequence of choices.

7 The Alternating-Bit Protocol

In this section we study the effects of applying the the maximal strategy of the program to a nontrivial example: the alternating-bit protocol.

The purpose of the alternating-bit protocol (originally presented in [BSW69]) is to provide reliable data transmission over an imperfect medium. Figure 1 shows the general structure of the protocol. It consists of three modules: a sender, a medium and a receiver. There are several versions of this protocol; we will begin by studying the protocol as presented in [MB83]. There,

[2] Actually, it checks against the original goal rather than the current goal; this has turned out to be more efficient in practice.

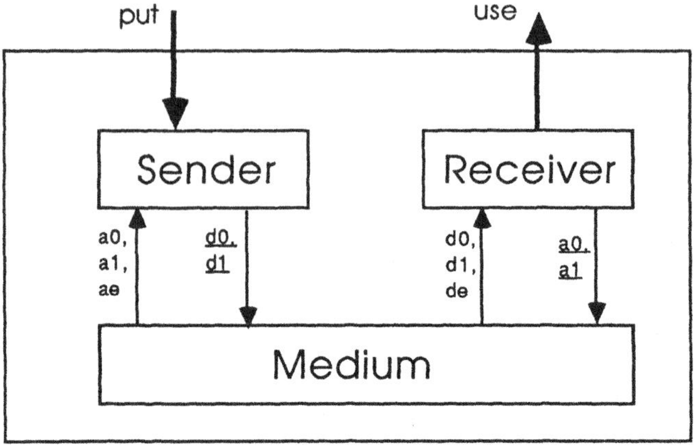

Notation:

put / *use* submitting/receiving a message to/from protocol
$\underline{d_i}$ / d_i transmitting/receiving a message to/from medium
$\underline{a_i}$ / a_i transmitting/receiving an acknowledgment to/from medium
d_e / a_e receiving corrupt message/acknowledgment from medium

Figure 1: The structure of the modules in the alternating-bit protocol.

the medium can corrupt but not lose messages. A message is delivered to the sender through the primitive *put*, and accepted from the receiver through the primitive *use*. The service of the protocol is that of a perfect one place buffer, i.e. *put* and *use* alternate:

$$Service \mapsto put.use.Service$$

Figure 2 depicts state transition diagrams for the modules in the protocol. We will in this section consistently use such diagrams to represent agents; the transformation between diagrams and a system of recursive agent identifier definitions is trivial.

The protocol works as follows. The sender adds a one bit sequence number to an incoming message (starting with 0 for the first message) and transmits it to the medium. We will not explicitly represent message contents, but the sequence numbers are important for the synchronisation properties of the protocol. Thus, we use $\underline{d_0}$ to represent transmission of messages with sequence number 0, and $\underline{d_1}$ for messages with sequence number 1. Following a transmission, the sender awaits an acknowledgment (actions a_0 and a_1) with the same sequence number. After reception of the correct acknowledgment, the procedure is repeated: a new message can be accepted for transmission. This time the sequence number is inverted. If the sender receives an acknowledgment with wrong sequence number, or a corrupt acknowledgment (action a_e), then it retransmits the last message.

Our model of the sender differs from that in [MB83] in one respect: in the states where acknowledgments are not expected, the sender may accept and discard spurious acknowledgments.

The receiver acknowledges all messages (d_0, d_1) by transmitting an acknowledgment with the same sequence number as the message ($\underline{a_0}, \underline{a_1}$). If the sequence number differs from the preceding one, then the message is not a retransmission, and is delivered to the user through the primitive *use*. If a corrupt message arrives (d_e), then the last acknowledgment is retransmitted.

The medium can contain at most one message or acknowledgment at a time, i.e. it is half duplex. Thus, following an action $\overline{\underline{d_i}}$ (the inverse of $\underline{d_i}$), it either delivers the message through $\overline{d_i}$

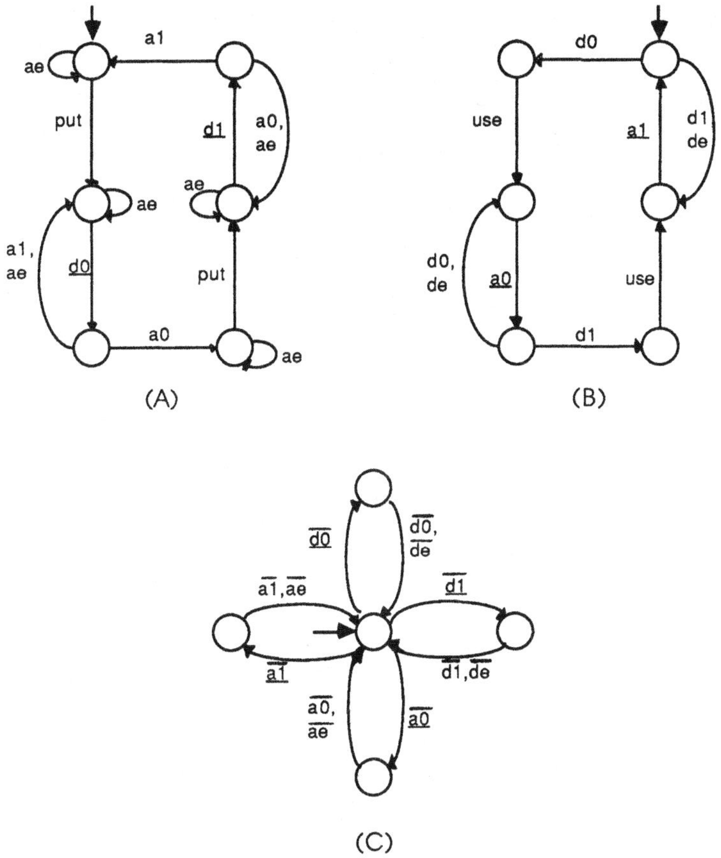

Figure 2: The modules in the alternating bit protocol. (*A*) The Sender. (*B*) The Receiver. (*C*) The Medium.

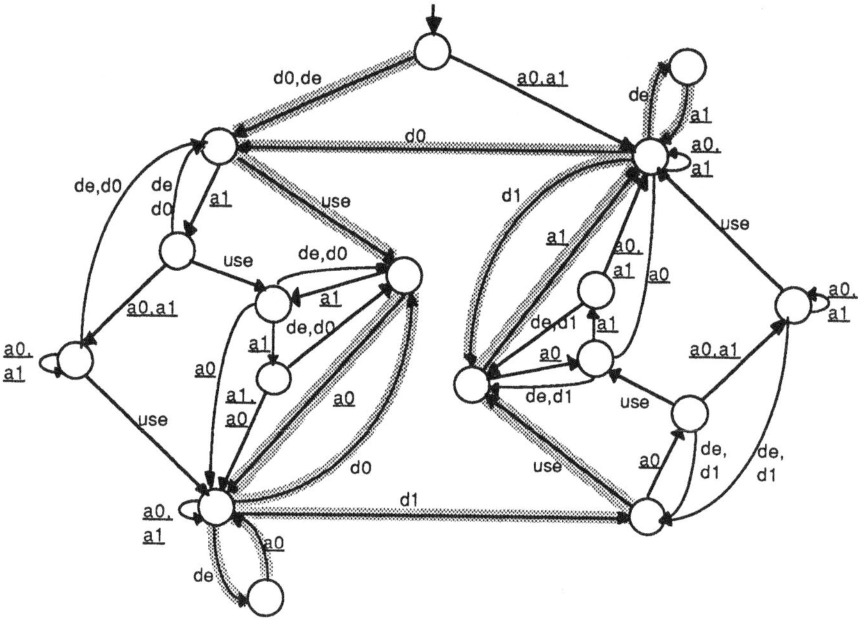

Figure 3: A most general receiver.

or delivers a corrupt message through $\overline{d_e}$. Similarly, acknowledgments may be corrupted.

The program for equation solving can be used to generated any one unknown module of the protocol. As an example, we have generated the receiver by solving the equation

$$(Sender|Medium) \parallel X \approx Service$$

Here, $\parallel$ means parallel composition and restriction over the internal actions ($\underline{d_i}$ and $\underline{a_i}$ for $i = 0$ and 1; d_i and a_i for $i = 0$, 1, and e). When applying the maximal strategy to solve the equation, the result is the rather surprising receiver in figure 3.

This receiver is a most general receiver in the sense that from any state, additional actions will either never be exercised or will lead to inadmissible behaviour of the protocol. It is clear that it is much more general than the expected solution in figure 2. For example, in the initial state, the receiver may begin by transmitting any sequence of acknowledgments. Of course, in a real implementation this would be ridiculous. Nevertheless, the receiver satisfies the formal problem. Indeed, with the medium being half duplex and of capacity one element, these extra acknowledgments are harmless: when the receiver has not accepted any message and it transmits an acknowledgment, then no message has been sent, and hence the sender is in a state where it discards the incoming acknowledgments. There are other similar paradoxical aspects of the behaviour of this receiver. Note, however, that the expected solution is contained as a subgraph (highlighted transitions). We take this example as a good illustration of our point: a completely automatic procedure for generating submodule behaviours is not always desirable.

A variation on the alternating-bit protocol is to use a full-duplex medium, with capacity one element in each direction, and ability to lose messages. For simplicity, we assume that messages are either lost or delivered intact (this is a realistic assumption; there might be an error detection mechanism that discards all corrupt messages). The medium can be modelled as the parallel composition of two independent simplex media, where τ actions correspond to message loss. The sender and receiver modules are modified by deleting all transitions dealing with corrupt messages (d_e and a_e), and by adding timeout transitions to the sender (τ transitions leading from states where the sender waits for acknowledgments to states where it can do retransmissions). These modules are shown in figure 4.

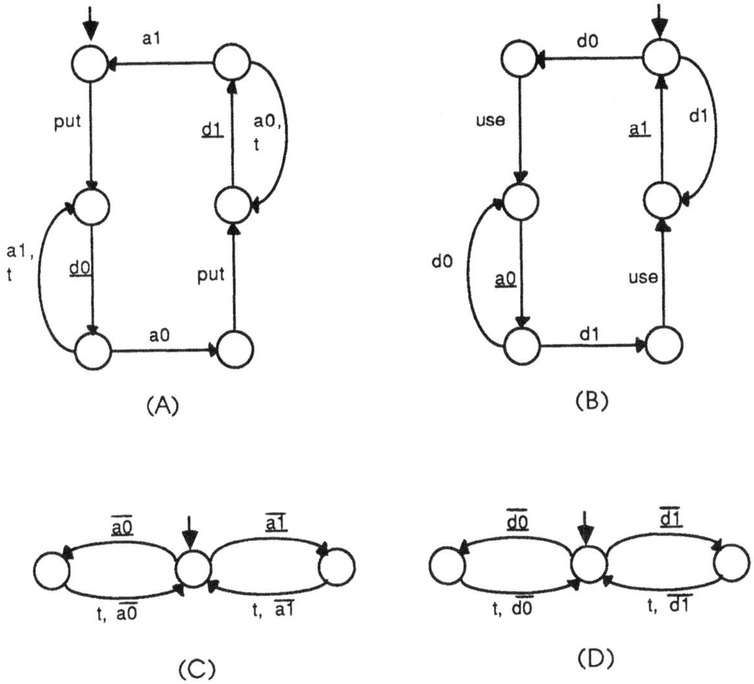

Figure 4: Second version of the modules in the alternating-bit protocol. (A) The Sender. (B) The Receiver. (C, D) Simplex media. The Medium in the protocol consists of these two media in parallel.

Again, using the maximal strategy to solve the equation where the receiver is unknown, yields a most general solution as shown in figure 5. This solution does not depart very much from the expected solution. The initial state is unreachable from the other states (in the initial state there is no useful d_1 action), and in all states it is harmless to retransmit the last acknowledgment or accept a duplicate of the last accepted message.

In a similar way, and with similar results, the sender of the protocol can be generated when the receiver is known. It is even possible to generate a medium if both sender and receiver are known. A most general medium for the protocol in figure 4 is depicted in figure 7. Naturally, it is unlikely that the medium is unknown in a real protocol design project. Instead, this result indicates the worst possible conditions under which the protocol will work. As can be seen in figure 7, the medium may not only lose messages, but also generate spurious messages in certain situations, without harming the protocol.

8 Conclusions and Comparisons with Related Work

We have in this paper indicated one way to give meaning to CCS equations of type $(A|X)\backslash L \approx B$, and presented a method for solving such equations. The method is based on a general tableau framework. Within this framework, we have formulated the transformations necessary for deriving solutions. These transformations form a basis for an implementation, which has been applied to generating the receiver of different versions of the alternating-bit protocol.

Our experience is that a completely automatic procedure for solving equations is not always desirable. Typically, an equation $(A|X)\backslash L \approx B$ has many solutions. Even if it has a unique most general solution (i.e. a solution which simulates every other solution), it is not certain that this solution is suitable for implementation. Thus, when generating a solution, some criteria for what

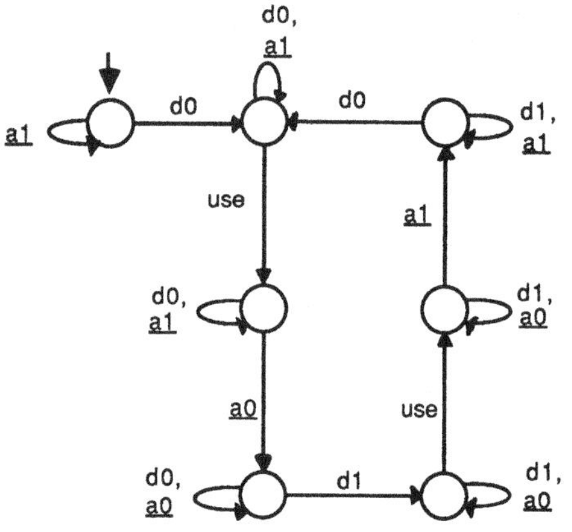

Figure 5: A most general receiver of the second version of the protocol.

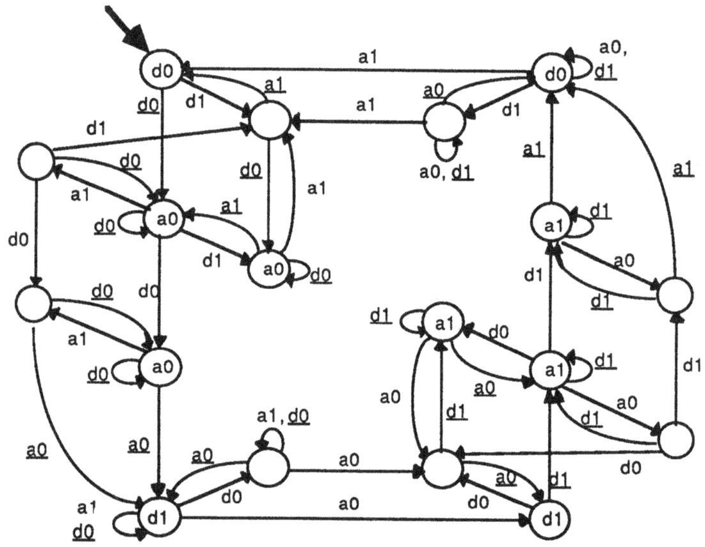

Figure 6: A most general medium of the second version of the protocol. To improve readability we have omitted the bars denoting inverted actions. In contrast with the previous solutions we here also indicate the non useful transitions. From each unlabelled state, actions which are not already labels of (useful) transitions are labels of non useful transitions. The same convention holds for labelled states, with the exception that the label of the state is not a label of a non useful transition. Since such transitions will never be exercised, their target states are unimportant.

constitutes a good solution must be used. Obviously, such criteria are dependent on the particular equation to be solved. With our method, the program performs some of the transformations automatically, but a user can effect critical transformations in order to guide the program towards a suitable solution.

One interesting way to extend this work is to consider a larger class of equations. Already, the method is sufficiently powerful to treat several equations simultaneously. Hence, it can be used to solve problems as "find an X such that $A_1 \parallel X \approx B_1$ and also $A_2 \parallel X \approx B_2$". Similarly, the method could handle nonlinear equations (e.g. "$X \parallel X \approx B$") or even systems of nonlinear equations (e.g. "find X and Y such that $X \parallel X \parallel Y \approx B$ and $X \parallel Y \parallel Y \approx C$"). However, for the nonlinear case our methods for determining admissible and useful actions would not apply.

Another way to extend the scope of this method is to consider other operators and other types of equivalences. For example, in TCSP ([BHR84]) there are other types of parallel operators, other types of nondeterministic choices, and a different equivalence relation. Also, the testing equivalences from [NH84] could be used in this context. We conjecture that the tableau method would work well also in these systems. A congruence property of guarded sum would be sufficient for a sound splitting transformation. For a completeness result, a counterpart of lemma 6 is needed.

It would be exciting to extend our method to include communication with value passing. The tableau transformation is easily extended by including events with value parameters and parametrised identifiers in the instantiations. The difficulty would be to provide good heuristics for choosing the value expressions in the output events.

Since there is a vast literature on generating modules of complex systems, we will here only comment on some approaches related to our method. To our knowledge, the only work on solving CCS equations is [Shi86b] and [Shi86a]. There, equations of type $(A|X)\backslash L \approx B$ are called "interface equations". For the case that B is deterministic, and under some requirements (not very restrictive) on the sorts of A and B, necessary and sufficient conditions for the existence of solutions of such equations are given. In the case that there exist solutions, an explicit construction of a solution is presented. This construction, and also the requirements for existence of a solution, are formulated in terms of the state spaces of A and B. There is, however, no indication that this method can be used interactively and guided towards solutions which are suitable for implementation.

We have already mentioned the work in [MB83]. There, a similar problem is considered with finite automata instead of agents, and trace equivalence instead of observation equivalence. Also, the definition of parallel composition is slightly different in that the simultaneous execution of two actions does not always result in an unobservable action. Within this formalism, the authors derive a solution in terms of the "complement" operation on automata (the complement of an automaton A accepts the complement of the language accepted by A). They apply this method to generate the receiver of the alternating-bit protocol, and remark that the most general solution is not always the best one. Their suggested remedy is to start by generating a most general solution, and proceed by deleting states and transitions which are unnecessary (i.e. can be deleted while preserving trace equivalence of the system). Also, they remark that trace equivalence is not sufficient to demonstrate properties like deadlock freedom.

The recent [BG86] goes one step further. There, the authors present a method to automatically partition an overall system behaviour B into submodules $A_1, \ldots, A_n$. These submodules, when composed in parallel, yields a behaviour which is trace equivalent with B. The idea is to partition the set of actions in B into different locations, and generate one module A_i for each location. The method assumes that the modules communicate over unbounded perfect channels.

In [ZWR*80], a semi automatic procedure is given on how to complete partly specified modules into a system which will be guaranteed to be free of certain unwanted properties such as deadlocks. In [GY84], an algorithm is presented for generating one module of a protocol when a second module is given. However, in neither of these is there any formal specification of the expected service of the combined system. Algorithms for synthesis of concurrent programs from service specifications in temporal logic are presented in [EC82] and [MW84]. A new direction is taken in [APP86]. There, specifications are formulated in knowledge logic (where assertions can be of type "module A knows the contents of message m").

Our method is based on transformation of tableaux. The main inspiration for this is [MW80], where (sequential) functional programs are generated in a similar way by transforming predicate logic formulas. Later, this idea was extended to synthesis of asynchronously communicating networks ([JMW86]). The approach is to first generate one single module, defined as a functional program, and subsequently transform this module into several modules working in parallel. This transformation is specifically aimed at generating dataflow networks.

Acknowledgments

I am grateful to Bengt Jonsson, Robin Milner, Colin Stirling, and David Walker for a critical reading of the manuscript. This work was carried out under a grant from the British Science and Engineering Research Council

References

[APP86] Foto Afrati, Christos Papadimitriou, and George Papageorgiou. The synthesis of communication protocols. In *Proceedings of the fifth ACM SIGACT-SIGOPS Symposium on Principles of Distributed Computing*, pages 263–271, 1986.

[BG86] Gregor von Bochmann and Reinhard Gotzhein. Deriving protocol specifications from service specifications. In *Proceedings of the ACM SIGCOM Symposium*, pages 148–156, 1986.

[BHR84] S. Brookes, C.A.R. Hoare, and W. Roscoe. A theory of communicating sequential processes. *J. ACM*, 31(3):560–599, 1984.

[BSW69] K Bartlett, R Scantlebury, and P Wilkinson. A note on reliable full-duplex transmissions over half duplex lines. *Communications of the ACM*, 2(5):260–261, 1969.

[EC82] E. Emerson and E. Clarke. Using branching time temporal logic to synthesize synchronization skeletons. *Science of Computer Programming*, 2(3):241–266, 1982.

[GY84] Mohamed Gouda and Yao-Tin Yu. Synthesis of communicating finite-state machines with guaranteed progress. *IEEE Transactions on Communications*, COM-32(7):779–788, 1984.

[JMW86] Bengt Jonsson, Zohar Manna, and Richard Waldinger. Towards deductive synthesis of dataflow networks. In *Proceedings of Symposium on Logic in Computer Science*, pages 26–37, 1986.

[MB83] Philip Merlin and Gregor von Bochmann. On the construction of submodule specifications and communication protocols. *ACM Transactions on Programming Languages and Systems*, 5(1):1–25, 1983.

[Mil80] Robin Milner. *A Calculus of Communicating Systems*. Volume 92 of *Lecture Notes of Computer Science*, Springer Verlag, 1980.

[Mil84] Robin Milner. A complete inference system for a class of regular behaviours. *J. of Computer System Science*, 28:439–466, 1984.

[MW80] Zohar Manna and Richard Waldinger. A deductive approach to program synthesis. *ACM Transactions on Programming Languages and Systems*, 2(1), 1980.

[MW84] Zohar Manna and Pierre Wolper. Synthesis of communicating processes from temporal logic specifications. *ACM Transactions on Programming Languages and Systems*, 6(1):68–93, 1984.

[NH84] R de Nicola and M. Hennessy. Testing equivalences for processes. *Theoretical Computer Science*, 34:83–133, 1984.

[Shi86a] M W Shields. *Extending the Interface Equation.* Technical Report SE/079/3, Electronic Engineering Laboratories, University of Kent at Canterbury, August 1986.

[Shi86b] M W Shields. *Solving the Interface Equation.* Technical Report SE/079/2, Electronic Engineering Laboratories, University of Kent at Canterbury, July 1986.

[ZWR*80] P Zafiropulo, C H West, H Rudin, D D Cowan, and D Brand. Towards analyzing and synthesizing protocols. *IEEE Transactions on Communications*, COM-28(4):651–661, 1980.

COMPUTATIONS IN UNDISTINGUISHED NETWORKS

SHAJI BHASKAR
Department of Computer Science
State University of New York
Stony Brook, New York 11794

GAEL N. BUCKLEY
Department of Computer Science
University of Texas
Austin, Texas 78712

Abstract

The correctness of most distributed algorithms depends on the existence of a unique name for each computer in the network. Several authors have investigated the consequences of the absence of such names on the sort of computations that can be performed on a network. It has been shown that it is not always possible to perform even relatively simple distributed computations such as determining the network topology or electing a leader if the number of nodes in the network is not known.

We make an additional assumption: that the number of nodes in the network is known to each node. We demonstrate distributed decision procedures to determine whether it is possible to compute network topology or carry out elections. The decision procedures can be modified into algorithms to determine topology and elect unique leaders in those topologies where it is possible to do so.

1 Introduction

The correctness of most distributed algorithms depends on the existence of a unique name or *id* for each computer or *node* in the network. This name is used by the computers for purposes such as identifying the origins and destinations of messages and the breaking of symmetry in election algorithms. Several authors (Angluin [1], Itai and Rodeh [6]) have explored the consequences of the non-existence of such unique names in a network in problems such as elections.

Most attention has been concentrated on the problems of determining network topology and that of carrying out elections. The latter is interesting because if election is possible, then nodes can be uniquely named, and most published distributed algorithms can then be implemented on the network. The former problem is a strictly simpler problem, because in any network where elections are possible, the topology can also be determined.

Angluin showed that there is no distributed algorithm to elect a leader when the underlying topology is unknown. She proved that in a ring where nodes have no names, the election of a unique leader is not possible. Her proof follows from the observation that in the absence of unique names, all nodes in the ring could behave in the same fashion. Whenever one node sends a message, all nodes send the same message. If the communication mechanism is reliable and preserves message order, it follows that when a node receives some message, all nodes in the ring receive the same message. Therefore, if any one node were to elect itself the leader, all nodes in the ring would elect themselves leader, making the algorithm incorrect. It is easy to conclude that either the algorithm fails to terminate, or it terminates incorrectly (either no leader is elected, or all nodes elect themselves leader, violating the requirement that the leader be unique).

Itai and Rodeh [6] investigated the possibility of applying probabilistic techniques to break this kind of symmetry in rings. Their approach was to assume independent random number generators at each node. When the total number of nodes in the ring is globally known, they demonstrated, there exists a probabilistic distributed election algorithm that terminates with probability equal to one and elects a unique leader. The approach was for each node to pick a random number as its name, and verify that the largest name was unique. Assuming there exists a means for each node to determine when an election is required, the following algorithm suffices. The algorithm is simpler to understand if one assumes that all nodes start the election algorithm at the same instant, and thereafter proceed in lock-step. Each node picks its name and circulates it around the ring in the left to right direction, recording and forwarding to its right the names it receives from its left. If the number of nodes in the ring is N, the N *th* name a node receives will be the one it originated. If, after receiving all N names the largest name is found to be unique, then the node with that name is considered the leader. If not, the election process starts all over again, with each node picking another name at random. It is easy to see that with probability 1 the algorithm will terminate, and that, upon termination, a unique leader would have been elected.

However, they also were able to show that in a ring of unknown size, no probabilistic algorithm can guarantee that it will eventually terminate, and that upon termination, a unique leader will have been elected. In fact, they were able to show that it is not even possible for a probabilistic algorithm to guarantee that *if and when* it terminates, it will assure even a *non-zero* probability that the leader elected is unique.

We investigate deterministic solutions to these problems in arbitrary topologies, under the assumption that the number of nodes in the network is globally known. Even with this assumption, we show that there exist topologies that cannot be computed by any distributed deterministic algorithm, and therefore, no election is possible in such topologies. However, if the number of nodes in the network is known, we present an algorithm to decide whether the topology can be determined, and, if possible, to actually determine the topology. We give an informal proof of the correctness of our algorithm. We also show how our algorithm can be modified to determine whether distributed election is possible in a particular topology, and to actually elect a leader if possible.

The rest of this paper is organized as follows. In Section 2, we introduce terminology used in the rest of the paper. Section 3 presents and proves certain properties of synchronous distributed computations. Section 4 extends the results obtained in Section 3 to asynchronous algorithms. Section 5 applies our results from the previous two sections to the problems of determining network topology and electing a leader. Our results are summarized in Section 6.

2 Terminology

A network consists of computers or *nodes* and point-to-point, bidirectional communication lines. Each end of a communication line is called a *port*. At a node that has k ports, each port is identified by a unique local *port number*, an integer between 1 and k. The nodes of the network do not have names.

Formally, a network is represented by a finite, connected undirected graph $G = < V_G, E_G >$ where V_G is the set of vertices of G and E_G is the set of edges of G. The vertices of G correspond to the nodes of the network, and the edges of G represent the communication lines of the network. Since communication lines end in numbered ports, each element of E_G is an unordered pair $(< x, i >, < y, j >)$, representing a communication line between port i of vertex x and port j of vertex y. Two such graphs are shown in Figure *I*. Although the vertices in G have unique names, these names are not available to the nodes of the network and do not affect their behavior. We use the names only to describe network behavior.

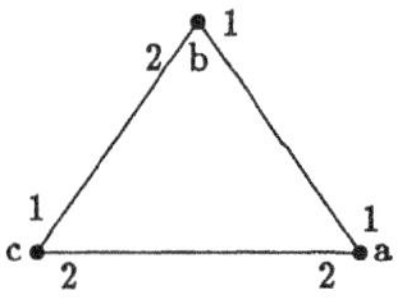

Figure I(a)

Figure I(b)

The *degree* of vertex v in V_G (denoted by degree(v)) is the number of edges incident on v in G. Vertices x and y are said to be *neighbors* if there is an edge $(< x, i >, < y, j >)$ in G. We say there is a *path* from vertex v to vertex w in G if there exists a sequence of edges $(< v, i_1 >, < x_2, j_2 >)$,$(< x_2, i_2 >, < x_3, j_3 >)$,...,$(< x_n, i_n >, < w, j_{n+1} >)$ in E_G. We denote this path by $(v; p; w)$ where p is the sequence of port numbers $i_1, i_2, i_3, ..., i_n$. This notation, though unconventional, is sufficient to reconstruct the sequence of edges that constitute the path. Thus, in Figure $I(a)$, $(a; 2; c)$, $(a; 1, 2; c)$, $(a; 2, 1, 1, 2; c)$ all represent paths from vertex a to vertex c. The *length* of a path $(v; p; w)$ is the count of port numbers in p. By definition, a path of length zero leads from each node to itself, i.e., for all v in V_G, $(v; ; v)$ is a path. A *loop* or *cycle* is a path of length greater than zero from any node to itself.

Graph G_1 is *isomorphic* to graph G_2 if there exists a one-to-one mapping $f : V_{G_1} \rightarrow V_{G_2}$ such that replacing all occurrences of each vertex v in G_1 by $f(v)$ yields G_2. The definition of isomorphism is the conventional definition of graph isomorphism with respect to vertex renaming. Note that under our definition of isomorphism, port numbers cannot be altered. The isomorphism relation is symmetric.

Although a network and the graph modeling it are conceptually distinct, we shall use the terms "node" and "vertex" interchangeably where there is no ambiguity.

To motivate the terminology that we introduce now, let us consider a potential distributed algorithm that attempts to compute the topology of any network that it is run on. (We shall take up this algorithm again in Section 5.) Consider the algorithm to be executing on the network shown in Figure II(a).

The algorithm proceeds in phases, with each node exchanging with all its neighbors the knowledge that it has about the topology in each phase. The messages received are then used to improve the information each node has about the topology.

Before the first phase, each node knows only its own degree. During the first phase, every node v sends out messages on all its ports. On port i, node v sends the values of i and degree(v). Once all these messages have been sent, node v receives the messages sent to it in the first phase by its neighbors. (There will be one received message per port.) From the contents of the messages and the numbers of the ports they were received on, each node v can compute the port numbers on both ends of the edges incident on v as well as the degrees of all of v's neighbors. In other words, for each edge $(< v, i >, < w, j >)$, v knows the values of j and degree(w). This improved information is exchanged between all nodes in the second phase.

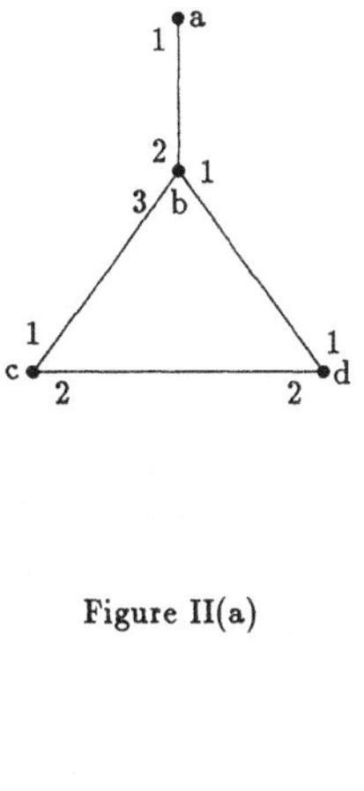

Figure II(a)

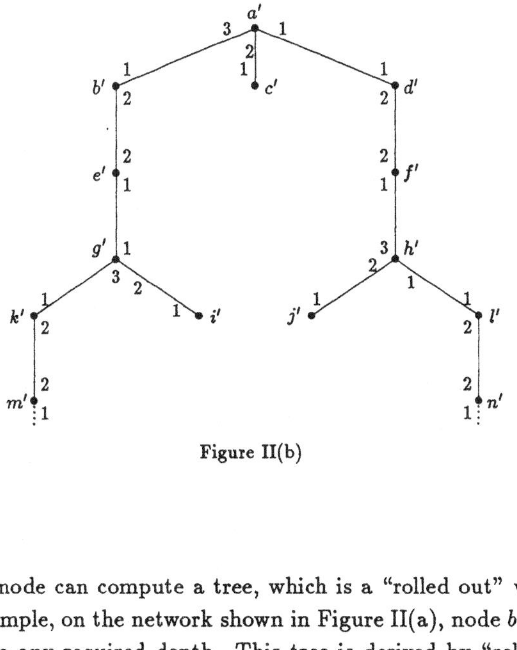

Figure II(b)

In several such phases, each node can compute a tree, which is a "rolled out" version of the topology of the network. For example, on the network shown in Figure II(a), node b can compute the tree shown in Figure II(b) to any required depth. This tree is derived by "rolling out" the graph in Figure II(a) at node b. In other words, all loops in Figure II(a) have been eliminated, but each node in Figure II(a) has been represented more than once in Figure II(b). Vertex a' represents b, vertex b' represents c, vertex c' represents a, and so on. Vertices a', g' and h' all represent vertex b.

We shall show later that two nodes v_1 and v_2 in graphs G_1 and G_2 will behave in identical fashion if the "rolled out" trees at v_1 and v_2 are isomorphic. To do so, we need to formalize three concepts. The first defines what it means for two nodes to "look alike". Then we define a derived or "rolled out" tree, and finally, we formalize the idea of having more than one node in a derived tree "represent" the same node in the graph the tree is derived from.

A vertex x in graph G_1 *matches* a vertex y in graph G_2 if $degree(x) = degree(y)$, and for each edge $(< x, i >, < q, j >)$ in E_{G_1} there is an edge $(< y, i >, < r, j >)$ in E_{G_2}.

This relation is symmetric. Two vertices match each other when they cannot be distinguished by either their degrees or the port numbering (on both ends) of the edges incident on them. In Figure I(b), the two vertices match each other. Vertex b in Figure II(a) does not match vertex b' in Figure II(b) because the two have different degrees. No two vertices match in Figure I(a). For example, vertex b does not match vertex a because although they have the same degree, port 1 of vertex a is connected to a port numbered 1, whereas port 1 of vertex b is connected to a port numbered 2.

The tree T with root r is said to be *derived* from vertex v of graph G if whenever there is a path $(v; p; w)$ in G, there is also a path $(r; p; u)$ in T, and u matches w. Vertex w is said to be the *underlying* vertex in G of vertex u.

Tree T is obtained from G by "unrolling" G at v. A direct result of this definition is that whenever there is a path $(r; q; u)$ in T, there is also a path $(v; q; w)$ in G, and u matches w. In general, if a finite graph has at least one loop, all trees derived from it are infinite. Any two trees derived from the same vertex v of graph G are isomorphic.

In Figure II(b), which shows part of an infinite tree derived from vertex b of Figure II(a), vertex b is the underlying vertex of vertex a' in Figure II(b), since there is a path of zero length from a to itself, and the path of zero length from vertex b' leads to itself. Vertex h' also has vertex b as its underlying vertex, since there exists $(b; 1, 2, 1; b)$ is a path in Figure II(a), and path $(a'; 1, 2, 1; h')$ in Figure II(b). It is easy to see that every vertex u of a tree T derived from a vertex v of G has exactly one underlying vertex w in G. More than one vertex in T will have the same underlying vertex in the graph G if and only if G contains one or more cycles of non-zero length.

To summarize, *matches* is a relation between pairs of vertices which are not necessarily from the same graph, and *derived* is a relation between a graph G, a vertex v of G and a tree T. *Underlying* is a relation between a vertex v of a graph G and a vertex w in a tree T that is derived from G.

We present next a model of deterministic synchronous computations on such a network. On each network, a finite set A of communication *symbols* is defined. Let Z_k denote the set $\{1, 2, ..., k\}$.

Definition: For a network with N nodes, a process that runs on a node of degree k, $P_{(k,N)}$, is denoted by $(Q_{(k,N)}, q_{(k,N)}, S_{(k,N)}, F_{(k,N)}, MO_{(k,N)}, MS_{(k,N)})$. For clarity, we shall omit the subscripts (k, N) in the following explanation of the notation and thereafter unless necessary, with the understanding that whenever we refer to a process P as executing on some node, P has been tailored to the degree of the node and the number of nodes in the network.

Q is a (possibly infinite) set of states of process P, partitioned into two disjoint subsets S and F called the set of *active states* and set of *final states* respectively. One state in Q, q, is designated the *initial state*.

MO: $S \longrightarrow A^k$ is the output function. If $MO(\hat{q}) = (a_1, a_2, ..., a_k)$ then process P in state q outputs symbol a_i on port i.

MS: $S \times A^k \longrightarrow Q$ is the state transition function. If $MS(\hat{q}, (a_1, a_2, ..., a_k)) = q'$, then P

in state $\hat{q}$ moves into state q' on receiving k symbols $a_1, a_2, ..., a_k$ on ports numbered 1 through k respectively.

A process that enters a final state remains in that state without any input-output activity.

Definition: A *network program* or a *distributed algorithm* is a set $\{P_{(1,N)}, P_{(2,N)}, ...\}$ of processes.

Definition: The *state* C_i *of a network program* executing on some network is an assignment to each node of the network a state of the process running on that node. We consider only those computations in which all processes that execute on nodes of the same degree are in the same state initially.

Definition: A *computation step* is a pair (C_i, C_{i+1}) where C_i and C_{i+1} are states of the network program, and C_{i+1} follows from C_i by the process on each node sending symbols to all its neighbors in accordance with its output function, receiving messages from all its neighbors, and moving into a next state in accordance with its state transition function. All these activities occur in one atomic action at each tick of a global clock.

Definition: A *network computation* is a sequence of network states where all processes are in their initial states in the first network state, and each network state in the sequence follows from the previous network state by a single step of computation.

Definition: A network computation *terminates* if the process on each node enters a final state.

3 Properties

In this section, we lay the groundwork for a deterministic test of whether two derived trees are isomorphic. We also show that in any network program, processes executing on nodes that have isomorphic derived trees go through exactly the same sequence of states.

Theorem I: Let v_1 be a vertex in a graph G_1 with N_1 vertices, and v_2 a vertex of graph G_2 with N_2 vertices. Let p be the shortest sequence such that $(v_1; p; w_1)$ is a path in G_1, $(v_2; p; w_2)$ is a path in G_2, and vertex w_1 does not match vertex w_2. If such p exists, the length of p is no more than $N_1 + N_2 - 1$.

Proof: The theorem can be reformulated in terms of the problem of recognizing equivalent states in two deterministic finite automata (DFAs). A graph G corresponding to a network can be transformed into a non-deterministic finite-state automaton ($NDFA$). The states of the NDFA are the vertices of G and the input alphabets of the NDFA are the port numbers of G. There is a transition from state v to state w of the NDFA on input alphabet a if and only if port a of vertex v is connected to vertex w. (In other words, there is an edge $(< v, a >, < w, x >)$ in G).

There is no real nondeterminism in such NDFAs, since no state has more than one outgoing edge labeled with the same symbol. This follows from the fact that port numbers are unique at any given vertex in a graph. They are not necessarily DFAs, however, because some vertices may not have outgoing edges for one or more symbols of the input alphabet. (This situation arises when not all vertices have the same degree.)

The NDFA derived from graph G can be converted to a DFA D with the addition of at most one state d, which is a "dead state". If any state v does not have an outgoing edge for some particular symbol, an edge with that symbol is added that goes from v to d. From d, transitions on every symbol lead back to d itself.

The DFAs D_1 and D_2 corresponding to G_1 and G_2 respectively can be converted to Moore machines by the assigning output symbols to each state. The dead states d_1 of D_1 and d_2 of D_2 are both assigned the same output alphabet λ which is not assigned to any other state. The remaining states of the two DFAs are the vertices of the corresponding graphs. Two states u and v (not necessarily both from the same graph) are assigned the same output alphabet if and only if vertex u matches vertex v.

The sequence p is now a shortest input sequence that can distinguish between the states v_1 and v_2. Since d_1 and d_2 are indistinguishable from each other but distinguishable from all other states (They have the same unique output alphabet, and once a dead state is entered, the DFA remains in that state) a simple argument on the lines of Kohavi [7], shows that if p exists, then the length of p is at most $N_1 + N_2 - 1$. ∎

The next theorem specifies an upper bound on an integer L such that two trees T_1 and T_2 derived from vertices v_1 and v_2 of graphs G_1 and G_2 are isomorphic if and only if there exists an isomorphism between finite trees T_1' and T_2' constructed from T_1 and T_2 respectively by deleting all nodes (and edges incident on them) whose path from the root is longer than L. The following lemma is useful:

Lemma I: If two trees T_1 and T_2 (with roots r_1 and r_2) are not isomorphic, than there exists a sequence p such that $(r_1; p; y_1)$ and $(r_2; p; y_2)$ are paths in T_1 and T_2 respectively, and y_1 does not match y_2.

Proof: If whenever $(r_1; q; w_1)$ is a path in T_1 and $(r_2; q; w_2)$ is a path in T_2, w_1 matches w_2, then it is fairly simple induction on the depth of the tree shows that T_1 and T_2 are isomorphic under the function $f(w_1) = w_2$. Since T_1 and T_2 are *not* isomorphic, there must exist at least one sequence of port numbers q such that one of the following conditions must hold.

Case 1: $(r_1; q; w_1)$ is a path in T_1 and there is no corresponding path with sequence q starting from r_2 in T_2. In this case, let us consider the longest prefix p of q such that $(r_1; p; y_1)$ and $(r_2; p; y_2)$ are paths in T_1 and T_2 respectively. Then y_1 cannot match y_2. If y_1 does match y_2, then p cannot be the longest prefix.
Case 2: $(r_2; q; w_2)$ is a path in T_2 and there is no corresponding path with sequence q starting from r_1 in T_1. This is analogous to Case 1.
Case 3: $(r_1; q; w_1)$ and $(r_2; q; w_2)$ are paths in T_1 and T_2 respectively such that w_1 does not match w_2. In this case, setting $q = p$, $w_1 = y_1$, and $w_2 = y_2$ proves our lemma. ∎

In the next theorem, T_1 and T_2 are trees (with roots r_1 and r_2 respectively) derived from vertices v_1 and v_2 of graphs G_1 and G_2 with N vertices each. Also, T_1' and T_2' are finite trees constructed from T_1 and T_2 by deleting from T_1 and T_2 those vertices (and all edges associated with deleted vertices) whose paths to the root are longer than $2N$.

Theorem II: T_1' and T_2' are isomorphic to each other if and only if T_1 and T_2 are isomorphic to each other.

Proof: The "if" part is trivial, given the method of constructing T_1' and T_2'. We prove the "only if" part using the method of contradiction. Let us assume that the trees T_1' and T_2' are isomorphic, but that T_1 and T_2 are not. By Lemma I, since T_1 and T_2 are not isomorphic, there exists p such that $(r_1; p; y_1)$ is a path in in T_1, $(r_2; p; y_2)$ is a path in T_2 and vertex y_1 does not match y_2. Also, the length of p must be greater than $2N-1$ since T_1' is isomorphic to T_2', and the tree T_i is identical to tree T_i' to a depth of $2N-1$.

Let u_1 and u_2 be the nodes underlying y_1 and y_2 respectively. Then u_1 matches y_1 and u_2 matches y_2. Since y_1 does not match y_2, u_1 does not match u_2. Since T_1 and T_2 are derived trees, $(v_1; p; u_1)$ and $(v_2; p; u_2)$ must be paths in G_1 and G_2 respectively. But, by Theorem I, the existence of such a p would imply that there exists another q such that $(v_1; q; u_1)$ and $(v_2; q; u_2)$ are paths of length no more than $2N-1$. By the definition of derived trees, there must exist nodes w_1 and w_2 such that $(r_1; q; w_1)$ and $(r_2; q; w_2)$ are paths in T_1' and T_2' such that w_1 matches u_1 and w_2 matches u_2. Obviously, w_1 does not match w_2. Since these paths have lengths no more than $2N-1$, trees T_1' and T_2' could not be isomorphic. ∎

Theorem II shows that it is possible to determine whether two derived trees are isomorphic by testing the finite trees constructed from them for isomorphism. The next theorem shows a sufficient condition for network processes executing on two nodes to follow exactly the same sequence of states.

In Theorem III, T_1 and T_2 are isomorphic trees derived from vertices v_1 and v_2 of graphs G_1 and G_2 respectively with N nodes each. Let $f : V_{T_1} \rightarrow V_{T_2}$ be the isomorphism function. Let y_1 in T_1 and y_2 in T_2 be two vertices such that $f(y_1) = y_2$. Also, let the underlying vertices of y_1 and y_2 be u_1 and u_2 respectively. The same network program is assumed to run on both networks.

Theorem III: The processes P^1 and P^2 running on nodes u_1 and u_2 will be in the same state at all steps of any network computation.

Proof: By induction on the number n of steps of the computation.

Basis: $n = 0$: Since u_1 is the underlying vertex of y_1, it must match u_1 and thus have the same degree as y_1. Similarly, u_2 must have the same degree as y_2. Since $f(y_1) = y_2$, both y_1 and y_2 must have the same degree. Thus, degree(u_1) = degree(u_2), implying that nodes u_1 and u_2 have the same network process, P_k running on them, where k =degree(u_1). At $n = 0$, the processes are in the same state.

Induction: $n > k \geq 0$: Assume that the hypothesis is true for $n = k$. Therefore, the nodes underlying any two vertices that correspond to each other are in the same state at $n = k$. In particular, P^1 and P^2 are in the same state at $n = k$. Let $(< y_1, i >, < z_1, j >)$ and $(< y_2, i >, < z_2, j >)$ be edges of trees T_1 and T_2 respectively. Since $f(y_1) = y_2$, $f(z_1) = z_2$. The nodes underlying z_1 and z_2 are in the same state at $n = k$. This means that the node underlying z_1 exchanges the same pair of symbols with u_1 as the node underlying z_2 does with u_2. Node u_1 must therefore receive the same symbol on each port i that node u_2 receives. The next state is uniquely determined by the current state and the symbols received on each port. This means that P^1 and P^2 move into the same state at $n = k + 1$. ∎

4 Asynchronous Algorithms

The theorems presented in the previous section can be extended to asynchronous networks. Our view of an asynchronous network is one where processes communicate with their neighbors using symbols from some set A. A process sending a symbol does not wait for it to be delivered to its neighbor. Symbols arriving at each port are maintained in a FIFO buffer in the order in which they are received, which (since the communication lines preserve message order and are reliable) is the order in which they were sent. A process that wants to receive a symbol on one of its ports will wait till the corresponding buffer is non-empty. It then picks up and removes the first entry in the buffer.

Definition: In a network with N nodes, a process that runs on a node of degree k, (called $P_{(k,N)}$) is denoted by $(Q_{(k,N)}, q_{(k,N)}, I_{(k,N)}, O_{(k,N)}, F_{(k,N)}, MP_{(k,N)}, MI_{(k,N)}, MO_{(k,N)})$
where (again dropping the subscripts (k, N) for clarity),

Q is a (possibly infinite) set of states of the process, which is divided into three disjoint subsets I (the set of *input states*), O (the set of *output states*) and F (the set of *final states*). A special state q in Q is designated the *initial state*.

MP: $I \bigcup O \longrightarrow Z_k$. If $MP(\hat{q}) = p$ then a process in state $\hat{q}$ performs its input-output activity on port p.

MI: $I \times A \longrightarrow Q$. If $MI(\hat{q}, a) = q'$ then a process in input state $\hat{q}$ on receiving symbol a through port $MP(\hat{q})$ moves into state q'.

$MO : O \longrightarrow S \times A$. If $MO(\hat{q}) = (q', a)$ then a process in output state $\hat{q}$ sends symbol a on port $MP(\hat{q})$ and moves into state q'.

We assume that once a process enters a final state it does not make any further state transitions but becomes quiescent. We also assume that all processes running on nodes with the same degree are initially in the same state. We shall continue to drop the process subscripts (k, N) with the understanding that all processes we refer to have been tailored to the degree of the node it executes on as well as to the number of nodes in the network. The definitions of a network program, the state of a network program and of program termination given in Section 2 hold for asynchronous processes as well.

Definition: An *event* is a transition in the state of any process in a network program in accordance with its process definition.

Definition: A computation step is a pair (C_i, C_j) where C_i and C_j are states of the network, and C_i follows from C_j by the simultaneous occurrence of a non-empty set of events. Since the events are concurrent and individual processes strictly serial, the set of events that constitute a computation step can have at most one event from each process.

In this asynchronous model, all of Section 3 remains valid, except Theorem III, which is restated and proven below. In the new version of Theorem III, T_1 and T_2 are isomorphic trees derived from vertices v_1 and v_2 of graphs G_1 and G_2 respectively. Both G_1 and G_2 have N nodes. Vertices y_1 in T_1 and y_2 in T_2 are any two vertices that map to each other under the isomorphism function, f. The underlying vertices of y_1 and y_2 are u_1 and u_2 respectively. The same network program is assumed to execute on both topologies.

Theorem III (for asynchronous networks): There exists at least one computation in which processes P^1 and P^2 running on nodes u_1 and u_2 are in the same state after each step of any network computation. At each step of this computation, the sequence of pending input symbols on each port of u_1 is the same as the sequence of pending input symbols at the identically numbered port of u_2.

Proof: We demonstrate one such computation. It is not necessary that this same sequence of steps occur in every computation, but since we are only interested in showing the possibility of a certain type of computation, we are free to consider any *possible* sequence of computation steps of the network program.

Initially, the process running on at least one of the nodes must make a transition (which must be the sending of a symbol since all message buffers are empty). Let us assume that there are m such processes. The first step of the computation consists of all these m transitions. We assume that before a computation step occurs, all symbols sent in the previous step have reached their destinations. In the second and subsequent steps, all processes that are in an input state q_i and have a symbol in the buffer for the port $MP(q_i)$ make their transitions, as do all processes that are in an output state. In other words, all processes capable of making a transition do so concurrently.

Induction on the number of computation steps completes the proof. An argument similar to the one used to prove Theorem III in Section 3 suffices. ∎

5 Applications

Let us take up first the problem of determining network topology. We state and prove the necessary and sufficient conditions under which there exists a distributed program to determine the topology of the network. We then consider the necessary and sufficient conditions for the existence of a distributed election algorithm.

5.1 Determining Network Topology

Two non-isomorphic topologies with the same number of nodes cannot be distinguished by a network program if their graphs G_1 and G_2 have vertices v_1 and v_2 respectively where the derived trees corresponding to v_1 and v_2 are isomorphic. By Theorem III, any network program that attempts to determine the topology in which it executes will take the processes running on v_1 and v_2 through exactly the same sequence of states. When any network program written to determine topology terminates, the processes on v_1 and v_2 will compute the same topology, and at least one of the two must therefore have computed the wrong topology.

We present a deterministic program which can compute the graph topology whenever possible. The number of nodes in the network, N, is assumed to be known globally. Each process first computes its derived tree to a depth of $2N$. This tree, called the *computed tree*, can be constructed in $2N$ phases of the algorithm described in Section 2. Details of how this can be implemented in synchronous and asynchronous networks are omitted.

Since we consider only connected graphs, no node is at a distance greater than $N-1$ from any other, the maximum degree of a node in the topology must be the maximum degree of the vertices in the tree constructed by each process. The finite set W of all graphs which are connected, have N vertices none of which has degree higher than the maximum degree computed, and are unique (i.e., not isomorphic to any other graph in W) is effectively enumerated in some order using standard enumeration techniques as in Rogers [11]. Each process then computes the set S of candidates for the topology. This is done by removing from W those graphs where no node can derive a tree which, when restricted to those nodes whose path to the root is no more than $2N$ long, is isomorphic to the finite tree computed by the process. (In many instances, it is not necessary to go through such an elaborate enumeration procedure. It is often possible to work backwards from the constructed tree to the set of candidate topologies. In Figure II, for example, it is relatively simple to reconstruct Figure II(a) from Figure II(b).)

Our correctness criteria for this algorithm are that if there exists any distributed algorithm to compute the topology of the network correctly, then S must contain exactly one element, and that element must be the graph representing the topology of the network. If on the other hand there exists no distributed algorithm to determine the topology, the algorithm must give us a set of topologies S, no two elements of which are distinguishable by a distributed algorithm. One member of S is the actual topology.

If there are no loops in the graph, then the correctness is obvious. A finite tree will be computed at each node, and that tree must correspond to the correct topology. We next consider the correctness of the algorithm when executed on a graph with loops.

We informally prove the correctness of our algorithm in two steps. In the first step, we show that no possible candidate for the topology is overlooked. In other words, there is no graph that could represent the actual topology that is not in S. In the second part , we show that if S contains more than one element, there exists no deterministic algorithm to distinguish between the elements of S.

Each node examines all possible topologies. Each graph that can possibly represent the topology must have a vertex where the derived tree when restricted to a depth of $2N$ is isomorphic to the constructed tree. Therefore, no graph that possibly represents the topology could be missing from S. This also implies that S contains at least one element, the graph that corresponds to the actual topology of G.

We now proceed to the second part of our proof of correctness. It can also be shown from Theorem II and Theorem III that if more than one topology remains in set S, it is not possible to distinguish between them. At each node v in the network, The set S contains those graphs G_i where there exists a node v_i such that the finite tree T_i' derived from v_i is isomorphic to the constructed tree. By Theorem II, then, the infinite tree derived from those vertices v_i and the graphs G_i must be isomorphic to each other and to the infinite tree that is actually derived from node v in its correct topology. If it were possible that there existed a deterministic algorithm that could distinguish between the graphs, then the computation would have terminated after some n steps. But, from Theorem III, all the nodes v_i must then be in the same state, and must have computed the same topology. At most one of them can have computed the correct topology. In other words, there is no distributed algorithm to distinguish between members of S.

Consider the two graphs in Figure III. The graphs are not isomorphic. But infinite trees derived from all vertices are isomorphic to each other, meaning that any network computation must leave all nodes in both graphs in the same state upon termination. Thus, if in some algorithm, a vertex in Figure III(a) computes the topology correctly, then all nodes (in both Figure III(a) and Figure III(b)) must compute the topology to be that of Figure III(a). The nodes in Figure III(b) therefore have computed the wrong topology, and the algorithm is incorrect.

Even if the topology can be uniquely determined, it may not be possible for a node to uniquely place itself in the graph. For example, in Figure I(b), it is not possible for a node to determine whether it is represented by vertex a or vertex b in the topology. Another example of a topology in which this situation can arise is a ring. This can lead to situations in which it is not possible for a unique leader to be elected, even though the topology can be uniquely determined. We take up this problem in greater detail in the next subsection.

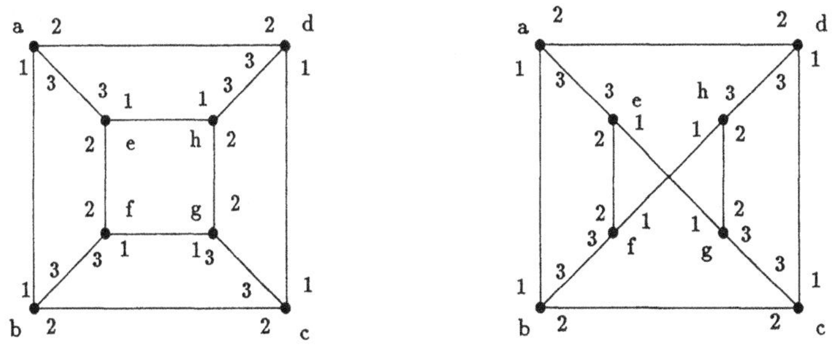

Figure III

5.2 Election Algorithms

The problem of determining whether there exists a deterministic algorithm for the election of a leader in a graph where the number of vertices known is solvable.

A leader can be elected by a deterministic program if and only if the topology can be uniquely determined, (i.e., there exists exactly one element G in S) and there exists a node v in G whose derived tree is not isomorphic to the derived tree at any other node in G.

We first consider the "if" part. If there exists more than one such v, a lexicographic ordering of such vertices that is known to all processes can be used to determine a unique leader. For example, if all nodes use the same standardized internal representation for trees, with the children arranged from left to right in order of the port number at the parent's end of the edge connecting parent and child, the constructed trees themselves can be used as names. A total order on names (such as the order imposed by comparison of the internal representations of the trees) is used to elect the node with the largest unique name. Figure IV shows one instance where the tree derived from each vertex is distinct. The binary value of the internal representation of the derived trees can be used to pick a unique leader in this instance.

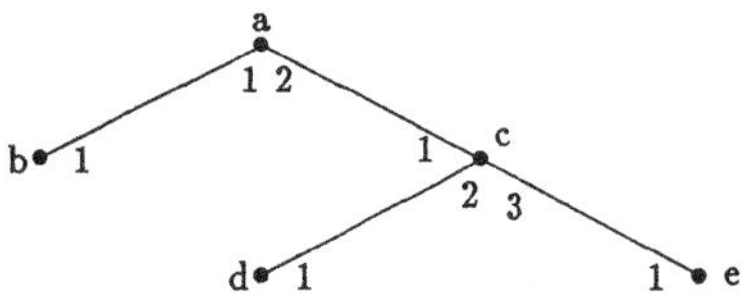

Figure IV

Let us now consider the "only if" part of the proof. Either the topology can be uniquely determined, or it cannot. If the topology cannot be uniquely determined, then there exists no deterministic algorithm to elect a leader. We prove the contrapositive of the previous statement. This proof is a generalization of a similar argument in [2] for ring topologies. Once a unique leader has been elected, each node can be uniquely named. Once this is done, conventional techniques can be employed to determine the topology.

The other situation that can occur is that S has exactly one element G, but for each vertex v in E_G there is at least one other vertex w in E_G such that the derived trees at v and w are isomorphic. Elections are not possible in this topology because by Theorem II, if node v elects itself leader in some n steps, node w would also elect itself leader in n steps. An example is Figure I(b).

6 Conclusions

Knowledge of the number of nodes in a network often makes topology detection and elections possible. However, such information is not sufficient to guarantee the existence of a distributed algorithm that can always elect a leader or determine the topology and. If the graph is a tree, then the topology can always be determined, even if the number of nodes is not known. However, even in trees, elections are not always possible (Figure I(b) is an example).

If the network contains multiple loops, the problem seems to be inherently difficult. Placing simple constraints such as planarity of topology or global knowledge of the number of edges does not appear to yield a class of networks in which elections or determining topology are always possible.

We have demonstrated the conditions under which a network program can be expected to yield the same result when run on different topologies. Using these conditions (that the derived trees are isomorphic) we have developed distributed algorithms to decide whether it is possible to determine network topology or elect a leader. These algorithms have been modified to determine the topology and elect a leader in those topologies whenever possible.

REFERENCES

1. ANGLUIN, D. *Local and Global Properties in Networks of Processors.* Proceedings of the 12th. Annual ACM Symposium on the Theory of Computing, (April 1980), pp 82-93.

2. ATTIYA, C., SNIR, M., AND WARMOUTH, M. *Computing on an Anonymous Ring.* Proceedings of the 4rth Annual ACM Symposium on Principles of Distributed Computing, (August 1985), pp 196-203.

3. CHANG, E. AND ROBERTS, R. *An Improved Algorithm for Decentralized Extrema-Finding in Circular Configurations of Processors.* Comm. ACM 22 5, (May 1979), pp. 281-283.

4. GARCIA-MOLINA, H. *Elections in a Distributed Computing System.* IEEE Transactions on Computers, C-31 1, (January 1982), pp 48-59.

5. HIRSCHBERG, D.S., AND SINCLAIR, J.B. *Decentralized Extrema-Finding in Circular Configurations of Processors.* Comm. ACM 23 11, (Nov. 1980), pp. 627-628.

6. ITAI, A., AND RODEH, M. *Symmetry Breaking in Distributive Networks.* Proceeding of the 22nd Symposium on the Foundations of Computer Science, IEEE, (October 1981), pp 150-158.

7. KOHAVI., Z. Switching and Finite Automata Theory. McGraw-Hill, 1970

8. LELANN, G. *Distributed Systems - Towards a Formal Approach.* Information Processing vol. 77, Elsevier Science, New York, pp. 155-160.

9. PETERSON, G.L. *An O(n log n) Unidirectional Algorithm for the Circular Extrema Problem.* ACM Transactions On Programming Languages and Systems, 4 4, (Oct. 1982), pp. 758-762.

10. PACHL, J., KORACH, E., and ROTEM, D. *Lower Bounds For Distributed Election Algorithms in Circular Configurations of Processors.* Research Report CS-81-33, Department of Computer Science, University of Waterloo, (Nov. 1981).

11. ROGERS, H. *The Theory of Recursive Functions and Effective Computability.* McGraw-Hill Book Company, 1967.

A DISTRIBUTED ALGORITHM TO IMPLEMENT N-PARTY RENDEZVOUS[1]

Rajive Bagrodia

Computer Science Department, 3531 Boelter Hall
University of California at Los Angeles, Los Angeles, CA 90024.

ABSTRACT

The concept of n-party rendezvous has been proposed to implement synchronous communication among an arbitrary number of concurrent, asynchronous processes. The problem of implementing n-party rendezvous captures two central issues in the design of distributed systems: exclusion and synchronization. This paper describes a simple, distributed algorithm, referred to as the event manager algorithm, to implement n-party rendezvous. It also compares the performance of this algorithm with an existing algorithm for this problem.

1. Introduction

Some recent research efforts [Charlesworth 87, Forman 87, Milne 85, Back 84, Francez 86] have focused on the utility of communication primitives that model synchronous communication between an arbitrary number of asynchronous processes; this form of communication is referred to as an **n-party rendezvous**. The synchronization and exclusion problems associated with implementing n-party rendezvous for a set of concurrent processes are illustrated by Chandy & Misra [Chandy 87] in the following anthropomorphic description of this problem:

> ... Professors in a certain university have organized themselves into committees. Each committee has an unchanging membership roster of one or more professors; each professor is in zero or more committees. From time to time, a professor ... starts waiting to attend some committee meeting and remains waiting until a meeting of a committe, of which he is a member, is convened. All meetings terminate in finite time. The restrictions on convening a meeting are as follows: (1) meeting of a committee is convened only if all its members are waiting, and (2) no two committees convene meetings simultaneously if they have a common member. The problem is to devise a protocol that ensures that ... if all members of a committee are waiting, then a meeting involving some member of this committee is convened.

We consider two recent proposals for distributed programming, Script [Francez 86] and Raddle [Forman 87], that incorporate communication mechanisms that can be represented by the committee-coordination problem. The *script* notation was proposed as an abstraction mechanism for communication patterns. A *script* defines a communication pattern among a set of *roles*, where a *role* is a formal process parameter of a *script*. In order to participate in a particular type of communication, processes *enroll* themselves in an instance of the corresponding *script*. If script enrollment is allowed within the guard of an alternative command, the problem of deciding which script-instance may be executed, reduces to the committee-coordination problem as follows: a script-instance represents a committee and an *enrolling* process a professor. Since script enrollment is allowed within a guard, a process may be ready to enroll in any one of many different script-instances. A script-instance (committee) may be executed (convened) if the required set of processes (professors) are waiting to *enroll*.

---

[1]The research was initiated while the author was with the Microelectronics & Computer Technology Corporation, Austin. It was partially supported by a grant from the IBM Corporation.

Raddle proposes the use of *teams* as an encapsulation mechanism to define the behavior of a set of *roles*, some of which may be formal process parameters of a *team*. The *roles* within a *team* communicate via *interactions*; an *interaction* specifies synchronous communication among a set of *roles*. Raddle provides a guarded construct, called a *rule*, which allows an *interaction* in the guard. An *interaction* may be executed only when all *roles* named within it are *ready*. Once again, the problem of selecting *interactions* for execution reduces to the committee-coordination problem as follows: an *interaction* is a committee and *roles* are professors. A particular *role* (professor) may be ready to execute (attend) any one of many *interactions* (meetings). An *interaction* (committee) may be executed (convened), when all the *roles* (professors) named in the *interaction* (committee) are waiting.

The n-party rendezvous is an extension of the binary rendezvous that has been suggested for CSP [Hoare 78] and Ada [Ada 82]. In a binary rendezvous, a communication involves the synchronization of exactly two processes. A number of algorithms have been suggested to implement binary rendezvous [Bernstein 80, Buckley 83, Van De Snepscheut 81, Natarajan 86, Schneider 82, Bagrodia 86]. Chandy & Misra [Chandy 87] have proposed an elegant distributed algorithm, referred to as the committee coordination algorithm to implement n-party rendezvous in the context of the committee coordination problem. In this paper, we present a simple algorithm to implement n-party rendezvous and compare its performance with the committee coordination algorithm.

Section 2 presents a detailed description of the problem. Section 3 introduces our solution. Sections 4 and 5 present centralized and distributed implementations of the solution. Section 6 presents a brief description of the committee coordination algorithm. Section 7 compares the performance of the three algorithms discussed in this paper. Section 8 is the conclusion.

2. The Problem

Let **P** be a set of **n** *processes* such that $\mathbf{P} = \{p_1, p_2, \ldots, p_n\}$ and **E** be a set of **m** *events* such that $\mathbf{E}=\{e_1, e_2, \ldots, e_m\}$. Each process participates in zero or more events. The set of events in which a process p_i participates is called its *event-set* and is referred to as E_i; each E_i is a subset of **E**. Each event, say e_k is associated with a set of one or more processes; this set is called the *process-set* of the event and is referred to as P_k; each P_k is a subset of **P**. Two events e_k and e_j are said to be in *conflict* if $P_k \cap P_j \neq \{\ \}$. The process-set of an event and the event-set of a process are both *static* sets, whose membership does not change.

A process is either *idle* or *active*. An *active* process autonomously makes the transition to become *idle*. An *idle* process p_i is waiting to **commit** to any one of the events in E_i. A process commits to some event e_k, only when it determines that all other processes that belong to P_k will also do so. An *idle* process may commit to at most one event at any time. Every process in the system satisfies the following two conditions:

- An *idle* process remains *idle* until it commits to some event C1
- An *idle* process becomes *active* if it commits to some event C2

An event is either *enabled* or *disabled*. An event e_k is *enabled* iff all processes that belong to P_k are *idle*; e_k is *disabled* if there exists some process $p_i \in P_k$, such that p_i is *active*. We use the phrase 'an event e_k is executed' to mean that each process that belongs to P_k has committed to e_k. We are required to devise an algorithm which allows an *idle* process to commit to an *enabled* event such that the following safety and liveness properties are satisfied:

1. Safety(Exclusion): An *idle* process may commit to at most one event. In other words, conflicting events cannot be executed simultaneously.

2. Liveness:

a. Synchronization: If process p_i commits to event e_k, then all processes that belong to P_k will eventually commit to event e_k.

b. Progress: If all processes that belong to the process-set P_k of some event e_k are *idle*, then eventually some p_j that belongs to P_k must become *active*. This property ensures that if an event e_k is *enabled*, then eventually, e_k is *disabled.*

In the above discussion, we have assumed that when a process is *idle* it is waiting to commit to any event from its event-set. In general, a process may be waiting to commit to any one of only a subset of the events from its event-set. As indicated subsequently, the algorithm presented in this paper can be easily extended to the general problem.

This paper does not impose any semantic association with events or their execution. We consider the communication primitives associated with CSP and Ada to indicate the possible semantics that may be associated with events and their execution. In CSP, an event represents a pair of *matched* CSP communication statements. Execution of an event corresponds to a message being sent by one process and received by another. For instance, consider an event e_k that represents synchronous communication between two processes, say p_1 and p_2; the process-set of e_k is $\{p_1,p_2\}$. In this context, the term process p_1 commits to event e_k, may imply that p_1 *synchronously* sends a message to process p_2. Similarly, in Ada, an event represents a remote procedure call; execution of an event corresponds to the execution of a *procedure call* statement in one task (process) and a corresponding *accept* statement in another task. In the context of Ada, the term process p_i commits to an event may imply that a particular **accept** statement was executed in task p_i.

3. A Solution

For every process p_i in the system, we introduce two variables as follows:

- w_i: number of times process p_i has been *idle*; also refered to as the *idle-count* for p_i.
- n_i: number of times process p_i has been *active*; also refered to as the *active-count* for p_i.

We temporarily ignore the problem of overflow, which is addressed subsequently. We assume that initially, every process is *active*, and variables n_i and w_i are initialized to 0 for every p_i. In order to satisfy the safety condition, the following invariant must be satisfied by every process in the system:

$$n_i \leq w_i \leq n_i+1 \qquad \text{I1}$$

We further claim that an event e_k can be executed if the following condition is satisfied for all processes that belong to its process-set:

$$\forall p_i \in P_k,\ w_i = n_i+1 \qquad \text{P1}$$

The condition P1 is henceforth referred to as the progress condition, and is used to ensure that all processes in the process-set of a given event are *idle*.

In the following sections, we present various implementations that maintain the invariant and ensure that eventually an event that satisfies the progress condition is selected for execution.

4. Centralized Algorithm

The simplest solution to the problem of n-party rendezvous is to designate a single process as a centralized manager for the system; this manager is referred to as **M**. We assume that **M** has access to the process-set of each event in the system and stores the *idle-count* and *active-count* for each process. All counters are initialized to zero. When any process p_i in the system becomes *idle*, it sends a *ready* message to **M**. On receiving a *ready* message from some p_i, the manager increments the idle-count of p_i by 1 and tries to find an event that satisfies the progress condition P1 defined above. If such an event exists, the manager increments the active-count n_i, for every p_i that belongs to P_k by 1, and informs each p_i to commit to the event[2]. It can be shown that the above algorithm does not violate invariant I1 and the exclusion, synchronization and progress properties are trivially satisfied. Although this algorithm may be suitable for certain architectures, in general, the concerns of performance and reliability argue for a distributed algorithm.

5. Distributed Algorithm

5.1. Informal Description

The previous algorithm may be distributed by using multiple managers located at different processes. The distributed implementation is refered to as the event-manager algorithm. The set of managers is represented by M; m_j represents an element of M. Each m_j is assigned a set of events refered to as *e-set*$_j$. A manager may only select events for execution from its e-set. Each manager is also associated with a set of processes refered to as its *p-set*. The *p-set* of a manager is the union of the process-sets of all events in its e-set. The managers cooperate with one another to select events for execution without violating the safety property. We note that no restrictions are imposed on the composition of an e-set for a manager. In particular, a given event e_k may be managed by more than one manager, and two events e_j and e_k in the e-set of a manager may be in conflict with each other. Conflicts between two events in the e-set of a manager may be resolved locally by the manager. Conflicts between different managers are resolved by using a circulating token. A manager may select an event for execution only when it possesses the token. Various strategies may be defined whereby a manager that owns the token may determine the current state of processes in its p-set. One possibility may be to assign a maximal set of non-conflicting events to each manager. On receiving the token, the manager may poll processes in parallel for their *idle* and *active* counts, and choose events for execution that satisfy the progress condition. The algorithm discussed here extends the idea of the centralized algorithm in a simple manner. Each manager stores the idle-count for every process in its p-set. The idle-count for process p_i stored by manager m_j is represented as $nr_j(p_i)$ and is refered to as its *ready-count*. Due to the asynchronous nature of the system, the ready-count of a process with a manager may be less than its idle-count. We prove subsequently that the following is an invariant for every manager m_j and process p_i:

$$nr_j(p_i) \leq w_i \qquad \text{I2}$$

The active-count for all processes in the system is carried by the token, with the count for process p_i refered to as $nx(p_i)$. On receiving the token, a manager selects events for execution that satisfy the progress condition. This condition may be redefined in terms of the local ready-count of a manager and the active-count carried by the token as follows:

$$\forall p_i \in P_k,\ nr_j(p_i) = nx(p_i) + 1 \qquad \text{P2}$$

Once a manager selects an event e_k for execution, $\forall p_i \in P_k$, it increments the active-count for p_i carried in the token by 1, informs p_i to commit to event e_k, and sends the token to the next manager. For brevity, we say that manager m_j executes event e_k to imply that the manager has determined that e_k can be executed and has informed each process in P_k accordingly. Finally, in the distributed implementation, the invariant I1 for every process may be redefined in terms of the active-count carried by the token as follows:

$$nx(p_i) \leq w_i \leq nx(p_i)+1 \qquad \text{I3}$$

---

[2]The centralized algorithm may be implemented more simply by using a single bit in the manager to represent the current state of each process. The above implementation is suggested as it can be generalized in a simple manner to a distributed implementation.

The synchronization property is guaranteed by the algorithm, since a manager either informs all or none of the processes in the process-set of an event, to commit to the event. The ready-count of a process with a manager is used to satisfy the exclusion property as follows: after an event e_k is executed by a manager m_j, for every p_i in P_k, $nr_j(p_i)$ is exactly equal to the active-count $nx(p_i)$ carried in the token. This implies that when the token reaches another manager m_l, for every p_i in P_k, the ready-count $nr_l(p_i)$ can be at most *equal* to the active-count $nx(p_i)$ for the process. Thus the progress condition P2 cannot be satisfied for any event that conflicts with e_k and manager m_l cannot execute any event that conflicts with e_k. The proof for the exclusion property is presented in the next section.

Correctness of this algorithm only requires that each event be present in the e-set of *at least* one manager. As long as the above property is satisfied, the allocation of events among managers does not affect the correctness of the algorithm. In fact, the algorithm will work correctly even if there is only one manager, in which case the implementation of the algorithm will reduce to a centralized implementation. On the other hand, the number of managers may be equal to the number of processes, with the e-set of each manager containing the entire list of events in the system. This corresponds to having a fully replicated event-list. In the distributed implementations with more than one manager, the performance of the algorithm improves as the number of managers is increased. However, the improved performance is achieved at the cost of heavier message traffic, since a larger number of *ready* messages need to be sent to the various managers. Any arbitrary allocation of events to the managers can be considered in the distributed implementation, in order to optimize the response-time/message-count trade off for a given network configuration. However, in general, for a given number of managers, performance will be enhanced if the events are allocated among the managers in a manner such that the e-set of each manager includes a maximal set of non-conflicting events. The performance issues are examined in greater detail subsequently.

5.2. Algorithm

We now give a precise description of the algorithm described above. The algorithm uses the following three types of messages:

- **ready**(p_i): message sent by a process p_i to a manager to indicate that the process is *idle*.
- **execut**(e_k) : message sent by a manager to a process to inform the process to commit to event e_k.
- **token**(*nx* : array [1..*p*] of **integer**) : This message represents the circulating token. *p* represents the total number of processes in the system; $nx(p_i)$ is the active-count for process p_i.

Each process continuously alternates between being *idle* or *active*. When a process p_i is *idle*, it sends a *ready* message to each manager in its manager-list. Process p_i then waits to receive an *execut* message from some manager at which point it becomes *active*. In addition to variables w_i and n_i introduced earlier, we introduce variables $idle_i$ and array variable com_i.

- w_i: integer variable that counts the number of times process p_i has been *idle*.
- n_i: integer variable that counts the number of times process p_i has been *active*.
- $idle_i$: boolean variable set to *true* when the process becomes idle; *false* otherwise.
- com_i : $com_i(e_k)$ is set to *true* when the process commits to event e_k; *false* otherwise.

The code executed by a process is expressed in the form of rules P1 and P2 given below. The two rules constitute a single guarded command. We reiterate that a process p_i autonomously sets $idle_i$ to *true* when it becomes idle. Initially each process is assumed to be *active* ($idle_i$ is set to *false*), and variables w_i and n_i are initialized to 0. The subscripts on variables have been dropped for ease of readability.

P1: Sending a *ready* message:

```
n=w ∧ idle ⇒
        ∀e_k∈ E_i,  com(e_k) :=false;
        send ready message to each manager in manager_list of p_i;
        w:=w+1;
```

P2: Receiving an *execut* message:

```
Upon receiving an execut(e_k) message ⇒
        com(e_k) :=true;
        idle:=false;
        n:=n+1;
```

The code executed by a manager is expressed in the form of the rules R1 and R2 given below. Each manager m_j has an integer array nr_j, where $nr_j(p_i)$ counts the number of *ready* messages received by manager m_j from process p_i. Once again the subscripts on local variables have been dropped for ease of readability. For every manager m_j, the array nr_j is initialized to *0*.

R1: Receiving a *ready* message:

```
Upon receiving a ready(p_i) message ==>
                      nr(p_i) :=nr(p_i)+1;
```

R2: Executing an event:

```
Upon receiving the token =>
       for every event e_k in the manager's e-set
            if (∀p_i∈ P_k, nr(p_i) =nx(p_i)+1) then
                  (∀p_i∈ P_k, send execut(e_k) message to p_i);
                  (∀p_i∈ P_k, nx(p_i) :=nr(p_i);
             end_if;
        end_for;
        send token to next manager;
```

5.3. Correctness

5.3.1. Exclusion

Lemma 1: For every manager m_j and process p_i, $0 \le nr_j(p_i) \le w_i$

Proof: From R1, $nr_j(p_i)$ counts the number of times a *ready* message is received by manager m_j from process p_i. From P1, w_i counts the number of times process p_i has sent a *ready* message to any of its managers. Since we assume that the channels are error-free, the number of *ready* messages received by a manager from some process p_i may be at most equal to the number of *ready* messages sent to that manager by p_i.

Lemma 2: If a manager m_j executes an event e_k, then $\forall p_i \in P_k$, $nx(p_i) = nr_j(p_i)$.

Proof: Follows directly from rule R2 for a manager.

Lemma 3: For any process p_i, if $w_i = k_i$, and a manager m_j executes an event e_k such that $p_i \in P_k$, then $nr_j(p_i) = k_i$.

Proof: Consider a process p_l. From P1, we note that w_l is incremented only when p_l becomes *idle* and sends a *ready* message. We use induction on the number of *ready* messages sent by p_l to prove the above lemma.

From the initial value for *nx* and rule R2 (the only rule that modifies the value of this variable), we conclude that $nx(p_l) \ge 0$ and increases monotonically. A1

Base Case: Let $w_l=1$. Assume that some manager m_j executes an event e_k, such that $p_l \in P_k$. From the rule for executing an event (R2), it follows that in order for manager m_j to execute event e_k, the following condition must be satisfied:

$$nr_j(p_l)=nx(p_l)+1$$

Since w_l is assumed to be 1, due to lemma 1, $nr_j(p_l)$ is either 0 or 1. If $nr_j(p_l)$ is 0, the above condition is satisfied only if $nx(p_l)$ is -1, which is impossible due to A1 above. It follows that $nr_j(p_l)$ must be 1, and thus equal to w_l.

Induction Hypothesis: Let $w_l=k_l$ (i.e. p_l has sent exactly k_l *ready* messages) and assume that some manager m_j executes an event e_k, such that $p_l \in P_k$. Then $nr_j(p_l)=k_l$.

From the above hypothesis and lemma 2, it also follows that

$$nx(p_l)=k_l \qquad \text{A2}$$

Induction Step: We show that if $w_l=k_l+1$ (i.e. process p_l has sent k_l+1 *ready* messages), and some manager m_j executes event e_k, such that $p_l \in P_k$, then $nr_j(p_l)$ is also equal to k_l+1.

Since w_l is assumed to be k_l+1, it follows from lemma 1 that $nr_j(p_l) \leq k_l+1$. In order for event e_k to be executed by manager m_j, due to R2, $nr_j(p_l)=nx(p_l)+1$. Due to A1 and A2, $nx(p_l) \geq k_l$. Thus $nr_j(p_l) \geq k_l+1$. Earlier, we showed that $nr_j(p_l) \leq k_l+1$. The two conditions can simultaneously be satisfied only if $nr_j(p_l)=k_l+1$.

Theorem 1: Exclusion: If a process p_i commits to an event e_k, no process in P_k may commit to another event. In other words

$$com_i(e_k) \Rightarrow (\forall e_l \neq e_k, \forall\, p_j \in P_k),\ \neg com_j(e_l))$$

ProofFrom rule P2, $com_i(e_k)$ is set to *true*, only if process p_i receives an *execut*(e_k) message from some manager. From rule R2, a manager m_j sends an *execut*(e_k) message to a process p_i, only if $p_i \in P_k$, and m_j executes e_k. Thus if we can show that *conflicting* events cannot be executed simultaneously, the result of the theorem follows directly. Assume that a manager m_j executes an event e_k. We show that no manager may simultaneously execute another event that conflicts with e_k.

When manager m_j executes event e_k, due to lemmas 2 and 3 the following relation must hold:

$$\forall p_i \in P_k,\ nr_j(p_i)=nx(p_i)=w_i=k_i \text{ (say)} \qquad \text{A3}$$

Further, from lemma 1 and A3 above, it follows that

$$(\forall m_l, \forall p_i \in P_k),\ nr_l(p_i) \leq k_i \qquad \text{A4}$$

Thus, if an event e_k is executed by a manager, due to A3 and A4, the following relation must hold for any manager that subsequently receives the token:

$$(\forall m_l, \forall p_i \in P_k)\ nr_l(p_i) \leq nx(p_i)$$

Due to the above relation, the progress condition P2 specified in rule R2 for the execution of an event, cannot be satisfied for any event that conflicts with event e_k. We conclude that if a manager executes an event, no other manager in the system can simultaneously execute a conflicting event.

5.3.2. Liveness

Lemma 4: For any process, say p_i, in the system, $n_i \leq nx(p_i) \leq n_i+1$

From rule R2, $nx(p_i)$ counts the number of *execut* messages sent to p_i and from P2, n_i counts the number of *execut* messages received by p_i. Since message-transmission is assumed to be error-free, the first part of the inequality is trivially satisfied. The exclusion condition in theorem 1 guarantees that conflicting events are not executed simultaneously, which implies that there may be at most one *execut* message in transit to any process. The result of the lemma follows directly.

Corollary: If p_i is *active*, $n_i = nx(p_i)$

If p_i is *active* and $nx(p_i) = n_i+1$, it implies that a manager has executed some event e_k, such that $p_i \in P_k$. This violates the exclusion condition proven in theorem 1. Due to the result of the above lemma, it must be that $nx(p_i) = n_i$.

Lemma 5:The *idle-count* of a process is equal to or at most one more than its *active-count* carried by the token. Stated otherwise: $\forall p_i,\ nx(p_i) \le w_i \le nx(p_i)+1$

Proof: We consider two cases: process p_i is *idle* or p_i is *active*.

Case i: p_i is *active*. The corollary to lemma 4 implies that if p_i is *active*, $nx(p_i) = n_i$, and no *execut* message is in transit to the process. From rules P1,P2 and the exclusion theorem, it also follows that if p_i is *active*, $n_i = w_i$. The two relations imply that $w_i = nx(p_i)$ and the invariant is satisfied.

Case ii: p_i is *idle*. From P1, when p_i is *idle*, $w_i = n_i+1$. Further, from lemma 4, either $n_i = nx(p_i)$ or $n_i = nx(p_i)-1$. In either case, $w_i = nx(p_i)+1$, or $w_i = nx(p_i)$ and the invariant is satisfied.

Lemma 6: For any process p_i, if $w_i = nx(p_i)$, then p_i is *active* or eventually becomes *active*.

Proof: Assume that p_i is *idle* and $w_i = nx(p_i)$. If process p_i is idle, due to rule P1, it must eventually send a *ready* message and increment w_i, such that $w_i = n_i+1$. From the assumption of the lemma, this implies that $nx(p_i) = n_i+1$. Due to R2 and P2, $nx(p_i) = n_i+1$ implies that an *execut* message has been sent to process p_i, but has not been received. Since message-transmission is assumed to be error-free, the *execut* message must eventually be received by p_i, causing it to become *active* due to rule P2.

Theorem 2: Liveness: If an event, say e_k is *enabled*, then eventually some p_i that belongs to P_k must become *active*.

Proof: Consider an event e_k, such that $\forall p_i \in P_k$, p_i is *idle*. Due to P1, each p_i must have sent a *ready* message to its manager(s) and due to P2, no process in P_k has received an *execut* message.

For every p_i that belongs to P_k, let $w_i = k_i$. Since message delivery can take only finite time, eventually for every manager m_j, of a process p_i that belongs to P_k, we must have

$$nr_j(p_i) = k_i \qquad \text{A5}$$

Further, due to lemma 5, for every p_i that belongs to P_k, we also have $nx(p_i) = k_i$ or $nx(p_i) + 1 = k_i$. If for any p_i that belongs to P_k, $nx(p_i) = k_i$, then due to the lemma 6, p_i must eventually become *active* and the liveness property will be satisfied. We assume, for every p_i that belongs to P_k:

$$nx(p_i) + 1 = k_i \qquad \text{A6}$$

If the processes remain *idle*, then due to A5 and A6 eventually, we must have some manager m_l, such that when m_l receives the token, for every p_i that belongs to P_k:

$$nx(p_i) + 1 = nr_l(p_i)$$

The above represents the progress condition included in rule R2 for the execution of an event by a manager. It follows that manager m_l must execute event e_k causing processes that belong to P_k to become *active*.

5.4. Extension

In the general case of the n-party rendezvous problem, on becoming *idle*, a process may be waiting to commit to only a subset of the events in its event-set. The algorithm described above can be extended to apply to the general case. The condition for the execution of an event e_k by a manager is modified as follows: the ready-count of every process in the process-set of event e_k must be one more that its active-count; in addition, each process in P_k must be waiting to commit to event e_k. Recall that when a process is *idle*, it sends a *ready* message to a manager. On receiving the message, the manager implicitly assumes that the process is waiting to commit to any one of the events from its event-set. The *ready* message is modified to include explicit information that indicates the specific events, to any one of which the process is waiting to commit. In particular, every *ready* message carries a boolean array *elist*; *elist*(k) is *true* if the process sending the message is waiting to commit to event e_k and is *false* otherwise. In addition, we define a boolean array *status* for every manager. On receiving a *ready* message from process p_i, *status*(i,k) is set to *true* if process p_i is waiting to commit to event e_k and is set to *false* otherwise. With an appropriate modification to the manager's data-structures, the condition specified above can be easily incorporated into the rule for execution of an event by a manager.

5.5. Overflow

In the description of the event-manager's algorithm, we have ignored the problem of overflow. We present a simple solution to ensure that no variable exceeds the maximum permissible value for an integer. The algorithm uses the following counters for each process:

- w_i: represents the idle-count for process p_i.
- n_i: represents the active-count for process p_i.
- $nr_j(p_i)$: counts the number of times manager m_j has received *ready* messages from process p_i.
- $nx(p_i)$: represents the active-count carried by the token for process p_i.

The values of the counters for each process are tightly coupled. If $nx(p_i)$ is monitored for overflow, then we can guarantee that neither of w_i, n_i or $nr_j(p_i)$ will overflow as follows: let **maxInt** be the maximum permissible value for an integer. Define a variable **max** such that **max**<**maxInt**. As long as $nx(p_i)<$**max**, due to lemma 4, $n_i<$**max**, and due to lemma 5, $w_i<$**maxInt**; this in turn implies $\forall(m_j)$, $nr_j(p_i)<$**maxInt**, due to lemma 1. We describe a technique that monitors the value of $nx(p_i)$ to prevent overflow errors. We define two new types of messages:

- *reset*: sent to a manager/process to reset its counters.
- *ack*: sent by a manager to indicate that its counters have been reset.

From the algorithm, we note that $nx(p_i)$ is incremented only when a manager possesses the token and executes some event e_k, such that $p_i \in P_k$ (Rule R2). On executing an event e_k, if a manager m_j determines that $\exists p_i : p_i \in P_k$ and $nx(p_i)=$**max**-1, m_j initiates the scheme to reset all counters; henceforth, m_j is referred to as the **initiator**. The **initiator** resets array *nx* to zero and sends a *reset* message to *all processes in the system*. The initiator does not transmit the token until it has received an *ack* message from all other managers in the system. This ensures that no events in the system are executed until all counters have been reset. On receiving a *reset* message, each process sets its active-count to zero; it resets its idle-count to 1 if it is *idle* or to 0 if it is *active*. A process then sends a reset message containing its idle-count to each manager. On receiving a reset message from p_i, a manager m_j sets $nr_j(p_i)$ to the idle-count carried in the message. After receiving reset messages from all processes in its p-set, the manager sends an ack message to the initiator. The algorithm proceeds normally after the initiator has received ack messages from all managers in the system. We note that invariant I3 is temporarily violated from the time a manager resets array *nx* until the processes receive the *reset* messages. However, since no events can be executed while the reset procedure is underway, and the invariant is restored on the completion of the reset procedure, correctness of the algorithm is not affected.

6. Committee-Coordination Algorithm

In this section, we briefly describe the algorithm suggested by Chandy & Misra [8]. This algorithm, referred to as the committee coordination algorithm splits the problem of n-party rendezvous into two sub-problems:

exclusive selection of one among many conflicting events, and the determination of the state of each process in the process-set of the selected event. The exclusion problem is solved by appropriately mapping the n-party rendezvous problem onto the dining philosopher's problem. The synchronization problem is solved by a judicious use of tokens. The committee coordination algorithm postulates a special process, called a coordinator for every event in the system. Two coordinators c_i and c_j are neighbours if the corresponding events e_i and e_j conflict with each other. Every pair of neighbours share a unique fork. Each process in the system is initially assigned a fixed number of tokens, whose count is equal to the number of events in the event-set of that process. When a process becomes *idle*, it sends a *token* to the coordinator for every event in its event-set. On receiving tokens from all processes in the process-set of its event, a coordinator requests forks from all its neighbours. The algorithm guarantees that every coordinator that requests forks will eventually receive all the forks from its neighbours. Once a coordinator has received all its forks, it determines if all processes in its process-set are still *idle*. (This is required since a neighboring coordinator may have executed a conflicting event.) The algorithm defines a scheme based on shuffling tokens among the coordinators to allow a coordinator to determine whether a conflicting event has been executed. The algorithm thus works in two steps: in the first step, a coordinator obtains the exclusive right to execute its event by requesting forks from its neighbours. In the second step, a coordinator that has obtained all the forks determines the current state of processes by requesting tokens from its neighbours. In the next section, we compare the performance of this algorithm with the event manager algorithm.

7. Performance

Two metrics are used in this paper to measure the performance of algorithms: message-count and response time. The response time for each algorithm is measured from the instant that an event becomes *executable* (as viewed by a global observer) to the instant that it is selected for execution by the algorithm. The two components that determine the total response time for an algorithm are:

1. Synchronization time: The time taken by the algorithm to ascertain that a given event is *executable* (i.e. all processes in the process-set of the event are *idle*).
2. Selection time(T_s): The time taken by an algorithm to select one of many *conflicting* executable events for execution.

The two algorithms discussed in this paper use different techniques to implement selection and synchronization. The event manager (EM) algorithm uses a message counting technique to determine when an event is executable. Selection among conflicting events is achieved by using a token that circulates among managers. The response time for this algorithm is determined primarily by the average time required by the token to travel between two managers whose e-lists contain an event e_i. For simplicity, we assume that the e-list of each manager contains the list of all events in the system. We further assume that the number of managers is equal to the number of processes, with each manager being located at a unique process. Under these assumptions, the response time for the algorithm is determined primarily by the average message transmission time between two managers (processes) in the system.

In the committee coordination (CC) algorithm, the auxiliary resources (forks and tokens) are transmitted only between the coordinators for conflicting events. The coordinators for events that do not conflict with each other do not exchange any messages. As a result, the response time for this algorithm is determined primarily by the average message transmission time between coordinators for *conflicting* events.

A performance study was undertaken to isolate the effects of the above techniques on the response time for each algorithm. The detailed performance study has been described in [4]. In this paper, we present a brief summary of some significant results. Two different process configurations were identified for the study: uniform configurations, in which all processes are equidistant from each other, and non-uniform configurations in which processes are organized into clusters, with the distance between processes in the same cluster being much less than that between processes in different clusters. We define the *cardinality* of an event as the number of processes in the process-set of that event, and the *degree of conflict* as the average number of events that are in conflict with each other in the system. The experiments were restricted to synchronization patterns between processes, where each event had the same cardinality and degree of conflict. Simulation models were constructed for each algorithm using the MAY [5] simulation language. Approximate analytical models were constructed for a restricted version of each algorithm to validate the results of the simulation. The results for the uniform process configurations are presented in figures 8-1 and 8-2. This set of experiments studied the effect of varying the cardinality (*c*) and degree of conflict (*d*) of an event on the message-count and response time for the algorithms. As can be seen from the figures, the response time for the event-manager algorithm was less by a factor of 1/3 over the committee coordination algorithm, whereas the message-count for the event-manager algorithm was approximately twice that of the committee coordination algorithm.

In the case of non-uniform process configurations, two types of synchronization patterns were identified: *localized synchronization*(LS), where processes interact primarily with other processes in the same cluster; and *uniform synchronization*(US), where processes interact uniformly with other processes, regardless of their

Number of processes=number of events = 10.
Average message transmission time between two processes = 5000.

c	*d*	Response Time	
		CC	EM
2	2	18444	6915
3	4	20574	6962
4	6	21516	7060
5	8	22059	6986

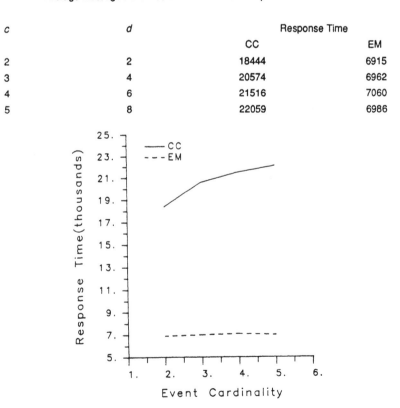

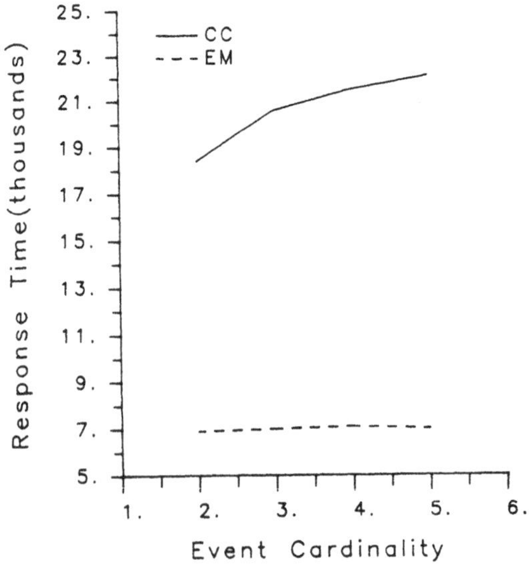

Figure 8-1: Comparison of CC and EM Algorithms: Response Time

location. Figure 8-3 presents a non-uniform process configuration comprising of two clusters. The transmission time for a message from one process to another in the same cluster is assumed to be τ_1 units, and the transmission time for messages from one cluster to another is τ_2, where $\tau_2 = 5\tau_1$. The results for this experiment are presented in tables 8-1 and 8-2, which compares the performance of the two algorithms for both LS and US configurations. In the case of the EM algorithm, the response time was the same in both configurations, since the topology of the network remained unchanged. For the CC algorithm in the LS configuration, the coordinators for *conflicting* events are relatively close to each other, and the response time was small. However, in the US configuration, the distances between coordinators for *conflicting* events included the large separation between different clusters causing the response time of the algorithm to increase significantly. As seen from the results in tables 8-1 and 8-2, in the LS configuration, the response time for the CC algorithm was much superior to that of the EM algorithm, whereas in the US configuration, the EM algorithm performed better.

8. Conclusion

This paper discussed the problem of synchronizing asynchronous processes, where each synchronization may involve an arbitrary, though pre-determined number of processes. This problem is referred to as the n-party rendezvous problem. This paper described a distributed algorithm, referred to as the event-manager algorithm, to

Number of processes=number of events = 10.
Average message transmission time between two processes = 5000.

c	*d*	Message Count CC	Message Count EM
2	2	5086	13593
3	4	10627	20579
4	6	17098	27818
5	8	24770	32944

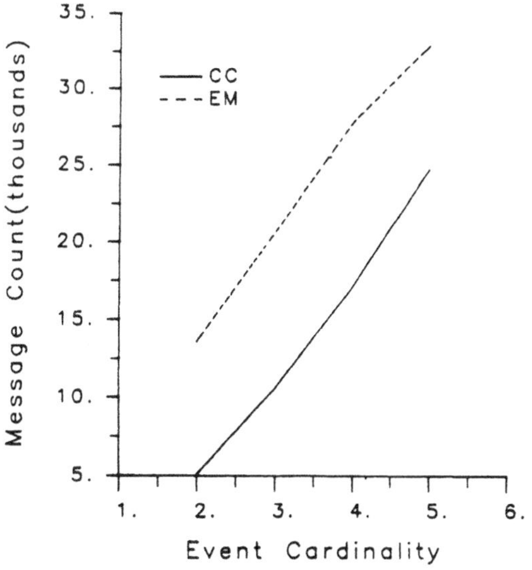

Figure 8-2: Comparison of CC and EM Algorithms: Message Count

implement n-party rendezvous among a group of concurrent, asynchronous processes. The n-party rendezvous problem is a non-trivial problem that captures the two central issues in the design of distributed systems: synchronization and exclusion. In general, a variety of centralized and distributed techniques exist to solve each of the two problems. For instance, synchronization may be solved by means of polling, message-counts, or using auxiliary resources like tokens; the exclusion problem may be solved by using timestamps, unique process-ids, auxiliary resources(forks), or probability-based techniques. The event manager algorithm presented in this paper used message-counts to implement synchronization and a circulating token to implement exclusion. The committee coordination algorithm used auxiliary resources (tokens and forks) to implement synchronization and exclusion. Other known techniques to solve synchronization and exclusion problems may be combined with each other to suggest different ways to implement n-party rendezvous. The variety of possible solutions indicates the

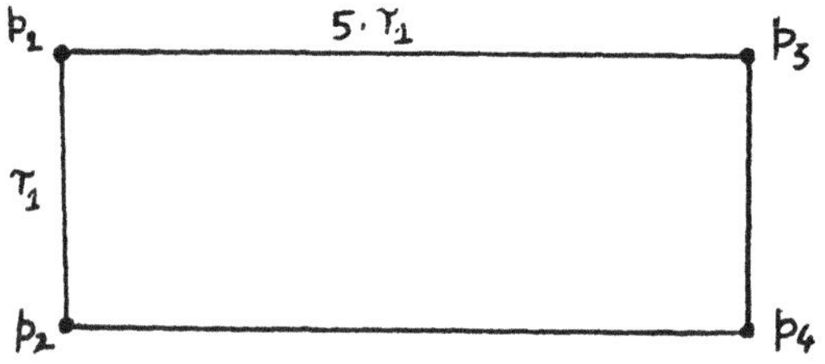

Figure 8-3: Network of Two Clusters

Number of processes = 4.
Number of events = 2; $e_1 = \{p_1, p_2\}$; $e_2 = \{p_3, p_4\}$.
Message transmission times : $\tau_1 = 5000$; $\tau_2 = 25000$.

Algorithm	Message Count	Response Time
CC	1002	2775
EM	8116	25135

Table 8-1: Comparison of CC and EM Algorithms : LS Configuration

Number of processes = 4.
Number of events = 4; $e_1=\{p_1,p_2\}$; $e_2=\{p_3,p_4\}$; $e_3=\{p_1,p_3\}$; $e_4=\{p_2,p_4\}$.
Message transmission times : $\tau_1 = 5000$; $\tau_2 = 25000$.

Algorithm	Message Count	Response Time
CC	4964	82445
EM	6404	25074

Table 8-2: Comparison of CC and EM Algorithms : US Configuration

strong need for some performance metrics that can be used to identify the suitability of a specific algorithm for a specific type of network configuration. The paper presented a brief performance study of the event-manager(EM) and committee coordination (CC) algorithms. Results from the study were used to identify the process configurations for the best-case and worst-case performance of each algorithm. It was determined that in uniform process configurations, the response time for the EM algorithm was better than that for the CC algorithm. In non-uniform configurations, where processes are not equidistant from each other, the performance of the algorithm depended on the pattern of interaction among the processes.

Acknowledgements

I am grateful to Ira Forman for initial discussions on this problem. I am also indebted to Professors K.M.Chandy and J.Misra for their invaluable input in the formulation of the algorithm.

References

[Ada 82] *Reference Manual for the Ada Programming Language*
United States Department Of Defense, 1982.

[Back 84] Back, R. and Kurki-Suonio, R.
Cooperation in Distributed Systems Using Symmetric Multi-Process Handshaking.
Technical Report No. Ser. A, No. 34, Department of Information Processing and Mathematics, Swedish University of Abo, Finland, 1984.

[Bagrodia 86] Bagrodia, R.
A Distributed Algorithm To Implement The Generalized Alternative Command of CSP.
In *Proccedings of 6th International Conference on Distributed Systems.* Cambridge, May, 1986.

[Bagrodia 87a] Bagrodia, R.
An Environment For the Design and Performance Analysis of Distributed Systems.
PhD thesis, Dept. of Computer Sciences, University of Texas, Austin, Tx 78712., May, 1987.

[Bagrodia 87b] Bagrodia, R., Chandy, K.M., and Misra, J.
A Message-Based Approach To Discrete-Event Simulation.
IEEE Transactions on Software Engineering , June, 1987.

[Bernstein 80] Bernstein, A.J.
Output guards And Non-determinism in Communicating Sequential Processes.
ACM TOPLAS 2(2):234-238, April, 1980.

[Buckley 83] Buckley, G. and Silberschatz, A.
An Effective Implementation Of The Generalized Input-Output Construct of CSP.
ACM TOPLAS 5(2):223-235, April, 1983.

[Chandy 87] Chandy, K.M. and Misra,J.
Synchronizing Asynchronous Processes:The Committee Coordination Problem.
Technical Report, Dept. of Computer Sciences, University of Texas, Austin, Tx 78712., 1987.
In Preparation.

[Charlesworth 87] A. Charlesworth.
The Multiway Rendezvous.
ACM Trans. on Programming Languages and Systems 9(3):350-366, 1987.

[Forman 87] Forman, I.R.
On the Design of Large Distributed Systems.
Technical Report No. STP-098-86, Microelectronics and Computer Technology Corp, Austin, Texas, January, 1987.
Preliminary version in Proc. First Int'l Conf. on Computer Languages, Miami, Florida, October 25-27, 1986.

[Francez 86] Francez, N., Hailpern, B. and Taubenfeld, G.
Script:A Communication Abstraction Mechanism.
Science of Computer Programming 6(1), January, 1986.

[Hoare 78] Hoare, C.A.R.
Communicating Sequential Processes.
CACM 21(8):666-677, August, 1978.

[Milne 85] Milne, George.
CIRCAL and the Representation Of Communication, Concurrency and Time.
ACM TOPLAS 7(2), April, 1985.

[Natarajan 86] Natarajan,N.
A Distributed Synchronization Scheme for Communicating Processes.
The Computer Journal 29(2):109-117, 1986.

[Schneider 82] Schneider,F.
Synchronization In Distributed Programs.
ACM TOPLAS 4(2):125-148, April, 1982.

[Van De Snepscheut 81]
Van De Snepscheut, J.L.A.
Synchronous Communication Between Asynchronous Components.
IPL 13(3):127-130, December, 1981.

Merge and Termination in Process Algebra

J.C.M. Baeten,
*Dept. of Computer Science, University of Amsterdam,
P.O. Box 41882, 1009 DB Amsterdam, The Netherlands*

R.J. van Glabbeek,
*Dept. of Software Technology, Centre for Mathematics and Computer Science,
P.O. Box 4079, 1009 AB Amsterdam, The Netherlands*

Abstract: In VRANCKEN [14], the empty process ε was added to the Algebra of Communicating Processes of BERGSTRA & KLOP [3, 4]. Reconsidering the definition of the parallel composition operator merge, we found that it is preferable to explicitly state the termination option. This gives an extra summand in the defining equation of merge, using the auxiliary operator $\surd$ (tick). We find that tick can be defined in terms of the encapsulation operator ∂_H. We give an operational and a denotational semantics for the resulting system ACP$\surd$, and prove that they are equal. We consider the Limit Rule, and prove it holds in our models.
Note: Partial support received from the European Communities under ESPRIT contract no. 432, An Integrated Formal Approach to Industrial Software Development (Meteor).

1. INTRODUCTION

Having been introduced to the Algebra of Communicating Processes of BERGSTRA & KLOP [3, 4], many people ask the question why there is no neutral element for the sequential composition $\cdot$. The neutral element for alternative composition + is the constant δ, that is used to denote deadlock, unsuccessful termination. A constant ε satisfying the laws $\varepsilon \cdot x = x \cdot \varepsilon = x$ must stand for an **empty process**, a process that terminates immediately and successfully. The investigation of what happens when we want to add such a constant to ACP was started by KOYMANS & VRANCKEN [9]. It turned out that the constant ε is very useful, but that the technicalities involved were substantial. For instance, the just quoted paper contained a non-associative merge operator. This problem was remedied in VRANCKEN [14], where the theory ACP was modified and extended to ACP$^\varepsilon$. In practice, the constant ε already showed its usefulness in BERGSTRA, KLOP & OLDEROG [5], where ε was needed to define the constant Δ denoting divergence.

This paper was motivated by a reconsideration of the interaction of merge and empty process in the papers [9], [14]. Merge is the parallel composition operator $\|$. Not considering communication for the moment, the merge of processes x and y will interleave the actions of x and y. In $x\|y$, there are three possibilities: a step from x can be executed, or a step from y, or the process can terminate (only if both x and y have that option). These options are present in the defining axiom of merge:

$$x\|y = x \mathbin{|\!\!\lfloor} y + y \mathbin{|\!\!\lfloor} x + \surd(x)\cdot\surd(y).$$

Here, we use the auxiliary operators $\mathbin{|\!\!\lfloor}$ (left-merge) and $\surd$ (used to indicate termination). Now, in [9] and [14], the left-merge is used also to indicate the termination possibility. We think that a separation of the two notions makes a more refined treatment possible, and can lead to a better understanding of the issues involved.

In section 2, we first discuss termination in a setting without communication, using the free merge. In section 3, we add communication, and prove some theorems, such as the elimination theorem and the expansion theorem. We also briefly discuss infinite processes. In section 4, we discuss different semantics for our theory, namely a term model and two graph models. The term model is based on action relations, is operational (cf. MILNER [11], PLOTKIN [13]), while the second graph model is denotational. We prove that these models are isomorphic.

In these models, guarded recursive specifications have unique solutions. We prove that these models are complete for our theory w.r.t. closed terms, i.e. we have a complete axiomatisation for them. A short proof of this fact was not published before, even for the theory ACP without empty process.

Finally, in section 5, we consider the Limit Rule of BAETEN & BERGSTRA [1], and prove that a restricted version holds in our models. The Limit Rule says that if we have an equation that holds for all finite processes, then it holds for all processes.

ACKNOWLEDGEMENT. The authors express their gratitude to Jan Bergstra and Henk Goeman, for help in developing the concepts defined in this paper.

2. PROCESS ALGEBRA WITH FREE MERGE

In this section, we consider the case of merge without communication, the so-called *free merge*.
Our starting point is the theory PA as defined in BERGSTRA & KLOP [2], without empty process ε.
For other algebraical theories of concurrency, see e.g. MILNER [10] or HOARE [8].

2.1 Process algebra starts from a collection of given objects, called atomic actions, atoms or steps. These actions are taken to be indivisible, usually have no duration and form the basic building blocks of our systems. The first two compositional operators we consider are $\cdot$, denoting sequential composition, and + for alternative composition. If x and y are two processes, then $x \cdot y$ is the process that starts the execution of y after the completion of x, and $x+y$ is the process that chooses either x or y and executes the chosen process (not the other one). Each time a choice is made, we choose from a *set* of alternatives (see axioms A1-3 below). We do not specify whether a choice is made by the process itself, or by the environment. We leave out $\cdot$ and brackets as in regular algebra, so $xy + z$ means $(x \cdot y) + z$. $\cdot$ will always bind stronger than other operators, and + will always bind weaker.
On intuitive grounds $x(y + z)$ and $xy + xz$ present different mechanisms (the moment of choice is different), and therefore, an axiom $x(y + z) = xy + xz$ is not included.
Next, we have the parallel composition operator $\|$, called merge. The merge of processes x and y will interleave the actions of x and y. In $x \| y$, either a step from x can be executed, or a step from y. These options are present in axiom M1. Here, we use the auxiliary operator $\lfloor\!\lfloor$ (left-merge). Thus, $x \lfloor\!\lfloor y$ is $x \| y$, but with the restriction that the first step comes from x, and likewise for $y \lfloor\!\lfloor x$. Axioms M2-4 give the laws for $\lfloor\!\lfloor$.

2.2 DEADLOCK. We enlarge the signature of PA, by adding the special constant δ, denoting deadlock, the acknowledgement of a process that it cannot do anything anymore, the absence of any alternative (see BERGSTRA & KLOP [3, 4]). δ has axioms A6-7. A process that ends in δ terminates unsuccessfully. The theory PA plus δ is called PA_δ.

2.3 SIGNATURE AND AXIOMS. A is a given (finite) set of atomic actions. All elements of A are constants of PA_δ. Further, PA_δ has binary operators $+, \cdot, \|, \lfloor\!\lfloor$, and a constant δ ($\delta \notin A$).
The axioms of PA_δ are presented in table 1. There $a \in A \cup \{\delta\}$, and x,y,z are arbitrary processes.

$x + y = y + x$	A1	$x \| y = x \lfloor\!\lfloor y + y \lfloor\!\lfloor x$	M1
$(x + y) + z = x + (y + z)$	A2	$a \lfloor\!\lfloor x = ax$	M2
$x + x = x$	A3	$ax \lfloor\!\lfloor y = a(x \| y)$	M3
$(x + y)z = xz + yz$	A4	$(x + y) \lfloor\!\lfloor z = x \lfloor\!\lfloor z + y \lfloor\!\lfloor z$	M4
$(xy)z = x(yz)$	A5		
$x + \delta = x$	A6		
$\delta x = \delta$	A7		

Table 1. PA_δ.

2.4 EMPTY PROCESS. Now we add the empty process ε, giving us the theory $PA\surd$. ε is the neutral element of sequential composition, so has axioms $\varepsilon x = x\varepsilon = x$ (A8,9). In a sum, as in $x + \varepsilon$, it tells us that the process can terminate immediately and successfully. We introduce the operator $\surd$ to indicate whether or not a process can terminate immediately: $\surd(x) = \varepsilon$ if x has the termination option, and $\surd(x) = \delta$ otherwise. Axioms Te1-4 give an axiomatisation of $\surd$: we just rename all atomic actions into δ, and distribute $\surd$ over + and $\cdot$.

Now, in $x\|y$, there are three possibilities: we can start with a step from x, or with a step from y, or the process can terminate, if both x and y have this option. A simple case distinction learns us that the termination summand of $x\|y$ can be represented by $\surd(x)\cdot\surd(y)$ ($= \surd(y)\cdot\surd(x)$). See axiom MT1. Finally, axioms EM2-4 are the laws for left-merge.

2.5 SIGNATURE AND AXIOMS. We have in the signature of theory PA$\surd$ as constants all elements of $A\cup\{\delta,\varepsilon\}$, the binary operators $+,\cdot,\|,\lfloor\!\lfloor$, and the unary operator $\surd$. The axioms are presented in table 2 below. There $a \in A\cup\{\delta\}$, and x,y,z are arbitrary processes.

$x + y = y + x$	A1	$\delta + \varepsilon = \varepsilon$	A6
$(x + y) + z = x + (y + z)$	A2	$\delta x = \delta$	A7
$\varepsilon + \varepsilon = \varepsilon$	A3	$\varepsilon x = x$	A8
$(x + y)z = xz + yz$	A4	$x\varepsilon = x$	A9
$(xy)z = x(yz)$	A5		
$x\|y = x\lfloor\!\lfloor y + y\lfloor\!\lfloor x + \surd(x)\cdot\surd(y)$	MT1	$\surd(\varepsilon) = \varepsilon$	Te1
$\varepsilon\lfloor\!\lfloor x = \delta$	EM2	$\surd(a) = \delta$	Te2
$ax\lfloor\!\lfloor y = a(x\|y)$	EM3	$\surd(x + y) = \surd(x) + \surd(y)$	Te3
$(x + y)\lfloor\!\lfloor z = x\lfloor\!\lfloor z + y\lfloor\!\lfloor z$	EM4	$\surd(xy) = \surd(x)\cdot\surd(y)$	Te4

Table 2. PA$\surd$.

2.6 REMARKS. In PA$\surd$, we have different versions of the axioms A3 and A6 of PA$_\delta$. Using axioms A4,7,8, it can be seen that the new versions are equivalent to the old ones. As we will see in section 3, the axiom M2 of PA$_\delta$ is derivable from PA$\surd$ if we add the extra axiom $\varepsilon\|x = x$. It is debatable whether or not this axiom $\varepsilon\|x = x$ should be included in PA$\surd$. We have chosen not to, since it is derivable for all closed terms (see section 3). PA$\surd$ differs from PA$^\varepsilon$ of VRANCKEN [14], by the use of the termination operator $\surd$. In [14], the termination option is represented by $\varepsilon\lfloor\!\lfloor x$.

Originally, we considered a binary operator $\downarrow$ instead of the unary operator $\surd$. $\downarrow$ is the so-called "termination merge", and $x\downarrow y = \varepsilon$ iff both x and y have the termination option, and δ otherwise. In this case, the axiom MT1 would read $x\|y = x\lfloor\!\lfloor y + y\lfloor\!\lfloor x + x\downarrow y$. The operator $\downarrow$ can be axiomatised by the following laws:

$$x\downarrow y = y\downarrow x,\quad \varepsilon\downarrow\varepsilon = \varepsilon,\quad ax\downarrow y = \delta,\quad (x + y)\downarrow z = x\downarrow z + y\downarrow z.$$

The idea to use a unary operator came from Jan Bergstra.

Before we discuss some consequences of PA$\surd$, we first introduce communication in section 3. Results for the system PA$\surd$, so without communication, can be obtained from the results in section 3 by forgetting the communication function.

3. ALGEBRA OF COMMUNICATING PROCESSES

We introduce the communication of the system ACP (Algebra of Communicating Processes) of BERGSTRA & KLOP [3, 4]. If two processes simultaneously execute two atomic actions that can communicate, the result is a communication action. In $x\|y$, we will add a fourth summand: the execution of a communication action, with components from x and y. Below we define the system ACP$\surd$.

3.1 SIGNATURE AND AXIOMS. A is a given (finite) set of atomic actions. On A, we assume that a **communication function** γ is given: γ is a partial binary function, that is commutative and associative, i.e. for all $a,b,c \in A$:

$$\gamma(a,b) = \gamma(b,a)$$
$$\gamma(\gamma(a,b),c) = \gamma(a,\gamma(b,c)),$$

(and each side of these equations is defined just when the other side is). If $\gamma(a,b)$ is defined (we write $\gamma(a,b)\downarrow$), and $\gamma(a,b) = c$, it means that actions a and b can communicate, and their communication is c; if $\gamma(a,b)$ is not defined, we say that a and b do not communicate.
All elements of A are constants of ACP$\surd$. Further, ACP$\surd$ has binary operators $+,\cdot,\|,⌊\!⌊,|$, unary operators ∂_H, ε_K (for $H,K \subseteq A$) and constants δ,ε.
The axioms of ACP$\surd$ are listed in table 3 below.
There, $a \in A\cup\{\delta\}$, $H,K \subseteq A$ and x,y,z are arbitrary processes.

$x + y = y + x$	A1	$\delta + \varepsilon = \varepsilon$		A6
$(x + y) + z = x + (y + z)$	A2	$\delta x = \delta$		A7
$\varepsilon + \varepsilon = \varepsilon$	A3	$\varepsilon x = x$		A8
$(x + y)z = xz + yz$	A4	$x\varepsilon = x$		A9
$(xy)z = x(yz)$	A5			
		$a \mid b = \gamma(a,b)$	if $\gamma(a,b)\downarrow$	CF1
		$a \mid b = \delta$	otherwise	CF2
$x\|y = x⌊\!⌊y + y⌊\!⌊x + x \mid y + \surd(x)\cdot\surd(y)$	EM1	$x \mid y = y \mid x$		EM5
$\varepsilon⌊\!⌊x = \delta$	EM2	$x \mid \varepsilon = \delta$		EM6
$ax⌊\!⌊y = a(x\|y)$	EM3	$x \mid ay = (x \mid a)⌊\!⌊y$		EM7
$(x + y)⌊\!⌊z = x⌊\!⌊z + y⌊\!⌊z$	EM4	$x \mid (y + z) = x \mid y + x \mid z$		EM8
$\partial_H(\varepsilon) = \varepsilon$	D0	$\varepsilon_K(\varepsilon) = \varepsilon$		E0
$\partial_H(a) = a$ if $a \notin H$	D1	$\varepsilon_K(a) = a$ if $a \notin K$		E1
$\partial_H(a) = \delta$ if $a \in H$	D2	$\varepsilon_K(a) = \varepsilon$ if $a \in K$		E2
$\partial_H(x + y) = \partial_H(x) + \partial_H(y)$	D3	$\varepsilon_K(x + y) = \varepsilon_K(x) + \varepsilon_K(y)$		E3
$\partial_H(xy) = \partial_H(x)\cdot\partial_H(y)$	D4	$\varepsilon_K(xy) = \varepsilon_K(x)\cdot \varepsilon_K(y)$		E4

Table 3. ACP$\surd$.

$|$ is the **communication merge**: $x \mid y$ is just like $x\|y$, but with the restriction that the first step must be a communication action, with components from x and y. Now if $\gamma(a,b) = c$, we can calculate that $a\|b = ab + ba + c$; if we do not want the a,b to occur separately, but only in the communication, we have to encapsulate them, using the **encapsulation operator** ∂_H: if $H = \{a,b\}$, we get $\partial_H(a\|b) = c$. ∂_H blocks all atomic actions from $H \subseteq A$, by renaming them into δ. Lastly, ε_K is also a renaming operator, that erases all actions from $K \subseteq A$, by renaming them into ε.
We did not list $\surd$ as an operator of ACP$\surd$, because it has become definable: $\surd$ is just ∂_A, the operator that renames *all* atomic actions into δ. This fact was pointed out to us by Henk Goeman. We will still use the notation $\surd$, though.

3.2 REMARKS. Axioms Te1-4 of PA$\surd$ are just the axioms D0,2,3,4 for the operator ∂_A. ACP$\surd$ differs from ACP$^\varepsilon$ of VRANCKEN [14], by the use of the termination operator. Other differences are that in [14], γ is a total function from $A\times A$ to $A\cup\{\delta\}$, while in this paper, γ is a partial function from $A\times A$ to A. Also, in the axioms in [14], a varies over A, not over $A\cup\{\delta\}$, which necessitates more axioms. Lastly, we left out the axiom $(x \mid y) \mid z = x \mid (y \mid z)$, as we saw no reason for its inclusion (it will be an axiom of Standard Concurrency, see below).

The system ACP^{ε} itself differs in several aspects from the system ACP of BERGSTRA & KLOP [3]. Most of these differences were a consequence of the addition of the constant ε. Another difference is the inclusion of axiom EM5, the commutativity of the communication merge, which decreased the number of axioms needed.

3.3 LEMMA. The following equations are derivable from the system $ACP\surd$ ($a,b \in A \cup \{\delta\}$):
1. $ax \| by = by \| ax$ 2. $x \mid \delta = \delta$
PROOF: Straightforward. For 2, use EM6,8 and A6.

3.4 LEMMA. In the system $ACP\surd$ plus extra axiom $\varepsilon \| x = x$ the following equations are derivable ($a,b \in A \cup \{\delta\}$):
1. $x = x \lfloor\!\lfloor \varepsilon + \surd(x)$ 2. $x \| \varepsilon = x$ 3. $a \lfloor\!\lfloor x = ax$
4. $a \mid bx = ax \mid b = (a \mid b)x$ 5. $ax \mid by = (a \mid b)(x \| y)$
PROOF: Straightforward.

3.5 Note that equation 3.4.1 states that we can write each process as the sum of its termination option ($\surd(x)$) and the summands that start with an atomic action ($x \lfloor\!\lfloor \varepsilon$). Equations 3.4.3-5 are axioms of ACP. In the next lemma, we focus on another equation that is of special interest, namely the assertion that $\surd(x)$ must be either ε or δ (note that $x = x + \varepsilon$ amounts to saying that x has an ε-summand):

$\surd(x) = \varepsilon$ iff $x = x + \varepsilon$, and $\surd(x) = \delta$ otherwise (Te5).

3.6 LEMMA. In the system $ACP\surd$ plus extra axiom Te5 the following equations are derivable:
1. $x \| y = y \| x$ 2. $\surd(x) \lfloor\!\lfloor y = \delta$ 3. $\surd(x) \mid y = \delta$
PROOF: Straightforward.

3.7 DEFINITION. A **basic term** is a closed term of the form

$$t = a_0t_0 + \dots + a_{n-1}t_{n-1} + b_0 + \dots + b_{m-1} \ (+\ \varepsilon)$$

for certain $n,m \in \mathbb{N}$, certain $a_i,b_j \in A \cup \{\delta\}$, basic terms t_i and the summand ε may or may not occur. If the summand ε does not occur, we must have $n+m > 0$.
We usually abbreviate such expressions, in this case to $t = \Sigma_{i<n} a_it_i + \Sigma_{j<m} b_j \ (+\ \varepsilon)$. Note that we can always write $t = \Sigma_{i<n} a_it_i + \Sigma_{j<m} b_j + \surd(t)$, for it is easy to see that $\surd(t) = \varepsilon$ iff t has a summand ε, and $\surd(t) = \delta$ otherwise.
The set of basic terms **BT** can be inductively built up as follows (working modulo laws A1-3 and A9):
1. $\varepsilon \in$ BT
2. if $a \in A \cup \{\delta\}$ and $x \in$ BT, then $ax \in$ BT
3. if $x,y \in$ BT, then $x+y \in$ BT.
Alternatively, if $\Sigma_{i<0}\, x_i$ denotes δ, we can build up BT as follows:
– If $n \in \mathbb{N}$, $a_i \in A \cup \{\delta\}$ and $t_i \in$ BT (for $i<n$), then $\Sigma_{i<n} a_it_i \ (+\ \varepsilon) \in$ BT.
Both these inductive schemes can be used in proofs.

3.8 DEFINITION. Let p be a process. We say p has a **head normal form** if there is an $n \in \mathbb{N}$, processes p_i ($i<n$), and constants $a_i \in A \cup \{\delta\}$ such that $p = \Sigma_{i<n} a_ip_i \ (+\ \varepsilon)$.
Note that by definition, all basic terms have a head normal form. It is easy to prove that all processes that have a head normal form satisfy Te5 of 3.5, and the following equations:
1. $\surd(x \lfloor\!\lfloor y) = \surd(x \mid y) = \delta$ 2. $\surd(\surd(x)) = \surd(x)$.

3.9 THEOREM. For every closed ACP√-term t there is a basic term s such that ACP√ ⊢ t = s.
This is the so-called **elimination theorem**.
PROOF: Let RACP√ be the full system ACP√, excluding axioms A1-2 and EM5, but including equation a⌊⌊x = ax, used as a rewrite system (from left to right), modulo axioms A1-2 and EM5. Working *modulo* axioms A1-2 and EM5 means that we consider terms that are equal using these axioms, to be identical. Note that a⌊⌊x = ax follows from A9, EM3 and ε‖x = x. Below we will prove that, using RACP√, any closed term t can be rewritten to a basic term s, and moreover ACP√ ⊢ ε‖t = t for closed terms t. From this the elimination theorem follows.
Let RACP√–E denote the system RACP√ without the rewrite rules E0-4.
We start by proving that RACP√–E is a terminating rewrite system on ε_K-free terms, and all its normal forms are basic terms. We first need some definitions. We define the **length** and **width** of a closed ACP√-term t without occurrences of the ε_K-operator inductively in table 4 below. As an auxiliary operator, we also define Te(t), the number of termination possibilities of t. The awkward expression for w(u‖v) is the result of working out the four summands of EM1.
Roughly, the length of a term indicates the maximal number of steps that can occur when the term is executed, and the width gives the number of alternatives at the start of the execution, multiplied by 2 for every renaming operator ∂_H around the term. Finally, we define the **size** of t, **s(t)**, to be the pair <l(t), w(t)>, with pairs ordered alphabetically.

t =	Te(t)	l(t)	w(t)
ε	1	1	1
a ∈ A∪{δ}	0	1	1
u + v	Te(u) + Te(v)	max(l(u),l(v))	w(u) + w(v)
u·v	Te(u)·Te(v)	l(u) + l(v)	w(u) + Te(u)·w(v)
u‖v	Te(u)·Te(v)	l(u) + l(v)	3·w(u) + (1 + 2·Te(u))·w(v) + w(u)·w(v)
u⌊⌊v	0	l(u) + l(v)	w(u)
u|v	0	l(u) + l(v)	w(u)·w(v)
∂_H(u)	Te(u)	l(u)	2·w(u)

Table 4. Termination count, length and width of an ε_K-free ACP√-term.

The proof now proceeds via a number of claims.
CLAIM 1: Let t be a closed ACP√-term with no ε_K-operator. Then:
i. application of A1-2, EM5 or a rewrite rule does not increase the size of t;
ii. any proper subterm of t has a smaller size than t.
PROOF: Easy.
CLAIM 2: The rewrite system RACP√–E is (strongly) terminating for closed ACP√-terms without ε_K-operator.
PROOF: Suppose it is not terminating. Let t be a closed ACP√-term of minimal size, such that there is an infinite reduction sequence $t \to t_1 \to t_2 \to$ ..... A reduction on t_i is called **external** (outermost) if it works on the main operator of t_i, and **internal** if it works on a proper subterm of t_i. From claim 1 it follows that it is not possible that from some i∈ℕ on, the sequence consists of internal reductions only. Therefore, there must be infinitely many external reductions in this sequence. Now note the following facts:
• Among these external reductions there are no reductions A3, A6-9, CF1-2, EM2,6 or D0-2, since they decrease the size of the term, contradicting the minimality of t.
• Therefore, there are no external reductions in the sequence, working on a term u + v, and hence there are no external reductions resulting in a term u + v.
• Thus, all external reductions in the sequence are from the list A5, EM3,7, D4 and a⌊⌊x = ax, so result in a term u⌊⌊v or u·v.

• The allowed external reductions working on a term $u \lfloor\!\lfloor v$ (EM3 and $a \lfloor\!\lfloor x = ax$) result in a term $u' \cdot v'$.
• The only allowed external reduction working on a term $u \cdot v$ is A5. It results in another term $u' \cdot v'$, but with u' having a smaller size than u.
Thus, apart from the first two, all external reductions must be A5-reductions. Therefore, in $t \to t_1 \to t_2 \to \dots$ we have, from some i on, $t_i = u_i \cdot v_i$, with $s(u_i)$ decreasing with each external reduction. This is impossible, and so claim 2 is proved.
CLAIM 3: All closed terms without ε_K-operator, which are normal forms w.r.t. the rewrite system RACP√–E, are basic terms.
PROOF: By induction on the structure of closed normal forms t. t must be a constant $a \in A$, ε, δ, or a term $u+v$, $u \cdot v$, $u \| v$, $u \lfloor\!\lfloor v$, $u \mid v$ or $\partial_H(u)$. Since also u and v are normal forms, we may assume that they are basic terms. If $t = u \cdot v$ with $u \notin A$, if $t = u \| v$, $u \lfloor\!\lfloor v$, $u \mid v$ or $\partial_H(u)$, or if t has more than one ε-summand, then t cannot be a normal form. In the other cases t is a basic term.
CLAIM 4: Using RACP√, any closed term t can be rewritten to a basic term s.
PROOF: For terms without ε_K-operator this follows from claims 2 and 3. For the general case it suffices to prove that for all basic terms t there is a basic term s such that $\varepsilon_K(t)$ reduces to s in RACP√. This only requires a straightforward induction on the structure of basic terms.
CLAIM 5: ACP√ $\vdash \varepsilon \| t = t$ for closed terms t.
$+ \sum_{j<m} b_j\ (+\ \varepsilon)$. For any application of $a \lfloor\!\lfloor x = ax$ in this process, claim 1 learns that x has a smaller size than t. Thus ACP√ $\vdash a \lfloor\!\lfloor x = a\varepsilon \lfloor\!\lfloor x = a(\varepsilon \| x) = ax$ (by induction) and therefore ACP√ $\vdash t = s$. Thus ACP√ $\vdash \varepsilon \| t = \varepsilon \| s = \varepsilon \lfloor\!\lfloor s + s \lfloor\!\lfloor \varepsilon + \varepsilon \mid s + \surd(\varepsilon)\surd(s) = \delta + \sum_{i<n} a_i(s_i \| \varepsilon) + \sum_{j<m} b_j(\varepsilon \| \varepsilon) + \delta + \surd(s) = \sum_{i<n} a_i s_i + \sum_{j<m} b_j \varepsilon + \surd(s)$ (by induction) $= s = t$.
The elimination theorem now follows from claims 4 and 5.
Note that as a consequence of the elimination theorem, all closed terms have a head normal form.

3.10 PROPOSITION. For all closed ACP√-terms x,y,z we have the following laws of **standard concurrency**:

$\varepsilon \| x = x$
$\surd(x) = \varepsilon$ iff $x = x + \varepsilon$, and $\surd(x) = \delta$ otherwise
$\surd(x \| y) = \surd(x) \cdot \surd(y)$
$x \mid (y \mid z) = (x \mid y) \mid z \qquad (x \lfloor\!\lfloor y) \lfloor\!\lfloor z = x \lfloor\!\lfloor (y \| z)$
$(x \mid y) \lfloor\!\lfloor z = x \mid (y \lfloor\!\lfloor z) \qquad x \| (y \| z) = (x \| y) \| z.$

PROOF: The first one is proved in 3.9. The second and third are easy to prove for all head normal forms, and therefore hold for all closed terms by 3.9.
For the others, note that because of the elimination theorem we can assume that x,y,z are basic terms. We use the second induction scheme in 3.7. Write

$x = \sum_{i\le n} a_i x_i\ (+\ \varepsilon)$, $y = \sum_{j\le m} b_j y_j\ (+\ \varepsilon)$ and $z = \sum_{k\le p} c_k z_k\ (+\ \varepsilon)$

$(a_i, b_j, c_k \in A \cup \{\delta\})$. By induction hypothesis, we can assume that the proposition holds for all triples (x_i,y,z), (x_i,y_j,z), (x_i,y_j,z_k). Then:
1. $x \mid (y \mid z) = \sum_{i,j,k} (a_i \mid (b_j \mid c_k))(x_i \| (y_j \| z_k))$ (EM6, 3.4.5) $= \sum_{i,j,k} ((a_i \mid b_j) \mid c_k)((x_i \| y_j) \| z_k)$ (definition of γ, induction hypothesis) $= (x \mid y) \mid z$.
2. $(x \lfloor\!\lfloor y) \lfloor\!\lfloor z = (\{\sum_i a_i x_i\ (+\ \varepsilon)\} \lfloor\!\lfloor y) \lfloor\!\lfloor z = \sum_i (a_i(x_i \| y)) \lfloor\!\lfloor z = \sum_i a_i((x_i \| y) \| z) = \sum_i a_i(x_i \| (y \| z))$ (induction hypothesis) $= \sum_i a_i x_i \lfloor\!\lfloor (y \| z) = x \lfloor\!\lfloor (y \| z)$.
3. $(x \mid y) \lfloor\!\lfloor z = (\sum_{i,j} (a_i \mid b_j)(x_i \| y_j)) \lfloor\!\lfloor z = \sum_{i,j} (a_i \mid b_j)((x_i \| y_j) \| z) =$
$= \sum_{i,j} (a_i \mid b_j)(x_i \| (y_j \| z))$ (induction hypothesis) $= \sum_{i,j} a_i x_i \mid b_j(y_j \| z) = x \mid (y \lfloor\!\lfloor z)$.
4. $x \| (y \| z) = x \lfloor\!\lfloor (y \| z) + (y \| z) \lfloor\!\lfloor x + x \mid (y \| z) + \surd(x) \cdot \surd(y \| z) =$ (using 3.6.2-3)
$= x \lfloor\!\lfloor (y \| z) + (y \lfloor\!\lfloor z) \lfloor\!\lfloor x + (z \lfloor\!\lfloor y) \lfloor\!\lfloor x + (y \mid z) \lfloor\!\lfloor x + x \mid (y \lfloor\!\lfloor z) + x \mid (z \lfloor\!\lfloor y) + x \mid (y \mid z) + \surd(x) \cdot \surd(y \| z) =$
$= (x \lfloor\!\lfloor y) \lfloor\!\lfloor z + y \lfloor\!\lfloor (z \| x) + z \lfloor\!\lfloor (y \| x) + (y \mid z) \lfloor\!\lfloor x + (x \mid y) \lfloor\!\lfloor z + (x \mid z) \lfloor\!\lfloor y + (x \mid y) \mid z + \surd(x)\surd(y)\surd(z) =$
(using 3.6.1 and EM5)
$= (x \lfloor\!\lfloor y) \lfloor\!\lfloor z + y \lfloor\!\lfloor (x \| z) + z \lfloor\!\lfloor (x \| y) + (z \mid y) \lfloor\!\lfloor x + (x \mid y) \lfloor\!\lfloor z + (z \mid x) \lfloor\!\lfloor y + z \mid (x \mid y) + \surd(x)\surd(y)\surd(z) =$

$= (x \lfloor\!\lfloor y) \lfloor\!\lfloor z + (y \lfloor\!\lfloor x) \lfloor\!\lfloor z + z \lfloor\!\lfloor (x \| y) + z \mid (y \lfloor\!\lfloor x) + (x \mid y) \lfloor\!\lfloor z + z \mid (x \lfloor\!\lfloor y) + z \mid (x \mid y) + \sqrt{}(x \| y) \cdot \sqrt{}(z) =$
$= (x \| y) \lfloor\!\lfloor z + z \lfloor\!\lfloor (x \| y) + z \mid (x \| y) + \sqrt{}(x \| y) \cdot \sqrt{}(z) = (x \| y) \| z.$

3.11 NOTE. We usually assume that the laws of Standard Concurrency hold for all processes. Therefore, they are often called the *axioms* of Standard Concurrency.
Often, we also assume the following **Handshaking Axiom**:

$$x \mid y \mid z = \delta \qquad \text{(HA)}.$$

It says, that all communication is *binary*, i.e. only involves two communication partners.

3.12 PROPOSITION. In ACP$\sqrt{}$ with standard concurrency and handshaking axiom we have the following **expansion theorem** ($n \geq 1$):

$$\mathop{\|}_{i \leq n} x_i = \sum_{i \leq n} x_i \lfloor\!\lfloor \Big(\mathop{\|}_{k \leq n, k \neq i} x_k \Big) + \sum_{i < j \leq n} (x_i \mid x_j) \lfloor\!\lfloor \Big(\mathop{\|}_{k \leq n, k \neq i,j} x_k \Big) + \prod_{i \leq n} \sqrt{}(x_i)$$

(Where $\|_{i \leq n} x_i$ means $x_0 \| \ldots \| x_n$, and $\prod_{i \leq n} x_i$ means $x_0 \cdot \ldots \cdot x_n$.)
PROOF: This follows from the axioms of standard concurrency and the handshaking axiom similar to the case of ACP (BERGSTRA & TUCKER [6]) or ACP$^{\varepsilon}$ (VRANCKEN [14]). The only difference is, that we have to keep track of the termination option.
We use induction on n. The case $n=1$ is exactly the axiom EM1. The induction step is as follows:
$\|_{i \leq n+1} x_i = (\|_{i \leq n} x_i) \| x_{n+1} =$
$= (\|_{i \leq n} x_i) \lfloor\!\lfloor x_{n+1} + x_{n+1} \lfloor\!\lfloor (\|_{i \leq n} x_i) + (\|_{i \leq n} x_i) \mid x_{n+1} + \sqrt{}(\|_{i \leq n} x_i) \sqrt{}(x_{n+1}).$
We consider these four terms in turn, and use the induction hypothesis. The first:
$(\|_{i \leq n} x_i) \lfloor\!\lfloor x_{n+1} =$
$= \Sigma_{i \leq n} (x_i \lfloor\!\lfloor (\|_{k \leq n,\, k \neq i} x_k)) \lfloor\!\lfloor x_{n+1} + \Sigma_{i<j \leq n} ((x_i \mid x_j) \lfloor\!\lfloor (\|_{k \leq n,\, k \neq i,j} x_k)) \lfloor\!\lfloor x_{n+1} + \delta$ (by 3.6 and EM4) =
$= \Sigma_{i \leq n} x_i \lfloor\!\lfloor ((\|_{k \leq n,\, k \neq i} x_k) \| x_{n+1}) + \Sigma_{i<j \leq n} (x_i \mid x_j) \lfloor\!\lfloor ((\|_{k \leq n,\, k \neq i,j} x_k) \| x_{n+1})$ (use 3.10) =
$= \Sigma_{i \leq n} x_i \lfloor\!\lfloor (\|_{k \leq n+1,\, k \neq i} x_k) + \Sigma_{i<j \leq n} (x_i \mid x_j) \lfloor\!\lfloor ((\|_{k \leq n+1,\, k \neq i,j} x_k).$
The second term is equal to $x_{n+1} \lfloor\!\lfloor (\|_{k \leq n+1,\, k \neq n+1} x_k)$, and the third:
$(\|_{i \leq n} x_i) \mid x_{n+1} =$
$= \Sigma_{i \leq n} (x_i \lfloor\!\lfloor (\|_{k \leq n,\, k \neq i} x_k)) \mid x_{n+1} + \Sigma_{i<j \leq n} ((x_i \mid x_j) \lfloor\!\lfloor (\|_{k \leq n,\, k \neq i,j} x_k)) \mid x_{n+1} + \delta$ (by 3.6 and EM8) =
$= \Sigma_{i \leq n} (x_i \mid x_{n+1}) \lfloor\!\lfloor (\|_{k \leq n,\, k \neq i} x_k) + \Sigma_{i<j \leq n} (x_i \mid x_j \mid x_{n+1}) \lfloor\!\lfloor (\|_{k \leq n,\, k \neq i,j} x_k)$ (use 3.10) =
$= \Sigma_{i<n+1} (x_i \mid x_{n+1}) \lfloor\!\lfloor (\|_{k \leq n+1,\, k \neq i,n+1} x_k)$ (by handshaking axiom).
Finally, the fourth term is equal to $\prod_{i \leq n+1} \sqrt{}(x_i)$ by the third axiom of standard concurrency.
Adding the obtained expressions gives the desired result.

3.13 Until now, we have mainly looked at closed terms. However, most processes encountered in practice cannot be represented by a closed term, by an element of the initial algebra of ACP$\sqrt{}$, but will be specified recursively. Therefore, we are interested in models that also contain infinite processes, processes that can perform infinitely many actions consecutively. The algebraic way to represent such processes is by means of recursive specifications. In this section, we introduce some terminology.

3.14 DEFINITION. A **recursive specification** over ACP$\sqrt{}$ is a set of equations $\{X = t_X : X \in V\}$, with V a set of variables, and t_X a term over ACP$\sqrt{}$ and variables V. No other variables may occur in t_X. There is exactly one equation $X = t_X$ for each variable X.
A **solution** of the recursive specification E (in a certain domain) is an interpretation of the variables of V as processes such that the equations of E are satisfied.
The **Recursive Definition Principle (RDP)** says that every recursive specification has a solution. In section 4, we will discuss models of ACP$\sqrt{}$ that satisfy RDP.
Recursive specifications are used to define (or specify) processes. If E has a unique solution, and $X \in V$, let $\langle X \mid E \rangle$ denote the X-component of this solution. If E has more than one solution, $\langle X \mid E \rangle$ denotes 'one of the solutions of E', and can be regarded as a kind of variable, ranging over these

solutions. If E has no solutions (possible in a model, not satisfying RDP), then no meaning can be attached to $<X \mid E>$. In a recursive language, the syntactical constructs $<X \mid E>$ may appear in the construction of terms. This limits the class of models of the language to the ones satisfying RDP.
If $E = \{X = t_X : X \in V\}$ is a recursive specification, and t a term, then $<t \mid E>$ denotes the term t in which each occurrence of a variable $X \in V$ is replaced by $<X \mid E>$. Thus, the assumption that the terms $<X \mid E>$ are solutions of E may be stated as follows ($X \in V$):

$$<X \mid E> = <t_X \mid E>.$$

Note that we cannot have that *every* recursive specification has a unique solution, for $E = \{X = X\}$ has every process as a solution. Therefore, we formulate the condition of guardedness below, and will claim that in the models of section 4, every guarded recursive specification does have a unique solution.

3.15 DEFINITION. i. Let t be a term over ACP√ without ε_K-operator, and X a variable in t. We call the occurrence of X in t **guarded** if X is *preceded* by an atomic action, i.e. t has a subterm of the form $a{\cdot}s$, with $a \in A$, and this X occurs in s. Otherwise, we call the occurrence of X **unguarded**.
ii. A recursive specification $\{X = t_X : X \in V\}$ is **guarded** if no ε_K-operator appears and each occurrence of a variable in each t_X is guarded.
iii. The **Recursive Specification Principle (RSP)** is the assumption that every guarded recursive specification has at most one solution. Thus, in a model satisfying RDP and RSP, each guarded recursive specification has a unique solution. Also note that each solution of a guarded recursive specification has a head normal form, so results 3.6 hold for such processes.

3.16 NOTE. In section 5, we will formulate the **Limit Rule (LR)**, and we will prove that a restricted version holds in the models of section 4. The Limit Rule says that any equation that holds for all closed terms, holds for all processes.
As a corollary, we find that the axioms of Standard Concurrency of 3.10 hold in the models.

4. SEMANTICS

We consider different semantics for ACP√. First, we define a term model (using the syntactical constructs $<X \mid E>$ of 3.14) by means of action relations. Action relations appear in MILNER [11], PLOTKIN [13] and in the setting of process algebra, in VAN GLABBEEK [7].

4.1 DEFINITION. Let $\mathbb{P}$ be the set of **process expressions**, closed terms over the signature of ACP√ and recursion constructs $<X \mid E>$ of 3.14. On $\mathbb{P}$, we define binary predicates $\to^a$ for each $a \in A$, and a unary predicate $\downarrow$, generated by the rules in table 5 below.

$a \to^a \varepsilon$	$\varepsilon\downarrow$
$x \to^a x' \Rightarrow x+y \to^a x' \;\&\; y+x \to^a x'$	$x\downarrow \Rightarrow (x+y)\downarrow \;\&\; (y+x)\downarrow$
$x \to^a x' \Rightarrow xy \to^a x'y$	
$x\downarrow \;\&\; y \to^a y' \Rightarrow xy \to^a y'$	$x\downarrow \;\&\; y\downarrow \Rightarrow (xy)\downarrow$
$x \to^a x' \Rightarrow x\|y \to^a x'\|y,\; y\|x \to^a y\|x' \;\&\; x \lfloor\!\lfloor y \to^a x'\|y$	$x\downarrow \;\&\; y\downarrow \Rightarrow (x\|y)\downarrow$
$x \to^a x' \;\&\; y \to^b y' \;\&\; \gamma(a,b) = c \Rightarrow x\|y \to^c x'\|y' \;\&\; x \mid y \to^c x'\|y'$	
$x \to^a x' \;\&\; a \notin H \Rightarrow \partial_H(x) \to^a \partial_H(x')$	$x\downarrow \Rightarrow \partial_H(x)\downarrow$
$x \to^a x' \;\&\; a \notin K \Rightarrow \varepsilon_K(x) \to^a \varepsilon_K(x')$	$x\downarrow \Rightarrow \varepsilon_K(x)\downarrow$
$x \to^a x',\; a \in K \;\&\; \varepsilon_K(x') \to^b y \Rightarrow \varepsilon_K(x) \to^b y$	$x \to^a x',\; a \in K \;\&\; \varepsilon_K(x')\downarrow \Rightarrow \varepsilon_K(x)\downarrow$
$<t_X \mid E> \to^a y \Rightarrow <X \mid E> \to^a y$	$<t_X \mid E>\downarrow \Rightarrow <X \mid E>\downarrow$

Table 5. Action relations.

The intuitive meaning is as follows:

- $x \to^a y$ means that x can evolve into y by executing the atomic action a,
- $x\downarrow$ means that x has a termination option.

Note that we defined the action relations in such a way that $x \to^a x'$ iff $\varepsilon x \to^a x'$, and $x\downarrow$ iff $\varepsilon x\downarrow$. This is why we can consider the process expression p to be identical to the expression εp, i.e. we consider process expressions modulo axiom A8. This identification makes the following proofs easier.

4.2 DEFINITION. A **bisimulation** is a binary relation R on $\mathbb{P}$, satisfying (for $a \in A$):

1. if R(p,q) and $p \to^a p'$, then there is a q' such that $q \to^a q'$ and R(p',q');
2. if R(p,q) and $q \to^a q'$, then there is a p' such that $p \to^a p'$ and R(p',q');
3. if R(p,q), then $p\downarrow$ if and only if $q\downarrow$.

If there exists a bisimulation R with R(p,q), we say p and q **are bisimilar**, and write $p \underline{\leftrightarrow} q$.

The notion of bisimulation was introduced by PARK [12]. Also see MILNER [11], BERGSTRA & KLOP [4] and VRANCKEN [14].

4.3 THEOREM. $\underline{\leftrightarrow}$ is a congruence on ACP√-terms.

PROOF: We have to check the following:

1. $p \underline{\leftrightarrow} p$ 2. $p \underline{\leftrightarrow} q \Rightarrow q \underline{\leftrightarrow} p$ 3. $p \underline{\leftrightarrow} q$ & $q \underline{\leftrightarrow} r \Rightarrow p \underline{\leftrightarrow} r$
4. $p \underline{\leftrightarrow} p'$ & $q \underline{\leftrightarrow} q' \Rightarrow p\Box q \underline{\leftrightarrow} p'\Box q'$ for $\Box = +,\cdot,\|,\lfloor\!\lfloor,|$; $\partial_H(p) \underline{\leftrightarrow} \partial_H(p')$, likewise for ε_K.

Now, let $p,q,r,p',q' \in \mathbb{P}$ and let R,S be bisimulations on $\mathbb{P}$.

We define the following relations on $\mathbb{P}$.

I: I(p,p) for $p \in \mathbb{P}$.
R^{-1}: $R^{-1}(p,q)$ iff R(q,p).
$R \circ S$: $R\circ S(p,r)$ iff $\exists q \in \mathbb{P}$: R(p,q) and S(q,r).
$R\cdot q$: $R\cdot q(p\cdot q, p'\cdot q)$ iff R(p,p').
$R\|S$: $R\|S(p\|q, p'\|q')$ iff R(p,p') and S(q,q').
$\partial_H(R)$, $\varepsilon_K(R)$: $\partial_H(R)(\partial_H(p), \partial_H(q))$ iff R(p,q), and similarly for ε_K.

Now 1,2 and 3 follow since I, R^{-1} and $R\circ S$ are bisimulations (as can be checked easily).

For 4, suppose R(p,p') and S(q,q').

+: $R \cup S \cup \{(p+q, p'+q')\}$ is a bisimulation relating p + q and p' + q';
· $R\cdot q \cup S$ is a bisimulation relating $p\cdot q$ and $p'\cdot q$';
$\|$: $R\|S$ is a bisimulation relating $p\|q$ and $p'\|q'$;
$\lfloor\!\lfloor$: $R\|S \cup \{(p\lfloor\!\lfloor q, p'\lfloor\!\lfloor q')\}$ is a bisimulation relating $p\lfloor\!\lfloor q$ and $p'\lfloor\!\lfloor q'$;
$|$: $R\|S \cup \{(p|q, p'|q')\}$ is a bisimulation relating $p|q$ and $p'|q'$;
∂_H, ε_K: $\partial_H(R)$ is a bisimulation relating $\partial_H(p)$ and $\partial_H(p')$, and $\varepsilon_K(R)$ one relating $\varepsilon_K(p)$ and $\varepsilon_K(p')$.

4.4 THEOREM. $\mathbb{P}/\underline{\leftrightarrow}$ is a model of ACP√.

PROOF: Straightforward.

4.5 THEOREM. ACP√ is a complete axiomatisation of $\mathbb{P}/\underline{\leftrightarrow}$ for closed terms (without recursion constructs <X|E>).

PROOF: We have to show that if $t \underline{\leftrightarrow} s$ holds for closed terms t,s, then ACP√ $\vdash t = s$. Since $\mathbb{P}/\underline{\leftrightarrow}$ is a model for ACP√, the elimination theorem tells us that we only have to prove this for basic terms t,s. For basic terms, this follows by means of a structural induction argument (using the second inductive scheme from 3.7) from the following two observations, that are not hard to prove:

i. $t \to^a t'$ iff t has a summand at';

ii. $t\downarrow$ iff t has a summand ε.

4.6 THEOREM. RDP holds in $\mathbb{P}/\underline{\leftrightarrow}$.
PROOF: This is immediate: the $\underline{\leftrightarrow}$-congruence class of $<X \mid E>$ is the X-component of a solution of E in $\mathbb{P}/\underline{\leftrightarrow}$.

It takes some more work to prove that the principles RSP and LR hold in $\mathbb{P}/\underline{\leftrightarrow}$. Therefore, we will skip this here, and treat this in section 5.
In the sequel, we describe a graph model for ACP$\surd$, that can be considered as a visualisation of the model $\mathbb{P}/\underline{\leftrightarrow}$ above.

4.7 DEFINITIONS. In this paper, a **graph** is a *rooted, countably branching, directed multigraph.* An edge goes from a node to another (or the same) node. We consider only countably branching graphs, so each node has only a countable number of outgoing edges. Graphs need not be finite (have finitely many nodes and edges), but we must be able to reach every node from the root in finitely many steps. An **endnode** of a graph is a node with no outgoing edges. A **path** π in a graph g is a finite alternating sequence of connected nodes and edges of g. A **tree** is a graph in which the root has no incoming edge, and all other nodes have exactly one incoming edge. Note that a tree has no **cycles**, no path from a node back to the same node. The **zero graph** $\mathbb{0}$ consists of a single node and no edges.
A **process graph** is a graph in which each edge is labeled with an element of A, the set of atomic actions, and nodes may have a label $\downarrow$. Such nodes are called **termination nodes.** $\mathbb{G}_\downarrow$ is the set of all process graphs. An **a-step** in a process graph from s to s' is an edge going from s to s' with label $a \in A$, notation $s \rightarrow^a s'$.

4.8 DEFINITION. We define a map graph from the set of process expressions $\mathbb{P}$ to the set of process graphs $\mathbb{G}_\downarrow$ as follows. Let $p \in \mathbb{P}$. graph(p) has a node for each $q \in \mathbb{P}$ that is reachable from p (i.e. there is a series of atomic actions $a_1,\ldots,a_n$ such that $p \rightarrow^{a_1} \ldots \rightarrow^{a_n} q$). The node corresponding to p itself will be the root of graph(p). There is an edge labeled a between two nodes exactly when the a-labeled action relation holds between the corresponding process expressions. A node receives an $\downarrow$-label exactly when the corresponding process expression can terminate.
Conversely, we define a map term from $\mathbb{G}_\downarrow$ to $\mathbb{P}$ as follows. Let $g \in \mathbb{G}_\downarrow$. We define a guarded recursive specification E as follows: take a variable $X \in V$ for every node in g. Then, if the node X has outgoing edges labeled $a_1,\ldots,a_n$, to nodes $X_1,\ldots,X_n$ respectively, we take as equation for X in E:

$$X = a_1X_1 + \ldots + a_nX_n \ (+\ \varepsilon),$$

with the summand ε appearing iff X has a $\downarrow$-label. If X has no outgoing edges, and no $\downarrow$-label, we put $X = \delta$. Then, if X_0 is the variable of the root of g, we define term(g) = $<X_0 \mid E>$.
Next, the notion of bisimulation translates easily to the present case, as we see below.

4.9 DEFINITION. Let $g,h \in \mathbb{G}_\downarrow$, and let R be a relation between the nodes of g and the nodes of h. R is a **bisimulation** between g and h, notation R: $g \underline{\leftrightarrow} h$, iff
1. the roots of g and h are related;
2. if R(s,t) and $s \rightarrow^a s'$ is an edge in g (with $a \in A$, s,s' nodes of g and t a node of h), then there is a node t' in h such that $t \rightarrow^a t'$ and R(s',t');
3. if R(s,t) and $t \rightarrow^a t'$ is an edge in h, then there is a node s' in g such that $s \rightarrow^a s'$ and R(s',t');
4. if R(s,t), then $s\downarrow$ (node s has a $\downarrow$-label) if and only if $t\downarrow$.
If there exists a bisimulation between g and h, we say g and h **are bisimilar**, and write **g $\underline{\leftrightarrow}$ h**.

4.10 PROPOSITION. i. If $p,q \in \mathbb{P}$ then $p \underline{\leftrightarrow} q$ iff graph(p) $\underline{\leftrightarrow}$ graph(q);
ii. If $g,h \in \mathbb{G}_\downarrow$ then $g \underline{\leftrightarrow} h$ iff term(g) $\underline{\leftrightarrow}$ term(h);

iii. For $g \in \mathbb{G}_\downarrow$ graph(term(g)) ≡ g, for $p \in \mathbb{P}$ term(graph(p)) $\underline{\leftrightarrow}$ p.

PROOF: In iii, g ≡ h means that g and h are isomorphic. This is the case if there exists a bijective bisimulation between them. Let N be the set of nodes of graph $g \in \mathbb{G}_\downarrow$. Then $\{X_i : i \in N\}$ is the set of variables, used in the construction of term(g) and $\{\langle X_i \mid E\rangle : i \in N\}$ is the set of $q \in \mathbb{P}$, reachable from term(g) = $\langle X_0 \mid E\rangle$. This gives a bijective mapping between the node sets of g and graph(term(g)), which is clearly a bisimulation. So we have proved the first part of iii. Now i. is trivial and ii. as well as the second part of iii. follow easily:

– g $\underline{\leftrightarrow}$ h ⇔ graph(term(g)) $\underline{\leftrightarrow}$ graph(term(g)) ⇔ term(g) $\underline{\leftrightarrow}$ term(h),

– graph(term(g)) $\underline{\leftrightarrow}$ g, so graph(term(graph(p))) $\underline{\leftrightarrow}$ graph(p), so term(graph(p)) $\underline{\leftrightarrow}$ p.

4.11 From 4.10 we can conclude that we can define all operators on $\mathbb{G}_\downarrow$ as the image of the same operators on $\mathbb{P}$ (i.e. g + h = graph(term(g) + term(h)), etc.). It is also possible to define the operators explicitly on $\mathbb{G}_\downarrow$, but we will not do so here. Now, the models $\mathbb{G}_\downarrow/\underline{\leftrightarrow}$ and $\mathbb{P}/\underline{\leftrightarrow}$ become isomorphic models, and thus, $\mathbb{G}_\downarrow/\underline{\leftrightarrow}$ is a sound and complete model of ACP√, in which RDP and RSP hold.

4.12 EXAMPLES. In fig. 1, we use an incoming arrow without a label to indicate the root of a graph, and an outgoing arrow without a label to indicate a termination node. In i, we see graph(δ) = graph(<X | X=X>); in ii, graph(ε); in iii. graph(<X | X = aX>); in iv, graph(a + ε), in v, graph(ab + ac), and in vi, graph(a(b + c)) (for a,b,c ∈ A). Note that the graphs in v, vi do not bisimulate.

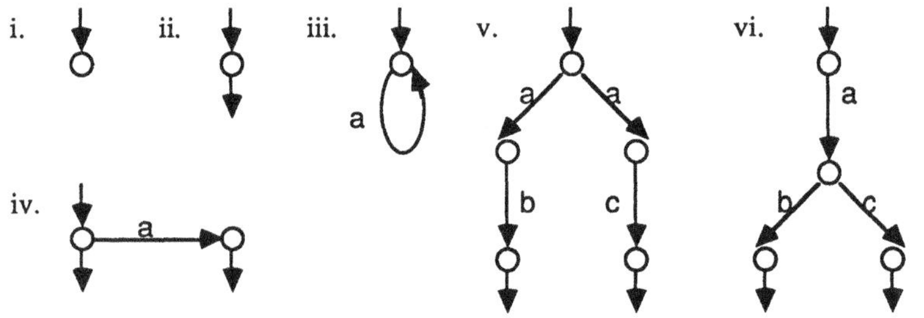

Fig. 1.

Although the graph model $\mathbb{G}_\downarrow/\underline{\leftrightarrow}$ is very useful, we still want to present another graph model $\mathbb{G}_{\varepsilon\delta}/\underline{\leftrightarrow}_\varepsilon$, which is more denotational. In this second graph model, we also have edges with label ε and δ. This increases the expressive power, and simplifies the definition of operators + and ε_K, but makes the definition of bisimulation and the operators ||,⌊⌊,| harder. The model $\mathbb{G}_{\varepsilon\delta}/\underline{\leftrightarrow}_\varepsilon$ is essentially the same model as the graph model of VRANCKEN [14].

4.13 DEFINITION. A process graph in the set $\mathbb{G}_{\varepsilon\delta}$ differs from a graph in $\mathbb{G}_\downarrow$ in three aspects: first, graphs must be finitely branching, second, edges are labeled with elements of $A \cup \{\delta, \varepsilon\}$, and third, we have no node labels. We will see that the restriction to finitely branching graphs is not a real restriction.

4.14 DEFINITION. We define the notion of an ε-bisimulation on $\mathbb{G}_{\varepsilon\delta}$ as in VRANCKEN [14]. In this definition, we need the following notation: $\twoheadrightarrow^\varepsilon$ stands for a path of ε-edges, a connected series of 0 or more ε-steps (so $\twoheadrightarrow^\varepsilon$ is the transitive and reflexive closure of $\rightarrow^\varepsilon$).

Let g,h be process graphs, and let R be a relation between nodes of g and nodes of h. R is an ε-**bisimulation** between g and h, notation R: g $\underline{\leftrightarrow}_\varepsilon$ h, iff

1. The roots of g and h are related.
2. If R(s,t) and from s, we can do a generalized ε-step followed by an a-step to a node s' ($s \twoheadrightarrow^{\varepsilon} \rightarrow^{a} s'$) with $a \in A$ (so $a \neq \varepsilon$, $a \neq \delta$), then from t in h, we can do a generalized ε-step, followed by an a-step to a node t' with R(s',t'), so $t \twoheadrightarrow^{\varepsilon} \rightarrow^{a} t'$.
3. Vice versa: if R(s,t) and $t \twoheadrightarrow^{\varepsilon} \rightarrow^{a} t'$ is a path in h with $a \in A$, then, in g, there is a node s' such that $s \twoheadrightarrow^{\varepsilon} \rightarrow^{a} s'$ and R(s',t').
4. If R(s,t), s' is an endnode in g, and $s \twoheadrightarrow^{\varepsilon} s'$, then, in h, there is a node t' such that t' is an endpoint and $t \twoheadrightarrow^{\varepsilon} t'$.
5. Vice versa: if R(s,t), t' is an endnode in h, and $t \twoheadrightarrow^{\varepsilon} t'$, then, in g, there is a node s' such that s' is an endpoint and $s \twoheadrightarrow^{\varepsilon} s'$.

Graphs g and h are **ε-bisimilar**, $g \leftrightarrow_{\varepsilon} h$, if there is an ε-bisimulation between g and h.

4.15 EXAMPLES. See fig. 2 below. We have $a,b \in A$, so $\neq \delta,\varepsilon$.

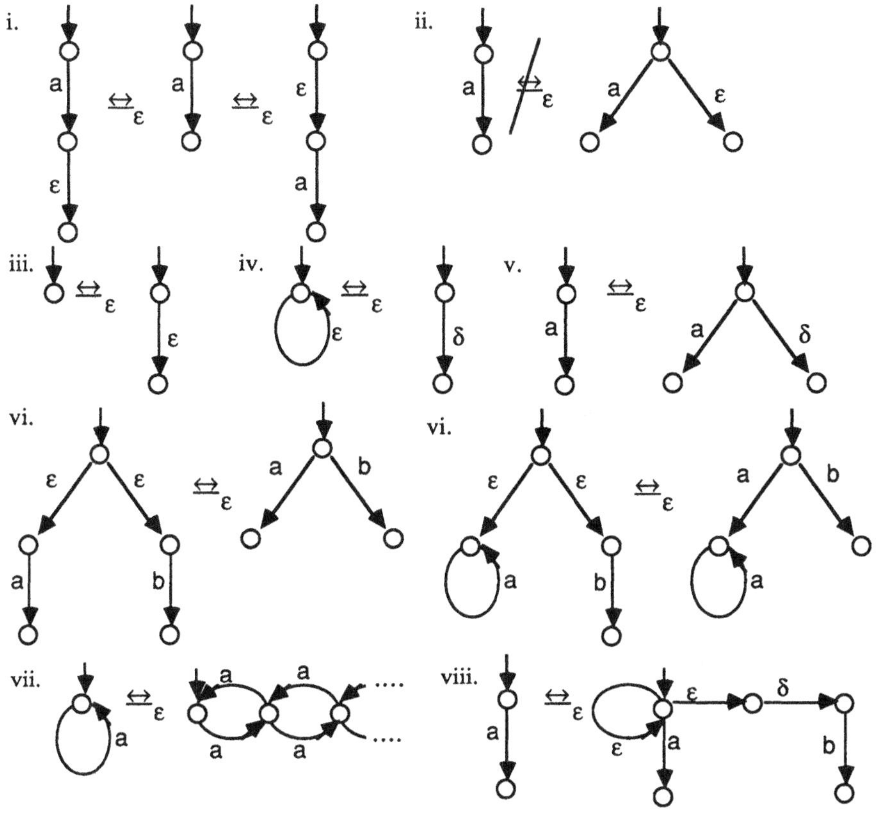

Fig. 2.

4.16 LEMMA. $\leftrightarrow_{\varepsilon}$ is an equivalence relation on $\mathbb{G}_{\varepsilon\delta}$.
PROOF: Straightforward.

4.17 LEMMA. Each $\leftrightarrow_{\varepsilon}$-equivalence class contains a nonzero process tree.
PROOF: Let g be a process graph. We find a tree h that is ε-bisimilar to g by *unrolling* g, i.e. we have a node in h for each path from the root in g. Edges and labels in h are defined in the obvious way; the root

of h corresponds to the empty path in g. We leave the details of this construction, and the verification of the ε-bisimilarity, to the reader. We use the notation tree(g) for the tree obtained by unrolling g. If h turns out to be the zero graph $\mathbb{0}$, we use the second tree in 4.15.iii instead.

4.18 $\mathbb{G}_{\varepsilon\delta}/\underline{\leftrightarrow}_{\varepsilon}$ will be the domain of the graph model for ACP√. The interpretation of a constant $u \in A\cup\{\delta,\varepsilon\}$ is the equivalence class of the graph with two nodes and a single edge between them labeled u. What remains is the definition of the operators of ACP√ on $\mathbb{G}_{\varepsilon\delta}/\underline{\leftrightarrow}_{\varepsilon}$. We will define these operators on $\mathbb{G}_{\varepsilon\delta}$ (the parallel operators only on process *trees*) and will then show that $\underline{\leftrightarrow}_{\varepsilon}$ is a congruence relation w.r.t. them.

4.19 DEFINITIONS. 1. +. If $g,h \in \mathbb{G}_{\varepsilon\delta}$, graph g+h is obtained by taking the graphs of g and h and adding one new node r, that will be the root of g+h. Then, we add two edges labeled ε: from r to the root of g, and from r to the root of h.
EXAMPLE:

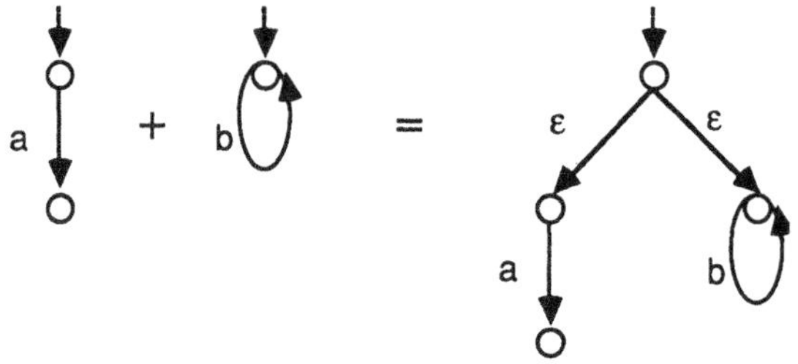

Fig. 3.

Note that it doesn't work to just identify the roots of g and h: if we do that in the example, it is possible to do an a-step after having done some b-steps. This fact is also illustrated in example 4.15.vi, and complicates the explicit definition of + in $\mathbb{G}_{\downarrow}$.
2. ·. If $g,h \in \mathbb{G}_{\varepsilon\delta}$, graph g·h is obtained by identifying all endpoints of g with the root node of h. If g has no endpoints, the result is just g. The root of g·h is the root of g.
EXAMPLE:

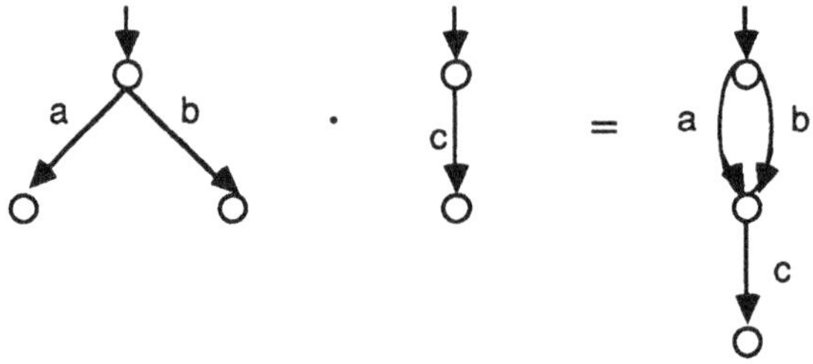

Fig. 4.

3. ||. The definition of the merge on $\mathbb{G}_{\varepsilon\delta}$ is rather complicated. Therefore, we will only define the merge on nonzero process *trees*. Using lemma 4.17, this definition can be extended to $\mathbb{G}_{\varepsilon\delta}$.
If g,h are nonzero process trees, graph g||h is the cartesian product graph of graphs g and h, with 'diagonal' edges added for communication steps, and with non-ε-edges 'orthogonal' to an incoming ε-step turned into δ-steps. By this, we mean the following: if (s,t) is a node in g||h, then it has the following outgoing edges ($u,v \in A\cup\{\delta,\varepsilon\}$, $a,b \in A$):
i. an edge $(s,t) \to^{u} (s',t)$ if $s \to^{u} s'$ is an edge in g, and $u = \varepsilon$ or h has no edge $t'' \to^{\varepsilon} t$;
ii. an edge $(s,t) \to^{\delta} (s',t)$ if $s \to^{u} s'$ is an edge in g, $u \neq \varepsilon$ and h has an edge $t'' \to^{\varepsilon} t$;

iii. an edge $(s,t) \rightarrow^{v} (s,t')$ if $t \rightarrow^{v} t'$ is an edge in h, and $u = \varepsilon$ or g has no edge $s'' \rightarrow^{\varepsilon} s$;
iv. an edge $(s,t) \rightarrow^{\delta} (s,t')$ if $t \rightarrow^{v} t'$ is an edge in h, $u \neq \varepsilon$ and g has an edge $s'' \rightarrow^{\varepsilon} s$;
v. an edge $(s,t) \rightarrow^{\gamma(a,b)} (s',t')$ if $s \rightarrow^{a} s'$ is an edge in g, $t \rightarrow^{b} t'$ is an edge in h and $\gamma(a,b)$ is defined (these are the *diagonal* edges).
The root of $g||h$ is the pair of roots of g and h.
Edges $(s,t) \rightarrow^{u} (s',t)$ are called *vertical* edges, and edges $(s,t) \rightarrow^{u} (s,t')$ are *horizontal* edges.
EXAMPLE: Suppose $\gamma(a,b) = c$, and $\gamma(d,b)$ is not defined. See fig. 5.

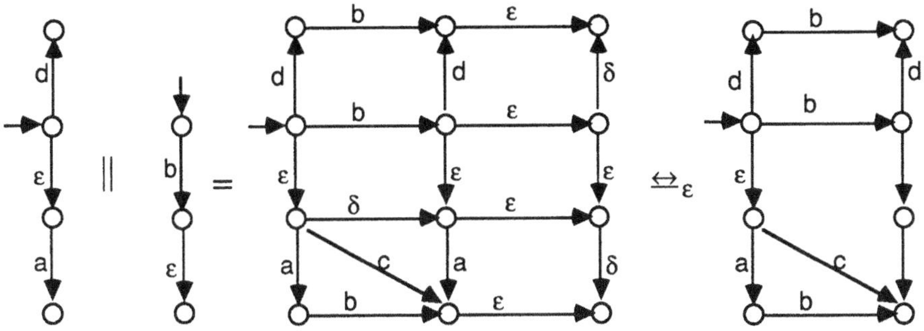

Fig. 5.

In this example, we see why some edges must be blocked, must be turned into δ: we have to make the one b-step δ, for if we start with a b-step, a d-step must still be possible.
4. $\lfloor\lfloor$. If g,h are nonzero process trees, graph $g \lfloor\lfloor h$ is obtained from graph $g||h$ by turning all horizontal and diagonal edges, that are reachable from the root by a generalized ε-step, into δ-edges.
EXAMPLE: the last example turns into:

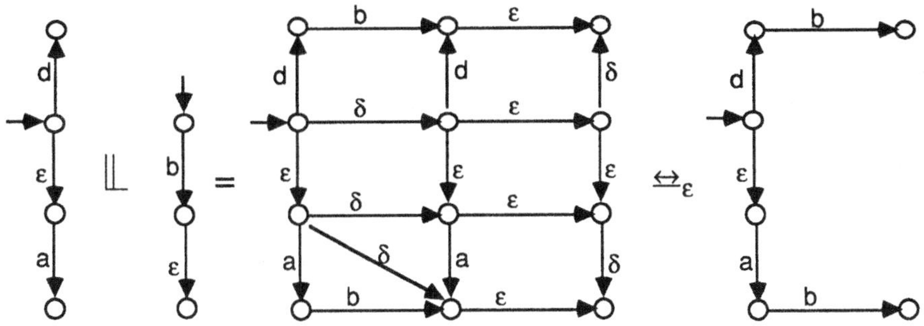

Fig. 6.

5. $|$. Similar to 4: If g,h are nonzero process trees, graph $g\,|\,h$ is obtained from graph $g||h$ by turning all horizontal and vertical edges, that are reachable from the root by a generalized ε-step, and do not have label ε, or do have label ε but lead to an endpoint, into δ-edges.
EXAMPLE: we use the same example. See following page.

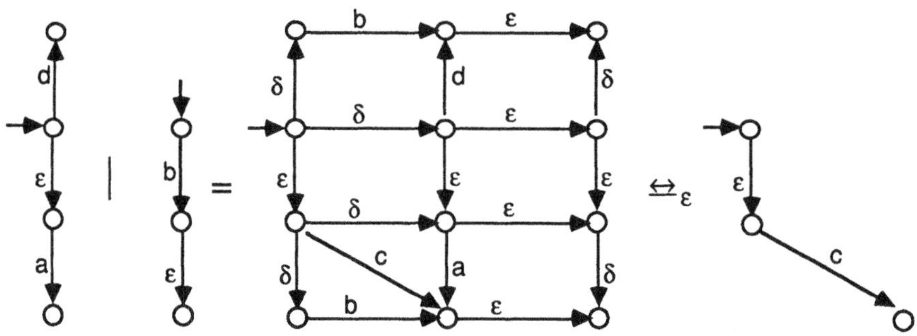

Fig. 7.

6. ∂_H, ε_K. If $g \in \mathbb{G}_{\varepsilon\delta}$, obtain $\partial_H(g)$ by replacing all labels in g from H by δ, and obtain $\varepsilon_K(g)$ by replacing all labels from K by ε.
This finishes the definition of the operators of ACP√ on $\mathbb{G}_{\varepsilon\delta}$. Then we also have the operators on $\mathbb{G}_{\varepsilon\delta}/\underline{\leftrightarrow}_{\varepsilon}$, if we use the following theorem 4.21.

4.20 NOTE. In VRANCKEN [14], the parallel operators $\|, \lfloor\!\lfloor, |$ are defined on a wider class of graphs, a class which is closed under these operators. This makes proofs of statements about them much easier.

4.21 THEOREM. $\underline{\leftrightarrow}_{\varepsilon}$ is a congruence relation on $\mathbb{G}_{\varepsilon\delta}$.
PROOF: As in VRANCKEN [14].

4.22 THEOREM. $\mathbb{G}_{\varepsilon\delta}/\underline{\leftrightarrow}_{\varepsilon}$ is a model of ACP√.
PROOF: As in VRANCKEN [14].

4.23 REMARK. We also obtain models of ACP√, if instead of limiting ourselves to finitely branching graphs, we allow all countably branching graphs, the set $\mathbb{G}_{\varepsilon\delta}{}^{\infty}$. Also, the set $\mathbb{R}$ of all finite (or *regular*) process graphs modulo $\underline{\leftrightarrow}_{\varepsilon}$ and the set $\mathbb{F}$ of all finite and acyclic process graphs modulo $\underline{\leftrightarrow}_{\varepsilon}$ form models of ACP√.
As we already stated in 4.13, it does not matter that we limit ourselves to finitely branching graphs instead of countably branching graphs. This is the content of the following lemma.

4.24 LEMMA. Let $g \in \mathbb{G}_{\varepsilon\delta}{}^{\infty}$. Then there is a graph $h \in \mathbb{G}_{\varepsilon\delta}$ such that $g \underline{\leftrightarrow}_{\varepsilon} h$.
PROOF: The proof is visualised in fig. 8 below: we can replace an infinite branching by a "spine" of ε-steps with the summands branching off consecutively.

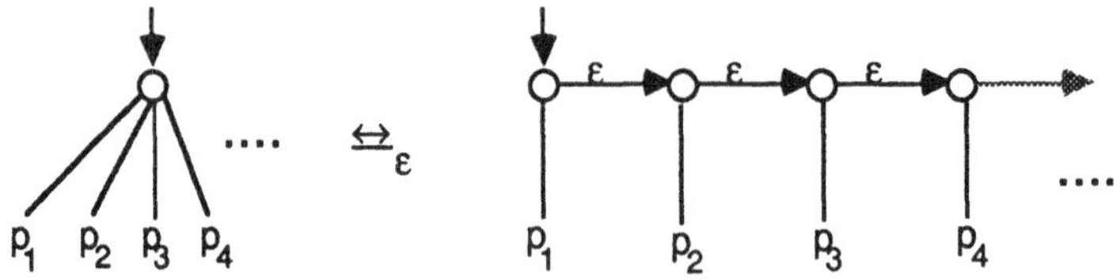

Fig. 8.

4.25 DEFINITION. Now we show that the models $\mathbb{G}_{\varepsilon\delta}/\underline{\leftrightarrow}_{\varepsilon}$ and $\mathbb{P}/\underline{\leftrightarrow}$ are isomorphic. A map from $\mathbb{G}_{\varepsilon\delta}$ to $\mathbb{G}_{\downarrow}$ is defined in three steps, as follows. Let $g \in \mathbb{G}_{\varepsilon\delta}$.

1. Unroll g to a tree, as defined in 4.17. This gives tree(g).
2. Leave out all intermediate ε-steps, i.e. if $s \to^{\varepsilon} t$ is an edge in tree(g), and t is not an endpoint, then leave out the edge and identify s and t; this gives int(tree(g)). The operation int may cause infinite branchings to appear, so we can only say $\text{int(tree(g))} \in \mathbb{G}_{\varepsilon\delta}{}^{\infty}$.
3. Leave out all remaining ε-edges, leaving a node-label ↓ for each removed edge, i.e. if $s \to^{\varepsilon} t$ is an edge (so t is an endpoint), remove it and attach a label ↓ to s. Furthermore, attach a label ↓ to each endnode. Then, leave out all δ-edges, and remove all nodes and edges that cannot be reached any more from the root. This gives end(int(tree(g))). Note that $\text{end(int(tree(g)))} \in \mathbb{G}_{\downarrow}$.

4.26 LEMMA. 1. Let $g \in \mathbb{G}_{\varepsilon\delta}$. Then: $g \underline{\leftrightarrow}_{\varepsilon} \text{tree}(g) \underline{\leftrightarrow}_{\varepsilon} \text{int(tree(g))}$.
2. Let $g,h \in \mathbb{G}_{\varepsilon\delta}{}^{\infty}$ with no intermediate ε-edges. Then: $g \underline{\leftrightarrow}_{\varepsilon} h \Leftrightarrow \text{end}(g) \underline{\leftrightarrow} \text{end}(h)$.
PROOF: 1. The first bisimulation is motivated in 4.17. Note that the second only holds in case we are dealing with trees: we must have that an ε-edge does not have any 'neighbours', there must be no other edges between the same two nodes. In case we do have trees, the bisimulation is easy, for the endpoints of ε-steps need not be related at all.
2. This is easy.

4.27 We can conclude from lemma 4.26 that the models $\mathbb{G}_{\downarrow}/\underline{\leftrightarrow}$ and $\mathbb{G}_{\varepsilon\delta}/\underline{\leftrightarrow}_{\varepsilon}$ are isomorphic models (since it is not hard to see that the resulting mapping from $\mathbb{G}_{\varepsilon\delta}/\underline{\leftrightarrow}_{\varepsilon}$ to $\mathbb{G}_{\downarrow}/\underline{\leftrightarrow}$ is a surjective homomorphism w.r.t. the operators), and thus, $\mathbb{G}_{\varepsilon\delta}/\underline{\leftrightarrow}_{\varepsilon}$ is a sound and complete model of ACP√, in which RDP and RSP hold.

4.28 THEOREM. The theory ACP√ is a conservative extension of the theory ACP of BERGSTRA & KLOP [3], i.e. for all closed ACP-terms s,t we have:

$$\text{ACP}\surd \vdash s = t \Leftrightarrow \text{ACP} \vdash s = t.$$

PROOF: The theory ACP consists of axioms A1-7 of PA_{δ} (see 2.3), axioms CF1,2, EM3,4,8 and D1-4 of ACP√ (see 3.1), the equations in 3.4.3,4,5, axiom EM1 of ACP√ without the last summand, and the axiom $(x + y) \mid z = x \mid z + y \mid z$. As in 4.5 (using ii. $t \to^{a} \varepsilon$ iff t has a summand a), we can show that ACP is a complete axiomatisation of $\mathbb{P}/\underline{\leftrightarrow}$ for closed terms, i.e. for closed ACP-terms t,s we have $t \underline{\leftrightarrow} s$ iff ACP $\vdash t = s$. Together with 4.5, this gives the conservativity.

5. LIMIT RULE

In this section, we discuss the Limit Rule, introduced in BAETEN & BERGSTRA [1]. Furthermore, we present the Fresh Atom Principle (FAP), first mentioned in VAANDRAGER [15]. We show that FAP, a restricted version of the Limit Rule, and also the Recursive Specification Principle of 3.15 hold in our models.

5.1 DEFINITION. Let $s(x_1,...,x_n)$, $t(x_1,...,x_n)$ be ACP√-terms with variables among $x_1,...,x_n$. Let $s(p_1,...,p_n)$, $t(p_1,...,p_n)$ be the terms obtained after substituting $p_1,...,p_n$ for $x_1,...,x_n$, respectively. Then the Limit Rule reads:

LR: $\quad s(p_1,...,p_n) = t(p_1,...,p_n)$ for all $p_1,...,p_n \in BT \Rightarrow s(x_1,...,x_n) = t(x_1,...,x_n)$.

We leave as an open question whether LR holds in the models of section 4. Next, we formulate a restricted version of LR, LR^{-}, that will be shown valid in these models.

5.2 DEFINITION. In order to formulate LR^{-}, we should realize that the theory ACP√ has the set of atomic actions A, and the communication function γ on A, as parameters. Thus, whenever we state that ACP√ $\vdash p = q$, we mean that for every choice of parameters A and γ (A containing at least the atoms occurring in p,q), we can derive $p = q$. Also, the models are parametrised by A and γ, so when we state that $p = q$

holds in a model, we mean that it holds for every choice of parameters. This practice can lead to misunderstandings, however, when we have an implication, as in the Limit Rule. The Limit Rule as stated, means:

for every choice of parameters A,γ:
if $s(p_1,...,p_n) = t(p_1,...,p_n)$ for all $p_1,...,p_n \in$ BT, then $s(x_1,...,x_n) = t(x_1,...,x_n)$.

The restricted version LR$^-$ will have two restrictions: first we will limit ourselves to terms not involving ε_K-operators, and second, we will put the quantification over all parameters in a different place:

Let $s(x_1,...,x_n)$, $t(x_1,...,x_n)$ be ACP$\surd$-terms without ε_K-operator.
LR$^-$: If for every choice of parameters A,γ and for all $p_1,...,p_n \in$ BT we have
$s(p_1,...,p_n) = t(p_1,...,p_n)$,
then (for every choice of parameters A,γ) $s(x_1,...,x_n) = t(x_1,...,x_n)$.

5.3 DEFINITION. The **Fresh Atom Principle (FAP)** says that we can use new (or 'fresh') atomic actions in proofs. In fact, using FAP (without justification!) is already standard practice in many writings on process algebra. FAP was introduced informally in VAANDRAGER [15], although the name was used earlier by Jan Willem Klop.
Here again, it is important to mention the parameters explicitly.
Suppose we have an atomic action set A and communication function γ given. Then we add an atom $f \notin A$, and extend γ to $A \cup \{f\}$, yielding γ^*. Now FAP says, that an equation $p = q$ over the signature with parameters (A,γ) may be proved using the parameters $(A \cup \{f\}, \gamma^*)$ in the proof.
Semantically, we can formulate this as follows.
Let $\mathfrak{A}$ be a model of ACP$\surd$, i.e. for every choice of parameters A,γ, we have a model $\mathfrak{A}(A,\gamma)$ for the theory ACP$\surd$ with parameters A,γ. Now a (parametrised) model $\mathfrak{A}$ satisfies FAP, if such an embedding $(A, \gamma) \to (A \cup \{f\}, \gamma^*)$ can be extended to an injective homomorphism $\mathfrak{A}(A,\gamma) \to \mathfrak{A}(A \cup \{f\},\gamma^*)$.

5.4 PROPOSITION. $\mathbb{P}/\underline{\leftrightarrow}$ satisfies FAP.
PROOF: We have to prove that if $p \underline{\leftrightarrow} q$ in $\mathbb{P}(A \cup \{f\})$ and p,q are process expressions over A, then also $p \underline{\leftrightarrow} q$ in $\mathbb{P}(A)$.
So let p,q be process expressions over A. Then all action relations starting from p and q have labels from A, and all process expressions reachable from p and q are again expressions over A. Thus, any bisimulation on $\mathbb{P}(A \cup \{f\})$ relating p and q can be restricted to $\mathbb{P}(A)$, and $R \subseteq \mathbb{P}(A) \times \mathbb{P}(A)$ is a bisimulation over action relations $\{\to^a : a \in A \cup \{f\}\}$, iff R is a bisimulation over action relations $\{\to^a : a \in A\}$.

5.5 LEMMA. Let f be an atomic action such that for all $a,b \in A$ $\gamma(a,f)\uparrow$ (is not defined) and $\gamma(a,b) \neq f$.
Then:
$\varepsilon_{\{f\}}(x \,\square\, y) = \varepsilon_{\{f\}}(x) \,\square\, \varepsilon_{\{f\}}(y)$ for $\square = +, \cdot, \|, \lfloor\!\lfloor, |$, and $\varepsilon_{\{f\}}(\partial_H(x)) = \partial_H(\varepsilon_{\{f\}}(x))$ for $H \subseteq A$.
PROOF: Straightforward.

5.6 DEFINITION. In order to show that LR$^-$ and RSP hold in $\mathbb{P}/\underline{\leftrightarrow}$ we need some auxiliary notions, that may also be interesting in their own right. First we define the **projections** of a process. To that end, we enlarge the signature of ACP$\surd$ with unary operators π_n, for $n \in \mathbb{N}$. Then we add the axioms PR (for $a \in A \cup \{\delta\}$) (on the following page).

$\pi_n(\varepsilon) = \varepsilon$
$\pi_0(ax) = \delta$
$\pi_{n+1}(ax) = a \cdot \pi_n(x)$
$\pi_n(x + y) = \pi_n(x) + \pi_n(y)$

Table 6. Projection.

We see that the operator π_n cuts off the process after it has executed n (atomic) steps; the remaining steps are replaced by δ. In order to define the operators π_n on the models $\mathbb{P}/\underline{\leftrightarrow}$ and $\mathbb{G}_{\downarrow}/\underline{\leftrightarrow}$, we provide the following action rules for π_n:

$$x \to^a x' \Rightarrow \pi_{n+1}(x) \to^a \pi_n(x') \qquad x\downarrow \Rightarrow \pi_n(x)\downarrow.$$

It is easy to check that $\underline{\leftrightarrow}$ remains a congruence on $\mathbb{P}$ and $\mathbb{P}/\underline{\leftrightarrow}$ satisfies the axioms of table 6.

5.7 PROPOSITION. The following equations are derivable for closed ACP$\surd$-terms. Moreover, they hold in $\mathbb{P}/\underline{\leftrightarrow}$.

1. $\pi_n(x \,\square\, y) = \pi_n(\pi_n(x) \,\square\, \pi_n(y))$ for $\square = +, \cdot, \|, \lfloor\!\lfloor, |$.
2. $\pi_n(\partial_H(x)) = \partial_H(\pi_n(x))$ for $H \subseteq A$.

PROOF: Straightforward, using one of the inductive schemes in 3.7. Note that the analogous statement for the operator ε_K does *not* hold.

5.8 DEFINITION. The process $g \in \mathbb{G}_{\downarrow}/\underline{\leftrightarrow}$ is **finitely branching** if there is a finitely branching graph in its equivalence class. Since $\mathbb{P}/\underline{\leftrightarrow}$ and $\mathbb{G}_{\varepsilon\delta}/\underline{\leftrightarrow}_{\varepsilon}$ are isomorphic to $\mathbb{G}_{\downarrow}/\underline{\leftrightarrow}$, this property carries over to the other models.

5.9 PROPOSITION. The domain of finitely branching processes (inside one of our models) is closed under the operators $+, \cdot, \|, \lfloor\!\lfloor, |, \partial_H$, but *not* under ε_K.
PROOF: Straightforward.

5.10 PROPOSITION. Let $p \in \mathbb{P}/\underline{\leftrightarrow}$ be finitely branching, and let $n \in \mathbb{N}$. Then there is a basic term q_n such that
$\pi_n(p) = q_n$ holds in $\mathbb{P}/\underline{\leftrightarrow}$.
PROOF: This is easiest to see in the model $\mathbb{G}_{\downarrow}/\underline{\leftrightarrow}$, and transfers by isomorphism to $\mathbb{P}/\underline{\leftrightarrow}$.

5.11 PROPOSITION. For any process $p \in \mathbb{P}(A)/\underline{\leftrightarrow}$, and fresh atom $f \notin A$, there is a finitely branching process $q \in \mathbb{P}(A \cup \{f\})/\underline{\leftrightarrow}$ such that $\varepsilon_{\{f\}}(q) = p$.
PROOF: This follows by considering fig. 8 in 4.24: replace every infinite branching by a spine of f-steps to obtain q; renaming f into ε gives a process that bisimulates with p.

5.12 DEFINITION. The **Restricted Approximation Induction Principle (AIP$^-$)** says that a finitely branching process is completely determined by its finite projections, i.e. if p is finitely branching, and q is such that $\pi_n(p) = \pi_n(q)$ for all n, then $p = q$.
The "–" refers to a version of AIP without the restriction to finitely branching processes. For more information on AIP$^-$, see VAN GLABBEEK [7].

5.13 THEOREM. AIP$^-$ holds in $\mathbb{P}/\underline{\leftrightarrow}$.
PROOF: As in VAN GLABBEEK [7]. There, a version of AIP$^-$ is used, which is less restrictive, with bounded processes instead of finitely branching processes. It is easy to see that a finitely branching processes is bounded in the sense of [7].

5.14 THEOREM. The Recursive Specification Principle RSP holds in $\mathbb{P}/\underline{\leftrightarrow}$.

PROOF: Let E be a guarded recursive specification over variables V, and $X \in V$. Since all variables have a head normal form (3.15), process $p = \langle X \mid E\rangle/\underline{\leftrightarrow}$ is finitely branching. By 5.10, the finite projections of p are equal to basic terms. But it is easy to see that these basic terms only depend on the equations in E, and not on the particular solution. So, any solution must have the same finite projections, and hence is equal to p by AIP$^-$.

5.15 THEOREM. The Restricted Limit Rule LR$^-$ holds in $\mathbb{P}/\underline{\leftrightarrow}$.

PROOF: Let $s(x_1,...,x_n)$, $t(x_1,...,x_n)$ be ACP$\surd$-terms without ε_K-operator such that for every choice of parameters A,γ, and any $p_1,...,p_n \in$ BT we have $s(p_1,...,p_n) = t(p_1,...,p_n)$ holds in $\mathbb{P}(A)/\underline{\leftrightarrow}$. We have to show that $s(x_1,...,x_n) = t(x_1,...,x_n)$ holds in $\mathbb{P}/\underline{\leftrightarrow}$. This is the case if for every choice A,γ we have $s(p_1,...,p_n) \underline{\leftrightarrow} t(p_1,...,p_n)$ for all $p_1,...,p_n \in \mathbb{P}(A)$.

So let A,γ be given and suppose $p_1,...,p_n \in \mathbb{P}(A)$. Let f be a fresh atom. Choose (using 5.11) finitely branching $q_1,...,q_n \in \mathbb{P}(A\cup\{f\})$ such that $\varepsilon_{\{f\}}(q_i) = p_i$ $(1\leq i\leq n)$. For each $k \in \mathbb{N}$, choose (using 5.10) basic terms $r_1{}^k,...,r_n{}^k$ such that $\pi_k(q_i) = r_i{}^k$. Now by 5.7 we have for each $k \in \mathbb{N}$

$$\pi_k(s(q_1,...,q_n)) = \pi_k(s(\pi_k(q_1), ..., \pi_k(q_n))) = \pi_k(s(r_1{}^k,...,r_n{}^k)) =$$
$$= \pi_k(t(r_1{}^k,...,r_n{}^k)) = \pi_k(t(q_1,...,q_n)).$$

Thus, by AIP$^-$ and 5.9, we have $s(q_1,...,q_n) = t(q_1,...,q_n)$, and hence, by 5.5,

$$s(p_1,...,p_n) = s(\varepsilon_{\{f\}}(q_1), ..., \varepsilon_{\{f\}}(q_n)) = \varepsilon_{\{f\}}(s(q_1,...,q_n)) = \varepsilon_{\{f\}}(t(q_1,...,q_n)) = t(p_1,...,p_n).$$

REFERENCES

[1] J.C.M.BAETEN & J.A.BERGSTRA, *Global renaming operators in concrete process algebra,* report CS-R8521, Centre for Math. & Comp. Sci., Amsterdam 1985. To appear in Inf. & Computation.

[2] J.A.BERGSTRA & J.W.KLOP, *Fixed point semantics in process algebras,* report IW 206, Mathematical Centre, Amsterdam 1982.

[3] J.A.BERGSTRA & J.W.KLOP, *Process algebra for synchronous communication,* Inf. & Control 60 (1/3), pp. 109 - 137, 1984.

[4] J.A.BERGSTRA & J.W.KLOP, *Algebra of communicating processes,* in: Proc. CWI Symp. Math. & Comp. Sci. (J.W.de Bakker, M.Hazewinkel & J.K.Lenstra, eds.), pp. 89 - 138, North- Holland, Amsterdam 1986.

[5] J.A.BERGSTRA, J.W.KLOP & E.-R. OLDEROG, *Failures without chaos: a new process semantics for fair abstraction,* in: Proc. IFIP Conf. on Formal Description of Programming Concepts - III, Ebberup 1986, (M.Wirsing, ed.), North-Holland, Amsterdam, pp. 77 - 103, 1987.

[6] J.A.BERGSTRA & J.V.TUCKER, *Top down design and the algebra of communicating processes,* Sci. of Comp. Progr. 5 (2), pp. 171 - 199, 1985.

[7] R.J.VAN GLABBEEK, *Bounded nondeterminism and the approximation induction principle in process algebra,* in: Proc. STACS 87 (F.J.Brandenburg, G.Vidal-Naquet & M.Wirsing eds.), Springer LNCS 247, pp. 336 - 347, 1987.

[8] C.A.R.HOARE, *Communicating sequential processes,* Prentice Hall 1985.

[9] C.P.J.KOYMANS & J.L.M.VRANCKEN, *Extending process algebra with the empty process ε,* report LGPS 1, Dept. of Philosophy, State University of Utrecht, The Netherlands 1985.

[10] R.MILNER, *A calculus of communicating systems,* Springer LNCS 92, 1980.

[11] R.MILNER, *Lectures on a calculus of communicating systems,* in: Seminar on concurrency (S.D.Brookes, A.W.Roscoe & G.Winskel, eds.), Springer LNCS 197, pp. 197 - 220, 1985.

[12] D.M.R.PARK, *Concurrency and automata on infinite sequences,* in: Proc. 5th GI Conf. (P.Deussen, ed.), Springer LNCS 104, pp. 167 - 183, 1981.

[13] G.PLOTKIN, *An operational semantics for CSP,* in: Proc. Conf. Formal Description of Progr. Concepts II (D.Bjørner, ed.), pp. 199 - 223, North-Holland, Amsterdam 1982.

[14] J.L.M.VRANCKEN, *The algebra of communicating processes with empty process,* report FVI 86-01, Dept. of Comp. Sci., Univ. of Amsterdam 1986.

[15] F.W.VAANDRAGER, *Process algebra semantics of POOL,* report CS-R8629, Centre for Math. & Comp. Sci., Amsterdam 1986.

Parallelism and Programming: A Perspective*

K. Mani Chandy
Jayadev Misra
Department of Computer Sciences
University of Texas at Austin
Austin, TX 78712

1. The Unity of the Programming Task

This talk is about parallel programs; however, this talk is primarily about programs and secondarily about parallelism. The diversity of architectures and consequent programming constructs (send and receive, await, fork and join...) must be placed in the proper perspective with respect to the unity of the programming task. By stressing the differences, we are in danger of losing sight of the similarities. The central thesis of this talk is that the unity of the programming task is of primary importance; the diversity is secondary.

The basic problem in programming is managing complexity. We cannot address that problem as long as we lump together concerns about the core problem to be solved, the language in which the program is to be written, and the hardware on which the program is to execute. Program development should begin by focusing attention on the problem to be solved and postponing considerations of architecture and language constructs.

Some argue that in cases where language and hardware are specified as part of a problem, concerns about the core problem, language, and hardware are inseparable. For instance, programs executing on a distributed network of computers must employ some form of message passing; in such cases concerns about message passing appear inseparable from concerns about the core problem. Similarly, since the presence or absence of primitives for process creation and termination in the programming language influence the program, it appears that language issues are inseparable from others. Despite these arguments, we maintain that it is not only possible but important to separate these concerns; indeed it is even more important to do so for parallel programs because parallel programs are less well understood than sequential programs.

Twenty-five years ago, many programs were designed to make optimum use of some specific

---

* This material will appear as Chapter One in the forthcoming book *A Foundation of Parallel Program Design*, by K. Mani Chandy and Jayadev Misra, copyright ©1988 by Addison-Wesley Publishing Co., Inc., and is reproduced by permission.

feature of the hardware. Programs were written to exploit a particular machine language command or the number of bits in a computer word. Now, we know that such optimizations are best left to the last stages of program design or left out altogether. Today, parallel programs are designed much like sequential programs were designed in the 1950's: to exploit the message passing primitives of a language or the network interconnection structure of an architecture. A quarter-century of experience tells us that such optimizations are *best postponed* until the very end of program development. We now know that a physicist who wishes to use the computer to study some phenomenon in plasma physics, for instance, should not begin by asking whether communicating sequential processes or shared-memory is to be used, any more than whether the word size is 32 or 60 bits. Such questions have their place, but concerns must be separated. The first concern is to design a solution to the problem; the later concern is to implement the solution in a given language on a particular architecture. Issues of performance on a specific architecture should be considered, but only at the appropriate time.

Programs outlive the architectures for which they were designed initially. A program designed for one machine will be called upon to execute efficiently on quite dissimilar architectures. If program designs are tightly coupled to the machines of today, program modifications for future architectures will be expensive. Experience suggests that we should anticipate requests to modify our programs to keep pace with modifications in architecture—witness attempts to parallelize sequential programs. It is prudent to design a program for a flexible abstract model of a computer with the intent of tailoring the program to suit future architectures.

An approach to exploiting new architectural features is to add features to the computational model. However, a baroque abstract model of a computer only adds to the complexity of programming. On the other hand, simple models such as the Turing Machine do not provide the expressive power needed for program development. What we desire is a model that is simple and has the expressive power necessary to permit the refinement of specifications and programs to suit target architectures.

The emphasis on the unity of the programming task is a departure from the current view of programming. Currently, programming is fragmented into subdisciplines, one for each architectural form. Asynchronous distributed computing, in which component processes interact by messages, is considered irrelevant to synchronous parallel computing. Systolic arrays are viewed as hardware devices and, hence, traditional ideas of program development are deemed inapplicable to their design.

The goal of our approach is to show how programs may be developed in a systematic manner for a variety of architectures and applications. A criticism of this approach is that its fundamental premise is wrong because programmers should *not* be concerned with architecture—compilers should. Some styles of programming—e.g., functional and logic programming—are preferred precisely because architecture is not their concern. Our response to this criticism is twofold. First, programmers who are not concerned with architecture should not have to concern themselves with it—they should stop early in the program development process with a program which may or may not map efficiently to the target architecture. Second, there are some problems in which programmers have to be concerned with architecture either because the problem specifies the architecture (e.g., the design of a distributed command and control system) or because performance is critical; for these problems the refinement process is continued until efficient programs for the target architectures are obtained.

2. A Search for a Foundation of Parallel Programming

We seek a small theory that is applicable to programming for a wide range of architectures and applications. The issues that we consider central to such a theory are: nondeterminism, absence of control flow, synchrony/asynchrony, states and assignments, proof systems that support program development by stepwise refinement of specifications, and the decoupling of correctness from complexity, i.e., of programs from architectures. These issues are elaborated on next.

2.1 Nondeterminism

How can we develop programs for a variety of architectures through a series of refinements? *By specifying program execution at an appropriate level of detail: by specifying little in the early stages of design, and by specifying enough in the final stages to ensure efficient executions on target architectures.* Specifying little about program execution means that our programs may be nondeterministic. Different runs of the same program may execute statements in different orders, consume different amounts of resources and even produce different results.

Nondeterminism is useful in two ways. First, nondeterminism is employed to derive simple programs, where simplicity is achieved by avoiding unnecessary determinism; such programs may be optimized by limiting the nondeterminism, i.e., by disallowing executions unsuitable for a given architecture. Second, some systems, e.g., operating systems and delay-insensitive circuits, are inherently nondeterministic; programs that represent such systems have to employ some nondeterministic constructs.

2.2 Absence of Control Flow

The notion of sequential control flow is pervasive in computing. Turing Machines and von Neumann computers are examples of sequential devices. Flow charts and early programming languages were based on sequential flow of control. Structured programming retained sequential flow of control and advocated problem decomposition based on sequencing of tasks. The prominence of sequential control flow is partly due to historical reasons. Early computing devices and programs were understood by simulating their executions sequentially. Many of the things we use daily, such as recipes and instructions for filling out forms, are sequential; this may have influenced programming languages and the abstractions used in program design.

The introduction of co-routines was an indication that some programs are better understood through abstractions that are not related to control flow. A program structured as a set of processes is a further refinement: it admits multiple sequential flows of control. However, processes are viewed as *sequential* entities—note the titles of two classic papers in this area, "Cooperating Sequential Processes" in Dijkstra [1968] and "Communicating Sequential Processes" in Hoare [1978]. This suggests that sequential programming is the norm, and parallelism, the exception.

Control flow is not a unifying concept. Programs for different architectures employ different forms of control flow. Program design at early stages should not be based on considerations of control flow; it is a later concern. It is easier to restrict flow of control in a program having few restrictions than to remove unnecessary restrictions from a program having too many.

The issue of control flow has clouded several issues. Let us review one. Modularity is generally accepted as a Good Thing. What is a module? A module implements a set of related concerns, it has clean narrow interfaces, and the states of a system when control flows into and out of the module are specified succinctly. Now, a clean, narrow interface is one issue and control flow into and out of a module is another. Why not separate them? In our program model, we retain the concept of module as a part of a program that implements a set of related concerns. Yet, we have no notion of control flow into and out of a module. Divorcing control flow from module construction results in an unconventional view of modules and programming—though a useful one, we believe, for the development of parallel programs.

2.3 Synchrony and Asynchrony

Synchronous and asynchronous events are at the core of any unified theory of parallel programming. For instance, all events in a systolic array are synchronous: at each clock tick all processors in the array carry out a computational step. On the other hand, a data network spanning the globe has no common clock; processes at different nodes of the network execute steps asynchronously. Some systems have synchronous components interconnected by asynchronous channels—an example of such a system is an electronic circuit consisting of synchronous subcircuits interconnected by wires with arbitrary delays. Partitioning systems into synchronous and asynchronous varieties is artificial; a theory should include synchrony and asynchrony as fundamental concepts.

2.4 States and Assignments

A formal model employed by computing scientists, control theorists, communication engineers, circuit designers, and operations researchers (among others) is the state transition system. Computing scientists use state transition models in studying formal languages. Control theorists represent the systems they study as continuous or discrete state transition models—a typical control problem is to determine an optimal trajectory in a state space. Markov processes, employed by communication engineers and operations researchers, are state transition systems. Communication engineers represent communication protocols as state transition systems. Physical systems are often described in terms of state transitions. Therefore, it appears reasonable to us to propose a unifying theory of parallel programming based on state transition systems; indeed, it is our hope that the theory will be helpful to engineers and natural scientists as well as to programmers. However, treating a program as a state transition system—a set of states, an initial state, and a state transition function—offers little for a methodology of program development. Too much of the semantics of a problem is lost when it is represented as a set of states and transitions. Therefore, we wish to employ the theory of state transition systems while enjoying the representational advantages of programming languages. One way of doing so is to employ variables and assignments in the notation.

A starting point for the study of assignments is the following quote from Backus [1978]:

> "... the assignment statement splits programming into two worlds. The first world comprises the right sides of assignment statements. This is an orderly world of expressions, a world that has useful algebraic properties (except that those properties are often destroyed by side effects). It is the world in which most useful computation takes place.
>
> The second world of conventional programming languages is the world of statements. The primary statement in that world is the assignment statement itself. All the other statements of the language exist in order to make it possible to perform a computation that must be based on this primitive construct: the assignment statement.
>
> This world of statements is a disorderly one, with few useful mathematical properties. Structured programming can be seen as a modest effort to introduce some order into this chaotic world, but it accomplishes little in attacking the fundamental problems created by the word-at-a-time von Neumann style of programming, with its primitive use of loops, subscripts, and branching flow of control."

One cannot but agree that disorderly programming constructs are harmful. But there *is* an orderly world of assignments. The problems of imperative programming may be avoided while retaining assignments.

Word-at-a-time bottleneck: Multiple assignments allow assignments to several variables simultaneously; these variables may themselves be complex structures.

Control flow: Assignment can be divorced from control flow. We propose a program model that has assignments but no control flow.

Mathematical properties: A program model based on assignments and without control flow has remarkably nice properties.

2.5 Extricating Proofs from Program Texts

One way of proving the correctness of a sequential program is to provide an annotation of it; the proof consists of demonstrating that a predicate holds at a point in the text of the program—thus the proof is inextricably intertwined with the program text. We seek a proof system that allows the proof to be extricated from the program text. This would allow us to develop and study a proof in its own right.

Much of program development in our methodology consists of refining specifications, i.e., adding detail to specifications. Given a problem specification, we begin by proposing a general solution strategy. Usually the strategy is broad; it admits many solutions. Next we give a specification of the solution strategy and prove that the solution strategy (as specified) solves the problem (as specified). When we consider a specific set of target architectures, we may choose to narrow the solution strategy, which means refining the specification further. At each stage of strategy refinement, the programmer is obliged to prove that the specification proposed is indeed a refinement of a specification proposed at an earlier step. The construction of a program is begun only after the program has been specified in extensive detail. Usually, the proof that a program fits the detailed specification is straightforward because much of the work associated with proofs is carried out in earlier stages of stepwise refinement. We seek methods of specification and proof that do not require a skeleton of the program text to be proposed until the final stages of design. This is a departure from conventional sequential program development, where it is quite common to propose a skeleton of the program text early in the design, and where refinement of a specification proceeds hand-in-hand with the addition of flesh to the program skeleton.

2.6 Separation of Concerns: Correctness and Complexity

A point of departure of our work from the conventional view of programming is this: We attempt to decouple a program from its implementation. A program may be implemented in many different ways—a program may be implemented on different architectures, and even for a given computer, a program may be executed according to different schedules. The correctness of a program is independent of the target architecture and the manner in which the program is executed; by contrast, the efficiency of a program execution depends on the architecture and manner of execution. Therefore, we do not associate complexity measures with a program but rather with a program *and a mapping* to a target computer. A mapping is a description of how programs are to be executed on the target machine and a set of rules for computing complexity measures for programs when executed on the given target machine. A programmer's task, given a specification and a target architecture, is to derive a program with its proof, select a mapping that maps programs to the given target architecture, and then evaluate complexity measures.

The operational model of a program—how a computer executes a program—is straightforward for programs written in conventional sequential imperative languages, such as PASCAL, executing on conventional sequential machines. Indeed, many sequential imperative languages (so-called von Neumann languages) have been designed so that the manner in which von Neumann machines execute programs, written in these languages, is self-evident. The complexity measures (i.e., metrics of efficiency) of a program written in such a language are the amounts of resources, such as time and memory, required to execute the program on a von Neumann architecture. Usually, when computing scientists refer to complexity measures of a program, they implicitly assume a specific operational model of a specific architecture—in most cases the architecture is the traditional, sequential architecture and its abstract model is the Random Access Machine or RAM.

The tradition of tightly coupling programming notation to architecture, inherited from von Neumann languages and architectures, has been adopted in parallel programming as well. For instance, programmers writing in Communicating Sequential Processes (CSP) notation usually have a specific architecture in mind, *viz.* an architecture that consists of a set of von Neumann computers that communicate by means of message passing.

3. Introduction to the Theory

We propose a theory—a computational model and a proof system—called UNITY. We choose to view our programs as Unbounded Nondeterministic Iterative Transformations—hence the term UNITY. In the interest of brevity, the phrase "a UNITY program" is preferred to "a program in unbounded nondeterministic iterative transformation notation." We are not proposing a programming language. We adopt the minimum notational machinery to illustrate our ideas about programming. This section is (even as introductions go) incomplete.

3.1 UNITY Programs

A program consists of a declaration of its variables, a specification of their initial values, and a set of multiple assignment statements. A program execution starts from any state satisfying the initial condition and goes on forever; in each step of execution some assignment statement is selected nondeterministically and executed. Nondeterministic selection is constrained by the following "fairness" rule: every statement is selected infinitely often.

Our model of programs is simple; in fact it may appear too simple for effective programming. Our experience shows that our model is adequate for the development of programs in general and parallel programs in particular. Now, we give an informal and very incomplete description of how this model addresses some of the issues described in section 2.

3.2 Separating Concerns: Programs and Implementations

A UNITY program describes *what* should be done in the sense that it specifies what the initial state and the state transformations (i.e., the assignments) are. A UNITY program does not specify precisely *when* an assignment should be executed—the only restriction is a rather weak fairness constraint: every assignment is executed infinitely often. Nor does a UNITY program specify *where*, i.e., on which processor in a multiprocessor system, an assignment is to be executed, or to which process an assignment belongs. Also, a UNITY program does not specify *how* assignments are to be executed or *how* an implementation may halt a program execution.

UNITY separates concerns between *what* on the one hand and *when, where* and *how* on the other. The *what* is specified in a program, whereas the *when, where* and *how* are specified in a mapping. By separating concerns in this way, a simple programming notation is obtained that is appropriate for a wide variety of architectures. Of course, this simplicity is achieved at the expense of making mappings immensely more important and more complex than they are now.

3.3 Mapping Programs to Architectures

In this section, we give a brief outline of mappings of UNITY programs to several architectures. We consider the von Neumann architecture, synchronous shared-memory multiprocessors, and asynchronous shared-memory multiprocessors. The description given here is sufficient for understanding how the example programs of the next section are to be executed on various architectures. Though we describe mappings from UNITY programs to architectures, UNITY programs can also be mapped to programs in conventional programming languages.

A mapping to a von Neumann machine specifies the schedule for executing assignments and the manner in which a program execution terminates. The implementation of multiple assignments on sequential machines is straightforward and is not discussed here. We propose a mapping in which an execution schedule is represented by a finite sequential list of assignments in which each assignment in the program appears at least once. The computer executes this list of assignments repeatedly forever (but, see below). We are obliged to prove that the schedule is fair, i.e., that every assignment in the program is executed infinitely often. Since every assignment in the program appears at least once in the list, and since the list is executed forever, it follows that every assignment in the program is executed infinitely often.

Given that a UNITY program execution does not terminate, how do we represent traditional programs whose executions do terminate (in the traditional sense)? We regard termination as a feature of an implementation. A cleaner theory is obtained by distinguishing program execution—an infinite sequence of statement executions—from its implementation—a finite prefix of the sequence.

A state of a program is called a *fixed point* if and only if execution of any statement of the program, in this state, leaves the state unchanged. A predicate, called FP (for fixed point), characterizes the fixed points of a program. It is the conjunction of the equations that are obtained by replacing the assignment operator by equality in each of the statements in the program. Therefore, FP holds if and only if values on left and right sides of each assignment in the program are identical. Once FP holds, continued execution leaves values of all variables unchanged, and therefore, it makes no difference whether the execution continues or terminates. One way of implementing a program is to halt the program after it reaches a fixed point.

A *stable predicate* or *stable property* of a program is a predicate that continues to hold, once it holds. Thus, FP is a stable property.

In a synchronous shared-memory system, a fixed number of identical processors share a common memory which can be read and written by any processor. There is a common clock, where in each clock tick, every processor carries out precisely one step of computation. The synchrony inherent in a multiple assignment statement makes it convenient to map such a statement to this architecture: each processor computes the expression on the right side of the assignment corresponding to one variable and then assigns the computed value to this variable. This architecture is also useful for computing the value of an expression which is defined by an associative operator, such as sum, minimum or maximum, applied to a sequence of data items.

An asynchronous shared-memory multiprocessor consists of a fixed set of processors and a common memory, but there is no common clock. If two processors access the same memory location simultaneously, then their accesses are made in some arbitrary order. A UNITY program can be mapped to such an architecture by partitioning the statements of the program among the processors. In addition, a schedule of execution for each processor should be specified that guarantees fairness of execution for each partition. Observe that if execution for every partition is fair, then any fair interleaving of these executions determines a fair execution of the entire program. Our suggested mapping assumes a coarse grain of atomicity in the architecture: two statements are not executed concurrently if one modifies a variable that the other one uses. Hence, the effect of multiple processor execution is the same as a fair interleaving of their individual executions.

To evaluate the efficiency of a program executed according to a given mapping, it is necessary to describe the mapping—the data structures and the computational steps—in detail. Descriptions of architectures and mappings can be made extremely detailed. Memory caches, I/O devices and controllers can be described if it is necessary to evaluate efficiency at that level of detail. What we wish to emphasize is the separation of concerns: programs are concerned with *what* is to be done whereas mappings are concerned with the implementation details of *where, when,* and *how.*

3.4 Modeling Conventional Programming Language Constructs and Architectures

In this section, we show that conventional programming language constructs that exploit different kinds of parallelism have simple counterparts in UNITY. This is not too surprising because the UNITY model incorporates both synchrony—a multiple assignment assigns to several variables synchronously—and asynchrony—nondeterministic selection leaves unspecified the order of executions of statements.

A synchronous system is one in which there is a global clock variable that is incremented with every state change. Multiple assignments model parallel synchronous operations.

A statement of the form **await** B **do** S in an asynchronous shared-variable program is encoded as a statement in our model which does not change the value of any variable if B is *false* and otherwise has the same effect as S. A Petri net, another form of asynchronous system, can be represented by a program in which a variable corresponds to a *place*, the value of a variable is the number of *markers* in the corresponding place, and a statement corresponds to a *transition*. The execution of a statement decreases values of variables corresponding to its input places by 1 (provided they are all positive) and increases values of variables corresponding to its output places by 1, in one multiple assignment.

Asynchronous message-passing systems with first-in-first-out error-free channels may be represented by encoding each channel as a variable whose value is a sequence of messages (representing the sequence of messages in transit along the channel). Sending a message is equivalent to appending the message to the end of the sequence and receiving a message to removing the head of the sequence.

We cannot control the sequence in which statements are executed. However, by using variables appropriately in conditional expressions, we can ensure that the execution of a statement has no effect (i.e., does not change the program state) unless the statement execution occurs in a desired sequence.

4. An Example: Scheduling a Meeting

The goal of this example is to give the reader *some* idea of how we propose to develop programs. The thesis of our approach is unusual and the computational model even more so; skeptical readers may want to get a rough idea of how we propose to design programs before investing their time any further—this example is to satisfy their need.

4.1 The Problem Statement

The problem is to find the earliest meeting time acceptable to every member of a group of people. Time is integer-valued and nonnegative. To keep notation simple, assume that the group consists of three people called F, G, and H. Associated with persons F, G, H are functions f, g, h (respectively) that map times to times. The meaning of f is as follows (and the meanings of g, h follow by analogy). For any t, $f(t) \geq t$; person F can meet at time $f(t)$ and cannot meet at any time u where $t \leq u < f(t)$. Thus, $f(t)$ is the earliest time at or after t at which person F can meet. (Note: From the problem description, f is a monotone nondecreasing function of its argument and $f(f(t)) = f(t)$. Also, $t = f(t)$ means that F can meet at t.) Assume that there exists some common meeting time z. In the interest of brevity we introduce a boolean function *com* (for *com*mon meeting time) over nonnegative integers defined as follows:

$$com(t) \equiv [t = f(t) = g(t) = h(t)]$$

Problem Specification

Note: All variables r, t, z, referred to in the specification, are nonnegative integers. □

Given integer-valued functions f, g, h, where for all t :

$$f(t) \geq t \ \wedge \ g(t) \geq t \ \wedge \ h(t) \geq t \ \wedge$$

$$f(f(t)) = f(t) \ \wedge \ g(g(t)) = g(t) \ \wedge \ h(h(t)) = h(t)$$

and given a z such that $com(z)$, design a program that has the following as a stable predicate:

$$r = \min\{t \mid com(t)\}$$

Furthermore, the program establishes this stable predicate within a finite number of steps of execution.

Discussion

There are many ways of attacking this problem. One approach is to structure the solution around a set of processes, one process corresponding to each person; the behavior of people provides guidelines for programming these processes. We propose an alternate approach based on our theory. We describe both methods as applied to this problem starting with the operational view.

4.2 Operational, Process-Oriented Viewpoint

Here we describe only person F's behavior; the behaviors of G and H follow by analogy. Consider persons seated at a round table and a letter containing a proposed meeting time (initially 0), passed around among them. Person F, upon receiving the letter with time t, sets the proposed time to $f(t)$ and passes the letter to the next person. If the letter makes one complete round without a change in the proposed meeting time then this time is the solution.

Another strategy is to use a central coordinator to whom each person reports the next time at which he can meet. The coordinator broadcasts t, the maximum of these times, to all persons and F then sends $f(t)$ back to the coordinator. These steps are repeated until the coordinator receives identical values from all persons.

Yet another solution is to divide the persons into two groups and recursively find meeting times for each group. Then the maximum of these times is used as the next estimate for repeating these steps, unless the two values are equal.

Another approach is to use a bidding scheme where an auctioneer calls out a proposed meeting time t, starting at $t = 0$, and F can raise the bid to $f(t)$ (provided this value exceeds t). The common meeting time is the final bid value, i.e., a value that can be raised no further. The reader may develop many other solutions by casting the problem in a real-world context. Different solutions are appropriate for different architectures.

4.3 The UNITY Viewpoint

We take the specification as the starting point for program design. For this example, we will merely propose programs and argue that they meet their specifications. Our next concern, after designing a program, is to refine it further so that it can be mapped to a target architecture for efficient execution. We may have to consider alternate refinements of the same program, or even alternate programs, if we are unable to find a mapping with the desired efficiency.

A Simple Program

The problem specification suggests immediately the following program. The syntax is as follows: the assignment statements are given under **assign**. Declarations of variables have been omitted.

Program P1

assign $\quad r := \min\{u \mid (0 \leq u \leq z) \wedge (com(u))\}$

end {P1}

This program's correctness needs no argument. Now, we consider how best to implement P1 on different architectures.

For a von Neumann machine, computation of the right side of the assignment—i.e., finding the first u for which $com(u)$ holds—can proceed by checking the various values of u, from 0 to z, successively. The program is entirely straightforward. The number of steps of execution is proportional to the value of r; in the worst case, it is $O(z)$.

For a parallel synchronous machine the minimum over a set of size z can be computed in $O(log\ z)$ steps by $O(z)$ processors and, in general, in $O(z/k + log\ k)$ steps by $O(k)$ processors.

For parallel asynchronous shared-memory systems, a similar strategy can be employed for the computation of the minimum.

Discussion

We showed a very simple program, the correctness of which is obvious from the specification. We described, informally, how the program could be mapped to different architectures. It is possible to refine this program so that the mappings correspond more directly to its statements and variables. For instance, to describe the mapping to an asynchronous message-passing system, we may refine this program by introducing variables to represent communication channels and statements to simulate sending and receiving from these channels; then, we can describe the mapping by specifying which statements are to be executed by which processors and which channels connect which pairs of processors.

We make some general observations about Program P1 independent of the architecture on which it is implemented. We note that $com(u)$ has to be evaluated for *every* u, $0 \leq u \leq z$. This may be wasteful because from the problem statement we can deduce that no u can be a common meeting time—i.e., $com(u)$ does not hold—if $t \leq u < f(t)$. Therefore, it is not necessary to evaluate $com(u)$ for any u in this interval. Such an approach is taken in the next program.

Another Simple Program

The program that we propose is so straightforward that we give it without a prior detailed discussion. The symbol $[\!]$ is used to separate the assignment statements in the following program; the initial condition is specified under **initially**.

Program P2

initially $r = 0$

assign $r := f(r) \;[\!]\; r := g(r) \;[\!]\; r := h(r)$

end {**P2**}

The program has three assignments: $r := f(r)$, $r := g(r)$, and $r := h(r)$. Computation proceeds by executing any one of the three assignments selected nondeterministically. The selection obeys the fairness rule: every assignment is executed infinitely often.

This program may be understood as follows. Initially, the proposed meeting time is zero. Any one of the participants—F, G, or H—increases the value of the proposed meeting time, if he cannot meet at that time, to the next time at which he can meet; in this sense, this program is similar to the bidding scheme outlined in section 4.2. At fixed point, r is a common meeting time.

Proof of Correctness

We divide the correctness argument into three parts.

(1) We claim that the following predicate is true at all points during program execution; such a predicate is called an invariant.

invariant $(0 \le r) \land \langle \text{for all } u \text{ where } 0 \le u < r \;::\; \neg com(u)\rangle$

In words, the invariant says that r is nonnegative and that there is no common meeting time earlier than r. Using the specification and this invariant, it is seen that $r \le z$ is always true, because there is a common meeting time at z.

To prove the invariant, we show that it is true initially and execution of any statement preserves its truth. Initially, $r = 0$. Hence, the first conjunct in the invariant is true and the second conjunct holds, vacuously. Now consider execution of the statement $r := f(r)$. We know before execution of this statement, from definition, that F cannot meet at any u, $r \le u < f(r)$. Hence, $\neg com(u)$ holds for all u, $r \le u < f(r)$. Also, from the invariant, we may assume that $\neg com(u)$ holds for all u, $0 \le u < r$. Trivially, $0 \le f(r)$. Therefore,

$$(0 \le f(r)) \land \langle \text{for all } u \text{ where } 0 \le u < f(r) \;::\; \neg com(u)\rangle$$

holds prior to execution of $r := f(r)$. The effect of execution of this statement is to set r to $f(r)$. Replacing $f(r)$ by r in the above predicate, we see that the invariant continues to hold after execution of this statement.

Due to symmetry among the statements, similar arguments show that the invariant is preserved by executing any statement.

(2) From the definition, FP for this program (which is the conjunction of the equations obtained by replacing := by = in every statement) is

$$FP \equiv r = f(r) \land r = g(r) \land r = h(r) .$$

From the definition of $com(r)$ it follows that $FP \equiv com(r)$.

Combining the results proved in parts (1) and (2), we claim that if Program P2's execution reaches a fixed point then the value of r is the earliest meeting time. Our remaining task is to show that every execution of Program P2 does, indeed, reach a fixed point; this is shown below.

(3) We show that if $\neg FP \wedge r = k$ holds at any point during computation then $r > k$ holds at some later point. Thus, r keeps on increasing as long as $\neg FP$ holds. We showed in part (1) that r cannot increase beyond z. Therefore, eventually FP holds. The proof of the claim that r increases if $\neg FP$ holds, is as follows. From the FP given in part (2),

$$\neg FP \wedge (r = k) \quad \equiv \quad k < f(k) \vee k < g(k) \vee k < h(k)$$

Suppose $k < f(k)$ (similar reasoning applies for the other cases). From the fairness requirement, the statement $r := f(r)$ is executed some time later. Since the value of r never decreases, just prior to execution of this statement, $r \geq k$ (r may have increased in the meantime) and hence,

$$f(r) \geq f(k) > k \ .$$

The effect of the execution of the statement is to set r to $f(r)$, and hence r increases beyond k.

This completes the proof.

Mapping Program P2 to Various Architectures

We propose a mapping from Program P2 to a von Neumann machine. The mapping is described by a list of assignments (see section 3.3). The list we propose is:

$$r := f(r) \ ; \ r := g(r) \ ; \ r := h(r)$$

This list of assignments is executed repeatedly until a fixed point is detected—a fixed point is detected when three consecutive assignments do not change the value of r. This program corresponds to a token, containing r, being passed in a circular fashion from F to G to H and then back to F, with each person setting r to the next time at or after r at which he can meet. When the token passes by all three persons without being modified, the program terminates.

Now suppose the functions f, g, h are such that it is more efficient to apply f twice as often as g or h. Therefore we wish to repeatedly execute the following cycle: apply f, then g, then f again and then h. So we employ a different mapping from P1 with the execution schedule represented by the following list of assignments:

$$r := f(r) \; ; \; r := g(r) \; ; \; r := f(r) \; ; \; r := h(r)$$

The point of showing two different mappings is to emphasize that P2 describes a family of programs, each one corresponding to a different schedule. By proving P2, we have proved the correctness of all members in the family. Observe that each member of the family can also be represented as a UNITY program. For instance, the first schedule corresponds to a program with a single assignment statement:

$$r := h(g(f(r)))$$

and the second one to a program with the assignment statement:

$$r := h(f(g(f(r)))) \; .$$

Program P2 can be implemented on asynchronous multiprocessors by partitioning its statements among the processors. For instance, we may employ three processors, each executing one statement, and r's value resides in the common memory.

We show yet another program whose correctness can be established in the same manner as for $P2$.

Program P3

initially $r = 0$

assign $r := \max(f(r), g(r), h(r))$

end {**P3**}

This program is similar in spirit to the central coordinator scheme outlined in section 4.4. It is a suitable starting point for programming parallel synchronous multiprocessors. If the number of persons is N ($N = 3$ in this case), the maximum on the right side of the assignment can be computed in $O(log\ N)$ steps using $O(N)$ processors.

Discussion

It is possible to develop yet other programs and show alternate schedules and mappings to various architectures. We have attempted to illustrate only that certain concerns, particularly dealing with architectures, may be ignored at higher levels of design, and introduced at lower levels based on considerations of efficiency.

5. Summary

We have proposed a unifying theory for the development of programs for a variety of architectures and applications. The computational model is unbounded nondeterministic iterative transformations of the program state. In our approach, transformations of the program state are represented by multiple assignments. The theory attempts to decouple the programmer's thinking about a program and its implementation on an architecture, i.e., separate the concerns of *what* from those of *where, when,* and *how.* Details about implementations are considered in mappings of programs to architectures. We believe that we can develop, specify and refine solution strategies independent of architectures.

Bibliographic Notes

UNITY was first discussed at the Conference on The Principles of Distributed Computing in Vancouver, B.C. in August 1984 in Chandy [1984]. The basic idea has not changed since then. Applications of UNITY in the literature include termination detection algorithms, Chandy and Misra [1986a], systolic programs, Chandy and Misra [1986b] and van de Snepscheut and Swenker [1987], and self stabilizing programs, Brown [1987].

The idea of modeling programs as state-transition systems is not new. Work of Pnueli [1981], Manna and Pnueli [1983], and Lamport and Schneider [1984] on using transition systems to model distributed systems are particularly relevant. Lynch and Tuttle [1987] use transition systems to develop distributed programs by stepwise refinement. A state based model of distributed dynamic programming is in Bertsekas [1982]. A stimulus-response based approach for program specification is proposed in Parker et al. [1980].

The idea of using mappings to implement programs on different architectures is not new either. The work, since the 1960's, of recognizing parallelism in sequential programs is an instance of employing mappings to parallel architectures. The point of departure of UNITY is to offer a different computational model from which to do the mapping. Formal complexity models of architectures are in Goldschlager [1977], Pippenger [1979], Aho et al. [1983], and Cook [1983]. A survey of concurrent programming constructs is in Andrews and Schneider [1983].

The importance of nondeterminism was stressed by Dijkstra [1976], and he proposed the nondeterministic construct—the guarded command. The guarded command is used extensively in Hoare [1984] which contains a definitive treatment of program structuring using Communicating Sequential Processes. A comprehensive treatment of fairness is in Francez [1986]. In its use of nondeterminism, UNITY is similar to expert-system languages such as OPS5, Brownston et al. [1985]. Milner [1983] contains a general theory of synchrony and asynchrony. Finally, we wish to point out that some of the initial motivation for UNITY came from difficulties encountered in using spreadsheets, a notation that has not received much attention from the computing sciences community.

Bibliography

Aho, A. V., J. E. Hopcroft, and J. D. Ullman [1983]. *Data Structures and Algorithms*, Reading, Massachusetts: Addison-Wesley, 1983.

Andrews, G. R., and F. B. Schneider [1983]. "Concepts and Notations for Concurrent Programming," *Computing Surveys*, **15**:1, March 1983, pp. 3-43.

Backus, J. [1978]. "Can Programming be Liberated from the von Neumann Style? A Functional Style and its Algebra of Programs," *C.ACM*, **21**:8, August 1978, pp. 613-641.

Bertsekas, D. P. [1982]. "Distributed Dynamic Programming," *IEEE Transactions on Automatic Control*, **AC-27**:3, June 1982, pp. 610-616.

Brown, G. M. [1987]. "Self Stabilizing Distributed Resource Allocation," Ph.D. thesis, University of Texas at Austin, Austin, Texas, 1987.

Brownston, L., et al., [1985]. *Programming Expert Systems in OPS5*, Reading, Massachusetts: Addison-Wesley, 1985.

Chandy, K. M. [1984]. "Concurrent Programming for the Masses," (invited address) *3rd Annual ACM Symposium on Principles of Distributed Computing*,Vancouver, Canada, August 5-7, 1984. (The text appears in *Proc. of the 4th Annual ACM Symposium on Principles of Distributed Computing*, 1985, pp. 1-12.)

Chandy, K. M., and J. Misra [1986a]. "An Example of Stepwise Refinement of Distributed Programs: Quiescence Detection," *ACM TOPLAS*, **8**:3, July 1986, pp. 326-343.

Chandy, K. M., and J. Misra [1986b]. "Systolic Algorithms as Programs," *Distributed Computing*, **1**, 1986, pp. 177-183.

Cook, S. A. [1983]. "The Classification of Problems Which Have Fast Parallel Algorithms," *Proc. of 24th IEEE Symposium on the Foundations of Computer Science*, 1983.

Dijkstra, E. W. [1976]. *A Discipline of Programming*, Englewood Cliffs, New Jersey: Prentice-Hall, 1976.

Dijkstra, E. W. [1968]. "Cooperating Sequential Processes," (in) *Programming Languages*, (ed.) Genuys, New York: Academic Press, 1968, pp. 43-112.

Francez, N. [1986]. *Fairness*, New York: Springer-Verlag, 1986.

Goldschlager, L. M. [1978]. "Synchronous Parallel Computation," Ph.D. thesis,

University of Toronto, Toronto, Ontario, (1977); see also *Proc. of 10th ACM Symposium on the Theory of Computing*, 1978, pp. 89-94 and *J.ACM*, **29**:4, October 1982, pp. 1073-1086.

Hoare, C. A. R. [1984]. *Communicating Sequential Processes*, London: Prentice-Hall International, 1984.

Hoare, C. A. R. [1978]. "Communicating Sequential Processes," *C.ACM*, **21**:8, August 1978, pp. 666-677.

Lamport, L., and F. B. Schneider [1984]. "The 'Hoare Logic' of CSP, and All That," *ACM TOPLAS*, **6**:2, April 1984, pp. 281-296.

Lynch, N. A., and M. R. Tuttle [1987]. "Hierarchical Correctness Proofs for Distributed Algorithms," *Proc. of 6th Annual ACM Symposium on Principles of Distributed Computing*, Vancouver, Canada, 1987.

Manna, Z., and A. Pnueli [1983]. "How to Cook a Temporal Proof System for Your Pet Language," *Proc. of the 10th Annual ACM Symposium on Principles of Programming Languages*, Austin, Texas, 1983.

Milner, R. [1983]. "Calculi for Synchrony and Asynchrony," *Theoretical Computer Science*, **25**, 1983, pp. 267-310.

Parker, R. A., et al., [1980]. "Abstract Interface Specifications for the A-7E Device Interface Module," *U.S. Navy Research Laboratories Memorandum Report 4385*, November 1980.

Pippenger, N. [1979]. "On Simultaneous Resource Bounds," *Proc. of 20th IEEE Symposium on Foundations of Computer Science*, 1979, pp. 307-311.

Pnueli, Amir [1981]. "The Temporal Semantics of Concurrent Programs," *Theoretical Computer Science*, **13**, 1981, pp. 45-60.

van de Snepscheut, J. L. A., and J. B. Swenker [1987]. "On the Design of Some Systolic Algorithms," *JAN 131a*, The Netherlands: University of Groningen, 1987.

ON OPTIMAL PARALLELIZATION OF SORTING NETWORKS

Ethan Gannett   Suraj C. Kothari   Hsu-Chun Yen
Department of Computer Science, Iowa State University
Ames, Iowa 50011, U.S.A.

1. Introduction

In his third volume of the *Art of Computer Programming*, Knuth has presented *sorting networks* for "constrained" type of sorting. A node in a sorting network is a *comparator module* which takes elements as inputs, compares them and, if necessary, interchanges them into ascending order. Knuth has also introduced a suitable representation for a sorting network. The representation for insertion sort with four inputs is shown in Figure 1. The elements enter from the left. The comparator modules are represented by vertical connections between two horizontal lines which correspond to elements of the sequence. The numbers come out at right, in ascending order from top to bottom. Knuth presents sorting networks for several sorting algorithms. He also introduces the *Zero-one* principle to prove the validity of a sorting network.

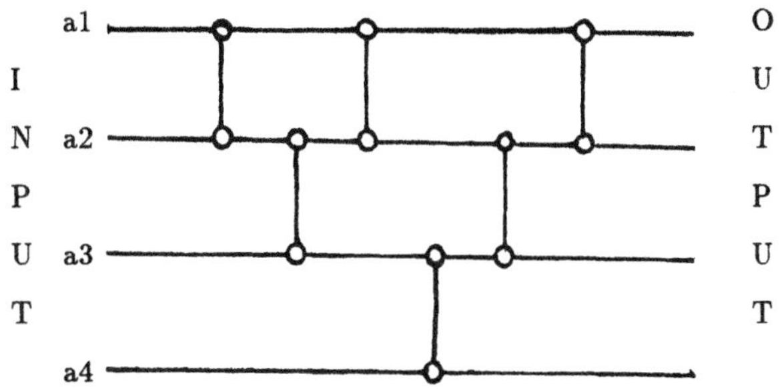

Figure 1: Sorting Network without Overlap for Insertion Sort, delay=6

An important advantage of sorting networks is the possibility to overlap operations of comparator modules to minimize the *delay* through the network. For example the sorting network shown in Figure 1, performs all comparisons in sequential order and the delay is 6. However the delay can be reduced to 5 by overlapping the operations of two comparator modules as shown in Figure 2. Note that each comparison is done at the earliest possible time in this new "concurrent" network. The *Ravel Transform* discussed later achieves this effect for the general case of a sorting network. In the context of a sorting network the problem of optimal concurrency is to find the maximal overlap of comparator modules without changing the underlying semantics of the network. Knuth has discussed the question of concurrency informally. Recently, Lengauer and Huang have provided automated proofs of optimal concurrency for the bitonic sort [2] and the insertion sort [6]. Since their work was a motivation for this paper, we provide a brief summary of their work. They apply a programming methodology [4,5] which can deal formally with concurrency. The method proceeds by attempting to successively parallelize the program execution steps based on certain properties of the program, that allow changes in the sequential executions without changing the semantics. In case of a sorting network the successive parallelization is attempted by the Ravel transform discussed later. The *commutativity* and the *idempotence* of comparator module operations are the properties used to change the order of sequential execution in order to parallelize. The program executions are called *traces*. They introduce Ravel transform which transforms a sequential trace of a sorting network into a parallel trace. By using the Boyer-Moore theorem prover [1] they give a mechanical proof that the transformation achieves optimal concurrency.

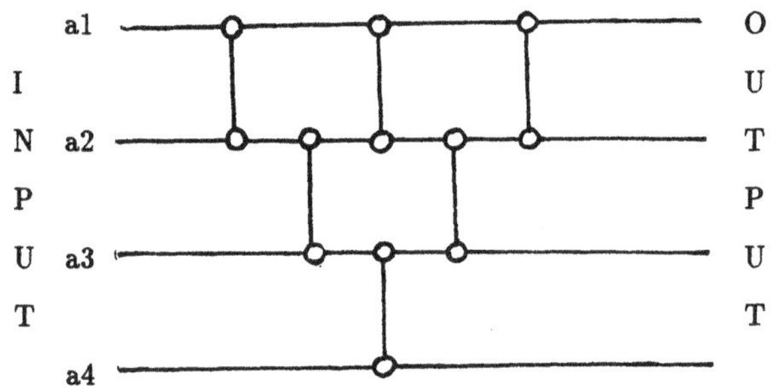

Figure 2: Sorting Network with Overlap for Insertion Sort, delay=5

This paper includes a "mathematical" proof of optimal concurrency in place of a mechanical proof. We use the formalism developed by Lengauer and Huang and provide the necessary extensions to make the mathematical proof possible. We feel that a mathematical proof provides more insight into the problem versus a mechanical proof where certain ideas are hidden in a black box, namely the theorem prover. The insight has enabled us to prove new results. Instead of separate proofs as in [2] and [6] for two different sorting networks, we provide a unifying proof technique which works in general. In fact our proof of optimality holds for any network of comparator modules.

Section 2 describes the necessary formalism and the notation. The main result and proofs are described in Section 3.

2. Traces and Their Transformations

Following Knuth [3], *cs(x,y)* denotes the comparator module that accesses the array a[0...n] of elements and compares elements a[x] and a[y] ($0 \leq x, y \leq n$) and then interchanges them into order if necessary. A simple comparator module *cs(x)* ($1 \leq x \leq n$) compares adjacent array elements a[x] and a[x-1]. For ease of understanding, we will use simple comparator modules in our examples; the extension to regular comparator modules is straightforward. The sequential trace of a sorting network will consist of a sequential list of comparator modules.

2.1 Trace Representation and Execution Time

Following the work of Lengauer and Huang [6], we use multilevel lists which allow us to represent parallel executions. A comparator module *cs(i)* will be represented as i in the lists. In a multilevel list, alternate list levels represent sequential execution and parallel execution in turn. The outermost list level (level 1) and all odd list levels will always denote sequential execution. The first nested list level (level 2) and all even list levels of a multilevel list will represent parallel execution. Hence, our representation of a sequential insertion sort trace on a six element array is :

(1 2 1 3 2 1 4 3 2 1 5 4 3 2 1)

If we restrict the execution time of a sorting network to be solely dependent on the execution time of a comparator module and we assert a unit execution time for each comparator module, the sequential insertion sort has execution time $n(n+1)/2$.

A parallel trace of the insertion sort example would be :

(1 2 (3 1) (4 2) (5 3 1) (4 2) (3 1) 2 1)

In Section 3, such a trace will be written as:

$$(1\ 2\ \langle 3\ 1 \rangle\ \langle 4\ 2 \rangle\ \langle 5\ 3\ 1 \rangle\ \langle 4\ 2 \rangle\ \langle 3\ 1 \rangle\ 2\ 1)$$

or

$$(1\ 2 \left\langle \begin{matrix} 3 \\ \\ 1 \end{matrix} \right\rangle \left\langle \begin{matrix} 4 \\ \\ 2 \end{matrix} \right\rangle \left\langle \begin{matrix} 5 \\ 3 \\ 1 \end{matrix} \right\rangle \left\langle \begin{matrix} 4 \\ \\ 2 \end{matrix} \right\rangle \left\langle \begin{matrix} 3 \\ \\ 1 \end{matrix} \right\rangle 2\ 1)$$

where '$\langle\rangle$' denotes parallel execution. The transformation that yielded this trace can be performed on any size array and results in an execution time of $2n-1$ (assume instantaneous forks and joins).

Thus, the transformation has improved the execution time of the insertion sort from quadratic to linear in the length of the array.

With this representation, we can determine the execution time of any multilevel trace by use of the following recursive Lisp-like function as presented by Lengauer and Huang [6] :

```
(EXECTIME FLAG L)
    =
(IF (NLISTP L)
    (IF L=NIL
        0
        1)
    (IF FLAG='PAR
        (MAX (EXEC-TIME 'SEQ (CAR L))
                (EXEC-TIME 'PAR (CDR L)))
        (PLUS (EXEC-TIME 'PAR (CAR L))
                (EXEC-TIME 'SEQ (CDR L)))))
```

where L is the trace, *FLAG* is the mode of execution ('SEQ or 'PAR) and *NLISTP* is the negation of *LISTP*. Note that the first call to *EXECTIME* has *FLAG = 'SEQ*.

2.2 Semantic-Preserving Operations and Parallelization

The intent of a semantic-preserving operation on a sequental trace is to transform it to a semantically equivalent trace. The semantic properties of comparator modules are :

- Idempotence: A comparator module that can be executed once or any number of times consecutively with the same effect is *idempotent*.
- Commutativity: Two comparator modules that can be executed in any order with the same effect are said to be *commutative*.

We can use these properties to perform semantic-preserving operations on a trace. That is, for commutative comparator modules C_i and C_j:

- $(C_i \; C_i) \rightarrow (C_i)$

  {Deletion of a comparator module by idempotence}

- $(C_i) \rightarrow (C_i \ C_i)$

  {Duplication of a comparator module by idempotence}

- $(C_i \ C_j) \rightarrow (C_j \ C_i)$

  {Commuting comparator modules}

The reader may note that all comparator modules are idempotent. Idempotence allows comparator modules to be introduced into or deleted from a trace.

A *semantic-preserving transformation* $\mathcal{F}$ on a sequential trace T is defined as a composition of finitely many semantic-preserving operations which possibly yields some new trace T'. We write : $T \xrightarrow{\mathcal{F}} T'$.

Semantic-preserving operations provide a means of transforming a sequential trace into some other sequential trace. The objective of a parallelizing transformation is to transform a sequential trace to a possibly parallel trace. To do so, we must examine the dependence between comparator modules in a trace since independent modules could be executed in parallel. The notion of *dependence* between two comparator modules can be defined as follows:

Let C_1 and C_2 be comparator modules of the form:

$$C_1 = cs(i,j), \quad C_2 = cs(k,l).$$

We define $C_1 \sim C_2$ (read as C_1 is dependent on C_2) if and only if:

$C_1 \sim C_2 \Leftrightarrow \{i,j\} \cap \{k,l\} \neq \emptyset$ *and* $C_1 \neq C_2$. Note that if $C_1 = C_2$, we consider these comparator modules independent.

Two comparator modules are said to be *independent* if they are not dependent. The reader may note that two consecutive comparator modules in a trace are commutative if and only if they are independent.

Similarly, we may define a *linearly dependent sequence.* Given a sequential trace $T = (C_1 C_2 \ldots C_k)$, T is called linearly dependent if and only if $C_i \sim C_{i+1}$ $(1 \leq i \leq k-1)$.

A *parallelizing transform* $\mathcal{G}$ turns a sequential trace T into a possibly multilevel list T' by exploiting independence of comparator modules and grouping those modules together into parallel lists. We write: $T \xrightarrow{\mathcal{G}} T'$.

2.3 Semantic Equivalency and Minimal (Parallel) Execution Time

Through the use of semantic preserving transforms and parallelizing transforms, we can define a semantically equivalent trace.

A multilevel trace T'' is said to be *semantically equivalent* to a sequential trace T if and only if T'' is obtained from T by a semantic preserving transform and/or a parallelizing transform. We write: $T \xrightarrow{\mathcal{F}} T' \xrightarrow{\mathcal{G}} T''$ or $T \xrightarrow{\mathcal{G}} T' \xrightarrow{\mathcal{F}} T''$ where $\mathcal{F}$ and/or $\mathcal{G}$ may be the identity transformation.

We write: $T'' \equiv_S T$ (to be read as T'' is semantically equivalent to T).

Consider the trace $T = (\ 1\ \ 5\ \ 7\ \ 1\ \ 2\ \ 3\ \ 6\ )$. The following are examples of traces semantically equivalent to T:

1. (1 5 7 2 3 6)

   {The transformation involves commuting 1 with 7 and 5, then by idempotence the 1 may be deleted }

2. (1 5 7 1 2 (3 5) 6)

   {By idempotence, we may introduce a second 5 and commute it with 7,1,2,3, but not 6. 3 and 5 may be executed in parallel due to their independence}

3. ((1 5 7 (1 2 3)) 6)

   {Note that (1 2 3) is in sequence. 1,5,7 and the sequence (1 2 3) are in parallel}

whereas the following are not semantically equivalent to T:

4. (1 5 7 1 2 3)

   {6 is missing}

5. (1 5 7 (1 3) 2 6)

   {2 is not commutative with 3}.

6. (1 5 7 ((1 2) 6 3))

   {3 is not independent from (1 2) and cannot be executed in parallel with it}.

2.4 Subsequences

Our proof of an optimally concurrent transform for sorting networks involves the analysis of a subsequence of a trace. A *subsequence* of a sequential trace $T = (C_1 C_2 \ldots Cn)$ is of the type: $(C_{j_1} C_{j_2} C_{j_3} \ldots C_{j_k})$ where $\forall_i\ 1 \leq j_i \leq n$ and $j_i < j_{i+1}$

Therefore, a list of any comparator modules taken from a trace is a subsequence if the original sequential order of those modules is preserved in that subsequence.

The definition of a linearly dependent sequence can now easily be applied to subsequences to provide the notion of a *linearly dependent subsequence.* Additionally, the *maximum linearly dependent subsequence* of a trace T is defined as a linearly dependent subsequence of T with the maximum length (i.e. the maximum number of dependent comparator modules). This length will be denoted by $l(T)$.

2.5 The Optimal Transformation

The objective of an optimally concurrent transform T'', which is semantically equivalent to the sequential trace T, is to provide the minimal (parallel) execution time of T such that:

$$EXECTIME\ (\ FLAG\ \ T''\ ) \ = \ MIN\{EXECTIME\ (\ FLAG\ \ T'\ )|\ T' \equiv_S T\}$$

The optimal transformation as proposed by Lengauer and Huang [6] consists of two functions: *RAVEL* and *RAVEL-TRANSFORM.*

The function *(RAVEL I T')* adds a comparator module I to a two-level trace T' as described below. Since T' is a two-level trace, T' is a sequential list consisting of parallel lists ($T' = (L_1 L_2 \ldots L_n)$). *RAVEL* places I into either:

1. The last parallel list L_n if I is commutative with all comparator modules in T' and I is not previously encountered in T'.

2. Some parallel list L_i such that I is dependent on some comparator module in parallel list L_{i+1}, I is commutative with all comparator modules in $L_j \ \ j \leq i$ and I is not previously encountered in T'.

3. A new parallel list at the left hand side of T' is created to hold I if I is dependent on some comparator module in L_1 or I is the first element raveled into T'.

4. I is encountered in T' and by idempotence I is not added to T'.

As an example, consider (RAVEL 7 ((1)(2)(3 6))). The new T' is: ((1)(2 7)(3 6)). The 7 is commutative with 1 and 2, but is dependent on 6 because 7 accesses array elements 7 and 6. Hence, 7 is placed in parallel with 2.

(RAVEL-TRANSFORM T) ravels the sequential trace T element after element by recursively calling *RAVEL*. The comparator modules from T are raveled into T' starting from the rightmost module in T and working leftward.

Using *RAVEL-TRANSFORM* on the trace $T = (\ 1\ \ 5\ \ 7\ \ 1\ \ 2\ \ 3\ \ 6\ )$ results in the concurrent trace $T' = (\ (\ 1\ )\ (\ 5\ \ 7\ \ 2\ )\ (\ 3\ 6\ )\ )$.

3. The Main Result

In this section, we show that *RAVEL-TRANSFORM* is "optimal" in the sense that it produces a parallel trace with minimal execution time, from a given sequential trace. Although a similar result was shown in [2, 6] using a mechanical theorem prover, we feel, however, that a mathematical proof provides more insight into the problem vs. a mechanical proof where certain key ideas are hidden in a black box, namely the theorem prover. To show the main result, a sequence of lemmas are required. First, we have the following easily shown lemma:

Lemma 3.1: *RAVEL-TRANSFORM* is a semantic preserving and parallelizing transform.
Proof. The proof follows directly from the definition of *RAVEL-TRANSFORM.*

□

In what follows, we show that for every multilevel list, there exists a semantically equivalent 2-level list which has exactly the same execution time. For ease of expression, (...) and ⟨...⟩ are used to denote sequential and parallel lists, respectively, through the rest of this paper (i.e., terms in (...) and ⟨...⟩ are executed in sequence and in parallel, respectively). Before presenting the detailed proof, we consider examples of converting a 3-level list into a semantically equivalent 2-level list with the same execution time. This, hopefully, will allow the reader to have a better understanding of the proof. Now, consider a 3-level sequential list $(\ \langle\ (a\ b)\ (c\ d)\ \rangle\ \langle\ (e\ f)\ (g\ h)\ \rangle\ )$, where $a, b, ..., h$ are comparator modules. In this list, one can see that

- $\langle\ (a\ b)\ (c\ d)\ \rangle$ and $\langle\ (e\ f)\ (g\ h)\ \rangle$ are executed in sequence,
- $(a\ b)$ and $(c\ d)$ (also $(e\ f)$ and $(g\ h)$) are executed in parallel,
- a and b (also c and d, e and f, g and h) are executed in sequence.

So, $\langle\ (a\ b)\ (c\ d)\ \rangle \equiv_S (\ \langle\ a\ c\ \rangle\ \langle\ b\ d\ \rangle\ )$ and $\langle\ (e\ f)\ (g\ h)\ \rangle \equiv_S (\ \langle\ e\ g\ \rangle\ \langle\ f\ h\ \rangle\ )$. As a result, $(\ \langle\ (a\ b)\ (c\ d)\ \rangle\ \langle\ (e\ f)\ (g\ h)\rangle\ ) \equiv_S (\ \langle\ a\ c\ \rangle\ \langle\ b\ d\ \rangle\ \langle\ e\ g\ \rangle\ \langle\ f\ h\ \rangle\ )$, i.e.,

$$\left(\left\langle \begin{matrix} (a\ b) \\ (c\ d) \end{matrix} \right\rangle \left\langle \begin{matrix} (e\ f) \\ (g\ h) \end{matrix} \right\rangle \right) \equiv_S \left(\left\langle \begin{matrix} a \\ c \end{matrix} \right\rangle \left\langle \begin{matrix} b \\ d \end{matrix} \right\rangle \left\langle \begin{matrix} e \\ g \end{matrix} \right\rangle \left\langle \begin{matrix} f \\ h \end{matrix} \right\rangle \right).$$

Now, consider a 3-level parallel list $\langle\ (\ \langle\ a\ b\ \rangle\ \langle\ c\ d\ \rangle\ )\ (\ \langle\ e\ f\ \rangle\ \langle\ g\ h\ \rangle\ )\ \rangle$. In this case, $\langle\ a\ b\ \rangle$ and $\langle\ c\ d\ \rangle$ (also $\langle\ e\ f\ \rangle$ and $\langle\ g\ h\ \rangle$) are executed sequentially, while a,b (also c,d etc.) are executed in parallel. It is then reasonably easy to see that $\langle\ (\ \langle\ a\ b\ \rangle\ \langle\ c\ d\ \rangle\ )\ (\ \langle\ e\ f\ \rangle\ \langle\ g\ h\ \rangle\ )\ \rangle \equiv_S$ $(\ \langle\ a\ b\ e\ f\ \rangle\ \langle\ c\ d\ g\ h\ \rangle\ )$, i.e.,

$$\left\langle \begin{pmatrix} \left\langle \begin{matrix} a \\ b \end{matrix} \right\rangle \left\langle \begin{matrix} c \\ d \end{matrix} \right\rangle \\ \left\langle \begin{matrix} e \\ f \end{matrix} \right\rangle \left\langle \begin{matrix} g \\ h \end{matrix} \right\rangle \end{pmatrix} \right\rangle \equiv_S \left(\left\langle \begin{matrix} a \\ b \\ e \\ f \end{matrix} \right\rangle \left\langle \begin{matrix} c \\ d \\ g \\ h \end{matrix} \right\rangle \right).$$

In general, we have:

Lemma 3.2: For every multilevel list, there exists a semantically equivalent 2-level list with the same execution time.

Proof. The proof is done by induction on the number of levels (n). Let L be an n-level list.

(Induction Base:) The case n=1 or 2 is trivial.

(Induction Hypothesis:) Assume that the assertion is true for k-level lists, where k $\geq$ 2. In other words, given an arbitrary k-level list L, there exists a 2-level list L$'$ such that L $\equiv_S$ L$'$ and EXECTIME(L)=EXECTIME(L$'$).

(Induction Step:) Consider the case when n=k+1.

Let $\overline{L}$ be a level (depth) k-1 sublist of L i.e., $\overline{L}$ consists of 3 alternations of sequential and parallel executions). In what follows, we show how to rewrite the 3-level list $\overline{L}$, using semantic preserving operations, as a 2-level list with the same execution time. Now, one of the following two cases is true:

- ($\overline{L}$ is sequential)

  Let $\overline{L}$=$(L_1 L_2 ... L_m)$, where $L_1, L_2, ..., L_m$ are executed sequentially and EXECTIME($\overline{L}$) = $\sum_{i=1}^{m} EXECTIME(L_i)$. Each L_i is a parallel list of the form $\langle L_{i,1} L_{i,2} ... L_{i,d_i} \rangle$, for some $d_i \geq 1$, and each $L_{i,j}$ is a sequential list of the form $(C_{i,j,1} ... C_{i,j,f_{i,j}})$, for some $f_{i,j} \geq 1$, where each $C_{i,j,l}$ is a comparator module which requires a unit execution time. Without loss of generality, we may further assume that for every i, j and j$'$, $f_{i,j} = f_{i,j'} = h_i$ (i.e., for every i, $L_{i,j}, 1 \leq j \leq d_i$, contains the same number of comparator modules). (Otherwise, an equivalent list satisfying this requirement can easily be constructed using idempotence operations.) Note that EXECTIME($\overline{L}$)= $\sum_{i=1}^{m} h_i$. At this moment, one should be able to observe that for every 1$\leq i \leq m$ and $1 \leq l \leq h_i$, $C_{i,1,l}, C_{i,2,l}, ..., C_{i,d_i,l}$ can be executed in parallel. Based on this observation, it is reasonably easy to see that the 2-level list $\overline{L}' =$

$(...\langle C_{i,1,1}C_{i,2,1}...C_{i,d_i,1}\rangle\langle C_{i,1,2}C_{i,2,2}...C_{i,d_i,2}\rangle...\langle C_{i,1,h_i}C_{i,2,h_i}...C_{i,d_i,h_i}\rangle...)$ is semantically equivalent to $\overline{L}$. Furthermore, EXECTIME($\overline{L}'$) = $\sum_{i=1}^{m} h_i$ (= EXECTIME($\overline{L}$)). Hence, there exists a k-level list which is semantically equivalent to L and both have the same execution time. The assertion then follows directly from the induction hypothesis.

- ($\overline{L}$ is parallel)
  Let $\overline{L}=\langle L_1L_2...L_m\rangle$, where $L_1, L_2, ..., L_m$ are executed in parallel and EXECTIME($\overline{L}$)= $Max_{1\leq i\leq m}$ {EXECTIME(L_i)}. Each L_i is a sequential list of the form $(L_{i,1}L_{i,2}...L_{i,d_i})$, for some $d_i \geq 1$, while each $L_{i,j}$ is a parallel list of the form $\langle C_{i,j,1}...C_{i,j,f_{i,j}}\rangle$, for some $f_{i,j} \geq 1$. Without loss of generality, we can assume that $d_i = d$, for all i. Note that EXECTIME($\overline{L}$)= $Max_{1\leq i\leq m}$ $\{d_i\} = d$. Let $L'_j = \langle C_{1,j,1}C_{1,j,2}...C_{1,j,f_{1,j}}...C_{i,j,1}C_{i,j,2}...C_{i,j,f_{i,j}}...C_{k,j,1}C_{k,j,2}...C_{k,j,f_{k,j}}\rangle$, $1 \leq j \leq d$. Then $\overline{L}' = (L'_1L'_2...L'_d)$ is semantically equivalent to $\overline{L}$. Furthermore, EXEC-TIME ($\overline{L}'$) = d (= EXECTIME ($\overline{L}$)). Hence, there exists a k-level list which is semantically equivalent to L with the same execution time. The assertion then follows directly from the induction hypothesis.

□

In what follows, we show that in an attempt to parallelize a sequential trace T, a maximum linearly dependent subsequence of T plays a crucial role. More precisely, the length ($l(T)$) of a maximum linearly dependent subsequence provides a lower bound for the parallel execution time under a semantic preserving transformation. To show this, first recall that a linearly dependent subsequence $C_1, C_2, ..., C_k$ of a sequence trace T is a subsequence in which $C_i \sim C_{i+1}$, 1≤ i < k. In other words, C_i and C_{i+1}, 1≤ i < k, can not commute with each other. Also recall that a semantically equivalent trace of T is obtained by applying a finite number of idempotence and/or commutative operations on T. As a consequence, the order $C_1, C_2, ..., C_k$ must be preserved in any semantically equivalent trace (of T) (otherwise, an invalid commutative operation involving C_i and C_{i+1} would have been performed). Therefore, we have:

Lemma 3.3: Let $C_1, C_2, ..., C_k$ be a linearly dependent subsequence of a sequential trace T. For every sequential trace T′, if T′ $\equiv_S$ T, then T′ must also contain $C_1, C_2, ..., C_k$ as a subsequence.

Lemma 3.4: Given an arbitrary sequential trace T, let L be a semantically equivalent multilevel list (of T). Then the (parallel) execution time of L is greater than or equal to $l(T)$.

Proof. According to Lemma 3.2, there exists a 2-level semantically equivalent list L′ of L with the same execution time. Let L′=$(L_1L_2...L_m)$, for some m, and let $L_i = \langle C_{i,1}C_{i,2}...C_{i,d_i}\rangle$, 1≤ i ≤m.

Then EXECTIME(L′)=m. Let $C_1, C_2, ..., C_k$ be a maximum linearly dependent subsequence of the sequential trace T. Clearly, $l(T)$=k. According to Lemma 3.3, any corresponding sequential trace of L′ must also contain $C_1, C_2, ..., C_k$. Now suppose k > m. According to the Pidgeon-hole principle, there must exist i, $1 \leq i < k$, such that C_i and C_{i+1} are in some L_t, for some $1 \leq t \leq m$. Hence, C_i and C_{i+1} are independent – a contradiction. This completes the proof of the lemma.

□

Lemma 3.5: Given a sequential trace T, *RAVEL-TRANSFORM* produces a 2-level list with execution time $l(T)$.

Proof. Let L=$(L_1 L_2 ... L_k)$ be the output of *RAVEL-TRANSFORM* on T. Clearly, EXECTIME(L)= k. According to the definition of *RAVEL-TRANSFORM*, there must exist $C_1, C_2, ..., C_k$ in $L_1, L_2, ..., L_k$, respectively, such that $C_1, C_2, ..., C_k$ are linearly dependent. Consequently, $l(T)$ (the length of the maximum linearly dependent subsequence) is no less than k. This together with the result of Lemma 3.4 yield the result that *RAVEL-TRANSFORM* produces a list with execution time $l(T)$.

□

The following theorem follows immediately from Lemmas 3.4 and 3.5:

Theorem 3.1: Given an arbitrary sequential trace T, the minimum (parallel) execution time of T is $l(T)$.

Corollary 3.1: *RAVEL-TRANSFORM* is an optimal parallel transform.

Acknowledgment: We would like to thank Anil Sharma for many helpful discussions concerning this paper and the referees for their thoughtful suggestions and comments.

References

[1] R.S. Boyer and J.S. Moore, *A Computational Logic*, Academic Press, 1979.

[2] C.-H. Huang and C. Lengauer, The automated proof of a trace transformation for a bitonic sort, *Theoretical Computer Science*, 46, (1986), pp. 261-284.

[3] D.E. Knuth, *The Art of Computer Programming, Vol. 3, Sorting and Searching*, Addison-Wesley, Reading, MA,(1973).

[4] C. Lengauer, A methodology for programming with concurrency: The formalism, *Sci. of Comput. Programm.*, 2, (1), (1982), pp. 19-52.

[5] C. Lengauer and E.C.R. Hehner, A methodology for programming with concurrency: An informal presentation, *Sci. of Comput. Programm.*, 2, (1), (1982), pp. 1-18.

[6] C.Lengauer and C.-H. Huang, A mechanically certified theorem about optimal concurrency of sorting networks, *Proc. 13th Ann. ACM Symp. on Principles of Programming Languages*, (1986), pp. 307-317.

Parallel Algorithms for Approximate Edge Colouring of Simple Graphs*

O.A. Ogunyode
Rhea Computer Systems, Inc., 5250 W. Century Blvd. #428
Los Angeles, CA 90045, USA.

ABSTRACT

Two parallel algorithms for edge-colouring simple graphs are presented. One takes $O(m\log n)$ time using a polynomial number of processors on an SIMD parallel computer which allows read conflicts but no write conflicts. The second algorithm uses the first in a divide-and-conquer setting and takes $O(n\log^2 n)$ time at the cost of a factor of n extra processors on the same model of computation. How to obtain improved time bounds from these algorithms for some special types of graph is also discussed.

Either algorithm uses no more than Ψ_e+1 colours where Ψ_e is the edge-chromatic number of the graph being coloured. Moreover the expected performance of each of the algorithms is optimal.

Keywords: edge-colouring, graphs, algorithm: approximation, probabilistic, parallel, SIMD computer

1. Introduction

A number of scheduling problems that arise in applications can be formulated in terms of colouring the vertices or edges of a graph. Finding a vertex colouring which uses a minimum number of colours is *NP*-hard. This suggests that the earlier result due to Vizing is probably the best achievable in the serial realm [14]. In this paper we present two parallel approximation algorithms for edge-colouring simple graphs on a PRAM which allows simultaneous reads but no simultaneous writes. We also discuss some results derived from these

*This work was done while a research student at Warwick University, Coventry, UK.

algorithms for some special types of graph.

By G we denote a simple graph with n vertices, m edges and whose maximum vertex degree is Δ. The edge-chromatic number Ψ_e of G is the minimum number of colours required for a proper edge-colouring of G. For standard graph theoretic terminology see Gibbons [6].

The motivation for the work discussed in this paper is the apparent lack of algorithms for solving *NP*-complete problems in parallel polynomial-time using polynomial number of processors. Essentially, we show that colouring an edge in a partially $(\Delta+1)$-coloured simple graph is in *NC*. In Section 2 we present a *polylog*-time parallelisation of a procedure for colouring an edge using polynomial number of processors. Our first algorithm uses this to colour the edges of a given graph in a sequential manner. In Section 3 we present our second algorithm which uses the first as a subprocess in a divide-and-conquer setting and in effect has an improved time bound.

Throughout this paper we assume without loss of generality that a graph has vertices $V=1,\ldots,n$, the set of colours used is $C=1,\ldots,\Delta+1$, and all logarithms are to base two unless otherwise stated. Also without loss of valuable information we write "$O(t)$ time using p processors" instead of "$O(t)$ time using $O(p)$ processors".

2. An $O(m\log n)$ Parallel Algorithm

Our $O(m\log n)$ parallel algorithm, PEDGE-COLOUR, for $(\Delta+1)$-edge-colouring uses an $O(\log n)$ parallel version of a *linear* serial implementation of the procedure used in the proof of Vizing's theorem [14] to assign an appropriate colour to each edge in turn. The parallel version, PEDGECOLOUR, is outlined in Figure 1.

In the serial implementation, stacks are used to ensure constant time determination and retrieval of a colour absent at a given vertex [11]. This together with further efficiency owing to the use of some special data structures reduce to $O(n)$, the complexity of the mechanism for constructing edge- and colour-sequences (the most expensive operation in the $O(m^2)$ direct implementation [11]). This appears to be the lowest bound for this operation even for parallel computation because determining a new element in an edge-sequence is dependent on information from the immediately previous one. So one may be tempted to think that it is an inherently sequential operation. Another operation which appears intrinsically sequential is the construction of the Kempe subgraphs (paths) $H_{v_j}(c_0,c_j)$ and $H_{v_j}(c_0,c_j)$

```
process PEDGECOLOUR (v0,v1)ξ
begin
if a common colour is absent at both v0 and v1
then colour (v0,v1)ξ with such a colour
else begin
    EDGESEQ(v0,v1)
    if TC[v1]='no edge coloured LASTC[v1]'
    then for all v in ES[v1] pardo
        colour (v0,v) with CM[v]
      odrap
    if TC[v1]='LASTC[v1] colours an edge (v0,vk[v1]) already in
      sequence'
    then begin {*recolour (v0,vi),1≤i<k with CM[vi]*}
      for all v in ES[v1]:RANK[v]<RANK[vk[v1]] pardo
        colour (v0,v) with CM[v]
      odrap
      uncolour (v0,vk[v1])
      KEMPSUB(CM[v0],LASTC[v1])
      if LASTVPc0[vk[v1]]≠v0{*v0 not on Hvk(c0,c1)*}
      then begin
            if LASTVPc0[vk[v1]]≠vk[v1]{*c0 not absent on vk*}
            then FLIP(vk[v1]){*Interchange c0 and cj on
              Hvk(c0,cj)*}
            colour (v0,vk[v1]) with CM[v0]
            end
      else begin {*recolour (v0,vi),k≤i<j with CM[vi]*}
            for all v in ES[v1]:RANK[vk[v1]]≤RANK[LASTV[v1]]
              pardo
                colour (v0,v) with CM[v]
            odrap
            if LASTVPc0[LASTV[v1]]≠LASTV[v1]{*c0 not absent on
              vj*}
            then FLIP(LASTV[v1]){*Interchange c0 and cj on
              Hvj(c0,cj)*}
            colour (v0,LASTV[v1]) with CM[v0]
            end
        end
    end
end {*of process*}
```

Figure 1: An Outline of the Parallel Version of EDGECOLOUR

induced by edges coloured c_0 or c_j. However, we prove this otherwise by designing *polylog* parallel implementations of these operations using the standard *doubling technique*.

While the time bound for our best serial implementations of Vizing's procedure is linear, we achieve a *polylog* parallel version, PEDGECOLOUR, on an SIMD machine with $\frac{n^2}{\log n}$ processors. Other operations that require parallelisation include: finding a colour commonly absent on two vertices of a partially coloured graph; recolouring the edges (by shifting) in a specified sublist of an edge-sequence; and interchanging of colours c_0 and c_j on either $H_{v_j}(c_0,c_j)$ or $H_{v_k}(c_0,c_j)$.

First, we define a number of data structures that, together with the colour stacks, contribute to the achievement of the *polylog* implementation of EDGECOLOUR. We assume these data structures are declared globally in the shared memory.

Arrays (i)A *C*olour-*V*ertex Matrix, *CVM*: A$(\Delta+1)\times n$ matrix used as a workspace to reflect the partial colouring produced so far. Each element in the matrix has two components. The first component (*ind* in the processes) is a Boolean field to indicate whether a given colour occurs on a specified vertex. The second component is an integer field to contain the vertex sharing a given colour with a specified vertex. If a colour is absent at a vertex, we store a dummy vertex (0) in this location. Each row is therefore a list of vertices at which a colour (the row index) is present while each column is a list of indicators to colours present at a vertex (the column index) and the vertices with which the indicated colours are shared. We shall show in Section 2.3.3 how $H_{v_k}(c_0,c_j)$ and $H_{v_j}(c_0,c_j)$ can both be traced from *CVM* and the terminal vertex compared with v_0 in $O(\log n)$ parallel time. In all processes, the phrase "colour (i,j) with c" means: begin $CVM[c,i].ind \leftarrow$ **true**; $CVM[c,i].vertex \leftarrow j$; $CVM[c,j].ind \leftarrow$ **true**; $CVM[c,j].vertex \leftarrow i$; update stacks by POPping and PUSHing; **end**. (ii) A *V*ertex-*V*ertex *M*atrix, *VVM*: An $n\times n$ Boolean matrix for resolving write conflicts likely in the construction of an edge sequence. The entries in the matrix are all reset to *zero* prior to edge sequence construction. The use of this structure will become clear later.

Lists (i) *E*dge *S*equence, *ES*: A list for each vertex v to contain vertices v_i for edges (v_0,v_i) on the sequence starting from v. (ii) *P*ath starting with c_0,Pc_0: A list for each vertex v to contain vertices v_i which are on the path (or subpath) or cycle starting with c_0 from v in $H(c_0,c_j)$. (iii) *P*ath starting with c_j,Pc_j: Similarly defined as Pc_0.

We use the symbols {} and // in the illustrated processes to represent a list and the operation *concatenate* respectively.

Vectors (i) *E*dge *C*oloured with, *EC*: A vector of neighbours of v_0 in a partially coloured graph indexed by colours assigned to the edges connecting them to v_0. The elements of this vector are determined prior to the edge sequence construction. Given a colour c, the edge (v_0,v) assigned c can be determined in constant time from this vector. Also one can decide in constant time whether there is an edge incident to v_0 that is assigned c. (ii) *Colour Missing on*, *CM*: A vector of colours indexed by the neighbours of v_0 in G on which they are missing. That is for each (v_0, v) in G, $CM[v]$ contains the top element in the stack for v. (iii) *Termination Condition*, *TC*: A vector of termination conditions each for the edge sequence starting from the indexing vertex.

The functions of all the other vectors used in the implementation can be easily understood from the context in which they are used.

2.1. Finding a Commonly Missing Colour

The first major operation in the process PEDGECOLOUR is finding (if it exists) a colour commonly absent at v_0 and v_1, the end points of the edge to be coloured. Such a colour can be obtained from *CVM* in $O(\log\Delta+1)$ parallel time using $\Delta+1$ processors. Assign one processor to each row of *CVM* to perform the Boolean operation, OR, on the entries corresponding to vertices v_0 and v_1, and enter the result in a linear list M. Thus $M[c]$ contains the result of the Boolean operation for colour c, $1 \leq c \leq \Delta+1$. Obviously this operation takes constant time. Next generate the sublist of colours with entries "false" in M using the doubling technique (see 11 for details). Choose the first colour in this sublist.

2.2. Construction of Edge Sequence

Unlike in the serial case, there is no need for constructing a colour sequence as the colours absent on the vertices in the required edge sequence can be readily obtained from *CM* in constant time. Therefore ranking of elements in an edge sequence is essential only if a two-part shifting of colours is anticipated. This is the case in the event that the second termination condition is satisfied (line 7, Figure 1). An outline of a process, EDGESEQ, for constructing an edge sequence can be found in Figure 3. Here we present a theory underlying the strategy used in its design.

Consider the following constant time operations: **for all** c, $1 \leq c \leq \Delta+1$ assign (in parallel) $CVM[c, v_0].vertex$ to $EC[c]$; and **for all** neighbours v of v_0 in G assign (in parallel) $EC[CM[v]]$ to $NEXTV[v]$. The resulting *NEXTV* gives a successor for each edge (v_0, v) of G and thus contains an edge sequence that start from each such edge. We require the edge sequence starting from $(v_0, v\ )$ the topology of which must be determined by tracing it out of *NEXTV*. We show how this can be done later. First we introduce an auxiliary graph henceforth referred to as a *C*olour *I*nduced *D*igraph (CID) whose properties provide a means of clarifying the strategy used for determining the topology of the required edge sequence.

A CID $G_1=(V_1,A_1)$ can be used to model the overall structure in *NEXTV*. Let each (v_0,v_i) in G be a vertex of G_1, and let there be an arc from (v_0,v_i) to (v_0,v_l) if $NEXTV[v_i]=v_l$. See Figure 2 for an illustration. Define a non-isolated vertex in a CID as *source* if the directed subpath or subloop starting from it is whole, otherwise define it as *target*. (A loop in this context means a path containing a cycle.) Also define a target vertex as *terminal* if it ends some path(s) in G . The relevant properties of a CID are summed up as follows.

Fact1: *The out-degree of every terminal vertex in a CID is zero while that of every non-isolated and non-terminal vertex is one.*

Proof: Follows from the standard definition of proper edge colouring. ■

Fact2: *A connected component in a CID is either an isolated vertex, a union of directed paths, a union of directed loops, or a circuit.*

Proof: Isolated vertices are likely in a CID because it is possible to have edges (v_0,v_i) with same colours missing on both endpoints. The rest of the **Fact** follows from **Fact1**. ■

Fact3: *The in-degree of every source vertex in a CID is zero while that of every target vertex is at least one.*

Proof: That the in-degree of a source vertex is *zero* in G_1 follows from definition. The in-degree of a target vertex is at least *one* because one or more neighbours of v_0 may have the same colour missing on them. ■

Fact4: *Given a loop L in a CID, there is only one vertex with exactly two incoming arcs in L. Each of the rest has at most one.*

Proof: Follows from the definition of a directed loop. ■

We are interested in the topology of the component induced by all the vertices that can be reached from (v_0,v_1) by following the directions of arrows on G_1. Tracing this component requires n processors to simultaneously double the pointers of all the vertices of G_1 $\lceil \log(\Delta+1) \rceil$ times. There are two cases:

(i) *The component is a directed path*. This corresponds to the termination situation when no edge is assigned the colour absent at the last vertex v_j.

(ii) *The component is a directed loop*. This corresponds to the

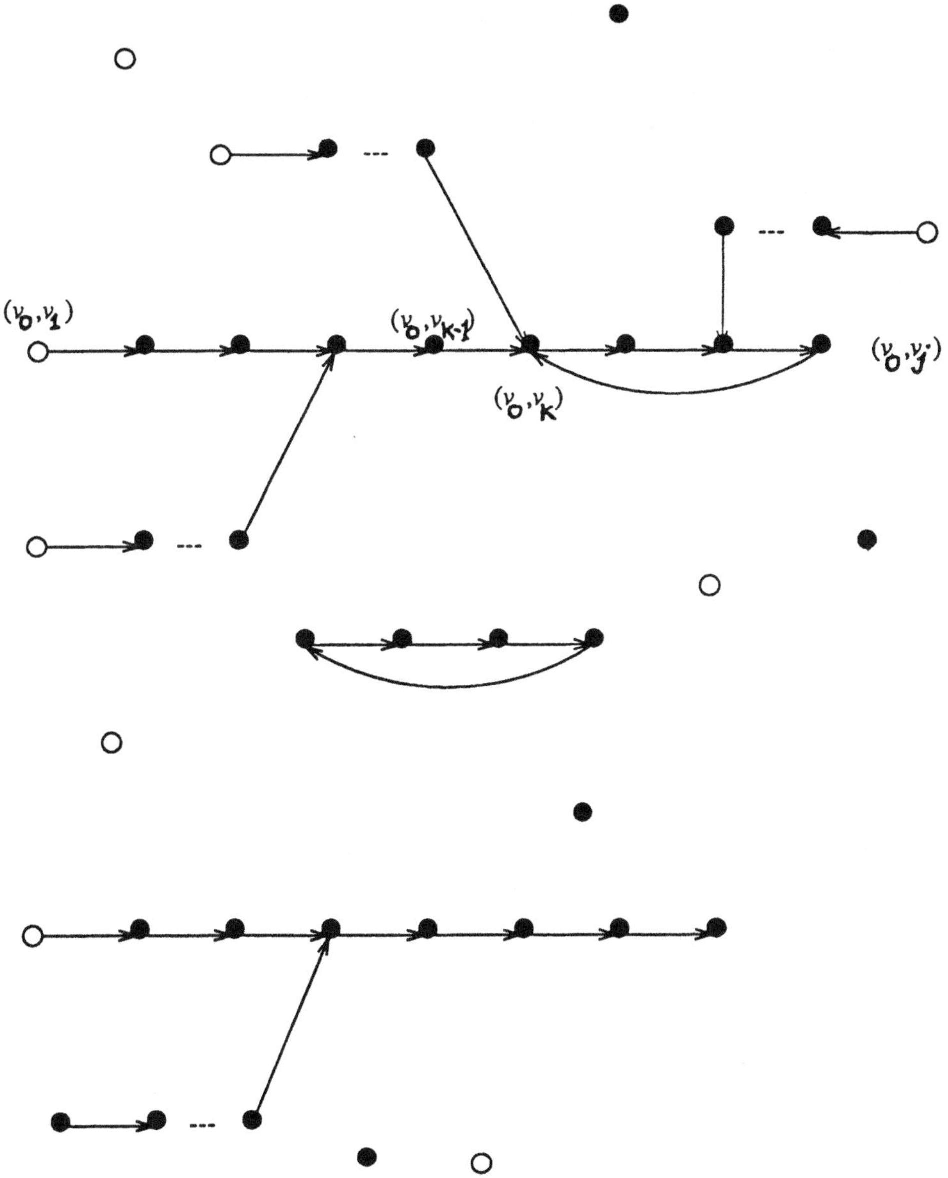

● corresponds to a coloured edge

○ corresponds to an uncoloured edge

Figure 2: The Structure of a Colour Induced Digraph

termination event when an edge appears previously in the edge sequence.

(Note that (v_0,v_1) cannot belong to a circuit by **Fact3.**) Determining which of the two termination conditions is satisfied is straight forward. What is more interesting is obtaining the parameters essential for later processing involving shifting of colours and construction of Kempe subgraph whenever condition (ii) is satisfied. We need to determine the last edge (v_0,v_j) in the sequence, the missing colour c_j associated with this edge, and the edge (v_0,v_k) that previously appears in the sequence and is assigned colour $c_j=c_{k-1}$.

Suppose the labelled loop in Figure 2 is the edge sequence traced from (v_0,v_1) after doubling pointers logarithmic times. It is easy to see that the last vertex pointed to could be any one of those in the loop's circuit, and its distance from (v_0,v_1) is 2^r for some r>0. Note that the loop's circuit might be 'traversed' more than once while doubling pointers. So the distance takes into account these possible several circuit 'traversals'. A favourable situation is when both the distance of (v_0,v_k) to (v_0,v_1) and the 'circumference' of the circuit are powers of two. In other words when both (v_0,v_k) and (v_0,v_1) point to (v_0,v_k) after the pointer-doubling operations. Determining v_k is relatively manifest and straightforward in this case.

In several pathological cases however, (v_0,v_1) does not point to (v_0,v_k), so we need some invariant property of a traced loop which renders this task feasible. We find this in **Fact4.** (Fortunately there is no loss of generality if we ignore the possibility of several 'traversals' in our treatment of such a situation.) Corresponding to (v_0,v_k) is the unique vertex with in-degree *two* on (v_0,v_1)'s loop. This vertex can be identified as follows. Suppose a location is reserved for each vertex for computing its in-degree in the loop. Instruct each vertex in the loop to add a 1 to the in-degree location for its immediate successor. Unfortunately a write conflict occurs here. We prevent this conflict by using the data structure *VVM* and $\frac{n^2}{\log n}$ processors and still remain within our $O(\log n)$ time bound. Each vertex v_i enters a 1 into $VVM[v_s,v_i]$ if v_s is its successor in the loop. Next each loop vertex computes in $O(\log n)$ time the sum of its row entries in *VVM* using $\frac{n}{\log n}$ processors, and enters the result into its in-degree location. Clearly the vertex with in-degree *two* can then be located in constant time from *VVM*. Once we have located (v_0,v_k), we can identify its two predecessors in the loop as follows.

Disconnect the circuit from the rest of the loop and turn the circuit into a path by making the two predecessors of (v_0,v_k) point to themselves. Mark these two predecessors. Then the last vertex (v_0,v_j) can be found in $O(\log n)$ time again using pointer doubling. After $\log n$ steps, (v_0,v_1) will be pointing to (v_0,v_{k-1}) the predecessor of (v_0,v_k) not in the circuit. Therefore the only marked vertex which is currently not the successor of (v_0,v_1) is the required one. Clearly its associated missing colour can be found in constant time from CVM.

Our detailed implementation of *polylog* edge sequence construction has two phases. One phase, illustrated in Figure 3, is the main process which performs the actual tracing of the required sequence. The other phase, shown in Figure 4 as TIDYUP, is a subprocess to tidy up an edge sequence with a cycle by ranking elements, and determining all the three parameters for later processing. Removal of possible duplicate edges is accomplished automatically while determining the parameters.

The process TIDYUP is essentially made up of a parallel do loop containing instructions to be executed for all vertices in $ES[v_1]$. It is easy to verify that the number of such vertices is at most $2^{\lceil \log(\Delta+1) \rceil}-1=O(2\Delta+1)$. Clearly TIDYUP requires $O(\log\Delta)$ time using $(\Delta+1)\frac{n}{\log n}$ processors. Therefore EDGESEQ requires $O(\log n)$ time using $\frac{n^2}{\log n}$ processors.

2.3. Construction of Kempe Paths $H_{v_k}(c_0,c_j)$ and $H_{v_j}(c_0,c_j)$

A straightforward approach to solving this problem is to apply existing algorithms of Tsin and Chin in [13]. Instruct each edge in G to signal in a duplicate data structure for G it if is assigned colour c_0 or c_j. After this operation which requires constant time using m processors, the duplicate data structure contains a Kempe subgraph $H(c_0,c_j)$. To find the required paths $H_{v_k}(c_0,c_j)$ and $H_{v_j}(c_0,c_j)$ do the following. Find a spanning forest of the Kempe subgraph using the $O(\log^2 n)$-time-$\frac{n^2}{\log n}$-processor algorithm in [13]. Clearly v_k, v_j, and v_0 are all of degree $\le$ *one* in the Kempe subgraph and hence could be made to be leaf vertices in the spanning forest by not using them as roots. Therefore determine which of v_k and v_j does not lie on the same path as v_0 using the $O(\log^2 n)$-time-$\frac{n^2}{\log n}$-processor lowest common ancestor algorithm in [13]. Then obtain the path

```
     process EDGESEQ (v0,v1)
     begin
     [*Initialise all structures*]
1.   for all v in G pardo
2.     CM[v]←POP(STACK[v])
3.     NEXTCM[v]←CM[v]
4.     TC[v]←'no termination condition met'
5.     ES[v]←{v}
6.     NEXTV[v]←LASTV[v]←v
7.     vk[v]←0
8.     LASTC[v]←CM[v]
     odrap
9.   for all c : 1≤c≤Δ+1 pardo
10.    EC[c]←0
11.    if CVM[c,v0].ind
12.    then EC[c]←CVM[c,v0].vertex
     odrap
     {*Trace the component for (v0,v1) into ES[v1]*}
13.  repeat ⌈log(Δ+1)⌉ times
     begin
14.  for all v in G pardo
15.    if TC[v]='no termination condition met'
16.    then if EC[NEXTCM[v]]=0
17.         then TC[v]←'no edge coloured LASTC[v]'
18.         else if EC[NEXTCM[v]]=v{*v in a circuit of "circumference"
              2^k for some k*}
                then begin
19.                   vk[v]←v
20.                   TC[v]←'LASTC[v] colours an edge (v ,vk[v]) already
                        in sequence'
                      end
                else begin
21.                   NEXTV[v]←EC[NEXTCM[v]]
22.                   ES[v]←ES[v]//ES[NEXTV[v]]
23.                   LASTV[v]←LASTV[NEXTV[v]]
24.                   LASTC[v]←LASTC[NEXTV[v]]
25.                   vk[v]←vk[NEXTV[v]]
26.                   TC[v]←TC[NEXTV[v]]
27.                   NEXTCM[v]←NEXTCM[NEXTV[v]]
                      end
     odrap
     end  *of repeat loop*
28.  if TC[v1]≠'no edge coloured LASTC[v1]
29.  then TIDYUP {*Remove duplicate edges from ES[v1] and rank its
       elements*}
     end {*of process*}.
```

Figure 3: The Process for Constructing Edge Sequence

containing v_k or v_j, whichever satisfies the test above, by using the $O(\log n)$-time-$\frac{n^2}{\log n}$-processor fundamental cycle algorithm in [13]. For each v such that (v_k,v) or (v_j,v) is not in $H(c_0,c_j)$ use dummy edges.

This approach clearly renders the construction of Kempe paths the most expensive operation in our algorithm since it contributes an extra factor of $\log n$ to the complexity obtained so far. To remain

```
process TIDYUP
begin
{*Determine v_k[v_1]*}
for all v in ES[v_1] pardo
 NEXTV[v]←EC[CM[v]]
 VVM[NEXTV[v],v]←1
 for all t in ES[v_1] pardo
    VVM[v,t]+VVM[v,v_0]→VVM[v,v_0]
 odrap
 if VVM[v,v_0]>1{*v has in-degree two in ES[v_1]*}
 then v→v_k[v_1]
 {*Determine the last edge LASTV[v_1] on ES[v_1],*}
 {*and its associated missing colour, LASTC[v_1]*}
 if NEXTV[v]=v_k[v_1]
 then begin
    NEXTV[v]←v
    mark v
    end
 while NEXTV[v_1] not marked do
    NEXTV[v]←NEXTV[NEXTV[v]]
 od
 if (v≠NEXTV[v_1]) and (v marked)
 then begin
    v→LASTV[v_1]
    CM[v]→LASTC[v_1]
    end
 {*Rank the elements of ES[v_1]*}
 if v=LASTV[v_1]
 then DIST[v]←0
 else begin
    NEXTV[v]←EC[CM[v]]
    DIST[v]←1
    end
 while NEXTV[v_1]≠LASTV[v_1] do
    DIST[v]←DIST[v]+DIST[NEXTV[v]]
    NEXTV[v]←NEXTV[NEXTV[v]]
 od
 RANK[v]←DIST[v_1]+1-DIST[v]
odrap
TC[v_1]←'LASTC[v_1] colours an edge (v_0,v_k[v_1]) already in sequence'
end {*of process*}.
```

Figure 4: The Process for Tidying up an Edge Sequence that Contains a Loop

within our target $O(m\log n)$-time bound requires a different approach.

A faster and much simpler way is to use a doubling mechanism. Here each vertex in the Kempe subgraph maintains in a doubling version, two lists of vertices (paths). One list, Pc_0, is the path starting from the particular vertex with c_0 if any, and the other list, Pc_j, is the path starting with c_j. To link a vertex's list to a successor's list, the last edge colour in the current list is used for determining which of two lists found it should be linked to. The process stops after log$n$ steps or when v_k and v_j stop. See Figure 5 for KEMPSUB, the process for constructing the Kempe paths.

After $O(\log n)$ steps, tracing of the required paths $Pc_0[v_k[v_1]]$ and $Pc_0[LASTV[v_1]]$ is completed by linking them with their respective start vertices v_k and $LASTV[v_1]$. Finally, the last vertex of each of the paths is determined by using a subprocess TVP which is outlined in Figure 6.

Clearly KEMPSUB takes $O(\log n)$ time using n processors.

2.4. Edge Recolourings

The two operations which remain to be parallelised are concerned with consistent recolouring of edges. One involves shifting colours in a specified sublist of an edge sequence while the other, interchanging of colours on a Kempe path.

Colour shifting can be done in constant time using Δ processors. Each vertex in the specified sublist assigns its missing colour to the edge connecting it with v_0 and updates its STACK accordingly. If we allow concurrent writes then it is easy to see that colour interchange can also be done in constant time using n processors. However our determination to remain with the CREW model renders this operation less trivial.

The trick we use here is to partition the vertices in the path into two sublists each with non-adjacent elements. Each vertex in one sublist then changes the colour of its incident c_0-edge to c_j, and each vertex in the other sublist changes the colour of its incident c_j-edge to c_0.

Since we have no means of identifying the immediate successor of each vertex in a Kempe path, we need an invariant property that can be used to partition its members into two groups. One such property which we use is derived from the following observation.

Fact5: *If the last vertex, $LASTVPc_0$, of a Kempe path is known and we double pointers $O(\log n)$ times, then the set of vertices whose Pc_0 end with $LASTVPc_0$ is a sublist of non-adjacent vertices.*

Proof: Suppose the assertion is not true. Then there exist two vertices x and y such that (x,y) is assigned colour c_0 in the Kempe path, and both $Pc_0[x]$ and $Pc_0[y]$ end with $LASTVPc_0$. Clearly this is impossible. ■

Using n processors, the partition operation takes $O(\log n)$ time. Colour interchange is done by the process FLIP depicted in Figure 7. Since its most expensive operation is the partition operation, FLIP

```
     process KEMPSUB (c0,cj)
     begin
1.   for all v in G pardo {*Initialise all structures*}
2.   LASTVPc0[v]←0
3.   NEXTCPc0[v]←CM[v0]
4.   NEXTCPcj[v]←LASTC[v1]
5.   NEXTVPc0[v]←CVM[CM[v0],v].vertex
6.   NEXTVPcj[v]←CVM[LASTC[v1],v].vertex
7.   Pc0←{NEXTVPc0[v]}
8.   Pcj←{NEXTVPcj[v]}
   odrap
9. repeat⌈logn⌉ times{*Construct the subgraph*}
   begin
10.for all v in G pardo
11.  ifNEXTVPc0[v]≠0
12.  then if NEXTCPc0[v]=CM[v0]
          then begin
13.                Pc0[v]←Pc0[v]//Pcj[NEXTVPc0[v]]
14.                NEXTCPc0[v]←NEXTCPcj[NEXTVPc0[v]]
15.                NEXTVPc0[v]←NEXTVPcj[NEXTVPc0[v]]
                   end
          else begin
16.                Pc0[v]←Pc0[v]//Pc0[NEXTVPc0[v]]
17.                NEXTCPc0[v]←NEXTCPc0[NEXTVPc0[v]]
18.                NEXTVPc0[v]←NEXTVPc0[NEXTVPc0[v]]
                   end
19.  if NEXTVPcj[v]≠0
20.  then if NEXTCPcj[v]=CM[v0]
          then begin
21.                Pcj[v]←Pcj[v]//Pcj[NEXTVPcj[v]]
22.                NEXTCPcj[v]←NEXTCPcj[NEXTVPcj[v]]
23.                NEXTVPcj[v]←NEXTVPcj[NEXTVPcj[v]]
                   end
          else begin
24.                Pcj[v]←Pcj[v]//Pc0[NEXTVPcj[v]]
25.                NEXTCPcj[v]←NEXTCPc0[NEXTVPcj[v]]
26.                NEXTVPcj[v]←NEXTVPc0[NEXTVPcj[v]]
                   end
   odrap
   end {*of repeat loop*}
27.Pc0[vk[v1]]←{vk[v1]}//Pc0[vk[v1]]
28.Pc0[LASTV[v1]]←{LASTV[v1]}//Pc0[LASTV[v1]]
29.TVP(vk[v1]) {*Find last vertex on Pc0[vk[v1]]*}
30.TVP(LASTV[v1]) {*Find last vertex on Pc0[LASTV[v1]]*}
   end {*of process*}.
```

Figure 5: The Process for Constructing Kempe Subgraphs $H_{v_k}(c_0,c_j)$ and $H_{v_j}(c_0,c_j)$

also takes (log$n$) time using n processors.

2.5. Remarks

In this section we have presented an algorithm for edge-

```
process TVP (V)
begin
for all v in Pc0[V] pardo
  if v≠0
  then if not CVM[CM[v0],v].ind
     then v→LASTVPc0[V]
  if (v≠0) and (v≠V)
  then if not CVM[LASTC[v1],v].ind
     then v→LASTVPc0[V]
odrap
end {*of process*}.
```

Figure 6: Process for Finding the Last Vertex on a Kempe Path

colouring a simple graph with n vertices and m edges in $O(m\log n)$ time on an SIMD computer with $\frac{n^2}{\log n}$ processors which allows concurrent reads but no concurrent writes. Therefore an optimal speedup from $O(mn^2)$ to $O(m\log n)$ is achieved for the direct implementation of the edge-colouring algorithm [11] at a cost of $\frac{n^2}{\log n}$ processors.

We sum up the results of this section by the following theorem.

Theorem1: *An edge in a graph G which is partially* $(\Delta+1)$*-coloured can be assigned one of the available colours in* $O(\log n)$ *time using* $\frac{n^2}{\log n}$ *processors on an SIMD computer that allows concurrent reads but no concurrent writes.* ■

Moreover it can be easily verified that if one uses PEDGECOLOUR appropriately as a subprocess in the algorithm based on complete colouring in [11] and introduce parallelism as necessary, then one will obtain a new parallel algorithm which can edge-colour a simple graph in $O(K(n)n\log n)$ time using $\frac{n^2}{\log n}$ processors. This parallel version is faster than PEDGE-COLOUR for the class of graphs that satisfy $n-(\Delta+1)=K(n)=K$ a fixed constant, or $K(n)=o(n^{\varepsilon})$ for every $\varepsilon>0$. A direct result of this is that graphs with spanning stars can be $(\Delta+1)$-edge-coloured in constant time on a CREW P-RAM using m processors.

3. An $O(n\log^2 n)$ Parallel Algorithm

We present our second algorithm which requires $O(n\log^2 n)$ time on a CREW SIMD computer with $\frac{n^2}{\log n}$ processors. The divide-and-conquer setting used is similar to that used by Gabow and Kariv in [5] to

```
      process FLIP (V)
      begin
1.    for all v in Pc₀[V] pardo
2.    if v≠0
      then begin
3.        NEXTCPc₀[v]←CM[v₀]
4.        NEXTCPcⱼ[v]←LASTC[v₁]
5.        if CVM[CM[v₀],v].ind
6.        then NEXTVPc₀[v]←CVM[CM[v₀],v].vertex
7.        else NEXTVPc₀[v]←v
8.        if CVM[LASTC[v₁],v].ind
9.        then NEXTVPcⱼ[v]←CVM[LASTC[v₁],v].vertex
10.       else NEXTVPcⱼ[v]←v
          end
11.   repeat ⌈logn⌉ times
      begin {*Partition path to two sublists of non adjacent vertices*}
12.   if v≠0
      then begin
13.       if (NEXTVPc₀[v]≠V) and (NEXTVPc₀[v]≠LASTVPc₀[V])
14.       then if NEXTCPc₀[v]=CM[v₀]
              then begin
15.               NEXTCPc₀[v]←NEXTCPcⱼ[NEXTVPc₀[v]]
16.               NEXTVPc₀[v]←NEXTVPcⱼ[NEXTVPc₀[v]]
                  end
              else begin
17.               NEXTCPc₀[v]←NEXTCPc₀[NEXTVPc₀[v]]
18.               NEXTVPc₀[v]←NEXTVPc₀[NEXTVPc₀[v]]
                  end
19.       if (NEXTVPcⱼ[v]≠V) and (NEXTVPcⱼ[v]≠LASTVPc₀[V])
20.       then if NEXTCPcⱼ[v]=CM[v₀]
              then begin
21.               NEXTCPcⱼ[v]←NEXTCPcⱼ[NEXTVPcⱼ[v]]
22.               NEXTVPcⱼ[v]←NEXTVPcⱼ[NEXTVPcⱼ[v]]
                  end
              else begin
23.               NEXTCPcⱼ[v]←NEXTCPc₀[NEXTVPcⱼ[v]]
24.               NEXTVPcⱼ[v]←NEXTVPc₀[NEXTVPcⱼ[v]]
                  end
          end
      end {*of repeat loop*}
25.   if (v≠0) and (v≠LASTVPc₀[V])
      then begin {*Interchange colours*}
26.       if NEXTVPc₀[v]=LASTVPc₀[V]
27.       then NEXTVPc₀[v]←CVM[CM[v₀],v].vertex
28.       else NEXTVPc₀[v]←CVM[LASTC[v₁],v].vertex
29.       if NEXTVPc₀[v]=LASTVPc₀[V]
30.       then colour (v,NEXTVPc₀[v]) with LASTC[v₁]
31.       else colour (v,NEXTVPc₀[v]) with  CM[v₀]
          end
      odrap
      end {*of process*}.
```

Figure 7: The Process for Interchanging Colours on a Kempe Path

obtain an efficient serial algorithm for edge colouring bipartite graphs. An NC equivalent of their algorithm has been presented by Lev et al in [10].

```
process PEULER-COLOUR (Gξ)
begin
Δ←degree of G
if Δ=1
then assign the same new colour to edges of G
else begin
     find an Euler partition of G
     use the Euler partition to divide G into two edge disjoint
       graphs G1 and G2
     for i:=1,2 pardo
        PEULER-COLOUR (Gi) using disjoint sets of colours
     odrap
     {*Reduce colours used to Δ+1 by recolouring edges*}
     if G has more than Δ+1 colours
     then begin
          if G has Δ+2 colours
          then let α1 be the colour with fewest edges
             in G and Eα the set of such edges
          else let α1 and α2 be the colours with fewest and
            second fewest edges in G and Eα the set of such edges
          for each e in Eα do
            PEDGECOLOUR (e)
          od
          end
     end
end {*of process*}.
```

Figure 8: An Outline of the Parallel Divide and Conquer Algorithm for Edge Colouring

Essentially our algorithm, PEULER-COLOUR, divides a given graph G of degree Δ into two edge-disjoint subgraphs $G1$ and $G2$. $G1$ and $G2$ are then coloured in parallel in a recursive manner. If $\Delta+1$ colours are used on G, no more processing is required. Otherwise one or two colours are removed from G and PEDGECOLOUR is applied to consistently recolour each of the edges now uncoloured choosing colours from the $\Delta+1$ remaining ones. See Figure 8.

An Euler partition is a partition of the edges of a graph G into open and closed paths such that each vertex of *odd* (*even*) degree is the end of exactly *one* (*zero*) open path. Such a partition can be used to divide G into two edge-disjoint subgraphs $G1$ and $G2$. Label alternate edges in each path with 1 and 2. Then let $G1$ contain all edges with label 1 and $G2$ all the remaining edges. It is easy to see that $G1$ and $G2$ each has degree $\lfloor \frac{1}{2}\Delta \rfloor$ or $\lfloor \frac{1}{2}\Delta \rfloor+1$.

Following tradition, define an Euler tour of a graph $G=(V,E)$ as a path (not necessarily simple) of G such that every edge in E appears on it exactly once. A graph which has an Euler tour is said to be Eulerian.

The Euler tour algorithm of Atallah and Vishkin [1] can be used to divide a graph into two edge-disjoint subgraphs in $O(\log^2 n)$ time on a CREW SIMD computer with $n+m$ processors. If G is Eulerian, apply the Euler tour algorithm to it directly. Otherwise, add a dummy vertex v_* to G and connect every odd-degree vertex to v_* using dummy edges. Then apply the Euler tour algorithm to the resulting Eulerian graph. Next label the edges of $G+v_*$ with 1 and 2 alternately following the route determined by its Euler tour using a doubling mechanism (See [11] for details). Once the labelling is completed, the dummy edges and vertex can be dropped, and the edge-disjoint subgraphs obtained in an obvious way.

The correctness of the above follows from the following well known Lemmas.

Lemma1: *A graph is Eulerian if it is connected and all vertices have even degrees, or exactly two vertices have odd degrees.* ■

Lemma2: *There are even number of odd-degree vertices in any given undirected graph.*

Our main results in this section are summed up in the following two theorems. ■

Theorem2: *Algorithm PEULER-COLOUR produces a $(\Delta+1)$-edge-colouring of an arbitrary graph G in $O(n\log^2 n)$ time on a CREW SIMD computer with $\frac{n^3}{\log n}$ processors.*

Proof: That the algorithm produces a $(\Delta+1)$-colouring is immediate from the consistent recolouring by PEDGECOLOUR and the fact that the degree of a subgraph $G1$ or $G2$ is either $\lfloor\frac{1}{2}\Delta\rfloor$ or $\lfloor\frac{1}{2}\Delta\rfloor+1$.

To prove the $O(n\log^2 n)$ time bound, we make use of a computation tree with root node at level 0 (see Figure 9). A node becomes active when it is assigned a subgraph by its parent node. Since our model of computation is SIMD, all same level nodes become active simultaneously.

Computation starts at the root node in a top-down fashion. When all the nodes at a particular level (i say) are activated, they perform lines 1-7 of the algorithm on their assigned subgraphs and activate their children accordingly. Each active node employs m processors in line 1 to determine the degree of its subgraph. The $d(v)$ edges incident with a given vertex v compute the degree of v in $O(\log d(v))$ time by finding the length of v's neighbour list. Then n vertices concurrently find the maximum of all $d(v_i)$ in $O(\log n)$ time. If $\Delta=1$ each edge of the subgraph performs line 3. Otherwise $n + m$ processors perform lines 4 and 5 in $O(\log^2 n)$ time as explained previously. Then the left and right sons are activated.

Based on the outcome of the computations done by its two sons,

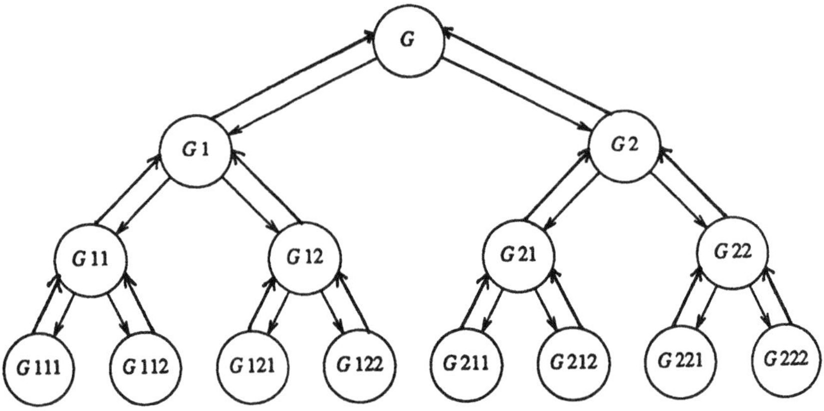

Figure 9: A Computation Tree for PEULER-COLOUR

a node decides whether recolouring is essential. If so, $\frac{n^2}{\log n}$ processors are employed to do it in $O(n\log n)$ time. Note that $|E_\alpha|=O(n)$.

The foregoing shows that there are two distinct phases in our algorithm. The first phase which involves the construction of edge-disjoint subgraphs proceeds top-down while the second phase which applies PEDGECOLOUR for recolouring proceeds bottom-up. So the algorithm terminates at the root node.

Since the depth of a computation tree is clearly $O(\log\Delta)$, the total time required by the algorithm to colour the edges of a graph of order n and size m is $(\log n+\log^2 n)\log\Delta+n\log n\log\Delta=O(n\log^2 n)$.

To prove the processor complexity claimed, we consider again a computation tree. It is not difficult to see from the foregoing discussion that the number of processors required at each node is $\frac{n^2}{\log n}$. Since we can have up to $2^{\log\Delta-1}=O(\Delta)$ nodes active at the same time (particularly at level $\log\Delta-1$), the maximum possible number of processors operating at a point in time is $\frac{n^2}{\log n}\Delta\le\frac{n^3}{\log n}$. ■

Theorem3: *Algorithm PEULER-COLOUR produces a* $(\Delta+1)$*-edge-colouring of an arbitrary planar graph with large degree in* $O(\log^2 n)$ *time on a CREW SIMD computer with* $\frac{n^3}{\log n}$ *processors.*

Proof: Observe that $|E_\alpha|=O(\frac{m}{\Delta})$. ■

Acknowledgements

I would like to thank Alan Gibbons, my Ph.D. supervisor, and the unknown referees for their useful suggestions.

References

[1] M. Atallah and U. Vishkin, "Finding Euler Tours in Parallel", *J. Comput. and Syst. Sciences* **29**, 330-337 (1984).
[2] R.D. Dutton and R.C. Brigham, "A new graph colouring algorithm", *Computer J.* **24**, 85-86 (1981).
[3] A.M. Frieze, "Parallel Algorithms for Finding Hamiltonian Cycles in Random Graphs", *Manuscript*, Department of Computer Science, Queen Mary College (March 1986).
[4] M.R. Garey and D.S. Johnson, *"Computer and Intractability: A Guide to the Theory of NP-completeness"*, Freeman (1979).
[5] H.N. Grabow and O. Kariv, "Algorithms for Edge Colouring Bipartite Graphs and Multigraphs", *SIAM J. Comput.* **11**, 117-129 (1982).
[6] A.M. Gibbons, *"Algorithmic Graph Theory"*, Cambridge University Press (1985).
[7] A.M. Gibbons and O.A. Ogunyode, "A Polynomial-Time Algorithm to Edge-Colour Almost All Graphs Using Ψ_e Colours", *Theory of Computation, Report No.* **68**, (September 1984).
[8] I. Holyer, "The NP-completeness of Edge-Colouring", *SIAM J. Comput.* **10**, 718-720 (1981).
[9] F.T. Leighton, "A graph coloring algorithm for large scheduling problems", *J. Res. Natn. Bur. Stand.* **84**, 489-506 (1979).
[10] G. Lev, N. Pippenger and L.G. Valliant, "A Fast Parallel Algorithm for Routing in Permutation Networks", *IEEE Trans. Comput.*, **C-30**, 93-110 (1981).
[11] O.A. Ogunyode, "Approximation and Parallel Algorithms for Some *NP*-Hard Problems", *Ph.D. Thesis*, Department of Computer Science, University of Warwick (August 1986).
[12] M.J. Quinn and N. Deo, "A Parallel Approximate Algorithm for the Euclidean Traveling Salesman Problem", *Report CS-83-105*, Computer Science Department, Washington State University, Pullman (1983).
[13] Y.H. Tsin and F.Y. Chin, "Efficient Parallel Algorithms for a Class of Graph Theoretic Problems", *SIAM J. Comput.* **13**, 580-599 (1984).
[14] V.G. Vizing, "On an estimate of the chromatic class of p-graph", *Diskret. Analiz.* **3**, 25-30 (1964).

An Optimal Randomized Routing Algorithm for the Mesh and A Class of Efficient Mesh-like Routing Networks

(Extended Abstract)

Sanguthevar Rajasekaran*
Thanasis Tsantilas†
Aiken Computation Laboratory
Harvard University
Cambridge, MA 02138, USA

Abstract

We present an optimal oblivious randomized algorithm for permutation routing on the MIMD version of Mesh. Our routing algorithm routes n^2 elements on an $n \times n$ Mesh in $2n + O(\log n)$ parallel communication steps with very high probability. Further, the maximum queue length at any node at any time is at the most $O(\log n)$ with the same probability. Since $2n$ is the distance bound for the Mesh, our algorithm is indeed optimal. Generalization of this result to k-dimensional (for any k) Meshes yields an algorithm that runs in time equal to the diameter of the Mesh. A lower bound result of [Schnorr and Shamir 86] states that sorting of n^2 elements takes at least $3n$ steps on an $n \times n$ MIMD Mesh (for indexing schemes of practical interest). Thus our algorithm demonstrates that routing is easier than sorting on the MIMD Mesh.

We also identify a class of Mesh-like networks (we call *circular meshes*) which have n^2 nodes but less than $2n$ diameter. These meshes have the property that they can be laid out on a chip with a physical diameter same as the model diameter. Our routing algorithm runs on these networks to route n^2 elements in $d + O(\log n)$ steps (d being the diameter of the network) with a very high probability. These circular meshes also have the potential of being adopted to run existing sorting and routing algorithms (on the regular SIMD and MIMD Meshes) with a corresponding reduction in their run times.

And finally we present a (possibly) non optimal oblivious routing algorithm for the Mesh that requires only $O(1)$ queue size for any node at any time. In particular we present a randomized oblivious constant queue size routing algorithm that runs in time $O(n^{1+\epsilon})$, for any $\epsilon > 0$.

*Supported in part by NSF Grant NSF-DCR-85-03251 and ONR contract N00014-80-C-0647
†Supported in part by NSF Grant NSF-DCR-86-00379

1 Introduction

1.1 Mesh Connected Computers

Mesh connected computers (MCCs) have drawn the attention of computer scientists in recent times, as revealed by the large number of algorithms in the literature proposed for these models, because of their many special properties. Some of the special features of MCCs are: 1) they have a simple interconnection pattern, 2) many problems have data which map naturally onto them, and 3) they are linear-scalable.

The basic topology of a 2-d MCC is an $n \times n$ square grid with one processor per grid point. Except for the processors at the boundary, every other processor is connected to its neighbours to the *left*, to the *right*, *above* and *below* through bidirectional links. Variations in this topology are possible depending on whether one or more of the following connections are allowed : 1) vertical wrap arounds, 2) horizontal wrap arounds, and 3) connections to diagonal neighbours. In this paper we are interested only in MCCs with the basic topology.

MCC computers can be categorized into two groups viz., SIMD (Single Instruction Multiple Data), and MIMD (Multiple Instruction Multiple Data) depending on the instruction streams allowed for the processors. In the context of MCCs, an instruction refers to an arithmetic operation, or a communication step with a neighbour in a specified direction. For example, 'communicate with the left neighbour' is a different instruction from 'communicate with the right (,below, or above) neighbour'.

The model we use in this paper is the MIMD MCC where each processor can communicate with all its four (or less) neighbours in a single step (see [Valiant and Brebner 81] and the lower bound result in [Schnorr and Shamir 86]).

1.2 Some Known Results

One of the earliest results on MCC was a sorting algorithm by [Thompson and Kung 77] who used the SIMD model. On this model, the trivial lower bound for sorting n^2 elements is $4n-4$, the distance bound (i.e., the number of steps needed to interchange two elements in opposite corners of the Mesh). [Thompson and Kung 77]'s algorithm sorted n^2 elements in $12n$ steps. Subsequently [Nassimi and Sahni 81], and [Kumar and Hirschberg] gave sorting algorithms on the SIMD model with run times $14n$ and $11n$ respectively. These two algorithms had a better performance for smaller n. Obtaining an optimal sorting algorithm on the SIMD model still remains an open problem.

For the MIMD model, [Schnorr and Shamir 86] have presented an optimal sorting algorithm. Their algorithm sorts n^2 elements in $3n$ (plus lower order terms) steps and they also prove a $3n$ lower bound for sorting. The MIMD model they use to prove the lower bound is stronger than the one we use in this paper, but for proving the upper bound they use a slightly weaker version. [Valiant and Brebner 81] gave a randomized algorithm for routing n^2 elements on an $n \times n$ MIMD MCC that runs in time $3n + O(n^\delta), \delta > 1/2$ with *high probability*.

[Ma, Sen, and Scherson 86] have presented an optimal sorting algorithm that runs in time $4n$ for a Mesh model that is stronger than SIMD but weaker than MIMD.

1.3 Some Definitions and Notations

The problem of *routing* on a parallel machine is defined as follows. Each node in the machine has a packet of information. Each packet has a destination address written on it that specifies the node to which it is to be sent. The task of the parallel machine is to send the packets to their correct destinations simultaneously so that at most one packet passes down any wire at any time and all of them arrive at their destinations quickly.

By *routing function* we mean a rule that specifies for each packet a directed path it should take and associates a *priority number* with each packet. Specification of priorities for packets is also called *queue discipline*. These priorities serve the purpose of resolving contentions for the same edge by more than one packets. The problem of routing is then the selection of a routing function.

We define the *queue size* of a routing algorithm to be the maximum number of packets that any processor will have to store at any time during the execution of the algorithm.

We say a probabilistic algorithm uses $\tilde{O}(g(n))$ amount of any resource (like time, space etc.) if there exists a constant c such that the amount of resource used is no more than $c\alpha g(n)$ with probability $\geq 1 - n^{-\alpha}$ on any input of size n.

By *high probability* we mean a probability $\geq 1 - n^{-\alpha}$ for any $\alpha \geq 1$.

By $B(n, p)$ we mean a binomial random variable with parameters (n, p). (For the definition of a binomial variable see appendix A).

The distance between two points (x_1, y_1) and (x_2, y_2) in the *manhattan metric* is defined to be $|x_1 - x_2| + |y_1 - y_2|$.

We say a sorting scheme is *linear* if in the final sorted order, the keys at nodes $(0, 0)$ and $(0, n-1)$ are $\leq n$ apart in rank.

1.4 Contents of this Paper

One of the important factors which determine the efficiency of any parallel machine is its speed of communication. A step of communication can be thought of as a routing task. Optimal algorithms on various versions of the MCC model can be found in the literature for the problem of sorting (and hence for permutation routing). Sorting, on some of these MCC models, has a lower bound greater than the distance bound. For example the MIMD version of MCC with n^2 elements has a distance bound of $2n$, but [Schnorr and Shamir 86] prove a $3n$ lower bound for sorting on this model (for linear indexing schemes).

Even for randomized algorithms this lower bound holds since this bound was obtained purely from distance arguments. In this paper we present an algorithm for permutation routing n^2 elements in time $2n + \tilde{O}(\log n)$ on the MIMD MCC. Thus routing is easier than sorting on the MIMD MCC (irrespective of the queue size allowed for individual processors) provided we require each key (or packet) to originate in a unique node and destine for a unique node and only a linear indexing scheme is allowed. Application of this algorithm for any k dimensional Mesh yields an algorithm that runs in time equal to the diameter of the Mesh. Our algorithm also applies to communication requests that form *partial permutations* or *partial h-relations* (defined in [Valiant and Brebner 81]).

MCCs do not have optimal diameter (in the manhattan metric). We identify in this paper a class of Meshes that have optimal or near optimal diameter. We also present a non optimal constant queue size routing algorithm. All our routing algorithms are distributed and *oblivious*, i.e., the route taken by each packet is determined entirely by itself.

In section 2 we state and solve some simple routing problems and in section 3 we present our optimal routing algorithm. In section 4, we describe the topology of circular meshes and compute their diameters and finally in section 5 we present our constant queue size routing algorithm.

2 Some Simple Routing Problems

In this section we state and solve two simple routing problems. These problems will give the reader a better understanding of the results to follow. The routing problems we consider here are on a linear n-array. In a linear array each processor can communicate with its left and right neighbours in a single step. Selection of a routing function, in the context of a linear array, only means selection of a *queue discipline*, since nothing is gained by routing packets along non-shortest paths. Some of the queue disciplines in use are:

Queue Discipline1. When on contention for an edge a random packet takes precedence over the others.

Queue Discipline2. The packet that has the farthest origin takes precedence [Valiant and Brebner 81].

Queue Discipline3. The packet that has the farthest destination takes precedence [Krizanc 86].

Now to the routing problems.

Problem1. Each node of a linear $n-$array has $k \geq 1$ packets initially and each node is the destination of exactly k packets. Send all the packets to their destinations sending at the most one packet along any edge in a single step.

Lemma 2.1 *If we use queue discipline2, problem1 can be solved in time* $\leq (k+1)n/2$.

Proof. Let the nodes of the array be numbered $0, 1, \ldots, n-1$ from left to right. Consider a packet at node i. W.l.o.g. assume its destination is to the right. This packet can be delayed by at the most $k(i+1)$ (the number of packets at and to the left of i) steps. Also, the delay is at the most $(n-1-i)k-1$ since only these many packets have destinations to the right of i. Therefore, the maximum delay for the packet at i is $\leq \min[k(i+1),\ (n-1-i)k]$. Thus, the maximum delay any packet suffers is $\leq \max_i[\min(k(i+1), (n-1-i)k)] = kn/2$ (for $i = n/2-1$). Therefore, all the packets can be routed in time $kn/2 + n/2 = (k+1)n/2$. □

Problem2. On an n-array, node i has k_i $(0 \le k_i \le n \; \& \sum_{i=0}^{n-1} k_i = n)$ packets initially (for $i = 0, 1, \dots, n-1$). Each node is the destination for exactly one packet. Route the packets.

Lemma 2.2 *If queue discipline3 is used the time needed for a packet starting at node i to reach its destination is no more than the distance between i and the boundary in the direction the packet is moving. That is if the packet is moving from left to right then this time is no more than $(n-i)$ and if the packet is moving from right to left the time is $\le i$. [Krizanc 86]*

Proof. Consider a packet q at node i and destined for j. Assume (wlog) it is moving from left to right. q can only be delayed by the packets with destinations $> j$ and which are to the left of their destinations. Let $k_0, k_1, \dots, k_{n-1}$ be the number of such packets (at the beginning) at nodes $0, 1, \dots, n-1$ respectively. (Notice that $\sum_{l=0}^{n-1} k_l \le n - j - 1$).

Let m be such that $k_{m-1} > 1$ and $k_{m'} \le 1$ for $m \le m' \le n-1$. Call the sequence $k_m, k_{m+1}, \dots, k_{n-1}$ *the free sequence*. Realize that a packet in the free sequence will neither delay nor be delayed by any other packet in the future. It is easy to see that at every time step, at least one new packet joins the free sequence. Thus, after $n - j - 1$ steps, all the packets that can possibly delay q would have joined the free sequence. q needs only an additional $j - i$ steps, at the most, to reach its destination. The case the packet moves from right to left is similar □

3 An Optimal Routing Algorithm

[Valiant and Brebner 81] gave a randomized algorithm for routing n^2 elements on an $n \times n$ MIMD MCC that runs in time $3n + \tilde{O}(n^\delta), \delta > 1/2$. This algorithm also has a maximum queue length of $\tilde{O}(\log n)$. In this section we present a routing algorithm for the MIMD MCC that runs in time $2n + \tilde{O}(\log n)$. The maximum queue length of our algorithm is also $\tilde{O}(\log n)$. Before describing our optimal algorithm we present a simple $(2+\epsilon)n$ (for any $\epsilon \ge 1/\log n$) time routing algorithm.

3.1 A $(2+\epsilon)n$ Routing Algorithm

[Valiant and Brebner 81]'s algorithm consists of three phases. Initially each node has a packet. Processors are named $(i,j), i = 0, \dots, n-1, \; j = 0, \dots, n-1$ with $(0,0)$ at the left top corner. Let q be any packet and let $(i,j)\&(k,l)$ be its origin and destination respectively.

Phase A sends q along the column j to a random node (i', j) in column j. Phase Z sends q to (i', l) along the row i'. And finally, phase B sends q to (k, l) along the column l.

Since there is one packet at each node at the beginning, phase A can be completed without any packet suffering any delay whatsoever by a continuous flow of packets along the columns. Phases Z and B use queue discipline2 (with ties broken arbitrarily). Analysis shows that phases Z and B can be implemented in time $n + \tilde{O}(n^\delta), \delta > 1/2$ each. The run time of the above algorithm can be improved to $(2+\epsilon)n, \epsilon \geq 1/\log n$ if in phase A, each packet is sent to a random position (along its column) within a distance of ϵn from its origin.

Assume wlog, ϵn divides n. Divide each column of the Mesh into slices of length ϵn as shown in figure-1. Modify phase A as follows. Every processor (i, j) chooses a random position in column j within the slice it is in and sends its packet to that position along column j.

Phases Z and B remain the same except that queue discipline3 is used in phase B.

Lemma 3.1 *The above modified algorithm runs in time* $(2+\epsilon)n + c\alpha n^\delta$*, for any* $\delta > 1/2$ *and some fixed constant c, with probability* $\geq 1 - n^{-\alpha}$.

Proof. The proof is very similar to [Valiant and Brebner 81]'s. Phase A can be implemented in time ϵn without any additional delay since there is one packet at each node initially.

Consider a packet that starts phase Z at (i', j). Wlog, assume it is moving to the right. Under the queue discipline2, this packet can be delayed by at the most the number of packets starting this phase in $\{(i', \bar{j}) | 1 \leq \bar{j} \leq j\}$.

At the starting of phase Z, for each node $(i', \bar{j})$ each of the ϵn packets originating in the slice $(i', \bar{j})$ is in has a probability $\frac{1}{\epsilon n}$ of being at $(i', \bar{j})$. Hence, for each set of nodes $\{(i', \bar{j}) | 1 \leq \bar{j} \leq j\}$ the number of packets at them in total at the beginning of phase Z is $B(\epsilon n j, 1/\epsilon n)$. The Chernoff bounds (in appendix A) imply that this number is at the most $j + n^\delta, \delta > 1/2$ with high probability. Since the packet has at the most $(n - j)$ steps to move, it will complete phase Z in $n + n^\delta$ steps with high probability.

In phase B we use queue discipline3. In any column since every node is the destination of a packet, phase B can be completed in time n (in accordance with lemma 2.2). □

Note that if in phase A, packets randomize over slices of length ϵn, then for the worst case input, queue size at the end of phase Z will be $\Omega(1/\epsilon)$. (An example is when all the packets that have to be routed to a particular column appear in the same row in the input). Thus ϵ has to be greater than $1/\log n$ if only $O(\log n)$ queue size is allowed.

3.2 Our Optimal Routing Algorithm

In the $(2+\epsilon)n$ algorithm above, let us say we overlap the three phases. That is, a packet that finishes phase A before ϵn steps can start phase Z without waiting for the other packets to finish phase A and so on. We expect some packets to finish faster now.

The only possible conflict between phases is between phases A and B. A packet that is doing its phase A and a packet that is doing its phase B might contend for the same edge. Always, under such cases, we give precedence to the packet that is doing its phase A. If a packet q doing its phase B contends for an edge with a packet that is doing its phase A, it means that q has completed its phases A and Z within ϵn steps. Since after ϵn steps from the start of the algorithm every packet will be doing either its phase Z or phase B,

q will reach its destination within $(1+\epsilon)n$ steps. Packets like q are not interesting to our analysis. Thus we won't mention them hereafter in any analysis. A packet doing its phase Z can not be delayed by packets doing their phase A or phase B and vice versa.

In summary, no packet suffers additional delays due to overlap of phases. It is also easy to see that the maximum queue length at any node does not increase due to overlap. Can some of the packets finish faster now? We answer this question next.

Consider a packet q initially at node (i,j) with (k,l) as its destination. Assume wlog, (k,l) is below (i,j) and to the right (the other cases can be argued in exactly the same lines). If in phase A q chooses a position (i',j) (in the slice (i,j) is in), then q will finish phase A in $|i-i'|$ steps. Also q will take at the most $l+n^{\delta}$ steps to finish phase Z (with high probability) and $(n-i')$ steps to finish phase B (see figure-2 and proof of lemmas 2.2 and 3.1).

Therefore q takes $|i-i'|+l+(n-i')$ (plus lower order terms) total steps to complete all the three phases. Call this sum the *normal path length* of q. We require the normal path length of every packet to be $\leq 2n$. This can be ensured if every packet moves in the direction of its destination in phase A, because then $|i-i'|+(n-i')$ will always be $\leq n$.

The normal path length of a packet is $\leq 2n$ also when the following condition holds: 'the origin of the packet is at least $2\epsilon n$ distance away from its nearest row or column boundary'. In the example of figure-2, if for example $i \geq 2\epsilon n$, even if the packet is sent ϵn away from its destination (in phase A), $|i-i'|+(n-i')$ will still be $\leq n$. Packets that satisfy the above condition are the ones that have their origins in the I region of figure-3. Call these packets the *inferior packets*. Packets that do not satisfy this condition are those that have their origins in the S region of figure-3. Call these packets the ***superior packets***. Superior packets have the potential of having a normal path length $> 2n$.

Our routing algorithm will route the inferior packets as usual using the $(2+\epsilon)n$ algorithm given above. Superior packets are given special treatment. We will route the superior packets such that those packets with a **potential** normal path length of $\geq 2n$ move in the direction of their destinations in phase A. Overlap of phases is assumed for both the types of packets. Details of the algorithm follow.

Algorithm for inferior packets

Inferior packets use the usual algorithm of section 3.1. Every column is divided into slices of length ϵn. In phase A, a packet at (i,j) with a destination (k,l) is sent to a random position (i',j) in its slice along the column j. In phase Z, the packet is sent to (i',l) along row i' and finally in phase B, the packet is sent to (k,l) along the column l.

Algorithm for superior packets

Each node (i,j) in the upper two S squares chooses a random i' in $\{2\epsilon n, 2\epsilon n+1, \ldots, 2\epsilon n+(1/4)n-1\}$ and sends its packet, q, to (i',j) along column j. If (k,l) is the destination of q, q is then sent to (i',l) along row i' and finally along column l to (k,l).

Each node (i,j) in the lower two S squares chooses a random i' in $\{n-2\epsilon n-1, n-2\epsilon n-2, \ldots, n-2\epsilon n-(1/4)n\}$ and sends its packet to (i',j) along column j. The packet is then sent to (i',l) along row i' and to (k,l), the packet's destination, along column l.

Queue Disciplines

- In phases A and B no distinction is made between superior and inferior packets.
- If a packet doing its phase A and a packet doing its phase B contend for the same edge, the packet doing its phase A takes precedence.
- Queue discipline3 is used for phase B.
- In phase Z, superior packets take precedence over inferior packets. Among superior (inferior) packets queue discipline2 is used.

Lemma 3.2 *The above algorithm runs in time $2n + \tilde{O}(\log n)$. Further, the maximum queue length at any node at any time is $\tilde{O}(\log n)$.*

Proof.
Superior packets

A superior packet does not suffer any delay in phase A.

A superior packet q starting its phase Z at (i',j) can be delayed by at the most the number of superior packets that will ever start their phase Z from a node to the left of (i',j) in row i' (assuming wlog, q is moving from left to right). The number of such packets is upper bounded by $B(j2\epsilon n, (4/n))$. If $j \geq \log n$, the Chernoff bounds affirm this delay will be $\leq j$ with probability $\geq 1 - n^{-\alpha}$ for any $\alpha \geq 1$ if we choose a proper constant ϵ. The delay will be $\tilde{O}(\log n)$ for $j < \log n$. Therefore, superior packets will complete phase Z in $n + \tilde{O}(\log n)$ steps.

A superior packet that moves in the direction of its destination in phase A spends at the most n steps in total in phases A and B (as was shown before). A packet that was moving in a direction opposite to its destination in phase A will complete phases A and B in a total of $2((1/4)n + 2\epsilon n)$ steps. Since ϵ is chosen to be < 1, this total is $\leq n$.

And hence all the superior packets will complete all the three phases in $2n + \tilde{O}(\log n)$ steps.

Inferior packets

Let q be a packet at (i,j) initially, that moves to (i',j) at the end of phase A, to (i',l) at the end of phase Z, and to (k,l) at the end of phase B.

q spends at the most ϵn steps in phase A.

In the following case analysis ignore the presence of superior packets.

case1: $i' \leq 2\epsilon n$ or $i' > n - 2\epsilon n$.

Delay for q in phase Z will be $\leq j - 2\epsilon n + n^{\delta}$ with high probability. This is because q is delayed by at the most the packets that will ever do their phase Z starting from a node to the left of (i', j) in row i' (assuming q moves from left to right), and in row i' packets in columns $0, 1, \ldots, 2\epsilon n - 1$ have been vacated. Therefore, q completes phase Z in $\leq n - 2\epsilon n + n^{\delta}$ steps.

q takes $\leq n$ steps to finish phase B. Thus, q takes $\leq \epsilon n + n - 2\epsilon n + n^{\delta} + n \ = \ 2n - \epsilon n + n^{\delta}$ steps to complete all the three phases if case1 is true.

case2: $n - 2\epsilon n \geq i' \geq 2\epsilon n$.

q takes $\leq n + n^{\delta}$ steps to complete phase Z with high probability.

In phase B q spends $\leq n - 2\epsilon n$ time since $n - 2\epsilon n$ is the maximum distance from row i' to any row boundary. Therefore q completes all the three phases in $\epsilon n + n + n^{\delta} + n - 2\epsilon n \ = \ 2n - \epsilon n + n^{\delta}$ steps.

The only unaccounted delay so far is the delay of inferior packets by the superior packets in phase Z. The number of superior packets that will ever do their phase Z in a given row i' is $B(8\epsilon^2 n^2, 4/n)$. The Chernoff bounds imply this number is $\leq g\alpha\epsilon^2 n$ with probability $\geq 1 - n^{-\alpha}$ for some fixed constant g. The number of superior packets that will delay an inferior packet doing its phase Z in row i' is therefore at the most $g\alpha\epsilon^2 n$. Hence, the inferior packet will complete all the three phases in time $\leq 2n - \epsilon n + n^{\delta} + g\alpha\epsilon^2 n \ \leq \ 2n$, for small enough ϵ.

Thus all the inferior packets will complete all the three phases in $\leq 2n$ steps with high probability.

It is easy to see that the queue length at any node will not exceed $\tilde{O}(\log n)$ at any time. Consider any node (i, j) in the mesh. During phase A, the only packets that can add to the queue size of (i, j) are those that start their phase Z from (i, j). The number of such packets is $\tilde{O}(\log n)$. During phase Z, the only packets that can contribute to the queue size of (i, j) are those that start their phase B form (i, j) and they are $\tilde{O}(\log n)$ in number. During phase B, the queue size of (i, j) can increase by at the most one (viz., by the packet whose destination is (i, j)). And hence the queue size of every node is $\tilde{O}(\log n)$.

Thus we have the following

Theorem 3.1 *Any permutation routing of n^2 elements on an $n \times n$ MIMD MCC can be completed in $2n + \tilde{O}(\log n)$ steps, the maximum queue length of no processor being $> \tilde{O}(\log n)$.*

4 A Class of Efficient Routing Networks

The reason why our routing algorithm runs optimally is the following. All the packets in the I region of figure 3 are less than $2n$ distance away from their destinations, and most of the nodes of the Mesh are in the I region. This suggests that if we somehow distribute the nodes of the S regions into the I region we will get an improved run time. This can be done by changing the topology of the Mesh as shown in figure 4.

Mesh1 of figure 4 is exactly like an $n \times n$ Mesh. Each node here also is connected to its four neighbours to the *left*, to the *right, above*, and *below* (except for the nodes in the boundary). The only difference is Mesh1 has a boundary shown in figure 4 rather than a square. If x is the maximum span along the vertical (or horizontal) direction of Mesh1, then the area of Mesh1 is $x^2 - 4\epsilon^2 x^2$. We require to place n^2 nodes in this Mesh. Therefore, we get $x = \frac{n}{\sqrt{1-4\epsilon^2}}$. Diameter d of this Mesh is $(2-2\epsilon)x$. Minimum of d (over all ϵ's) occurs for $\epsilon = 1/4$ and the minimum value is $\sqrt{3}n$.

The above idea can be extended further by choosing the boundaries shown in figure 5 for a Mesh. For these Meshes also minimum diameter occurs when $\epsilon = 1/4$. These have diameters $\sqrt{5/2}n$ and $1.5n$ respectively. These Meshes are all approximations to a rhombus inclined at 45° to the axes, which is a circle in the manhattan metric.

The limiting case in this class of networks is a rhombus with a diameter of $\sqrt{2}n$. This rhombus has $\sqrt{2}n$ rows. If the rows are numbered $-\frac{\sqrt{2}n}{2}, -(\frac{\sqrt{2}n}{2} - 1), \ldots, -1, 0, 1, \ldots, \frac{\sqrt{2}n}{2}$, then row 0 has $\sqrt{2}n$ nodes. Row $\pm i$ has $(\sqrt{2}n - 2i)$ nodes, for $1 \leq i \leq \frac{\sqrt{2}n}{2}$.

Our routing algorithm runs in time $d + \tilde{O}(\log n)$ in a circular Mesh of diameter d. The only modification needed to be made in the algorithm of section 3 is to define the inferior and superior packets of the circular Mesh accordingly. Thus we have the following

Lemma 4.1 *Routing algorithm of section 3 runs in time $d + \tilde{O}(\log n)$ on a circular Mesh of diameter d.*

The joker-zone argument of [Kunde 86] and [Schnorr and Shamir 86] can be used to prove the following lower bound for sorting on circular Meshes.

Lemma 4.2 *Any sorting algorithm using a linear indexing scheme needs at least $1.5d$ time to sort n^2 elements on a circular Mesh of diameter d if we require each key to originate in a unique node and destine for a unique node.*

We believe most of the sorting and routing alogorithms running on the regular Meshes can be run on the circular meshes with a corresponding reduction in their run times.

5 Constant Queue Size Oblivious Routing

One of the important performance criteria of any parallel communication scheme is its queue size. Algorithms discussed in the previous sections have $\tilde{O}(\log n)$ queue size. Even though $\log n$ is a slowly increasing function of n, even $\log n$ queue size might be prohibitive in practical parallel machines. In this section we present a non optimal oblivious routing algorithm for the MCCs that requires only $\tilde{O}(1)$ queue size. Previously, [Pippenger 84] has given a routing algorithm for the d-way digit exchange graph that routes N packets in time $\tilde{O}(\log N)$ with a queue size of $O(1)$. In some strict sense, this algorithm is not oblivious and also there is a nonzero probability of *dead lock*. If we do not require obliviousness, then any sorting algorithm can be used for permutation routing. The algorithm to be presented in this section is oblivious (and so are the ones in the previous sections).

We show that oblivious routing can be done in time $\tilde{O}(n^{1+\epsilon})$ for any $\epsilon > 0$ by a randomized algorithm of queue size $\tilde{O}(1)$. The problem of deadlock does not arise for this algorithm.

5.1 An $\tilde{O}(n^{1+\epsilon})$ Randomized Routing Algorithm

Let $N = n^2$ throughout. Assume wlog N^δ divides N (for $\delta < 1$). We route the packets in batches of size (roughly) N^δ. We route the batches sequentially one after the other. Each batch can be routed in time $\tilde{O}(n)$ using the 3 phase algorithm of [Valiant and Brebner 81] discussed in section 3. Therefore the whole algorithm takes time $\tilde{O}(n.N^{1-\delta})$ which is $\tilde{O}(n^{1+\epsilon}), \epsilon > 0$ for a proper δ. Details of the algorithm follow.

algorithm ROUTE;

begin

for batch $=$ *1 to* cn^ϵ *do*

begin

step1. Each node (i, j) that has one or more packets yet to be routed flips a coin for each such packet with a probability of *success* $= 1/N^{\epsilon'}, \epsilon' > 0$.

step2. Packets that have got *success* in the coin flips of step1 execute the 3 phase algorithm of section 3. A total time of $3n$ is given.

end

end;

Theorem 5.1 *The above algorithm runs in time $\tilde{O}(n^{1+\epsilon})$ for any $\epsilon > 0$ and further, the queue size is $\tilde{O}(1)$.*

The proof of this theorem depends on the following two lemmas.

Lemma 5.1 *On an n-array let node i have k_i packets (for $i = 0, 1, \ldots, n-1$) initially and let $k = \max_i(k_i)$. If queue discipline2 is used to route the packets, then no node will have more than $(2k+1)$ packets at any time during the execution of the algorithm (on the assumption that no more than k packets have the same destination).*

Proof. Route the packets in two phases. First route all the packets that have their destinations to the right of their origins. After $\sum_i k_i$ time, route the packets that have destinations to the left of their origins. In the first phase, once a packet starts moving it can not be delayed by any other packet. So if a packet enters a node, it will leave that node in the next step unless the destination of the packet is that node. Thus all the packets passing through any node can only increase that node's queue size by one. On the other hand, there might be a node with k nodes initially and none of these packets moves until all the k packets destined for this node (originating from left) reach this node. Therefore, a node can have a queue size of $(2k+1)$ and no more. The same arguments hold for the second phase. □

Lemma 5.2 *Any packet needs to make at the most cn^{ϵ} (where $\epsilon > 2\epsilon'$) coin flips before it gets success. Also the number of packets in any batch is at the most $\tilde{O}(N^{1-\epsilon'})$.*

Proof. The probability that a packet *fails* in a particular trial is $\leq 1 - \frac{1}{N^{\epsilon'}}$. Therefore, the probability that it fails in x successive coin flips is $\leq (1 - \frac{1}{N^{\epsilon'}})^x$. If x is cn^{ϵ} for any $\epsilon > 2\epsilon'$ then this probability is $\leq N^{-\alpha}$ for any $\alpha \geq 1$ and a proper c.

The number of packets in any *batch* is clearly $B(N, \frac{1}{N^{\epsilon'}})$. Using the Chernoff bounds, the second statement of lemma 5.2 follows. □

Proof of theorem 5.1. Lemma 5.2 immediately implies that the run time of our algorithm is $\tilde{O}(n.n^{\epsilon})$, since for routing packets in a *batch* we need only $\tilde{O}(n)$ time using the 3 phase algorithm. It remains to show that the queue size is $\tilde{O}(1)$.

Any batch B_l consists of at the most $N^{1-\epsilon'}$ packets. Notice that just after routing any *batch* of packets, no node will have more than 2 packets. The queue size of the whole algorithm is then determined by the queue size needed to route a single batch.

Consider a batch B_l. Initially each node consists of a single packet that is to be routed. Let q be a packet originating at (i,j) and destined for (k,l). The number of packets of B_l in column j is $B(N^{1-\epsilon'}, \frac{1}{\sqrt{N}})$. This number is $\tilde{O}(N^{0.5-\epsilon'})$. Let (i',j) be any node in column j. Each of the $\tilde{O}(N^{0.5-\epsilon'})$ packets originating in column j has a probability $\frac{1}{\sqrt{N}}$ of choosing node (i',j) in phase A. Therefore, the number of packets ending up at node (i',j) at the end of phase A is $B(N^{0.5-\epsilon'}, 1/\sqrt{N})$. This number is $\tilde{O}(1)$ using the Chernoff bounds if $\epsilon' > 0$.

Using the same argument, we can show that at the end of phase Z, no node will have more than $\tilde{O}(1)$ packets, and hence applying lemma 5.1, we conclude at no time during the running of the 3 phases will the queue size exceed $\tilde{O}(1)$. □

Acknowledgement

The authors would like to thank John Reif and Leslie Valiant for their constant encouragement and support. The authors also would like to thank Danny Krizanc for many fruitful discussions.

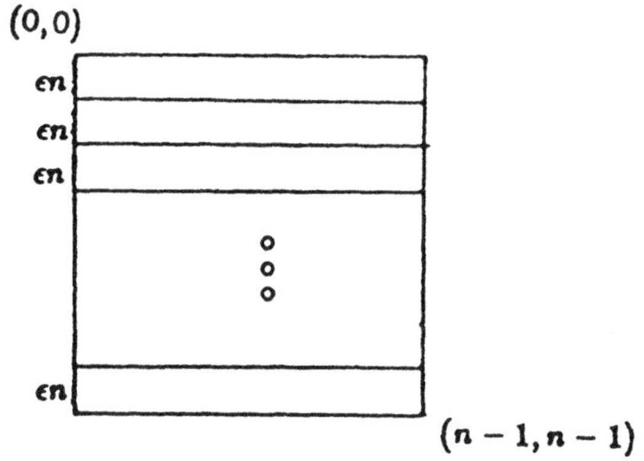

Figure 1: Partition of columns for the $(2+\epsilon)n$ algorithm

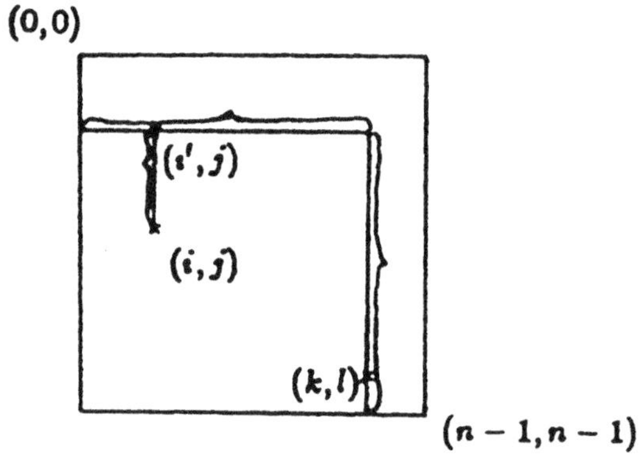

Figure 2: Normal path length of a packet

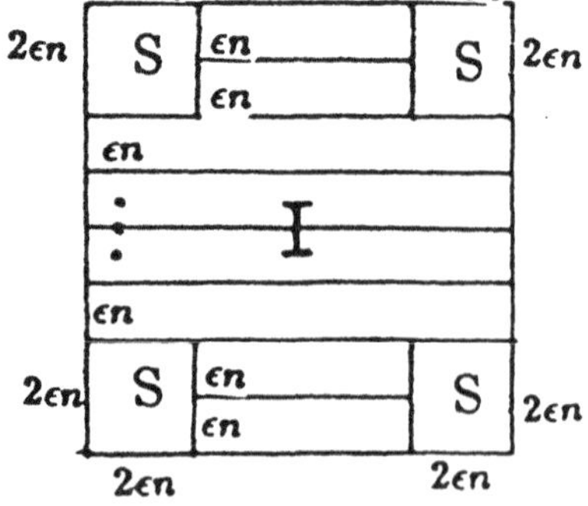

Figure 3: Superior and inferior packets

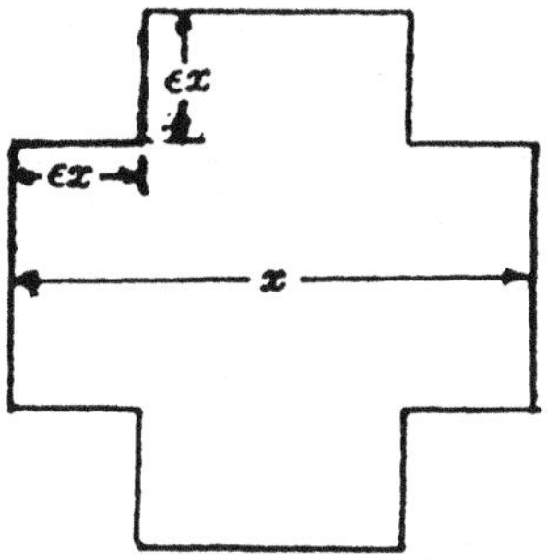

Figure 4: Mesh1 has a diameter of $\sqrt{3}n$

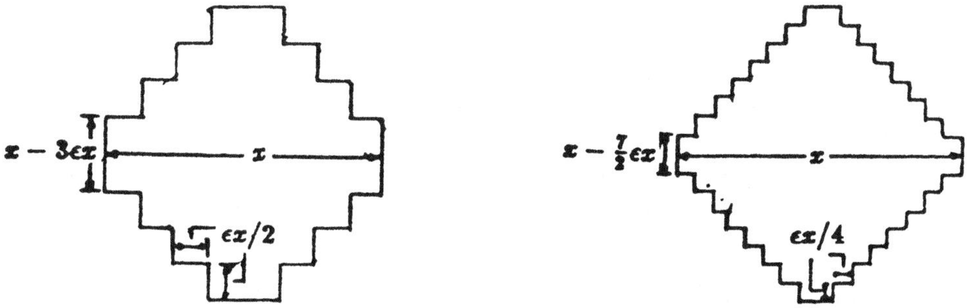

Figure 5: Mesh2 and Mesh3 have diameters $\sqrt{5/2}n$, and $1.5n$ resp.

REFERENCES

- Lang,H.-W. et al., "Systolic Sorting on a Mesh Connected Network," IEEE Transactions on Computers, volume c-34, no.7, 1985.
- Krizanc,D., Private Communication, 1986.
- Kumar,M., and Hirschberg,D.S., "An Efficient Implementation of Batcher's Odd-Even Merge Algorithm and its Application in Parallel Sorting Schemes," IEEE Transactions on Computers, volume c-32, 1983.
- Ma,Y., Sen,S., and Scherson,D., "The Distance Bound for Sorting on Mesh Connected Processor Arrays is Tight," Proc. of the IEEE FOCS, 1986.
- Nassimi,D., and Sahni,S., "Bitonic Sort on a Mesh Connected Parallel Computer," IEEE Transactions on Computers, volume c-27, no.1, 1979.
- Nassimi,D., and Sahni,S., "Data Broadcasting in SIMD Computers," IEEE Transactions on Computers, volume c-30, no.2, 1981.
- Pippenger,N., "Parallel Communication with Limited Buffers," Proc. IEEE Symposium on FOCS, 1984, pp. 127-136.
- Sado,K., and Igarishi,Y., "Some Parallel Sorts on a Mesh Connected Processor Array and their Time Efficiency," to appear in Journal of Parallel and Distributed Computing, 1987.
- Schnorr,C.P., and Shamir,A., "An Optimal Sorting Algorithm for Mesh Connected Computers," Proc. of the ACM STOC, 1986.
- Thompson,C.D., and Kung,H.T., "Sorting on a Mesh Connected Parallel Computer," Communications of the ACM, volume 20, no.4, 1977.
- Thompson,C.D., "The VLSI Complexity of Sorting," IEEE Transactions on Computers, volume c-32, no.12, 1983.
- Valiant,L.G., and Brebner,G.J., "Universal Schemes for Parallel Communication," Proc. of the ACM STOC, 1981.

APPENDIX A: Probabilistic Bounds

We say a random variable X *upper bounds* another random variable Y (equivalently, Y *lower bounds* X) if Probability($X \leq x$) $\leq$ Probability($Y \leq x$) for all x.

A *Bernoulli trial* is an experiment with two possible outcomes viz. *success* and *failure*. The probability of success is p.

A *binomial variable* X with parameters (n,p) is the number of successes in n independent Bernoulli trials, the probability of success in each trial being p.

The *distribution function* of X can easily be seen to be

$$\text{Probability}(X \leq x) \; = \; \sum_{k=0}^{x} \binom{n}{k} p^n (1-p)^{n-k}.$$

[Chernoff 52] and [Angluin and Valiant 79] have found ways of approximating the tail ends of a binomial distribution. In particular, they have shown that

Lemma A.1 *If X is binomial with parameters (n,p), and $m > np$ is an integer, then*

$$Probability(X \geq m) \; \leq \; \left(\frac{np}{m}\right)^m \; e^{m-np}. \tag{1}$$

Also,

$$Probability(X \leq \lfloor (1-\epsilon)pn \rfloor) \; \leq \; exp(-\epsilon^2 np/2) \tag{2}$$

and

$$Probability(X \geq \lceil (1+\epsilon)np \rceil) \; \leq \; exp(-\epsilon^2 np/3) \tag{3}$$

for all $0 < \epsilon < 1$.

An $O(n^2)$ Algorithm for Fan-Out Free Query Optimization

Pratul Dublish S.N. Maheshwari

Department of Computer Science & Engineering
Indian Institute of Technology, Delhi
New Delhi - 110016

Abstract: An optimization algorithm for fan-out free queries, which form an untyped subclass of conjunctive queries, based on the implication graph technique is presented. The algorithm takes $O(n^2)$ steps where n is the size of the query. This algorithm subsumes all known algorithms for optimizing subclasses of fan-out free queries.

Introduction

The problem of query optimization in relational databases has been studied extensively in the past. One of the criteria used for optimizing relational queries has been to minimize the number of joins to be performed for query evaluation [ASU, CM, DM, JK, MM, MDM, Sag]. The pioneering work in this area was done by Chandra and Merlin [CM]. They introduced the class of conjunctive queries and showed that the optimization of conjunctive queries was NP-hard.

Since then attempts have been made to identify subclasses of conjunctive queries which can be optimized in polynomial time. The initial approaches had been to identify typed subclasses like simple tableaux [ASU], queries in which a conjunct is covered by atmost one other conjunct and queries in which a conjunct has atmost one repeated non-distinguished variable [Sag]. Sagiv [Sag] has given $O(n^2)$ optimization algorithms for these three classes. His method is to first convert the given query into a quasi-minimal tableau, for which he gives a **separate** $O(n^2)$ algorithm for each of the above classes. He then optimizes the resulting quasi-minimal tableau by using another $O(n^2)$ optimization algorithm.

Johnson and Klug [JK] were first to identify an untyped subclass, called fan-out free queries, for which they gave an $O(n^3)$ optimization algorithm. Considering that the above typed subclasses can be optimized in $O(n^2)$ time, it is natural to ask whether fan-out free queries can also be optimized in $O(n^2)$ time. The technique of [Sag] does not naturally extend to fan-out free queries, the major stumbling block being the inability to convert a fan-out free query into an untyped quasi-minimal tableau in $O(n^2)$ time. In this paper we present an $O(n^2)$ optimization algorithm for fan-out free queries, based on the work of Johnson and Klug, which uses certain structural properties of implication closures for fan-out free queries to achieve the quadratic time bound. Since the class of fan-out free queries properly contains the class of simple tableaux and the class of queries in which a conjunct is covered by atmost one other conjunct [JK], our algorithm subsumes the two **separate** quadratic algorithms given in [Sag] for these classes. The algorithm developed here can be considered to be an extension of the $O(n^2)$ optimization algorithm, presented in [DM], for an untyped subclass of fan-out free queries.

Definitions

While we assume familiarity with the theory and results presented in [JK], for the sake of readability and completeness we give certain definitions. Definitions of terms not defined can be found in [JK,Mai,Ull].

A **conjunctive query** is an existential first order formula of the form

$$(x_1,x_2,\dots,x_p) \exists\, y_1\, y_2 \cdots y_q\; c_1 \wedge c_2 \wedge \cdots \wedge c_r \;.$$

The free variables x_is are the **distinguished variables (DVs)** and the quantified variables y_is are the **non-distinguished variables (NDVs)**. Each **conjunct** c_i, $1 \le i \le r$, is an atomic formula of the form $R_i(c_i[1],c_i[2],\dots,c_i[m])$ where R_i, also denoted by $R(c_i)$, is some relation from the underlying relation scheme having m attributes and each $c_i[k]$, $1 \leq k \leq m$, is either a DV or a NDV or a **constant**, i.e., an element from the domain of the kth attribute of R_i. A conjunctive query is said to be **typed** if each variable is associated with a unique attribute. Otherwise the query is said to be **untyped**, i.e., a variable may be associated with one or more attributes. A conjunctive query can be looked upon as a function that takes a database as its argument and outputs a p-ary relation (provided the query is well defined on the database). Two conjunctive queries are said to be equivalent iff their respective functions are equivalent. The problem of conjunctive query optimization is, given a conjunctive query Q find an equivalent query Q' with **minimum** number of conjuncts. The query Q' can be found by deleting some conjuncts from Q [CM].

For a conjunctive query Q, let C_Q denote the set of its conjuncts and U_Q be the union of DVs, NDVs and constants occuring in Q. Let Q' be some other conjunctive query such that $C_{Q'} \subseteq C_Q$ and each DV and constant occuring in Q also occurs in Q'. Then a **symbol mapping** from Q to Q' is a function **f** : $U_Q \rightarrow U_{Q'}$ which preserves all DVs and constants. We say $c_2 \in C_{Q'}$ **covers** $c_1 \in C_Q$ if $R(c_1) = R(c_2)$ and there is a symbol mapping from Q to Q' which maps c_1 to c_2. A **conjunct mapping** is a function **g** : $C_Q \rightarrow C_{Q'}$ such that **g**(c_1) covers c_1 for each $c_1 \in C_Q$. A **self-homomorphism h** from Q to Q' is a tuple (**f**,**g**), where **f** is a symbol mapping from Q to Q' and **g** is a conjunct mapping from Q to Q' such that **f** induces **g** and vice versa. A conjunct $c_2 \in C_{Q'}$ is said to be in the **range** of **h** if there is some $c_1 \in C_Q$ such that **g**$(c_1) = c_2$. The self-homomorphism is said to be **shrinking** if $C_{Q'} \subset C_Q$. The importance of shrinking self-homomorphism comes from the fact that if $C_{Q'} \subset C_Q$, then Q and Q' are equivalent iff there is a shrinking self-homomorphism from Q to Q' [CM].

Johnson and Klug [JK] introduced the notion of implication graph for finding shrinking self-homomorphisms. For a conjunctive query Q, the **implication graph** of Q is a bipartite graph G[Q] = (V[Q],E[Q]) defined as follows :
The vertices of G[Q] correspond to the potential elements of homomorphisms. The set of vertices V[Q] consists of $V_C[Q]$, a set of **conjunct-pair vertices (CPVs)**, and $V_S[Q]$, a set of **symbol-pair vertices (SPVs)**. $V_C[Q]$ contains a vertex $\langle c_1,c_2 \rangle$ for each pair of conjuncts in C_Q such that c_2 covers c_1 and a special vertex $\langle \Theta \rangle$, which indicates that no homomorphism is possible. $V_S[Q]$ contains a vertex

$\langle s_1,s_2\rangle$ for each NDV $s_1 \in U_Q$ and each $s_2 \in U_Q$ such that for some CPV $\langle c_1,c_2\rangle$ and some j, $1 \le j \le length(c_2)$, $c_1[j] = s_1$ and $c_2[j] = s_2$. Each edge in E[Q] joins a CPV to a SPV. There is an edge between $\langle s_1,s_2\rangle$ and $\langle \theta\rangle$ iff there is a conjunct c_1 such that $c_1[j] = s_1$ and for each conjunct c_2 covering c_1, $c_2[j] \ne s_2$. There is an edge between $\langle s_1,s_2\rangle$ and $\langle c_1,c_2\rangle$ iff for some j, $c_1[j] = s_1$ and $c_2[j] = s_2$. A conjunctive query and its implication graph are shown in Figure 1(a) and 1(b) respectively.

$$Q = (x1,x2) \exists\, y1\ y2\ y3\ y4\ y5\ y6\ y7\ (c1 \wedge c2 \wedge c3 \wedge c4 \wedge c5 \wedge c6)$$

$$c1 = R(c_1,y1,y5) \qquad c2 = R(c_1,y2,y7)$$

$$c3 = R(x1,y1,y3) \qquad c4 = R(x1,y2,y4)$$

$$c5 = R(c_2,y6,y3) \qquad c6 = R(c_2,x2,y4)$$

Figure 1(a)

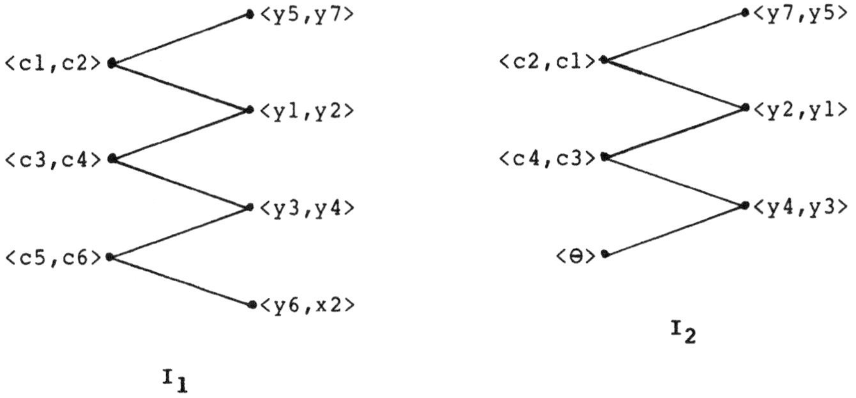

Figure 1(b)

The implication graph is used to find self-homomorphisms in the following way. Suppose we wish to know whether a self-homomorphism mapping a conjunct c_1 to c_2 is possible. Let **h** = (**f**,**g**) be such a homomorphism. Then **g** has the CPV $\langle c_1,c_2\rangle$ (we shall consider **g** to be a set of CPVs and **f** to be a set of SPVs). Since **f** and **g** induce each other, **f** must contain the symbol mappings induced by mapping c_1 to c_2. Note that these mappings are given by the SPVs adjacent to $\langle c_1,c_2\rangle$. We add all such SPVs to **f**. Let $\langle s_1,s_2\rangle$, $s_1 \ne s_2$, be any SPV adjacent to

$\langle c_1, c_2\rangle$. Then all the conjunct mappings induced by $\langle s_1, s_2\rangle$ must be added to **g**. If $\langle s_1, s_2\rangle$ is adjacent to $\langle \theta\rangle$, then we know that no homomorphism is possible. We stop after adding $\langle \theta\rangle$ to **g**. If all CPVs adjacent to $\langle s_1, s_2\rangle$ have the same first component, then since $\langle c_1, c_2\rangle$ has already been added to **g** no other CPV adjacent to $\langle s_1, s_2\rangle$ needs to be added to **g**. If all CPVs adjacent to $\langle s_1, s_2\rangle$ have distinct first component then all of them must be added to **g**. If however $\langle s_1, s_2\rangle$ has CPVs $\langle c_3, c_4\rangle$ and $\langle c_3, c_5\rangle$ adjacent to it, $c_4 \neq c_5$ and $c_3 \neq c_1$, then only one of $\langle c_3, c_4\rangle$ or $\langle c_3, c_5\rangle$ can be added to **g**, but we do not know which choice would eventually lead to a homomorphism. The availability of such choices can cause the optimization problem to become NP-hard [MDM]. To eliminate such choices, Johnson and Klug introduced the class of fan-out free queries. A SPV $\langle s_1, s_2\rangle$ is said to be **fan-out free** if either all its neighbours have the same first component or all its neighbours have distinct first components. A conjunctive query is said to be **fan-out free** iff each SPV $\langle s_1, s_2\rangle$, $s_1 \neq s_2$, in its implication graph is fan-out free. For example, the query shown in Figure 1(a) is fan-out free. Note that when a SPV is examined while building a homomorphism one of its neighbouring CPV has already been added to **g**. Thus for a fan-out free query we either add all the other neighbouring CPVs to **g** or add none of them. The above process continues till no more vertices can be added to **f** and **g**.

Based on the above discussion, the concept of **implication** can be introduced to capture the notion of **f** inducing **g** and vice versa. A CPV **implies** all its neighbouring SPVs. A SPV $\langle s_1, s_1\rangle$ implies nothing and a SPV adjacent to $\langle \theta\rangle$ only implies $\langle \theta\rangle$. A SPV $\langle s_1, s_2\rangle$, $s_1 \neq s_2$, implies a neighbouring CPV $\langle c_1, c_2\rangle$ iff $\langle c_1, c_2\rangle$ is the only CPV adjacent to $\langle s_1, s_2\rangle$ having c_1 as its first component. The **implication closure** (**IC**) of a CPV $\langle c_1, c_2\rangle$ is the smallest superset of $\{\langle c_1, c_2\rangle\}$ closed under implication. For example, in Figure 1(b), I_1 is the IC of $\langle c1,c2\rangle$. It is also the IC of $\langle c3,c4\rangle$ and $\langle c5,c6\rangle$. The importance of ICs arises from the following fact (Theorem 3.2 in [JK]). For a fan-out free query if an IC does not contain $\langle \theta\rangle$ and a conjunct (NDV) appears as the first component of atmost one CPV (SPV) in the IC, then the IC induces a self-homomorphism **h**= (**f**,**g**) where

$$\mathbf{f} = \{\langle s_1, s_2\rangle : \langle s_1, s_2\rangle \in \text{IC or else } s_1 = s_2\}$$
$$\mathbf{g} = \{\langle c_1, c_2\rangle : \langle c_1, c_2\rangle \in \text{IC or else } c_1 = c_2\}.$$

Note that I_1, in Figure 1(b), induces a shrinking self-homomorphism but I_2 fails to induce a self-homomorphism since it contains $\langle \theta\rangle$. Thus to verify whether there is an homomorphism mapping c_1 to c_2, we construct the IC $\{\langle c_1,c_2\rangle\}$ and check whether it induces a self-homomorphism.

Given a fan-out free query Q, let v_s and v_t be two distinct vertices not adjacent to each other in G[Q].An **implication path** from v_s to v_t is an alternating sequence of CPVs and SPVs $v_1,v_2,\ldots,v_k$ such that v_s implies v_1, v_i implies v_{i+1}, $1\leq i\leq k-1$, and v_k implies v_t. If v_s is a CPV (SPV) then v_1 is a SPV (CPV). For example, in Figure 1(b), the implication path from <c1,c2> to <c5,c6> is <y1,y2>, <c3,c4>, <y3,y4>. If v_s and v_t are both CPVs, then by reversing the implication path from v_s to v_t we obtain an implication path from v_t to v_s. Hence there is an implication path between any two CPVs in an IC. This statement is not true, in general, for SPVs. To see this consider the case when v_t is an SPV. Then it is quite possible that v_t does not imply any of its neighbours and in particular does not imply v_k. Thus the implication path cannot be reversed. But if v_t implies all its neighbouring CPVs (v_s already does so since it implies v_1) then the implication path can be reversed. Hence there is an implication path **between** any two SPVs in an IC provided both the SPVs imply all their neighbouring CPVs. Note that a CPV (SPV which implies all its neighbours) has an implication path to each vertex in the IC in which the CPV (SPV) lies and it does not have any implication path to a CPV (SPV, except of type <y,y>,) which lies in some other IC.

The Optimization Algorithm

The fan-out free query optimization algorithm of [JK] can essentially be summarized to the following :

repeat

1. Construct the implication graph **G** for the query **Q**;
2. **if** $\exists$ an IC **I** in **G** inducing a shrinking self-homomorphism **h**
   then
   delete from Q the conjuncts not in the range of **h**
   else
   exit;

forever

G has $O(n^2)$ edges and can be constructed in $O(n^2)$ time [JK]. The search for **I** can be carried out in time proportional to the size of **G** [JK]. Thus in each iteration of the **repeat** loop, step 1 and step 2 may take $O(n^2)$ time each. Since, in the worst case, the **repeat** loop may have to be iterated $O(n)$ times, the above algorithm runs in $O(n^3)$ time.

Note that an iteration, say the jth one, of the **repeat** loop starts with an query Q^j and obtains a reduced query Q^{j+1} by deleting some conjuncts from it. In the $(j+1)^{th}$ iteration, step 1 constructs $G[Q^{j+1}]$. Note that each conjunct (symbol) present in Q^{j+1} is also present in Q^j, therefore each CPV (SPV) present in $G[Q^{j+1}]$ is also present in $G[Q^j]$. It is, therefore, natural to consider whether $G[Q^{j+1}]$ could be obtained by simply deleting from $G[Q^j]$ those CPVs and SPVs such that at least one of their components does not appear in Q^{j+1}. However, it is not obvious whether the above deletion will always result in $G[Q^{j+1}]$ since a non <θ>-adjacent SPV in $G[Q^j]$ may become <θ>-adjacent in $G[Q^{j+1}]$ or a <θ>-adjacent SPV in $G[Q^j]$ may become non <θ>-adjacent in $G[Q^{j+1}]$. We shall now show that by carefully choosing **I**, in step 2, $G[Q^{j+1}]$ can be obtained from $G[Q^j]$ by the above deletion process.

Central to our approach is the notion of a **disjoint** IC which is defined as follows. An IC is said to be **disjoint** if the set containing conjuncts which appear as first component of CPVs in the IC and the set containing conjuncts which appear as the second component of CPVs in the IC, are disjoint. For example the ICs I_1 and I_2, shown in Figure 1(b), are disjoint. Let Q1 be a fan-out free query and let I1 be a disjoint IC in G[Q1] which induces a shrinking self-homomorphism h_1. Since I1 is disjoint, each conjunct appearing as the first component of some CPV in I1 does not appear in the range of h_1. Let Q2 be the query obtained from Q1 by deleting the conjuncts not in the range of h_1. We now show that G[Q2] can effectively be obtained from G[Q1] by deleting from it each CPV <c1,c2> such that c1 or c2 does not appear in the range of h_1.

Note that each CPV (SPV) in G[Q2] also appears in G[Q1]. The above deletion process deletes all CPVs involving conjuncts which do not appear in Q2. However if both components of a CPV are in Q2 then that CPV is not deleted. Hence the CPVs remaining after deletion are precisely the CPVs in G[Q2]. The CPV deletion causes SPVs with atleast one symbol not in Q2 to have all their adjacent CPVs to be deleted. Such SPVs, therefore, become isolated and cannot appear in any IC in G[Q2]. Hence we do not bother about SPV deletion. To complete the proof, we must show that <θ>-adjacency structure is preserved across G[Q1] and G[Q2], i.e., if a SPV <s1,s2> appears unisolated in G[Q2] then <s1,s2> is <θ>-adjacent (not <θ>-adjacent) in G[Q2] iff it is <θ>-adjacent (not <θ>-adjacent) in G[Q1].

Consider the case when <s1,s2> is <θ>-adjacent in G[Q1]. Then there is a conjunct c1 in Q1 which is not mappable to any conjunct under any symbol mapping which maps s1 to s2. If c1 appears in Q2 then <s1,s2> is <θ>-adjacent in G[Q2]. If c1 does not appear in Q2, then since <s1,s2> is not isolated there is atleast one conjunct in Q2 in which s1 occurs. Since c1 does not appear in Q2, c1 appears as the first component of some CPV, say <c1,c3>, in I1. Note that <c1,c3> implies the SPV <s1,s1>. To see this consider the case when <c1,c3> implies a SPV <s1,s3>, s1≠s3. Since <s1,s3> is not <θ>-adjacent, each conjunct in Q1, in which s1 occurs, occurs as the first component of some CPV implied by <s1,s3>. Since I1 is disjoint, no conjunct in which s1 occurs can be present in Q2. This contradicts the fact that <s1,s2> is an unisolated SPV in G[Q2]. Since c3 appears in Q2 and c3 is not mappable to any conjunct under any symbol mapping which maps s1 to s2 (otherwise c1 would also be mappable to that conjunct) therefore <s1,s2> is <θ>-adjacent in G[Q2]. The proof of the remaining cases can also be carried out similarly.

We shall show later that the optimization of fan-out free queries can be carried out by using only disjoint ICs, i.e., in each iteration I, the IC discovered in step 2, is always disjoint. Then it follows from the above discussion that the algorithm of [JK] can be modified to the following :

1. Construct the implication graph **G** for the query **Q**.
2. **while** ∃ an IC **I** in **G** inducing a shrinking self-homomorphism **h**
   do
   begin
   delete from Q the conjuncts not in the range of **h**;
   delete from **G** each CPV <c1,c2> such that c1 or c2 does not appear in the range of **h**;
   end;

However, it is not obvious that the above modification will result in an $O(n^2)$ algorithm since step 2 may still take $O(n^3)$ time. To see this consider the following. Each iteration of the **while** loop (in step 2) scans **G** searching for an IC which induces a shrinking self-homomorphism. Suppose during the jth iteration of the **while** loop ICs $I_1, I_2, \ldots, I_k$ are scanned before discovering **I**, the IC inducing a shrinking self-homomorphism. Clearly ICs I_i, $1 \leq i \leq k$, do not induce shrinking self-homomorphisms in the jth iteration. Now consider the effect of the CPV deletion in the jth iteration on I and each I_i. Since **I** is disjoint, the CPV deletion would delete each conjunct in it. So no CPV in **I** will be scanned in any future iteration. If each CPV in I_i is deleted then clearly no CPV in I_i will ever be scanned in any future iteration. If only some CPVs in I_i are deleted, then I_i may split up into a number of ICs. It is possible that a resultant fragment of I_i may induce a shrinking self-homomorphism and so in the $(j+1)^{th}$ iteration, we may have to rescan the fragments of I_i, $1 \leq i \leq k$. Of course, if no CPV in I_i is deleted then I_i need not be scanned in the $(j+1)^{th}$ iteration since it cannot induce a shrinking self-homomorphism. However, we cannot rule out the possibility of I_i splitting into fragments in some future iteration and the fragments being scanned again. Since the size of the parts being rescanned can be $O(n^2)$ and the **while** loop may have to be iterated $O(n)$ times, in the worst case, step 2 can take $O(n^3)$ time.

We now show that for each I_i, scanned in the jth iteration while searching for **I**, the CPV deletion in the jth iteration either deletes all its CPVs and hence no fragment is formed or the resultant fragments also do not induce a shrinking self-homomorphism.

<u>Lemma 1</u>: Let **Q** be a fan-out free query and let G be its implication graph. Let **I** be a disjoint IC in **G** inducing a shrinking self-homomorphism **h**. Let <c1,c2> be any CPV in **I**. Let I1 be any other IC in **G**. Then

(i) if <c3,c1> $\in$ I1, then each conjunct appearing as the second component of some CPV in I1 does not appear in the range of **h**

(ii) if <c1,c3> $\in$ I1, then each conjunct appearing as the first component of some CPV in I1 does not appear in the range of **h** provided one of the following holds

(a) No SPV in **I** is of the form $<\bar{s},\bar{s}>$

(b) If **I** does have a SPV $<\bar{s},\bar{s}>$, then the SPV in I1 having $\bar{s}$ as its first component is either $<\theta>$-adjacent or does not imply any CPV.

<u>Proof</u> : Note that since <c1,c2> ∈ **I** and **I** is disjoint, c1 does not appear in the range of **h.**

(i) Let <s3,s1> be any SPV adjacent to <c3,c1> in I1 such that <s3,s1> implies at least one other CPV besides <c3,c1>. Note that <c1,c2> in **I** cannot have <s1,s1> adjacent to it otherwise <c3,c2> would be adjacent to <s3,s1> making <s3,s1> an fan-out vertex. Hence <c1,c2> has <s1,s2>, s1 ≠ s2, adjacent to it in **I.** Now for each $\langle c_z, c_x \rangle$ adjacent to <s3,s1> in I1 there exists a CPV $\langle c_x, c_y \rangle$, $c_x \neq c_y$, adjacent to <s1,s2> in **I.** If not then <s1,s2> is <Θ>-adjacent violating the assumption that **I** induces a shrinking self-homomorphism. Since **I** is disjoint each conjunct c_x, such that $\langle c_z, c_x \rangle$ is adjacent to <s3,s1> in I1 and $\langle c_x, c_y \rangle$ is adjacent to <s1,s2> in **I**, does not appear in the range of **h.** By inductively applying the same argument at CPVs $\langle c_x, c_y \rangle$ ∈ **I** and $\langle c_z, c_x \rangle$ ∈ I1 we can show that each conjunct appearing as the second component of some CPV in I1 does not appear in the range of **h.**

(ii) Let <s1,s3> be any SPV adjacent to <c1,c3> in I1 such that <s1,s3> implies at least one other CPV besides <c1,c3>. Note that <c1,c2> in **I** cannot have <s1,s1> adjacent to it, since it would lead to the violation of (a) or (b). Hence <c1,c2> in **I** has <s1,s2>, s2≠s1 and s2≠s3, adjacent to it. Now for each CPV $\langle c_x, c_z \rangle$ adjacent to <s1,s3> in I1 there is a CPV $\langle c_x, c_y \rangle$, $c_y \neq c_x$ and $c_y \neq c_z$, adjacent to <s1,s2> in **I.** If not then <s1,s2> is <Θ>-adjacent, violating the assumption that **I** induces a shrinking self-homomorphism. Since **I** is disjoint, each conjunct c_x such that $\langle c_x, c_z \rangle$ is adjacent to <s1,s3> does not appear in the range of **h.** By inductively applying the same argument at CPVs $\langle c_x, c_z \rangle$ ∈ I1 and $\langle c_x, c_y \rangle$ ∈ **I**, we can show that each conjunct appearing as the first component of some CPV in I1 does not appear in the range of **h.** ∎

Lemma 1 specifies the conditions under which all the CPVs of an IC, say I1, can be deleted in an iteration of the **while** loop, provided that **I** is disjoint. Suppose that I1 does not induce a shrinking self-homomorphism and also does not obey the conditions of Lemma 1. If no CPV of I1 is deleted in this iteration then I1 cannot induce a shrinking self-homomorphism in the next iteration. However, if part (ii) of Lemma 1 holds but the conditions (a) and (b) do not hold, then we cannot guarantee that all the CPVs in I1 will be deleted in this iteration. To see this consider the situation when a CPV

<c1,c2> in **I** has a SPV <s1,s1> adjacent to it. Let I1 have a CPV <c1,c3>, c1≠c3, which implies <s1,s3>, s1≠s3. Assume **wlg** that I1 does not obey the conditions in part (i) of Lemma 1 (otherwise each CPV in I1 can be deleted). Although we can delete the CPV <c1,c3>, we cannot guarantee the deletion of the other CPVs implied by <s1,s3> since <s1,s3> may imply $<c_x,c_y>$ such that both c_x and c_y appear in the range of **h**. Therefore if (a) and (b) do not hold then I1 could undergo a partial deletion which could cause it to split into a number of ICs, which we term as **fragments** of I1. It is not immediately clear whether these fragments can or cannot induce a shrinking self-homomorphism in the next iteration. We now show that if **I** is a disjoint IC then the fragments of I1 continue to have the properties of I1. Note that if the fragments are to result then <s1,s3> must imply atleast one other CPV besides <c1,c3>. In particular it must imply a CPV whose first component is c2 since <c1,c2> is adjacent to <s1,s1>. We claim that this CPV is <c2,c3>, because if <s1,s3> implies $<c2,c_x>$, $c_x \neq c3$, then <s1,s3> also implies $<c1,c_x>$ making it a fan-out vertex. Note that <c2,c3> cannot be deleted since both c2 and c3 appear in the range of **h**. Suppose I1 splits into two or more fragments. Let I_p and I_q be any two fragments of I1. Then we can find a CPV $<c_p,\bar{c}_p>$ in I_p and a CPV $<c_q,\bar{c}_q>$ in I_q which had an implication path between them in I1 such that no vertex on this implication path is in I_p, except the SPV implied by $<c_p,\bar{c}_p>$, and no vertex on this implication path is in I_q, except the SPV implied by $<c_q,\bar{c}_q>$. Let $<s_p,\bar{s}_p>$ ($<s_q,\bar{s}_q>$) be the SPV implied by $<c_p,\bar{c}_p>$ ($<c_q,\bar{c}_q>$). Since the CPV implied by $<s_p,\bar{s}_p>$ on the implication path is deleted but $<s_p,\bar{s}_p>$ is not isolated therefore **I** must have the SPV $<s_p,s_p>$ (remember **I** is disjoint). Similarly it can be shown that **I** also has the SPV $<s_q,s_q>$. Note that since $<s_p,\bar{s}_p>$ and $<s_q,\bar{s}_q>$ lie on an implication path in I1, they imply all their neighbouring CPVs. Hence there is an implication path between them in I1. In fact this implication path can be obtained by deleting these SPVs from the implication path between $<c_p,\bar{c}_p>$ and $<c_q,\bar{c}_q>$.

Consider the case when I1 induces an identity homomorphism in the current iteration. Then if a conjunct appears as the first component of some CPV in I1 it also appears as the second component of some CPV in I1. Hence whenever a CPV of I1 is deleted part (i) of Lemma 1 is applicable. Therefore all the CPVs in I1 are deleted.

In the following we assume that I1 stands for an IC which does not induce a homomorphism in the current iteration of the **while** loop and it does not obey the conditions of Lemma 1, i.e., not all CPVs of I1 are deleted by the CPV deletion caused by **I**. Further **I** is assumed to be disjoint.

<u>Lemma 2</u> : Let the CPV deletion, caused by **I**, result in I1 splitting into fragments $I_1, I_2, \ldots, I_f$, $f \geq 2$. Then each fragment of I1 contains $\langle \theta \rangle$.

<u>Proof</u> : Note that for any fragment I_p we can always find another fragment I_q, $1 \leq p \neq q \leq f$, and SPVs $\langle s_p, \bar{s}_p \rangle$, $s_p \neq \bar{s}_p$, and $\langle s_q, \bar{s}_q \rangle$, $s_q \neq \bar{s}_q$, in I_p and I_q respectively such that no vertex on the implication path between $\langle s_p, \bar{s}_p \rangle$ and $\langle s_q, \bar{s}_q \rangle$ (such a path must have existed in I1) lies in any fragment I_r, $1 \leq r \leq f$. Let the implication path between $\langle s_p, \bar{s}_p \rangle$ and $\langle s_q, \bar{s}_q \rangle$ in I1 be as shown in Figure 2(a). Note that the

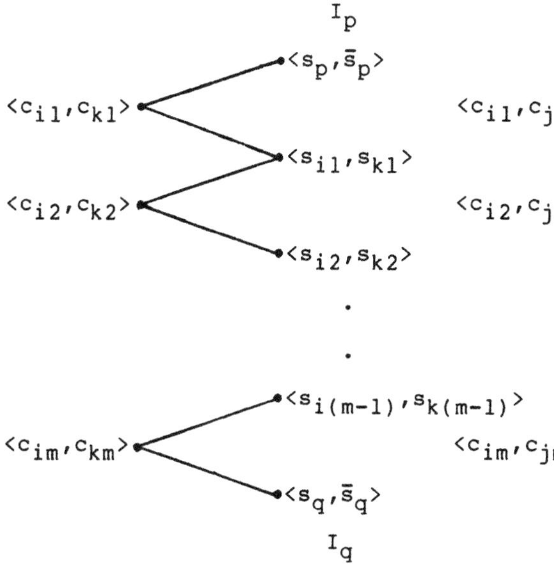

Figure 2(a)

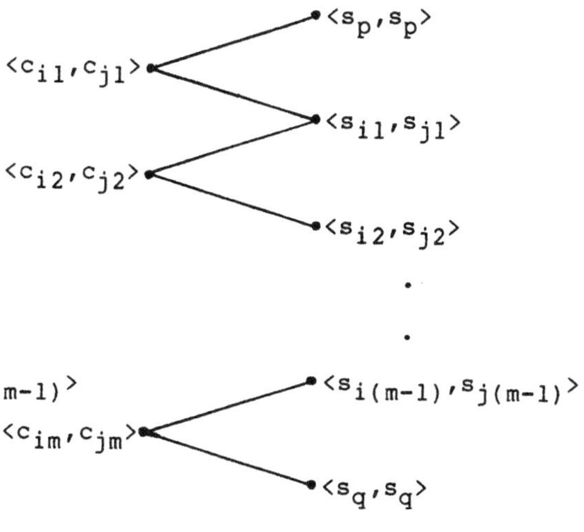

Figure 2(b)

CPV deletion caused by I deletes each CPV $\langle c_{it}, c_{kt} \rangle$ on this path, $1 \leq t \leq m$, and isolates each SPV $\langle s_{iu}, s_{ku} \rangle$, $1 \leq u \leq m-1$. Since $\langle c_{i1}, c_{k1} \rangle$ is deleted therefore **I** must have a CPV $\langle c_{i1}, c_{j1} \rangle$, $c_{i1} \neq c_{j1}$. Since the SPV $\langle s_p, \bar{s}_p \rangle$ is not isolated therefore in **I** the CPV $\langle c_{i1}, c_{j1} \rangle$ implies the SPV $\langle s_p, s_p \rangle$. We claim that $\langle c_{i1}, c_{j1} \rangle$ also implies the SPV $\langle s_{i1}, s_{j1} \rangle$,

$s_{i1} \neq s_{j1}$. Consider the case when $\langle c_{i1}, c_{j1} \rangle$ implies $\langle s_{i1}, s_{i1} \rangle$. Then in I1 the SPV $\langle s_{i1}, s_{k1} \rangle$ must imply a CPV whose first component is c_{j1}. This CPV is not deleted by the CPV deletion caused by I since c_{j1} appears in the range of **h**. Hence $\langle s_{i1}, s_{k1} \rangle$ is not isolated, a contradiction. Since the conjunct c_{i2} contains the symbol s_{i1} (see Figure 2(a)) hence in I the SPV $\langle s_{i1}, s_{j1} \rangle$ must imply a CPV $\langle c_{i2}, c_{j2} \rangle$ or else $\langle s_{i1}, s_{j1} \rangle$ would be $\langle \Theta \rangle$-adjacent violating the assumption that I is disjoint. By repeatedly applying the above argument we can show that there is an implication path in I (see Figure 2(b)) corresponding to the implication path between $\langle s_p, \bar{s}_p \rangle$ and $\langle s_q, \bar{s}_q \rangle$ in I1.

Suppose that I_p does not contain $\langle \Theta \rangle$. Since the NDV s_p occurs in the conjunct c_{j1} (see Figure 2(b)) therefore in I_p the SPV $\langle s_p, \bar{s}_p \rangle$ must imply a CPV whose first component is c_{j1}. From arguments immediately preceding this lemma it follows that this CPV is $\langle c_{j1}, c_{k1} \rangle$. Since c_{j1} appears in the range of **h**, the CPV $\langle c_{j1}, c_{k1} \rangle$ is not deleted by the CPV deletion caused by **I**. Hence $\langle c_{j1}, c_{k1} \rangle$ is in I_p. Note that $\langle c_{j1}, c_{k1} \rangle$ implies the SPV $\langle s_{j1}, s_{k1} \rangle$. Since I_p does not contain $\langle \Theta \rangle$ therefore $\langle s_{j1}, s_{k1} \rangle$ must imply the CPV $\langle c_{j2}, c_{k2} \rangle$ which in turn implies the SPV $\langle s_{j2}, s_{k2} \rangle$. Since c_{j2} appears in the range of **h**, therefore $\langle c_{j2}, c_{k2} \rangle$ is also in I_p. By repeatedly applying this argument we can show that I_p contain the CPV $\langle c_{jm}, c_{km} \rangle$ and the SPV $\langle s_q, \bar{s}_q \rangle$. This contradicts our assumption that I_p and I_q are two distinct fragments, since $\langle s_q, \bar{s}_q \rangle$ has an implication path to each vertex in I_q. Therefore I_p must contain $\langle \Theta \rangle$. ∎

As a result of Lemma 2, if I1 splits up into two or more fragments then none of these fragments can induce a homomorphism in the next iteration of the **while** loop. We now show that this also holds if only a single fragment is formed from I1 due to CPV deletion in the current iteration of the **while** loop. Lemma 3 considers the case when I1 contains $\langle \Theta \rangle$ and Lemma 4 the case when I1 contains two distinct CPVs having the same first component.

<u>Lemma 3</u>: Let I_1 be the single fragment of I1. If I1 contains $\langle \Theta \rangle$ then I_1 also contains $\langle \Theta \rangle$.

<u>Proof</u>: Suppose I_1 does not contain $\langle \Theta \rangle$. Then we can find a SPV $\langle s1, s2 \rangle$ in I_1 which had an implication path to $\langle \Theta \rangle$ in I1 such that no vertex on this implication path lies in I_1 (see Figure 3(a)). By arguments similar to those used in Lemma 2, we can show that there is an

corresponding implication path in **I** (see Figure 3(b)). Note that $s_{im} \neq s_{jm}$ or else the SPV $\langle s_{im}, s_{km} \rangle$ (see Figure 3(a)) would not be isolated contradicting the assumption that I_1 is the only fragment of I1. Since I_1 does not contain $\langle \Theta \rangle$, the SPV $\langle s1, s2 \rangle$ must imply the CPV

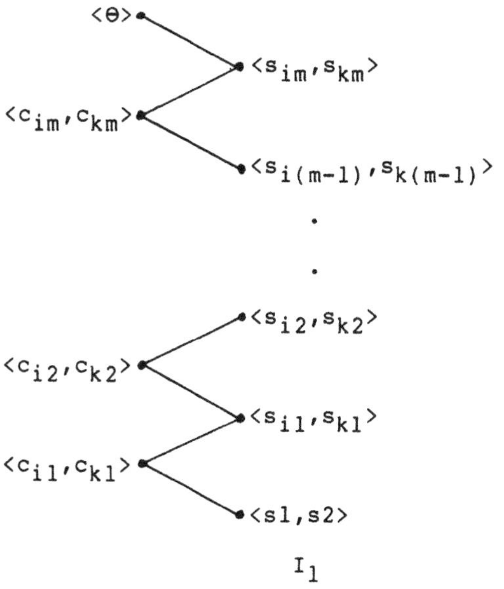

Figure 3(a)

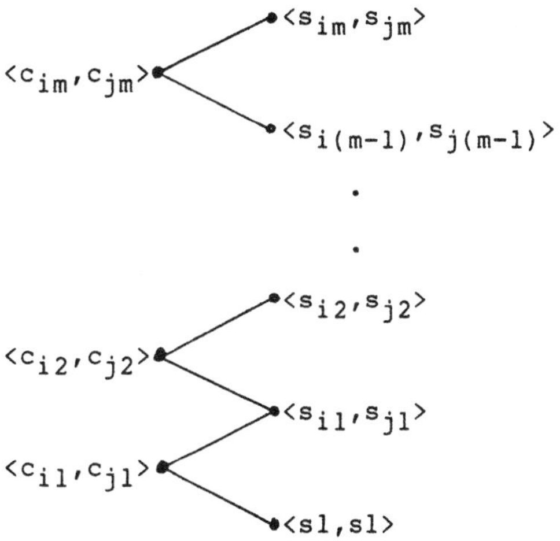

Figure 3(b)

$\langle c_{j1}, c_{k1} \rangle$. Since c_{j1} appears in the range of **h**, hence $\langle c_{j1}, c_{k1} \rangle$ must be in I_1. By arguments similar to those used in Lemma 2, we can show that I_1 contains the CPV $\langle c_{jm}, c_{km} \rangle$ and the SPV $\langle s_{jm}, s_{km} \rangle$. Since I_1 does not contain $\langle \Theta \rangle$, therefore $\langle s_{jm}, s_{km} \rangle$ is not $\langle \Theta \rangle$-adjacent. Since **I** is disjoint , $\langle s_{im}, s_{jm} \rangle$ is also not $\langle \Theta \rangle$-adjacent. But then $\langle s_{im}, s_{km} \rangle$ in I1 also cannot be $\langle \Theta \rangle$-adjacent, contradicting the assumption that I1 contained $\langle \Theta \rangle$. Hence I_1 must contain $\langle \Theta \rangle$. ∎

Lemma 4: Let I1 contain CPVs $\langle c_p, c_q \rangle$ and $\langle c_p, c_r \rangle$, $c_q \neq c_r$. Then I_1, the single fragment of I1, also contains two distinct CPVs having the same first component.

Proof: **Wlg** assume that I1 does not contain $\langle \Theta \rangle$. Suppose that the statement of this lemma does not hold for I_1. Then I_1 does not contain the CPVs $\langle c_p, c_q \rangle$ and $\langle c_p, c_r \rangle$. Note that it is not possible for I_1 to contain only one of these CPVs since I_1 is the only fragment of I1 and the CPV deletion either deletes both these CPVs or deletes none of

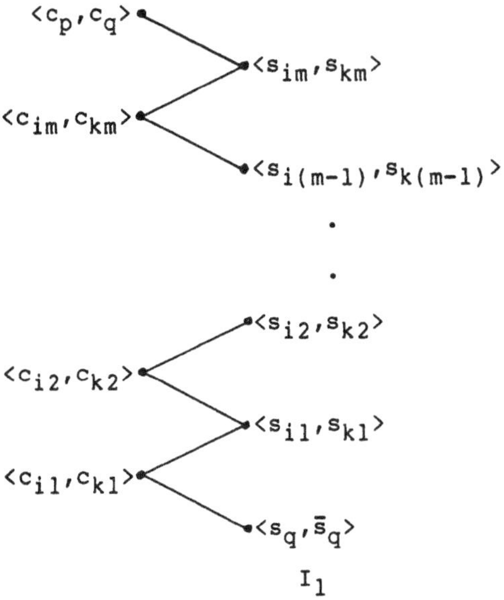

Figure 4(a)

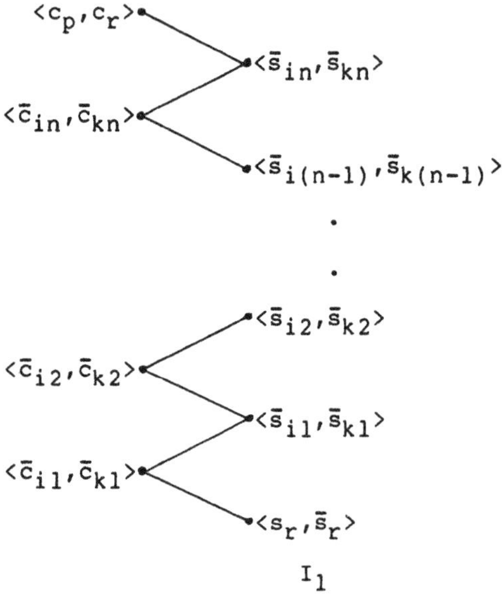

Figure 4(b)

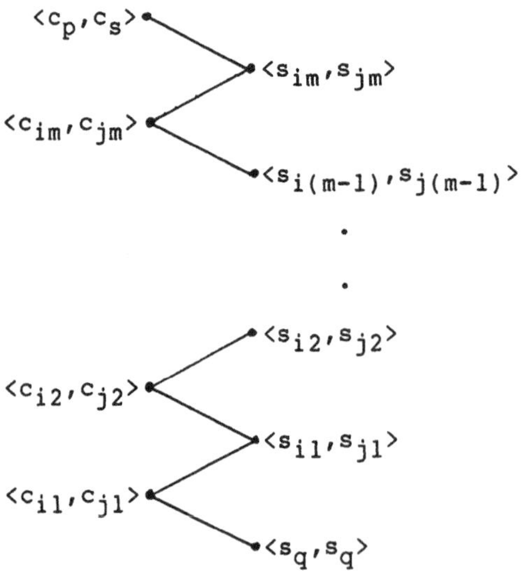

Figure 4(c)

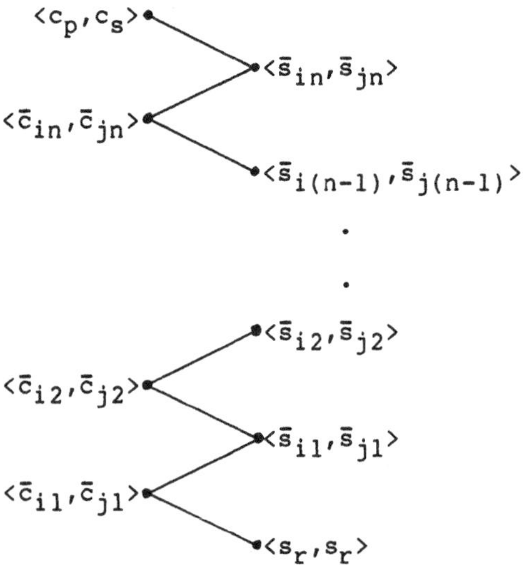

Figure 4(d)

them. In I_1 we can find a SPV $<s_q,\bar{s}_q>$, $s_q \neq \bar{s}_q$ ($<s_r,\bar{s}_r>$, $s_r \neq \bar{s}_r$), which had an implication path to $<c_p,c_q>$ ($<c_p,c_r>$) in I1 such that no vertex on this implication path is in I_1 (see Figures 4(a) and 4(b) respectively). Note that these two implication paths may be overlapping and the SPVs $<s_q,\bar{s}_q>$ and $<s_r,\bar{s}_r>$ may indeed be the same. Since $<c_p,c_q>$ and $<c_p,c_r>$ are deleted hence **I** must have a CPV $<c_p,c_s>$, $c_p \neq c_s$. By arguments similar to those used in Lemma 2 we can show that **I** has implication paths from $<c_p,c_s>$ to $<s_q,s_q>$ and $<s_r,s_r>$ as shown in Figures 4(c) and 4(d) respectively. By applying the argument used in Lemma 2 to Figures 4(a), 4(c) and Figures 4(b), 4(d) respectively we can show that I_1 contains the CPVs $<c_s,c_q>$ and $<c_s,c_r>$. ∎

We have shown that if in an iteration of the **while** loop the IC **I** used is disjoint then for any other IC I1, such that I1 does not induce a shrinking self-homomorphism in the same iteration, either all its CPVs are deleted in the current iteration or none of its fragments can induce a shrinking self-homomorphism in the next iteration. Further all the CPVs of **I** are also deleted in the current iteration. Hence if it was possible to use a disjoint IC in each iteration then parts of G scanned once need not be scanned again. This would result in step 2 taking $O(n^2)$ time and thereby give us an $O(n^2)$ optimization algorithm. We now show that fan-out free query optimization can be carried out by only using disjoint ICs.

Consider an IC which induces a shrinking self-homomorphism in an iteration of the **while** loop but is not disjoint. Then there are atleast two distinct CPVs in the IC such that the first component of one of them is the second component of the other. Therefore one of the following must hold

(i) the IC has a **chain**, i.e., it has CPVs <c1,c2> and <c2,c3> such that c3 does not appear as the first component of any CPV in the IC. Note that c1 **may** occur as the second component of some CPV in the IC.

(ii) the IC has a **cycle**, i.e., it has CPVs $\{<c_i,c_{i+1}>, <c_k,c_1> : 1 \leq i<k$ and $k \geq 2\}$ where all conjuncts c_j, $1 \leq j \leq k$, are distinct. Note that a conjunct c_i, $1 \leq i \leq k$, **may** occur as the second component of some other CPV in the IC which is not in this cycle.

The following lemma rules out chains in ICs inducing shrinking self-homomorphisms.

<u>Lemma 5</u> : For a fan-out free query, every IC inducing a shrinking self-homomorphism is free from chains.

<u>Proof</u> : Suppose an IC inducing a shrinking self-homomorphism has a chain and let <c1,c2> and <c2,c3> be the components of the chain. Since <c1,c2> and <c2,c3> are in the same implication closure there exists an implication path from <c1,c2> to <c2,c3> containing p distinct SPVs and p-1 distinct CPVs, $p \geq 1$ (see Figure 5). Since

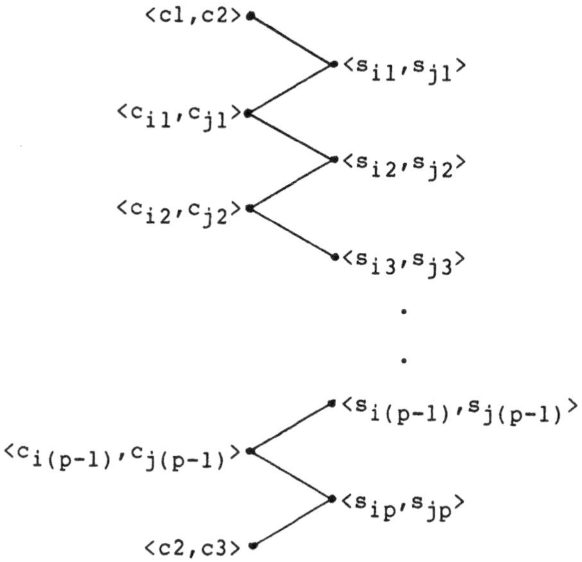

Figure 5

<c1,c2> implies $\langle s_{i1}, s_{j1} \rangle$, $s_{i1} \neq s_{j1}$, hence <c2,c3> must imply a SPV whose first component is s_{j1}. This SPV cannot be $\langle s_{j1}, s_{j1} \rangle$ or else <c1,c3> is adjacent to $\langle s_{i1}, s_{j1} \rangle$ making it a fan-out vertex. If $\langle s_{j1}, s_{i1} \rangle$ is adjacent to <c2,c3> then either <c3,c4> is adjacent to $\langle s_{i1}, s_{j1} \rangle$ or $\langle s_{i1}, s_{j1} \rangle$ is $\langle \Theta \rangle$-adjacent, a contradiction in either case. Hence $\langle s_{j1}, s_{k1} \rangle$ is adjacent to <c2,c3>, $s_{k1} \neq s_{i1}$ and $s_{k1} \neq s_{j1}$. Now $\langle c_{j1}, c_{k1} \rangle$, $c_{j1} \neq c_{k1}$, must be adjacent to $\langle s_{j1}, s_{k1} \rangle$ or else this SPV is $\langle \Theta \rangle$-adjacent. By applying the same logic to $\langle c_{i1}, c_{j1} \rangle$ and $\langle c_{j1}, c_{k1} \rangle$ we can show that the CPV $\langle c_{j2}, c_{k2} \rangle$, $c_{k2} \neq c_{j2}$, also occurs in the IC. By repeating this argument we can show that the IC has a CPV <c3,c4>, $c4 \neq c3$, which is a contradiction. ∎

However, for fan-out free queries we cannot rule out the existence of cyclic ICs which induce a shrinking self-homomorphism.

Figures 6(a) and 6(b) illustrate one such query and its cyclic IC.

$$Q = \exists\ s1\ s2\ s3\ s4\ s5\ s6\quad c1 \wedge c2 \wedge c3 \wedge c4 \wedge c5$$

c1 = R(s1,s5,s6)   c2 = R(s1,s5,c)

c3 = R(s2,s4,c)   c4 = S(s1,s4)

c5 = S(s2,s5)

Figure 6(a)

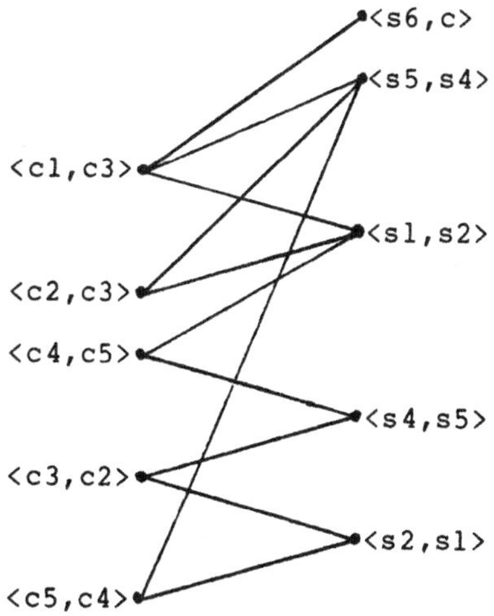

Figure 6(b)

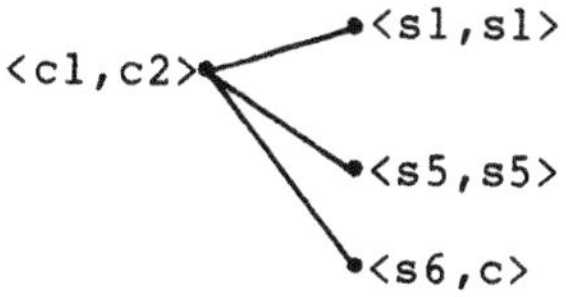

Figure 6(c)

Note that the cyclic IC shown in figure 6(b) causes the deletion of conjunct c1 only. The same deletion can also be obtained by using a disjoint IC as shown in figure 6(c). We formalize this observation to show that fan-out free queries can be optimized **without** using cyclic ICs. Lemmas 6 and 7 prove some structural properties of cyclic ICs. Lemma 8 uses these properties to show that optimization can be carried out without using cyclic ICs.

<u>Lemma 6</u> : For a fan-out free query, let I_c be a cyclic IC inducing a shrinking self-homomorphism. Let the cycle in I_c be $\{<c_i,c_{i+1}>, <c_k,c_1> : 1 \le i < k \text{ and } k \ge 2\}$. Let $<s_1,s_2>$ be any SPV adjacent to $<c_1,c_2>$. Then

(i) if $s_1=s_2$, then each CPV in the cycle has the SPV $\langle s_1,s_1\rangle$ adjacent to it

(ii) if $s_1\neq s_2$, then for each i, $2\leq i<k$, $\langle s_i,s_{i+1}\rangle$ is adjacent to $\langle c_i,c_{i+1}\rangle$ such that $s_{i+1}\neq s_j, \forall\ j\leq i$.

<u>Proof</u> : (i) Since $\langle s_1,s_1\rangle$ is adjacent to $\langle c_1,c_2\rangle$, $\langle c_2,c_3\rangle$ must imply a SPV whose first component is s_1. To avoid non-homomorphism, this SPV must also be $\langle s_1,s_1\rangle$. By repeating the same argument at each CPV in the cycle, the proof follows.

(ii) Suppose $s_{i+1}=s_j$ for some $j\leq i$. If $j=i$, then $\langle c_i,c_{i+1}\rangle$ has $\langle s_i,s_i\rangle$ adjacent to it. Then from part (i) it follows that each CPV in the cycle has $\langle s_i,s_i\rangle$ adjacent to it. This contradicts the assumption that $\langle c_1,c_2\rangle$ has $\langle s_1,s_2\rangle$, $s_1\neq s_2$, adjacent to it. If $j<i$, then assume **wlg** that $s_j\neq s_{j+1}$. To avoid non-homomorphism $s_{i+2}=s_{j+1}$ must hold. Since each conjunct occuring in a cycle is mappable to all other conjuncts in the cycle, $\langle s_{i+1},s_{i+2}\rangle$ is a fan-out vertex because it has $\langle c_j,c_{j+1}\rangle$, $\langle c_j,c_{i+2}\rangle$, $\langle c_{i+1},c_{i+2}\rangle$ and $\langle c_{i+1},c_{j+1}\rangle$ adjacent to it. This contradicts the assumption that the query is fan-out free. ∎

<u>Lemma 7</u> : For a fan-out free query, if an IC with a cycle induces a shrinking self-homomorphism then each conjunct appearing as the second component of some CPV in the IC is in some cycle belonging to the IC.

<u>Proof</u> : Let $\{\langle c_i,c_{i+1}\rangle,\ \langle c_k,c_1\rangle\ :\ 1\leq i<k \text{ and } k\geq 2\}$ be a cycle in the IC. Let $\langle s_1,s_2\rangle$, $s_1\neq s_2$, be any SPV adjacent to $\langle c_1,c_2\rangle$. Then from Lemma 6, each CPV $\langle c_i,c_{i+1}\rangle$ has $\langle s_i,s_{i+1}\rangle$ adjacent to it such that all the s_is are distinct.

Case 1 : Let $\langle c_{p1},c_{p2}\rangle$ be an arbitrary CPV, $c_{p1}\neq c_1$, implied by by $\langle s_1,s_2\rangle$. If c_{p2} is in some cycle which lies in the IC then we are done. Therefore assume that c_{p2} is not in any cycle which lies in the IC. In particular $c_{p2}\notin\{c_i\ :\ 1\leq i\leq k\}$. Then, to avoid $\langle\theta\rangle$-adjacency, $\langle c_{pi},c_{p(i+1)}\rangle$ must be adjacent to $\langle s_i,s_{i+1}\rangle$, $2\leq i<k$, and $\langle c_{pk},c_x\rangle$ must be adjacent to $\langle s_k,s_1\rangle$. Since all the s_is are distinct (Lemma 6(ii)) hence all c_{pi}s are also distinct. We now claim that $\langle s_i,s_{i+1}\rangle$ implies $\langle c_{pi},c_{p(i+1)}\rangle$, $1\leq i<k$, and $\langle s_k,s_1\rangle$ implies $\langle c_{pk},c_x\rangle$. Otherwise let some $\langle s_i,s_{i+1}\rangle$ ($\langle s_k,s_1\rangle$) not imply $\langle c_{pi},c_{p(i+1)}\rangle$ ($\langle c_{pk},c_x\rangle$). Since the query is fan-out free this is only possible if $c_{pi}=c_i$ ($c_{pk}=c_k$). But then $\langle c_{p1},c_2\rangle$ is adjacent to $\langle s_1,s_2\rangle$ making it a fan-out vertex, a contradiction. If $c_x=c_{p1}$ then we are done. If $c_x\neq c_{p1}$, then $\langle c_x,c_y\rangle$ must be implied by $\langle s_1,s_2\rangle$ or else $\langle s_1,s_2\rangle$ is $\langle\theta\rangle$-adjacent. If $c_y\neq c_{p2}$,

then $\langle c_{p1},c_y\rangle$ is also adjacent to $\langle s_1,s_2\rangle$, making it a fan-out vertex. Hence , in both cases, c_{p2} occurs in a cycle and this cycle lies in the IC.

Note that in Case 1, $\langle c_{p1},c_{p2}\rangle$ may not occur in any cycle. Therefore, to complete the proof, we must also consider :

Case 2 : Let $\langle c_{q1},c_{q2}\rangle$ be a CPV implied by a SPV $\langle \bar{s}_{q1},s_{q2}\rangle$ adjacent to $\langle c_{p1},c_{p2}\rangle$. If c_{q2} belongs to some cycle in the IC then we are done. Assume that c_{q2} is not in any cycle which lies in the IC. Clearly $\langle c_{p2},c_{p3}\rangle$ cannot imply $\langle s_{q2},s_{q2}\rangle$ or else $\langle c_{p1},c_{p3}\rangle$ is adjacent to $\langle \bar{s}_{q1},s_{q2}\rangle$ making it a fan out vertex. Hence $\langle c_{p2},c_{p3}\rangle$ implies $\langle s_{q2},s_{q3}\rangle$, $s_{q2}\neq s_{q3}$. Note that $s_{q3}\neq \bar{s}_{q1}$ or else $\langle \bar{s}_{q1},s_{q2}\rangle$ would be adjacent to $\langle c_{p3},c_{p4}\rangle$, which is in a cycle, and this case would become the same as Case 1. From Lemma 6(ii) it follows that $\langle c_x,c_{p2}\rangle$ implies $\langle s_{q1},s_{q2}\rangle$, $\langle c_{pi},c_{p(i+1)}\rangle$ implies $\langle s_{qi},s_{q(i+1)}\rangle$, $2\leq i<k$, and $\langle c_{pk},c_x\rangle$ implies $\langle s_{qk},s_{q1}\rangle$. Furthermore all the s_{qi}s are distinct. By the argument used in Case 1 above, $\langle c_{qi},c_{q(i+1)}\rangle$ must be implied by $\langle s_{qi},s_{q(i+1)}\rangle$, $2\leq i<k$, and $\langle c_{qk},c_z\rangle$ must be implied to $\langle s_{qk},s_{q1}\rangle$. As in Case 1, we can show that $\langle c_z,c_{q2}\rangle$ is implied by $\langle s_{q1},s_{q2}\rangle$. Hence c_{q2} is in a cycle which lies in the IC.

By repeatedly applying the arguments outlined in Case 1 and Case 2, as the need may be, we prove the lemma. ∎

<u>Lemma 8</u>: Consider a cyclic IC I_c inducing a shrinking self-homomorphism h_c in an iteration of the **while** loop. Let $\langle \bar{c},c_2\rangle \in I_c$ such that $\langle \bar{c},c_2\rangle$ is not in any cycle. Let the cycle in which c_2 lies be $\{\langle c_i,c_{i+1}\rangle,\langle c_k,c_1\rangle : 1\leq i<k \text{ and } k\geq 2\}$. Then

(i) I1, the IC of $\langle \bar{c},c_1\rangle$, does not have any cycles and it induces a shrinking self-homomorphism h_1 in the same iteration of the **while** loop. Further, for each CPV $\langle c_x,c_y\rangle \in$ I1, I_c has CPVs $\langle c_x,c_z\rangle$ and $\langle c_y,c_z\rangle$ such that $\langle c_x,c_z\rangle$ is not in any cycle but $\langle c_y,c_z\rangle$ is in some cycle.

(ii) Let I2 be the IC of $\langle c_i,c_j\rangle$, I2 being distinct from I1, such that I_c has CPVs $\langle c_i,c_k\rangle$ and $\langle c_j,c_k\rangle$ where $\langle c_i,c_k\rangle$ is not in any cycle but $\langle c_j,c_k\rangle$ is in a cycle. Let $\langle c_{p1},c_{q1}\rangle$ and $\langle c_{p2},c_{q2}\rangle$ be arbitrary CPVs in I1 and I2 respectively. Then $c_{p1}\neq c_{p2}$, $c_{p1}\neq c_{q2}$ and $c_{q1}\neq c_{p2}$.

<u>Proof</u>: (i) Consider the CPV $\langle \bar{c},c_1\rangle$. No SPV adjacent to $\langle \bar{c},c_1\rangle$ can imply $\langle\theta\rangle$. If it were so then some SPV in I_c would be $\langle\theta\rangle$-adjacent thus violating the assumption that I_c induces a shrinking self-

homomorphism. If each SPV implied by $\langle \bar{c}, c_1 \rangle$ does not imply any other CPV then the assertion is seen to hold immediately.

Let $\langle \bar{s}, s_1 \rangle$, $\bar{s} \neq s_1$, be an arbitrary SPV, adjacent to $\langle \bar{c}, c_1 \rangle$ in I1, implying at least one other CPV. Now consider the CPV $\langle \bar{c}, c_2 \rangle$ in I_c. Since $\bar{s}$ occurs in the conjunct $\bar{c}$ a SPV with $\bar{s}$ as its first component must be adjacent to $\langle \bar{c}, c_2 \rangle$. Suppose $\langle \bar{c}, c_2 \rangle$ has $\langle \bar{s}, \bar{s} \rangle$ adjacent to it. Clearly $\langle c_1, c_2 \rangle$ implies $\langle s_1, \bar{s} \rangle$. Since $\langle c_1, c_2 \rangle$ is in a cycle, it follows from Lemma 6(ii) that some CPV in the cycle will imply $\langle \bar{s}, s_j \rangle$, $\bar{s} \neq s_j$. But then I_c cannot induce a homomorphism, a contradiction. Therefore $\langle \bar{c}, c_2 \rangle$ must imply $\langle \bar{s}, s_2 \rangle$, $\bar{s} \neq s_2$. Note that $s_2 \neq s_1$ since $s_2 = s_1$ would either imply that I contains the CPV $\langle \bar{c}, c_1 \rangle$ or that $\langle \bar{s}, s_1 \rangle$ does not imply any CPV, a contradiction in either case. Note that $\langle c_1, c_2 \rangle$ implies $\langle s_1, s_2 \rangle$, $s_1 \neq s_2$. Hence from Lemma 6(ii) it follows that each CPV $\langle c_i, c_{i+1} \rangle$ implies $\langle s_i, s_{i+1} \rangle$, $1 \leq i < k$, and all the s_is are distinct. We claim that $s_i \neq \bar{s}$, $1 \leq i \leq k$. Consider the case when some $s_j = \bar{s}$. Since I_c contains the SPV $\langle \bar{s}, s_2 \rangle$ and all s_is are distinct therefore to avoid non-homomorphism $\bar{s} = s_1$, which contradicts the assumption that $\bar{s} \neq s_1$. By a similar argument we can show that $\langle \bar{s}, s_2 \rangle$ cannot be adjacent to any CPV which is in some cycle in I_c. Therefore for each conjunct c_x in which $\bar{s}$ occurs there is a CPV $\langle c_x, c_z \rangle$ implied by $\langle \bar{s}, s_2 \rangle$ such that $\langle c_x, c_z \rangle$ is not in any cycle. From Lemma 7 there is a CPV $\langle c_y, c_z \rangle$ in I_c such that $\langle c_y, c_z \rangle$ is in some cycle. It is easy to show that $\langle c_y, c_z \rangle$ implies $\langle s_1, s_2 \rangle$. Hence the SPV $\langle \bar{s}, s_1 \rangle$, in I1, implies the CPV $\langle c_x, c_y \rangle$. By repetitively applying the above argument we can show that I1 does not contain $\langle \Theta \rangle$ and that for each CPV $\langle c_x, c_y \rangle$ in I1 there exist in I_c the CPVs $\langle c_x, c_z \rangle$, which is not in any cycle, and $\langle c_y, c_z \rangle$, which is in a cycle.

Suppose that I1 has a cycle. Then it must have CPVs $\langle c_p, c_q \rangle$ and $\langle c_q, c_r \rangle$. This implies that in I_c c_q occurs in a CPV which is in some cycle and also not in any cycle, a contradiction. Now suppose that I1 fails to induce a homomorphism. Since I1 does not contain $\langle \Theta \rangle$ then it must contain two distinct CPVs $\langle c_p, c_q \rangle$ and $\langle c_p, c_r \rangle$. This implies that I_c has CPVs $\langle c_p, c_s \rangle$, which is not in any cycle, $\langle c_q, c_s \rangle$ and $\langle c_r, c_s \rangle$, which are both in some cycles. Since a conjunct occurs in only one cycle (or else the IC is non-homomorphic) and within the cycle it occurs as the second component of exactly one CPV, we have a contradiction.

(ii) Let $c_{p1} = c_{p2}$. Since I1 and I2 are distinct, therefore $c_{q1} \neq c_{q2}$. But then I_c has a cycle containing $\langle c_{q1}, c_r \rangle$ and another cycle containing

$<c_{q2},c_r>$, a contradiction. If $c_{p1}=c_{q2}$, then we have the contradiction that I_c has a CPV, with c_{p1} as its first component, which is simultaneously in some cycle and not in any cycle. Similarly we can show $c_{q1} \neq c_{p2}$. ∎

As a corollary to Lemma 8 we have

Corollary 1 : Let I_c be a cyclic IC inducing shrinking self-homomorphism h_c. Then there exist cycle-free ICs I_i, $1 \leq i \leq k$ for some k, inducing shrinking self-homomorphisms h_is such that

$$h_c = h_{p(1)} \circ h_{p(2)} \circ \cdots\cdots \circ h_{p(k)}$$

for all permutations p over $\{1,2,3,...,k\}$.

Proof: The proof follows immediately from Lemma 8. ∎

Based on the above Lemmas, the optimization algorithm for fan-out free queries is straightforward and is given below.

Algorithm Optimize_fan_out_free_queries

1. Construct G, the implication graph of the query Q.
2. Delete all CPVs belonging to the ICs which do not induce a shrinking self-homomorphism on Q or which have cycles.
3. **While** ∃ an IC I inducing a shrinking self-homomorphism **h**
   do
   begin
   delete from Q all conjuncts not in the range of **h**;
   delete all CPVs <c1,c2> such that c1 or c2 does not appear in the range of **h**;
   end;

Theorem 1 : The above algorithm correctly optimizes fan-out free queries in $O(n^2)$ time.

Proof: The correctness of the above algorithm follows from Lemmas 1 to 8. Note that step 1 can be easily implemented in $O(n^2)$ time. In step 2 we construct an IC and delete it if it has a cycle or does not induce a homomorphism. The total time for constructing the ICs and checking whether they should be deleted is $O(n^2)$ [JK]. The deletion can be easily carried out in $O(n^2)$. Similarly step 3 can also be implemented in $O(n^2)$ time since if a CPV is scanned in an iteration of the **while** loop it is also deleted in the same iteration. ∎

References

[ASU] A.V.Aho,Y.Sagiv and J.D.Ullman, Efficient optimization of a class of relational expressions, ACM Trans. on Database Systems, Vol. 4, No. 4, Dec 1979.

[CM] A.K.Chandra and P.M.Merlin, Optimal implementation of conjunctive queries in relational databases, Proc. 9th Annual Symposium on Theory of Computation, May 1977.

[DM] P.Dublish and S.N.Maheshwari, Optimization of a subclass of fan-out free queries, Unpublished Manuscript, Feb 1987.

[JK] D.S.Johnson and A.Klug, Optimizing conjunctive queries that contain untyped variables, SIAM Journal on Computing, Vol. 12, No. 4, Nov 1983.

[MM] B.N.S.Murthy and S.N.Maheshwari, Optimization of a class of relational expressions, Proc. 2nd Annual Conference on Foundations of Software Technology and Theoretical Computer Science, Bangalore, 1982.

[MDM] B.N.S.Murthy, P.Dublish and S.N.Maheshwari, Some negative results on the optimization of conjunctive queries, Technical Report TR 85/01, Deptt. of Computer Science and Engg., IIT Delhi, Dec 1985.

[Mai] D.Maier, The Theory of Relational Database, Computer Science Press, 1983.

[Sag] Y.Sagiv, Quadratic algorithms for minimizing joins in restricted relational expressions, SIAM Journal on Computing, Vol. 12, No. 2, May 1983.

[Ull] J.D.Ullman, Principles of Database Systems, Computer Science Press, 1982.

Weak Consistency of Read-Only Transactions: A Tool to Improve Concurrency in Heterogeneous Locking Protocols

R. C. Hansdah and L. M. Patnaik
Department of Computer Science and Automation
Indian Institute of Science
Bangalore 560 012
INDIA

Abstract.

Three different types of consistencies, viz., semiweak, weak, and strong, of a read-only transaction in a schedule s of a set **T** of transactions are defined and these are compared with the existing notions of consistencies of a read-only transaction in a schedule. We present a technique that enables a user to control the consistency of a read-only transaction in heterogeneous locking protocols. Since the weak consistecy of a read-only transaction improves concurrency in heterogeneous locking protocols, the users can help to improve concurrency in heterogeneous locking protocols by supplying the consistency requirements of read-only transactions. A heterogeneous locking protocol P' derived from a locking protocol P that uses exclusive mode locks only and ensures serializability need not be deadlock-free. We present a sufficient condition that ensures the deadlock-freeness of P', when P is deadlock-free and all the read-only transactions in P' are two phase.

1. Introduction

One of the problems of <u>database management systems</u> is to ensure the <u>consistency</u> of the <u>database</u> when it is accessed by several asynchronously running user transactions. A <u>transaction</u> is a user program that preserves the consistency of the database if executed alone on an initially consistent database. One of the approaches to preserve the consistency of the database is to ensure that a concurrent execution of transactions behaves as if the transactions have been executed in some serial order, i.e., the concurrent execution is <u>serializable</u>[6].

A transaction is usually modeled by a finite sequence of <u>atomic</u>

operations on data items of the database and a concurrent execution of a set **T** of transactions is modeled by a schedule. A schedule of a set **T** of transactions is a merging of the operations of the transactions in **T** preserving the order of operations present in each transaction. Since the execution of an arbitrary schedule may not preserve the consistency of the database, the concurrency control algorithm of the database management system intercepts the operations of the transactions and reorders them so that the resulting schedule is serializable.

Locking has been widely used as a concurrency control mechanism to ensure serializability[2,6,11,17,18]. In a locking protocol, a transaction locks a data item x in exclusive(**X**) mode if it intends to update x and it locks x in shared(**S**) mode if it intends to read x. A transaction unlocks a data item after reading or updating it.

There are basically two classes of locking protocols, viz., (i) two phase locking protocols[6,12,14], and (ii) non-two phase locking protocols[2,5,10,11,12,14,17,18]. Locking protocols that use both **X** and S mode locks are further grouped into two calsses, viz., homogeneous locking protocols[11,14] and heterogeneous locking protocols[1,10,11]. In homogeneous locking protocols, a transaction can request locks both in **S** and **X** modes. In heterogeneous locking protocols, an update transaction can request locks only in mode **X** and a read-only transaction can request locks only in mode **S**. In this paper, we are concerned with heterogeneous locking protocols only. A locking protocol P that consists of update transactions only is made heterogeneous by including in P read-only transactions that also follow the locking protocol P. In the rest of this section, we assume that P is a locking protocol that consists of update transactions only and ensures serializability.

All the locking protocols referred to above aim to achieve serializability only. In [8], we show that a heterogeneous locking protocol P' derived from P ensures update serializability. A schedule s of a set **T** of transactions is update serializable iff (i) the schedule s' obtained from s after deleting all the read-only transactions is serializable, and (ii) every read-only transaction in s is weakly consistent. A read-only transaction T_i is weakly consistent in a schedule s of a set **T** of transactions iff the schedule s' obtained from s after deleting all the read-only transactions except T_i is serializable. Hence , if the users are satisfied only with weak consistency of read-only transactions, a heterogeneous locking protocol P' derived from P can be used to improve concurrency. However, if a set **T'** of read-only transactions requires strong consistency, one cannot use the heterogeneous locking protocol P'. A set **T'** $\subseteq$ **T** of read-only transactions is strongly consistent in a schedule s of the set **T** of transactions iff the schedule s' obtained from s after deleting all the read-only transactions except those in **T'** is serializable.

In this paper, we propose a solution to the above problem by which a user can control the consistency of read-only transactions in a heterogeneous locking protocol. If a set **T'** of read-only transactions that follow the locking protocol P requires strong consistency, then every read-only transaction of **T'** is executed as a two phase transaction. However, if a read-only transaction T does not belong to a set of transactions requiring strong consistency, then it is executed as a non-two phase transaction if possible. This follows from the fact that a heterogeneous locking protocol P' derived from P ensures serializability if all the read-only transactions in P' are two phase. We prove this result later in this paper.

The rest of the paper is organized as follows. In section 2, we define update serializability. A heterogeneous locking protocol P' derived from P ensures update serializability if the original locking protocol P ensures serializability. This result has earlier been reported in [8] and for the sake of continuity we state it again in section 3. In section 3, we also prove that P' ensures serializability if all the read-only transactions in P' are two phase. We also present in section 3 a sufficient condition that ensures the deadlock-freeness of P', when P is deadlock-free and all the read-only transactions in P' are two phase. Section 4 concludes this paper.

2. Update Serializability

In the following , we define a series of terms leading to the definition of update serializability. A transaction is a finite sequence of steps $T_i = (T_{i1}, \ldots, T_{in})$, where each step T_{ij} is either a read operation or a write operation on some data item x. A read operation $R_i[x]$ on a data item x by a transaction T_i reads the current value of the data item x. A write operation $W_i[x]$ on a data item x by a transaction T_i writes a new value for the data item x. We assume that each transaction reads and/or writes a data item at most once and that a transaction does not read a data item x after it has written x. The value written by a transaction is a function of the values of the data items read by it so far. A transaction is an update transaction if it contains at least one write operation ; otherwise it is a read-only transaction.

A schedule s of a set **T** of transactions is a merging of the operations of the transactions in **T** such that T_{ij} precedes T_{ik} in s iff j<k. A schedule s is serial if the operations of the different transactions are not interleaved, i.e., an operation of a transaction T_i does not lie between two operations of some other transaction T_j in s. A schedule s of a set **T** of transactions is view serializable (VSR) if there is a serial schedule s' of **T** such that, for every initial state of the database and for every interpretation of the various functions computed by the transactions, each transaction of **T** receives the same view of the database in s and s' and the execution of s or s' will leave the database in the same final state[21]. From now on, by a serializable schedule, we mean a view serializable schedule.

In the following, we define various types of consistencies of a read-only transaction T_i in a schedule s of a set **T** of transactions.

Definition 2.1. A read-only transaction T_i is semiweakly consistent in a schedule s of a set **T** of transactions iff the transaction T_i sees a consistent view of the database in s.

This definition of semiweak consistency of a read-only transaction is identical to that of weak consistency given in [7]. We introduce the term semiweak consistency as the full power of weak consistency defined in [7] is not realizable in heterogeneous locking protocols. The term weak consistency is redefined below.

Definition 2.2. A read-only transaction T_i is weakly consistent in a schedule s of a set **T** of transactions iff the schedule s' obtained from s after deleting all the read-only transactions except T_i is serializable.

Note that a weakly consistent read-only transaction is always semiweakly consistent. However, a semiweakly consistent read-only transaction need not be weakly consistent. The example below clarifies this point.

Example 2.1. Consider the schedule s shown below.

$R_2[b]R_4[b]W_2[b]R_1[a]R_1[b]R_1[c]R_3[c]W_3[c]R_4[c]W_1[a]$

There is only one read-only transaction in s,viz., T_4. The schedule s is not serializable, and hence T_4 is not weakly consistent. However, T_4 sees the consistent database obtained from the initial database by the execution of update transaction T_3 and the schedule s' obtained from s after deleting T_4 is view-equivalent to the serial schedule $T_2T_1T_3$, i.e., s' is serializable. Hence, T_4 is semiweakly consistent in s.

The notion of strong consistency applies to a set of read-only transactions and the definition given below is a generalization of the definition given in [7].

Definition 2.3. A set **T'** of read-only transactions, where **T'** is a subset of a set **T** of transactions, is <u>strongly consistent</u> in a schedule s of the set **T** of transactions iff the schedule s' obtained from s after deleting all the read-only transactions except those in **T'** is serializable.

The above definition of strong consistency is a generalization of the definition given in [7], because, in [7], a schedule can have only one set of strongly consistent read-only transactions. Note that the weak consistency of a read-only transaction T_i is a special case of strong consistency when the set containing T_i is a singleton set. The following lemma states the relationship between strong consistency and weak consistency of a read-only transaction in a schedule s.

Lemma 2.1. If a set **T'** of read-only transactions, where **T'** is a subset of a set **T** of transactions, is strongly consistent in a schedule s of the set **T** of transactions, then every read-only transaction of **T'** is weakly consistent in s.

<u>Proof.</u> The proof immediately follows from the definitions 2.2 and 2.3.

The notion of strong consistency is important one, since the various users in a group may require that a set **T'** of read-only transactions which are originated by the users in the group is strongly consistent and a set **T"** of read-only transactions is not required to be strongly consistent if it contains read-only transactions of the users who belong to different groups. This situation may actually arise in practice in a distributed database system, where it may be necessary that the set of read-only transactions at a particular site is strongly consistent and any set of read-only transactions which are from different sites is not required to be strongly consistent. One can probably make use of this information to enhance concurrency in distributed concurrency control algorithms.

Definition 2.4. A schedule s of a set **T** of transactions is <u>weak update serializable</u> iff (i) the schedule s' obtained from s after deleting all the read-only transactions is serializable, and (ii) every read-only transaction in s is semiweakly consistent.

Definition 2.5. A schedule s of a set **T** of transactions is <u>strong update serializable</u> iff (i) the schedule s' obtained from s after deleting all the read-only transactions is serializable, and (ii) every read-only transaction in s is weakly consistent.

A weak update serializable schedule is not necessarily strong update serializable, but a strong update serializable schedule is always weak update serializable. The schedule of example 2.1 is weak update serializable but is not strong update serializable. The notion of update serializability has been used earlier to improve concurrency in concurrency control algorithms presented in [3,7,19]. However, in these concurrency control algorithms, it is not clear whether they can realize schedules which are weak update serializable but are not strong update serializable.

In this paper, by an update serializable schedule, we mean a strong update serializable schedule. The definition of update serializability given in [8] is identical to that of strong update serializability. An update serializable schedule is not necessarily serializable but is always state serializable. In addition, there are schedules which are state serializable but are not update serializable. The examples to show these facts can be found in [8]. The definition of state serializability can be found in [16,21]. A locking protocol that ensures update serializability provides more concurrency than the one that ensures serializability, because the size of the set correct schedules that is output by a lock manager implementing the former protocol is larger then that output by a lock manager implementing the latter one[13].

3. Heterogeneous Locking Protocols

In the following, we define terminologies that are necessary to state and prove the results in this section.

A lock mode **A** is compatible with another lock mode B if a transaction T is allowed to acquire a lock in mode **A** on a data item which is locked by some other transaction in mode **B**. An **X** mode lock is neither compatible with itself nor with an **S** mode lock; however, an **S** mode lock is compatible with itself. A transaction is <u>well-formed</u> if it locks every data item it accesses , and unlocks only those data items which it has previously locked. The definition of a schedule of a set **T** of well-formed locked transactions is identical to that of the unlocked transactions. A schedule s of a set **T** of well-formed locked transactions is <u>legal</u> if, in the schedule s, two incompatible lock operations are not requested on a data item x simultaneously. From now on , by a transaction we mean a well-formed locked transaction unless otherwise stated.

A locking protocol may require that only **X** mode locks be used even to read a data item. A <u>heterogeneous locking protocol</u>(HTLP) allows two types of transactions, viz., *update transactions* which can request locks only in mode **X** and *read-only transactions* which can request locks only in mode **S**. In this paper, we are concerned with heterogeneous locking protocols only, and hence from now on, the terms update transaction and read-only transaction are understood as defined above unless otherwise stated. If the **X** mode lock operations of an update transaction T_i are replaced by **S** mode lock operations, then the read-only transaction so obtained is said to be *derived* from T_i. A heterogeneous locking protocol P' is *derived* from a locking protocol P that permits update transactions only by allowing read-only transactions that can be derived from the update transactions of P.

A transaction T' that is derived from a transaction T by shifting the unlock operations of T to the end of T follows the locking protocol which T follows. In this way, we can get a two phase transaction from a non-two phase transaction and the two phase transaction so derived follows the locking protocol which the non-two phase transaction follows.

A *partial* schedule s' of a set **T** of transactions is a legal schedule of those operations of the transactions which have been executed by the lock manager, i.e., in case of lock operation, lock has been granted, and in case of unlock operation, lock has been released. The partial schedule s' preserves the order of operations present in each transaction.

Let s be a schedule of a set **T** of transactions and $\mathbf{T'} \subseteq \mathbf{T}$. A *subschedule* s' of s consisting of the transactions in **T'** is obtained by deleting the transactions belonging to **T-T'** from s.

The share lock, exclusive lock, and unlock operation of a transaction T_i on a data item e are denoted by $<T_i,LS,e>$, $<T_i,LX,e>$, and $<T_i,UN,e>$ respectively.

The *suffix* of a transaction T_i starting with the lock operation $<T_i,A_i,e>$ on a data item e is obtained by deleting from T_i (i) all the lock operations preceding $<T_i,A_i,e>$, and (ii) all the unlock operations corresponding to the lock operations deleted in step (i).

We define the "precedes" relations $<-_e$ and $<-$ in a legal schedule s of a set **T** of transactions as follows:

$T_i <-_e T_j <=> T_i$ locks the data item e before T_j locks it in s and at least one of the lock requests is in mode **X**. In addition, in the schedule s, there is no other transaction T_k that locks the data item x in mode **X** between the unlock operation of T_i on e and the lock operation of T_j on e.

$T_i <- T_j <=> \exists\, e[T_i <-_e T_j]$.

We define the "waits-for" relations $\rightarrow_e$ and $\rightarrow$ in a set **T** of transactions which are executing as follows:

$T_i \rightarrow_e T_j \iff T_j$ holds a lock on a data item e in mode **L** and T_i waits to lock e in a mode which is incompatible with the mode **L**.

$T_i \rightarrow T_j \iff \exists\, e[T_i \rightarrow_e T_j]$.

Proposition 3.1. A legal schedule s of a set **T** of transactions is serializable iff the associated "precedes" relation <- in s is acyclic.

Proof. See[20,theorem 11.3].

Definition 3.1. A locking protocol P ensures serializability (update serializability) if all the legal schedules of any set **T** of transactions obeying the locking protocol P are serializable (update serializable).

In the following, we state the guard locking protocol(GLP)[18], as it is used to illustrate the sufficient condition that we have proposed for the deadlock-freeness of a heterogeneous locking protocol. In the GLP protocol, the database is organised as a directed acyclic graph(DAG) $\mathbf{G}=(\mathbf{V},\mathbf{E})$, where **V** is the set of vertices and **E** is the set of arcs. Data items in the database are in one to one correspondence with vertices; so we use the terms data item and vertex interchangeably. An arc $(v_i,v_j) \in \mathbf{E}$ represents the relationship between the data items v_i and v_j (logical or physical). We say that a DAG **G** is a guarded graph iff with each $v \in \mathbf{V}$ there is associated a (possibly empty) set of pairs:

$$\text{guard}(v)=\left\{\langle A_1^v,B_1^v\rangle,\langle A_2^v,B_2^v\rangle,\ldots,\langle A_k^v,B_k^v\rangle\right\}$$

satisfying the conditions:

(1) $\emptyset \neq B_i^v \subseteq A_i^v \subseteq \mathbf{V}$, for $1 \leqslant i \leqslant k$.

(2) $\forall x \in A_i^v$, x is a parent of v and $1 \leqslant i \leqslant k$.

(3) If $A_i^v \cap B_j^v = \emptyset$, then there is no biconnected component[1] of **G** including the vertices from both A_i^v and B_j^v.

Each pair $\langle A_i^v,B_i^v\rangle$ is called a subguard of v. We say that the subguard $\langle A_i^v,B_i^v\rangle$ is <u>satisfied</u> in lock mode **M** by a transaction T if T currently holds a lock in mode **M** on all the vertices in B_i^v and it has locked (and possibly unlocked) all the vertices in $A_i^v - B_i^v$ in mode **M**. The rules

---

[1]A biconnected component of a graph consists of maximal collections of vertices $u_1,u_2,\ldots,u_p$ such that either p>3 and for each pair (u_i,u_j) there exits two or more disjoint chains between u_i and u_j or p=2 and u_1 and u_2 share an arc.

of the GLP protocol on a guarded graph are [18]:

(1) A transaction T may lock any vertex first in mode **X**.

(2) A transaction T may lock a subsequent vertex v in mode **X** only if T has not previously locked it and there exists a subguard $<A_i^v,B_i^v>$ satisfied in mode **X** by T.

(3) A transaction may unlock a vertex any time.

The GLP protocol ensures serializability and is deadlock-free[18].

In the following, we prove results that enable a user to control the consistency of the read-only transactions in the heterogeneous locking protocols that are derived from a locking protocol ensuring serializability. We also present a sufficient condition that ensures the deadlock-freeness of these heterogeneous locking protocols.

It is not necessary that every locking protocol when generalized to a HTLP protocol would produce update serializable schedules which are not serializable. For example, the heterogeneous two phase locking protocol produces only serializable schedules[12,14]. The example to illustrate that a HTLP protocol produces update serializable schedules which are not serializable can be found in [8].

If the original locking protocol P is deadlock-free, then a deadlock cycle resulting due to the concurrent execution of transactions following a HTLP protocol P' derived from P contains at least two read-only transactions. The example to illustrate that the deadlock-freeness of a locking protocol may not be preserved when it is generalized to a HTLP protocol can be found in [8].

In the following, we state and prove the main results of this paper.

Theorem 3.1. Let P be a locking protocol that uses **X** mode locks only and ensures serializability, and P' be a heterogeneous locking protocol derived from P. Then the following holds:

(a) P' ensures update serializability.

(b) If P is deadlock-free, then a deadlock cycle in P' involves at least two read only transactions.

Proof. See[8].

If the read-only transactions are two phase in a heterogenous locking protocol P' derived from a locking protocol P that ensures serializability, then P' ensures serializability. In addition, if P is deadlock-free and satisfies an additional condition, called DF, to be defined below, then P' is also deadlock-free.

Definition 3.2. Let P be a locking protocol that uses **X** mode locks only and **T** be the set of all update transactions which obey P.

Let T_i and T_j be any two transactions in **T** that access a common data item x. In addition, T_i is two phase. Let $B(T_k,x)$ be the set of all data items on which T_k holds locks before the operation $\langle T_k,LX,x\rangle$. The DF condition is defined as follows: If $B(T_j,x)\neq\emptyset$ and $B(T_i,x) \cap B(T_j,x)=\emptyset$, then the suffix of T_i starting from the lock operation $\langle T_i,LX,x\rangle$ (after deleting the unnecessary unlock operations which correspond to the lock operations preceding $\langle T_i,LX,x\rangle$ in T_i) also belongs to **T**, i.e., the transaction derived in such a way also follows the locking protocol P.

Definition 3.3. A locking protocol P that uses **X** mode locks only satisfies DF if for any pair of transactions T_i and T_j that follow P, the DF condition is true for all data items that are locked by both T_i and T_j.

Example 3.1. The GLP protocol on a rooted DAG satisfies DF.

Let T_i and T_j be two transactions that lock a common data item x following the GLP protocol on a rooted DAG. In addition, let T_i be two phase. Let T_i lock the data item x using the subguard $\langle A_i^x,B_i^x\rangle$ and T_j lock the data item x using the subguard $\langle A_j^x,B_j^x\rangle$. Since the DAG is rooted, we have $A_i^x \cap B_j^x\neq\emptyset$ if $A_i^x\neq\emptyset$ and $B_j^x\neq\emptyset$. Hence, the DF condition is satisfied, as $B(T_j,x)=B_j^x$, $B(T_i,x)=A_i^x$, and T_i is two phase.

The results discussed above are stated and proved in the following theorem.

Theorem 3.2. Let P be a locking protocol that uses **X** mode locks only and ensures serializability. Let P' be a heterogeneous locking protocol derived from P such that every read-only transaction obeying the heterogeneous locking protocol P' is two phase. Then the following holds:

(a) P' ensures serializability.

(b) If P is deadlock-free and satisfies DF, then P' is also deadlock-free.

Proof. (a) Let **T'** be a set of read-only and update transactions that follow the heterogeneous locking protocol P'. Consider a legal schedule s of the transactions in **T'** that contains the following cycle in its "precedes" relation <-.

$$T_0 \leftarrow_{a_1} T_1 \leftarrow_{a_2} T_2 \leftarrow_{a_3} \cdots \leftarrow_{a_{n-1}} T_{n-1} \leftarrow_{a_0} T_0.$$

Assume that this cycle contains k read-only transactions and is minimal. That is, there is no legal schedule s" of a set **T** of transactions that follow P' such that there is a cycle in the "precedes" relation <- of s" containing less than k read-only transactions. Now, from s delete all the transactions which do not occur in the above cycle. The new schedule s' obtained in this way consists of the transactions $T_0, T_1, \ldots, T_{n-1}$ and is legal. Moreover, the cycle in the "precedes" relation <- of s remains unchanged. In the above cycle, no two consecutive transactions can be read-only transactions. Hence, we have $n \geqslant 2k$. We shall prove by induction on the number k of read-only transactions in s' that there is no minimal cycle in the "precedes" relation <- of s' containing k read-only transactions. Before we do so, we modify the schedule s' as follows.

Consider a read-only transaction T_i in s'. Let A be the first unlock operation of T_i. Move all the unlock operations of T_i in s' from the right side of A so that between A and any other unlock operation of T_i, there is no other operation of any other transaction T_j. This modification of T_i in s' would change neither the legality of s' nor the "precedes" relation <- of s', since T_i is two phase. Similarly, the lock operations of the read-only transaction T_i are grouped together close to its last lock operation so that, between any two lock operations of T_i, there is no other operation of any other transaction T_j. In addition, this grouping together of the lock operations of T_i must not change the relative order of the lock operations of T_i. This modification of T_i also would change neither the legality of s' nor the "precedes" relation <- of s', since T_i is two phase. After these two modifications, the schedule s' would look like the schedule shown in fig. 1.

--- lock operations of T_i --- unlock operations of T_i ---

Fig. 1. The schedule s' after compacting the lock and unlock operations of T_i.

The operations of other transactions occuring between the lock and unlock operations of T_i are shifted out as follows.

The lock and unlock operations of a read-only transaction T_j are shifted out either to the right side of the unlock operations of T_i or to the left side of the lock operations of T_i. This shifting is done without changing the relative order of the operations of T_j. Most importantly, this shifting is done only to one side, i.e., either to the left side of T_i or to the right side of T_i. The lock and unlock operations of an update transaction are also shifted out without changing their relative order. Next, this process is repeated for each read-only transaction. At the end of this process, the schedule s' is legal and its "precedes" relation <- remains unchanged. Each transaction of s' obeys the heterogeneous locking protocol P' and the read-only transactions are two phase. Moreover, the operations of a read-only transaction in s' now occur together. That is, between any two operations of a read-only transaction T_i, there is no other operation of any other transaction T_j. Next, we prove by induction that a minimal cycle in the "precedes" relation <- of s' with k read-only transactions is impossible.

k=0. In this case, a cycle in s' is not possible, as all the transactions obey the locking protocol P and all of them are update transactions.

k=1. In this case also, a cycle in s' is not possible, as the lone read-only transaction can be treated as an update transaction. Hence, the above cycle is not possible.

k>1. Since k>1 , we have $n \geq 2k \geq 4$. In s', change one of the read-only transactions to an update transaction by converting all its **S** mode locks to **X** mode locks. The schedule s' continues to be legal, as each read-only transaction occurs at exactly one place in s'. Now, the schedule s' consists of n transactions with a cycle in its "precedes" relation <- which contains k-1 read-only transactions. This contradicts the assumption about the minimality of the number of read-only transactions in a cycle of the "precedes" relation <- of any schedule s in the heterogeneous locking protocol P'. Hence, part (a) of the theorem is proved.

(b) When the transactions obeying the heterogeneous locking protocol P' are executing, assume that there arises a deadlock cycle of the form

$$T_0 \rightarrow_{a_1} T_1 \rightarrow_{a_2} T_2 \rightarrow_{a_3} \cdots \rightarrow_{a_{n-1}} T_{n-1} \rightarrow_{a_0} T_0.$$

Now, delete all the transactions which are not in the deadlock cycle. No transaction in the deadlock cycle will be affected. That is, the partial schedule s' of the transactions in the deadlock cycle has been obtained without violating the heterogeneous locking protocol P'. Assume that there are k read-only transactions in the deadlock cycle and the deadlock cycle is minimal. That is, when the transactions obeying the heterogeneous locking protocol P' are executing, a deadlock cycle with k-1 or less number of read-only transactions is not possible. In the deadlock cycle, no two consecutive transactions can be read-only transactions. Hence, we have $n \geq 2k$. Before we prove by induction on the number k of read-only transactions that there is no minimal deadlock cycle with k read-only transactions, we shall slightly modify the partial schedule s'.

None of the read-only transactions in the deadlock cycle has released any lock, as all of them are in the process of acquiring locks and all of them are two phase. Consider a read-only transaction T_i. Let the last granted lock operation of T_i be A_i. Move all the lock operations of T_i close to A_i so that between any two lock operations of T_i there is no other operation of any other transaction T_j. We can assume that all the lock operations which cause waiting occur only after the partial schedule s'. Hence, this modification will change neither the legality of the partial schedule s' nor the deadlock cycle, as T_i is two phase.

Consider a read-only transaction T_i. Since T_{i-1} is an update transaction, and it holds a lock on the data item a_{i-1} and waits at the data item a_i for T_i, we have $B(T_{i-1},a_i)\neq\emptyset$, and $B(T_{i-1},a_i)\cap B(T_i,a_i)=\emptyset$. Since the locking protocol P satisfies the DF condition defined in definition 3.2, the suffix of T_i starting with the lock operation $\langle T_i,LS,a_i\rangle$ (after deleting the unlock operations which correspond to the lock operations preceding $\langle T_i,LS,a_i\rangle$) can be considered as a complete transaction obeying the heterogeneous locking protocol P'. So we delete from s' the lock operations of T_i which occur before the lock operation $\langle T_i,LS,a_i\rangle$, and the corresponding unlock operations. This modification would change neither the legality of the partial schedule s' nor the deadlock cycle, since the cycle is minimal and T_i is two phase. However, the read-only transaction T_i does get modified as some of its operations are deleted. We modifiy all the read-only transactions in this way as the locking protocol P satisfies the DF condition defined in definition 3.2. After these modifications, a read only transaction T_i would start locking the data item a_i in the partial schedule s' and the transaction T_{i-1} would wait at the data item a_i in the deadlock cycle. Now, we prove by induction that a minimal deadlock cycle with k read-only transactions is not possible. Let $L(T_i)$ denote the set of data items on which T_i holds locks at the time of deadlock.

<u>k=0</u>. In this case, all the transactions in the deadlock cycle are update transactions and follow the locking protocol P. Hence, a deadlock cycle is not possible according to the statement of the theorem.

<u>k=1</u>. In this case also, the lone read-only transaction can be treated as an update transaction following the locking protocol P. Hence, the deadlock cycle is not possible.

<u>k>1</u>. In this case, we have $n\geqslant 2k\geqslant 4$. Since an **S** mode lock is compatible with itself, only the read-only transactions may hold locks on common data items. Accordingly, we consider the following two cases:

(1) There is a read-only transaction T_i such that $L(T_i)\cap L(T_j)=\emptyset$ for all the read-only transactions $T_j\neq T_i$ in the deadlock cycle.

Convert the transaction T_i to an update transaction. The partial schedule s' continues to remain legal and the deadlock cycle remains unchanged. Moreover, all the transactions in the deadlock cycle follow the heterogeneous locking protocol P'. However, in the deadlock cycle, there are only k-1 read-only transactions. This contradicts the assumption about the minimality of the number of read-only transactions in a deadlock cycle in the heterogeneous locking protocol P'.

(2) For each read-only transaction T_i, there exists a read-only transaction $T_j \neq T_i$ in the deadlock cycle such that $L(T_i) \cap L(T_j) \neq \emptyset$.

Let T_i be a read-only transaction in the partial schedule s'. The data item a_i is not locked by any other read-only transaction T_k; otherwise, T_{i-1} would also wait for T_k and the number of read-only transactions in the deadlock cycle will not be minimal. Let a_m be the first data item locked by T_i such that it is also locked by some other read-only transaction T_j. Convert the read-only transaction T_i to an update transaction by replacing **S** mode locks by **X** mode locks. Remove from s' those lock operations of T_i which occur after the lock operation $\langle T_i, LX, a_m \rangle$ and let $\langle T_i, LX, a_m \rangle$ occur after s'. Then, we have $T_i \rightarrow_{a_m} T_j$. So we get a deadlock cycle which has fewer than k read-only transactions(since T_i is now an update transaction) and which has been obtained following the heterogeneous locking protocol P'. This contradicts the assumption about the minimality of the number of read-only transactions in a deadlock cycle in the heterogeneous locking protocol P'. Hence, part (b) of the theorem is proved.

The heterogeneous guard locking protocol on a rooted DAG ensures serializability and is deadlock-free if the read-only transactions are two phase. This follows from example 3.1 and theorem 3.2.

In view of theorem 3.2, the read-only transactions are classified into two classes:(i) The first class consists of the read-only transactions which would like to see a common serilizable schedule of the update transactions, and (ii) the second class consists of the read-only transactions whose members need not agree on a common serializable schedule of the update transactions. The read-only transactions of the first type form a strongly consistent set and the read-only transactions of the second type are weakly consistent. A read-only transaction has the choice of strong consistency just by remaining two phase. If a read-only transaction is non-two phase, then it is just weakly consistent. Hence, if it is known that a read-only transaction is satisfied with weak consistency, it can be executed as a non-two phase transaction, and this fact helps to improve concurrency. Concurrency is also improved, because of the fact that update serializable schedules may be generated if non-two phase read-only transactions are allowed.

4. Conclusions

The notion of consistency of a read-only transaction in a schedule s of a set **T** of transactions is important one, since the users can supply this information to the database management system and the database management system can take advantage of this information to improve concurrency. In this paper, we have defined three different types of consistencies, viz., semiweak, weak, and strong, of a read-only transaction in a schedule s of a set **T** of transactions. The no consistency requirement of a read-only transaction defined in [7] is not discussed in this paper as we believe that no extra effort is required by the database management system to achieve it. Further research is required to exploit the fact that a read-only transaction is semiweakly consistent or weakly consistent and it is not a member of any set **T** of transactions, which is strongly consistent, for improving concurrency in concurrency control algorithms for both centralized and distributed database management systems. The notion of strong consistency of a set **T** of read-only transactions may be useful to improve concurrency in distributed database management systems and further research is required in this direction.

We have shown that a heterogeneous locking protocol P' derived from a locking protocol P ensures update serializability if P ensures serializability. In addition, P' ensures serializability if the read-only transactions in P' are two phase. The condition for serializability given in [11] for heterogeneous locking protocols is that if any two update transactions T_i and T_j lock some data items which are also locked by a read-only transaction T_k, then there are data items which are locked by both T_i and T_j. The condition for serializability given here is much simpler than the condition given in [11] and is easier to implement; in addition, it allows the safety of transaction systems not permitted by the condition given in [11]. However, the condition given in this paper does not allow non-two phase read-only transactions. It follows from the theorem 3.1(a) and 3.2(a) that a read-only transaction which is just weakly consistent, i.e., whose membership in any set **T** of transactions which is strongly consistent is not needed, can be executed as a non-two phase transaction concurrently with the two phase read-only transactions without affecting the strong consistency of the set of two phase read-only transactions. We have also presented a sufficient condition that ensures the deadlock-freeness of the heterogeneous locking protocol P', when the locking protocol P is deadlock-free, and all the read-only transactions following P' are two phase. Such a condition has been defined for the first time and it is an important contribution of this paper. However, it is not known whether the condition DF is also necessary for the deadlock-freeness of heterogeneous locking protocols and further research is required in this direction.

References

1. Buckley, G. N., Silberschatz, A.: On the heterogeneous guard locking protocol. The Computer Journal, 27, 1 (1984), pp.86-87.
2. Buckley, G. N., and Silberschatz, A.: Beyond two phase locking. J. ACM, 32,2(Apr. 1985),314-326.
3. Chan, A., and Gray, R.: Implementing distributed read-only transactions. IEEE Trans. Soft. Eng. SE-11, 2(Feb. 1985), 205-212.
4. Casanova, M. A.: The concurrency control problem for database systems. Lecture Notes in Computer Science, vol. 116, Berlin-Heidelberg-New York, Springer 1981.
5. Dasgupta, P., and Kedem, Z. M.: A non-2-phase locking protocol for general databases. In Proc. of the 8th Int. Conference on Very Large Databases, Oct. 1983, 92-96.
6. Eswaran, K. P., Gray, J. N., Lorie, R. A.,and Traiger, I. L.: The notions of consistency and predicate locks in a database system. Comm. ACM, 19,11(Nov. 1976),624-633.
7. Garcia-Molina, H.: Read-only transactions in distributed databases. ACM Trans. Database Syst., 7, 2(Jun. 1982),209-234.
8. Hansdah, R. C., and Patnaik, L. M.: Update serializability in locking. In Proc. of the International Conference on Database Theory, Rome, Italy, Sept. 1986(Lecture Notes in Computer Science, vol. 243, pp. 171-185).
9. Kedem, Z. M., and Silberschatz, A.: A characterization of database graphs admitting a simple locking protocol. Acta Informatica, 16, 1(1981), 1-13.
10. Kedem, Z. M., and Silberschatz, A.: Non-two phase locking protocols with shared and exclusive locks. In Proc. of the 6th Int. Conf. on VLDB, Montreal, 1980,309-317.
11. Kedem, Z. M., and Silberschatz, A.: Locking protocols from exclusive to shared locks. J. ACM, 30, 4(Oct.1983),787-804.
12. Korth, H.: Locking protocols: general lock classes and deadlock freedom. Ph.D. Thesis, Princeton University, Jun. 1981.

13. Kung, H. T., and Papadimitriou, C. H.: An optimality theory of concurrency control in databases. Acta Informatica, 19, 1(1983), 1-12.

14. Mohan, C.: Strategies for enhancing concurrency and managing deadlocks in database locking protocols. Ph.D. Thesis, Dept. of Computer Science, University of Texas at Austin, 1981.

15. Mohan, C., Fussel, D., and Silberschatz, A.: Compatibility and commutativity of lock modes. Information and control,61,1(April 1984), 38-64.

16. Papadimitriou, C. H.: The serializability of concurrent database updates. J. ACM, 29,4(Oct. 1979), 631-653.

17. Silberschatz, A., and Kedem, Z. M.: Consistency in hierarchical database systems. J. ACM, 27,1(Jan. 1980), 72-80.

18. Silberschatz, A., and Kedem, Z. M.: A family of locking protocols for database systems that are modeled by directed graphs. IEEE Trans. Soft. Engg., SE-8,6(Nov. 1982), 558-602.

19. Stearns, R. E., Lewis, P. M. II, and Rosenkrantz, D. Z.: Concurrency control for database systems. In Proc. of the 17th Symp. on Foundations of Computer Science, Oct.1976, 19-32.

20. Ullman, J. D.: Principles of database systems. Computer Science Press Inc., Potomac, Md., 1982.

21. Yannakakis, M.: Serializability by locking. J. ACM, 31, 2(Apr. 1984), 227-244.

OPTIMIZING JOIN QUERIES IN DISTRIBUTED DATABASES

Sakti Pramanik
Michigan State University

David Vineyard
University of Michigan - Flint

ABSTRACT

A reduced cover set of the set of full reducer semijoin programs for an acyclic query graph for a distributed database system is given. An algorithm based on this reduced cover set is then presented which determines the minimum cost full reducer program. We show that the computational complexity of finding the optimal full reducer for a single relation is of the same order as that of finding the optimal full reducer for all the relations. The optimization algorithm is able to handle query graphs where more than one attribute is common between the relations. We also present a method for determining the optimum profitable semijoin program. The computational complexities of finding the optimum cost semijoin program is high. We present a low cost algorithm which determines a near optimal profitable semijoin program. We do this by converting a semijoin program into a partial order graph. This graph also allows us to maximize the concurrent processing of the semijoins. It is shown that the minimum response time is given by the largest cost path of the partial order graph. We can use this reducibility as a post optimizer for the SDD-1 query optimization algorithm. Finally, it is shown that the least upper bound on the length of any profitable semijoin program is $N * (N - 1)$ for a query graph of N nodes.

Index terms: Full reducer semijoin program, distributed databases, profitable semijoin, partial order graph.

1. INTRODUCTION

An important performance issue in distributed database systems is the implementation of logical relationships of data elements stored across sites. An example of this is the high cost of performing the join of relations stored at different sites. The straight forward approach to implement the join is to send one of the join participating relations to the site of the other relation and perform the join at that site. This requires much movement of data between sites. The objective of join query optimization is to reduce the cost of this inter site data transmission and to move data in parallel so as to minimize the response time.

Several distributed query optimization algorithms have been proposed that minimize the amount of this data transmission [1,3-6,8,10-12]. Wong has proposed a greedy algorithm that is based on selecting the most profitable semijoin at each step [10]. This has been implemented in SDD-1 [4]. Yao and Hevner [1] have proposed an algorithm which is optimal for a class of queries in which only one attribute is common to all the relations in the join. They have considered optimizing the response time of a query. There are other query optimization strategies for distributed database systems some of which are extensions of centralized query processing [6,8].

To minimize the amount of data transmission between sites an approach using semijoin programs has been proposed [4]. Instead of performing joins in one step, semijoins are performed first to reduce the size of the relations. In the next step joins are performed on the reduced relations. Semijoins are also used in performing joins for database machines [2,7,9].

In this paper we consider query optimization using semijoins. It has been shown that a class of queries called tree queries, or acyclic queries, can be answered by using a sequence of semijoins called a semijoin program [3]. Cyclic queries, however, require more elaborate data transmission for reduction, and in some cases semijoins cannot reduce the join relations at all. In this paper we first consider optimum cost semijoin programs for acyclic queries and then extend this to compute a low cost profitable semijoin program. Optimum cost semijoin strategies have been studied by Yu [12] and Chiu [3]. Their strategies handle query graphs where at most one attribute is common to two relations. In this paper we derive optimal semijoin programs for acyclic queries where the relations can have more than one common attribute. Finally, we give a low cost algorithm which converts any profitable semijoin program into a partial order graph. This graph enables us to derive a semijoin program with much reduced total cost while at the same time allowing maximum possible parallel execution of the semijoin program.

2. TREE QUERIES AND SEMIJOIN PROGRAMS

The *semijoin* [4] of a relation R_j by another relation R_i over a set of common attributes is defined as the projection of the result of taking the equijoin of R_i with R_j over the attributes of R_j. The semijoin of R_j by R_i denoted (i,j) is computed by transmitting the projection of R_i on the common attributes to the site of R_j and then performing the join of this projection with R_j. In evaluating a relational database query, in general many semijoins are required. We call a sequence of semijoins a semijoin program.

In finding an optimal cost semijoin program it is helpful to consider a *query graph*

$G_Q = (V_Q, E_Q)$ where

$V_Q = \{$set of relations referenced by the query Q$\}$

$E_Q = \{(i,j) \mid i \neq j$ and query Q has a join of relations i with j$\}$

An example of a query graph is given in figure 1.

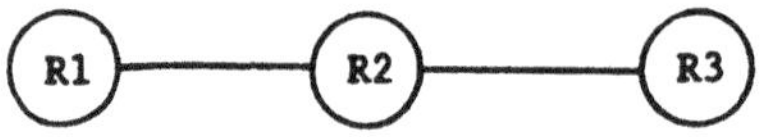

Figure 1. Query Graph

A *query Q is called acyclic* either if its query graph is acyclic or if it is equivalent to a query whose query graph is acyclic. Otherwise, Q is called a cyclic query [3]. For some cyclic query graphs equivalent acyclic query graphs exist. For example, the cyclic query graph G_Q of figure 2a is reducible to the query graph $G_{Q'}$ of the equivalent query Q' (see figure 2b.) The algorithm to convert G_Q into $G_{Q'}$ is given below [3].

Step 1. Find the transitive closure graph, G_Q+, corresponding to the transitive closure, Q^+, of Q. Essentially, we are adding edges to G_Q corresponding to the implied joins of the query. In our example

$G_Q+ = G_Q$.

Step 2. Find the join graph, J_Q+, for Q^+ by taking the edges from G_Q+ over exactly one attribute per component of J_Q+. This is shown in figure 2c.

Step 3. Now construct an acyclic query graph from J_Q+ by constructing the spanning forests of J_Q+. If any one of these spanning forests correspond to an acyclic query qraph, name that graph $G_{Q'}$.

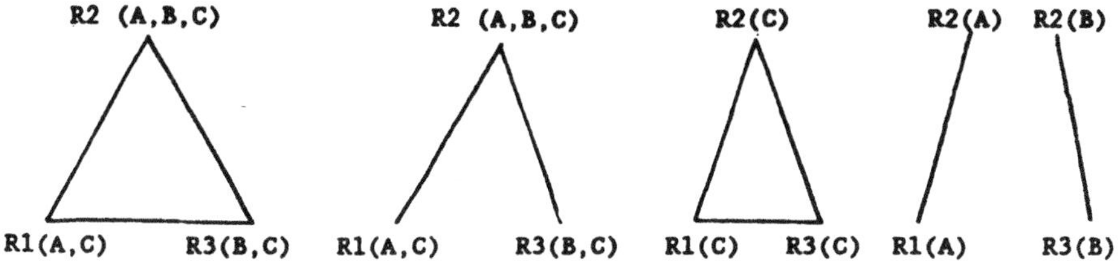

Figure 2a. G_Q Figure 2b. $G_{Q'}$ Figure 2c. J_Q+.

Figure 2. Equivalent query graphs

Please note that step 3 is different from that in Bernstein [3] because we allow more than one attribute in common between two relations. In the rest of this paper we apply our algorithms and theorems to the equivalent acyclic query graph of an acyclic query.

3. REDUCED COVER OF SEMIJOIN PROGRAMS

We denote a *semijoin program* of n semijoins by the sequence $\{(a_i,b_i)\}_{i=1,n}$.

An *embedded chain* is defined to be any subsequence of the semijoin program as follows:

$$\{(a_{j_r},b_{j_r})\}_{r=1,m} \text{ where } m\leq n,\ r<s \text{ implies } j_r<j_s,\ 1\leq j_r\leq n, \text{ and } a_{k+1}=b_k$$

For example, in the semijoin program

(1,2) (1,3) (4,5) (3,6) (5,7) (8,9)

the following semijoin programs are embedded chains

(1,3) (3,6) and (4,5) (5,7).

In words, the embedded chain is a subsequence which preserves the order of semijoins in the original semijoin program, and in which any two contiguous semijoins operate on the same relation, the earliest occurring semijoin reduces that relation and the next semijoin uses that reduced relation to reduce another.

We say that a relation R_i is *reduced* by a relation R_j in a semijoin program if the semijoin program has an embedded chain $\{(a_i,b_i)\}_{i=1,m}$ such that $a_1=R_j$ and $b_m=R_i$.

A relation R_i is said to be *fully reduced* in a query graph if given any relation R_j in the query qraph such that $i \neq j$, R_i is reduced by R_j.

A *full reducer program* for a query graph is a semijoin program which reduces each relation in the query graph fully.

An example of a full reducer program for the query graph of figure 1 follows:

(1,2), (3,2), (2,3), (2,1)

Here R_2 is fully reduced since R_2 is reduced by both R_1 and R_3, similarly, R_1 and R_3 have been fully reduced.

There are many full reducer programs for a given query graph. The number of such programs grows combinatorially with the number of edges of the query graph. For the simple query graph of figure 1, there are 28 unique full reducer programs in which each semijoin reduces some relation nontrivially. Our objective is to find the full reducer program of an acyclic query graph which has the least cost. This least cost full reducer program will depend on the cost model, and on the specific data for the relations in the query graph. An algorithm to determine an optimal cost semijoin program for a chain query has been given in [4]. We will propose an algorithm which works for any acyclic query graph. Further, the cost model used can be very general in our algorithm. In fact, this cost model depends only on the size of the relation used to do the reducing. We will apply this model to find a subset of the set of full reducer programs which have less cost than those full reducer programs not in the subset. This subset is considerably smaller than the set of all possible full reducer programs for the query graph in which each semijoin is nontrivial.

In this paper, we concentrate on reducing the communications cost. We assume that the local processing cost has a negligible contribution to the total cost. Thus we need to consider only the cost of transmitting the data. We assume that the transmission cost is given by

$$\text{cost}(n) = c_0 + c_1 * n$$

where n is the amount of data transmitted and c_0 and c_1 are constants [12]. The value of n changes dynamically with the execution of the sequence of semijoins in the semijoin program. The effectiveness of the algorithms given in this paper depends on the accuracy of determining the values of n. Some work to compute the values of n is given in [4,11].

We will use the following three properties of semijoins to derive the reduced cover for a query graph:

Property 1: Applying the same semijoin twice in succession does not reduce the relation more than a single application of that semijoin. That is, (j,i), (j,i) does not reduce i any more than (j,i).

Property 2: Given two successive steps of a semijoin program where a given relation, say i, is always the rightmost (leftmost) of the pair, these steps may be performed in any order with no effect on the cost of the semijoin program.

Property 3: If a semijoin program has two consecutive steps of the type (k,i), (j,k) then the semijoin program found by reversing their order is less expensive if $i \neq j$.

Under Property 2 we can commute the order of performing semijoins without altering the cost of the semijoin program. Property 3 allows us to commute steps in order to derive a less costly semijoin program. In fact, by successively applying the three properties above, we can derive a less costly semijoin program. For example, each step of the following full reducer program for figure 1 reduces some relation.

(2,3), (2,1), (1,2), (2,3), (3,2), (2,1)

By applying the above properties we will derive a semijoin program which has less cost. The above semijoin program is equivalent by property 2 to

(2,1), (2,3), (1,2), (2,3), (3,2), (2,1)

now apply property 3 to derive the less expensive program

(2,1), (1,2), (2,3), (2,3), (3,2), (2,1)

apply property 1 to eliminate one of the (2,3)

(2,1), (1,2), (2,3), (3,2), (2,1)

The above has less cost than the original full reducer semijoin program. From now on we will consider two semijoin programs which can be derived from each other by using property 2 to be the same semijoin program.

The *data state* is defined to be the current values of the tuples of each relation of the database. For one particular data state, one full reducer program may have the minimum cost; but for another data state there may be another full reducer which has less cost.

A reduced cover, C_G, for the full reducer programs of a query graph, G, is a set of full reducer programs which has the property that no other full reducer program can have less cost than one of the elements of this set for any data state. Furthermore, no two elements in C_G have the same cost for every data state.

A reduced cover of full reducers for figure 1 is given in figure 3.

1. (1,2), (3,2), (2,1), (2,3)
2. (1,2), (2,3), (3,2), (2,1)
3. (3,2), (2,1), (1,2), (2,3)
4. (2,1), (1,2), (2,3), (3,2), (2,1)
5. (2,3), (3,2), (2,1), (1,2), (2,3).

Figure 3: Reduced Cover for the Query Graph of Figure 1.

Our objective is to produce an algorithm which will give us a reduced cover for a general query graph. Using this reduced cover will greatly reduce the complexity of the problem of finding the minimal cost full reducer program of a query graph.

4. MINIMAL COVER OF SINGLE REDUCER PROGRAMS

A *single reducer program* for relation i of a query graph is a semijoin program in which i is the only relation which is fully reduced. For example:

(2,3), (3,2), (1,2)

is a single reducer program for relation 2 of the query graph of figure 1.

A *Prefix* of a semijoin program is the first n steps of a semijoin program. The number n is arbitrarily chosen such that $1 <= n <= m$, the number of steps in the program.

Lemma 1:

For any full reducer program there is a unique prefix which is a single reducer program.

Proof:

A full reducer program is a finite number of semijoins executed in succession. Each semijoin reduces at most one relation. Thus exactly one of the relations in the query graph is fully reduced first. □

A *minimal cover*, S_G, of single reducer programs for a query graph, G, is a set of single reducer programs which has the property that no other single reducer program can have less cost than one of the elements of this set for any data state. Furthermore, no two elements in this set have the same cost for each data state.

For example, (1,2), (3,2) is in S_G but (2,3), (3,2), (1,2) is not. The later is not in S_G though it reduces only R_2 fully. This is because the program (1,2), (2,3) is in S_G and it costs less for every data state. Note that (1,2), (2,3) reduces node R_3, which is a different node from the original node reduced (R_2).

The theorems and propositions we will discuss depend upon the properties of graphs and trees. We will therefore use the terms node and relation interchangeably.

Theorem 1:

A single reducer program for node i in S_G does not reduce node j by i for any j in G.

Proof:

We number the nodes of the query graph so that i is now 1 and its children are nodes 2, 3, ... ,m. Assume without loss of generality that node 2 is reduced by node 1. Now since node 1 must be reduced by nodes 3,4, . . . , m, by property 3 it is better to perform semijoins (3,1), (4,1), . . . (m,1), first. Now node 2 is fully reduced before node 1. This is a contradiction. □

For example, (1,2), (3,2) is in S_G and node 2 does not reduce any node. On the other hand (2,3), (3,2), (1,2) is a single reducer for node 2, but node 2 also reduces node 3. Thus this program is not in S_G.

Lemma 2:

A single reducer program in the minimal cover can be extended to a unique full reducer program by the following:

1. Consider the query graph as a tree with the fully reduced node i as the root.

2. For each child, j, of i, reduce j by i.

3. For each subtree with root j, rename j to i and proceed with step 2.

4. Stop when all relations of the query graph have been reduced.

Proof:
Given in Bernstein [3]. □

Theorem 2:

There is a one-to-one correspondence between S_G and C_G for a given query graph, G.

Proof:
Let N be the number of full reducer programs in C_G. Let M be the number of single reducer programs in S_G. $N <= M$ since, by Lemma 1, for each semijoin program in C_G there is a unique prefix which is a single reducer program. This single reducer program is in the minimal cover S_G else by replacing it with a single reducer program of S_G and extending this to a full reducer program by lemma 2, we have a less costly full reducer program. This is a contradiction since the full reducer program was chosen from C_G.

$M <= N$ since for each single reducer program in S_G, we may append a sequence of steps to create a minimal cost full reducer program by lemma 2. This full reducer program is in C_G by lemma 2.

We have shown that $N <= M$ and that $N >= M$, hence $N = M$. □

The semijoin programs of figure 4 form a minimal cover for the query graph of figure 1. Note that there is a one to one correspondence between the semijoin programs of figure 4, the minimal cover, and the semijoin programs of figure 3, the reduced cover. In fact, each semijoin program of figure 4 is a prefix of a semijoin program in figure 3.

1. (1,2), (3,2)
2. (1,2), (2,3)
3. (3,2), (2,1)
4. (2,1), (1,2), (2,3)
5. (2,3), (3,2), (2,1)

Figure 4. Minimal Cover of Single Reducer Programs of the Query Graph of Figure 1.

5. ALGORITHM TO DERIVE REDUCED COVER

Define $S_i \subseteq S_G$ to be the set of all single reducers in S_G for the node i and define C_i^j to be the set of full reducer programs in the reduced cover for the subtree of G with root j, where G is considered to be rooted at i.

Proposition 1:

$$|S_i| = \prod_{j \in \{child(i)\}} |C_j^i|$$

Proof:

By theorem 1, the node i must be fully reduced before any other node is reduced by i. In particular, each child j of i must be fully reduced in the subtree of which j is the root before i is reduced by j. The semijoin programs for the subtrees are independent, and since there is only one way to reduce i by j once j is reduced, the number of ways to reduce i is the product of the number of ways to reduce the nodes j in their various subtrees. □

By theorem 2 we know that

$$|C_G| = \sum_{i \in V} |S_i|.$$

Thus using proposition 1 we have that

$$|C_G| = \sum_{i \in V} \left(\prod_{j \in \{child(i)\}} |C_j^i| \right).$$

The above is the formula for computing the number of semijoin programs in C_G. We can derive the semijoin programs in C_G similarly. The query graph of figure 5 has 16 semijoin programs in C_G, $|S_1| = |S_3| = |S_4| = 5$, $|S_2| = 1$.
Elements of C_G associated with S_1 from the query graph of figure 5 are:

(3,2), (4,2), (2,1), (1,2), (2,3), (2,4)
(4,2), (2,3), (3,2), (2,1), (1,2), (2,3), (2,4)
(2,4), (4,2), (2,3), (3,2), (2,1), (1,2), (2,3), (2,4)
(3,2), (2,4), (4,2), (2,1), (1,2), (2,3), (2,4)
(2,3), (3,2), (2,4), (4,2), (2,1), (1,2), (2,3), (2,4).

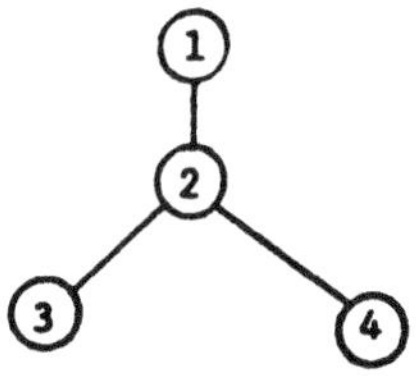

Figure 5. Query Graph

6. MINIMUM COST FORMULAE

In this section we derive a formula for the minimal cost full reducer program. We will use a cost function K(i,G) which gives the minimal cost single reducer program in S_i for node i in G. Note that K(i,G) depends on the data state, but we will not make this explicit in the definition for K(i,G).

The cost is a function of a semijoin program and is defined as the sum of the costs of the semijoins in the semijoin program. Under this interpretation, the parameters we consider are the query graph and the node in the graph which is fully reduced.

Proposition 2:

$$K(i,G) = \sum_{j \in \{child(i)\}} (\mathrm{Min}_{p \in G_j}\{K(p,G_j) + K'(p,j)\} + K'(j,i))$$

where G is a tree rooted at i, G_j is the subtree of G rooted at j, and K'(r,s) is the cost of the semijoin program to reduce s by r.

Proof:

From the proof of Proposition 1, for each j where j is a child of i, take the least cost semijoin program which fully reduces j in G_j, then add the cost to reduce i by j.□

We will illustrate the process of finding K(1,G1) for the graph G1 in figure 6. Our cost model will be defined by the cost, $c_{i,j}$, for the semijoin (i,j) where i and j are the unreduced relations. Assume that there is a factor $d < 1$ such that if relation i is reduced by k other relations, the size of relation i is d^k times its original size. Make the assumptions $d = .6$, $c_{1,2} = 50$, $c_{2,1} = 100$, $c_{2,3} = 150$, $c_{3,2} = 300$, $c_{2,4} = 200$, and $c_{4,2} = 250$.

K(1,G1) = Min{K(2,G2),K(3,G2)+K'(3,2),K(4,G2)+K'(4,2)} + K'(2,1)

K(3,G2) = Min{K(2,G3),K(4,G3)+K'(4,2)} + K'(2,3)

K(2,G3) = K(4,G4) + K'(4,2) = K'(4,2) = $c_{4,2}$ = 250

K(4,G3) = K(2,G5) + K'(2,4) = K'(2,4) = $c_{2,4}$ = 200

thus K(3,G2) = Min{250, 200 + 150} + 90 = 340

similarly K(1,G1) = Min{550, 340 + 108, 420 + 90} + 36 = 484.

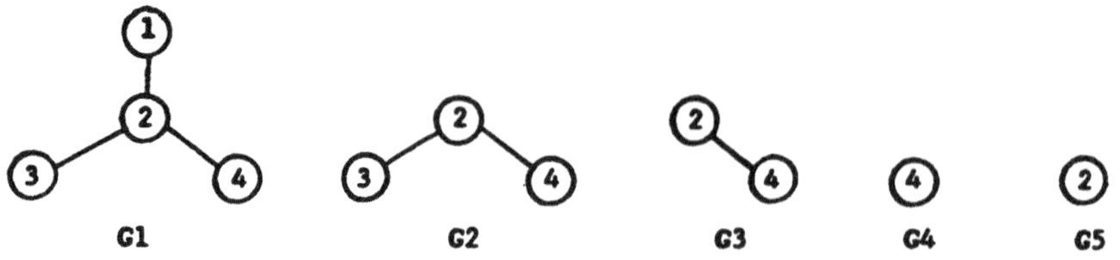

Figure 6. Query Graph and Subtrees

Proposition 2 can be used to find |V| least cost single reducer programs in S_G, one for each of the nodes of G. We will use this result to find the minimal cost full reducer program for G, $M(C_G)$. By Lemma 2, once we have a single reducer program in S_i, there is a unique extension which makes this a full reducer program in C_G. Call this extension X_i. Define $K''(X_i)$ to be the cost of this extension.

Proposition 3:

$$M(C_G) = \min_{i \in G}\{K(i,G) + K''(X_i)\}.$$

Proof:

By proposition 2 K(i,G) has minimal cost. $K''(X_i)$ has minimal cost by lemma 2. Therefore $M(C_G)$ has minimal cost. □

It is often useful to know the minimal cost to reduce a certain node, say n, fully, independently of the cost of reducing any other node. This is a similar problem to finding $M(C_G)$. Use M(n,G) to represent the minimal cost to reduce node n in G. Use $X_{i,n}$ to represent the extension of any single reducer for node i in S_i to the semijoin program which reduces node n fully. Define K''' as the cost of this extension.

Proposition 4:

$$M(n,G) = \min_{i \in G}\{K(i,G) + K'''(X_{i,n})\}.$$

Proof:

This follows from proposition 2 and lemma 2. □

7. PROFITABLE SEMIJOIN PROGRAMS

In the previous sections we have considered full reducers, i.e, reducing the relations fully. It may cost more to reduce relations fully than to send the partially reduced relations to the destination site. Thus, we define a profit in performing a semijoin $\sigma = (I, J)$ as

P(σ) = (cost of sending the relation J to the destination site)
- ((cost of sending the common attributes of relations I and J to the site of J) + (cost of sending the reduced relation J to the destination site))

Note that P(σ) can be negative. We define the profit of a semijoin program $\{ \sigma_i \}$ as

$$\sum_i P(\sigma_i)$$

Thus the profit of a semijoin program is the sum of all the profits of all the semijoins taken in the semijoin program. In SDD-1 only profitable semijoins are considered. Note, however, that the semijoin program with optimal overall profit may have locally unprofitable semijoins. In the following section we describe a method for determining the optimal profitable semijoin program.

The profit of a semijoin program can only increase or stay the same if the semijoins are pairwise reordered by using properties 2 and 3. After reordering, some profitable semijoins may become unprofitable. These unprofitable semijoins can not be removed from the semijoin program because that may reduce the overall profit. For example, assume that all the semijoins in (3,2), (1,2), (2,5), (4,3) are profitable. Then reordering can make (1,2) unprofitable even though (4,3), (3,2), (1,2), (2,5) is a more profitable semijoin program. Removing a profitable (or adding an unprofitable) semijoin to the semijoin program may increase the profit of that program. Therefore, we have to consider semijoin programs consisting of all possible combinations of all the semijoins as long as the ordering of the semijoins satisfy properties 2 and 3. Thus in finding the optimum profitable semijoin program we consider the full reducers of C_G because they are already ordered by properties 2 and 3. However, a profitable semijoin program does not have to be a full reducer. Thus we determine the optimum profitable semijoin program by considering all possible subsequences of all the semijoin programs of C_G . The subsequence with the highest profit is the optimum profitable semijoin program. Some of the subsequences in a semijoin program do not have the right ordering according to properties 2 and 3. But equivalent subsequences with the right order exist in another semijoin program of the C_G.

The cost of finding the optimal profitable semijoin program is high. However, there are inexpensive algorithms to find a suboptimal profitable semijoin program such as that in SDD-1. Now we will transform any profitable semijoin program into a more profitable semijoin program.

Proposition 5:

If there exist semijoins (a_i,b_i) and (a_j,b_j) in a semijoin program such that $b_j = a_i$ and $i < j$, then moving semijoin (a_j,b_j) before (a_i,b_i) in the semijoin program will reduce cost of (a_i,b_i).

Proof:

The proposition follows from the fact that (a_j,b_j) is a profitable semijoin and therefore reduces node a_i. □

Note that the cost of (a_j,b_j) in the new semijoin program may be greater than in the old semijoin program. For example, if there is some node (a_k,b_k) in the old semijoin program with $b_k = a_j$ and $i < k < j$ then (a_j,b_j) is reduced in the old semijoin program by (a_k, b_k) but not in the new semijoin program.

Theorem 3:

If semijoins (a_i,b_i) and (a_j,b_j) are not part of the same embedded chain of the sequence of semijoins $\{(a_k,b_k)\}$, $i <= k <= j$, then semijoin (a_j,b_j) and all the embedded chains of which (a_j,b_j) is the trailing semijoin may be moved before (a_i,b_i) without increasing the cost of any semijoin in the semijoin program. (embedded chain has been defined in section 3)

Proof:

By proposition 5 the cost of (a_i,b_i) is reduced. Now assume that the cost of some semijoin is increased. Then that semijoin must be performed before a semijoin which had previously reduced its cost. Thus an embedded chain has been broken. This is a contradiction since the only semijoin which has explicitly been caused to be performed after the embedded chain is (a_i,b_i) and this semijoin is by assumption not part of the embedded chain. □

We see that the cost of (a_i,b_i) is reduced if (a_j,b_j) is moved before (a_i,b_i) by theorem 3. By applying theorem 3 iteratively to a semijoin program, we will reduce the cost further. We will formalize this procedure in algorithm 1.

Algorithm 1 below derives a new semijoin program from a given program such that the overall profit is increased. The method used is a combination of rearranging of semijoins using theorem 3 and the addition of profitable semijoins. It uses a partial order graph, P, to describe the order of performing semijoins. The nodes of P are the semijoins of the semijoin program. The directed edges of P determine the order of semijoins in the derived program. We will use the idea of level of a node for P. Level 0 nodes are source nodes of P. A node (i_k,j_k) which is the terminating node of some edge is at the level Max{ level of node (i_r,j_r) such that (i_r,j_r) (i_k,j_k) is an edge of P} + 1.

Algorithm 1.

Step 1. [Initialize P]. Make P the null graph.

Step 2. [Add semijoin nodes to P]. For each semijoin (i_k,j_k) in the semijoin program order do:

Step 2.a If P is the null graph, then P becomes the graph of one node, (i_k,j_k).

Step 2.b If P is not null then do:

Step 2.b.1 For each node (i_r,j_r) in P such that $j_r = i_k$, if an edge from (i_r,j_r) to (i_l,j_l) is not in P where (i_l,j_l) is a previous occurrence of semijoin (i_k,j_k) in P, then form the edge in P from (i_r,j_r) to (i_k,j_k).

Step 2.b.2 For each node (i_r,j_r) in P such that $i_r=j_k$, if there is no path from (i_r,j_r) to (i_k,j_k), form the edge from (i_k,j_k) to (i_r,j_r) in P.

Step 2.b.3 If no semijoins (i_r,j_r) as described in steps 2.b.1 and 2.b.2 exist in P then make (i_k,j_k) a separate component of P.

Step 3. [Add new semijoins to P]. For each node (i_k, j_k) in P do the following:

Step 3.a [Find semijoin]. Consider a semijoin (i_r, j_r) from the original query graph which does not appear as the head of an edge in P to (i_k, j_k), but in which $j_r = i_k$. Consider the node i_k from the query graph as having been reduced by all semijoins above (i_k, j_k) in P except for those semijoins forming edges (i_n, j_n) (i_k, j_k) in P. If semijoin (i_r, j_r) is not profitable go to step 3.d

Step 3.b [Add]. Let $\sigma = \vee$ Profit((i_n, j_n)) where (i_n, j_n) (i_k, j_k) is an edge in P. Let $\sigma' = \vee$ Profit((i_n, j_n)) where (i_n, j_n) (i_k, j_k) is an edge in P or $(i_n, j_n) = (i_r, j_r)$. If $\sigma' >= \sigma$ then add (i_r, j_r) to P and form the edge (i_r, j_r) (i_k, j_k).

Step 3.c [Attach]. For any node (i_m, j_m) in P such that $j_m = i_r$, if there is no edge from (i_m, j_m) to (i_s, j_s) where (i_s, j_s) is another occurrence of semijoin (i_r, j_r) then form the edge (i_m, j_m) (i_r, j_r). Now if a cycle has been formed in P, delete this edge.

Step 3.d Continue step 3.a with another (i_r, j_r) if one exists. Else continue step 3.a with another node (i_k, j_k) in P.

Step 3.e Halt when no profitable semijoins (i_r, j_r) exist.

Step 4. Write the derived semijoin program from the graph P in the following manner: For level 0 to Max{level(node)| node ϵ P} list the nodes of P in level order.

In words, algorithm 1 is used to determine the embedded chains found by reordering the semijoins of the original semijoin program. Step 2 places the semijoins in the graph P so that embedded chains are formed, but in a manner which prevents cycles in P from being created. Step 3 is used to place semijoins in P which are profitable in the data state corresponding to P but which were not in the original semijoin program. Figure 7 below gives an example of a derived semijoin program.

With modifications, this algorithm can be used to generate a semijoin program. Essentially, use some method to choose a profitable semijoin to add to the new program (instead of taking the semijoin from a given semijoin program) and add this semijoin to the graph P. One method would be to choose the locally most profitable semijoin as in SDD-1 to add to the graph.

Semijoin Program:

(4,5),(6,8),(5,6),(9,14),(1,2),(13,12),(3,4),(12,9),(2,4),(9,11),(5,7)

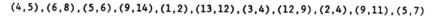

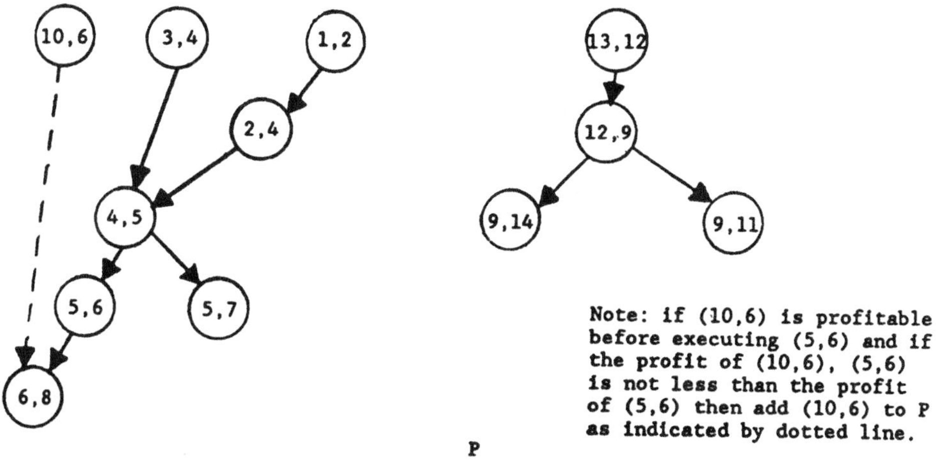
10,6
3,4
1,2
2,4
4,5
5,6
5,7
6,8
13,12
12,9
9,14
9,11
Note: if (10,6) is profitable before executing (5,6) and if the profit of (10,6), (5,6) is not less than the profit of (5,6) then add (10,6) to P as indicated by dotted line.

P

Derived Semijoin Program:

(1,2),(3,4),[(10,6)],(13,12),(2,4)(12,9),(4,5),(9,14),(9,11),(5,6),(5,7),(6,8)

Figure 7. Semijoin program and partial order graph P

Proposition 6:

Algorithm 1 gives a derived semijoin program which is at least as profitable as the original program. That is, algorithm 1 has the inclusion property.

Proof:

Step 2 corresponds to rearranging the semijoins according to properties 2 and 3 and can not decrease the profitability by theorem 3. Step 3 guarantees that the global profit will not decrease. Therefore, the derived semijoin program is at least as profitable as the original program.□

Note that as a result of step 2 we may have locally unprofitable semijoins in the semijoin program. These semijoins were part of a profitable semijoin program before applying step 2 and are now part of a more profitable program. Step 3 is used to place semijoins in the program which were made unprofitable by the inclusion of another semijoin in the program. This only occurs if the semijoin placed in the program by step 3 does not reduce the profitability of the already occuring semijoins significantly.

It is quite possible for a hill climbing algorithm for semijoin programs to create a semijoin program which violates properties 1, 2, or 3. These same algorithms can also, by order of inclusion, prevent profitable semijoins from being included in the semijoin program. Our algorithm will give us a better, although not the optimal in many cases, semijoin program.

Proposition 7:

Algorithm 1 will stop after a finite number of steps.

Proof:

By proposition 11 we know that the number of semijoins is bounded in a semijoin program in which each semijoin reduces some relation. Algorithm 1 adds nodes to P, each corresponding to a semijoin which reduces some relation. Therefore, the number of steps executed by algorithm 1 is bounded.□

Proposition 8:

Let N be the maximum number of semijoins possible for a given query, Q. Then the worst case computational complexity of algorithm 1 applied to a semijoin program for Q is $O(N^2)$

Proof:

Algorithm 1 consists of placing the semijoins on P as nodes. For each of the at most N semijoins, this involves a scan of P. Therefore, for the worst case, algorithm 1 has complexity $O(N^2)$.□

8. CONCURRENCY IN A SEMIJOIN PROGRAM

A semijoin program is a linear structure, it implies a linear processing of the semijoins. The graph P is a two dimensional structure. If we consider the graph P to be a data flow graph, then P is a schedule of the concurrent semijoin processing of the semijoin program. In fact, the graph P gives the maximum concurrency allowed in a given semijoin program while achieving the best reduction in the total cost.

Given a semijoin program, the partial order graph P gives the minimal cost of performing these semijoins. For this minimal cost semijoin program P provides the minimal response time. The minimal cost comes from increasing the size of embedded chains. The minimal response comes from executing these semijoins concurrently.

The minimal response time is given by the maximal cost path from a source node to a sink node of the graph, assuming that the response time is directly proportional to the cost. This follows directly from the properties of data flow graphs.

9. LONGEST PROFITABLE SEMIJOIN PROGRAM

There are algorithms which determine the low cost semijoin program by choosing locally optimal profitable semijoins. These algorithms may select a semijoin program which is not in the set of optimal profitable semijoin programs. For example, using figure 1, (2,1) (3,2),(2,3),(1,2),(2,1), (2,3) is not in the optimal set, but each semijoin in the program reduces a node and thus can be profitable. This is the longest such semijoin program for figure 1. The following propositions give the longest profitable semijoin programs for a given query graph.

Proposition 9:

An upper bound on the number of profitable semijoins in a semijoin program for an acyclic query graph of N nodes is N*(N-1).

Proof:

Consider any semijoin (A,B) in a semijoin program. If (A,B) is profitable then B must be reduced by at least one node. Obviously, if each semijoin reduces its terminal node by exactly one node, this is the worst case for minimizing the number of semijoins. If each semijoin reduces its terminal node by one node, it takes N-1 semijoins to fully reduce any given node. Therefore, N*(N-1) is an upper bound on the number of profitable semijoins for a query graph of N nodes. □

Proposition 10:

There is a semijoin program which takes N*(N-1) profitable semijoins for an acyclic query graph of N nodes.

Proof:
The proof is by induction on the number of nodes of the query graph.

Basis: For N=2 with nodes A and B, the semijoins (A,B), (B,A) reduce the graph fully.

Induction hypothesis: Assume that the proposition is true for N = K.

Induction step: Consider an acyclic query graph with N=K+1 nodes. Consider any leaf node of the graph, call it B and call its parent node A. Remove B from the graph, then by our hypothesis there is a semijoin program of K*(K-1) nodes for the resulting K node graph. Extend this program to the entire graph as follows:

Step 1: (A,B) is the first semijoin in the new program.

Step 2: After any semijoins (X,A) insert the semijoin (A,B)

Step 3: At the end of the old program insert the semijoins (B,A) followed by all (A,X), followed by all (X,Y), etc. until all nodes have been reduced by B.

The number of semijoins in this extended program is (K+1)*K.□

Proposition 11:

The least upper bound on the number of profitable semijoins in a semijoin program for a graph of N nodes is N*(N-1).

Proof:
Follows from propositions 9 and 10.□

10. CONCLUSION

An algorithm to find the minimal cost full reducer and single reducer semijoin programs is given. The computational complexities of this algorithm is high. This algorithm has lead to the development of a better heuristic to compute the near optimal profitable semijoin program. The partial order graph used in this heuristic enables us to exploit the parallel execution of the semijoins in the program.

ACKNOWLEDGEMENTS

The authors would like to thank the reviewers for their helpful comments.

REFERENCES

1. P. Apers, A. Hevner, and S. B. Yao, "Optimization algorithms for distributed queries," IEEE Trans. on Software Engineering, vol. SE-9 No. 1 , pp. 57-68, Jan. 1983.

2. E. Babb, "Implementing a relational database by means of specialized hardware," ACM Trans. Database Syst.,vol. 4 No. 1, pp. 1-29, March 1979.

3. P. Bernstein and D. Chiu, "Using semijoins to solve relational queries," Journal of the ACM, vol. 28 No. 1, pp. 25-40, January 1981.

4. P. Bernstein, N. Goodman, E. Wong, C. Reeve, and J. Rothnie, "Query processing in a system for distributed databases (SDD-1)," ACM Trans. on Database Systems, vol. 6 No. 4, pp. 602-625, December 1981.

5. D. Chiu and Y. Ho, "A methology for interpreting tree queries into optimal semi-join expressions," in Proc. ACM SIGMOD, May 1980, pp. 169-178.

6. R. Epstein, M. Stonebraker, and E. Wong, "Distributed query processing in a relational database system," in Proc. ACM SIGMOD, May 1978, pp. 169-180.

7. S. Pramanik, and F. Fotouhi, "An index database machine- an efficient m-way join processor," The Computer Journal, vol.29 No. 5, pp. 430-445, October 1986.

8. M. Stonebreaker, and E. Neuhold, "A Distributed database version of INGRESS," in Proc. second Berkeley workshop on Dist. Data Management and Computer Networks, 1977, pp. 19-36.

9. S. Su, L. Nguyen, A. Emam, and G. Lipovskky, "The Architectural Features and Implementation Techniques of the Multicell CASSM," IEEE Trans. on Computers, vol. C-28(6), pp. 430-445, June 1979.

10. E. Wong, "Retrieving dispersed data from SDD-1 : A system of distributed databases," in Proc. second Berkeley wordshop on Dist. Data Management and Computer Networks, 1977, pp. 217-235.

11. C. Yu, and C. Chang, "Distributed query processing," ACM computing surveys, vol. 16 No. 4, pp. 399-433, Dec. 1984

12. C. Yu, Z. Ozsoyoglu, and K. Lam, "Optimization ofdistributed tree queries," Journal of computer and system sciences, vol. 29 No. 3 pp. 409-445, Dec. 1984.

Reasoning in Systems of Equations and Inequations

Chilukuri K. Mohan **Mandayam K. Srivas**
Computer Science Department, State University of New York
Stony Brook, NY-11794-4400, U.S.A.

Deepak Kapur
General Electric Co., Corporate Research and Development
Schenectady, NY-12301, U.S.A.

ABSTRACT: Reasoning in purely equational systems has been studied quite extensively in recent years. Equational reasoning has been applied to several interesting problems, such as, development of equational programming languages, automating induction proofs, and theorem proving. However, reasoning in the presence of explicit inequations is still not as well understood. The expressive power of equational languages will be greatly enhanced if one is allowed to state inequations of terms explicitly. In this paper, we study reasoning in systems which consist of equations as well as inequations, emphasizing the development of *forward,* i.e., non-refutational, techniques for deducing valid inequations, similar to those for equational inference. Such techniques can be used as a basis for developing execution strategies for equational and declarative languages. We develop an inference system and show that it is complete for deducing all valid inequations. The inference system is used to develop a goal-directed semi-decision procedure which uses a narrowing technique for proving inequations. This semi-decision procedure can be converted into a decision procedure when certain additional conditions are satisfied.

1. INTRODUCTION

Reasoning in purely equational systems has received considerable attention in recent years. Since the well known completeness result of Birkhoff [Birk35], equational reasoning has been applied to several interesting problems: for designing decision procedures for solving word problems in equational theories [KnBe70], for designing equational programming languages [HoOd82], for automating induction proofs [Muss80, HuHu80, JoKo86, KaNZ86, KaMu87], and for theorem proving in the First Order Predicate Calculus [HsDe83, KaNa84]. Some of the results in equational systems have also been extended to systems with conditional equations. A completeness result similar to that of Birkhoff's was obtained by Selman for conditional equational systems [Selm72]. Recently, several researchers have studied equational reasoning in conditional rewriting systems [Kapl83, ZhRe85, BeKl86, MoSr86].

The expressive power of equational languages will be greatly enhanced if one is allowed to state non-equality of terms explicitly as axioms (or as part of an axiom). For example, axiomatic specifications for data types and functions can be expressed more elegantly and concisely using explicit *inequations* (negations of equations). For instance, a specification of the *fetch* operation on an array-like data type is best expressed as follows:

$$i = j \Rightarrow \text{fetch}(\text{assign}(a, i, x), j) = x$$
$$i \neq j \Rightarrow \text{fetch}(\text{assign}(a, i, x), j) = \text{fetch}(a, j).$$

It is necessary to understand reasoning in systems of equations and inequations before one can study such conditional definitions. Even while reasoning with purely equational specifications of functions, it might be necessary to make use of the fact that certain terms are not equal: the free constructor assumption (eg., *nil* is not equal to *cons* (x, y)) is often used in reasoning about specifications. Most current equational languages get around this situation by treating the inequational relation as the logical negation of an explicitly defined equality predicate. This method, while not being generally applicable, leads to unnatural specifications. For example, an approach adopted in the AFFIRM system [Muss79] avoids inequations by explicitly defining a separate Boolean-valued equality predicate for each domain which is then used to write axioms; an artificial distinction is thus made between the equality predicate for the domain and the equality predicate in the logical language. We feel that such an approach is not so elegant because there should not be any reason to define the equality predicate separately; instead, the definition of the equality predicate can be obtained directly from the axioms.

In this paper, we study reasoning in systems which consist of equations and inequations. We assume that the variables in the axioms are (implicitly) universally quantified. Current approaches to studying inequations broadly fall into the following categories:

(1) refutational techniques which derive a contradiction after adding the negation of the goal to the system [WoMc86, HsRu86],

(2) default assumption of two terms being not equal when their equality cannot be proved using a reasonable inference system [MoSr87], and

(3) finding a ground substitution for the variables which solves a system of equations and inequations (an inequation $s \neq t$ is *solved* by a ground substitution σ if $s\sigma, t\sigma$ are distinct terms) [Colm84, LaMM86, Como86, KiLe87].

In this paper, we investigate a new *forward* approach to deriving inequational consequences, similar to the one for deriving equational consequences. Our approach is different from (2) and (3) in that we derive inequations which hold in <u>every</u> model of a given system. It is different from (1), the refutational approach, in that inequations are deduced directly using inference rules which allow us to explicitly infer inequations from existing ones. We refer to such proofs of inequations as *forward* proofs as opposed to refutational proofs. In a forward proof, the given system cannot be altered by adding new literals, and reductio ad absurdum arguments are not used. By contrast, the refutational proof of a literal is obtained by adding its skolemized negation to the system and showing that a contradiction results. A set of inference rules R is *forward complete* if every valid consequence of any system S is deducible by repeatedly applying the rules of R to the members of S. We explore the forward completeness of sets of inference rules applied to systems containing equations and inequations.

For purely equational systems, forward proofs of equational consequences can be constructed using the traditional equality inference rules: reflexivity, symmetry, transitivity, and substitutivity. Inference rules (I_k) for inequations are constructed as contrapositives of the equational inference rules (E_k), by the following schema (where A_i are equations):

$$(E_k)\frac{\{a=b\}\cup\{A_i\}}{c=d} \quad \longrightarrow \quad (I_k)\frac{\{c\neq d\}\cup\{A_i\}}{a\neq b}$$

For example, from the substitutivity inference rule of equality, one can construct an analogous inference rule for inequations as follows:

$$\frac{s_1=t_1,\ s_2=t_2}{f(s_1, s_2)=f(t_1, t_2)} \quad \longrightarrow \quad \frac{s_1=t_1,\ f(s_1, s_2)\neq f(t_1, t_2)}{s_2\neq t_2}$$

There are several reasons for preferring forward proofs of inequations to refutational proofs. Unlike refutational proofs, forward proofs do not *perturb* the environment by adding a skolemized literal. Such perturbation complicates matters when the property being proved is just a subgoal in a larger proof; such as when it is necessary to prove the antecedent of a conditional rewrite rule which contains inequations. If refutational methods were used, all other consequences of adding the new (skolemized) literal would need to be discarded before continuing with the rest of the proof. Forward proofs are conceptually simpler, and have a more appealing constructive flavor which is missing in refutational proofs that survive on excluded middles. Forward proofs serve as a basis for developing decision procedures (where possible) for inequations. It is important to have such decision procedures when the task is one of evaluation rather than a property to be proved, since the result is not known a priori. This is often the case in applicative and functional programming evaluations. Forward proof methods are more compatible with existing equational reasoning, functional and applicative programming systems.

The main results of the paper are the following:

(i) A basic inference system obtained by taking the contra-positive of each of the equational inference rules is not forward complete. In other words, not all inequational consequences are deducible using this inference system. The main reason for its incompleteness is that the contra-positive of the substitutivity inference rule is not general enough to deduce all valid inequations. For example, although we can deduce $f(s,t)=f(t,s)$ from $s=t$ using the substitutivity inference rule, we cannot deduce $s \neq t$ from $f(s,t) \neq f(t,s)$ using its contrapositive.

(ii) We develop a forward complete inference system by generalizing the substitutivity inference rule for inequations. This is done by introducing a mechanism for *deriving conditional consequences* which intuitively means deducing equality of terms assuming that two given terms are equal. Using this mechanism, a new inequation $l \neq r$ is deduced from an inequation $m \neq n$ and the conditional consequence $m=n$ obtained assuming $l=r$.

(iii) The result in (ii) is strengthened by showing that the above forward complete inference system is strong and powerful enough, so that there is a proof of every valid inequation using exactly one inequational axiom which is used at the very beginning.

(iv) The result in (iii) gives us a semi-decision procedure for proving inequations, much like a semi-decision procedure for proving equations.

(v) Finally, if Ξ is the subset of equations in the given system S, and if the equational theory of $\mathcal{E}\cup\{skolem\,(s=t)\}$ has a decidable unification algorithm, then we can decide whether or not $s\neq t$ is a consequence of S.

NOTE: Proofs omitted due to space constraints may be found in [MoSK87].

2. PRELIMINARIES

In this section, we present the definitions, notation and equational inference rules used in the rest of the paper, and state the forward completeness result for equational inference rules in the presence of inequational axioms.

A *term* is either a variable from a denumerably infinite set V of symbols, or consists of a function symbol from a set F (disjoint from V) and a finite (possibly empty) sequence of terms (*arguments*). Terms without variables are *ground terms*. A *substitution* is a mapping from variables to terms. The result of *applying* a substitution σ to a term t is another term obtained by replacing all occurrences of the variables in t by the terms to which σ maps them. *Skolemization* of a term t is the application of a substitution '*skolem*' from all variables of t to new constants (nullary function symbols not in F). An *equation* is a two-tuple of terms written with the infix operator '='. Similarly, an *inequation* is a two-tuple of terms separated by the '$\neq$' symbol. A *literal* is either an equation or an inequation. We denote by $p\equiv q$ that two terms are syntactically identical. We write 'p[q]' to indicate that q is a proper subterm of p. Two terms are *unifiable* iff a substitution *(unifier)* can be applied to them making them identical; σ is a most general unifier (*mgu*) for p and q if every other unifier for p,q is an instance of σ (i.e., every unifier of p,q is obtained by composing σ with some other substitution).

• A system is a set of equations and inequations. An *equational* system contains only equations, while an *inequational* system contains only inequations.

• A Forward Proof of a literal P with respect to a set of inference rules R and a system of equations and inequations S is a proof tree whose root is that literal P, whose leaves are axioms of S, such that every non-leaf node of the tree is a literal obtained by applying one of the inference rules in R to the literals that are the children of that node. When such a forward proof of P exists, we say $S\vdash_R P$ ('S derives P using R'), dropping the subscript when the context is clear.

• A Refutation Proof of a literal P with system S and set R of inference rules is the forward proof of $\Box$ (or some instance of $x \neq x$), from the system $S \cup \{\neg skolem(P)\}$ using R.

• A set of literals is consistent if it does not contain contradictory literals $(m = n)$, $(m \neq n)$ for any terms m, n. An *E-interpretation* for a system S is a consistent superset of ground instances of literals in S that satisfies the reflexive, symmetric, transitive and substitutive axioms for the equality relation [ChLe73]. We say $S \models P$ ('S entails P') if P holds in every E-interpretation of S.

• A system S is E-unsatisfiable (or inconsistent) if it has no E-interpretation. Otherwise, S is E-satisfiable (or consistent). By definition, it follows that every equational system is consistent.

• A set of inference rules R is (forward) ***complete*** if $S \models P \supset S \vdash_R P$, for every system S and every literal P, whereas R is *refutationally complete* if $S \models P \supset S \cup \{\neg skolem(P)\} \vdash_R \Box$.

Given below is a set (E) of simple equational inference rules that are conventionally used for deducing equations from other equations. Other equivalent formulations for the inference rules for equations also exist. In the following, p, q, r, p_i, q_i can be any arbitrary terms, f is any function of arity n, and σ is any substitution for variables.

Reflexive: (E0) $\dfrac{\{\}}{p = p}$ Symmetry: (E1) $\dfrac{p = q}{q = p}$

Transitive: (E2) $\dfrac{p = q,\ q = r}{p = r}$ Instance: (E3) $\dfrac{p = q}{p\sigma = q\sigma}$

Superterm: (E4) $\dfrac{p_1 = q_1,\ \ldots,\ p_n = q_n}{f(p_1, \ldots, p_n) = f(q_1, \ldots, q_n)}$

Proposition 2.1 : The set of equational inference rules E={E0,E1,E2,E3,E4} is forward complete for deducing the equational consequences of any consistent system.

3. STRUCTURE OF PROOFS

Inequational inference rules typically use one inequation and zero or more equations to deduce another inequation. Generally, such inference rules are of no use in deriving equations. The following observation hence becomes significant.

Proposition 3.1 : Let R be any inference system containing the inference rules in E={E0,E1,E2,E3,E4} as well as any other inference rules with the following structure:

$$\frac{m \neq n\ ,\ s_1 = t_1, s_2 = t_2,\ \ldots\ ,\ s_k = t_k}{p \neq q}$$

where m, n, s_i, t_i, p, q are arbitrary terms. Then, for any system A, and terms p, q,

(1) IF $A \vdash_R p = q$ THEN there is a proof of $p = q$ which invokes no inequational axiom.

(2) IF $A \vdash_R p \neq q$ THEN there is a proof of $p \neq q$ which invokes exactly one inequation among the axioms (it may invoke other equational axioms). The proof tree has a unique chain of inequations, from the root to a leaf.

As a special case, substitute p for q in (2) above: IF $A \vdash_R p \neq p$ THEN there is a proof of $p \neq p$ which invokes zero or more equations and exactly one inequation in A. So if there are no inequational axioms, $p \neq p$ cannot be deduced. Commonly, we abbreviate $p \neq p$ as $\square$. Since $p = p$ is an instance of the equational reflexivity axiom, any derivation of $\square$ using sound inference rules indicates that the system is inconsistent.

4. INFERENCE RULES WITH INEQUATIONS

We first introduce inference rules for deducing inequations which are similar to the equational inference rules given earlier, and a proposition demonstrating the duality between certain proofs of equations and inequations. The refutational completeness of a basic set of inference rules R_0 is shown. We then prove a theorem central to the proof of the main result of the paper, showing that every inconsistent system contains an inequational axiom an instance of whose negation can be derived using R_0.

The following are inference rules that derive inequations with an inequation among the premises. I0, I1, I2, $I4^I$ are formulated as the contrapositives of the equational inference rules with the same number. There is no useful contrapositive of E3: instead we have another instantiation rule (I3).

Refutation: (I0) $\dfrac{p \neq p}{\square}$ Symmetry: (I1) $\dfrac{p \neq q}{q \neq p}$

Transitive: (I2) $\dfrac{p \neq q\ ,\ q = r}{p \neq r}$ Instance: (I3) $\dfrac{p \neq q}{p\sigma \neq q\sigma}$

Subterm: $(I4^I)\ \dfrac{[\forall i \neq k.\ p_i = q_i], f(p_1, \ldots, p_n) \neq f(q_1, \ldots, q_n)}{p_k \neq q_k}$

We first consider the *Basic Set* of inference rules $R_0 = E \cup \{I0, I1, I2, I3\}$ which is shown to be refutationally complete; and $R_1 = R_0 \cup \{I4^I\}$ which is the first set of inference rules we formulate toward the goal of forward completeness. To help reason about easily transformable proof subtrees, we also consider subsets of R_0, viz., R_{cons} ={E1,I1,E2,I2,E3,I3} and R_{trans} ={I0,E1,I1,E2,I2}; proofs using R_{cons}, R_{trans} are referred to as *conservative* and *transitive* proofs respectively.

The duality between equations and inequations is reflected in an interesting property of equational proofs which do not use the reflexivity (E0) or superterm (E4) inference rules. From the result that follows, the proof of certain properties of the proof tree of an equation in R_{cons} or R_{trans} is adequate to justify the claim that similar properties hold for the proof tree of an inequation. The corollary establishes the converse which holds for R_0 as well.

Proposition 4.1 : Suppose P is a conservative (or transitive) proof tree of an equation. Let P' be a tree obtained by replacing in P every equation $l_i = r_i$ along a path from the root of P to one of its leaves by the inequation $l_i \neq r_i$. Then, P' is also a conservative (or transitive) proof tree.

PROOF: From proposition 3.1(1), proofs of equations in R_{cons}, R_{trans} do not use inequations at any stage. For each step in the chain of literals in the proof tree in which inequations are substituted for the equations, the new inference remains valid: instances of E1, E2, and E3 become respectively transformed to instances of I1, I2, and I3. Other inferences are untouched. So the transformed tree continues to represent a proof in R_{cons} or R_{trans} respectively. The new proof uses axioms from a different system, and derives a different theorem than the original proof.

Corollary 4.1.1 : In any proof tree using R_0 (or R_{trans} or R_{cons}), if all inequations $l_i \neq r_i$ are replaced by the corresponding equations $l_i = r_i$, the resulting structure continues to be a proof tree in R_0 (or R_{trans} or R_{cons}, respectively).

THEOREM 4.2 : (Refutational Completeness for R_0)

IF $S \models s \neq t$, *THEN* $S \cup \{skolem(s=t)\} \vdash_{R_0} \Box$.

Proof: If $S \models s \neq t$, then $S \cup \{s\sigma = t\sigma\}$ is unsatisfiable, where σ is a skolemizing substitution for s and t. Therefore, $\Box$ can be derived from $S \cup \{s\sigma = t\sigma\}$ using positive hyper-resolution and hyper-paramodulation, together with the functionally reflexive axioms (by proposition 4.2.1). We show that every application of hyper-resolution and hyper-paramodulation on equations and inequations has an equivalent proof using the inference rules of R_0. Refutational completeness of R_0 follows because there is a R_0-proof corresponding to every inference that can be accomplished using a known refutationally complete strategy.

The functionally reflexive axioms as well as x=x can be obtained simply by invoking rule E0. Paramodulation and resolution derive <u>only</u> single-literal clauses in systems consisting of equations and inequations. Resolution between equations and inequations is just the final refutation step: a proof of □ from an equation and inequation, given by rule I0, possibly after first instantiating (E3,I3) the literals resolved. Positive hyper-paramodulation between equations and inequations has the equivalent proof in R_0 shown below.

Positive Hyper-paramodulation: $\dfrac{f\,[t\,]=g\,[t\,],\quad r=s\,,\quad \sigma \text{ is the m.g.u. of } t \text{ and } r}{f\,[s\,]\sigma=g\,[s\,]\sigma}$

Equivalent proof using R_0:

```
          r=s
(E1)   ----------
          s=r
(E4)   ----------
       f[s]=f[r]                f[t]=g[t]                  r=s
(E3)   ----------       (E3)  ---------------    (E4)  ------------
       f[s]σ=f[r]σ              f[t]σ=g[t]σ               g[r]=g[s]
(E2)   ----------------------------------------   (E3)  ---------------
             f[s]σ=g[t]σ                                 g[r]σ=g[s]σ
     (E2)   --------------------------------------------------------    {since tσ≡rσ}
                              f[s]σ=g[s]σ
```

Q.E.D.

Proposition 4.2.1 [ChLe73]: For an E-unsatisfiable set of clauses S, there is a hyper-refutation with resolution and paramodulation from $S \cup \{x=x\} \cup F$, where F is the set of the functionally reflexive axioms for S.

Corollary 4.2.2 : Any set of inference rules containing {E0,E1,E2,E3,E4,I0,I3} is refutationally complete for systems of equations and inequations.

THEOREM 4.3 : *IF* $A \vdash_{R_0} \square$ *THEN there is some inequation* $(p \neq q) \in A$ *and some* *substitution* ρ, *such that* $A \vdash_{R_0} (p\,\rho = q\,\rho)$.

PROOF: We show that whenever $A \vdash_{R_0} \Box$, any R_0-proof of $\Box$ from A can be transformed to the following form, which includes as a subtree the R_0-proof of $p\,\rho = q\,\rho$ for some substitution ρ, where $p \neq q \in A$.

$$\dfrac{\begin{matrix}\vdots\\ p\,\rho = q\,\rho\end{matrix} \qquad \dfrac{p \neq q}{p\,\rho \neq q\,\rho}\,(\text{I3})}{\Box}\,(\text{I0})$$

First, any proof of $\Box$ can be transformed to another derivation in which instantiation and superterm proof steps can be 'bubbled' towards the leaves of the proof tree, so that these proof steps (E3,I3,E4) are successively performed in the first few inferences from the axioms of A, leaving the rest of the derivation as a transitive proof (see lemma 4.3.1 below). Second, any transitive proof can be transformed, pulling down any leaf until it is utmost one hop away from the root (see lemma 4.3.3 below). There is a unique inequation $p \neq q \in A$ invoked in the R_0-derivation of $\Box$ (from proposition 3.1(2)), which can hence be pulled down in the proof tree using these transformations until it is no more than two inference-steps (I3,I0) away from the root. The only way in which $\Box$ can be derived is by using rule I0, hence the resulting proof tree has the desired structure, with $p\,\rho = q\,\rho$ and $p\,\rho \neq q\,\rho$ as the nodes immediately above the root.

Lemma 4.3.1 : IF $A \vdash_{R_0} p \neq q$ THEN there is a proof of $p \neq q$ in which all instantiation steps (E3,I3) are performed immediately after axioms are invoked, and all superterm substitutions (E4) are performed immediately thereafter, leaving the rest of the tree containing only transitivity (and symmetry) steps.

Proposition 4.3.2 : A proof tree of p=q using $R \supset E$ can be transformed to another proof in which inference rules of instantiation (E3) and superterm substitution (E4) are first performed on the axioms (leaves) in the proof tree, leaving the rest of the tree as a transitive proof.

Lemma 4.3.3 : If P is any literal occurring at the leaf of a transitive proof tree T deriving $\Box$, then T can be transformed to an equivalent transitive proof tree such that P is the premise in the last step (I0) of the proof of $\Box$.

5. A FORWARD-COMPLETE INFERENCE SET

In this section we develop a forward-complete set of inference rules R_ω which is a superset of R_0. The incompleteness of forward derivations of inequations using the basic set R_0 comes as no surprise since R_0 does not contain the subterm rule contrapositive to the superterm rule (E4). However, R_1, which includes the subterm rule $I4^I$, is also shown to be forward incomplete; so are sets of inference rules which include generalized versions of $I4^I$. We notice, however, that the subterm rule can be made progressively more general: we have forward completeness in the limit, when we use R_ω which contains inference rules to compute conditional consequences.

Proposition 5.1 : R_1 *is not forward complete.*

The following example shows that $R_1 = R_0 \cup \{I4^I\}$ is incomplete with respect to forward derivations of inequations.

Example 5.1.1 : $S=\{f(s,t)\neq f(t,s)\}$

None of the inference rules I2,I3,I4 can be applied to infer any new inequation from S in this example. Hence, $s\neq t$ is not derivable, although $\{s=t\}\vdash_{R_0} f(s,t)=f(t,s)$.

5.2. A First Attempt

• Two terms m,n are <u>l,r-identical</u> (denoted $m \underset{l,r}{\approx} n$) if m and n can be made syntactically identical by replacing in them zero or more occurrences of l by r, and r by l respectively.

Proposition 5.2.1 : If $\{l=r\}\vdash_{R_0} m=n$, **and** l,r are ground terms, **then** $m \underset{l,r}{\approx} n$ (i.e., two terms are l,r-identical if their equality is a consequence of a single ground equation $l=r$).

We now introduce a new inference rule: $$(I4^{II})\quad \frac{m\neq n\,,\ m \underset{l,r}{\approx} n}{l\neq r}$$

Using $R_2 = R_0 \cup \{I4^{II}\}$, which includes a generalization of the subterm rule, takes care of the previous counterexample (5.1.1). The next theorem (5.2.2) shows that R_2 is forward complete for the restricted class of inequational systems.

THEOREM 5.2.2: *If Q is a set of inequations, then $Q \models (s \neq t) \Rightarrow Q \vdash_{R_2} (s \neq t)$.*

<u>*PROOF*</u>: Let $Q \models (s \neq t)$, so that refutational completeness implies $Q \cup \{s\sigma = t\sigma\} \vdash_{R_0} \square$, where σ is a skolem substitution. By Theorem 4.3, $Q \cup \{s\sigma = t\sigma\} \vdash_{R_0} [p\rho = q\rho]$ for some $(p \neq q) \in Q$. Invoking proposition 3.1(1), we have $\{s\sigma = t\sigma\} \vdash_{R_0} p\rho = q\rho$. We conclude (from proposition 5.2.1 above) that $p\rho \underset{s\sigma, t\sigma}{\approx} q\rho$. Using inference rule $I4^{II}$, we infer $s\sigma \neq t\sigma$. Since σ is a skolemizing substitution, we conclude $Q \vdash_{R_2} s \neq t$.

Q.E.D.

Although several more inferences are possible now than before, R_2 is still not forward complete for systems containing equations as well as inequations, as shown by the following example.

Example 5.2.3 : $S = \{g(s) = h(s),\ g(t) \neq h(t)\}$

Here, while $S \cup \{s = t\}$ derives a contradiction, no other inequation is derivable from S even if we use $I4^{II}$. To account for this example, we may use $R_3 = R_0 \cup \{I4^{III}\}$, generalizing $I4^{II}$ to the stronger inference rule $I4^{III}$ defined below:

$$(I4^{III})\ \frac{m \neq n,\ m \underset{l,r}{\approx} m_1,\ n \underset{l,r}{\approx} n_1,\ m_1 = n_1}{l \neq r}$$

For the above example (5.2.3), we then have the proof

$$(I4^{III})\ \frac{g(t) \neq h(t),\ g(t) \underset{s,t}{\approx} g(s),\ h(t) \underset{s,t}{\approx} h(s),\ g(s) = h(s)}{s \neq t}$$

But even R_3 is incomplete, and sometimes does not succeed in deducing valid inequations from a system. The following example shows that there are inequations for which there is a refutational proof but no forward proof using the inference rules in R_3, i.e., it is possible that $S \cup \{s\sigma = t\sigma\} \vdash \square$ but $s \neq t$ is not derivable from S.

Example 5.2.4 : $S = \{f(s) = h(s),\ f(t) = g(t),\ g(s) \neq h(t)\}$.

$S' = \{s = t,\ f(s) = h(s),\ f(t) = g(t),\ g(s) \neq h(t)\} \vdash \square$, hence $S \models s \neq t$. But no other inequation can be inferred using the inference rules of R_3, and nor can any of the equations $g(s) = h(s)$, $g(t) = h(s)$, $g(t) = h(t)$. So we cannot use $I4^{III}$ to derive $s \neq t$. In trying to obtain stronger inequational inference rules, we need not stop with $I4^{III}$. For instance, in this example, we can infer $s \neq t$ using the inference rule $I4^{IV}$ given below:

$$(I4^{IV})\ \frac{m \neq n,\ m \underset{l,r}{\approx} m_1,\ n \underset{l,r}{\approx} n_1,\ m_1 = m_2,\ n_1 = n_2,\ m_2 \underset{l,r}{\approx} n_2}{l \neq r}$$

Incompleteness persists, eg. with $S = \{f(s) = h(s), f(t) = k(s), k(t) = g(t), g(s) \neq h(t)\}$, where s$\neq$t cannot be deduced using $R_0 \cup \{I4^{IV}\}$ although $S \models s \neq t$.

There is an infinite hierarchy of successively more powerful inference rules with which we can obtain forward proofs of increasingly larger sets of inequational consequences of systems. We can define $I4^{III}$, $I4^{IV}$, $I4^{V}$, . . . , ad infinitum, so that for any $I4^{N}$, we have a stronger inference rule $I4^{N+1}$ which helps prove more inequations. Each inference rule is obtained from the previous by incorporating one more instance of transitivity between $=$ and $\approx$. Whereas $m_{k-1}=n_{k-1}$ in $I4^{2k-1}$, we have $m_{k-1}=m_k \approx n_k = n_{k-1}$ in $I4^{2k}$; similarly, whereas $m_k \approx n_k$ in $I4^{2k}$, we have $m_k \approx m_{k+1} = n_{k+1} \approx n_k$ in $I4^{2k+1}$. The following progression illustrates this, showing the chain of reasoning which deduces l$\neq$r using each of $I4^{II}$-$I4^{V}$:

$\mathbf{I4^{II}}$	$\mathbf{I4^{III}}$	$\mathbf{I4^{IV}}$	$\mathbf{I4^{V}}$
$$\begin{array}{c} m \neq n \\ \approx \end{array}$$	$$\begin{array}{ccc} m & \neq & n \\ \wr & & \wr \\ m_1 & = & n_1 \end{array}$$	$$\begin{array}{ccc} m & \neq & n \\ \wr & & \wr \\ m_1 & & n_1 \\ \Vert & & \Vert \\ m_2 & \approx & n_2 \end{array}$$	$$\begin{array}{ccc} m & \neq & n \\ \wr & & \wr \\ m_1 & & n_1 \\ \Vert & & \Vert \\ m_2 & & n_2 \\ \wr & & \wr \\ m_3 & = & n_3 \end{array}$$

5.3. Conditional Consequence Mechanism

Each of the sets of inference rules $R_0 \cup \{I4^k\}$ can be shown to be incomplete. The apparent problem is that we do not have transitivity between $\underset{l,r}{\approx}$ and $=$ relations. To handle a proof with any number of occurrences of the skolemized literal, we need a rule that encapsulates all the rules $\{I4^i\}$.

We introduce below a new relation $\underset{l,r}{\sim}$ (pronounced l,r-equivalence), computed using inference rules analogous to the equational inference rules. We show that this defines a conditional equality, i.e. $S \cup \{l=r\} \vdash m=n \supset S \vdash m \underset{l,r}{\sim} n$ (lemma 5.3.2). We prove the forward completeness theorem for the new inference system R_ω obtained by adding these inference rules to R_0.

$$(E0^{\omega}_{l,r})\ \frac{m \underset{l,r}{\approx} n}{m \underset{l,r}{\sim} n} \qquad\qquad (I4^{\omega}_{l,r})\ \frac{m \underset{l,r}{\sim} n\ ,\ m \neq n}{l \neq r}$$

$$(\mathrm{E2}^{\omega}_{l,r})\frac{m=n}{m \underset{l,r}{\sim} n} \qquad (\mathrm{E5}^{\omega}_{l,r})\frac{m \underset{l,r}{\sim} n\ ,\ n \underset{l,r}{\sim} p}{m \underset{l,r}{\sim} p}$$

- The new inference system is $\mathbf{R}_{\omega}(\mathbf{l},\mathbf{r})=R_0 \cup \{E0^{\omega}_{l,r},\ E2^{\omega}_{l,r},\ E5^{\omega}_{l,r},\ I4^{\omega}_{l,r}\}$.

The following theorem states that every inequational consequence $s \neq t$ of a system S can be derived using $R_{\omega}(s,t)$. The proof uses refutational completeness of R_0, together with another previous result (4.3), to first show that there is an R_0-proof from $S \cup \{skolem\,(s=t)\}$ of some equation $p\,\rho = q\,\rho$ that contradicts an inequation $p \neq q$ in S. Using the lemma that follows, it can be concluded that there is a R_{ω}-proof of $p\,\rho \underset{skolem\,(s,t)}{\sim} q\,\rho$. Rule $\mathrm{I4}^{\omega}$ can now be applied, yielding a R_{ω}-proof of $skolem\,(s \neq t)$. This is equivalent to a proof of $s \neq t$, since any proof of a skolemized literal is practically a proof of the original literal, with the only difference that uninstantiated variables replace skolem constants throughout the proof.

THEOREM 5.3.1 : **If** $S \models s \neq t$ **then** $S \vdash_{R_{\omega}(s,t)} s \neq t$.

PROOF: Let $S \models s \neq t$. Since R_0 is refutationally complete (from Theorem 4.2), we have the following where σ is a skolemizing substitution for the variables in s and t.

$$S \models s \neq t \supset S \cup \{s\,\sigma = t\,\sigma\} \vdash_{R_0} \Box.$$

From Theorem 4.3, there is an inequation $p \neq q \in S$ and some substitution ρ such that

$$S \cup \{s\,\sigma = t\,\sigma\} \vdash_{R_0} \Box \ \supset\ S \cup \{s\,\sigma = t\,\sigma\} \vdash_{R_0} p\,\rho = q\,\rho.$$

From the lemma that follows (5.3.2), we have

$$S \cup \{s\,\sigma = t\,\sigma\} \vdash_{R_0} p\,\rho = q\,\rho \ \Rightarrow\ S \vdash_{R_{\omega}(s\,\sigma,t\,\sigma)} p\,\rho \underset{s\,\sigma,\ t\,\sigma}{\sim} q\,\rho.$$

Since $p \neq q \in S$ and since the instantiation rule (I3) is in $R_{\omega}(s\,\sigma,t\,\sigma)$, we have:

$$S \vdash_{R_{\omega}(s\,\sigma,t\,\sigma)} p\,\rho \neq q\,\rho$$

Hence, applying the new inference rule $\mathrm{I4}^{\omega}_{s\,\sigma,t\,\sigma}$ to $[p\,\rho \underset{s\,\sigma,\ t\,\sigma}{\sim} q\,\rho]$ and $[p\,\rho \neq q\,\rho]$, we have:

$$S \vdash_{R_{\omega}(s\,\sigma,t\,\sigma)} s\sigma \neq t\sigma.$$

Since σ only substitutes distinct skolem constants for variables in s and t, the proof of $s\sigma \neq t\sigma$ in $R_{\omega}(s\,\sigma,t\,\sigma)$ will also be a proof of $s \neq t$ in $R_{\omega}(s,t)$.

Hence, we have $\mathrm{S} \models \mathrm{s} \neq \mathrm{t} \supset \mathrm{S} \vdash_{R_{\omega}(s,t)} \mathrm{s} \neq \mathrm{t}$.

Q.E.D.

Lemma 5.3.2 : If l,r are ground terms, then

$$S \cup \{l = r\} \vdash_{R_0} m = n \Rightarrow S \vdash_{R_\omega(l,r)} m \underset{l,r}{\sim} n$$

Proof: Let T be any proof tree for $m = n$ from $S \cup \{l = r\}$ using R_0. We transform T to another proof tree in which all non-transitive proof steps occur at the top two levels next to each leaf (as in proposition 4.3.2). If equation $a = b$ results from applying inference rules E1,E3,E4 to a leaf node $l = r$, (i.e., if $\{l = r\} \vdash_{R_0} a = b$), then by proposition 5.2.1, a and b must be l,r-identical, i.e. $a \underset{l,r}{\approx} b$, whence we can deduce $a \underset{l,r}{\sim} b$ using $E0^{\omega}_{l,r}$. If $S \vdash_{R_0} a = b$ (without invoking $l = r$), then $a \underset{l,r}{\sim} b$ can be derived using inference $E2^{\omega}_{l,r}$. Other (transitive) proof steps can be replaced by $E5^{\omega}_{l,r}$. We now have a $R_\omega(l,r)$-proof of $m \underset{l,r}{\sim} n$, which does not use $l = r$ as an axiom, i.e. $S \vdash_{R_\omega(l,r)} m \underset{l,r}{\sim} n$.

• *Forward Completeness of* R_ω: We now have $S \models s \neq t \Rightarrow S \vdash_{R_\omega(s,t)} s \neq t$ by the above theorem 5.3.1. By an earlier result (proposition 2.1), $S \models (m = n) \Rightarrow S \vdash_{R_0} (m = n)$. Hence R_ω is forward complete, where the proof of each inequation $m \neq n$ is understood to use the inference rules of $R_\omega(m, n)$.

The next proposition illustrates that conditional consequences could also be computed with a different set of inference rules E_ν. Derivations in this new system (which is also forward complete) are interesting in that conditional consequences (terms related by $\underset{l,r}{\sim}$) occur only in one chain of nodes in the proof tree (between a leaf and the root).

Proposition 5.3.3 : If $S \vdash_{R_\omega(l,r)} p \underset{l,r}{\sim} q$ then there is also a proof for $p \underset{l,r}{\sim} q$ from S using $E^{l,r}_\nu = E \cup \{E0^{\omega}_{l,r}, E6^{\omega}_{l,r}, E7^{\omega}_{l,r}\}$, where the latter two rules are defined below:

$$(E6^{\omega}_{l,r})\frac{m \underset{l,r}{\sim} n,\quad n \underset{l,r}{\approx} n'}{m \underset{l,r}{\sim} n'},\qquad (E7^{\omega}_{l,r})\frac{m \underset{l,r}{\sim} n,\quad n = n'}{m \underset{l,r}{\sim} n'}.$$

Lemma 5.3.3.1 : A $R^{l,r}_\omega$-proof subtree of $p \underset{l,r}{\sim} q$ in which every node is a conditional consequence $p_i \underset{l,r}{\sim} q_i$ can be transformed to another $R^{l,r}_\omega$-proof subtree with the same leaves and root such that there is only one node in the tree with two leaves as children.

6. PROCEDURE FOR DERIVING INEQUATIONS

In the previous section, we have proved that every inequational consequence of a system can be derived using the inference rules in R_ω. However, it is not immediately obvious as to how these rules may be applied in a goal-directed way to derive a desired consequence. We do not know which axioms (members) of S must be picked for a successful proof, and which sequence of inference rules would be most fruitful. We now outline a goal-directed semi-decision procedure for deducing inequational consequences of a system S. To ensure fairness, we follow a breadth-first strategy.

We have shown earlier that if $s \neq t$ is a consequence of a system S, then S contains an inequation $p_i \neq q_i$ such that for some ρ we can derive $p_i \rho \underset{skolem(s,t)}{\sim} q_i \rho$ using R_ω. Hence we devise a semi-decision procedure which <u>starts</u> from the inequations in S, and finds the appropriate substitution ρ, by deriving the *conditional inequations* $[p \underset{skolem(s,t)}{\not\sim} q]$. Analogous to the $\underset{l,r}{\sim}$ relation, the $\underset{l,r}{\not\sim}$ relation is defined so that $p \underset{l,r}{\not\sim} q$ implies $(l = r \Rightarrow p \neq q)$. In the procedure, conditional inequations are computed using a variant of the narrowing mechanism [Lank75, Hull80] defined below:

- A term p <u>*equationally narrows*</u> to p' by $l = r$ if there is a subterm m of p which unifies with l, and p' is $p[m \leftarrow r]\rho$, the result of replacing the occurrence of m in p by r, and instantiating with ρ, the most general unifier of m and l.
- A conditional inequation $p \underset{l,r}{\not\sim} q$ is $\underset{l,r}{\sim}$**-narrowed** by S to $p' \underset{l,r}{\not\sim} q'$ if

  <u>either</u> p and q equationally narrow to p' and q' using some equation in S

  <u>or</u> there is a most general substitution ρ such that $p\rho \underset{l,r}{\approx} p'$, and $q\rho \underset{l,r}{\approx} q'$.

procedure *ProveInequation* $(s,t : terms;\ S : system)$;
  let σ be a skolem substitution for variables in s, t;
  $C := \{p \underset{s\sigma,t\sigma}{\not\sim} q \mid p \neq q \in S\}$;
  while true do
    if $r \underset{s\sigma,t\sigma}{\not\sim} r' \in C$ such that $\exists \rho . r\rho \equiv r'\rho$
      then return with SUCCESS concluding $s \neq t$;
    let α be a member of C that has been left unnarrowed for the longest time;
    $C := C - \{\alpha\} \cup \{\xi \mid \alpha \underset{s\sigma,t\sigma}{\sim}$-narrows to $\xi\}$;
  end while ;
end procedure .

Proposition 6.1 : The above procedure is complete for proving inequations, i.e., **if** $S \models s \neq t$, **then** *ProveInequation* (s, t, S) terminates with success.

PROOF: Completeness of procedure *ProveInequation* follows from the forward completeness of R_ω proved in section 5. From Theorem 5.3.1, if $S \models s \neq t$, there must be some inequation $p \neq q \in S$ such that $p\rho \underset{s\sigma,t\sigma}{\sim} q\rho$ can be derived using R_ω (or using $E_\nu^{s\sigma,t\sigma}$, from proposition 5.3.3). It can be shown (via proof tree transformations given below) that whenever there is such a R_ω-proof of $s \neq t$ there must be a derivation of $m \underset{s\sigma,t\sigma}{\not\sim} n$ obtained by repeatedly $\underset{s\sigma,t\sigma}{\sim}$-narrowing some inequation in S, where m, n are unifiable. The breadth-first strategy used by procedure *ProveInequation* guarantees that every possible $\underset{s\sigma,t\sigma}{\sim}$-narrowing from every inequation eventually gets generated after a finite number of iterations through the while-loop of the procedure. Hence, $m \underset{s\sigma,t\sigma}{\not\sim} n$ will also be generated at some stage, and since m, n are unifiable, the procedure returns with success concluding $s \neq t$. Details of the full proof may be found in [MoSK87].

6.2. Towards a Decision Procedure

It is possible to convert the semi-decision procedure described in the previous section into a decision procedure for proving a restricted class of inequational consequences of a system. The decision procedure uses a complete procedure for *T-Unification,* i.e., unification with respect to an equational theory T (finding a substitution which when applied makes two terms equal in the theory T). It can be shown that if there is a decidable unification procedure for T={*skolem* $(s = t)$}∪{equations in S}, then we can decide whether or not $S \models s \neq t$. This can be done by checking whether there is any inequational axiom in S, whose arguments can be unified with respect to T.

Hullot [Hull80] has developed a criterion for the decidability of T-unification for any equational theory described by a term rewriting system T. A narrowing is ***basic*** if each narrowing step affects a non-variable subterm of the original term from which narrowing began (this is a paraphrase of the actual technical definition in [Hull80]). A rewriting system T satisfies Hullot's criterion iff T is canonical (i.e., has a decision procedure for equations) and if every basic narrowing derivation from the right hand side of every rule in T terminates. There is a complete decision procedure for T-

unification with respect to every equational theory described by a TRS which satisfies Hullot's criterion. Based on this result, we have the following condition: we can decide whether or not $s \neq t$ is an inequational consequence of S, if the equations in a system S together with *skolem* $(s = t)$ can be represented by a term rewriting system which satisfies Hullot's criterion.

Some simple sufficient conditions can be given for Hullot's criterion to hold. For example, when the equations in $S' = S \cup skolem(s = t)$ can be represented by a canonical rewriting system in which, for every rule, the *rhs* is a ground term or a proper subterm of the *lhs*, T-unification terminates [KaNO87] and we can decide whether or not $S \models s \neq t$. If a rewriting system representing the equations in S is known to satisfy Hullot's criterion, and if the *lhs* of no rewrite rule contains a non-variable subterm that unifies with $s\sigma$ or $t\sigma$, then there is a rewriting system satisfying Hullot's criterion with respect to the augmented equational theory (of equations in S'), hence decidability of $s \neq t$.

7. CONCLUDING REMARKS

In this paper we have explored reasoning in systems of equations and inequations giving special emphasis to developing a forward reasoning method for proving valid inequations. We developed an inference set R_ω, and proved its forward completeness. We used the completeness result to construct a goal-directed semi-decision procedure for proving valid inequations. Decidability of an inequational consequence $s \neq t$ obtains if criteria are met for the decidability of T-unification of the equational part of the system together with *skolem* $(s = t)$.

The motivation for this work came from a study of conditional equations and rewriting systems, with the goal of incorporating equations as well as inequations in the antecedents of conditional equations and rules. The expressive power of declarative languages and systems will be greatly enhanced if inequations can be stated explicitly. To develop evaluation strategies for such programming and specification languages it is important to study forward reasoning techniques for checking inequations. We believe that the completeness result and the inference system developed here can serve as a basis for developing better strategies and decision procedures for proving inequations whenever possible.

7.1. Conditional Consequences vs. Refutational Proofs

Proofs in R_ω resemble some refutation proofs, the major difference being that the latter explicitly invoke $s\sigma = t\sigma$ while the former derives equations which hold **if** $s\sigma = t\sigma$ holds. Proofs in R_ω are preferable to refutational proofs for reasons of clarity and efficiency. Firstly, unlike refutational proofs, no new equations are introduced into the system by R_ω-proofs: every conditional consequence $m \underset{l,r}{\sim} n$ is visibly different from the equational consequences of the system. Secondly, whenever there is a R_0-refutation proof, there is a forward proof of the same or lesser complexity using R_ω, where complexity is measured by the size of the proof tree. Finally, since there is no transitivity inference rule between the relations $\neq$ and $\underset{s,t}{\sim}$, the number of (minimal) R_ω-proofs of a literal from a given system is no greater (generally less) than the number of (minimal) refutational proofs.

7.2. Relation to Selman's work

The forward completeness result for R_ω is analogous to a special case of Selman's completeness result [Selm72] for a language of *equation implications*. Thus $m \underset{l,r}{\sim} n$ is equivalent to $l = r \supset m = n$, and $l \neq r$ is equivalent to $l = r \supset \mathbf{T} = \mathbf{F}$ for special symbols **T**,**F**. Selman gives an inference system which is forward complete for deducing every equation implication $a = b \supset c = d$ which is a consequence of the equational implication system S. Hence every inequation $a = b \supset \mathbf{T} = \mathbf{F}$ is deducible if it is a consequence of S. However, since Selman is concerned with a more general formalism than just equations and inequations, his inference rules are much more complex, and include modus ponens and transitivity of implication.

REFERENCES

[BeKl86] J.A.Bergstra, J.W.Klop, Conditional Rewrite Rules: Confluence and Termination, *Journal of Computer & System Sciences 32,* No.3, June 1986.

[Birk35] G.Birkhoff, On the Structure of Abstract Algebras, Proc. Cambridge Philos. Soc. 31, 433-454, 1935.

[ChLe73] C.L.Chang, R.C.Lee, *Symbolic Logic and Mechanical Theorem Proving,* Academic Press, New York, 1973.

[Colm84] A.Colmerauer, Equations and Inequations on Finite and Infinite Trees, Proc. Intl. Conf. on Fifth Generation Computer Systems, ICOT, Japan, 1984.

[Como86] H.Comon, Sufficient Completeness, Term Rewriting Systems, and 'Anti-Unification', Eighth Conference on Automated Deduction, Oxford, LNCS 230, Springer Verlag, July 1986.

[HoOd82] C.M.Hoffman, M.J.O'Donnel, Programming with equations, ACM TOPLAS, Vol. 4, No. 1, 83-112, 1982.

[HsDe83] J.Hsiang, N.Dershowitz, Rewrite Methods for Clausal and Nonclausal Theorem Proving, Proc. 10th ICALP, July 1983.

[HsRu86] J.Hsiang, M.Rusinowitch, On Word Problems in Equational Theories, Computer Science Dept., SUNY at Stony Brook, New York, Aug. 1986 (also in Proc. 14th ICALP, Karlsruhe, July 1987).

[HuHu80] G.Huet, J.M.Hullot, Proofs by Induction in Equational Theories with Constructors, Proc. 21st FOCS, 96-107, 1980.

[Hull80] J.M.Hullot, Canonical Forms and Unification, Proc. 5th CADE, LNCS 87, Springer Verlag, also Tech.Rep. CSL-114, SRI Int'l, April 1980.

[JoKo86] J.-P.Jouannaud, E.Kounalis, Proofs by induction in equational theories without constructors, Proc. of Logic in Computer Science Conference, Cambridge, MA, June 1986.

[KaMu87] D.Kapur, D.Musser, Proof by Consistency, *Artificial Intelligence 31,* Feb. 1987.

[KaNZ86] D.Kapur, P.Narendran, H.Zhang, Proof by induction using test sets, Proc. of CADE-8, Oxford, England, July 1986.

[Kapl83] S.Kaplan, Fair Conditional Term Rewriting Systems: Unification, Termination, and Confluence, Rapport de Recherche, No. 194, Universite de Paris-Sud, Orsay, France, Dec. 1983.

[KaNa84] D.Kapur, P.Narendran, An equational Approach to Theorem Proving in FOPC, Technical Report, GE Corp. Res. and Dev. Center, Schenectady, NY 12345, April 1984.

[KaNO87] D.Kapur, P.Narendran, F.Otto, On Ground Confluence of Term Rewriting Systems, Technical Report 87-06, GE Corp. Res. and Dev. Center, Schenectady, NY 12345, 1987.

[KiLe87] C.Kirchner, P.Lescanne, Solving Disequations, Proc. 2nd IEEE Symp. on Logic in Computer Science, 1987.

[KnBe70] D.E.Knuth, P.B.Bendix, Simple word problems in Universal Algebras, in

J.Leech, Ed., *Computational Problems in Abstract Algebras,* Pergamon, 1970.

[LaMM86] J-L.Lassez, M.J.Maher, K.Marriott, Unification Revisited, IBM T.J.Watson Research Center, Yorktown Heights, New York, USA, 1986.

[Lank75] D.S.Lankford, Canonical Inference, Report ATP-32, Dept. of Math. and Comp. Sci., Univ. of Texas at Austin, Dec. 1975.

[MoSK87] C.K.Mohan, M.K.Srivas, D.Kapur, On Proofs in Systems of Equations and Inequations, Tech.Rep.87/02, Computer Science Dept., SUNY at StonyBrook, New York, Jan.1987.

[MoSr86] C.K.Mohan, M.K.Srivas, Function Definitions in Term Rewriting and Applicative Programming, *Information and Control,* Vol.71, No.3, Academic Press, Dec.1986.

[MoSr87] C.K.Mohan, M.K.Srivas, Conditional Specifications Using Inequality Assumptions, First International Workshop on Conditional Term Rewriting Systems, Univ. of Paris-Sud, Orsay, France, July 1987.

[Muss79] D.R.Musser, Abstract Data Type Specification in the AFFIRM System, Specifications of Reliable Software Conference, Boston, April 1979.

[Muss80] D.R.Musser, On Proving Inductive Properties of Abstract Data Types, Proc. 7th POPL, Las Vegas, 1980.

[Selm72] A.Selman, Completeness of Calculii for Axiomatically Defined classes of Algebras, *Algebra Universalis,* Vol.2, 20-32, 1972.

[WoMc86] L.Wos, W.McCune, Negative Paramodulation, Eighth Conference on Automated Deduction, Oxford, England, July 1986.

[ZhRe85] H.Zhang, J.L.Remy, Contextual Rewriting, First Conference on Rewriting Techniques and Applications, Dijon, France, 1985.

SPECIFICATION = PROGRAM + TYPES

Lee Naish

Department of Computer Science
University of Melbourne, Parkville 3052
Australia

ABSTRACT

It has been claimed that logic programs are equivalent to or consequences of specifications. We argue this is generally not correct. Programs often make implicit assumptions about types, leading to the possibility of incorrect answers. If the assumptions are made explicit, so that the program is equivalent to the specification, the program is less efficient. We define when programs with type declarations are *type correct* and show all well typed answers returned by such programs are correct.

As well as making to relationship between programs and specifications clear, this type scheme can be used to detect certain programming errors. The semantics we define for type declarations can also be applied to other type schemes. This leads to a simple characterization of what errors are detected by these schemes, and a way to generalize these schemes to allow arbitrary type definitions. One such implementation is discussed.

1. INTRODUCTION

This paper first examines the relationship between logic programs and specifications. We argue that the relationship is more complex than has been suggested previously. Specifications should have explicit type information, but in programs this information is often absent, for reasons of efficiency. The result can be answers which are incorrect with respect to the specification. A formal model which involves types is proposed and we give sufficient conditions for ensuring correct answers. The conditions are satisfied by most reasonable programs.

This scheme is compared with other proposed types schemes for Prolog. It can be used directly, to detect certain programming errors. The semantics we give to type declarations can also be applied to other schemes. This provides greater understanding and points to a way of generalising them. We describe a simple implementation of this kind which accepts arbitrary type definitions. The possibility of combining different styles of type checking in one system and other areas for further research are breifly mentioned.

2. SPECIFICATION = PROGRAM

In many places in the logic programming literature there is reference to the relationship between logic programs and specifications. It is often claimed that programs are typically implied by specifications, equivalent to (complete) specifications or even indistinguishable from specifications. This provides an elegant framework for proving programs are partially correct with respect to the specification and deriving programs from specifications [Clark 77, Clark 84, Hogger 81, Kowalski 85, Tamaki 84].

The following two simple examples illustrate many of the points we will discuss. The first is the standard `append` predicate. The specification is given informally in English. This is done elsewhere in the literature: the highest level of specification can never be made completely formal.

Specification: `append(A,B,C)` is true iff `C` is the list `B` concatenated onto the list `A`.

Program:

```
append([], A, A).
append(A.B, C, A.D) :- append(B, C, D).
```

The second example is the subset predicate, from [Kowalski 85], where sets are represented as lists. The specification is given in logic. We use the syntax of NU-Prolog for this [Naish 86, Thom 86].

Specification:

```
subset(A, B) :- all X member(X, B) => member(X, A).
```

Program:

```
subset([], A).
subset(A.B, C) :- member(A, C), subset(B, C).
```

3. SPECIFICATION ≠ PROGRAM

If we examine the two examples above in detail, a more complex picture of the relationship between programs and specification emerges. The specification of `append` implicitly states that the arguments are lists. However the program may succeed when the second and third arguments are not lists. The `append` program is not equivalent to the specification; it is not even a consequence of the specification. This can lead to answers which are wrong (with respect to the specification). In the program below `false` succeeds when it should fail.

```
false :- append([], a, a).
```

The `subset` program is a consequence of the specification (though not equivalent to it). It is a standard way to implement `subset`. However, this formal specification is not the intuitive specification of `subset`, which states that both arguments must be sets. We believe the specification given is not what is actually intended. Since no type information is given for the arguments of `subset`, `subset(fred,2)` is a consequence of the specification (with the standard equality theory), though not of the program. The program is not a consequence of the intuitive specification either, since `subset([],2)` can be concluded from the program.

If programs should be equivalent to specifications (or even consequences of them) then either the programs everyone has been using should be changed or we should not use the most natural specifications. If the programs are changed then the definition of `append` would become:

```
append([], A, A) :- list(A).
append(A.B, C, A.D) :- append(B, C, D).
```

The cost of the extra test whenever `append` (or `subset`, `member`, `delete`, et cetera) is called is highly undesirable. In most calls to `append` the arguments must be lists and in other cases, separate calls to `list` can be used.

In the natural specification of `append`, all arguments must be lists. If this is to be altered, several possible specifications come to mind:

(1) If `A`, `B` and `C` are lists then `C` is `B` concatenated onto `A`. This implies that if `append` is called the first two arguments lists, any non-list can be returned as the third argument.

(2) If `A` and `B` are lists then `C` is `B` concatenated onto `A`. This specification implies that if `append` is called the last argument a list, any non-lists can be returned as the first two arguments.

(3) If `A` and `B` or `C` are lists then `C` is `B` concatenated onto `A`. This specification is sufficient for all reasonable calls to `append`. It is not equivalent to the program however; it implies that `append(a,b,c)` is true. Also, this specification seems to reflect how `append` is used, rather than being purely declarative.

(4) The high level specification which is equivalent to the program is as follows: `A` is a list, `B` is a list if and only if `C` is a list and `C` has the same "elements" as `A` and `B` in that order. The definition of an element must be extended to non-lists. The asymetry of the specification with respect to the first two arguments reflects the implementation of lists. If the representation of lists allowed access to the last element faster than access to the first element then the specification of an inefficient `append` procedure would be different.

Specifications should be precise, intuitive, as high level and as independent of use and implementation details as possible. Programs should be efficient. We conclude that desirable logic programs are not generally consequences of their natural specifications.

4. SPECIFICATION = PROGRAM + TYPES

Despite the dubious relationship between programs and specifications, with careful programming and some restriction on goals, incorrect answers can be eliminated. Programs which use `append` are not normally plagued by incorrect answers to reasonable goals. The differences between programs and specifications generally stem from the treatment of type information. Type information is often absent from Prolog programs. It should be present in specifications, though it is sometimes implicit or inadvertently left out of completely. We now propose a formal model of the relationship between programs and (complete) specifications which takes account of the role of type information.

We assume the specification is equivalent to a set of *general program clauses* S. General program clauses have a single atom as the *head* and zero or more positive or negative literals constituting the *body*. This gives the expressibility of full first order logic [Lloyd 84a]. The precise details of the equivalence with the specification does not concern us, as we will be dealing with S rather than the specification. Logical equivalence with the completion of S is an obvious candidate and [Maher 86] examines several other possibilities.

Clauses about some subset of the predicates defined by S have explicit type information and are in the form

```
p(t1,...,tn) :- Body, p_type(t1,...,tn).
```

The *program* P is the same as S, except the explicit calls to the type predicates are absent. For example, the standard append procedure could be obtained from the following clause set S by deleting the calls to append_type.

```
append([], A, A) :- append_type([], A, A).
append(A.B, C, A.D) :- append(B, C, D), append_type(A.B, C, A.D).

append_type(A, B, C) :- list(A), list(B), list(C).

list([]).
list(A.B) :- list(B).
```

The type predicates (append_type in this example) are defined by clauses in S in the same way as any other predicate. For the purposes of our model, there are no restrictions on these definitions. P and S can be represented more concisely by a single set of clauses with *type declarations*. The following syntax allows arbitrary definitions of types.

```
?- append(A,B,C) type list(A), list(B), list(C).
append([], A, A).
append(A.B, C, A.D) :- append(B, C, D).
```

Any goal can be used in the body of a type declaration. This goes beyond the traditional view of what constitutes a type [Cardelli 85]. For example, many Prolog predicates assume some input list is sorted. This seems a reasonable extension to the list type. Elements of sorted lists are not independent and their relationship cannot be expressed by conventional type definitions. Our scheme allows the following type declaration.

```
?- merge(A,B,C) type sorted(A), sorted(B), sorted(C).
```

Similarly, the terms allowed in different arguments of a procedure call may not be independent. With some implementations of sets, the union operation is more efficient if the lists are known to be disjoint. This could be expressed by the following declaration.

```
?- disj_union(A,B,C) type set(A), set(B), set(C), disjoint(A,B).
```

It would be possible to have more concise but less flexible declarations (and type definitions) also. Using the following syntax, the type information of each argument must be independent.

```
type append(list, list, list).
type merge(sorted, sorted, sorted).
type subset(set, set).
```

Whatever syntax is used for type declarations, they are simply a shorthand used for defining the program S, which gives the semantics.

This scheme allows us to have efficient programs, as before, but still explicitly state the assumptions the program makes. The program and type declarations define a set S which is equivalent to the natural specification of the problem. We now examine the correctness of answers returned by the program.

5. PROGRAM CORRECTNESS

As we have seen, P may return answers which are incorrect with respect to the specification. By restricting programs and goals we can eliminate incorrect answers but still maintain efficiency.

The restrictions on programs are not severe: we argue they do not exclude reasonable, bug-free programs. The restriction on goals does not affect users at all. Extra conjuncts can be added to the goal by the logic programming system automatically, without affecting correct answers.

More specifically, the program must be such that if an ill typed literal is constructed at some inner level of the computation then the computation fails or returns an ill typed literal at the top level. The top level goal must be such that it only returns well typed answers. These two conditions ensure that only consequences of S are returned. At least when no negation is present, this result can be obtained fairly simply by examining the operational semantics of Prolog: SLD resolution. We take the more general approach of the declarative semantics: model theory. We first consider programs without negation then extend the definitions and (some) proofs for negation.

5.1. Definite Clauses

Definition the ground atoms p(t1,...) and p_type(t1,...) are *well typed* if p_type(t1,...) is true in all models of S.

Definition a ground negation free goal (or clause body) G is *well typed* if each atom in it is well typed.

Definition a negation free program P is *type correct* if for all ground clause instances H:-B, if H is well typed and B is true in some model of P then B is well typed.

Theorem (Model Correspondence 1) If P is type correct and free of negation and M_P is a model of P then $M_S = \{A \mid A \in M_P \text{ and A is well typed}\}$ is a model of S.

Proof Models correspond to the fixed points of the function T associated with the program:

$$T_P(M_P) = M_P$$

T_P is monotonic (since there is no negation) and $M_S \subseteq M_P$ so

$$T_P(M_S) \subseteq T_P(M_P) = M_P$$

Since P is type correct, no well typed atom is derived in one step from any ill typed atoms in a model. All well typed atoms in $T_P(M_P)$ are derived from well typed atoms in M_P, so

$$M_S \subseteq T_P(M_S)$$

S derives in one step any well typed atom in M_P which P derives in one step, so

$$M_S \subseteq T_S(M_S)$$

P derives in one step any atom which S derives in one step, so

$$M_S \subseteq T_S(M_S) \subseteq T_P(M_S) \subseteq M_P$$

S derives in one step only well typed atoms from M_S (from the definition of well typed), so

$$T_S(M_S) = M_S$$

So M_S is a model of S. □

Thus any well typed goal which is true in a model of P is true in a model of S. Rather than considering arbitrary models, we could just consider the least model. This corresponds to the answers returned by Prolog, which are logical consequences (true in all models) of the program.

Theorem (Model Correspondence 2) If P is type correct and free of negation and M_S is a model of S then there exists a model for P, M_P such that $M_S = \{A \mid A \in M_P$ and A is well typed$\}$.

Proof Consider T_P applied to the set M_S plus zero or more ill typed atoms. Since P is type correct and M_S is a fixed point of T_S, the set of well typed atoms in the result is the same as the input: M_S. The function preserves the set of well typed atoms and is monotonic. Thus, the least fixed point of T_P containing M_S is a model of P with the desired property. □

Thus we have a bijection between models in S and models in P. In particular, the least models of S and P correspond. If a well typed atom A is in either least model then it is true in all models of S and P.

Theorem (Soundness) If P is a type correct negation free program and G is a goal then any well typed instance of G returned by P (using SLD resolution) is a logical consequence of S.

Proof Follows from the model correspondence properties and the soundness of SLD resolution (see [Lloyd 84b]). □

Theorem (Strong Completeness) If P is a type correct negation free program and G is a goal then any instance of G which is a logical consequence of S will be returned by P.

Proof Follows from the model correspondence properties and the strong completeness of SLD resolution (see [Lloyd 84b]). □

If P is not type correct then there is some ''incorrect'' derivation which results in a well typed answer. This is a direct consequence of the definition of type correct programs: there must be a ground clause instance with a well typed head and an ill typed body which is true in the least model. However, the head of the clause is not necessarily false. It might be derivable from another clause. If the program is such that there is never more than one successful derivation of a ground atomic goal then the answer returned by an incorrect derivation must be false. Programs which are not type correct usually return incorrect well typed answers and always have incorrect derivations. Thus we claim most reasonable programs are type correct and fit into our model.

5.2. Negation

If negation is present, the previous definition of type correct is not strong enough: type correct programs could return incorrect but well typed answers. For example, the following definition of `false` succeeds when it should fail.

```
false :- not t.

t :- not append([], a, a).
```

To avoid incorrect answers, we must ensure that answers to negated calls are well typed.

Definition a program P is *type correct* if for all ground clause instances H:-B, if H is well typed and B is true in some model of P then B is well typed and all negated atoms in B which are true in some model of P are well typed.

Theorem (Model Correspondence 1) If P is type correct and M_P is a model of P then $M_S = \{A \mid A \in M_P$ and A is well typed$\}$ is a model of S.

Proof We can use the same proof as previously, except that due to the presence of negation, T_P may not be monotonic. We must prove that if $T_P(M_P) = M_P$ and $M_S \subseteq M_P$, then $T_P(M_S) \subseteq T_P(M_P)$.

Suppose $A \in T_P(M_S)$, then a set X of atoms A depends on positively are in M_S and a set Y of atoms A negatively depends on are not in M_S. M_P contains all atoms in X, since $M_S \subseteq M_P$, and no atoms in Y, since M_P is a model and negated atoms must be well typed. Therefore, $A \in T_P(M_P)$. Hence $T_P(M_S) \subseteq T_P(M_P)$. □

Thus any well typed goal which is true in a model of P is true in a model of S, even when negation is present. This gives a weak form of soundness. The second model correspondence theorem does not hold when arbitrary negation is present. In the following program, there is a model for S (`p(a)` and `q(b)` are both false) but no model for P.

```
?- p(X) type X=b.
p(a) :- not q(b).

?- q(X) type X=a.
q(b) :- not p(a).
```

It is worth considering for what class of programs with negation the second model correspondence theorem holds. For this class we have the stronger form of soundness and if we have SLDNF completeness for P, we also have completeness for S. An obvious candidate is *stratified* programs [Apt 86], in which there can be no recursion through negation. The result of most practical significance is would be the following.

Conjecture If P is type correct then G is a logical consequence of the completion of S if and only if G is well typed and G is a logical consequence of the completion of P.

Correspondence of the individual models is not needed but there is the added complexity of using completions. We are currently investigating these ideas.

5.3. An Example

Consider a typical permutation program:

```
type perm(list, list).
type delete(term, list, list).

perm([], []).
perm(A.B, C) :- delete(A, C, D), perm(B, D).

delete(A, A.B, B).
delete(A, B.C, B.D) :- delete(A, C, D).
```

Because delete can succeed with non-lists, perm could potentially return wrong answers. To show the program is type correct we need to prove that for all ground instances of

```
perm(A.B, C) :- delete(A, C, D), perm(B, D).
```

where `A.B` and `C` are lists and the body is true in some model (true if the body succeeds), `B` and `D` are also lists; and to prove that for all ground instances of

```
delete(A, B.C, B.D) :- delete(A, C, D).
```

where `B.C` and `B.D` are lists and the body is true in some model, `C` and `D` are also lists. The proofs for unit clauses are always trivial, since they have no bodies.

The proof for the delete clause is simple, using the definition of `list`. Whenever all the variables in a clause appear in the head (as in `delete`, `append` and `subset`) the proof of type correctness deals only with simple analysis of the types of ground terms. For the perm clause, a more complex analysis is needed. `B` is obviously a list. We can show `D` is a list by proving (by induction) that if the second argument of delete is a list then the third argument is a list in any successful call.

5.4. Testing Goals For Well-typedness

All incorrect answers returned by a type correct program are ill typed. Therefore, if we just use goals which only succeed when they are well typed, all answers will be correct. This can be acheived automatically by the logic programming system. Whenever a goal is executed at top level, extra calls to type predicates can be added to check the answers are well typed. For example, if the following goal was typed

```
?- append([],a,X).
```

`list([]), list(a), list(X)` would be run also. This causes the goal to correctly fail.

The extra overhead is not significant for expensive goals, since it only occurs at the top level. Even this overhead can be reduced sometimes if more analysis is done. The type analysis of [Mycroft 83] ensures that if some instance of a goal is well typed then all answers returned will have a well typed instance. In this case, all ground answers are correct if some instance of the goal is well typed. Goals containing variables can be misleading however. `?- append([],X,X)` succeeds without binding X, but is only true if X is a list. Efficiency could also be improved by coroutining between the original goal and the type goal. This can reduce the time spent executing the type goal and also detects failures more quickly.

6. TYPE SCHEMES FOR PROLOG

So far we have discussed the relationship between specifications and programs. This prompted a theory of types. Although the motivation behind our type scheme is unusual, it can also be applied to the same areas as other type schemes. Checking type correctness can be used to detect errors in programs and the semantics we give to type declarations can be applied to other type schemes, resulting in greater flexibility. Our scheme is also being applied to run-time type checking.

6.1. Type Correctness

The main use of types is for detecting certain kinds of errors at compile time. In functional languages such as ML [Milner 78] the saying ''well typed programs do not go wrong'' has a well understood meaning. In the logic programming framework, it is not clear what ''going wrong'' means. The direct analog is that calls never have arguments of the wrong type. This is embodied in the proposal of [Mycroft 83]. To handle the meta level primitives of Prolog, such as univ, the scheme needs some extensions, since the checking is very strict. The desirability of strict type checking in Turbo Prolog [Hankley 87] has aroused debate in the logic programming community.

In the context of our scheme, ''going wrong'' means that incorrect but well typed answers are returned. Analysis of programs which are not type correct should result in warnings or errors. No algorithm for this task is complete. The question of whether a program is type correct is undecidable (we leave the proof as an exercise for those who like proving such things). This is not to say that our scheme finds fewer errors than other schemes. They lose information by approximating sets of terms by restricted types (typically regular trees), whereas our scheme only loses information from the incomplete decision procedure.

Rather than aiming at a system which verifies that programs are type correct (which is a difficult task), we should aim at a system which attempts to find clauses which are not type correct. The system should consider all clauses `H:-B` and attempt to find a solution to goals of the form `well_typed(H), B, not well_typed(B)`. We discuss how this might be done later.

6.2. Detecting failure

In other proposed type schemes for Prolog, "going wrong" is said to mean *a clause always fails* [Bruynooghe 82, Zobel 87]. That is, for all calls, the head does not match or the body fails. Similarly, [Mishra 84] discusses predicates which always fail (and the analysis also reveals individual failing clauses). The converse of the original saying is used: ill typed programs always go wrong.

[Bruynooghe 82] gives a scheme based on polymorphic type declarations. As an example, the types for `append` are:

```
append(list(Any), list(Any), list(Any)).
```

`Any` is a type variable. [Mishra 84] shows how (non-polymorphic) types can be derived automatically. The possibility of using optional type declarations is mentioned but no details are given. [Zobel 87] derives polymorphic types automatically and also shows how type declarations can be used in the analysis. The same type declaration for `append` is given as an example. The semantics of a program with type declarations is not discussed in these papers. It is assumed that type declarations do not affect the semantics.

The three schemes (as well as [Mycroft 83]) associate a type with each argument of each predicate and each variable instance. A clause is well typed if the functors are legal and the types associated with the instances of each variable are compatible. Two types are compatible unless they are disjoint (have no terms in common). The presence of variables complicates these type schemes considerably and we will not go into details. Several kinds of errors can be detected by the three schemes.

(1) There is an illegal functor in the head of a clause (implying that any answer the clause returns will be ill typed).

(2) There is an illegal functor in the body of a clause (implying some call will always be ill typed; possibly implying it will fail).

(3) Different instances of a variable which appears in the clause head have incompatible types. This implies that all solutions returned are ill typed or some call in the body returns an ill typed answer (assuming that the variable is ground by the time the answer is returned).

(4) Different instances of a variable which appears only in the clause body have incompatible types. This implies the body always fails (this is the only case detected without type declarations) or some call in the body returns an ill typed answer (assuming that the variable is

ground by the time the answer is returned).

If the semantics we have given for type declarations is used, these errors can be summarized as follows: a clause in P always fails or P is not equivalent to S. More precisely:

If a clause is ill typed then the corresponding clause in S always fails.

Although our scheme was devised for a different reason, the semantics is apropriate for the other schemes. In fact, the errors other schemes detect using type declarations do not generally indicate a clause in the program always fails, as is the stated intention. Our first `append` example is treated as an error, even though it succeeds. The simplest explanation of these schemes seems to be that they detect (some) clauses *in S* which always fail. It is not possible to detect all failing clauses and guarantee termination (we leave the proof as an exercise, for those who enjoyed the previous one).

Given that we can define S using arbitrary type declarations, we should obviously consider this style of type checking with arbitrary type declarations. The types can express all the assumptions the program makes and also redundant information, to help detect more errors. We outline one simple implementation we are working on.

6.3. An Implementation

The input is a NU-Prolog program with (optional) type declarations. The output is a list of clauses corresponding to clauses in S which always fail. Clauses with disjunctions are expanded into several clauses, to allow more potential errors to be found. Clauses which must fail due to an explicit call to `fail` are not printed, since this obviously does not indicate an error. Other cases are generally errors or unreadable code. It is always possible to add a call to `fail` at the end of such clauses. This improves readability and has virtually no overhead.

The core of the type checker is a meta-interpreter for NU-Prolog. We have experimented with several different interpreters. The only requirement is that they must be sound with respect to finite failure. The interpreter can be unsound with respect to success, which simplifies many things. Most importantly, it means that an incomplete search may be done, so termination can be guaranteed. Rather than attempting to prove a subgoal, we can simply ignore the call as if it succeeded.

Ingoring calls is very useful for dealing with many system predicates. Input and output predicates are ignored, since it is not reasonable to call them. All calls which could fail due to the incomplete search are ignored. This includes non-logical predicates and all negative subgoals, such as `not` (if-then-else is simplified to a disjunction). Negative goals could also be handled by a call to a meta-interpreter which is sound with respect to success (this may be useful for checking type correctness). Assert, retract, clause and calls to ''dynamic'' predicates are ignored, for similar reasons. Cut is also ignored, simplifying the interpreter. Calls to predicates such as univ (=..), `is` and `name` may be insufficiently instantiated due to the incomplete search. This is handled in NU-Prolog by delaying the execution. In other systems insufficiently instantiated calls fail, so they must be ignored.

The bodies of most clauses succeed very quickly. As soon as the first solution is found, we know the clause is well typed. No more solutions are considered. The search for the first solution can generally be made quicker by considering facts before rules. Since non-logical predicates such as cut are ignored, we simply assert all facts at the start of a procedure and all rules at the end of the procedure. Clauses which fail are the most time consuming, since more of the search space is examined. This is acceptable however, since these are the clauses which have bugs. Substantial time savings can be made by deleting (or never asserting) clauses which are known to always fail.

Several incomplete search strategies have been tried. There is always a compromise between the time spent and the number of possible errors detected. The simplest strategy was a depth bound on the search tree. This can result in a combinatorial explosion even with a shallow search. A method which we have found to be better is to limit the depth of recursive calls, rather than all calls. Other strategies, including a form of bottom up evaluation, are being investigated.

All the methods we have tried use the standard Prolog computation rule (with the exception of some delaying system predicates). Although this rule is normally unfair (resulting in incompleteness with respect to finite failure), in the context of an incomplete search it is fair. Thus there does not seem to be any advantage in using a rule such as breadth first, which is complete in general but slower.

Many enhancements could be made to the system but we believe it has shown the feasibility of this generalized type scheme. It accepts NU-Prolog with no restrictions and arbitrary type declarations and is reasonably fast (reading and storing the input takes a significant fraction of the time).

6.4. Combining Type Schemes

Because of the common theoretical basis, it would be possible to combine checking for type correctness and checking for clauses in S which fail. This would detect more errors than either scheme alone. We now give some examples of errors which could be detected by the different methods.

Consider the previous `perm` program with following fact:

```
perm([], a).
```

The program is type correct and the clause in P succeeds, but the corresponding clause in S fails.

Consider `perm` again, with following fact for `delete`:

```
delete(A, A.B, C).
```

This does not cause a failure in P or S or have an illegal functor. However, the program is not type correct. The following two clause instances can be used to derive a well typed atom from ill typed atoms.

```
perm(b.a.[], b.c.[]) :- delete(b, b.c.[], a.d), perm(a.[], a.d).
perm(a.[], a.d) :- delete(a, a.d, []), perm([], []).
```

In the following `perm` program, the second clause for `perm` must fail. This can be detected by execution of the clause or the analysis of [Zobel 87] without type declarations.

```
perm([], []).
perm(A.B, C.D) :- delete(A, C.D, E), perm(B, E).

delete(A, cons(A,B), B).
delete(A, cons(B,C), cons(B,D)) :- delete(A, C, D).
```

The following program illustrates the generality of the type checker we have implemented. It detects that `p` has no solutions (assuming `append` has the correct type declaration).

```
p :- loop, q(X), X =.. [F,A1,A2,A3], append(A1, A2, A3).

q(f([1], [2], [])).
q(g([1], [2], [3])).
q(h([], a, a)).

loop :- loop.
loop.
```

7. CONCLUSIONS

The relationship between typical efficient logic programs and natural specifications is not as simple as has been suggested previously. By incorporating the idea of type information, a realistic model has been developed. The model is applicable to the class of type correct programs, which includes most reasonable programs. The semantics of type declarations in this scheme can be applied to other type schemes also, despite their different origins. This gives a characterisation of what errors are detected by the other schemes and generalizes the notion of what a type is.

We are working on further development of the theory of type correct programs containing negation and the implementation of type checkers. Others are investigating the use of our scheme to reduce overheads of run-time type checking. Further work should also be done on how this work affects the derivation (as opposed to verification) of programs from specifications.

REFERENCES

[Apt 86]

K. R. Apt, H. A. Blair, and A. Walker, Towards a theory of declarative knowledge, *Preprints of the Workshop on Foundations of Deductive Databases and Logic Programming*, Washington, D.C., August 1986, pp. 546-628.

[Bruynooghe 82]

M. Bruynooghe, Adding redundancy to obtain more reliable and more readable Prolog programs, *Proceedings of the First International Logic Programming Conference*, Faculte des Sciences de Luminy, Marseille, France, September 1982, pp. 129-133.

[Cardelli 85]

L. Cardelli, and P. Wegner, On understanding types, data abstraction, and polymorphism, *ACM Computing Surveys*, 17:471-522 (December 1985).

[Clark 77]

K. Clark, and S. Sickel, Predicate logic: a calculus for the formal derivation of programs, *Proceedings of the Fifth International Joint Conference on Artificial Intelligence*, Cambridge,

Massachusetts, August 1977, pp. 419-420.

[Clark 84]

K. Clark, The synthesis and verification of logic programs, *Proceedings of the Conference on Logic and Computation, Vol. II*, Melbourne, January 1984.

[Hankley 87]

W. Hankley, Feature analysis of Turbo Prolog, *SIGPLAN Notices*, 22:111-118 (March 1987).

[Hill 74]

R. Hill, Lush-Resolution and its completeness, DCL Memo 78, Department of Artificial Intelligence, University of Edinburgh, Edinburgh, Scotland, August 1974.

[Hogger 81]

C. J. Hogger, Derivation of logic programs, *Journal of the ACM*, 28:372-392 (April 1981).

[Kowalski 85]

R. Kowalski, The relationship between logic programming and logic specification, in: A. Hoare, and J. Shepherdson (eds.), *Mathematical logic and programming languages*, Prentice Hall, 1985.

[Lloyd 84a]

J. W. Lloyd, and R. W. Topor, Making Prolog more expressive, *Journal of Logic Programming*, 1:225-240 (1984).

[Lloyd 84b]

J. W. Lloyd, *Foundations of logic programming*, Springer-Verlag, New York, 1984.

[Maher 86]

M. J. Maher, Equivalences of logic programs, *Proceedings of the Third International Conference on Logic Programming*, Imperial College of Science and Technology, London, England, July 1986, pp. 410-424.

[Milner 78]

R. Milner, A theory of type polymorphism in programming, *Journal of Computer and System Sciences*, 17:348-375 (December 1978).

[Mishra 84]

P. Mishra, Towards a theory of types in Prolog, *Proceedings of the IEEE International Symposium on Logic Programming*, Atlantic City, New Jersey, February 1984, pp. 289-298.

[Mycroft 83]

A. Mycroft, and R. O'Keefe, A polymorphic type system for Prolog, *Proceedings of the Logic Programming Workshop*, Algarve, Portugal, 1983, pp. 107-122.

[Naish 86]

L. Naish, Negation and quantifiers in NU-Prolog, *Proceedings of the Third International Conference on Logic Programming*, Imperial College of Science and Technology, London, England, July 1986, pp. 624-634.

[Tamaki 84]

H. Tamaki, and T. Sato, Unfold/fold transformation of logic programs, *Proceedings of the*

Second International Logic Programming Conference, Uppsala University, Uppsala, Sweden, July 1984, pp. 127-138.

[Thom 86]

J. Thom, and J. Zobel (eds.), NU-Prolog reference manual, version 1.0, Technical Report 86/10, Department of Computer Science, University of Melbourne, Melbourne, Australia, 1986.

[Zobel 87]

J. Zobel, Derivation of polymorphic types for Prolog programs, *Proceedings of the Fourth International Conference on Logic Programming*, Melbourne, Australia, May 1987.

Paraconsistent Logic Programming

Howard A. Blair, V.S.Subrahmanian
Logic Programming Theory Group
School of Computer & Information Science
313 Link Hall
Syracuse University
Syracuse, NY 13244.

Abstract

This paper makes two contributions. Firstly, we give a semantics for sets of clauses of the form $L_0 \Leftarrow L_1 \& \ldots \& L_n$ where each L_i is a literal. We call such clauses generally-Horn clauses. Any such endeavour has to give a coherent, formal treatment of inconsistency (in the sense of two-valued logic). Thus, as a second contribution, we give a *robust* semantics for generally-Horn programs that allows us to "make sense" of sets of generally-Horn clauses that are inconsistent (in the two-valued logic sense). This applies to the design of very large knowledge bases where inconsistent information is often present.

1. Motivation

Over the past few years, several researchers have made attempts to allow programming with sets of non-Horn clauses [NA86,PG86]. However, there has been relative lack of success in giving model-theoretic and fixpoint semantics to such extensions. The main reason for this lack of success has been due to the fact that sets of non-Horn clauses may be inconsistent. Thus, certain programs may mean "nothing" simply because they have no models.

However, if logic programming is to be a *pragmatic* tool for the development of knowledge bases, it must have some means for dealing with inconsistent knowledge. Take for example an expert system developed by a team of logic programmers. Each programmer might have acquired information from various domain experts. It is very common for experts to disagree (often strongly and violently). Thus, the knowledge base so developed might contain inconsistent information.

Pioneering work has been done on reasoning in the presence of inconsistent information by Newton da Costa [CA74,77,81,87] and Nuel Belnap,Jr. [BE77]. Logics of this kind are normally labelled *paraconsistent logics.* Recently, in a landmark paper, Fitting [FI85] has given a declarative semantics for reasoning in the presence of inconsistent information. Under Fitting's semantics, the sentence $A \& \neg A$ would not be falsified by the interpretation that assigns the truth value $\perp$ to A (where $\perp$ is the truth value *unknown* of Kleene [LM85]).

Thus, $A\&\neg A$ has a *weak* Kleene model (see [K57,LM85]). We feel that the sentence $A\&\neg A$ should be assigned the truth value *inconsistent* (with respect to the intuition of two valued logic) rather than *unknown*. This distinction is made in great detail in [BE77].

Perlis [PE86,p.180] has argued that methods must be found for reasoning in the presence of inconsistent information. Paraconsistent [AR79] logics provide what seems to be the *only* way known thus far to declaratively characterize arbitrary sets of clauses (that may or may not be inconsistent). The first paraconsistent logic programming languages were developed in [AS87,S87a,b,BS87].

As in [S87a], we shall use the device of *annotated atoms (literals)* instead of using the negation symbol. It will be clear from Theorem 12 below that there is no loss of generality in doing so. In section 2, we shall introduce the class of generally Horn programs. We then investigate the semantics of generally Horn programs (sections 3,4). A decidable subset of the class of generally Horn programs is introduced in section 5 and it is shown that this class possesses some interesting model theoretic properties. The operational semantics of generally Horn programs is discussed in Sections 6 and 7.

2. Generally-Horn Logic Programs: Syntax

We assume the reader is familiar with the usual syntactic notions of terms, atoms and literals. Any undefined expressions used in this paper may be found in Lloyd [LL84].
The set $\mathcal{T} = \{\bot, \mathbf{t}, \mathbf{f}, \top\}$ is the set of ***truth values*** of our four-valued logic. The truth values $\bot, \mathbf{t}, \mathbf{f}, \top$ correspond respectively to the truth values $*, T, F, TF$ of Visser [VI84] and **None, T, F, Both** of Belnap [BE77] and stand respectively for "undefined", true (in the intuitive sense of two valued logic), false (also in the two valued sense), and "over-defined " (which may also be thought of as inconsistent in the intuition of two-valued logic). We define an ordering $\preceq$ on $\mathcal{T}$ as follows:

DEF 1:

$$(\forall x \in \mathcal{T}) x \preceq x$$

$$(\forall x \in \mathcal{T}) \bot \preceq x$$

$$(\forall x \in \mathcal{T}) x \preceq \top$$

The ordering $\preceq$ is represented by the Hasse diagram given below. We use the notation $x \succeq y$ iff $y \preceq x$ where $x, y \in \mathcal{T}$. Also, as usual, $\prec, \succ$ are the irreflexive restrictions of $\preceq$ and $\succeq$ respectively. The set $\mathcal{T}$ is a complete lattice under this ordering.

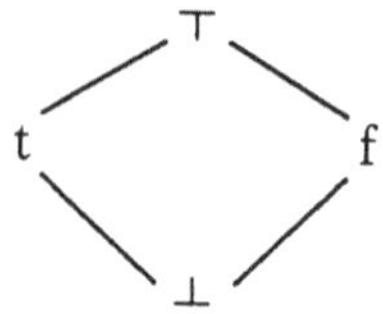

DEF 2: If A is a literal, then $A : \mu$ is called an *annotated literal*, where $\mu \in \mathcal{T}$. μ is called the *annotation* of A. If μ is one of $\mathbf{t}, \mathbf{f}$, then $A : \mu$ is called a *well-annotated* literal, and μ is called a *w-annotation*.

Intuitively, the annotated atom $A : \mathbf{t}$ may be thought of as the *modality* "A is *known* to be true ". Similarly, the annotated atom $A : \mathbf{f}$ may be regarded as saying "A is *known* to be false ". This is only meant as an aid to intuition, and we are not committing ourselves to any epistemic consequences of this point of view.

DEF 3: (1) Any annotated atom is a *formula*.

(2) If $A : \mu$ is an annotated atom, then $\neg A : \mu$ is a formula.

(3) If F_1, F_2 are formulas, then $F_1 \& F_2, F_1 \vee F_2, F_1 \Leftarrow F_2, F_1 \Leftrightarrow F_2$ are formulas.

(4) If F is a formula and x any variable symbol, then $(\forall x)F$ and $(\exists x)F$ are formulas.

DEF 4: If $A_0, \ldots, A_n$ are literals, and if $\mu_0, \ldots, \mu_n$ are w-annotations, then

$$A_0 : \mu_0 \Leftarrow A_1 : \mu_1 \& \ldots \& A_n : \mu_n$$

is called a *generalized Horn clause* (or gh-clause for short). $A_0 : \mu_0$ is called the *head* of the above gh-clause, while $A_1 : \mu_1 \& \ldots \& A_n : \mu_n$ is called the *body* of the above gh-clause. The notion of a substitution is similar to that in [LL84]. Applying a substitution θ to an annotated literal $A : \mu$ results in the annotated literal $A\theta : \mu$. The notion of applying a substitution is extended in the obvious way to a conjunction of annotated literals, and to gh-clauses. If $A : \mu$ and $B : \rho$ are annotated literals, then $A : \mu$ and $B : \rho$ are said to be unifiable (with mgu θ) iff A and B are unifiable (with mgu θ). Note that μ need not equal ρ as we are not defining the result of the unification yet.

DEF 5: A *generalized Horn program* (GHP) is a finite set of gh-clauses.

3. Generally-Horn Logic Programs: Semantics

In this paper, we will consider only "Herbrand-like" interpretations [LL84],i.e.the universe of individuals in the interpretation consists only of the ground terms of the language being interpreted. Unless explicitly specified otherwise, throughout the rest of this paper, the set of individuals in models and interpretations will be an Herbrand universe. We will consider an interpretation I as a function $I : B_L \rightarrow \mathcal{T}$ where B_L is the Herbrand base under consideration.

DEF 6: The *negation* of an annotation is defined as: $\neg(\mathbf{t}) = \mathbf{f}, \neg(\mathbf{f}) = \mathbf{t}, \neg(\bot) = \bot, \neg(\top) = \top$.†

DEF 7: A formula is said to be *closed* if it contains no occurrence of a free variable.

In this paper, we give a non-classical interpretation to the $\Leftarrow$ symbol,i.e. we do not treat it as classical material implication. In particular, the equivalence of $A \vee \neg B$ and $A \Leftarrow B$ does not hold. This is quite necessary because, in general, $A : \mathbf{t} \vee A : \mathbf{f}$ may not be a tautology. This formula asserts (in an *intuitionistic* fashion) the sentence

It is *known* that A is true OR it is *known* that A is false.

DEF 8: [*Satisfaction*] We write $I \models F$ to say that I satisfies F. An interpretation I

(1) satisfies the formula F iff I satisfies each of its closed instances, i.e. for each variable symbol x occurring free in F, and each variable free term t, $F(t/x)$ is satisfied by I. (Here $F(t/x)$ denotes the replacement of all occurrences of x in F by t).

(2) satisfies the variable-free annotated atom $A : \mu$ iff $I(A) \succeq \mu$.

(3) satisfies the variable-free annotated literal $\neg A : \mu$ iff it satisfies $A : \neg\mu$.

(4) satisfies the closed formula $(\exists x)F$ iff for some variable free term t, $I \models F(t/x)$.

(5) satisfies the closed formula $(\forall x)F$ iff for every variable free term t, $I \models F(t/x)$.

(6) satisfies $F_1 \Leftarrow F_2$ iff I does not satisfy F_2 or $I \models F_1$.

(7) satisfies the closed formula $F_1 \& \ldots \& F_n)$ iff $I \models F_i$ for all $i = 1, \ldots, n$.

(8) satisfies the closed formula $F_1 \vee \ldots \vee F_n$ iff $I \models F_i$ for some $1 \leq i \leq n$.

(9) satisfies $F \Leftrightarrow G$ iff $I \models F \Leftarrow G$ and $I \models G \Leftarrow F$.

DEF 9: An interpretation I satisfies a generalized Horn program G if it satisfies every gh-clause $C \in G$.

The $\preceq$ ordering on truth values is extended in the obvious way to interpretations. Given a GHP G, and Herbrand interpretations I_1, I_2, we say

$$I_1 \preceq I_2 \; iff \; (\forall A \in B_G) I_1(A) \preceq I_2(A)$$

where B_G is the Herbrand base of G.

† Our logic differs from that of Belnap [BE77] and Visser [VI86] with respect to our definition of negation. Their definition makes $\neg$(**Both**) = **None** and $\neg$(**None**) = **Both**. Our definition seems to be more appropriate with regard to the *known that* intuition given to the annotated atoms.

DEF 10: If C is a gh-clause in G, then the result of replacing all negated literals $\neg A : \mu$ in C by $A : \neg\mu$ is called the *positive counterpart* C^{pos} of C. The GHP G^{pos} obtained by replacing each gh-clause in the GHP G is called the *positive counterpart* of G.

Lemma 11: $I \models (\exists)\neg A : \mu$ iff $I \models (\exists)A : \neg\mu$.

Proof: $I \models (\exists)\neg A : \mu$

iff $I \models \neg A(\vec{t}/\vec{x}) : \mu$

iff $I \models A(\vec{t}/\vec{x}) : \neg\mu$

iff $I \models (\exists)A : \neg\mu$.

(where $\vec{t}$ is a tuple of variable free terms and $\vec{x}$ is a tuple of all the variable symbols occurring in A).

Theorem 12: I is a model of G iff I is a model of G^{pos}.

Proof: Immediate from Lemma 11. ∎

The above theorem assures us that the device of annotations is powerful enough to make the use of negated atoms unnecessary. Therefore, in future, we will always assume that GHPs do not contain any negated literals (with negations being *implicitly* present in the form of atoms annotated with **f**).

Example 13. Consider the GHP given below:

$$p(a) : \mathbf{t} \Leftarrow$$

$$p(a) : \mathbf{f} \Leftarrow$$

This GHP has exactly one model, viz. the interpretation that assigns the truth value $\top$ to $p(a)$. This is in keeping with our intuition which says that this program contains contradictory information (in the two valued sense).

Example 14. Consider the GHP G_1 given below. We intend that this GHP represent the sentence: *It is known that* $p(a) \vee p(b)$.

$$p(a) : \mathbf{t} \Leftarrow p(b) : \mathbf{f}$$

$$p(b) : \mathbf{t} \Leftarrow p(a) : \mathbf{f}$$

This GHP has several models. They are listed below:

$I_1 : I_1(p(a)) = \mathbf{t}; I_1(p(b)) = \mathbf{t}$
$I_2 : I_2(p(a)) = \mathbf{t}; I_2(p(b)) = \mathbf{f}$
$I_3 : I_3(p(a)) = \mathbf{f}; I_3(p(b)) = \mathbf{t}$
$I_4 : I_4(p(a)) = \bot; I_4(p(b)) = \bot$
$I_5 : I_5(p(a)) = \bot; I_5(p(b)) = \mathbf{t}$
$I_6 : I_6(p(a)) = \mathbf{t}; I_6(p(b)) = \bot$
$I_7 : I_7(p(a)) = \top; I_7(p(a)) = \top$

$I_8 : I_8(p(a)) = \mathbf{t}; I_8(p(b)) = \top$
$I_9 : I_9(p(a)) = \top; I_9(p(b)) = \mathbf{t}$

The proliferation of models may appear somewhat bewildering, but it is important to observe that the GHP G_1 has a least model (viz. I_4) and a greatest model (viz. I_7). The least model says that from G, it is not *known* that $p(a)$ is true and it is not *known* that $p(b)$ is true. Similarly, the model, I_3 says that if it is *known* that $p(a)$ is false then it is *known* that $p(b)$ is true. This is in keeping with our intuition that this GHP really represents the clause $p(a) \vee p(b)$. This provides a strong argument in favour of our notion of GHPs.

Having defined the models of GHP, we now proceed to define a certain monotone operator from interpretations to interpretations. We then relate the prefixpoints† of this operator with the models of Generalized Horn Programs.

4. (Pre) Fixpoint Semantics

It has now become a standard practice in logic programming research to try and characterize the models of a program in terms of the (possibly pre or post)†fixpoints of a certain monotone operator usually referred to as T_P.

DEF 15: Suppose G is a GHP. Then T_G is a mapping from the Herbrand intepretations of G to the Herbrand interpretations of G defined by: $T_G(I)(A) = lub\{\mu | A : \mu \Leftarrow B_1 : \mu_1 \& \ldots \& B_k : \mu_k$ is a ground instance of a gh-clause in G and $I \models B_1 : \mu_1 \& \ldots B_k : \mu_k\}$.

Example 16. Consider the GHP G_4 given below:

$$p(a) : \mathbf{t} \Leftarrow$$

$$p(a) : \mathbf{f} \Leftarrow p(a) : \mathbf{t}$$

and the interpretation I that assigns t to $p(a)$. Then $T_G(I)(p(a)) = \text{lub}\{\mathbf{t}, \mathbf{f}\} = \top$.

Theorem 17: T_G is monotonic.

Proof: Suppose $I_1 \preceq I_2$ where I_1, I_2 are interpretations. Suppose A is an arbitrary ground atom and that $T_G(I_1)(A) = \mu_1$.

Case 1: $[\mu_1 = \top]$ In this case, there are two gh-clauses $C_1, C_2 \in G$ that have ground instances of the form

$$A : \mathbf{t} \Leftarrow B_1 : \rho_1 \& \ldots \& B_k : \rho_k$$

$$A : \mathbf{f} \Leftarrow D_1 : \delta_1 \& \ldots \& D_m : \delta_m$$

† x is a pre (post) fixpoint of a function $f : L \rightarrow L$ where L is a lattice under the $\sqsubseteq$ ordering iff $f(x) \sqsubseteq x$ $(x \sqsubseteq f(x))$.

where $I_1 \models B_1 : \rho_1 \& \ldots \& B_k : \rho_k$ and $I_1 \models D_1 : \delta_1 \& \ldots \& D_m : \rho_m$. As $I_1 \preceq I_2$, it follows that for all annotated literals $E : \psi$, $I_1 \models E : \psi$ implies $I_2 \models E : \psi$. therefore, it follows that

$$I_2 \models B_1 : \rho_1 \& \ldots \& B_k : \rho_k$$

and

$$I_2 \models D_1 : \delta_1 \& \ldots \& D_m : \delta_m$$

whence, by definition, $T_G(I_2)(A) \succeq lub\{\mathbf{t}, \mathbf{f}\} = \top$. Thus, $T_G(I_1)(A) \preceq T_G(I_2)(A)$.
Case 2: $[\mu_1 = \bot]$ In this case, $T_G(I_2)(A) \succeq \bot$ is trivially true.
Case 3: $[\mu_1 = \mathbf{t}$ or $\mathbf{f}]$ In this case, there is a ground instance of some gh-clause $C \in G$ of the form

$$A : \mu_1 \Leftarrow B_1 : \beta_1 \& \ldots \& B_k : \beta_k$$

such that $I_1 \models B_1 : \beta_1 \& \ldots \& B_k : \beta_k$. As $I_1 \preceq I_2$, it follows that $I_2 \models B_1 : \beta_1 \& \ldots \& B_k : \beta_k$, whence $T_G(I_2)(A) \succeq \mu_1 = T_G(I_1)(A)$. ∎

Before proceeding to investigate the fixpoints of T_G, we show that the prefixpoints of T_G are exactly the models of G.

Theorem 18: I is a model of the GHP G iff $T_G(I) \preceq I$.

Proof: Suppose A is an arbitrary ground literal in B_G.
$(\rightarrow)$ Suppose I is a model of G and suppose $T_G(I)(A) = \mu$.
Case 1: $[\mu = \bot]$ Then $T_G(I)(A) = \bot \preceq I(A)$ holds trivially.
Case 2: $[\mu = \top]$ Then there are two ground instances of gh-clauses $C_1, C_2 \in G$ of the following form:

$$A : \mathbf{t} \Leftarrow B_1 : \beta_1 \& \ldots \& B_n : \beta_n$$

$$A : \mathbf{f} \Leftarrow D_1 : \rho_1 \& \ldots \& B_m : \rho_m$$

such that I satisfies the bodies of both the above gh-clauses. But then, as I is a model of G, it must satisfy both the above ground instances of C_1, C_2 and so it must be true that $I(A) \succeq lub\{\mathbf{t}, \mathbf{f}\} = \top$. Thus, in this case, $I(A) = \top = T_G(I)(A)$ and it follows that $T_G(I)(A) \preceq I(A)$.
Case 3 $[\mu = \mathbf{t}$ or $\mathbf{f}]$. In this case, there is a gh-clause $C_1 \in G$ having a ground instance of the following form:

$$A : \mu \Leftarrow B_1 : \beta_1 \& \ldots \& B_n : \beta_n$$

such that $I \models B_1 : \beta_1 \& \ldots \& B_n : \beta_n$. But then, as I is a model of G, it must satisfy the above ground instance of C_1, and so it must be true that $I(A) \succeq \mu$. Thus, $T_G(I)(A) = \mu \preceq I(A)$.
$(\leftarrow)$ Suppose $T_G(I)(A) \preceq I(A)$ for all $A \in B_G$. We will show then that I is a model of G. Suppose C is a ground instance of a gh-clause in G of the following form:

$$A : \mu \Leftarrow B_1 : \psi_1 \& \ldots \& B_k : \psi_k$$

It suffices to show that if $I \models B_1 : \psi_1 \& \ldots \& B_k : \psi_k$ then $I(A) \succeq \mu$. Suppose $I \models B_1 : \psi_1 \& \ldots \& B_k : \psi_k$. Then, by definition of T_G, we have that $T_G(I)(A) \succeq \mu$. But as $T_G(I)(A) \preceq I(A)$ (as I is a prefixpoint of T_G), it follows that $I(A) \succeq \mu$, which completes the proof. ∎

Theorem 18 assures us that the models of G are exactly the prefixpoints of T_G. The monotonicity of T_G assures us that T_G has a fixpoint, and hence a prefixpoint, and hence a model. In addition, as T_G is monotone, the least fixpoint and the least prefixpoint of T_G must coincide, thus giving us the proof of the following result.

Theorem 19: Any GHP G has a least model $\mathcal{M}_G$. In addition, this least model is identical to the least fixpoint $lfp(T_G)$ of T_G.

Unfortunately, monotonicity by itself does not guarantee us that the least fixpoint of T_G is semi-computable. We show, nevertheless, that this is indeed the case.

DEF 20: We define the special interpretation Δ to be the interpretation that assigns the value $\perp$ to all members of B_G. Similarly, the interpretation ∇ assigns the value $\top$ to all members of B_G.

DEF 21: The *upward iteration* of T_G is defined as follows:

$$T_G \uparrow 0 = \Delta$$

$$T_G \uparrow \alpha = T_G(T_G \uparrow (\alpha - 1))$$

$$T_G \uparrow \lambda = \sqcup\{T_G \uparrow \eta | \eta < \lambda\}$$

where α is a successor ordinal and λ is a limit ordinal.

The *downward iteration* of T_G is defined as:

$$T_G \downarrow 0 = \nabla$$

$$T_G \downarrow (\alpha) = T_G(T_G \downarrow (\alpha - 1))$$

$$T_G \downarrow \lambda = \sqcap\{T_G \downarrow \eta | \eta < \lambda\}$$

where α is a successor ordinal and λ a limit ordinal.

Remark: We observe that $T_G \uparrow 0 \preceq T_G \uparrow 1 \preceq \ldots \preceq T_G \uparrow \omega$ and that $T_G \downarrow 0 \succeq T_G \downarrow 1 \succeq \ldots \succeq T_G \downarrow \omega$.

Theorem 22: $T_G \uparrow \omega = \mathcal{M}_G$.

Proof: $[\mathcal{M}_G \preceq T_G \uparrow \omega]$ In order to prove this, it is sufficient to show that $T_G \uparrow \omega$ is a model of G. Suppose

$$A : \mu \Leftarrow B_1 : \psi_1 \& \ldots \& B_k : \psi_k$$

is a ground instance $C\theta$ of some gh-clause $C \in G$, and suppose

$$T_G \uparrow \omega \models B_1 : \psi_1 \& \ldots \& B_k : \psi_k$$

Then, it must be true that for some finite n,

$$T_G \uparrow n \models B_1 : \psi_1 \& \ldots \& B_k : \psi_k$$

But then, $T_G \uparrow (n+1) = T_G(T_G \uparrow n) \models A : \mu$ (by definition of T_G), whence it follows that $T_G \uparrow \omega \models A : \mu$ (by the remark preceding Theorem 22). Thus, $T_G \uparrow \omega$ is a model of G, and as $\mathcal{M}_G$ is the least such model, it follows that $\mathcal{M}_G \preceq T_G \uparrow \omega$.
$[T_G \uparrow \omega \preceq \mathcal{M}_G]$ Suppose $T_G \uparrow \omega(A) = \mu$ for some arbitrary A. Then for some finite n, $T_G \uparrow n(A) = \mu$. We will show by induction that for all n, $\mathcal{M}_G \succeq T_G \uparrow n$.
Base Case $[n = 0]$: In this case, $T_G(A) = \bot = \mu$, whence it is trivially true that $\mathcal{M}_G(A) \succeq \bot = \mu = T_G \uparrow 0(A)$.
Inductive Case $[n = r + 1]$: By the inductive hypothesis, $T_G \uparrow n \preceq \mathcal{M}_G$. Therefore, by monotonicity of T_G, it follows that $T_G \uparrow (n+1) \preceq T_G(\mathcal{M}_G)$. But $\mathcal{M}_G$ is a model of G and hence a prefixpoint of T_G (by Theorem 18), and therefore,

$$T_G \uparrow (n+1) \preceq T_G(\mathcal{M}_G \preceq \mathcal{M}_G$$

As $T_G \uparrow n \preceq \mathcal{M}_G$ for all $n < \omega$, it follows that $T_G \uparrow \omega \preceq \mathcal{M}_G$. ∎
Theorem 22 above assures us that the least fixpoint of T_G, and hence the minimal model of G is indeed semi-computable (since each $T_G \uparrow n (n \in \omega)$ is clearly semi-computable; indeed decidable). This assures us that if $lfp(T_G) \models A : \mu (A \in B_G)$, then it is indeed possible to show that $lfp(T_G) \models A : \mu$. The proof procedure will be discussed later in Sections 6 and 7.

5. Well-Behaved GHPs

Theorem 22 is likely to immediately raise the question: "Is $T_G \downarrow \omega$ identical to the greatest model ?" Unfortunately, as in the case of logic programs (cf.[LL84],p.31]), the answer to this question is negative. However, the reason for this is that $T_G \downarrow 0$ is the greatest model of *any* GHP whatsoever. Thus, we are led to ask:
Question What kind of models would we like GHPs to have, and in addition, what kind of GHPs should be qualified as being acceptable or decent ?

One answer is immediately forthcoming. We should like an *acceptable* GHP to be one that expresses consistent knowledge. Before proceeding to finish our answer to the above question, it is necessary to introduce a new definition.
DEF 23: An interpretation I of a GHP G is said to be *nice* if the following condition holds:

$$(\forall A \in B_G)\ I(A) \neq \top$$

We are therefore interested in those models of G that are nice. Now it should be apparent that in view of the fact that $\top$ is a formalization of the notion of *both true and false* which is exactly the notion of inconsistency, we should like to characterize the *acceptable* GHPs to be exactly those GHPs that possess a nice model. Thus, we have answered the preceding question in full now:

(1) The models of a GHP that interest us are the nice models.

(2) The GHPs that we shall be interested in are the acceptable ones.

It is appropriate, therefore, to identify a class $\mathcal{C}$ of GHPs that are guaranteed to possess nice models. In addition, it is desirable that $\mathcal{C}$ be decidable.

Theorem 24: In general, the set NICE(G) $= \{G|G$ is a GHP having at least one nice model$\}$ is undecidable.

Proof: The satisfiability problem for first order three valued logic directly reduces to the membership problem for NICE(G). (Any clause F of three valued logic can be converted to a formula F' in our system by replacing any positive atom A in F by $A : \mathbf{t}$, by replacing negated atoms $\neg A$ by $A : \mathbf{f}$. This entails that $NICE(G)$ is Π^0_1–hard). ∎

This is not a problem to worry about too much. We observe that deciding whether a normal logic program is canonical [JS86] (determinate) is Π^0_3-complete, (resp. Π^2_0-complete) [BL86]. Thus, we are forced to try and define recursive subsets of NICE(G). We now define such a class, viz. the *well-behaved* GHPs.

DEF 25: A GHP G is *well-behaved* iff the gh-clauses of G satisfy the following condition:

> If G_1, G_2 are gh-clauses in G such that their (respective) heads are $A_1 : \mu_1, A_2 : \mu_2$ and if A_1, A_2 are unifiable, then $\mu_1 = \mu_2$.

It remains to prove our claim that every well-behaved GHP has a nice model. We go one step further and show that for well-behaved GHPs, $T_G \uparrow \omega$ is nice. We already know that $T_G \uparrow \omega$ is a model of G; so this is sufficient to substantiate our claim.

Theorem 26: If G is a well-behaved GHP, then $T_G \uparrow \omega$ is nice.

Proof: Suppose G is well-behaved and $T_G \uparrow \omega$ is not nice. Then there is some $A \in B_G$ such that $T_G \uparrow \omega(A) = \top$. But then, there exists some finite n such that $T_Q \uparrow n(A) = \top (n > 0)$. But then there must exist two gh-clauses C_1, C_2 in Q of the form

$$A_1 : \mathbf{t} \Leftarrow B_1 : \psi_1 \& \ldots \& B_m : \psi_m$$

$$A_2 : \mathbf{f} \Leftarrow D_1 : \rho_1 \& \ldots \& D_k : \rho_k$$

such that A is an instance of A_1, A_2 and $T_G \uparrow (n-1) \models B_1 : \psi_1 \& \ldots \& B_m : \psi_m$ and $T_G \uparrow (n-1) \models D_1 : \rho_1 \& \ldots \& D_k : \rho_k$. As A is a common instance of A_1, A_2, it is true that A_1, A_2 are unifiable, thus contradicting the assumption that G is well-behaved. Therefore, $T_G \uparrow \omega$ must be nice. ∎

It is natural at this stage is to investigate the properties of $T_G \downarrow \omega$. For well-behaved GHPs, is $T_G \downarrow \omega$ nice ?

Theorem 27: If G is a well-behaved GHP, then $T_G \downarrow 1$ is nice; hence, $T_G \downarrow \omega$ is nice.
Proof: Suppose G is well-behaved and $T_G \downarrow 1$ is not nice. Then there is some $A \in B_G$ such that $T_G \downarrow 1(A) = \top$. Then there must be at least two gh-clauses C_1, C_2 in G having ground instances of the following form:

$$A : \mathbf{t} \Leftarrow D_1 : \rho_1 \& \ldots \& B_k : \rho_k$$

$$A : \mathbf{f} \Leftarrow E_1 : \psi_1 \& \ldots \& E_r : \psi_r$$

such that $T_G \downarrow 0$ satisfies the bodies of both the above instances of C_1 and C_2. But then the heads of C_1, C_2 are unifiable, but the annotations of the heads are distinct, thus contradicting the well-behavedness of G. Therefore, $T_G \downarrow 1$ is nice. By the remark preceding Theorem 22, it follows that $T_G \downarrow \omega$ is nice. ∎
In addition, for any GHP, $T_G \downarrow \omega$ is a model of G.
Theorem 28: If G is a GHP, then $T_G \downarrow \alpha$ is a model of G for every ordinal α.
Proof: By the remark preceding Theorem 22, all the $T_G \downarrow \alpha$'s are prefixpoints of T_G. Hence, by Theorem 18, all the $T_G \downarrow \alpha$'s are models of G. ∎
Corollary 29: If G is a well-behaved GHP, then $T_G \downarrow \omega$ is a nice model of G.
In order to give an idea of what the models $T_G \uparrow \omega$ and $T_G \downarrow \omega$ look like, we give an example.
Example 30. Consider the well-behaved GHP G_6 given below:

$$p(a) : \mathbf{t} \Leftarrow q(X) : \mathbf{t}$$

$$q(s(X)) : \mathbf{t} \Leftarrow q(X) : \mathbf{t}$$

In this case, $T_{G_6} \uparrow \omega = \Delta$, while

$$T_{G_6} \downarrow \omega(p(a)) = \mathbf{t}$$

For every ground atom $A \in B_{G_6}, A \neq p(a)$, $T_{G_6} \downarrow \omega(A) = \bot$.

The above example illustrates the fact that while $T_G \uparrow \omega$ is a fixpoint of T_G, $T_G \downarrow \omega$ may not be a fixpoint of T_G (of course, it is constrained to be a prefixpoint). But then, what *kind* of model of G is $T_G \downarrow \omega$? This is a perplexing question. In order to investigate this question, we borrow the notion of a supported model from [ABW86].
DEF 31: A model I of a GHP G is said to be *supported* if for every ground atom $A \in B_G$ such that $I(A) = \mu \neq \bot$, there is a gh-clause in G having a ground instance of the form:

$$A : \mu \Leftarrow B_1 : \psi_1 \& \ldots \& B_m : \psi_m$$

such that $I \models B_1 : \psi_1 \& \ldots \& B_m : \psi_m$. (Note that all literals occurring in a GHP are well annotated. Hence, $\mu \neq \top$. Thus, every supported model must be nice.)

We now investigate the relationship between the fixpoints of T_G and the supported models of G.

Lemma 31: If I is a supported model of the GHP G, then I is a fixpoint of T_G.

Proof: Suppose I is a supported model of G and $I(A) = \mu \neq \top$. Let $\Gamma =$

$$\{A : \rho^1 \Leftarrow B_1^1 : \psi_1^1 \& \ldots \& B_{k1}^1 : \psi_{k1}^1,$$
$$\cdots\cdots$$
$$A : \rho^m \Leftarrow B_1^m : \psi_1^m \& \ldots \& B_{km}^m : \psi_{km}^m, \ldots\}$$

be the set of all ground instances of gh-clauses with a head of the form $A : \rho$ in G such that I satisfies the body of each gh-clause in Γ. As I is supported, $m \geq 1$. As I is a supported model of G, $I(A) = \sqcup\{\rho^i | 1 \leq i \leq m\} \neq \top$. But by definition of T_G and the fact that I is supported, we must have $T_G(I)(A) = \sqcup\{\rho^i | 1 \leq i \leq m\} = I(A)$. ∎

Lemma 32: If I is a nice fixpoint of G, then I is a supported model of G.

Proof: Without loss of generality, assume $I(A) \neq \bot$. As I is nice, $I(A)$ must be in $\{\mathbf{t}, \mathbf{f}\}$.
Case 1: $[I(A) = \mathbf{t}]$ Therefore, since I is a fixed point of T_G, $T_G(I)(A) = \mathbf{t}$. That is, $\sqcup\{\mu | A : \mu \Leftarrow B_1 : \psi_1 \& \ldots \& B_k : \psi_k$ is a ground instance of a gh-clause in G and $I \models B_1 : \psi_1 \& \ldots \& B_k : \psi_k\} = \mathbf{t}$. But for the lub above to be $\mathbf{t}$, there must be a gh-clause in G having a ground instance of the $A : \mathbf{t} \Leftarrow B_1 : \psi_1 \& \ldots \& B_k : \psi_k$ and such that $I \models B_1 : \psi_1 \& \ldots \& B_k : \psi_k$, i.e. I is supported.
Case 2: $[I(A) = \mathbf{f}]$ Similar to case 1. ∎

Theorem 33: I is a supported model of the GHP G iff I is a nice fixpoint of G.

Proof: Follows immediately from Lemmas 31, 32 and the fact that every supported model is nice. ∎

Jaffar et.al. [JLM86] have introduced a *decency* thesis in conventional logic programming. Essentially, the decency thesis claims that all decent logic programs are canonical [JS86], i.e. $T_P \downarrow \omega = gfp(T_P)$ where T_P is defined as in Lloyd [LL84]. The term *decent* as used by Jaffar et al is intended to refer to programs that arise"naturally "in good programming practice. Under this criterion, the logic program obtained by deleting the annotations in Example 30 is *not* decent. We now give the definition of a canonical GHP.

<u>DEF 34</u>: A GHP G is *canonical* iff $T_G \downarrow \omega$ is the greatest fixpoint of T_G.

It follows immediately from Lemma 32 that if G is a well behaved program, then $T_G \downarrow \omega$ is a supported model of G. We are now in a position to state an interesting result.

Theorem 35: $T_G \downarrow \omega$ is the greatest (nice) supported model of G if G is a canonical well-behaved GHP.

Proof: Since G is canonical, $T_G \downarrow \omega$ is the greatest fixpoint of T_G. Since G is well-behaved, $T_G \downarrow \omega$ is nice. Thus, $T_G \downarrow \omega$ is the greatest supported model of G. ∎

With this, we conclude our declarative characterization of GHPs. The fact that $T_G \downarrow \omega$ is a supported nice model of G (G a canonical well-behaved GHP) is useful in characterizing the use of GHPs in reasoning about beliefs [BS87]. A more comprehensive discussion of decent GHPs is included in [BS87]. In addition, we have proved that the least model of a GHP is semi-computable (Theorem 22), and that when G is well-behaved, the least model of G coincides with the least nice model of G (Theorem 26). We now investigate the operational semantics of GHPs which is similar to the approach of Van Emden [VE86] for quantitative deduction.

6. Operational Semantics for GHPs

Van Emden [VE86] has given an operational semantics for and/or tree searching in the context of his quantitative rule sets. We give a similar operational semantics for GHPs. Suppose G is a GHP, $A \in B_G$ and μ an annotation. We define an and/or tree $\mathbf{T}(G, A : \mu)$ as follows:

(1) The root of $\mathbf{T}(G, A : \mu)$ is an or-node labelled $A : \mu$.
(2) If N is an or-node, then it is labelled by a single annotated literal.
(3) Each and-node is labelled by a gh-clause from G and a substitution.
(4) Descendants of an or-node are and-nodes and vice-versa.
(5) If N is an or-node labelled by $B : \alpha$ $(\alpha \neq \perp)$, and if $C\theta$ is an instance of a gh-clause C in G of the following form:

$$B : \beta \Leftarrow D_1 : \psi_1 \& \ldots \& B_k : \psi_k$$

where $\beta \succeq \alpha$, then there is a descendant of N labelled by C and θ. An or-node with no descendants is called an *uninformative node.*
(6) If N is an and-node labelled by the q-clause C and the substitution θ, then for every annotated literal $B : \gamma$ in the body of C, there is a descendant or-node labelled $B\theta : \gamma$. An and-node with no descendants is called a *success node.*

Associated with every node N in the and/or tree $\mathbf{T}(G, A, \mu)$ is a truth value $\nu(N)$ called the value of that node.

DEF 36: ν is defined as follows:

If N is a success node labelled $B : \psi$, then $\nu(N) = \psi$.

If N is an uninformative node, then $\nu(N) = \perp$.

If N is an or-node that is not uninformative and its descendants are $N_1, \ldots, N_k$, then $\nu(N) = lub\{\nu(N_1), \ldots, \nu(N_k)\}$.

If N is a non-terminal and-node labelled with the gh-clause $A : \rho \Leftarrow B_1 : \psi_1 \& \ldots \& B_k : \psi_k$, and if the value $\nu(N_i)$ of each of its descendant nodes N_i labelled B_i is such that $\nu(N_i) \succeq \psi_i$ for all $1 \leq i \leq k$, then $\nu(N) = \rho$, else $\nu(N) = \perp$.

Before proceeding to investigate the soundness and completeness of the and/or tree search procedure just described, we give an example.

Example 37. Consider the GHP G_7 given below:

$$p(a) : \mathbf{t} \Leftarrow$$
$$p(X) : \mathbf{t} \Leftarrow q(X) : \mathbf{f} \ \& \ r(X) : \mathbf{t}$$
$$r(a) : \mathbf{t} \Leftarrow$$
$$r(b) : \mathbf{t} \Leftarrow$$
$$q(a) : \mathbf{f} \Leftarrow$$
$$q(b) : \mathbf{f} \Leftarrow$$

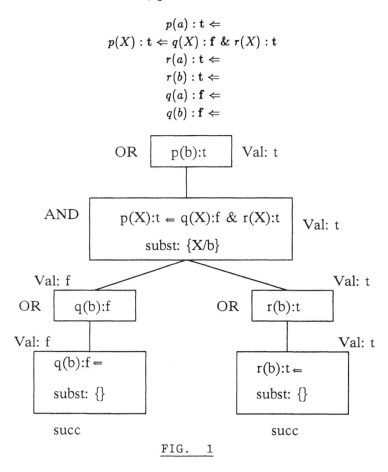

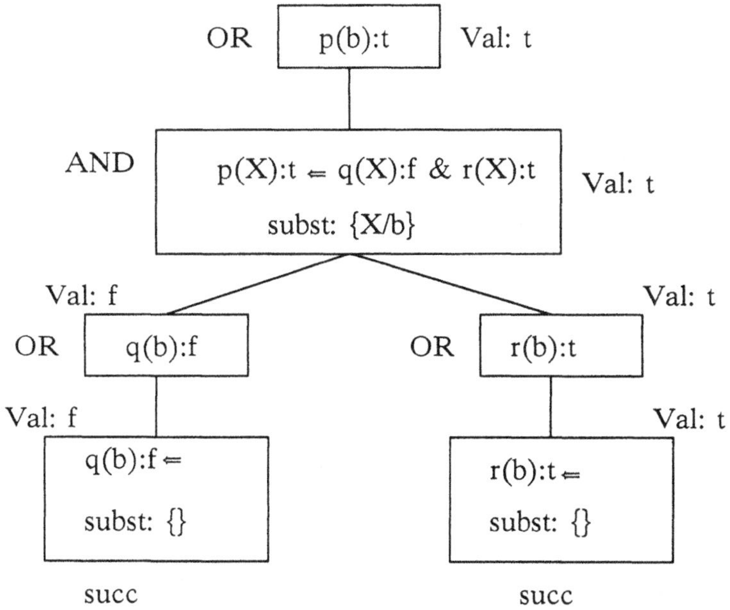

FIG. 1

Consider the problem of checking whether $p(b) : \mathbf{t}$ is satisfied by $T_{G_7} \uparrow \omega$. The and/or tree associated with this problem is shown in Fig.1. We see that the truth value of $p(b)$ in $T_{G_7} \uparrow \omega$ is $\mathbf{t}$.

DEF 38: A GHP G is said to be *covered* if every variable symbol that occurs in the body of a gh-clause $C \in G$ occurs in the head of C.

Theorem 39: If G is a covered GHP, $A \in B_G$ and if $\mathcal{T}(G, A : \mu)$ is finite with root R, then $\nu(R) \preceq T_G \uparrow \omega(A)$.

Proof: Similar to the proof of theorem 3.1′ of Van Emden [VE86]. Observe that the proof in [VE86] applies only to covered rule sets. ∎

Theorem 40:[Completeness] If G is a covered GHP, $A \in B_G$, and if $\mathcal{T}(G, A : \mu)$ is finite with root R, then $\nu(R) \succeq T_G \uparrow \omega(A)$.

Proof: Let R be the root of $\mathcal{T}(G, A : \mu)$. We will first prove by induction that

$$(\forall n \in \mathbf{N})\nu(R) \succeq T_Q \uparrow n(A)$$

(where **N** denotes the set of non-negative integers).

Base Case[n=0] Trivially true as $T_G \uparrow 0(A) = \bot$.

Inductive Case Suppose $T_G \uparrow (n+1)(A) = \alpha$.

Case 1:$[\alpha = \top]$ Then there are two ground instances $C_1\theta_1, C_2\theta_2$ of gh-clauses $C_1, C_2 \in G$ of the form

$$A : \mathbf{t} \Leftarrow B_1 : \psi_1 \& \ldots \& B_r : \psi_r$$

$$A : \mathbf{f} \Leftarrow D_1 : \rho_1 \& \ldots \& D_s : \rho_s$$

and $T_G \uparrow n$ satisfies the bodies of $C_1\theta_1$ and $C_2\theta_2$ respectively. As G is covered, and as $A \in B_G$, each B_i, D_j is ground, and therefore, by the induction hypothesis, $\nu(B_i') \succeq \psi_i$ and $\nu(D_j') \succeq \rho_j$ where B_i' and D_j' are the roots of the and/or trees $\mathcal{T}(G, B_i : \psi_i)$ and $\mathcal{T}(G, D_j : \rho_j)$ respectively. Therefore, the descendant nodes N_{C_1}, N_{C_2} of R that are labelled with C_1, C_2 respectively are such that $\nu(N_{C_1}) \succeq \mathbf{t}, \nu(N_{C_2}) \succeq \mathbf{f}$ respectively, whence, $\nu(R) \succeq lub\{\mathbf{t}, \mathbf{f}\} = \top$. This completes this case.

Case 2: $[\alpha = \bot]$ Trivial.

Case 3: $[\alpha = \mathbf{t}$ or $\mathbf{f}]$ In this case, the analysis is almost identical to that of the case when $\alpha = \top$ except that we consider only one gh-clause C_1 instead of two.

From the above arguments, we have shown that for all $n \in \mathbf{N}$, $\nu(R) \succeq T_G \uparrow n$. Now $T_G \uparrow \omega(A) = \alpha$ implies that $T_G \uparrow n(A) = \alpha, T_G \uparrow (n+1)(A) = \alpha, \ldots$ for some finite n, and so it follows that $\nu(R) \succeq T_G \uparrow \omega(A)$. ∎

Theorems 39 and 40 are respectively, the soundness and completeness (in the sense of Van Emden [VE86]) results for and/or tree searching. As in the case of [VE86], the restriction to finite and/or trees seems to be necessary. The following question then comes to mind:

Question 41: Can a SLD-resolution like proof procedure be given for GHPs ?

The answer to this question seems to be "NO". This is because a certain amount of breadth-oriented search seems necessary in order to compute $T_G \uparrow \omega(A)$ for $A \in B_G$. However, in the case of well-behaved GHPs, it does seem to be possible to define an SLD-resolution like proof procedure.

7. SLDnh-Resolution for Well-Behaved GHPs

A *query* is the existential closure of a conjunction of w-annotated literals. In future, when discussing queries, we will often write them as a conjunction of w-annotated literals and assume all variables in it to be implicitly existentially quantified.

DEF 42: A *nh-resolvent* with respect to $A_i : \rho_i$ of the query Q given by $A_1 : \rho_1 \& \ldots \& A_k : \rho_k$ and the gh-clause C of the form $D : \beta \Leftarrow B_1 : \psi_1 \& \ldots \& B_r : \psi_r$ is the query

$$(A_1 : \rho_1 \& \ldots \& A_{i-1} : \rho_{i-1} \& B_1 : \psi_1 \& \ldots \& B_r : \psi_r \& A_{i+1} : \rho_{i+1} \& \ldots \& A_k : \rho_k)\theta$$

where $\beta \succeq \rho_i$ and θ is the most general unifier of D and A_i. (Without loss of generality, we assume that C and Q contain no variable symbols in common i.e. we assume that they have been standardized apart, cf. Lloyd [LL84]). $A_i : \rho_i$ and $D : \rho$ are called "the literals nh-resolved upon"("nh"stands for "non-Horn"). Note that an nh-resolvent is always a query.

DEF 43: An *SLDnh-deduction* from the *initial* query Q_0 and the GHP G is a sequence

$$\langle Q_0, C_1, \theta_1 \rangle, \ldots, \langle Q_i, C_{i+1}, \theta_{i+1} \rangle, \ldots$$

where Q_{r+1} is the nh-resolvent of Q_r and C_{r+1} where C_{r+1} is a renamed version of some gh-clause $C \in G$ such that C_{r+1} has no variable symbols in common with any of $Q_0, \ldots, Q_r, C_1, \ldots, C_r$, and θ_{r+1} is the most general unifier of the literals nh-resolved upon.

DEF 44: An *SLDnh-refutation* of the initial query Q_0 is a finite SLDnh-deduction

$$\langle Q_0, C_1, \theta_1 \rangle, \ldots, \langle Q_n, C_{n+1}, \theta_{n+1} \rangle$$

with Q_{n+1} being the empty query (i.e. an empty conjunction). Associated with every SLDnh-refutation is a path called the *SLDnh-refutation path*. Fig.2 gives the SLDnh-refutation path associated with the above SLDnh-refutation.

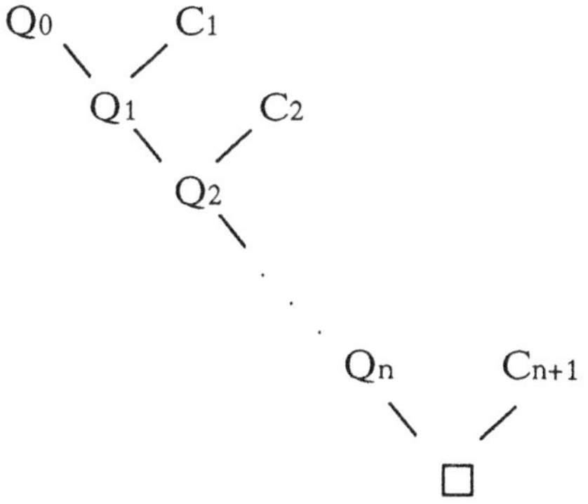

Fig. 2

We now address the soundness of SLDnh-resolution.
Theorem 45:[Soundness] If there exists an SLDnh-refutation of the initial query Q_0:

$$A_1 : \rho_1 \& \ldots \& A_m : \rho_m$$

from the GHP G, then

$$T_G \uparrow \omega \models \exists(Q_0)$$

Proof: Suppose there exists an SLDnh-refutation of the initial query Q_0 from G of the following form:

$$\langle Q_0, C_1, \theta_1 \rangle, \ldots, \langle Q_n, C_{n+1}, \theta_{n+1} \rangle$$

We will show by induction on n that $T_Q \uparrow \omega \models \exists(Q_0)$.
Base Case:[n=0] Then the nh-resolvent of Q_0 and C_1 is the empty query,i.e. Q_0 is a unit conjunction (i.e. $A_1 : \rho_1$) and C_1 is a unit gh-clause,i.e. C_1 is of the form

$$A' : \beta \Leftarrow$$

where $\beta \succeq \rho_1$ and $A_1\theta_1 = A'\theta_1$. As $T_G \uparrow \omega$ is a model of the GHP G, it must be a model of C_1, and so it must be true that for every ground instance A_2 of A', $T_G \uparrow \omega(A_2) \succeq \beta$. In particular, for every A_3 that is a ground instance of $A'\theta_1$, $T_G \uparrow \omega(A_3) \succeq \beta \succeq \rho_1$, whence $T_G \uparrow \omega \models \exists Q_0$.
Inductive Case: Suppose

$$\langle Q_0, C_1, \theta_1 \rangle, \ldots, \langle Q_n, C_{n+1}, \theta_{n+1} \rangle, \langle Q_{n+1}, C_{n+2}, \theta_{n+2} \rangle$$

is an SLDnh-refutation of Q_0. Then

$$\langle Q_1, C_2, \theta_2 \rangle, \ldots, \langle Q_n, C_{n+1}, \theta_{n+1} \rangle$$

is an SLDnh-refutation of Q_1. Therefore, by the induction hypothesis, it is true $T_G \uparrow \omega \models \exists(Q_1)$. But Q_1 is the nh-resolvent of Q_0 and C_1. So Q_1 is of the form:

$$(A_1 : \rho_1 \& \ldots \& A_{i-1} : \rho_{i-1} \& E_1 : \psi_1 \& \ldots \& E_r : \psi_r \& A_{i+1} : \rho_{i+1} \& \ldots \& A_m : \rho_m)\theta_1$$

where C_1 is the gh-clause

$$H : \delta \Leftarrow E_1 : \psi_1 \& \ldots \& E_r : \psi_r$$

such that $H\theta_1 = A_i\theta_1$ and $\delta \succeq \rho_i$ (by definition of nh-resolution). As $T_G \uparrow \omega \models (\exists)Q_1$ it follows that

$$T_G \uparrow \omega \models (E_1 : \psi_1 \& \ldots \& E_r : \psi_r)\theta_1$$

(as this is a sub-conjunct of Q_1). As $T_G \uparrow \omega$ is a model of G (Theorem 22), it must satisfy every gh-clause of G (and every renamed version of any gh-clause in G). In particular, $T_G \uparrow \omega$ must satisfy $C_1\theta_1$. As $T_G \uparrow \omega$ satisfies the body of $C_1\theta_1$, it must satisfy $H\theta_1 : \delta$. But $H\theta_1 = A_i\theta_1$; so $T_G \uparrow \omega \models A_i\theta_1 : \delta$. Therefore, as $\delta \succeq \rho_i$, $T_G \uparrow \omega \models A_i\theta_1 : \rho_i$. Thus,

$$T_G \uparrow \omega \models (\exists)(A_1 : \rho_1 \& \ldots \& A_m : \rho_m)\theta_1 \quad \blacksquare$$

Notice that the soundness theorem above does not restrict the GHP to covered GHPs. However, this restriction is needed for our completeness result.

Theorem 46: Suppose G is a covered, well-behaved GHP. Then if $Q_0 = A_1 : \rho_1 \& \ldots \& A_m : \rho_m$ is a ground query that is satisfied by $T_G \uparrow \omega$, then there is an SLDnh-refutation of Q_0 from G.

Proof: Suppose G is covered and well-behaved. Let $Q_0 = (A_1 : \rho_1 \& \ldots \& A_m : \rho_m)$ be a ground query that is satisfied by $T_G \uparrow \omega$. Then there must be some $n > 0$ (as $\rho_i \neq \perp$ for all i) such that $T_G \uparrow n \models Q_0$. We will prove by induction on n that an SLDnh-refutation of Q_0 from G exists.

<u>Base Case</u>: Suppose $T_G \uparrow 1 \models Q_0$. Then for each $1 \leq i \leq m$, there is a gh-clause C_i in G having a ground instance $C_i\theta_i$ of the form

$$A : \beta_i \Leftarrow$$

where $\beta_i \succeq \rho_i$. As Q_0 is ground, none of the substitutions θ_i affect it, and so

$$\langle A_1 : \rho_1 \& \ldots \& A_m : \rho_m, C_1, \theta_1 \rangle,$$

$$\langle A_2 : \rho_2 \& \ldots \& A_m : \rho_m, C_2, \theta_2 \rangle$$

$$\vdots$$

$$\langle A_m : \rho_m, C_m, \theta_m \rangle$$

is an SLDnh-refutation of Q_0.

<u>Inductive Case</u>: Suppose $T_G \uparrow (r+1) \models A_1 : \rho_1 \& \ldots \& A_m : \rho_m$. Then, for each A_i, there is a gh-clause C_i in G having a ground instance $C_i\theta_i$ of the form:

$$A_i : \beta_i \Leftarrow B_1^i \& \ldots \& B_{\kappa_i}^i$$

where $\beta_i \succeq \rho_i$, and $T_G \uparrow r \models B_1^i \& \ldots \& B_{\kappa_i}^i$. Now, as each A_i is ground, and as G is covered, $B_1^i \& \ldots \& B_{\kappa_i}^i$ is ground and so, by the induction hypothesis, there exists an SLDnh-refutation $\mathbf{R}_i$ of $B_1^i \& \ldots \& B_{\kappa_i}^i$. Therefore,

$$\langle A_i : \rho_i, C_i, \theta_i \rangle, \mathbf{R}_i$$

is a SLDnh-refutation of A_i. Denote the SLDnh-refutation tree of each $A_i : \rho_i$ by Γ_i. Then Fig.3 below gives an SLDnh-refutation tree for Q_0.

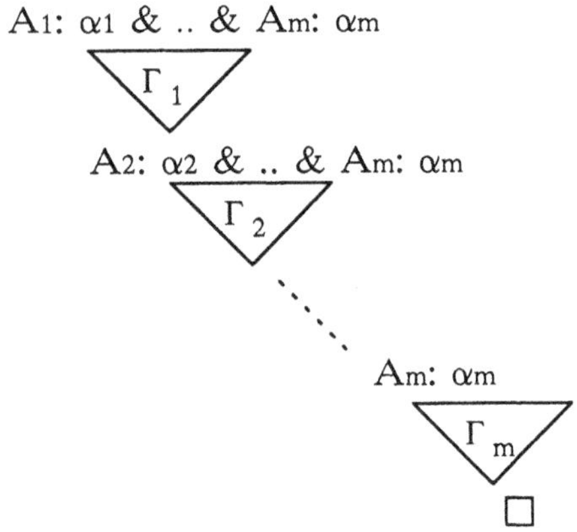

FIG. 3

Example 47. Consider the following covered, well-behaved GHP:

$$
\begin{aligned}
p(X) : \mathbf{t} &\Leftarrow q(X) : \mathbf{f} \& r(X) : \mathbf{t} \\
q(a) : \mathbf{t} &\Leftarrow \\
q(b) : \mathbf{f} &\Leftarrow \\
q(c) : \mathbf{f} &\Leftarrow \\
r(a) : \mathbf{t} &\Leftarrow \\
r(a) : \mathbf{f} &\Leftarrow \\
r(b) : \mathbf{f} &\Leftarrow \\
r(c) : \mathbf{t} &\Leftarrow
\end{aligned}
$$

and the queries $p(b) : \mathbf{t}$ and $p(c) : \mathbf{t}$. The latter succeeds, but the former does not. This is despite the fact that the above GHP expresses inconsistency via the fifth and sixth clauses.

8. Summary and Future Work

Let us now see how much progress we have made concerning the goals set out in Section 1 of this paper.

First of all, we have indeed succeeded in giving a fixpoint semantics for arbitrary sets of clauses. Based upon the intuitive connection between arbitrary sets of clauses and positive GHPs, we have given a means of associating a fixed point semantics with sets of arbitrary clauses. And lastly, it is quite clear that a GHP that expresses inconsistency via the annotations need not be classically inconsistent (in terms of having no models). Example 47 amply demonstrates this fact.

Some open problems remaining are:

Problem 1.: Can we find a recursive class of GHPs that (strictly) includes the class of well-behaved GHPs, while still guaranteeing existence of a nice model ?

Problem 2.: How much can the covering condition used in the completeness result of SLDnh-resolution be weakened ? In view of the very strong conditions imposed on completeness results for SLDNF-resolution for general logic programs [BM86a,b] it should not be surprising that we have such a restriction in Theorem 46.

Acknowledgements. We thank R. Anand for typesetting the diagrams.

References

[AS87] Anand,R.,Subrahmanian,V.S.(1987) FLOG: A Logic programming system based on a six-valued logic, *Proc. AAAI Intl. Symp. on Knowledge Engg.*, Madrid, Spain, April 1987.

[ABW86] Apt,K.,Blair,H,Walker,A.(1986) Towards a theory of declarative knowledge, to appear.

[AR79] Arruda,A.I.(1979) A Survey of paraconsistent logic, in *Mathematical Logic in Latin America*, (eds. Arruda,A.I., Chuaqui,R.,Da Costa,N.C.A.) Proc. 4th Latin American Symp. on Math. Logic, Santiago, Dec. 1978, pps. 1-41, D.Reidel.

[BM86a] Barbuti,R., Martelli,M. (1986) Completeness of the SLDNF-resolution for a class of logic programs, *Proc. Intl. Symp. on Logic Prog.*, London, Lecture Notes in Computer Science No.225, (ed.Shapiro,E.), pps 600-614.

[BM86b] Barbuti,R., Martelli,M. (1986) Completeness of SLDNF-resolution for structured programs, submitted for publication.

[BE77] Belnap,N.D. (1977) A Useful four-valued Logic, in *Modern Uses of Many-valued Logic* (eds. Epstein,G. , Dunn,J.M.), pps. 8-37, D.Reidel.

[BL86] Blair,H.A. (1986) Decidability in the Herbrand base, to appear.

[BS87] Blair,H.A.,Subrahmanian,V.S. (1987) A Logical Framework for Approximate Reasoning in Logic programming, in preparation.

[CA74] Costa, N.C.A.da (1974) On the theory of inconsistent formal systems, *Notre Dame J. of Formal Logic* 15, pps 497-510.

[CA77] Costa,N.C.A.da, Alves,E.H. (1977) A semantical analysis of the calculi C_n, *Notre Dame J. of Formal Logic* 18, pps 621-630.

[CA81] Costa,N.C.A.da, Alves,H.(1981) Relations between paraconsistent logic and Many-valued logic, *Bull. of the Section of Logic*, 10,pps 185-191.

[CA87] Costa,N.C.A.,Marconi,D. (1987) An Overview of Paraconsistent Logic in the 80's, to appear in *Logica Nova*, Akademie Verlag, Berlin.

[FI85] Fitting,M. (1985) A Kripke-Kleene semantics for logic programming, *J. of Logic Prog.* 4,pps 295-312.

[JLM86] Jaffar,J.,Lassez,J.-L.,Maher,M. (1986) Issues and trends in the Semantics of Logic Programming, *Proc. 3rd Intl. Conf. on Logic Programming*, Lecture Notes in Computer Sci., Vol. 225, Springer Verlag.

[JS86] Jaffar,J., Stuckey,P.J. (1986) Canonical Logic Programs, *J. of Logic Programming*, 3,2, pps 143-155.

[K57] Kleene,S.C. (1957) Introduction to Metamathematics, Van Nostrand Reinhold.

[LL84] Lloyd,J.W.(1984) Foundations of Logic Programming, Springer-Verlag.

[LM85] Lassez,J.-L.,Maher,M.(1985) Optimal fixed points of logic programs, *Theoret. Comput. Sci.*, 39, pps 115-125.

[NA86] Naish,L. (1986) Negation and quantifiers in NU-Prolog, *Proc. 3rd Intl. Conf. on Logic Prog.*, London, Lecture Notes in Comp. Sci., Vol. 225, pps 624-634, Springer-Verlag.

[PE86] Perlis,D. (1986) On the consistency of commonsense reasoning, *Computational Intelligence*, 2, pps 180-190.

[PG86] Poole,D.,Goebel,R. (1986) Gracefully adding negation and disjunction in Prolog, *Proc. 3rd Intl. Conf. on Logic Prog.*, London, Lecture Notes in Comp. Sci., Vol. 225, pps 635-641, Springer-Verlag.

[S87a] Subrahmanian,V.S. (1987) On the semantics of quantitative logic programs, *4th IEEE Symp. on Logic Prog.*, San Francisco, Sep. 1987, (accepted-to appear).

[S87b] Subrahmanian,V.S. (1987) Towards a theory of evidential reasoning in logic programming, *Logic Colloquium '87 (European Summer Meeting of the Association of Symbolic Logic)*, Granada, Spain, July 1987 (accepted-to appear).

[VE86] Van Emden,M. (1986) Quantitative deduction and its fixpoint theory, *J. of Logic Prog.*, 4,1,pps 37-53.

[VI86] Visser,A. (1984) Four valued semantics and the liar, *J. of Philosophical Logic*, 13,pps 181-212.

[VK76] Van Emden,M.,Kowalski,R.(1976) The semantics of predicate logic as a programming language, *JACM*, 23,4,pps 733-742.

SEMANTICS OF DISTRIBUTED HORN CLAUSE PROGRAMS

R.Ramanujam* +
The Institute of Mathematical Sciences
C.I.T. Campus, MADRAS 600 113.

Abstract: We study the semantics of a Horn clause program distributed over a fixed finite number of sites. We present a least fixed-point characterisation and then describe the operational semantics using refutation trees.

1. MOTIVATION

If we can accept the maxim

deduction = computation

of logic programming, we can attempt to extend the maxim and ask

concurrent deduction $\stackrel{?}{=}$ distributed computation.

That is, we venture to think of a system of several deductions proceeding concurrently as a system of distributed computations.

Let L be a logical language, p a sentence of L, and T a set of L - sentences. Write $T \vdash p$ to mean that there is a finite proof of p from T. Let Mod(T) denote the collection of all models of T. In logic programming, L is thought of as a programming language, T as a logic program and Mod(T) as the set of possible behaviours of T. The proof $T \vdash p$ is given an operational meaning(usually referred to as the procedural interpretation) and is seen as the 'execution' of program T resulting in a 'computation' of T.

Now, the question we would like to study is the following: let $p_1,\ldots,p_n$ be sentences of L and $T_1,\ldots,T_n$ be sets of L sentences. We look for a notion of $T_i \vdash p_i$ $(1 \leq i \leq n)$ standing for concurrent deductions, in such a way that $Mod(T_1),\ldots,Mod(T_n)$ can be described as the behaviour of a distributed system. This would give us the concept of a distributed logic program.

Following the tradition of automatic theorem proving, researchers in logic programming have considered the clausal form of predicate logic for L so that a program T is simply a set of clauses. Usually T is a set of Horn clauses, Herbrand models are considered for

---

* This research was done while the author was at: Computer Science Group, Tata Institute of Fundamental Research, Homi Bhabha Road, Bombay 400 005.

+ We thank Melvin Fitting and R.K.Shyamasundar for discussions, P.S.Thiagarajan and the referees for comments and T.V.Vasudevan for typing the manuscript.

Mod(T) and resolution is used to give proofs $T \vdash p$. This provides for a clean and elegant semantics of logic programs, without losing expressive power. The most remarkable gain of this approach is that given a logic program, all its consequences can be determined by examining a single model, which is the intersection of all its models. The semantics of logic programs has been extensively studied [van Emden and Kowalski], [Apt and van Emden 82], [Lassez and Maher 84], [Lloyd 84], [Fitting 85].

In the next section, we study the semantics of distributed Horn clause programs, using Herbrand models and giving a least fixed-point characterization in the style of [Apt and van Emden]. With each program, we associate a mapping on interpretations and show that the least fixed-point of the function is the same as the least model of the program. We give two different such functions, which differ in the way meanings are built locally and globally, but which agree on the least fixed-point.

In Section 3, we describe the operational semantics of distributed Horn clause programs using refutation trees. A refutation is a syntactic entity intended to demonstrate the unsatisfiability of a set of clauses. We prove that distributed derivations are sound and complete for success as well as finite failure a' ℓ'a [Lassez and Maher 84].

We conclude the paper with a discussion on various interesting issues that arise from this material. The work presented here is only part of [Ramanujam 87] to which the reader is referred to for more results on distributed logic programs.

2. SEMANTICS

Assume that we are given countable and disjoint sets of function symbols, predicate symbols and variables and with each function symbol and predicate symbol, an appropriate arity is associated. A zero-ary function symbol is called a constant. A term is a constant, a variable or of the form $f(t_1,\dots\dots,t_n)$, where f is a function symbol of arity n and $t_1,\dots,t_n$, are terms. An atom or atomic formula is of the form $P(t_1,\dots\dots,t_n)$ where P is a predicate symbol of arity m and $t_1,\dots\dots,t_m$ are terms.

Definition 2.1: A clause is of the form

$$A_1,\dots\dots,A_n \leftarrow B_1,\dots\dots B_m, \quad n \geq 0, \quad m \geq 0,$$

where $A_1,\dots\dots,A_n$, $B_1,\dots\dots,B_m$ are atoms. If $m = 0$ and $n = 1$, we call the clause an assertion or a fact (and omit the backward arrow symbol). If $n = 0$ and $m > 0$, then the clause is said to be a negative clause. If $m = n = 0$, we say it is an empty clause, denoted $\Box$. A Horn clause has $0 \leq n \leq 1$ and $0 \leq m$. A definite clause has $n = 1$ and $m \geq 0$. A logic program is a set of definite clauses.

Definition 2.2: Substitution θ is an operation, which given an expression (atom, clause) e replaces uniformly throughout e every occurrence of a variable v by a term t. If e is an expression and θ a substitution, the result of applying θ on e is written $e\theta$ and is called instance of e. We say that expressions e and e' are unifiable when there exists θ such that $e\theta \equiv e'\theta$ and θ is said to be a unifier of e and e'.

Assume the existence of a fixed finite number of sites, indexed by the set $\{1,\dots,n\}$. Associated with each site is a set of definite clauses. The set containing clauses from all sites defines the logic program.

Definition 2.3: A distributed logic program (DLP) is a tuple $< P_1,\dots,P_n >$ where P_i is the set of definite clauses associated with site i. Let $P = \bigcup_i P_i$. P is said to be the composite program, or system, and each of the P_i's is referred to as component programs.

Throughout this paper, we implicitly consider a DLP $<P_1,\dots,P_n>$ and we refer to P, P_i etc. to mean the composite and component programs in this system, respectively.

The Herbrand Base of P denoted HB(P) is the set of all variable-free atoms (called ground atoms) containing no predicate or function symbols other than those occurring in P. An interpretation is a tuple $(I_1,\dots,I_n)$, where for each j, I_j is a subset of HB(P). We use the letter I to denote the tuple $(I_1,\dots,I_n)$.

Definition 2.4: Given an interpretation $(I_1,\dots,I_n)$ the notion that I_j is a model of program P_j is defined as follows:

(a) an atom is true in I_j iff it belongs to I_j,

(b) a variable-free instance of a clause $B_0 \leftarrow B_1,\dots,B_m$, $m \geq 0$ is true in I_j iff B_0 is true in I_j or at least one of the B_k, $1 \leq k \leq m$, is not true in $I_1 \cup \dots \cup I_m$.

(c) a clause is true in I_j iff each of its variable free instances is true in I_j.

(d) I_j is a model of P_j iff each of the clauses in P_j is true in I_j.

The intersection of all models of a program P_j is said to be the least model of P_j (it can be readily verified that the intersection of all models is indeed a model). $(I_1,\dots,I_n)$ is the least model of DLP iff, for all j, I_j is the least model of P_j.

Let PH denote the set of all subsets of the Herbrand Base of the composite program P. Note that $(PH, \subseteq)$ is a complete lattice with the empty set $\emptyset$ as its bottom element and PH as its top element. Now let $I \leq I'$ iff $I_j \subseteq I'_j$ for all j. We also have $(PH^n, \leq)$ as a complete lattice with the bottom element $(\emptyset,\dots,\emptyset)$ and the top element (PH, ..., PH).

With each P_j, we associate a transformation F_j on interpretations from PH^n to PH.

Definition 2.5:

$A \in F_j(I)$ iff there exists a clause $B_0 \leftarrow B_1,\dots,B_m$, $m \geq 0$ in P_j such that for some θ, $B_0\theta = A$ and for all k, $1 \leq k \leq m$: there exists h, $1 \leq h \leq n$ such that $B_k\theta \in I_h$.

Let F be the transformation that 'collects' all the F_j's together:

Definition 2.6: F is a function from PH^n to PH^n such that

$$F(I) = (F_1(I),\dots, F_n(I)).$$

Fact 2.7: F is monotonic under $\leq$.

Since F is a monotonic operator on a complete lattice, it has a least fixed-point, which can be constructed as follows:

$$I^0 = (\emptyset,\dots,\emptyset)$$

$$I^{k+1} = F(I^k)$$

The least fixed-point of F is simply $\bigcup_k F(I^k)$.

Lemma 2.8: $F(I) \leq I$ iff I_j is a model of P_j, for all j.

Proof: Let $F_j(I) \subseteq I_j$. We show that I_j is a model of P_j. Suppose not. Therefore there is a clause in P_j which is not true in I_j. Let this clause be of the form $B_0 \leftarrow B_1,\dots B_m$, $m \geq 0$. If $m = 0$ then for some θ, $B_0\theta \notin I_j$. However, by definition of F_j every such $B_0\theta'$ is in $F_j(I)$

for every I, and hence, in particular, $B_0\theta \in F_j(I)$. Thus $B_0\theta \in F_j(I)$ and $B_0\theta \notin I_j$, contracting the assumption that $F_j(I) \subseteq I_j$.

If m > 0, then, for some θ, $B_0\theta \notin I_j$, and for all k, $B_k\theta$ is true in $I_1 \cup \ldots \cup I_n$; that is, for all k, $1 \leq k \leq m$, there exists h, $1 \leq h \leq n$, such that $B_k\theta \in I_n$. However, given this, by definition of F_j, $B_0\theta \in F_j(I)$. This again contradicts $F_j(I) \subseteq I_j$.

The converse readily follows from Definitions 2.4 and 2.5. QED

Lemmas 2.7 and 2.8 together give us the following theorem.

Theorem 2.9: The least model of a DLP is the same as the least fixed point of F associated with it. Moreover, this least fixed point can be constructed as $F^{\omega}(\emptyset, \ldots, \emptyset)$.

It may be instructive to analyse how F_j builds the meanings of the component programs P_j simultaneously. The input to F_j is not simply I_j, but the entire tuple I. Thus the 'global input' $(I_1, \ldots, I_n)$ is simultaneously made available to all $F_1, \ldots, F_n$. We can see the input interpretation as being shared by all the component programs.

Example 2.10: Consider the DLP: $\langle P_1, \ldots, P_n \rangle$

P_1 : 1. P(0)
2. Q(X) ← P(X)

P_2 : 1. R(X) ← P(X), Q(X)

Let $I_1 = I_2 = \emptyset$. Write P, Q, R for P(0), Q(0), R(0) respectively.

$F_1(\emptyset, \emptyset) = \{P\}$

$F_1(\{P\}, \emptyset) = \{P, Q\}$

$F_1(\{P, Q\}, \emptyset) = \{P, Q\}$

Thus $F_1(F_1(\emptyset, \emptyset), \emptyset) = \{P, Q\}$

$F_2(\emptyset, \emptyset) = \emptyset$

$F_2(\{P, Q\}) = \emptyset$

$F_2(\{P, Q\}, \emptyset) = \{R\}$

Thus, $F_2(F_1(F_1(\emptyset, \emptyset), \emptyset), \emptyset) = \{R\}$

$F(\emptyset, \emptyset) = (\{P\}, \emptyset)$

$F(F(\emptyset, \emptyset)) = (\{P, Q\}, \emptyset)$

$F(F(F(\emptyset, \emptyset))) = (\{P, Q\}, \{R\})$,

and this is the least fixed point.

We could alternatively consider a semantics, where the meanings are built 'locally' as far as possible. We would then expect that the meaning of a clause in P_j be specified only in terms of I_j. However, the defining clause for the premise of some clause in P_j may be in P_k, where $k \neq j$ and in this case, the meaning of that clause would also depend on clauses in P_k, and on I_k. Below we construct such functions.

Definition 2.11: L_j : PH → PH is the 'local' transformation defined as follows: (below $I \subseteq HB(P)$ and not a tuple interpretation)

A $\in L_j(I)$ iff for some clause $B_0 \leftarrow B_1, \ldots, B_n$ in P_j such that for some θ, $B_0\theta \equiv A$ and for all k, $1 \leq k \leq m$, $B_k\theta \in I$

L_j is also a montotone operator on (PH, $\subseteq$) and hence has a least fixed point, which is $L_j^{\omega}(\emptyset)$.

Given L_j, we now construct T_j, which builds meanings locally, and 'communicates' with T_k, $k \neq j$, stepwise.

Definition 2.12: $T_j : PH^n \times \{0, 1, \ldots\} \rightarrow PH$

$$T_j(I, 0) = L_j^{\omega}(I_j)$$

$$T_j(I, h+1) = L_j^{\omega}(I_j \cup \bigcup_r T_r(I,h)).$$

Example 2.13: Consider the DLP of Example 2.10:

$L_1^{\omega}(\emptyset) = \{P, Q\}$ $L_2^{\omega}(\emptyset) = \emptyset$

$T_1(\emptyset, h) = \{P, Q\}$ for all h.

$T_2(\emptyset, 0) = \emptyset$ and $T_2(\emptyset, h) = \{R\}$ for all $h > 0$. Note that for all h, if $I \leq J$ then $T_j(I, h) \subseteq T_j(J, h)$. Let E denote the empty interpretation $(\emptyset, \ldots, \emptyset)$.

Lemma 2.14: $\forall j \forall h$ $T_j(E, h) \subseteq T_j(E, h+1)$

Proof: The proof is by induction on h. For the base case, let $h = 0$. $A \in T_j(E,0)$. Since $I_j = \emptyset$, A must be the variable free instance of some clause in P_j without premises. Hence $A \in L_j^{\omega}(\emptyset)$ and by monotonicity, $A \in L_j^{\omega}(X)$ for $X \subseteq HB(P)$. Thus $A \in T_j(E, 1)$.

For the induction step, assume that $A \in T_j(E, h)$ but that $A \notin T_j(E, h+1)$. That is $A \notin L_j^{\omega}(\bigcup_r T_r(E, h))$, since $I_j = \emptyset$. Hence it may be that A does not unify with the conclusion of any clause in P_j, in which case, for all I, $A \notin L_j^{\omega}(I)$. Hence $A \notin T_j(E, k)$ for all k. In particular, $A \notin T_j(E, h)$ contradicting our assumption. Otherwise, $A = B_0\theta$ for some θ, and $B_0 \leftarrow B_1, \ldots, B_m$ is a clause in P_j such that for some k, $B_k\theta \notin \bigcup_r T_r(L, h)$. By induction hypothesis, $B_k\theta \notin T_r(E, \ell)$ for all $\ell < h$. In particular, $B_k\theta \notin \bigcup_r T_r(E, h-1)$. $A \notin T_j(E, h)$, giving the required contradiction. QED

Let T(I, h) denote the tuple $(T_1(I,h), \ldots, T_n(I, h))$ and let $T(I, \omega)$ denote the pointwise union $\bigcup_h T(I, h)$. Below we study the relationship between the F and T semantics.

Question 2.15: $\forall I.$ $T(I, \omega) \leq F^{\omega}(I)$?

Answer No. As a counter example, consider the DLP: $< P_1, P_2 >$

P_1 : 1. $P(X) \leftarrow Q(X), R(X)$ P_2 : 1. $Q(X) \leftarrow S(X)$

Again, write P, Q, R, S to mean P(0), Q(0), R(0), S(0) respectively. Let $I = (\{R\}, \{S\})$.
$F^{\omega}(I) = (\emptyset, \{Q\})$, $T(I,\omega) = (\{P\}, \{Q\})$. In fact, $T(I, 1) \not\leq F^{\omega}(I)$.

Question 2.16: $\forall I$ $F^{\omega}(I) \leq T(I, \omega)$?

Answer: No. As a counter example consider the DLP $< P_1, P_2 >$ below:

P_1 : 1. $P(0) \leftarrow Q(0)$ P_2 : 1. $R(0)$

Let $I = (\emptyset, \{Q, R\})$. $F(I) = (\{P\}, \{R\})$

We have for all h, $T_1(I, h) = \emptyset$ and $T_2(I, h) = \{R\}$. Thus, $F(I) \not\leq T(I, \omega)$.

Question 2.17: $F^{\omega}(I) = T(I,\omega)$ when I is a model of P ?

Answer: No. Consider the DLP in counter example 2.16 above.

Let $I = (\{P\}, \{Q, R\})$. Again $F(I) = (\{P\}, \{R\})$,

$T(I, \omega) = (\emptyset, \{R\})$.

Question 2.18: Is $F^{\omega}(I) = T(I,\omega)$ when I is a fixed-point of F ?

Answer: No. Consider $< P_1, P_2 >$ below.

P_1 : 1. $P(0) \leftarrow Q(0)$ $\qquad$ P_2 : 1. $Q(0) \leftarrow P(0)$

Let $I = (\{P(0)\}, \{Q(0)\})$. $F(I) = I$. But $T(I, \omega) = (\emptyset, \emptyset)$.

However all is not lost yet. Though F and T do not have the same fixed-points, they do agree on the least fixed-point. In the example above, the least model is in fact $(\emptyset, \emptyset)$ and for this, both F and T coincide. In the previous example (of 2.16 and 2.17), the least model is $(\emptyset, \{R\})$ and again $F(I) = T(I, \omega)$. The theorem below asserts that these are not mere accidents.

Recall that E stands for the 'everywhere empty' interpretation $(\emptyset,\ldots,\emptyset)$.

Theorem 2.19: $F^{\omega}(E) = T(E, \omega)$.

Proof: We can show by easy induction on k that for all j, $A \in F_j^{k+1}(E)$ iff $A \in T_j(E, k)$. QED

Thus we have shown two different ways of building the meaning of a distributed Horn clause program, both of which yield the same meaning when we treat the least fixed-point as the semantics of the program.

We now turn our attention to another aspect of logic program semantics. [Lassez and Maher 84] have shown that the complement of the greatest fixed-point of the transformation can be seen as an alternative definition of finite failure. We study a similar result in the context of distribited Horn clause programs.

Definition 2.20: $A \in HB(P)$ is finitely failed in P_i, denoted $A \in FF_i$, if and only if, for some $d \geq 0$, A is failed by depth d, denoted $A \in FF_i^d$, defined as follows:

$A \in FF_i^0$ iff for all clauses $B_0 \leftarrow B_1,\ldots,B_m$ in P_i, for all variable-free substitutions θ, $B_0\theta \neq A$.

$A \in FF_i^{d+1}$ iff for every clause $B_0 \leftarrow B_1,\ldots, B_m$ in P_i such that for some variable-free substitution θ, $B_0\theta = A$, for some k, $1 \leq k \leq m$, for all j, $1 \leq j \leq n$, $A \in FF_j^d$.

Note that by definition of FF_i, if $A \in FF_i^d$, then $A \in FF_i^{d+1}$ as well. We have the following theorem, where H denotes HB(P) and $\bar{X}$ denotes the complement of X in H.

Theorem 2.21: $FF_i = \overline{\bigcup_k F_i^k(H)}$

Proof: We show by induction on k that for all k, we have $FF_i^k = \overline{F_i^{k+1}(H)}$. For the base case, let k = 0. Suppose $A \in FF_i^0$. Clearly $A \notin F_i(H)$. Conversely suppose that $A \notin F_i(H)$. Then for all clauses in P_i, there is no matching conclusion for A, so $A \in FF_i^0$, or there is a clause $B_0 \leftarrow B_1,\ldots, B_m$ such that $B_0\theta = A$ but for some k, $B_k\theta \notin H$. If θ is a variable-free substitution, this case is not possible, since H is the Herbrand Base of P; otherwise by definition $A \in FF_i^0$.

For the induction step, assume that the theorem has been proved for all k' < k. If $A \in FF$ it follows from the definition of FF_i and the induction hypothesis that $A \notin F_i^{k+1}(H)$. Converse let $A \notin F_i^{k+1}(H)$. Then for every clause in P_i whose conclusion matches A for some θ, there is a premise B_j such that $B_j\theta \notin F_r^k(H)$. By induction hypothesis, then $B_j\theta \notin \bigcup_r FF_r^{k-1}$. By definition, then $A \in FF_i^k$. QED.

3. OPERATIONAL SEMANTICS

In a distributed logic program, we have a fixed number of sites, say n. With each site is associated a set of definite clauses. The operational understanding of these clauses as programs can be obtained by studying proof procedures, where various sites 'cooperate' in producing a proof.

Traditionally, operational semantics is given by describing configurations and transitions on them. In logic programs, the state of a program is the set of theorems derivable from the axioms(clauses) that comprise the program. Thus the state of a distributed logic program can be specified by determining the theorems derivable at each site. The inference rule of proof describes transitions, in the sense that new theorems are derived from old theorems.

For example, consider P_1 which has the clause 'A ← B' and P_2 which has 'B'. Now, 'A' is a theorem of P_1 and P_2 together but not individually. When proof proceeds by refutation, P_1 attempts to refute 'A' and finds that 'A' can be refuted provided 'B' can be refuted. P_2, in an attempt to refute 'B' finds a contradiction.

When we have definite clauses, we have atoms in clauses and hence we need to find terms instantiating variables. If we have a clause A ← B, C, then the refutation for A depends on those for B and C and we must ensure that all these refutations instantiate variables in a consistent manner. This gives us a notion of compatible substitutions.

Definition 3.1: Substitution θ_1 is said to be compatible with substitution θ_2 iff for all variables $\nu \in dom(\theta_1) \cap dom(\theta_2)$, $\nu\theta_1$ and $\nu\theta_2$ unify.

Note that compatibility is a reflexive and symmetric binary relation on substitutions. We will say that a set of substitutions S is compatible-closed, if compatibility is an equivalence relation on S. In this case, we denote the equivalence class of substitution θ by $[\theta]$. In general, we write $[\theta_1] = [\theta_2]$ to mean that θ_1 and θ_2 belong to the same equivalence class of compatibility.

Proposition 3.2: If a set of substitutions S is compatible-closed, then there exists a substitution θ such that for all $\theta' \in S$, $dom(\theta') \subseteq dom(\theta)$ and $[\theta] = [\theta']$.

Proof: The proof is easy by induction on finite subsets of S. If the result is true for some subset S' of S, and $\theta' \in S' - S$, from the induction hypothesis and by equivalence of compatibility, we get $[\theta] = [\theta']$. So there exists σ such that for all $\nu \in dom(\theta) \cap dom(\theta')$, $(\nu\theta)\sigma = (\nu\theta')\sigma$. Clearly $(\theta\sigma) \cup (\theta'\sigma)$ is a function. Let this be a new θ; we have $dom(\theta') \subseteq dom(\theta)$. QED

Example 3.3: Consider substitutions $\theta_1, \theta_2, \theta_3$ below:

$\theta_1 : x_1/g(y_1)\ ,\ x_2/f(x_3)$

$\theta_2 : x_2/f(4)\ ,\ y_1/6$

$\theta_3 : x_1/h(5)\ ,\ x_2/f(4)$

θ_1 and θ_2 are compatible, but θ_1 and θ_3 are not. Let $\theta : x_1/g(y_1)\ ,\ x_2/f(4)\ ,\ y_1/6$. θ is the substitution which is compatible with both θ_1 and θ_2 and whose domain includes that of θ_1 and θ_2.

The idea of compatible substitutions is that when variables shared among subgoals have to be instantiated, this is done in a consistent manner. We now define distributed refutations below.

Definition 3.4: Let $A \in HB(P)$. The distributed derivation of P_i for A is a tree with atoms and substitutions at its nodes as follows:

(i) the root of the tree contains the atom A.

(ii) there is a branch from a node x having atom A to a leaf node having □ only if there is a clause B in P_i without premises such that $B\theta \equiv A$ for some θ. Then the node x also has θ.

(iii) there is more than one branch from a node x having atom A only if there is a clause $B_0 \leftarrow B_1, \ldots, B_m$ in P_i, $m > 0$, and for all k, $1 \leq k \leq m$, there is a branch from node x to a node y_k which is the root of a distributed derivation for P_{k_j}, B_k, $1 \leq k_j \leq n$. The node x also has θ if for all k, the child node y_k has a substitution θ_k such that $B_0\ \theta \equiv A$ and $[\theta] = [\theta_1] \ldots = [\theta_m]$.

Definition: The distributed refutation of P_i for atom A is a distributed derivation which has a substitution θ at its root.

Operationally, atoms are sent to all sites to perform refutations concurrently. As soon as a contradiction is found for some instance at some site, the appropriate subgoal is solved and that substitution is passed up the tree. When all subgoals are satisfied, the 'correct' substitution is at the root of the tree.

Difinition 3.6: The success set of a DLP

$= \{A \in HB(P) \mid \text{for some } i, 1 \leq i \leq n, P_i \text{ has a distributed refutation for } A\}$.

We now show that the success set of a distributed logic program is the same as its least model. The proofs are very similar to those in [Ramanujam and Shyamasundar 84]. Assume again that E stands for the tuple of empty interpretations $(\emptyset, \ldots, \emptyset)$.

Theorem 3.7: The success set of a DLP is contained in its least model.

Proof: Let A be an atom and consider the distributed refutation of P_i for A. We show that for some k, $A \in F_i^k(E)$. Consider the root node. Let the clause associated be $B_0 \leftarrow B_1, \ldots, B_m$, $m \geq 0$. The proof proceeds by induction on the number of non-leaf nodes in the refutation tree having substitutions.

The base case is trivial. There is only one non-leaf node with a branch leading to the leaf node. Then m = 0 and the required k is 1.

For the induction step, we have m > 0 and by clause (iii) of Definition 3.4, there are m branches to nodes having B_j and θ_j such that B_0 such that $B_0\ \theta \equiv A$ and $[\theta] = [\theta_1] = \ldots = [\theta_m]$ and these nodes are roots of refutation trees P_{h_j} for B_j respectively. By induction hypothesis, there is a k_j such that $B_j\ \theta_j \in F_{h_j}^{k_j}(E)$. Let k be the maximum of all the k_j. Since F_{h_j} is monotonic, we have $B_j\ \theta_j \in F_{h_j}^{k}(E)$. By definition of compatible-closed substitutions, $B_j\ \theta\ \varepsilon\ F^k_{h_j}$ (E). Let $I = F^k$ (E). We have, for all j, $B_j\ \theta\ \varepsilon\ I_h$, for some h. By definition, $A\ \varepsilon\ F^{k+1}_i$ (E). QED

Theorem 3.8: The least model of a DLP is contained in its success set.

Proof: We have to show that for all k > 0, if $A\ \varepsilon\ F^k_i$ (E), for some i, then, P_i has a distributed refutation for A. Suppose $A\ \varepsilon\ F^k_i$ (E). Then there is a clause $B_0 \leftarrow B_1,..,B_m$, $m \geq 0$, in P_i such that $B_0\ \theta\ \equiv\ A$ for some θ.

The construction is straightforward. Associate a node with each of the atoms above. If $m = 0$, add another node with the empty clause □ and put θ in the parent node. Otherwise attach each of the $B_j\ \theta$ nodes to the roots of the respective refutation trees, which exist by the induction hypothesis. QED

We now show that distributed derivations are sound and complete, not only for success, but also for finite failure.

Definition 3.9: A distributed derivation is said to be finitely failed, when it is a finite tree and there is no substitution at the root node.

Theorem 3.10: Distributed derivations are sound with respect to finite failure.

Proof: Let A be an atom for which every derivation of P_i is finitely failed. We show that for some d, $A\ \varepsilon\ FF^d_i$, by induction on the number of nodes in the tree.

For the base case, we have only the root node, which is also the leaf node, having the atom A and no substitution. Then for every clause in P_i, the conclusion does not unify with A. By definition, $A\ \varepsilon\ FF^0_i$.

Assume that for every k-node finitely failed tree the theorem holds. Let A be such that every (k+1) - node derivation is finitely failed. (Rather, every derivation for A is finitely failed and k+1 is the number of nodes in the largest derivation tree). Now, the root has atom A and there are m branches to nodes having atoms B_j, $1 \leq j \leq m$, which are roots of derivations of P_h for B_j, $1 \leq h \leq n$. We can have two cases.

(i) there is a j such that the node having atom B_j has no substitution. That is, for some θ, such that $B_0\ \theta \equiv A$, P_h has a finitely failed derivation for B_j. This derivation has $\leq$ k nodes and by induction hypothesis, for some d, $B_j\theta\ \varepsilon\ FF^d_h$. By definition of FF, $A\ \varepsilon\ FF^{d+1}_i$, and we are done.

(ii) every one of these branches leads to a node having a substitution, but this set of substitutions $S = \{\theta_1,....,\theta_m\}$ is not compatible-closed. Let S' be the largest compatible-closed subset of S. (Trivially, S' could be a singleton, so it need not be empty.) Let θ be the substitution extending S' as in Proposition 3.2. Set all the other substitutions to θ. Now at least one of the derivations for $B_j\theta$, $1 \leq j \leq m$, must be finitely failed; otherwise we would get a contradiction to our assumption that every (k+1) - node derivation for A is finitely failed. We can apply the induction hypothesis to get $B_j\theta\ \varepsilon\ FF^d_h$, for some d, h and hence $A\ \varepsilon\ FF^{d+1}_i$.

QED

Theorem 3.11: Distributed derivations are complete with respect to finite failure.
Proof: Straight forward from the definition of FF_i^d and that of a finitely failed derivation, by induction on d. QED

These theorems demonstrate the equivalence of the operational semantics with the least fixed-point semantics of distributed Horn clause programs presented in the earlier section.

4. DISCUSSION

In the way the operational understanding of refutations is described above, the distributed nature of execution is quite hidden. Refutation proceeds at one site, and when a branch leads to a node having some atom, that atom is sent to all sites for finding derivations, and the first successful substitution is used for further proof. A message has to be sent to all other sites to discontinue finding more instantiations. Further, among sibling nodes there needs to be communication to ensure compatibility of substitutions.

One way of describing this would be in the style of giving semantics in the way traditionally followed in distributed computing: for example, the linear history semantics [Francez et.al.84] for communicating sequential processes [Hoare 78]. A similar scheme is described in [Ramanujam 87] and will be included in a more detailed version of this paper: where a set of histories is associated with each site and global histories are built using these. Further, a mapping is set up between refutation and histories.

As hinted at in the paragraph above, sibling nodes need to 'synchronize' their instantiation of shared variables to ensure compatibility. While leaving the entire detail for the level of implementation gives us a clear semantics, such an approach is of no use if we wish to study traditional synchronization problems of distributed computing using logic programs as specifications. While we have concentrated on distributedness, for synchronization, the works of [Falaschi et.al. 84] and [Pereira and Nasr 84] are far more suitable, where the subject is studied axiomatically. Similarly, axiomatizing essential ideas for distributedness can be done giving a concept of concurrent deductions in the general setting of sentences in a logical language and their models (as mentioned in Section 1). This is done using an intuitionistic model logic where a program is a set of sentences in first order logic (rather than Horn clauses) in [Ramanujam 87] and it will be the subject of a different paper.

Parallelism in logic program execution has been extensively studied, by [Conery and Kibler 85] who use dataflow graphs, using pipelining as in [Lindstrom and Panangaden 84], by clausal annotation as in the languages PARLOG of [Clark and Gregory 85] and concurrent Prolog of [Shapiro 83]. However all these concentrate on the aspects of implementing parallelism and do not study distribution of clauses in a distributed system. The only attempt at such a study has been in [Warren et.al. 84], where an Ethernet style broadcast network is studied. However no semantic issues are studied in their paper.

An important advantage one may expect of distributing Horn clause programs is that this would enable us to control the order of evaluation of clauses for matching conclusions. That is, try clauses at site first, then neighbours connected to that site, and so on, in the order specified by the connectivity of the distributed system. However this leads to incompleteness since a matching clause at a site earlier in this order can lead to a nonterminating derivation, though there are refutations using clauses at other sites. Some fairness notions can be introduced to study these problems as done in [Ramanujam 87].

A crucial topic for further research is a notion of complexity. Can distributing logic programs improve efficiency, and if yes, what kind of distributions are necessary to maintain some bound on the lengths of derivations?

5. REFERENCES

Apt K.R. and M.H. van Emden, Contributions to the Theory of Logic Programming, Journal of the ACM, 29: 841-862, 1982.

Clark K.L. and S. Gregory, PARLOG: Parallel Programming in Logic, ACM Transactions on Programming Languages and Systems, 8 : 1-49, 1986.

Conery J.S. and D.F. Kibler, AND - Parallelism and Nondeterminism in Logic Programs, New Generation Computing, 3 : 43-70, 1985.

van Emden M.H. and R.A. Kowalski, The Semantics of Predicate Logic as a Programming Language, Journal of the ACM, 23 : 733-742, 1976.

Falaschi M, G. Levi and C.Palamidessi, Synchronization Logic : axiomatics and formal semantics of Generalized Horn Clauses, Information and Control, 60 : 36-69, 1984.

Fitting M, A. Kripke-Kleene semantics for logic programs, Journal of Logic Programming, 4 : 295-312, 1985.

Francez N, D. Lehmann and A. Pnueli, A linear history semantics for languages for distributed programming, Theoretical Computer Science, 32 : 25-46, 1984.

Hoare C.A.R. Communicating Sequential Processes, Communications of the ACM, 21 : 666-677, 1978.

Lassez J-L and M.J.Maher, Closures and Fairness in the Semantics of Programming Logic, Theoretical Computer Science, 29 : 167-184, 1984.

Lindstrom G. and P. Panangaden, Stream based execution of logic Programs, Proc. of the Intl. Symp. on Logic Programming, Atlantic City, 168-176, 1984.

Lloyd, J.W. Foundations of Logic Programming, Springer-Verlag, New York, 1984.

Pereira, L.M. and R. Nasr, Delta-Prolog: A Distributed Logic Programming Language, Proc. of the Intl. Conf. on Fifth Generation Systems, Tokyo, 263-290, 1984.

Ramanujam R. and R.K. Shyamasundar, Process Specification of Logic Programs, Proc. FST and TCS 4, Springer Lecture Notes in Computer Sciences 181, 31-43, 1984.

Ramanujam R. Theories and Models of Distributed Logic Programs, Ph.D. Thesis submitted to the University of Bombay, Tata Institute of Fundamental Research, Bombay, 1987.

Shapiro, E. A subset of Concurrent Prolog and its interpretor, Tech. Rep. TR-003, ICOT, Tokyo, 1983.

Warren D.S., M. Ahamad, S.K. Debray and L.V. Kale, Executing distributed Prolog Programs on a broadcast network, Proc. of the Intl. Symp. on Logic Programming, Atlantic City, 12-21, 1984.

The Calculus of Constructions : State of the Art

Gérard Huet

INRIA

France

Abstract

The Calculus of Constructions is a higher-order natural deduction logical framework which uses the analogy of propositions and types. Proofs of logical propositions may be manipulated explicitly as λ-expressions. Higher-order quantification allows powerful abstractions to be expressed naturally.

The present talk describes the current status of the inference system and its implementation. We document the design of an abstract machine for proof-checking and synthesizing constructions. This abstract machine, implemented in the CAML functional language, has been used to develop numerous mathematical proofs. Such an example proof is presented and discussed.

The paper concludes by discussing current experiments for extracting computer programs from proofs of validity of their specifications.

MODULES FOR RE-USE

David Gries
Computer Science Department
Cornell University, Ithaca, New York 14853, USA

1. Introduction

Generally speaking, a 'module' is an encapsulation mechanism: it is used to tie together a set of declarations of variables and operations on them. This is supposed to make it easier to write a large program in a structured, hierarchical fashion and to use program segments over and over again. Examples of such encapsulation mechanisms are the CLU cluster, the Alphard form, the Ada package, and the Modula-2 module. We have created yet another encapsulation mechanism in a language that is under development.

The language contains a facility for defining new types in terms of the signatures of functions and statements using variables of the new type. Once a type is defined, because the language is to be strongly typed a program using variables of the new type can be checked for syntax and type-correctness. However, the type definition defines only the use and not the implementation of the type, so the program cannot be yet be compiled.

Separately, one writes a module that describes a —typically partial— implementation of variables of the type and gives 'an implementation directive' to indicate which module should be used to implement each variable (a default can also be used to reduce the number of such directives). Most importantly, different variables of the same type can be implemented by different modules.

We believe that our new notion of encapsulation strongly supports the notion of programming at a high level of abstraction and then dealing with efficient implementations. We believe that our notion of encapsulation can lead to more effective use of modules, perhaps even to more wide-spread programming using 'off-the-shelf' parts.

For example, suppose one writes a program in terms of a set variable s that can contain a set of integers, using statements like $s := \{\ \}$, $s := s \cup \{e\}$, $s := s - MIN(s)$, and $\#s$ (which denotes the size of s. Having written the program, one could search a library for modules that implement a set of integers and choose the one that makes the program most efficient, depending on what operations were used. Then, with a simple implementation directive one could direct that s should be implemented as a bit string, a hash table of one sort or another, a heap, a balanced tree, a binary search tree, and so forth. One could envision having 50 different modules that implement a set variable, each being more efficient under certain circumstances.

Time does not permit a full enough written explanation of our module concept, and the reader will have to be satisfied with a single example. There are various subtle issues dealing with modules, such as the automatic insertion of a conversion of a value from one implementation representation to another when necessary, that cannot be dealt with here. One's notion of type changes slightly from the conventional one; for example, I now think of *stack* and *queue* not as types but simply as restricted implementations of the sequence. Further, it is quite interesting to see how this concept can be used to change totally the structure of a program —we leave this surprise to the lecture itself.

2. An Example of a Module.

In what follows, we only outline the parts of the module and leave many details unsaid. The example is taken from [0], where it is explained fully; the data structure implemented by the module is due to Knuth (see [1]). Further details of our notion of module can be found in [2].

Having read the first part of the module (only), to use it to implement a set variable x one would insert in the program the implementation directive **Implement** x **by** *OrderedHash*.

The interface of the module. The first part of the module is a heading together with a description of the operations it implements. This is the part the user of a module would read to determine whether it was suitable in his context. Typically, a narrative description would be attached to help the reader understand the context in which the writer of the module thought it would be useful.

The module heading and list of implemented operations are shown below. Note the use of a *pattern* <**exp** *t:int*> to denote any expression of type integer and a similar pattern <**state** *S*> to denote any statement. Also, some statements have *preconditions* that describe the context in which they are implemented.

module *OrderedHash* (*R*,*N* : *int*) **implements** *s* : *set*(1..*N*);

Implemented operations.

$s := \{\}$	(Takes time $O(R)$)
$\#s$	(Takes constant time)
<**exp** *t:int*> $\in s$	(Time depends on load factor)
$\{\#(s \cup \{t\}) \leq R\}$ $s := s \cup \{$<**exp** *t:int*>$\}$	(Time depends on load factor)
for ordered $v \in s$ **do** <**state** *S*>	(Takes between R and $2*R$ probes to extract the set elements in ascending order.)

Restriction: the assignment $s := \{\}$ must be executed before any reference to s is made.

The concrete variables that implement s. The implementation uses the method of the paper *Ordered hash tables* by Amble and Knuth (*The Computer Journal 17* (May 1974), 135-142). The important point here is not the implementaiton itself but the fact that in this section of the module are declared the variables that are used to implement the abstract variable *s*. In this case, there are two of them, *size* and *b*, and two constants *A* and *H*.

const A : *real* $= R \,/\, N$;
const $H =$ **function** (i: 1..N): *int*; $H := floor(A*(i-1))$;

var *size*: *int*; {number of elements in *s*}
var *b* : **array** 0..$R-1$ **of** *int*; {the hash table}

A *coupling invariant* is given to describe how abstract variable s is represented in the concrete variables. First, *size* is the size of s as well as the number of nonzero elements of b:

(0) **Invariant:** $size = \#s = \mathbf{N}(i: 0 \le i < R: b.i \ne 0)$

Second, the placement in b of values of s is described:

(1) **Invariant:** Let $t \in s$. Then $t = b.k$, where k is the first value in the sequence $H.t$, $H.t \ominus 1$, $H.t \ominus 2$, $H.t \ominus 3$, ..., satisfying $b.k \le t$. ($\ominus$ is subtraction modulo R).

Our coupling invariant is then (0) and (1). Two theorems concerning values in b can be derived from (0), which we do not prove here.

Theorem. The values of s that are $> b.0$ are in ascending order in b: $b.0 < b.i < b.j \Rightarrow i < j$.

Theorem. Suppose there exists a value in s that is less than $b.0$. Let $t = b.j$ (say) be the minimum such value. Then the segment $b(j..R-1)$ contains no zeros and contains, in ascending order, all the values of s that are less than $b.0$.

The concrete operations. The final part of the module gives the concrete operations on the concrete variables corresponding to the implemented abstract operations:

$s := \{\}$	$size := 0$; **for** $(i: 0 \le i < R: b.i := 0)$
$\#s$	*size*
<**exp** t:*int*> $\in s$	**var** $k := H.t$; **do** $b.k > t \rightarrow k := (k-1)$ **mod** R **od**; $b.k = t$
$\{\#(s \cup \{t\}) \le R\}$ $s := s \cup \{$<**exp** t:*int*>$\}$	(Implementation not given here)
for ordered $v \in s$ **do** <**state** $S.v$>	(Implementation not given here)

References

[0] Gries, D. *Programming pearls* column on *CACM 30*, 4 (April 1987), 284-290.

[1] Knuth, D.E. *Programming Pearls* column in *CACM 29* (May 1986), 364-369.

[2] Gries, D., and J. Prins. A new notion of encapsulation. *Proc. SIGPLAN 85 Symp. on Language Issues in Programming Environments*, Seattle, June 1985, 131-139.

Hierarchical Refinement Of A Z Specification

Dave Neilson

Programming Research Group
Oxford University
Keble Road
Oxford 0X1 3QD

Abstract

In this paper we present a rigorous refinement method that transforms a hierarchically-structured Z specification into a correct implementation, using a set of transformation rules based on the pre- and post-conditions inherent in the specification language. The method allows for the full testing of each hierarchy of the specification, facilitating the early detection of specification error, and provides for a clear indication of the effect of specification change on the implementation, simplifying the task of program maintenance. The paper is based on the specification and implementation of a text editor.

1 Introduction

One of the most important developments in computer science has been that of data abstraction, which has enabled the specification of computer systems without regard to implementation detail, and has resulted in the development of many formal specification languages.

A formal specification may be regarded as a contract between the client and implementor of a system, providing a vehicle for discussion between the two, and although it will certainly provide for a greater understanding on both sides, it should not be regarded as an end in itself: it must ultimately be judged on whether it results in the production of better quality software or in the more efficient production of software [8].

A crucial problem in constructing a formal specification is to ensure correspondence with an initial (usually informal) set of requirements. One solution that has been proposed is to write the specification in an executable language [5],[17] enabling the specification to be tested as it is written. The nature of such declarative formulations, however, tend to be make them more difficult to read than those written in a non-executable specification language (since the latter need not provide the algorithmic solution that the former, by definition, requires) and also compromises the data abstraction qualities of the specification process. Whilst it is desirable that a formal specification should contain a body of theory to help to build confidence that the specification does indeed describe the model that it is meant to, the support of a rapid prototyping facility would be of considerable use in demonstrating that the formal specification conforms to the informal requirements.

The process of specification should, of course, permit a rigorous determination that any proposed implementation is consistent with its specification, and we present and demonstrate a rigorous transformational refinement method, using a partial formal specification drawn from the specification and implementation of a text editor [13], written in **Z** and using the Schema Calculus [4],[10],[14],[16]. We use a set of refinement rules based on the pre- and post- conditions inherent in the specification language, which ensure that the implementation so-produced is indeed correct with respect to its specification.

The specification that we consider is constructed in a hierarchical manner, each hierarchy conforming to an abstract data type comprising an abstract data representation, an initialisation operation and a family of operations. Each abstract representation is embellished to provide the next-level hierarchy, to which existing operations are "promoted" (i.e. are re-specified on the embellished state, retaining their original characteristics) and on which new operations may be defined. This structure enables each hierarchy to isolate and treat a specific aspect of the model.

Of course the goals of an abstract specification are not usually compatible with the design requirements of its implementation: the former seeks to express the relationship between the before- and after-states of a system rather than defining the algorithms underlying those relationships which the latter requires, the refinement rules providing the bridge between the two. We can, however, use the problem-isolating structure of the specification to advantage in the refinement process.

We may view each specification hierarchy (i.e. each abstract data type) as a candidate for refinement. It will not be necessary to pursue refinement on every level, since several hierarchies can usually be comfortably treated in a single refinement step. Once a specification hierarchy has been selected for refinement, we produce a complete implementation of that abstract data type; the next selected hierarchy will produce its corresponding implementation, and so on. Thus the series of implementations will be embedded in each other in an analogous way to that in which each abstract data type of the specification is embedded in the next highest level. Each specification hierarchy may therefore be fully tested before the next refinement phase is entered, and although this may not be regarded as a rapid prototyping facility, it does enable alterations to the specification to be made at an early stage in the development process with obvious cost benefits, since higher-level hierarchies will not have been implemented and thus cannot require alteration (as would be the case if an implementation of the complete specification had been made).

Although this refinement method results in each operation being implemented several times (once on its own hierarchy, and then each time a promotion occurs), the promotion from one hierarchy to the next will often involve no-change (new) state components, with correspondingly little change in the code being necessary, or, at worst, the consideration of a new aspect of the system which will typically be achieved by the sequential composition of the previous-level operation with one meeting the new requirements. Of course the final structure of each operation's implementation may not be optimal, but this may be rectified, if required, by program transformation techniques.

It may seem unusual that the structure of the implementation should closely match that of the abstract specification. The vast majority of existing computer implementations have been constructed without the aid of an abstract specification, and the structure of new implementations (even when an abstract specification has been made) will usually reflect that of previous implementations. However we have no reason to believe that the the final code that we produce is any less efficient than that produced by more traditional means, and hope that the method will be used in different application areas to test this belief.

The stimulus for this project was provided by [18], which closely followed the structure of the specification on which it was based [15], the idea for the structure of the implementation arising from discussion between the two authors. Although the code was produced informally from the specification, it was felt that the implementor had a greater control over the project than would otherwise have been possible, and that the structure of the implementation did not compromise its efficiency.

We present the partial specification in Section 2, the refinement rules in Section 3, data refinement in Section 4, the refinement of the partial specification to code (Dijkstra's language of Guarded Commands [2]) in Section 5, and our conclusions in Section 6.

2 The Specification

We assume a knowledge of the specification language **Z**, although we give a brief informal explanation of the meaning of the more obscure symbols as they are introduced. A feature of the language is that specifications consist of a combination of formal text and natural language text, the latter enabling the reader not familiar with the mathematics to follow the specification. We use the convention that a vertical alignment of predicates implies their logical conjunction.

We present a partial specification of the text editor presented in [13], which uses many of the ideas presented in [12], which, in turn, was motivated and heavily influenced by [15]. Our initial hierarchy is the *Doc1* state, in which we use a pair of sequences to capture both the content of a document and the current position, and we specify the operations to initialize the editor and delete a character to the left of the current position. We extend this abstract representation to the *Doc2* state which includes an unbounded display of the document and incorporates a two-dimensional cursor position, and promote the two specified operations to this hierarchy.

2.1 The Doc1 Hierarchy

We assume the set of characters, *Char*, and represent the document as a pair of sequences, one corresponding to the part of the document preceding the cursor, *Left*, and the other to that following the cursor, *Right*:

$$[Char]$$

$$Doc1 \mathrel{\widehat{=}} Left, Right : \mathrm{seq}\ Char$$

where "$\widehat{=}$" denotes syntactic equivalence. We use the symbol "Δ" to represent a before- and after-state on which operations are defined (the after-state components being dashed), and the symbol "Ξ" to represent a no-change Δ state:

$$\Delta Doc1 \mathrel{\widehat{=}} Doc1 \wedge Doc1'$$

$$\Xi Doc1 \mathrel{\widehat{=}} \Delta Doc1 \mid Left', Right' = Left, Right$$

The former is an example of schema conjunction, in which declarations are merged and predicate parts conjoined, and the latter shows a schema presented in horizontal form with the vertical bar separating the signature from the predicate.

Initially both sequences are empty:

$$Init_{Doc1} \mathrel{\widehat{=}} Doc1 \mid Left = Right = [\,]$$

We now specify the operation to delete a character to the left, in which the right sequence does not change and the left sequence has its last element removed. The operation, therefore, has the pre-condition that the left sequence must not be empty:

$$
\begin{array}{|l}
\textit{Del} \\
\hline
\Delta \textit{Doc1} \\
\hline
\textit{Left} \neq [\,] \\
\textit{Left}' = \mathsf{front}\ \textit{Left} \\
\textit{Right}' = \textit{Right} \\
\hline
\end{array}
$$

This is an example of a schema presented in horizontal form; $\Delta Doc1$ is "included" in the schema *Del* (the declarations of an included schema being merged with those of the defining schema, the predicate parts of the two being conjoined), and in this form the horizontal bar separates the signature and predicate parts.

We include a report (assumed to belong to the set *Report*) with each operation, indicating whether or not the operation has been successful, and define:

$$[\textit{Report}]$$

$$\textit{Success} \mathrel{\widehat{=}} \textit{rep}! : \textit{Report} \mid \textit{rep}! = \text{“OK”}$$

the "!" indicating that the value of *rep* is output by the operation.

In order to totalize the operation we define an error schema that deals with the case when the left sequence is empty, leaving the document unchanged and issuing an appropriate report message:

$$
\begin{array}{|l}
\textit{ErrotAtTop} \\
\hline
\Xi \textit{Doc1} \\
\textit{rep}! : \textit{Report} \\
\hline
\textit{Left} = [\,] \\
\textit{rep}! = \text{“At top of document”} \\
\hline
\end{array}
$$

We now specify the two total operations on the *Doc1* state by the use of logical conjunction and disjunction (note that *any* before-state for the initialization operation will suffice and so the operation will always succeed):

$$
\begin{array}{lcl}
\textit{Initialize}_{\textit{Doc1}} & \widehat{=} & \Delta \textit{Doc1} \wedge \textit{Init}_{\textit{Doc1}}{}' \wedge \textit{Success} \\
\textit{Delete}_{\textit{Doc1}} & \widehat{=} & (\textit{Del} \wedge \textit{Success}) \vee \textit{ErrorAtTop}
\end{array}
$$

where $\textit{Init}_{\textit{Doc1}}{}'$ is the same as $\textit{Init}_{\textit{Doc1}}$, but with all unprimed variables replaced with primed variables having the same name.

It is necessary to demonstrate the "plausibility" of the delete operation [1] - i.e. we assume that the state invariants hold before the operation commences and must demonstrate that they still hold upon termination. In this case the state invariant is provided by the signatures of the variables, which, clearly, will be maintained by the operation.

The operations to right delete a character, left and right delete a word or line, left and right move by a character, word or line, move to the top or bottom of the document, and insert a character may be similarly specified on the *Doc1* state.

2.2 The Doc2 Hierarchy

We extend the model to incorporate a display, and first define a *Line* as a sequence of characters not containing the newline character; a document may then be defined as a non-empty sequence of *Line* (and so an empty document, [[]], is the unit sequence comprising the empty sequence):

$$
\begin{array}{lcl}
nl & : & Char \\
Line & : & seq\ (Char - \{nl\}) \\
DocLines & : & seq\ Line - \ []
\end{array}
$$

We now characterise the unbounded display of the editor by a sequence of lines (displayed one above the other and aligned at their left hand end, with the first displayed at the top, the next immediately below it, and so on), together with a pair of numbers to model the cursor position (the top left hand position corresponding to the value $(0,0)$). Although the current position is defined as being between characters, the cursor will be displayed immediately to the right of that position. In order to ensure that the cursor can not move "outside" the document, the vertical co-ordinate must be less than the length of the sequence of lines, and the horizontal co-ordinate must not exceed the length of the $(Y+1)$th line of the sequence:

UnbDisplay

$$
\begin{array}{l}
DocLines : seq\ Line - \ [] \\
DocX, DocY : \mathbf{N} \\
\hline
DocY < |\ DocLines\ | \\
DocX \leq |\ DocLines\ (DocY + 1)\ |
\end{array}
$$

N is the set of non-negative integers, and $|\ a\ |$, for example, denotes the length of the sequence a.

In order to provide the connection between a sequence of lines of the *Doc2* model and a sequence of characters of the *Doc1* model we define a one-to-one function (FlattenLines) that converts the former into the latter by inserting the unit newline sequence between adjacent members of the line sequence, and then concatenating the resulting sequence:

$$
\begin{array}{l}
\mathsf{FL} : seq\ Line - \ [] \longrightarrow seq\ Char \\
\hline
\forall\ l : Line\ ;\ L_1, L_2 : seq\ Line \bullet \\
\quad \mathsf{FL}\ [l] = l \\
\quad \mathsf{FL}\ (L_1 \frown L_2) = \mathsf{FL}\ L_1 \frown [nl] \frown \mathsf{FL}\ L_2
\end{array}
$$

" $\frown$ " is the sequence concatenation operator. We now conjoin the *Doc1* and *UnbDisplay* states to obtain the *Doc2* state, cementing their relationship through an invariant:

$$
\begin{array}{|l}
\multicolumn{1}{l}{\textit{Doc2}} \\
\hline
\textit{Doc1} \\
\textit{UnbDisplay} \\
\hline
\textit{Left} \frown \textit{Right} = \mathsf{FL}\ \textit{DocLines} \\
\textit{DocY} = |\, \textit{Left} \rhd \{nl\} \,| \\
\textit{DocX} = |\, \textit{Left} \,| - \textit{StartIn} \\
\text{where} \\
\quad \textit{StartIn} \leq |\, \textit{Left} \,| \\
\quad \textit{StartIn} \neq 0 \Rightarrow \textit{Left}\ \textit{StartIn} = nl \\
\quad nl \notin \mathsf{rng}\ (\textit{Left}\ \mathbf{after}\ \textit{StartIn}) \\
\hline
\end{array}
$$

"$\rhd$" is the range restrict operator, and $[a, b, c, d]$ **after** *3*, for example, is $[d]$. *DocY* is equal to the number of newline characters in *Left*; if *DocY* is non-zero, *DocX* is equal to the number of characters in *Left* following its last newline character (pointed to by *StartIn*), and if *DocY* is zero, *DocX* is equal to the length of *Left* (in which case *StartIn* will be zero).

We promote the *Doc1* operations to the *Doc2* state by logically conjoining both with a before- and after-*Doc2* state:

$$
\begin{array}{lcll}
\textit{Initialize}_{\textit{Doc2}} & \widehat{=} & \textit{Initialize}_{\textit{Doc1}} & \wedge\ \Delta \textit{Doc2} \\
\textit{Delete}_{\textit{Doc2}} & \widehat{=} & \textit{Delete}_{\textit{Doc1}} & \wedge\ \Delta \textit{Doc2}
\end{array}
$$

Note that the *Doc2* invariant provided by the promotion schemas automatically ensures the correct update of the *UnbDisplay* components, and the plausibility of the delete operation follows.

3 Operational Refinement Rules

We give a set of refinement rules which is sufficient to implement the partial specification of Section 2, allowing us to proceed by either transforming the specification into an implementable form by repeated application of the rules, or, by using our intuition, produce what we feel is a refinement and prove it is so by appealing to the rules.

An operation B *refines* an operation A if it satisfies two conditions: the *Domain* condition, which requires that B must be applicable when A is (although B may be applicable for further states as well), and the *Safety* condition, which requires that when A is applicable the results produced by B must imply those produced by A (although B may do more than A). In other words, we may weaken the pre-condition and make the operation more deterministic. These requirements have been presented in [9]:

Definition [$\sqsubseteq$ 3.1]

$A \sqsubseteq B$

iff

$\mathsf{Pre}[A] \Rightarrow \mathsf{Pre}[B]$ *Domain*

$\mathsf{Pre}[A] \wedge B \Rightarrow A$ *Safety*

■

A corollary is that a total operation may be refined only by another total operation that does at least as much:

Corollary [$\sqsubseteq$ 3.2]

$\mathsf{Pre}[A]$

$\vdash$

$A \sqsubseteq B$

iff

$\mathsf{Pre}[B]$ *Domain*

$B \Rightarrow A$ *Safety*

■

The ordering is transitive, enabling a stepwise approach to refinement to be adopted:

Rule [$\sqsubseteq$ 3.3]

$(A \sqsubseteq B) \wedge (B \sqsubseteq C)$

$\vdash$

$A \sqsubseteq C$

■

The ordering is reflexive (by definition, $A \triangleq B$ if they are applicable for exactly the same set of states, and the results produced by one imply, and are implied by, the results produced by the other):

Rule [$\sqsubseteq$ 3.4]

$(A \sqsubseteq B) \wedge (B \sqsubseteq A)$

$\vdash$

$A \triangleq B$

■

Note that since every operation trivially refines itself, [$\sqsubseteq$ 3.3] and [$\sqsubseteq$ 3.4] imply that "$\sqsubseteq$" is a partial order.

We give a result which will enable the addition of predicates to the post-condition:

Rule [$\sqsubseteq$ 3.5]

$\mathsf{Pre}[A] \Rightarrow \mathsf{Pre}[B]$

$\vdash$

$A \sqsubseteq A \wedge B$

■

We give a result which we will use when refining an operation which is promoted from one abstract state to another by the use of logical conjunction. Suppose we wish to promote an operation A by logically conjoining it with D, and suppose further that a refinement, B, of A already exists. Then if B is refined to C, and C also refines the promotion schema D, then C will refine the promoted operation $(A \wedge D)$:

Rule [$\sqsubseteq$ 3.6]

$$A \sqsubseteq B$$
$$B \sqsubseteq C$$
$$D \sqsubseteq C$$
$$\vdash$$
$$A \wedge D \sqsubseteq C$$

■

The next rule will enable an operation to be split into a disjunction of smaller operations, typically dictated by a composite pre-condition:

Rule [$\sqsubseteq$ 3.7]

$$\vdash$$
$$A \sqsubseteq \bigvee_{i\,:\,1..n}(B_i)$$

iff

$\mathsf{Pre}[A] \Rightarrow \bigvee_{i\,:\,1..n}(\mathsf{Pre}[B_i])$ *Domain*

$\forall\, i : 1..n \bullet (\mathsf{Pre}[A] \wedge B_i \Rightarrow A)$ *Safety*

■

Having refined an operation into a disjunction of operations, we may wish to preserve the structure so-gained and pursue refinement on each disjunction:

Rule [$\sqsubseteq$ 3.8]

$$\forall\, i : 1..n \bullet A_i \sqsubseteq B_i$$
$$\forall\, i,j : 1..n \mid i \neq j \bullet \neg(\mathsf{Pre}[A_i] \wedge \mathsf{Pre}[B_j])$$
$$\vdash$$
$$\bigvee_{i\,:\,1..n}(A_i) \sqsubseteq \bigvee_{i\,:\,1..n}(B_i)$$

■

We now consider the decomposition of a total operation A into two operations B and C, such that their sequential composition will refine A: each will, in general, be a simpler operation than A, and will themselves be candidates for such refinement, enabling an operation to be refined into the sequential composition of several simpler operations:

Rule [$\sqsubseteq$ 3.9]

$$\mathsf{Pre}[A]$$
$$\vdash$$
$$A \sqsubseteq (B \mathbin{;} C)$$

iff

$\mathsf{Pre}[B]$ *Domain1*

$\mathsf{Post}[B][\_/\_'] \Rightarrow \mathsf{Pre}[C]$ *Domain2*

$(B \mathbin{;} C) \Rightarrow A$ *Safety*

■

We use $\mathsf{Post}[B][\_/\_']$ to denote the schema $\mathsf{Post}[B]$ (denoting all possible output states from B), whose dashed variables have been renamed to undashed variables (to coincide with the pre-condition variables of C).

Having shown how an operation may be refined into a sequential composition of other operations, we now give a result for the refinement of such a sequential composition:

Rule [$\sqsubseteq$ 3.10]

$$
\begin{array}{l}
\quad A \sqsubseteq B \\
\quad C \sqsubseteq D \\
\quad \mathsf{Post}[A][\_/\_'] \;\Rightarrow\; \mathsf{Pre}[C] \\
\vdash \\
\quad (A \,;\, C) \sqsubseteq (B \,;\, D)
\end{array}
$$

■

and when C is total:

Corollary [$\sqsubseteq$ 3.11]

$$
\begin{array}{l}
\quad A \sqsubseteq B \\
\quad C \sqsubseteq D \\
\quad \mathsf{Pre}[C] \\
\vdash \\
\quad (A \,;\, C) \sqsubseteq (B \,;\, D)
\end{array}
$$

■

Refinement To The Alternative Construct

We now consider refinement to the the "**if** ... **fi**" program construct [2], and may informally interpret the statement:

$$\textbf{if } (G_1 \longrightarrow B_1) \,\square\, (G_2 \longrightarrow B_2) \,\square\, \cdots \,\square\, (G_n \longrightarrow B_n) \textbf{ fi}$$

as " if guard G_i is true carry out B_i, and if not then if guard G_j is true carry out B_j, and if not ...". Clearly the construct will be non-deterministic if more than one of the guards holds, and if none hold (equivalent to a *FALSE* pre-condition) then we have the *Abort* operation. We have:

Rule [$\sqsubseteq$ 3.12]

$$
\begin{array}{lr}
\vdash & \\
\quad A \sqsubseteq \textbf{if } (G_1 \longrightarrow B_1) \,\square\, (G_2 \longrightarrow B_2) \,\square\, \cdots \,\square\, (G_n \longrightarrow B_n) \textbf{ fi} & \\
\qquad\qquad\qquad \textit{iff} & \\
\quad \mathsf{Pre}[A] \;\Rightarrow\; \bigvee_{i\,:\,1..n} (G_i) & \textit{Domain1} \\
\quad \forall\, i : 1..n \bullet (\mathsf{Pre}[A] \wedge G_i \;\Rightarrow\; \mathsf{Pre}[B_i]) & \textit{Domain2} \\
\quad \forall\, i : 1..n \bullet (\mathsf{Pre}[A] \wedge G_i \wedge B_i \;\Rightarrow\; A) & \textit{Safety}
\end{array}
$$

■

We may informally represent [$\sqsubseteq$ 3.12] by the following checklist, echoing the results in [3]:

When the pre-condition for A is satisfied:

- at least one of the guards must be true
- each body must be applicable when its guard holds
- the results produced by each body (when its guard is true) must imply those results produced by A

Refinement To The Iterative Construct

Finally we consider refinement to the "**do** ... **od**" construct [2]:

$$\textbf{do}\ (G \longrightarrow B)\ \textbf{od}$$

which we may informally interpret as "if guard G holds carry out B and then start the construct again; if G does not hold then finish".

An important concept in the proof of loop correctness is that of an invariant: a set of predicates which hold before the loop activates, after each iteration of the loop, and after the loop has terminated. We denote the invariant by I. It will be defined on *State*, on which A is assumed to be defined, and will usually employ the (fixed) initial values of the state variables. Since we wish to accomplish A, and I' must hold after termination of the loop, I must form part of A's pre-condition.

Another important consideration concerning loops is that of demonstrating *total* correctness - i.e. showing that the loop does terminate after a finite number of iterations. In order to do this we introduce a *bound* function, Bnd, which associates each state (satisfying A's pre-condition) with a natural number, and we require each iteration of the loop to reduce its value. We have:

Rule [$\sqsubseteq$ 3.13]

$$\mathsf{Pre}[A] \mathrel{\widehat{=}} \mathsf{Pre}[A] \land I$$

$$\mathsf{Bnd} : [\, State \mid \mathsf{Pre}[A]\,] \longrightarrow \mathbb{N}$$

$\vdash$

$$A \sqsubseteq \textbf{do}\ (G \longrightarrow B)\ \textbf{od}$$

iff

$\mathsf{Pre}[A] \land I \land G \Rightarrow \mathsf{Pre}[B]$	*Domain*
$\mathsf{Pre}[A] \land I \land G \land B \Rightarrow I'$	*Safety1*
$\mathsf{Pre}[A] \land I' \land \neg G' \Rightarrow A$	*Safety2*
$\mathsf{Pre}[A] \land I \land G \land B \Rightarrow \mathsf{Bnd}\,(State') < \mathsf{Bnd}\,(State)$	*Bound*

■

We may informally interpret [$\sqsubseteq$ 3.13] by the following checklist (similar to that given in [3]):

- identify an invariant (part of A's pre-condition)
- identify a non-negative bound function (on A's state)

and when the pre-condition for A (and, hence, the invariant) is satisfied:

- the body of the loop must be applicable when its guard holds

- each iteration of the loop must preserve the invariant
- when the guard no longer holds, A must be satisfied
- each iteration of the loop must decrease the bound function

4 Data Refinement On A Specification Hierarchy

Once an abstract hierarchy has been selected for refinement, the first step is to replace the abstract state by a concrete one that may be implemented using an existing programming language. We first consider the basis on which this replacement may proceed, and then derive results enabling data refinement to be applied to each operation of the specification hierarchy, producing the weakest concrete operation from each abstract specification [7]. This represents the starting point for the refinement of each operation, to which the refinement results of Section 3 may then be applied.

4.1 Data Refinement Of An Abstract State

We assume a *fully abstract* state, by which we mean that each abstract representation is unique in the sense that for any two states there exist a sequence of operations (defined on the abstract state) which enable the two states to be distinguished (in [9] this is referred to as "freedom from implementation bias"). We further assume the existence of the abstract object AS, and abs_inv, the invariant on the state, together with a design decision producing the corresponding concrete (implementable) object CS with its invariant conc_inv:

$$AbsState \;\widehat{=}\; AS \mid \mathsf{abs\_inv}\ AS$$
$$ConcState \;\widehat{=}\; CS \mid \mathsf{conc\_inv}\ CS$$

We require that each concrete configuration of the concrete state has an abstract counterpart, and a fully abstract representation means that each such abstract state will be unique. Thus it is necessary to demonstrate the existence of a concrete-to-abstract total function extract (which extracts the abstraction from the implementation details):

$$\mathsf{extract} : ConcState \longrightarrow AbsState$$

We may conveniently illustrate extract through the schema:

$$Rel \;\widehat{=}\; AbsState \wedge ConcState \mid AS = \mathsf{extract}\ CS$$

4.2 The Weakest Concrete Operation

We consider the implementation of the weakest concrete operation, *COP*, for the abstract operation *AOP*. The latter links a before-abstract state, *AbsState*, with an after-abstract state, *AbsState'*, and we assume a design decision in which *AbsState* and *AbsState'* correspond to *ConcState* and *ConcState'*; this may be represented in the following commuting diagram [6],[7]:

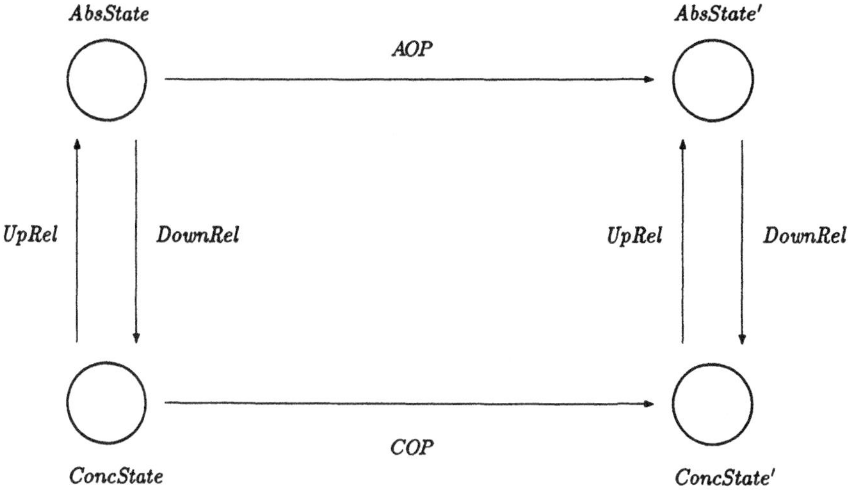

We label the operation linking the concrete states *COP*, and *UpRel* and *DownRel* are defined:

$$UpRel \mathrel{\widehat{=}} Rel[AbsState'/\ AbsState]$$
$$DownRel \mathrel{\widehat{=}} Rel[ConcState'/\ ConcState]$$

where "/" is the renaming operator: *S*[*new*/ *old*], for example, indicating that the component *old* is renamed to *new* in the signature, as is every free use of *old* within the predicate of *S*. Both schemas are similar to the schema *Rel*, except that the *direction* of the relationship is recognized, the former being concrete-to-abstract (and so *AbsState'* replaces *AbsState*), and the latter abstract-to-concrete (*ConcState'* replacing *ConcState*).

AbsState and *AbsState'* will be unique configurations of the abstract state, but it is possible that the corresponding concrete states will each be satisfied by more than one concrete configuration; in fact these configurations will each form an equivalence class (each member, of course, corresponding to the same abstract state), and the class may be calculated by computing:

$$ConcRel \mathrel{\widehat{=}} UpRel \ ⨟ \ DownRel$$

where " ⨟ " denotes schema composition, in which the output variables from the first are taken as the input variables to the second, for those variables sharing the same name. We return to this schema at the end of this section. If we consider the composition in reverse order, and compute:

$$AbsRel \mathrel{\widehat{=}} DownRel \ ⨟ \ UpRel$$

we should obtain the identity operation on the abstract state, indicating an *adequate* representation: in fact this will not always be the case (for example the limited storage capacity of a computer system will not normally be detailed in an abstract specification, but *AbsRel* will reflect such limited resources and will, in fact, define the *subset* of the abstraction that can be implemented). We return to this in Section 5. We may now calculate the weakest specification for *COP* by computing:

$$UpRel \; ⨾ \; AOP \; ⨾ \; DownRel$$

which simplifies to:

$$AOP[(\mathsf{extract}\ CS), (\mathsf{extract}\ CS') / AS, AS']$$

i.e. it is the same as *AOP*, but with ($\mathsf{extract}\ CS$) and ($\mathsf{extract}\ CS'$) replacing AS and AS' respectively, and for convenience we denote it by *AOPC*. Thus the weakest concrete operation may be derived from its abstract specification by replacing its abstract components by its concrete counterparts, obtained through the schema *Rel*. We have the result:

Rule [$\sqsubseteq$ 4.1]

Rel

$\vdash$

$AOP \ \sqsubseteq \ AOPC$

■

We now return to the schema defining the concrete equivalence class, *ConcRel*; efficiency considerations (for example) may dictate that a particular operation is best effected on a specific configuration of the concrete state. We assume the predicate Specific (defining the configuration required) and define:

$$Reconfigure\_Specific \ \widehat{=} \ ConcRel \mid \mathsf{Specific}\ CS'$$
$$AOPC\_Specific \ \widehat{=} \ AOPC \mid \mathsf{Specific}\ CS$$

We have the following result:

Rule [$\sqsubseteq$ 4.2]

$\vdash$

$AOPC \ \sqsubseteq \ Reconfigure\_Specific \ ⨾ \ AOPC\_Specific$

■

[$\sqsubseteq$ 3.3] and the above two results give:

Rule [$\sqsubseteq$ 4.3]

Rel

$\vdash$

$AOP \ \sqsubseteq \ Reconfigure\_Specific \ ⨾ \ AOPC\_Specific$

■

and [$\sqsubseteq$ 3.9] will now enable refinement to be conducted on the desired configuration.

Proofs of these results and those given in Section 3 may be found in [13].

5 Refinement Of The Specification

We first consider data refinement on the *Doc1* state, and refine two operations specified, and then data refinement on *Doc2*, indicating how both operation implementations may be promoted to this state.

5.1 Data Refinement On The Doc1 State

The abstract state *Doc1* comprises the two components *Left* and *Right*, and our representation is a character array, *Arr* (assumed to have a maximum length of *Max*), together with the pointers *LP* (*L*eft *P*ointer), *RP* (*R*ight *P*ointer), and *CP* (*C*ursor *P*ointer):

$$Max : \mathbb{N}$$

$$CharArray \mathrel{\widehat{=}} Arr : 1 \,..\, Max \longrightarrow Char$$

$$Pointers \mathrel{\widehat{=}} LP, RP, CP : 0 \,..\, Max \mid LP \leq RP$$

$$ConcDoc1 \mathrel{\widehat{=}} CharArray \wedge Pointers$$

The contents of the array from *1* to *LP* and from $(RP + 1)$ to *Max* represent the concatenation of the left and right character sequences, with *CP* providing the cursor position. Cursor-movement operations may therefore be accomplished by a change of *CP* (since the contents of the array will not change), thus avoiding "array shuffling".

We also consider the special case of representing the abstract document, in which the array contents from *1* to *LP* correspond to the left character sequence (and thus *CP* will be equal to *LP*), and the array contents from $(RP + 1)$ to *Max* correspond to the right character sequence. This *Standard* configuration will be used for the refinement of operations that change the content of the document; for example the left deletion of characters will commence at array position *LP*, with *LP* and *CP* being decremented accordingly.

Thus the content of the document is represented by the part of the array from *1* to *LP* and $(RP + 1)$ to *Max*, with *CP* equal to the length of the left character sequence, and for ease of reference, we define

$$ArrCont \mathrel{\widehat{=}} Arr \text{ for } LP \frown Arr \text{ after } RP$$

and the schema which relates the concrete representation to the abstract state (illustrating the existence of the total function $\mathsf{extract}_{Doc1}$):

```
┌─ Rel_Doc1 ──────────────────────────
│ Doc1
│ ConcDoc1
├──────────────
│ Left = ArrCont for CP
│ Right = ArrCont after CP
└─────────────────────────────────────
```

where $[a, b, c, d]$ for *3*, for example, is $[a, b, c]$. We have the special case:

$$\begin{array}{|l}
\hline
\multicolumn{1}{l}{Rel_{Doc1}_Standard} \\
\hline
Doc1 \\
ConcDoc1_Standard \\
\hline
Left = Arr \text{ for } LP \\
Right = Arr \text{ after } RP \\
\hline
\end{array}$$

AbsRel simplifies to produce:

$$AbsRel \mathrel{\widehat{=}} \Xi Doc1 \mid |Left \frown Right| \leq Max$$

indicating that we are not able to effect a full implementation of the abstraction, since it defines the subset of the abstraction that we are able to implement. Clearly, if the resources were unlimited, we would be able to fully implement *Doc1*, since, as *Max* increases, the predicate part of *AbsRel*, in the limit, becomes *TRUE*, and so *AbsRel* becomes $\Xi Doc1$, the identity operation on the state. We refer to this implementation as an ∞-refinement, and the interested reader is referred to [13] for a fuller treatment of the topic.

Further, we have, after simplification:

$$\begin{array}{|l}
\hline
\multicolumn{1}{l}{ConcRel_{Doc1}} \\
\hline
\Delta ConcDoc1 \\
\hline
ArrCont' = ArrCont \\
CP' = CP \\
\hline
\end{array}$$

and may informally interpret this equivalence class as those concrete states whose cursor pointers are the same, and whose arrays agree once the array positions not being used have been filtered out; thus *LP* and *RP* will not be uniquely defined, although their numerical difference must be equal to the difference between *Max* and the length of *ArrCont* for each member of the equivalence class.

5.1.1 Content-Changing Operations And The "Standard" State

Operations which change the document's content will be refined on a configuration in which the array from *1* to *LP* coincides with *Left*, and from $(RP + 1)$ to *Max* coincides with *Right*. We refer to this as the *Standard* configuration of the representation:

$$ConcDoc1\_Standard \mathrel{\widehat{=}} ConcDoc1 \mid LP = CP$$
$$Reconfigure_{Doc1}\_Standard \mathrel{\widehat{=}} ConcRel_{Doc1} \wedge ConcDoc1\_Standard'$$

Thus [$\sqsubseteq$ 4.3] enables the refinement of a content-changing operation to proceed on the *Standard* state, when pre-sequentially composed with this reconfigure operation. For such operations we maintain the *Standard* configuration after termination (and so when obtaining the weakest concrete operation, we may replace the before- and after-abstract components by their *Standard* concrete counterparts). In so doing, the refinement still holds, since we are making the operation more deterministic [$\sqsubseteq$ 3.1]. Finally [$\sqsubseteq$ 3.11] will enable the separate refinements of the reconfigure and content-changing operations (since the latter will be total).

Note that the reconfigure operation is itself a refinement of the schema defining the concrete equivalence class, *ConcRel*, since we are just selecting another member of that class on which to conduct refinement, and although we do not pursue the refinement here, we obtain the code:

do
| $(LP > CP) \longrightarrow Arr\ RP := Arr\ LP\ ;\ RP, LP := (RP - 1), (LP - 1)$
od ;
do
| $(LP < CP) \longrightarrow RP, LP := (RP + 1), (LP + 1)\ ;\ Arr\ LP := Arr\ RP$
od

5.1.2 Refinement Of "Initialize"

We have the abstract specification:

$$Initialize_{Doc1} \mathrel{\widehat=} \Delta Doc1 \wedge Init_{Doc1}' \wedge Success$$

which expands to:

Initialize$_{Doc1}$
$\Delta Doc1$
$rep! : Report$

$Left' = Right' = [\,]$
$rep! = \text{"OK"}$

The weakest concrete operation is obtained by replacing the abstract components by their concrete counterparts defined by Rel_{Doc1} [$\sqsubseteq$ 4.1]:

Initialize$_{Doc1}$C
$\Delta ConcDoc1$
$rep! : Report$

$ArrCont'\ \text{for}\ CP' = ArrCont'\ \text{after}\ CP' = [\,]$
$rep! = \text{"OK"}$

The predicate part simplifies to:

$$\left[\begin{array}{l} LP' = CP' = 0 \\ RP' = Max \\ rep! = \text{"OK"} \end{array}\right.$$

to give the code:

$rep! : Report$;

$LP, CP, RP, rep! := 0, 0, Max,$ "OK"

5.1.3 Refinement Of "Delete"

We have the abstract specification:

$$Delete_{Doc1} \mathrel{\widehat{=}} (Del \wedge Success) \vee ErrorAtTop$$

which we expand to:

```
Delete_Doc1 ______________________________
| ΔDoc1
| rep! : Report
|______________________
| Right' = Right
|     Left ≠ []
|     Left' = front Left
|     rep! = "OK"
| ∨
|     Left' = Left = []
|     rep! = "At top of document"
|__________________________________________
```

We obtain the weakest *Standard* concrete operation by replacing the abstract components by their concrete counterparts, defined by Rel_{Doc1}*_Standard* [$\sqsubseteq$ 4.3]:

```
Delete_Doc1 C_Standard ______________________________
| ΔConcDoc1_Standard
| rep! : Report
|______________________
| Arr' after RP' = Arr after RP
|     Arr for LP ≠ []
|     Arr' for LP' = front (Arr for LP)
|     rep! = "OK"
| ∨
|     Arr' for LP' = Arr for LP = []
|     rep! = "At top of document"
|_____________________________________________________
```

The predicate part simplifies to give:

$$\left[\begin{array}{l} RP' = RP \\ Arr' \text{ after } RP = Arr \text{ after } RP \\ \quad\quad LP \neq 0 \\ \quad\quad LP' = LP - 1 \\ \quad\quad Arr' \text{ for } LP - 1 = Arr \text{ for } LP - 1 \\ \quad\quad rep! = \text{"OK"} \\ \vee \\ \quad\quad LP' = LP = 0 \\ \quad\quad Arr' \text{ for } LP = Arr \text{ for } LP \\ \quad\quad rep! = \text{"At top of document"} \end{array}\right.$$

We use [$\sqsubseteq$ 3.8] to refine each disjunction, and [$\sqsubseteq$ 3.1] to keep the entire array unchanged in both cases, and so we have the refinement:

$$\left[\begin{array}{l} Arr' = Arr \\ RP' = RP \\ \quad\quad LP \neq 0 \\ \quad\quad LP' = LP - 1 \\ \quad\quad rep! = \text{"OK"} \\ \vee \\ \quad\quad LP' = LP = 0 \\ \quad\quad rep! = \text{"At top of document"} \end{array}\right.$$

Since we are refining on the *Standard* state, [$\sqsubseteq$ 4.3] suggests that we first perform the reconfigure operation. Our task is now completed by using [$\sqsubseteq$ 3.12] to produce the **if** construct, and appealing to [$\sqsubseteq$ 3.3] which allows for stepwise refinement, to give as the code for $Delete_{Doc1}$:

$rep! : Report$;

$Reconfigure_{Doc1}\text{-}Standard$;

$\{ LP, RP, CP, Arr = LP_o, RP_o, CP_o, Arr_o \}$

$\{ LP = CP = CP_o \}$

if

$|\ (LP \neq 0) \longrightarrow LP, CP, rep! := (LP - 1), (LP - 1), \text{"OK"}$

$\Box$

$|\ (LP = 0) \longrightarrow rep! := \text{"At top of document"}$

fi

$\{ LP, RP, Arr = CP, RP_o, Arr_o \}$

Note that the components of *ConcDoc1* constitute the global variables of the implementation, and so do not need to be declared. In an **{** *assertion* **}** we distinguish initial values by a subscripted "*0*".

5.2 Refinement On The Doc2 State

We embellish the abstract *Doc1* state with the components *DocLines, DocX,* and *DocY*, together with an invariant relationship that renders all of these components redundant (since each be calculated from the *Doc1* components). We include them in the specification for reasons of clarity and conciseness, but are at liberty to exclude such redundant components from the design, since we may build a complete model without them. However, efficiency considerations may dictate that such items are best included in the implementation (thereby, for example, obviating the need for the continual re-calculation of a particular value). These considerations may depend not only on the hierarchies up to the current level under consideration, but also on higher levels (not yet considered), and we note that a redundant component included in the design at a particular stage in the development, and subsequently found not to be required, may be removed from the implementation by methods of program transformation; of course, the alternative solution would be to redo the derivation without introducing the component.

Our design decision for *Doc2* comprises *ConcDoc1* logically conjoined with a concrete representation of the abstract co-ordinates *DocX* and *DocY*:

$$\begin{array}{lcl} \mathit{Coordinates} & \widehat{=} & X, Y : 0 \mathinner{..} \mathit{Max} \\ \mathit{ConcDoc2} & \widehat{=} & \mathit{ConcDoc1} \land \mathit{Coordinates} \end{array}$$

with special case:

$$\mathit{ConcDoc2\_Standard} \mathrel{\widehat{=}} \mathit{ConcDoc2} \mid \mathit{LP} = \mathit{CP}$$

We define the schema relating the abstract components to their concrete counterparts (and illustrating the existence of the $\mathsf{extract}_{Doc2}$ function):

$$\begin{array}{|l} \mathit{Rel}_{Doc2} \\ \hline \mathit{Doc2} \\ \mathit{ConcDoc2} \\ \mathit{Rel}_{Doc1} \\ \hline \mathit{DocLines} = \mathsf{FL}^{-1} \mathit{ArrCont} \\ \mathit{DocX}, \mathit{DocY} = X, Y \\ \hline \end{array}$$

with special case:

$$\mathit{Rel}_{Doc2}\mathit{\_Standard} \mathrel{\widehat{=}} \mathit{Rel}_{Doc2} \land \mathit{Rel}_{Doc1}\mathit{\_Standard}$$

We may readily verify that AbsRel_{Doc2} indicates an ∞-refinement on the *Doc2* state, and $\mathit{ConcRel}_{Doc2}$ is identical to $\mathit{ConcRel}_{Doc1}$, but with the addition of a no-change X and Y co-ordinate pair, which the reconfigure operation on the *Doc2* state must reflect, and we define:

$$\begin{array}{lcl} \mathit{ConcDoc2\_Standard} & \widehat{=} & \mathit{ConcDoc2} \mid \mathit{LP} = \mathit{CP} \\ \mathit{Reconfigure}_{Doc2}\mathit{\_Standard} & \widehat{=} & \mathit{ConcRel}_{Doc2} \land \mathit{ConcDoc2\_Standard}' \end{array}$$

5.2.1 Promotion Of "Initialize"

We have the abstract specification:

$$\mathit{Initialize}_{Doc2} \mathrel{\widehat{=}} \mathit{Initialize}_{Doc1} \land \Delta \mathit{Doc2}$$

We refine $\mathit{Initialize}_{Doc1}$ in such a way that it also serves as a refinement for $\Delta Doc2$, and then appeal to [$\sqsubseteq$ 3.6] to show that it also provides a refinement for $\mathit{Initialize}_{Doc2}$, and we do so by setting both X and Y to zero [$\sqsubseteq$ 3.1]:

$$\left[\begin{array}{l} LP' = CP' = 0 \\ RP' = Max \\ X' = Y' = 0 \\ rep! = \text{“OK”} \end{array}\right.$$

This represents a refinement for $\Delta Doc2$, since the predicate part of weakest concrete specification of the after-state of that promotion schema (after simplification) is:

$$\left[\begin{array}{l} Y' = |(Arr' \text{ for } CP') \rhd \{nl\}| \\ X' = CP' - Startln \\ \text{where} \\ \quad Startln \leq CP' \\ \quad Startln \neq 0 \Rightarrow Arr'\ Startln = nl \\ \quad nl \notin Arr \,(\!|\, Startln + 1 \,..\, CP' \,|\!) \end{array}\right.$$

and the refinement now follows by [$\sqsubseteq$ 3.2] ($Startln$, of course, being zero).

We thus have as the code for $\mathit{Initialize}_{Doc2}$:

$$rep! : Report \ ;$$
$$LP, CP, RP, X, Y, rep! := 0, 0, Max, 0, 0, \text{“OK”}$$

5.2.2 Promotion Of "Delete"

Abstract specification:

$$Delete_{Doc2} \ \widehat{=} \ Delete_{Doc1} \ \wedge \ \Delta Doc2$$

An intuitive approach suggests that only the new components of the *Doc2* state, X and Y, need be considered, since the refinement on *Doc1* will have dealt with all other components. This, in fact, was our approach for the promotion of the initialize operation, and is our approach here; in this case, however, there is slightly more work to be done and so we resort to sequential composition.

Thus our method of refinement is to specify and refine a concrete operation that updates X and Y, and show that post-sequential composition of this operation with $Delete_{Doc1}$ refines both $Delete_{Doc1}$ and the promotion schema $\Delta Doc2$. We then appeal to [$\sqsubseteq$ 3.6] to show that the sequential operation also refines $Delete_{Doc2}$.

We first specify the concrete operation updating X and Y, depending upon whether or not the character deleted by (a successful) $Delete_{Doc2}$ was a newline: if not, we must leave Y unchanged and decrement X, and if so, we must decrement Y and set X to the value dictated by the $ConcDoc2'$ invariant:

UpdXY

$$X, Y : 0 \mathinner{..} Max$$
$$ConcDoc2'$$
$$\Xi ConcDoc1$$

$$\begin{array}{l} \quad Arr(CP + 1) \neq nl \\ \quad X', Y' = (X - 1), Y \\ \vee \\ \quad Arr(CP + 1) = nl \\ \quad Y' = Y - 1 \\ \quad X' = CP - Startln \\ \quad \text{where} \\ \qquad Startln \leq CP \\ \qquad Startln \neq 0 \;\Rightarrow\; Arr\ Startln = nl \\ \qquad nl \notin Arr \llparenthesis\, Startln + 1 \mathinner{..} CP \,\rrparenthesis \end{array}$$

We refine to code by using [$\sqsubseteq$ 3.12] to produce the **if** construct, and [$\sqsubseteq$ 3.13] to give the **do** construct:

$$\{\, LP, RP, CP, Arr, X, Y = LP_o, RP_o, CP_o, Arr_o, X_o, Y_o \,\}$$
$$Startln : 0 \mathinner{..} Max \;;$$
if
$$\mid (Arr(CP + 1) \neq nl) \longrightarrow X := (X - 1) \quad \{\, Y = Y_o \,\}$$
$\square$
$$\begin{array}{l} \mid (Arr(CP + 1) = nl) \longrightarrow \\ \qquad Y, Startln := (Y - 1), CP \;; \\ \qquad \textbf{do} \\ \qquad \mid (Startln \neq 0 \wedge Arr\ Startln \neq nl) \longrightarrow Startln := (Startln - 1) \\ \qquad \quad \{\, \textsf{Invariant}\ \ nl \notin Arr \llparenthesis\, Startln + 1 \mathinner{..} CP \,\rrparenthesis \,\} \\ \qquad \quad \{\, \textsf{Bound}\ \ Startln \,\} \\ \qquad \quad \{\, \textsf{Guard}\ \ Startln = 0 \vee Arr\ Startln = nl \,\} \\ \qquad \textbf{od} \;; \\ \qquad X := (CP - Startln) \end{array}$$
fi
$$\{\, LP, RP, CP, Arr = LP_o, RP_o, CP_o, Arr_o \,\}$$

We now define the construct *UpdateXY* which acts on the report input by $Delete_{Doc1}$, and outputs that same report:

$$rep?, rep! : Report \;;$$
if
$$\mid (rep? = \text{“OK”}) \longrightarrow UpdXY$$
$\square$
$$\mid (rep? \neq \text{“OK”}) \longrightarrow Skip$$
fi ;
$$rep! := rep?$$

the "?" indicating that the report is input to the operation. Since *UpdXY* and, hence, *UpdateXY* do not change any component of *Doc1*, [$\sqsubseteq$ 3.2] together with [$\sqsubseteq$ 3.9] imply that:

$$\begin{array}{lcl} Delete_{Doc1} & \sqsubseteq & Delete_{Doc1} \,\text{;}\, UpdateXY \\ \Delta Doc2 & \sqsubseteq & Delete_{Doc1} \,\text{;}\, UpdateXY \end{array}$$

with [$\sqsubseteq$ 3.6] providing the required result:

$$Delete_{Doc2} \;\widehat{=}\; Delete_{Doc1} \wedge \Delta Doc2 \;\sqsubseteq\; Delete_{Doc1} \,\text{;}\, UpdateXY$$

As suggested in the introduction, simple program transformation will produce a (slightly) more efficient code structure, for example:

```
StartIn : 0 .. Max ; rep! : Report ;
Reconfigure_Doc1_Standard ;
if
  | (LP ≠ 0 ∧ Arr LP ≠ nl) ⟶
  |                 LP, CP, X, rep! := (LP − 1), (LP − 1), (X − 1), "OK"
□
  | (LP ≠ 0 ∧ Arr LP = nl) ⟶
  |                 LP, CP, Y, StartIn := (LP − 1), (LP − 1), (Y − 1), (LP − 1) ;
  |                 do
  |                 | (StartIn ≠ 0 ∧ Arr StartIn ≠ nl) ⟶ StartIn := (StartIn − 1)
  |                 od ;
  |                 X, rep! := (CP − StartIn), "OK"
□
  | (LP = 0) ⟶ rep! := "At top of document"
fi
```

However, our experience suggests that unless there is considerable gain in such transformation, the code is best left as originally implemented, since any changes made to a particular hierarchy of the specification will not affect the implementation of lower-level hierarchies, thus easing the task of changing the code to meet the new specification.

6 Conclusions

We have demonstrated a rigorous stepwise-refinement method that may be used to transform a **Z** specification into an implementation meeting its specification; although particularly suited to a hierarchical specification, it may also be applied to "flat" specifications. The structure of the method allows a greater degree of formality than that presented here: for example, the simplification steps following the derivations of weakest concrete operations could be supplemented by an appropriate theory of sequences, and a *formal* proof could be given that a particular refinement rule is applicable.

Our experience suggests that the method also permits a lesser degree of formality than presented: each abstract data type will usually contain many operations, some of which will be similar, and once one of a set of such operations has been rigorously refined, similar operations may be refined by grouping together like refinement steps into one single step.

The emphasis here has been on practicality, and on a rigorous, rather than formal, approach (for example the use of check lists, rather than the theory from which they were derived). It is based on work which will shortly be submitted for the degree of D. Phil., in which a sixty page **Z** specification is implemented using the methodology outlined in this paper. Although not yet complete, the dissertation does indicate that the errors that have occurred in the implementation have largely been of a trivial nature (typing errors and the like), that there have been no errors (yet!) of a "serious" nature (requiring the re-writing of large parts of the implementation), and that the facility to test each hierarchical level of the specification is of great value. Indeed it seems that for some projects the simultaneous development of specification and implementation might be a useful approach.

If formal methods are to gain a wider acceptance, those practicing in the field have a dual responsibility: to promote their approach by indicating the way in which it may be used in practical applications, and at the same time not to make unreasonable claims about what a particular methodology may achieve. Although one's intuition is not foolproof, many people would argue that it is a computer scientist's most valuable tool, and any methodology used may, at best, supplement it [11].

Some theoreticians may feel that the approach adopted here is somewhat simplistic, whilst those working in an industrial environment may feel intimidated by the formalism used. To the former we would say that whilst it is probable that the next generation of computer scientists will have a greater formal mathematical training than those currently working in the field, it must be recognized that change will always be resisted, and if formal methods are not made readily accessible to the current professional system designers and implementors, it will be all the more difficult for the next generation to put such methods to widespread use. And to the latter we point out that today the cost of software development often exceeds that of the hardware on which it will be used, and whilst there is no certain way to ensure the efficient production of error free software, formal methods does provide a better base from which to achieve that aim than many of the ad-hoc methods currently in use.

7 Acknowledgements

Ian Hayes stimulated my interest in formal specification and influenced the style of presentation, and Phil Wadler is currently supervising the D. Phil. project on which this paper is based, and has provided sound guidance.

References

[1] J.-R. Abrial, *Specification or how to give reality to abstraction*, Technology and Science of Informatics, vol. 3 no. 3, 1984.

[2] E. G. Dijkstra, *A Discipline of Programming*, Prentice-Hall, 1976.

[3] D. Gries, *The Science of Programming*, Springer-Verlag, 1981.

[4] I. J. Hayes (ed.), *Specification Case Studies*, Prentice-Hall, 1987.

[5] P. Henderson, *Functional Programming, Formal Specification, and Rapid Prototyping*, IEEE Trans. Soft. Eng., Vol. SE 12, No. 2, 1986.

[6] C. A. R. Hoare, *Proof of Correctness of Data Representations*, Acta Informatica 1, 1972.

[7] C. A. R. Hoare, He Jifeng, J. W. Sanders, *Data Refinement Refined*, to appear.

[8] J. J. Horning, *Putting Formal Specifications to Productive Use*, Proceedings of the Joint IBM/University of Newcastle upon Tyne Seminar, 1983.

[9] C. B. Jones, *Systematic Software Development Using VDM*, Prentice-Hall, 1986.

[10] C. C. Morgan, *The Schema Language*, Programming Research Group, Oxford University, 1984.

[11] P. Naur, *Intuition in software development*, Proc. Int. Joint. Conf. on Theory and Practice of Software Development (TAPSOFT), 1985 (LNCS 186).

[12] D. S. Neilson, *Formal Specification Of An Occam Editor*, Programming Research Group, Oxford University, 1985. M.Sc. Thesis.

[13] D. S. Neilson, *A Rigorous Refinement Method For Z*, Programming Research Group, Oxford University. D.Phil. Thesis, to appear.

[14] J.M.Spivey, *Understanding Z: A Specification Language and its Formal Semantics*, Programming Research Group, Oxford University, 1986. D.Phil Thesis.

[15] B. Sufrin, *Formal Specification of a Display Editor*, PRG-21, Programming Research Group, Oxford University, 1981.

[16] B. Sufrin, C. C. Morgan, I. H. Sørensen, I. J. Hayes, *Notes for a Z Handbook, Part 1 - Mathematical Language*, Programming Research Group, Oxford University, 1985.

[17] D. A. Turner, *Functional programs as executable specifications*, Mathematical Logic and Programming Languages (C.A.R.Hoare and J.C.Shepherdson eds.), Prentice-Hall, 1984.

[18] P.Wadler, *Implementation of the VED text editor*,, Programming Research Group, Oxford University, 1984.

Lazy pattern matching in the ML language

Alain Laville

I.N.R.I.A. (Projet FORMEL)
B.P. 105 78150 Le Chesnay CEDEX France
and Université de Reims
B.P. 347 51062 Reims CEDEX France

1 Introduction

Several of the recently developped programming languages include features that need some *pattern matching* mechanism. An important case of this use is the following : The language handles structured values and some function calls result in evaluating an expression which is determined by the way the argument (a structured value) has been built. The definition of such a function consists of couples whose first element is a structured value which may contain variables and the second one is an expression which may use the variables appearing in the first one. The meaning of such a definition is that, if the argument may be obtained by replacing the variables in the first element of a couple by suited values, then one has to evaluate the corresponding expression after doing the same replacement on the variables it contains. The first part of the couples are often called patterns and the pattern matching process determines which expression has to be evaluated. Such a mechanism may be found in languages which implement Term Rewriting Systems (such as HOPE, see [3]) but also in languages implementing Lambda Calculus (as is in particular the case of ML, see [12], or MIRANDA, see [15]).

In order to get deterministic calculations one may demand that every value can match at most one pattern in each function definition. This leads to tedious work to write such definitions and consequently this constraint is often relaxed, and, in order to maintain determinism, some rules are added which decide what expression has to be chosen when the argument matches more than one pattern. The rule used in ML is the following : the pairs (pattern, expression) are ordered and if the argument matches several patterns one uses the first of them for this ordering. Some other rules are used in different languages, for example choosing the "most defined" of the patterns that the argument matches (this implies some constraints on the set of patterns). We shall only deal in this paper with the case of the ML language.

Another important feature which is more and more implemented in programming languages is *lazyness* (also called call by need or normal order evaluation, see [13]). This means that a value is effectively computed only when it is needed to produce the result, and, for a structured value, that only the needed parts are evaluated. This ensures that the language is *safe*, i.e. if computation fails there was no way to avoid this failure. This moreover gives to the language the ability of handling infinite data structures as long as only finite parts of them are used in calculations. MIRANDA and at least two implementations of ML include this feature : Lazy CAML at INRIA (see [10] or [11]) and LML the implementation of Göteborg (see [1]).

However there are problems when using pattern matching in a lazy language. One wants that the process of finding which pattern the argument matches does not force the evaluation of parts of the argument that are not needed. As far as we know this has not yet been done. For example in his paper "A Compiler for Lazy ML" [1] L. Augustsson writes :

> This rather explicit top-down, left-right ordering is perhaps unfortunate, but some ordering must be imposed to avoid the necessity of parallel evaluation of the subparts of the expression that is to be matched.

It is well known that, even in very simple cases, it is not always possible to find a lazy pattern matching process. Classical examples of this fact are the "PARALLEL OR" or Berry's example (see section 3.2.2 below). This is the problem we address in this paper and we give a (effectively computable) characterisation of the sets of patterns for which such a lazy pattern matching is possible. Moreover this characterisation yields an effective algorithm to realize the pattern matching. This solution was known in the cases where the patterns are not ambiguous (i.e. no value may match two of them), we extend it to the general case of ML patterns (ambiguous ordered list of patterns with the priority rule induced by this ordering). Moreover, the method we give here could be modified to handle other priority rules.

In order to achieve this goal, we introduce the new notion of *minimally extended pattern* (see definition 11). It will give us the key tool to check the lazyness of the pattern matching process (see section 5). It allows us to replace the set of patterns with priority by a new set in which the priority rule is captured by the syntax of the patterns. This makes the priority rule much easier to handle mechanically.

Remark 1 Along this paper, when reference to an implementation of ML is done, it is to CAML the version of ML currently implemented at INRIA (see [11] or [14]).

A detailed version of this work is a part of the author's thesis ([9]), which contains furthermore a study of the implementation of this work in the CAML system.

2 Definitions and Notations

2.1 Patterns

Definition 1 A *pattern* is a term built from the pairing operator, some constructors of (already defined) concrete data types, variables and the special symbol "_". The meaning of "_" is that one doesn't care about what may appear at the place where it is used. CAML (as other ML implementations up to date) restricts patterns to be *linear* : no variable is allowed to appear twice in the same pattern.

Definition 2 A value of CAML is said to be an *instance* of a pattern if it can be obtained from the pattern by replacing all the variables and "_" by any values (compatible with the type discipline of ML but this will always be ensured by the type-checker, so that we don't care about typing). As usual, if σ is a function which maps variables into terms, we call *substitution* the extension of σ as a morphism from terms to terms. Thus, if a term is an instance of a pattern, and if one replaces all "_" by new distinct variables, then there exists a substitution σ which yields the term as image of the pattern (that is here the classical definition of instanciation). With a list of patterns $[\ p_1, \ldots, p_n\ ]$, we shall say that a value v of CAML *matches* the pattern p_i if p_i is the *first* pattern in the list, of which v is an instance.

Definition 3 We shall say that a function is *defined by pattern* if

1. Its definition consists of an ordered list of pairs (pattern, expression)
2. Its value when applied to an argument v is obtained in the following way : first find the first pattern, say p, in the list such that v is an instance of p by a substitution σ and then evaluate the result of applying σ to the corresponding expression.

2.2 Partial Terms and Occurrences

In this paper we shall only deal with the process of finding which pattern is matched by a given value (and not of the evaluation of the corresponding expression). As patterns are linear, this implies that we don't care about the subterms corresponding to variables. Moreover, in a lazy version of CAML, at a given time a term is only partially evaluated. It will thus be convenient to define a notion corresponding to terms of which only a part is known.

We assume given the definition by pattern of a function :

$$\Pi = \begin{cases} fun & p_1 & \rightarrow & exp_1 \\ \mid & p_2 & \rightarrow & exp_2 \\ \cdots & \cdots & \cdots & \cdots \\ \mid & p_n & \rightarrow & exp_n \end{cases}$$

where the p_i's are the patterns to be matched against the value to which one applies the function (if the function has arity greater than 1, the patterns p_i's are t-uples).

One defines a signature Σ containing all the constructors that appear in the patterns $p_1, \ldots, p_n$ and two other symbols : Ω, which will denote the "unknown" or "undefined", and $\mathcal{F}$, which denotes the function. As we want to extend methods of Terms Rewriting Systems theory which consider patterns as terms represented by trees, we shall sometimes have to use this representation. Since CAML (as other ML systems) does not allow function calls in the patterns, we shall only consider terms with root symbol $\mathcal{F}$ and such that $\mathcal{F}$ does not appear at another place in the term. This kind of restriction is known as "systems with constructors" in the Terms Rewriting Systems theory. We assume given a set of variables $\mathcal{V}$ containing all the variables that appear in the patterns $p_1, \ldots, p_n$. If one replaces the "_" of the p_i's by Ω's, then all the $\mathcal{F}(p_i)$ are terms of the algebra built over $\Sigma \cup \mathcal{V}$.

Definition 4 Since such terms will often denote partially known, or partially evaluated values, we shall call *partial term* every term built over Σ (with the restriction on the use of $\mathcal{F}$ stated above). We shall only use *term* to denote a partial term in which there is no symbol Ω (but we do not forbid to use "partial term" even in this case).

Partial terms provide us with a formalism suited for patterns (which are partially undefined terms) as well as for lazy values (which may be thought of as partially unknown since they are not completely evaluated). To avoid introducing new notation, we shall denote from now on by p_i the partial term obtained from $\mathcal{F}(p_i)$ by replacing all variables and "_" by Ω's. We shall denote by Π in the following the ordered sequence : $[\ p_1, \ldots, p_n\ ]$ (they are the p_i's we just defined).

We define a partial ordering (denoted by $\leq$) over the set of all partial terms as follows :

- For each partial term M : $\Omega \leq M$
- $F(M_1, \ldots, M_n) \leq F(N_1, \ldots, N_n)$ if and only if $M_i \leq N_i$ $(1 \leq i \leq n)$

We shall use the notation $M \uparrow N$ when M and N have a common upper bound (and we shall say that M and N are compatible), and the notation $M \sharp N$ if they don't have one (and we shall say that M and N are incompatible).

The ordering $\leq$ is a kind of prefix ordering with the meaning that a partial term is less than another if it is less defined (or less known).

Remark 2 Assume that a partial term M (representing here a lazy value of CAML) given as argument to $\mathcal{F}$ is sufficiently defined to decide which of the right hand side expressions defining $\mathcal{F}$, say exp_{i_0}, has to be evaluated after instantiation to return the desired value of the application. Then it is clear that the following must hold : $p_{i_0} \leq M$.

The converse, i.e. if $p_{i_0} \leq M$ then to get the value of $\mathcal{F}(\mathcal{M})$ one always has to evaluate exp_{i_0} is not true for all sets of patterns. It is true if and only if for each pair $(p_i,\ p_j)$ of patterns one has $p_i \sharp p_j$. The *if* part is obvious. For the *only if* part, assume $p_i \uparrow p_j$ with $i < j$ and let M be a common upper bound of p_i and p_j then, although $p_j \leq M$, exp_j is not the expression to evaluate.

Definition 5 When seeing partial terms as trees, we shall say that M_i is the ith *son* of the partial term $F(M_1, \ldots, M_n)$. We call *occurrence* an integer list which designates a subterm of a given partial term. For example, the occurrence [2; 3] points to the third son of the second son of the full partial term. The prefix ordering of occurrences will be denoted by $\leq$. For a given partial term M, we shall denote $O(M)$ the set of all occurrences in M, $\overline{O}(M)$ the set of occurrences in M where the symbol is not Ω and $O_\Omega(M)$ the set of occurrences in M where the symbol is Ω. The symbol in M at occurrence u will be denoted by $M(u)$.

2.3 Matching Predicates

We shall now define some predicates over the set of partial terms (i.e. functions with values in the set {tt, ff} of the truth values).

Definition 6 For each $i \in \{1, \ldots, n\}$, the predicate $match_i$ is defined by $match_i(M) = \text{tt}$ if and only if the following two conditions hold :

1. $p_i \leq M$
2. $\forall j < i \quad p_j \uparrow\!\!\!\!\uparrow M$

Remark 3 We recall that the patterns are ordered, and that matching searches for the *first* suitable pattern in the list (see definition 2). The meaning of the preceding definition is that $match_i(M) = \text{tt}$ iff M is sufficiently defined to decide that if M is the argument of $\mathcal{F}$ then one has to evaluate (after suitable instantiation) the expression number i.

We could have used as second condition in the above definition :

$\forall j < i \quad p_j \not\leq M$

The two definitions coincide on all terms (without any Ω). They may differ on some partial terms and we could lose the property of monotonicity for the predicates $match_i$ (see below proposition 1).

Example

With $\Pi = [\mathcal{F}(A);\ \mathcal{F}(\Omega)]$, the partial term $\mathcal{F}(\Omega)$ does not verify the predicate $match_2$ with the definition we choosed. It would have verify this predicate if we had choosen the second version. The term $\mathcal{F}(A)$, which is greater than $\mathcal{F}(\Omega)$, does not verify the predicate $match_2$ neither with the first definition nor with the second one.

Definition 7 We now define the predicate $match_\Pi$:
$match_\Pi(M) = \text{tt}$ if and only if $match_i(M) = \text{tt}$ for some $i \in \{1, \ldots, n\}$.

Remark 4 The meaning is of course that M is sufficiently defined to decide which right hand side has to be evaluated to get the value of $\mathcal{F}(M)$.

3 Properties of the Match Predicates

3.1 Monotonicity

The following lemma groups some useful characterizations and properties related with the ordering of partial terms.

Lemma 1

a) *$M \sharp N$ if and only if there exists an occurrence u in $\overline{O}(M) \cap \overline{O}(N)$ such that $M(u) \neq N(u)$.*

b) *$M \leq N$ if and only if for each $u \in O(M)$ either $M(u) = \Omega$ or $M(u) = N(u)$.*

c) *$M \uparrow N$ if and only if the two following hold :*

- *$\forall u \in O(M)$ either $M(u) = N(u)$ or $\exists v \leq u$ such that $N(v) = \Omega$*
- *$\forall u \in O(N)$ either $N(u) = M(u)$ or $\exists v \leq u$ such that $M(v) = \Omega$*

d) *The ordering $\leq$ over the partial terms is well founded (i.e. there exists no infinite strictly decreasing sequence).*

e) *If $match_i(M) = \mathrm{tt}$ then for all $j \neq i$ $match_j(M) = \mathrm{ff}$.*

Proof : a), b), c) and d) are straightforward. To get e) one simply remarks that if $j < i$ then $M \sharp p_j$, and if $j > i$ then one can not have $M \sharp p_i$, in both cases $match_j(M)$ is false. ■

Definition 8 We order the set of truth values by defining ff < tt. Using the ordering on partial terms this allows to define *monotonically increasing* predicates. For short, we call them simply *increasing* predicates.

Proposition 1 *The predicates $match_i$ and the predicate $match_\Pi$ are all increasing.*

Proof : The only case which could make false this proposition is if one could find two partial terms, say M and N, such that $match_i(M) = \mathrm{tt}$, $match_i(N) = \mathrm{ff}$ and $N \geq M$. Now assume that $match_i(M) = \mathrm{tt}$ and let $N \geq M$. By definition of $match_i$ one has $M \geq p_i$ and hence $N \geq p_i$. From the same definition we know that $M \sharp p_j$ for each $j < i$. Thus (from part a) of lemma 1)

$$\forall j < i\ \exists u_j \in \overline{O}(M) \text{ such that } \quad M(u_j) \neq \Omega \text{ , } p_j(u_j) \neq \Omega \text{ and } p_j(u_j) \neq M(u_j)$$

Since, from part b) of lemma 1, $N(u_j) = M(u_j)$, the result follows obviously for each predicate $match_i$.

It is now straightforward, from the definition, to reduce the case of $match_\Pi$ to the preceding one. ■

3.2 Sequentiality

3.2.1 Definition

We define here a formal property of increasing predicates, called sequentiality and due to G. Kahn and G. Plotkin (see [8]), and also to G. Berry and P.L. Curien (see [6]) which is strongly connected with the problem we address as will be shown later.

Definition 9 Definition is given in three steps as follows :

1. For a given partial term M and an increasing predicate $\mathcal{P}$, we shall say that an occurrence u in M is an *index* of $\mathcal{P}$ in M if the three following conditions hold :

   a) $M(u) = \Omega$

   b) $\mathcal{P}(M) = \text{ff}$

   c) $\forall N \geq M$ if $\mathcal{P}(N) = \text{tt}$ then $N(u) \neq \Omega$

2. For a given partial term M and an increasing predicate $\mathcal{P}$, we shall say that $\mathcal{P}$ is *sequential at M* if and only if the two conditions $\mathcal{P}(M) = \text{ff}$ and there exists $N \geq M$ such that $\mathcal{P}(N) = \text{tt}$ imply together that $\mathcal{P}$ has an index in M.

3. Finally we shall say that an increasing predicate $\mathcal{P}$ is *sequential* if it is sequential at every partial term.

3.2.2 Examples

We shall give examples, with the predicates $match_\Pi$ associated with various lists of patterns. We recall that $\mathcal{F}$ denotes the function associated with the pattern matching process. It has arity 2 in the first three examples, arity 3 in the last one. Hence this symbol is applied to couples in the first examples and to triples in the last one. The algebra Σ is built each time according to section 2.2 : it consists of the two symbols $\mathcal{F}$ and Ω together with the constructors that appear in the patterns ("a" and "b" or "true" and "false"). We recall furthermore that $\mathcal{F}$ is not allowed to appear at another place than the top of a pattern.

1. With $\Pi = [\mathcal{F}(a,a); \mathcal{F}(a,b); \mathcal{F}(b,a); \mathcal{F}(b,b)]$, if $match_\Pi(M) = \text{ff}$ and there exists $N \geq M$ such that $match_\Pi(N) = \text{tt}$, then M must belong to the set $\{\Omega, \mathcal{F}(\Omega,\Omega), \mathcal{F}(\Omega,a), \mathcal{F}(\Omega,b), \mathcal{F}(a,\Omega), \mathcal{F}(b,\Omega)\}$. It is easy to check that all the occurrences where Ω appears are indexes for $match_\Pi$, and thus that this predicate is sequential.

2. With $\Pi = [\mathcal{F}(a,\Omega); \mathcal{F}(\Omega,b)]$, if $match_\Pi(M) = \text{ff}$ and there exists $N \geq M$ such that $match_\Pi(N) = \text{tt}$, then M must belong to the set $\{\Omega, \mathcal{F}(\Omega,\Omega), \mathcal{F}(b,\Omega), \mathcal{F}(\Omega,b)\}$. The fourth element of this set may look rather surprising since it is one of the patterns but it is an example of the fact that $match_i(p_i)$ may be false.

The predicate $match_\Pi$ has trivially an index at Ω. One easily sees that if $match_\Pi(N) = \text{tt}$ then $N = \mathcal{F}(N_1, N_2)$ with $N_1 \neq \Omega$. Hence $match_\Pi$ has an index at $\mathcal{F}(\Omega,\Omega)$ and $\mathcal{F}(\Omega,\text{b})$. If $N \geq \mathcal{F}(\text{b},\Omega)$ then $match_1(N) = \text{ff}$ so that if $match_\Pi(N) = \text{tt}$ $match_2(N) = \text{tt}$ must hold. Hence $N([2]) = \text{b}$ and $[2]$ is an index of $match_\Pi$ at $\mathcal{F}(\text{b},\Omega)$ (see notations in definition 5) : $match_\Pi$ is sequential.

3. With $\Pi = [\mathcal{F}(\text{a,b});\ \mathcal{F}(\Omega,\Omega)]$, if $match_\Pi(M) = \text{ff}$ and there exists $N \geq M$ such that $match_\Pi(N) = \text{tt}$, then M must belong to the set $\{\Omega,\ \mathcal{F}(\Omega,\Omega),\ \mathcal{F}(\text{a},\Omega),\ \mathcal{F}(\Omega,\text{b})\}$. One easily checks that $match_\Pi$ has an index at Ω, $\mathcal{F}(\text{a},\Omega)$ and $\mathcal{F}(\Omega,\text{b})$. It has none at $\mathcal{F}(\Omega,\Omega)$ since both $\mathcal{F}(\text{b},\Omega)$ and $\mathcal{F}(\Omega,\text{a})$ verify $match_2$ and hence verify $match_\Pi$ too.

4. We give now a version of what is known as Berry's example : $\Pi = [\mathcal{F}(\text{true,false},\Omega);$ $\mathcal{F}(\text{false},\Omega,\text{true});\ \mathcal{F}(\Omega,\text{true,false})]$. One sees that there is no index for $match_\Pi$ at $\mathcal{F}(\Omega,\Omega,\Omega)$: since the three patterns are pairwise incompatible, each of them verifies $match_\Pi$ and one can find an Ω at every occurrence.

3.2.3 Sequentiality and Lazyness

We address now the question of choosing the right hand side when one needs to evaluate $\mathcal{F}(v)$ in a lazy version of ML, where v is any value (and hence may be only partially evaluated). We want that this process does not force the evaluation of any part of v which is not necessary to make the choice.

Definition 10 We call *pattern matching algorithm* any deterministic algorithm which matches any partial term against Π (see definition 2). As partial terms are trees and a pattern is a prefix of any partial term that matches it, this process has to work in a top-down way if it never does useless work.

We say that a pattern matching algorithm is *lazy* if it satisfies the preceding condition. We may express this constraint in the following way : Let U be the set of all occurrences in v where the symbol was evaluated during the pattern matching process. Denote v_Ω the partial term which coincides with v along U and is completed with Ω's according to the arities of the symbols used. Then we ask v_Ω to be less than or equal to (for the ordering of partial terms) every prefix of the full value v which is sufficient to choose the right hand side.

This property of lazy pattern matching is connected with sequentiality, as shows the following theorem.

Theorem 1 *Given a function defined by pattern, there exists an associated lazy pattern matching algorithm if and only if the predicate $match_\Pi$ is sequential.*

Proof : We shall only give a sketch of the proof.

Assume that the predicate $match_\Pi$ is sequential. Then it suffices at each step of the pattern matching process, to look in v at an occurrence that is an index for $match_\Pi$ in the prefix of v that was already explored.

Conversely, assume $match_\Pi$ not to be sequential and let M be a partial term with no index. Let run the pattern matching algorithm from Ω, getting the symbol at u in M as long as it looks at an occurrence $u \in \overline{\mathcal{O}}(M)$. Let u_0 be the first occurrence in $\mathcal{O}_\Omega(M)$ which the algorithm will look at. Since there is no index in M one can find a partial term N such that $\mathrm{N}(u_0) = \Omega$ and $match_\Pi(N) = \mathrm{tt}$. For this N the algorithm makes useless work, or in other words it may fail to recognize a matching by failing during the evaluation of a not needed part of the argument. ■

Remark 5 This kind of result could have been expected : The sequentiality of the predicate $match_\Pi$ means that there exists a sequential safe calculation that changes the value of the predicate from ff to tt, each time that this change is possible. It is well known that the trouble in lazy pattern matching comes from the inherent parallelism of this process in some cases (see for example the quotation of L. Augustsson in the introduction of this paper).

Remark 6 We gave the value ff as result of $match_\Pi$ when it is applied to an unsufficiently known value as well as when it is applied to a value which matches none of the patterns. This leads to have no constraint of lazyness when finding that the pattern matching process fails. We could have retain this constraint in the following way : Add to the set of truth values an "undefined" (denoted by $\perp$) and define the ordering over these values by $\perp < \mathrm{tt}$ and $\perp < \mathrm{ff}$ (tt and ff being not comparable). We now give another definition of $match_\Pi$:

- If there exists i such that $match_i(M) = \mathrm{tt}$ then $match_\Pi(M) = \mathrm{tt}$
- If for all $i \in \{1, \ldots, n\}$ $M \not\uparrow p_i$ then $match_\Pi(M) = \mathrm{ff}$
- Otherwise $match_\Pi(M) = \perp$

With this predicate $match_\Pi$, sequentiality means that one can find which pattern matches a value without useless work, and that failure of matching is recognized without useless work.

4 Equivalent Matching Predicate

4.1 Introduction

The sequentiality of the predicate $match_\Pi$ is not so easy to test. So we shall give an equivalent definition of this predicate the sequentiality of which can be studied in a more tractable way.

The idea is as follows : If $match_i(M) = \mathrm{tt}$, then M has to be incompatible with all the patterns p_j such that $j < i$. Thus we shall try to replace the single pattern p_i by a *set* of patterns, each of them greater than p_i and incompatible with all the preceding patterns. Then we shall replace the initial list of patterns by the longer one that we get from the replacement of each pattern by the set above. This new list may be constituted of pairwise incompatible patterns, and the matching against it may be studied by already known methods. The list may also contain two (or more) compatible patterns, and there is no sequential pattern matching algorithm for the initial definition (i.e. $match_\Pi$ is not sequential) as will be proved later.

Of course we have to show that we did not change the function call when modifying the set of patterns. Moreover, we have to take care that the *new* match predicates have the same sequentiality properties as the old ones. The trouble is the following : Assume we deal with the function AND over the booleans which may be defined by pattern matching with two cases, namely

$$\begin{array}{lccl} fun & (true, true) & \rightarrow & true \\ | & (x, y) & \rightarrow & false \end{array}$$

One can see that there is no sequential pattern matching in this case using the same argument as in the third example of 3.2.2. We could define the same function over the set of boolean values with incompatible patterns, for example by

$$\begin{array}{lccl} fun & (true, true) & \rightarrow & true \\ | & (false, x) & \rightarrow & false \\ | & (true, false) & \rightarrow & false \end{array}$$

But although this defines the same function over the booleans, we can easily see that this definition is not equivalent to the first one in a lazy system. Assume we give the AND function as argument a pair the first part of which fails to evaluate and the second part evaluates to false. Then, with the first definition, the function returns false and, with the last one, the function fails. Replacing the pattern (x, y) by the two patterns $(false, x)$ and $(true, false)$ introduced a precedence of the first part of the couple which was not in the first definition (one may check that there exists in the second case a lazy pattern matching algorithm : look first at first occurrence).

4.2 Minimally Extended Patterns

In the following lemma,we use the notation OCC_Π to denote the set of all the occurrences which may be useful to choose the pattern at least in one case, i.e.

$$OCC_\Pi = \bigcup_{i=1}^{n} \overline{\mathcal{O}}(p_i)$$

Lemma 2 *If* $match_\Pi(M) = \mathrm{tt}$, *there exists a prefix* M' *of* M *such that :*

1. $match_\Pi(M') = \mathrm{tt}$
2. $\overline{\mathcal{O}}(M') \subset OCC_\Pi$

Proof : If u is an occurrence in M not belonging to OCC_Π, there exists a maximal prefix of u, say v, in OCC_Π. In order to get M' we cut M at every such occurrence v and complete with Ω's according to the arities of remaining symbols. We easily get the property $match_\Pi(M') = \mathrm{tt}$, since, by lemma 1, we express it using only symbols at occurrences in OCC_Π and these symbols are the same in M and M'. ■

Definition 11 We shall call *minimally extended pattern* (associated with Π) any partial term t verifying the following two properties :

1. $match_\Pi(t) = \mathrm{tt}$
2. $\forall t' < t,\ match_\Pi(t') = \mathrm{ff}$

We shall denote the set of all minimally extended patterns by MEP_Π.

Remark 7 The elements of MEP_Π are the minimal points of the predicate $match_\Pi$ if this predicate may be viewed as a stable function (see [6] definition 2.4.1 and proposition 2.4.2).

Proposition 2 *The set MEP_Π is a finite set. Furthermore it is possible to effectively build this set from the initial list of patterns.*

Proof : From the second part of the definition, for each minimally extended pattern t, one has $\mathcal{O}(t) \subset OCC_\Pi$. Since we deal with (partial) terms over a finite signature, the results follow (all the calculations involved are finite). ■

4.3 Examples :

1. In the case of the AND function used above (see section 4.1), the set MEP_Π contains the extended pattern $\mathcal{F}$(true,true) coming from the first pattern, and the two ones $\mathcal{F}$(false,Ω) and $\mathcal{F}$(Ω,false) coming from the second pattern. One sees here a case where two elements of MEP_Π are compatible. As we said above, this is a case where no sequential pattern matching is possible. When we used this function (in the introduction above) the trouble with the sequentiality came from the following fact : we replaced then the second pattern by the set {$\mathcal{F}$(false,Ω), $\mathcal{F}$(true,false)}. In this set the second element is not a *minimally* extended pattern : it asks for too much information about the value.

2. If one wants to use the classical PARALLEL OR, and tries to define it as :

$$\begin{array}{lcll} fun & (true, x) & \rightarrow & true \\ \mid & (x, true) & \rightarrow & true \\ \mid & (x, y) & \rightarrow & false \end{array}$$

   the set MEP_Π will be {$\mathcal{F}$(true,Ω), $\mathcal{F}$(false,true), $\mathcal{F}$(false,false)}. This set contains only pairwise incompatible patterns, which correspond one to one to the initials ones. We shall discuss the meaning of that fact after giving the procedure to study the existence of a lazy pattern matching algorithm.

3. In the case of Berry's example (see 3.2.2), since the three patterns are pairwise incompatible, the set MEP_Π simply contains them.

4. We give now some abstract examples, using a signature Σ consisting of $\mathcal{F}$, Ω and three symbols (denoted a, b and c) each of arity zero. We shall not discuss here the question of sequentiality. We shall only do after giving the procedure to decide it.

- With initial patterns $p_1 = \mathcal{F}(a,\Omega,\Omega)$, $p_2 = \mathcal{F}(\Omega,b,\Omega)$ and $p_3 = \mathcal{F}(\Omega,\Omega,c)$, p_1 remains unmodified ; p_2 has to be replaced by $\{\mathcal{F}(b,b,\Omega), \mathcal{F}(c,b,\Omega)\}$ meaning that it can be recognized only after excluding a symbol "a" in first place ; similarly p_3 is replaced by the set $\{\mathcal{F}(b,c,c), \mathcal{F}(c,c,c), \mathcal{F}(b,a,c), \mathcal{F}(c,a,c)\}$ since one has to exclude at the same time "a" in first place and "b" in second place.
- With the list of patterns $[\mathcal{F}(a,\Omega,\Omega); \mathcal{F}(b,\Omega,\Omega); \mathcal{F}(\Omega,\Omega,c)]$, the first two are not modified, and the third is replaced by $\{\mathcal{F}(c,\Omega,c)\}$.
- With the list of patterns $[\mathcal{F}(a,\Omega,\Omega); \mathcal{F}(a,b,\Omega); \mathcal{F}(\Omega,\Omega,c)]$, the first one remains, the second one is discarded (replaced by the empty set) and the third one is replaced by $\{\mathcal{F}(c,\Omega,c), \mathcal{F}(b,\Omega,c)\}$.
- With the list of patterns $[\mathcal{F}(a,b,\Omega); \mathcal{F}(\Omega,a,\Omega); \mathcal{F}(\Omega,\Omega,c); \mathcal{F}(\Omega,\Omega,\Omega)]$ the first two remain, the third one is replaced by the set $\{\mathcal{F}(\Omega,c,c), \mathcal{F}(b,b,c), \mathcal{F}(c,b,c)\}$, and the last one by the set $\{\mathcal{F}(\Omega,c,a), \mathcal{F}(\Omega,c,b), \mathcal{F}(b,b,a), \mathcal{F}(b,b,b), \mathcal{F}(c,b,a), \mathcal{F}(c,b,b)\}$.
- We slightly change the list of patterns (only modifying the first symbol in the second pattern) getting the list $[\mathcal{F}(a,b,\Omega); \mathcal{F}(a,a,\Omega); \mathcal{F}(\Omega,\Omega,c); \mathcal{F}(\Omega,\Omega,\Omega)]$. Now the first two remain, the third one is replaced by $\{\mathcal{F}(\Omega,c,c), \mathcal{F}(b,\Omega,c), \mathcal{F}(c,\Omega,c)\}$ and the last one by the set $\{\mathcal{F}(\Omega,c,a), \mathcal{F}(\Omega,c,b), \mathcal{F}(b,\Omega,a), \mathcal{F}(b,\Omega,b), \mathcal{F}(c,\Omega,a), \mathcal{F}(c,\Omega,b)\}$.

4.4 New Definition of Matching Predicate

Definition 12 We call $match'_\Pi$ the predicate defined over the set of partial terms by : $match'_\Pi(M) = \text{tt}$ if and only if there exists an element t of MEP_Π such that $t \leq M$.

Proposition 3 *The two predicates $match'_\Pi$ and $match_\Pi$ are the same predicate over the set of all partial terms.*

Proof : Assume $match'_\Pi(M) = \text{tt}$, and let $t \in MEP_\Pi$ be such that $t \leq M$. From the definition of MEP_Π, one has $match_\Pi(t) = \text{tt}$. Since this predicate is increasing (proposition 1) we get $match_\Pi(M) = \text{tt}$.

Conversely, the result is straightforward since the ordering on partial terms is well founded (lemma 1 d). We may remark that nothing here ensures that for each partial term M verifying $match_\Pi(M) = \text{tt}$, there exists a unique $t \in MEP_\Pi$ such that $t \leq M$. In many cases this result will not hold. ∎

Corollary 1 *The predicate $match_\Pi$ is sequential if and only if $match'_\Pi$ is.*

5 Deciding Sequentiality

5.1 Incompatible Minimally Extended Patterns

When all the minimally extended patterns are pairwise incompatible, the sequentiality of $match'_{\Pi}$ is easily decided using already known methods. One only has to check if this predicate is sequential at every partial term which is a prefix of an element of MEP_{Π}. Moreover, one can exhibit a lazy pattern matching algorithm when the checking succeeds. These two goals are achieved by trying to build a "matching tree" (see for details Huet and Lévy [7] where this method is introduced). A matching tree is a tree of which each node contains a partial term M with an index u of $match'_{\Pi}$ in M, and the branches issued from a node are labelled with the symbols that may be placed at u in M in order to get a match. Leaves correspond to elements of MEP_{Π} which mean a success in the matching process. The root of the tree contains the partial term Ω with the trivial index of $match'_{\Pi}$ at this partial term. For an example of the building of such a matching tree see examples of section 5.3.

Given the matching tree, the lazy pattern matching algorithm is as follows : start at the root of the tree and when reaching a node look in the value at the occurrence contained in the node ; follow the branch of which the label is the symbol found in the value if there is one (if there is no such branch the matching process fails) ; when reaching a leave one ensures that the value is greater than one of the elements of MEP_{Π}, say p, the one corresponding to the leave. Hence the value matches the unique initial pattern p_i such that $match_i(p) = \text{tt}$.

5.2 Compatible Minimally Extended Patterns

We deal now with the case where there exists two (or more) compatible extended minimal patterns.

Lemma 3 *Let s and t be two compatible minimally extended patterns. By definition both verify the predicate $match_{\Pi}$. Hence there exists i and j such that $match_i(s) = \text{tt}$ and $match_j(t) = \text{tt}$. Then $i = j$.*

<u>Proof</u> : Let M be a partial term such that $s \leq M$ and $t \leq M$ (M exists since s and t are compatible). As all the predicates $match_k$ are increasing (proposition 1) one has $match_i(M) = \text{tt}$ and $match_j(M) = \text{tt}$. Since, for a given partial term, only one of the $match_k$ may be true (lemma 1 e) we get $i = j$. ∎

Examples

It is easy to see from the examples above (section 4.3), that one effectively can get compatible patterns and that the preceding proposition holds in these cases.

Proposition 4 *If MEP_{Π} contains two (or more) compatible patterns then the predicate $match_{\Pi}$ is not sequential. Hence there is no lazy pattern matching algorithm for the initial list of patterns.*

Proof : We give two proofs of this proposition. The first one is rather abstract but very short. It uses results of the theory of sequentiality (for definition and results see the monograph of P.L. Curien [6], chapter 2, sections 1 and 4).

Assume that $match_\Pi$ is sequential. Then this predicate is stable ([6] proposition 2.4.7). Hence its minimal points are pairwise incompatible ([6] proposition 2.4.2 (3)). Since the set MEP_Π is the set of minimal points of $match_\Pi$ (see remark 7 above) the result follows.

The second proof is a direct one. It is more complicated, but it exhibits an example of how sequentiality and lazyness are connected.

Assume that there exists two compatible minimally extended patterns s and t. As they are both minimal they are not comparable for the ordering over partial terms. Hence their greatest lower bound M (which always exists) is strictly less than both s and t. Hence one must have $match_\Pi(M) = \mathrm{ff}$ (from the definition of minimally extended pattern).

We shall prove that there exists no index for $match_\Pi$ in M. Let u be an occurrence of Ω in M and look at $s(u)$ and $t(u)$. There are two cases to consider :

- If s and t have the same symbol at occurrence u, this symbol must be Ω. Otherwise replacing the Ω at u in M by the same symbol as in s and t (extended with Ω's according with its arity) would give us a partial term less than s and t and strictly greater than M. This would contradict the assumption that M is the greatest lower bound of s and t.

- If s and t have distinct symbols at occurrence u, one of them has to be Ω. This is a consequence of the caracterisation of compatible partial terms given in lemma 1.

In all cases we get a partial term greater than M, for which the predicate $match_\Pi$ returns tt, and having a symbol Ω at occurrence u. Hence this occurrence is not an index of $match_\Pi$ in M. As this is true for every occurrence of Ω in M $match_\Pi$ is not sequential at M. ∎

Theorem 2 *The existence of a lazy pattern matching algorithm for a given list of patterns is decidable. Moreover we are able to effectively build such an algorithm if there exists one.*

Proof : Using the preceding results, the procedure is as follows : Build MEP_Π and check for compatible patterns in this set. If one can find such patterns, there is no lazy pattern matching algorithm. If such patterns do not exist one only has to try to build a matching tree. If this building succeeds it gives a lazy pattern matching algorithm, if it fails the predicate $match_\Pi$ is not sequential (the only failure may come from the lack of an index in one of the partial terms that are placed in the tree) and hence there exists no lazy pattern matching algorithm. ∎

5.3 Examples

We shall look now at the examples of section 4.3 from the point of view of lazy pattern matching.

- The set MEP_Π associated with the AND function contains two compatible patterns (both coming from the second rule, see section 4.3), hence there is no lazy pattern matching algorithm. In fact this is the obviously correct result, since the meaning of the function is : If either of the two arguments is "false" then the result is false. In an abstract sense this is exactly the PARALLEL OR (exchanging false and true) for which we expect no sequentiality to hold.

- We tried to define a PARALLEL OR by

$$\begin{array}{rcll} fun & (true, x) & \rightarrow & true \\ | & (x, true) & \rightarrow & true \\ | & (x, y) & \rightarrow & false \end{array}$$

  and got $\{\mathcal{F}(\text{true},\Omega); \mathcal{F}(\text{false},\text{true}); \mathcal{F}(\text{false},\text{false})\}$ as MEP_Π. In order to determine if a lazy pattern matching algorithm exists one has to build a matching tree.

  Starting from $\mathcal{F}(\Omega, \Omega)$, one has to look at its first argument. We can find here two symbols : getting true we match the first rule, getting false we have to look to the second argument; getting here true we match the second rule, getting false we match the third one. This means that there is here a sequential pattern matching algorithm. This is because the function we defined is not a parallel OR. In fact, due to the priority rule of ML when choosing which pattern the value matches, the function is OR(x,y) $\equiv$ if x then true else y.

- In Berry's example, although the initial patterns were pairwise incompatible (and hence the set MEP_Π too), one cannot find a lazy pattern matching algorithm since there is no index for $match_\Pi$ in $\mathcal{F}(\Omega,\Omega,\Omega)$. In fact, whatever the first place to look at would be, one can build a term M such that M matches one of the patterns and the value in M at that place is irrelevant.

- In the first abstract example, we have :
  $\Pi = [\mathcal{F}(a,\Omega,\Omega); \mathcal{F}(\Omega,b,\Omega); \mathcal{F}(\Omega,\Omega,c)]$
  and
  $MEP_\Pi = \{\mathcal{F}(a,\Omega,\Omega), \mathcal{F}(b,b,\Omega), \mathcal{F}(c,b,\Omega), \mathcal{F}(b,c,c), \mathcal{F}(c,c,c), \mathcal{F}(b,a,c), \mathcal{F}(c,a,c)\}$.
  All the patterns are pairwise incompatible. The matching tree is easily build : look at the first occurrence, if you find "a" then rule 1, else look at occurrence 2, if you find "b" then rule 2, else look at occurrence 3, if you find "c" then rule 3 else match fails.

- With $\Pi = [\mathcal{F}(a,\Omega,\Omega); \mathcal{F}(b,\Omega,\Omega); \mathcal{F}(\Omega,\Omega,c)]$ and $MEP_\Pi = \{\mathcal{F}(a,\Omega,\Omega), \mathcal{F}(b,\Omega,\Omega), \mathcal{F}(c,\Omega,c)\}$ the patterns are pairwise incompatible and the building of the matching tree is straightforward.

- With $\Pi = [\mathcal{F}(a,\Omega,\Omega); \mathcal{F}(a,b,\Omega); \mathcal{F}(\Omega,\Omega,c)]$ and $MEP_\Pi = \{\mathcal{F}(a,\Omega,\Omega), \mathcal{F}(b,\Omega,c), \mathcal{F}(c,\Omega,c)\}$ the patterns are pairwise incompatible and the building of the matching tree is straightforward.

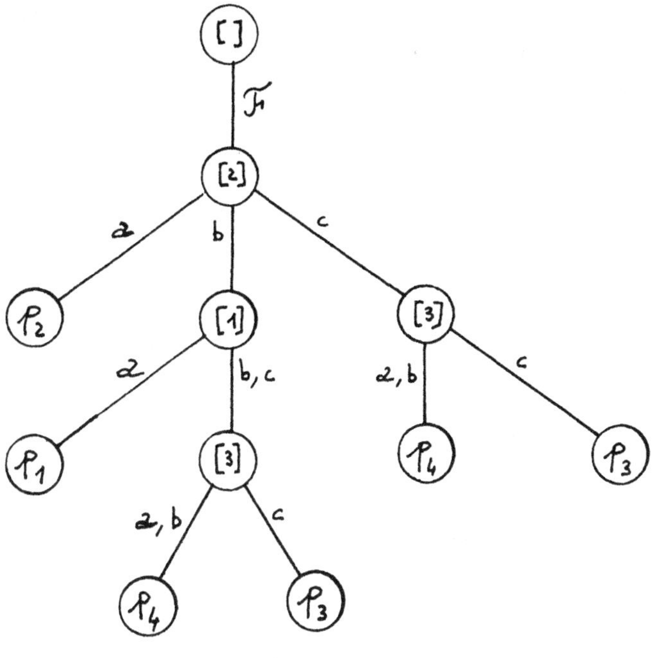

Figure 1: Matching tree

- With $\Pi = [\mathcal{F}(a,b,\Omega);\ \mathcal{F}(\Omega,a,\Omega);\ \mathcal{F}(\Omega,\Omega,c);\ \mathcal{F}(\Omega,\Omega,\Omega)]$, the set MEP_Π will consist of $\{\mathcal{F}(a,b,\Omega), \mathcal{F}(\Omega,a,\Omega), \mathcal{F}(\Omega,c,c), \mathcal{F}(b,b,c), \mathcal{F}(c,b,c), \mathcal{F}(\Omega,c,a), \mathcal{F}(\Omega,c,b), \mathcal{F}(b,b,a), \mathcal{F}(b,b,b), \mathcal{F}(c,b,a), \mathcal{F}(c,b,b)\}$. One can easily check that the extended patterns are pairwise incompatible and it remains to build the matching tree. In $\mathcal{F}(\Omega,\Omega,\Omega)$ the index is the second occurrence. If we find here the symbol "a" then we have to apply the second rule. If we find a "b" we have to look at the first occurrence : if there is a "a" apply the first rule, otherwise look at the third occurrence where a "c" leads to rule three and "a" or "b" to rule four. If, when looking at the second occurrence, one finds a "c" then one has to look at the third occurrence where a "c" leads to the third rule and "a" or "b" to the fourth. (see the matching tree, with some modifications in order to improve readability, in figure 1).

  Since the building of the matching tree succeeds, we get a lazy pattern matching algorithm. However this algorithm is not straightforward and some ingenuity would be needed for a compiler to derive it directly from the initial list of patterns.

- With $\Pi = [\mathcal{F}(a,b,\Omega);\ \mathcal{F}(a,a,\Omega);\ \mathcal{F}(\Omega,\Omega,c);\ \mathcal{F}(\Omega,\Omega,\Omega)]$ the set MEP_Π will consist of $\{\mathcal{F}(a,b,\Omega), \mathcal{F}(a,a,\Omega), \mathcal{F}(c,\Omega,c), \mathcal{F}(b,\Omega,c), \mathcal{F}(\Omega,c,c), \mathcal{F}(b,\Omega,a), \mathcal{F}(b,\Omega,b), \mathcal{F}(c,\Omega,a), \mathcal{F}(c,\Omega,b), \mathcal{F}(\Omega,c,a), \mathcal{F}(\Omega,c,b)\}$. In this case there are compatible minimally extended patterns (for example

$\mathcal{F}$(c,Ω,c) and $\mathcal{F}$(Ω,c,c) in the set replacing the third initial pattern) and we cannot find a lazy pattern matching algorithm. A trouble for example comes from the fact that in order to recognize the third rule, one has to find a "c" at the third occurrence and to discard the first two rules. But this second condition is achieved looking at the first occurrence in some terms and at the second one in others so that the occurrence to look at can not be choosen before looking at its symbol.

The very important difference between the last two examples is due to a little change in the set of initial patterns. It would be rather difficult to detect such differences without a mechanical process such as the one we give here.

- We end with a more realistic example. It is an ML function which simulates a piece of the Categorical Abstract Machine (C.A.M., see [5] or [11]).

```
let rec Exec = fun
  (pair(x,y), (car::CC), D) ->  Exec (x, CC, D)
| (pair(x,y), (cdr::CC), D) ->  Exec (y, CC, D)
| (T, (Cons::CC), (val(T')::D))
             ->  Exec (pair(T',T), CC, D)
| (pair(closure(x,y),z), (app::CC), D)
             ->  Exec (pair(y,z), x, (adr(CC)::D))
| (T, (cur(x)::CC), D)
             ->  Exec (closure(x,T), CC, D)
| (T, [], _) -> T;;
```

One can see the first element of each pattern as the register of the machine, the second one as the code (list of instructions) to be executed and the third one as a stack (implemented as a list). The above function describes what to do when getting each instruction at first place in the code or when code is empty. Of course in a real case there would be much more instructions and hence much more cases in the function definition.

In this case, we see that all the patterns are pairwise incompatible : they are all distinct in the code argument. However, what is interesting here is that the building of the matching tree shows that one has to look first at the second argument and if it is not the empty list to the first element of the list that one finds. This is sufficient to select the only rule which may be applied (it remains to verify the other conditions to apply it). All the already implemented pattern matching compilations fail to recognize this fact and give a code that does useless work (for the algorithms used see [1], [4] and [14]). This is, at least, true when the code is placed at a well chosen occurrence : for example, CAML would not do useless work if the code was placed at first place in the triple.

6 Conclusion

6.1 Implementation

In order to insert our method in a compiler for an ML system, one has to solve some other problems : for example ML accepts infinite signatures to build the patterns, allowing them to contain integers or strings. This may be solved since there is only a finite number of integers or strings that effectively appear in the patterns ; one only has to group other values as a single otherwise case. The same method is used to take into account that other constructors may appear in the value to match, than those that one find in the patterns. Some trouble may come from the internal representation of ML structured values, of which some parts are discarded for the sake of efficiency (see Suarez [14]) : this only leads to some complications in the algorithm. We also have to give a compilation of the pattern matching even in the cases where there is no lazy pattern matching algorithm : issuing a warning, we pick an occurrence that is useful at least in one case, and continue the building of a matching tree with this occurrence as if it was an index. This gives a pattern matching algorithm but of course lazyness is lost.

We are also led to address the point of efficiency in our compilation, and particularly when searching for indexes and building the set MEP_{Π}. However experimental versions of a pattern matching compiler produce CAM code from ML code using less than twice the time that the present compiler uses. On the other hand these versions use simpler internal representations of the patterns and one can expect some gain on the parsing time. Moreover the CAM code seems to be more compact and may run faster. Another possible improvement (that is still under test too) is the following : when our algorithm recognizes the expression to evaluate, the set of occurrences it looked at in the argument is known ; if we keep pointers at them the access to variables appearing in this expression may be significantly improved.

All these facts lead us to try to implement such a pattern matching compilation not only in the lazy version of the CAML system but also in the strict version. We expect some efficiency gain in the two cases (we recall here the example of the function simulating the C.A.M.). However some further experiment is needed to determine exactly what is really useful among the possible improvements we listed above.

For further information (including more realistic algorithms to generate the set of minimally extended patterns) on this part of the work, see author's thesis([9]).

6.2 Further work

Apart from the implementation work in progress, we want to look at some extensions of this paper.

The first one is to extend the theoretical results to other systems. This covers ambiguous pattern matching with other priority rule than ML, but also investigating the possibilities of extending them to Term Rewriting Systems with ambiguous left-hand-sides and priority meta-rules to ensure determinism of computation (as is proposed for example in [2]).

The second interesting extension of this work is strictness analysis. It has been introduced as a way of improving lazy systems by determining at compile time that some parts of the values are always needed and may be evaluated without "delaying" or "freezing" mechanism. If we know that the lazy pattern matching algorithm needs to evaluate some part of the argument of a function this gives us this kind of information. Moreover when compiling the expression associated with a pattern we can use the fact that some parts of the argument have been evaluated during the pattern matching process.

Strictness analysis has another connection with lazy pattern matching. In fact a lazy language does not need a lazy pattern matching algorithm : it only needs that the application of a function to its argument does not evaluate not needed part of the argument. Now look at a function using Berry's example :

$$\begin{array}{lll} fun & (true, false, x) & \rightarrow & x \\ | & (false, x, true) & \rightarrow & x \\ | & (x, true, false) & \rightarrow & x \end{array}$$

Since we did not modify the patterns there is no lazy pattern matching algorithm, but as the expression to evaluate in order to return the result is in each case that part of the argument that the pattern matching algorithm does not need, we see that the whole argument is always needed. Hence the function's result may be lazyly evaluated using any pattern matching algorithm. However there is no mean of deciding what part of a general ML expression will always be evaluated. So there is here much work to gain efficiency from the concept of strictness analysis, and finding a lazy pattern matching algorithm remains the only systematic way to ensure that the function evaluation will always be lazy.

References

[1] L. Augustsson "A Compiler for Lazy ML", A.C.M. Conference on Lisp and Functional Programming, Austin 1984, pp 218-225

[2] J. Baeten J. Bergstra J. Klop "Priority Rewrite Systems", Report CS-R8407, Center for Mathematics and Computer Science, Amsterdam

[3] R. Burstall D. MacQueen D. Sannella "HOPE : An Experimental Applicative Language", A.C.M. Conference on Lisp and Functional Programming, Stanford 1980, pp 136-143

[4] L. Cardelli "Compiling a Functional Language", A.C.M. Conference on Lisp and Functional Programming, Austin 1984, pp 208-217

[5] G. Cousineau P.L. Curien M. Mauny "The Categorical Abstract Machine", in J.P. Jouannaud ed. Functional Programming Languages and Computer Architecture, L.N.C.S. 201, Springer-Verlag 1985

[6] P.L. Curien "Categorical Combinators, Sequential Algorithms and Functional Programming", Research Notes in Theoretical Computer Science, Pitman Publishing Ltd 1986

[7] G. Huet J.J. Lévy "Call by Need Computations in Non Ambiguous Linear Term Rewriting Systems", Rapport IRIA Laboria 359, August 1979

[8] G. Kahn G. Plotkin "Domaines concrets", Rapport IRIA Laboria 336, December 1978

[9] A. Laville "Filtrage et Evaluation paresseuse", Thèse de Doctorat, Université Paris 7, to appear

[10] M. Mauny "Compilation des Langages Fonctionnels dans les Combinateurs Catégoriques, Application au langage ML", Thèse de 3ème cycle, Université Paris 7, 1985

[11] M. Mauny A. Suarez "Implementing Functional Languages in the Categorical Abstract Machine", A.C.M. Conference on Lisp and Functional Programming, Cambridge 1986, pp 266-278

[12] R. Milner "A Proposal for Standard ML", A.C.M. Conference on Lisp and Functional Programming, Austin 1984, pp 184-197

[13] G. Plotkin "Call-by-need, Call-by-value and the Lambda Calculus", T.C.S. Vol 1, pp 125-159, 1975

[14] A. Suarez "Une Implémentation de ML en ML", Thèse, Université Paris 7, to appear

[15] D. Turner "Miranda a Non Strict Functional Language with Polymorphic Types", in J.P. Jouannaud ed. Functional Programming Languages and Computer Architecture, L.N.C.S. 201, Springer-Verlag 1985

PROGRAM DEVELOPMENT USING LAMBDA ABSTRACTION

Alberto Pettorossi
IASI-CNR, Viale Manzoni 30
I-00185 Roma (Italy)

ABSTRACT

We study the problem of avoiding multiple traversals of data structures in functional programming. A solution proposed in [Bir84] makes use of lazy evaluation and local recursion. We show that analogous perfomances can be achieved using higher order functions and lambda abstractions. The solution we propose works for the call-by-value evaluation rule and it does not require local recursion. We also show through some examples that higher order functions allow us to simulate the use of pointers of a Pascal-like language. We finally spend a few words on a theory of strategies for program development.

1. INTRODUCTION

We address the problem of program derivation from specifications, or more precisely, the problem of deriving efficient programs by transformation and symbolic evaluation. In particular, we focus our attention on the strategies one may adopt for the development of functional programs. We analyze the problems involved in the construction of programs which avoid multiple traversals of data structures, and we propose a novel approach as an alternative to the one suggested in [Bir84], which need local recursion and lazy evaluation. Moreover, our approach suggests a specific methodology, and we think that, precisely for that respect, it is an improvement on the approaches of [Bir84, Tak87]. In those papers, in fact, no general methods are introduced for the definition of the new functions needed during the development of programs.

We show that using higher order functions and the lambda abstraction strategy (defined in the paper), one can derive through program transformation, one-pass algorithms from multi-pass ones. We also give suggestions to the programmer on how to invent the auxiliary functions needed for the derivations and how to apply the proposed strategy (together with the tupling strategy [Pet84]). Those suggestions are given through the study of some challenging examples.

In functional programs the efficient manipulation of data structures is considered to be a difficult problem to tackle, because pointers are not avalable. We will study that problem and we will present a clean solution which makes use of lambda expressions.

We will also analyze the relationship between the "shifting of data boundaries" in program development [JøS86] on one hand, and the composition and lambda abstraction strategies on the other hand. We will also compare the generation of new bound variables for the lambda expressions introduced using abstraction, with the use of extra arguments in Prolog-like programs.

Finally we will present some preliminary ideas for the study and the classification of various program derivation strategies.

2. THE PALINDROME EXAMPLE

As a first example of use of our proposed *lambda abstraction strategy* (also called *higher order generalization* strategy [PeS87], or simply, *abstraction* strategy) we will derive a program for testing whether or not a list of integers is palindromic. In this example we will also use the tupling strategy, which is already well known and often considered in the transformation methodology (for a brief account see [Fea86]). The *lambda abstraction strategy* consists in replacing the expression:

"e where x = e1" by the semantically equivalent expression: "(λx.e) e1".

Since the subexpression e1 occurring within e is replaced by the variable x, the application of the abstraction strategy may allow us to perform "folding steps" which are otherwise impossible.
It may also allow us to suspend computations because the evaluation of e is performed only when the lambda expression λx.e is applied to e1. This fact is very important, because often we may also want to simulate lazy evaluation using call-by-value.

For our palindrome problem we will obtain a one-pass algorithm whose execution is essentially the same as the one evoked by the program given in [Bir84], but it does not need either *local recursion* or *lazy evaluation*. We will achieve the same time × space performances via the use of the abstraction strategy. The bound variables will play the role of pointers and we will be able to manipulate them within the framework of functional languages in a referentially transparent way.

As in [Bir84] we start off from the following initial program version:

1. palindrome(*l*) = eqlist(*l*,rev(*l*))
2. eqlist([],[]) = true
3. eqlist(a:*l*1,b:*l*2) = (a=b) and eqlist(*l*1,*l*2)
4. rev([]) = []
5. rev(a:*l*1) = rev(*l*1) @ [a].

As usual ':' denotes the 'cons' operation on lists, @ denotes the concatenation of lists, and [] denotes the empty list. Now we may apply the composition strategy for the given expression of palindrome(*l*), that is, eqlist(*l*,rev(*l*)).
After a few unfolding steps we get:

palindrome([]) = true
palindrome(a:*l*) = eqlist(a:*l*, rev(a:*l*))
= a=hd(rev(*l*) @ [a]) and eqlist(*l*, tl(rev(*l*) @ [a]))
= a=hd(x @ [a]) and eqlist(*l*, tl(x @ [a])) where x=rev(*l*)

and by abstraction strategy we have:

palindrome(a:*l*) = λx.(a=hd(x @ [a]) and eqlist(*l*, tl(x @ [a]))) rev(*l*). (#)

Now, looking for a recursive definition of palindrome(*l*), it seems that our derivation process cannot proceed because we cannot fold eqlist(*l*,tl(x@[a])) as an instance of eqlist(*l*,rev(*l*)). At this point we use the "mismatch information" [Dar81] for choosing the strategy to apply.

In order to allow a folding step between eqlist(*l*, tl(x @ [a])) and eqlist(*l*,rev(*l*)) we need to *generalize* rev(*l*) to a variable, say z. (That generalization technique has been often used in the literature [Aub76, BoM75]). Then, by abstraction from eqlist(*l*,z) we get: λz.eqlist(*l*,z). Moreover, since rev(*l*) and λz.eqlist(*l*,z) both visit the same data structure *l* we can apply the *tupling strategy* [Pet84]. Thus we are led to the following definition of the auxiliary function:

Q(*l*) ≡ < λz.eqlist(*l*,z), rev(*l*) >. Its explicit definition is:

6. Q([]) = < λz.null(z), [] > (by unfolding);
7. Q(a:*l*)= < λz.eqlist(a:*l*,z), rev(a:*l*) >
   = < λz. a=hd(z) and eqlist(*l*, tl(z)), rev(*l*) @ [a] >
   = < λz. a=hd(z) and u(tl(z)), v@[a] > where <u,v>=Q(*l*) (by folding).

The final program consists of the above equations 6, and 7, together with:

1'. palindrome(*l*) = u v where <u,v> = Q(*l*).

Notice that the abstraction strategy together with the tupling strategy allows us to express Q(a:*l*) in terms of Q(*l*) only. Therefore a linear recursive definition of Q(*l*) is derived and the list *l* is visited only once. During that visit we test the equality of lists and at the same time, we compute the reverse of the given list.

The above algorithm requires essentially the same time and space resources needed in the algorithm presented in [Bir84], which we rewrite here for the reader's convenience:

B1. Bird-palindrome(*l*) = π1(p) whererec p = eqrev(x, π2(p), [])

B2. eqrev([], y, z) = < true, [] >

B3. eqrev(a:*l*, y, z) = < (a=hd(y)) and u, v > where <u,v>=eqrev(x, tl(y), a:z).

As usual, πi(p) denotes the i-th projection of p.

Two questions naturally arise at this point: i) in what sense the given list *l* is visited only once, and ii) what is the relation between our program and Bird's program.

Here is the sequence of Q calls for computing palindrome([1,2]) using our algorithm:

palindrome([1,2]) = u v where <u,v>=Q([1,2]):

l=[1,2]	Q(*l*) = < λz.1 =hd(z) and u([2]), v@[1] >	where <u,v> = Q(tl(*l*))
tl(*l*)=*l*'=[2]	Q(*l*') = < λz.2=hd(z) and u([]), v@[2] >	where <u,v> = Q(tl(*l*'))
tl(*l*')=*l*"=[]	Q(*l*") = < λz.null(z), [] >.	

During the visit of a given list *l*, a functional data structure u and a list data structure v are constructed as the first and second component of Q(*l*)=<u,v>. The final application (u v) could be considered as a second visit of the list rev(*l*) recorded in v, but it formally occurs without reference to hd or tl operations.

In any case the described behaviour is the same which is obtained using Bird-palindrome, but in Bird's approach it is necessary to compute using lazy evaluation. We are able to do without it, because the relevant computations are suspended via lambda abstractions.

Notice that the construction of one-pass algorithm depends on the 'access functions' which are available for the data structures under consideration. Indeed the one-pass palindrome algorithm would have been obvious if for any given list *l* we had the access functions 'last(*l*)' computing the last element of *l* and the function 'begin(*l*)' computing the list *l* without the last element.

The use of a one-pass algorithm for palindrome(*l*) allows 'on-line computations' in the sense that while the items of a given list are input in a left to right order, some computations can be performed, and at the end of the input, what it remains to be done is only a final function application. (That operation can be considered as an unexpensive task within an applicative language.)

Computer experiments in our ML implementation on VAX-VMS show that the derived program (1",6',7') runs faster than the original program (1,2,3,4,5) for lists of about 100 items or more.

The advantages we get with our higher order approach are the following ones:

i) we can explicitly manipulate bounded variables, which can be used like pointers. In Bird's approach pointers are implicitly used, and it is difficult to see that the derived programs preserve termination. In our approach termination is guaranteed by structural induction of the function definitions.

ii) We do not need the lazy evaluation mode, but call-by-value together with lambda abstraction is sufficient.

iii) The programmer is not required to learn any unfamiliar method. Bird himself says that his local recursive programs "require a little practice". For instance, it is not immediate to see that in Bird-palindrome the replacement of B3 by the following:
B3'. eqrev(a:*l*, b:y, z) = < (a=b) and u, v > where <u,v>=eqrev(x, y, a:z),
leads to a an infinite loop [Bir84].
On the contrary, we think that lambda expressions are familiar objects, and any functional programmer knows how to use functions as "first class citizens" (see [Bac78, Bir86]).

iv) In the derivation of the program B1-B2-B3, Bird does not give any fundamental reason for the introduction of new auxiliary function 'eqrev'. Sometimes in his paper analogous definitions are suggested by "little foresight" [Bir84, p. 245] or given without justification. Our aim is to provide methods for suggesting suitable function definitions: this is the essential role of the strategies we present and we will show through some examples that they work in a large variety of cases.

Let us finally remark that as in Bird's program we can perform the derivation using an "accumulator version" of the reverse function, that is, using rev(*l*) defined as rev1(*l*,[]) where:

rev1([],y) = y

rev1(a:*l*,y) = rev1(*l*,a:y), where the second argument behaves indeed as an accumulator.

In that case we use the function R(*l*,y) ≡ < λz.eqlist(*l*,z), rev1(*l*,y) > instead of the function Q(*l*) ≡ <λz.eqlist(*l*,z), rev(*l*)>.

The final program one can get is the following one:

1". palindrome(*l*) = u v where <u,v>=R(*l*,[]).

6'. R([],y) = < λz.null(z), y >

7'. R(a:*l*,y) = < λz.a=hd(z) and u(tl(z)), v > where <u,v>=R(*l*,a:y).

That program can be gotten by replaying the same derivation steps presented above. This fact also shows the power of the abstraction and tupling strategies. Notice that the given example is an evidence for the need of replaying program derivations. Indeed most existing program-derivation systems have that "replay" feature.

The reader should also notice that the generalization strategy *without* the lambda abstraction, is *not* powerful enough to solve our problem of obtaining a one-pass algorithm. In fact, if we do not use abstraction we have, instead of the function R, the function:

$R^*(l,z,y) \equiv \langle \mathrm{eqlist}(l,z), \mathrm{rev1}(l,y) \rangle$, whose explicit definition is:

8. $R^*([],z,y) = \langle \mathrm{null}(z),\ y \rangle$

9. $R^*(a{:}l,z,y) = \langle a{=}\mathrm{hd}(z)\ \underline{\mathrm{and}}\ u,\ v \rangle\quad \underline{\mathrm{where}}\ \langle u,v\rangle = R^*(l, \mathrm{tl}(z), a{:}y)$. We also have:

10. $\mathrm{palindrome}^*(l) = \pi 1\ R^*(l, \mathrm{rev1}(l,[]), [])$.

But, unfortunately, palindrome*(*l*) is not good enough for our purposes: it visits twice the list *l* in a call-by-value mode of evaluation. In fact, we need to compute first the value of the argument rev1(*l*,[]) and then we have to compute R*(*l*, rev1(*l*,[]), []), visiting again the list *l*. It was exactly this point which stimulated Bird's analysis in his paper.

3. MODIFYING AND SORTING LEAVES OF TREES

Let us consider some more examples of program derivation using the lambda abstraction strategy. Through those examples we hope that the reader may convince himself that the abstraction strategy is not an ad-hoc mechanism. Those examples were used also by Bird to show that circular programs and call-by-need are nice features to include in applicative languages for deriving very efficient programs. We do not contrast that view here, we only want to show that the same efficiency can be achieved if we allow ourselves functions which return functions as values.

We will also see that the lambda abstraction strategy allows the clean handling of pointers within the framework of applicative languages (via the use of the bound variables) and it makes it possible to suspend computations in a call-by-value semantics.

The first example is about the construction of the binary tree Min-tree(t) which is like a given tree t, except that all its leaves are equal to the minimum leaf of t.

Let tip: num→tree and ^: tree×tree→tree be the obvious constructors for binary trees. A two-pass algorithm is as follows:

Min-tree(t) = repl(t,minl(t)), where minl computes the minimum leaf value:

minl(tip(n)) = n

minl(t1^t2) = min(minl(t1),minl(t2)), and repl(t,m) replaces the leaf values of a given tree t by its minimum leaf value m:

repl(tip(n),m) = tip(m)

repl(t1^t2,m) = repl(t1,m) ^ repl(t2,m).

Looking for a one-pass algorithm we may try to apply the composition strategy by defining:

V(t) ≡ repl(t,minl(t)). However, having obtained:

V(tip(n)) = tip(n)

$V(t1 \wedge t2) = repl(t1, minl(t1 \wedge t2)) \wedge repl(t2, minl(t1 \wedge t2))$,

we cannot fold the two above recursive calls of repl. We may try to apply the generalization strategy [AbV84, Aub76] by defining: $V^*(t,t') \equiv repl(t, minl(t'))$, but the reader may check that it does not work. A possible way to proceed is to apply the lambda abstraction strategy, so that:

$V(t1 \wedge t2) = repl(t1,x) \wedge repl(t2,x)$ <u>where</u> $x = min(minl(t1), minl(t2))$

$= (\lambda x.(repl(t1,x) \wedge repl(t2,x)))$ $min(minl(t1), minl(t2))$.

Now we can apply the tupling strategy because repl and minl both visit the same data structure t1. We define: $W(t) \equiv < \lambda z.repl(t,z), minl(t) >$. We get:

M1. $W(tip(n)) = < \lambda z.tip(z), n >$

M2. $W(t1 \wedge t2) = < \lambda z.(repl(t1,z) \wedge repl(t2,z)), min(minl(t1), minl(t2)) >$

$= < (\lambda z.\ T1 \wedge T2), min(m1,m2) >$ <u>where</u> $<\lambda z.T1, m1> = W(t1)$

<u>and</u> $<\lambda z.T2, m2> = W(t2)$

M3. Min-tree(t) = f m <u>where</u> <f,m> = W(t).

The folding step for equation M2 is possible and the one-pass algorithm is obtained. In fact, $W(t1 \wedge t2)$ is defined in terms of W(t1) and W(t2) only. During the visit of a given tree t, we construct in the first component of W(t) a functional data structure which basically encodes a copy of t and therefore, we wast space. One may say that in the above algorithm time efficiency has been achieved at the expense of memory efficiency. However, at this point the *destructiveness analysis* [Myc81, Pet78] can be applied, so that the cells necessary for the first component of W(t) are obtained from the ones of the given tree t, which can be discarded 'on the fly', while the visit progresses.

We think that our derivation of the algorithm M1-M2-M3, which is essentially the same given by Bird, has its importance, because it clarifies the folding requirement in the invention of the relevant auxiliary functions. In Bird's paper those functions are introduced without much explanation, so that the reader may find difficult to use his proposed methodology in other programs.

The example we have considered above shows also a correspondence between *logical variables* in Prolog-like languages and *bound variables* of lambda abstractions, which we will now explain.

Let us look first at a solution to the above tree transformation problem written in Prolog. (For this version we thank A. Falkner and T. Frühwirth of the Technical University of Vienna).

P1. mintree(Intree, Outtree) ← visit(Intree, Outtree, Min, Min).

P2. visit(treeof(InL,InR), treeof(OutL,OutR), Inmin, Outmin)

← visit(InL, OutL, Inmin,MinL), visit(InR, OutR, Inmin, MinR), min(MinL, MinR, Outmin).

P3. visit(tip(N), tip(X), X, N).

min(M,N,X) binds X to the minimum value between M and N.

The above Prolog program is deterministic and it makes one visit only of the given input tree Intree when producing the output tree Outtree. It is the equality of the last two arguments of the initial call of the predicate 'visit' which realizes the desired tree modification.

The correctness of the program mintree is not too difficult to prove, but it is *not* given us for free, while the correctness of our program Min-tree is straightforward, because it was derived by transformation. It would be interesting to develop a program transformation method for Prolog programs in order to obtain, for instance, the above program P1-P2-P3 from a two-pass algorithm of the form:

P1'. mintree1(Intree, Outtree) ← minleaf(Intree, Min), build(Intree,Outtree,Min).

P2'. minleaf(treeof(L,R), Min) ← minleaf(L,MinL), minleaf(R,MinR), min(MinL,MinR,Min).

P3'. minleaf(tip(N), N).

P4'. build(treeof(InL,InR), treeof(OutL,OutR), Min)
← build(InL,OutL,Min), build(InR,OutR,Min).

P5'. build(tip(N), tip(Min), Min).

The Prolog program P1-P2-P3 shows the correspondence between the role of the extra logical variable which is used by the predicate 'visit' (with 4 arguments) w.r.t. the predicate 'build' (with 3 arguments) and the bound variable z in the first component of W(t), that is, λz.repl(t,z).

The flow of information during the execution of the program P1-P2-P3 shows also an interesting relationship between the Prolog programs we have presented and the evaluation of attributes in *Attribute Grammars*. Indeed the two arguments Inmin and Outmin of the predicate 'visit' in the equation P2 above, are respectively inherited and synthesized attributes.

Prof. Swierstra recently showed us an applicative program for computing Min-tree(t) which was derived (without using transformation techniques) by analysing the given problem from the attribute grammars point of view [Swi85]. The ability of writing a one-pass algorithm is related to the fact that for Knuthian semantic systems [ChM79] with synthesized and inherited attributes one can obtain equivalent systems in a purely synthesized form. ■

Let us consider now a second example. In this case we are asked to construct a tree which is like a given one, but its leaves should be ordered 'from left to right'. That construction should take place in one-pass only. A two-pass version of the program is as follows:

S1. Sort-tree(t) = replace(t,sort(leaves(t))),

where: i) leaves(t) computes the list of the leaves of the tree t,

ii) sort(*l*) rearranges the list *l* of leaf values in an ascending order from left to right, and

iii) replace(t,*l*) uses the leftmost k values of the list *l* to replace the k leaf values of the tree t, in the left to right order.

We assume, as Bird does, that sort is an 'a priori' given routine, whose performances have been already optimized. The definition of leaves and replace are as follows:

S2. leaves(tip(n)) = [n]

S3. leaves(t1^t2) = leveas(t1) @ leaves(t2)

S4. replace(tip(n),*l*) = tip(hd(*l*))

S5. replace(t1^t2,*l*) = replace(t1,*l*1) ^ replace(t2,*l*2) <u>where</u> <*l*1,*l*2>=cut(size(t1),*l*),

where: size(t) computes the number of leaves in a given tree t,

cut(k,*l*) produces from a given list *l* a pair of lists <*l*1,*l*2> such that *l*1@*l*2=*l* and length(*l*1)=k.

We assume that: 0≤k≤length(*l*) holds for any call of cut(k,*l*), and
size(t) ≤ length(*l*) holds for any call of replace(t,*l*).

For instance, size(tip(4)^tip(5))=2 and cut(4,[5,3,7,8,6])=<[5,3,7,8],[6]>. We have:

S6. size(tip(n)) = 1

S7. size(t1^t2) = size(t1) + size(t2)

S8. cut(0,*l*) = < [], *l* >

S9. cut(n+1,*l*) = < *l*1 @ [hd(*l*2)], tl(*l*2) > where <*l*1,*l*2>=cut(n,*l*).

For instance, if t ≡ ((6^3)(4^3))(1^(4^5)) (for simplicity we write n instead of tip(n)) then Sort-tree(t) ≡ ((1^3)(3^4))(4^(5^6)).

As usual, for deriving a one-pass algorithm from the equations S1-...-S9 we proceed by applying the composition strategy to the equation S1. Unfortunately it is impossible to make a folding step. We get, in fact:

replace(tip(n),sort(leaves(tip(n)))) = replace(tip(n),sort([n])) = tip(n)

replace(t1^t2,sort(leaves(t1^t2))) = replace(t1,*l*1) ^ replace(t2,*l*2) (♦)
where <*l*1,*l*2>=cut(size(t1), sort(leaves(t1^t2))),

and it is not possible to derive the recursive calls to Sort-tree(t1) and Sort-tree(t2). That fact is due to the existence of *relevant information* shared between the two recursive calls of replace. Therefore we may try to apply the abstraction strategy by defining: λx.replace(t,x).

Since λx.replace(t,x), sort(leaves(t)), and size(t) visit the same data structure t, the Tupling Strategy leads us to the definition of: Z(t) ≡ < λx.replace(t,x), sort(leaves(t)), size(t) >. We then have:

Z(tip(n)) = < λx.replace(tip(n),x), sort(leaves(tip(n))), size(tip(n)) >
= < λx.tip(hd(x)), [n], 1 >.

Z(t1^t2) = < λx.replace(t1^t2,x), sort(leaves(t1^t2)), size(t1^t2) >
= < λx.replace(t1,*l*1) ^ replace(t2,*l*2) where <*l*1,*l*2>=cut(size(t1), x),
merge(sort(leaves(t1)),sort(leaves(t2))), size(t1) + size(t2) >
= < λx.((A1 *l*1) ^ (B1 *l*2) where <*l*1,*l*2>=cut(A3, x)), merge(A2,B2), A3+B3 >
where <A1,A2,A3>=Z(t1) and <B1,B2,B3>=Z(t2)

HOSort-tree(t) = (A1 A2) where <A1,A2,A3>=Z(t).

In the definition of Z(t) merge(*l*1,*l*2) is regarded as a primitive function, and it gives us the ordered list which is the result of merging the two ordered list *l*1 and *l*2.

The above program HOSort-tree(t) is a one-pass program in the sense that Z(t1^t2) is defined in terms of Z(t1) and Z(t2) only. As in the Palindrome Example, during the visit of the tree t, information is collected in the components of Z(t), so that one visit only need to be made.
Computer experiments made in our VAX-VMS system using ML show that HOSort-tree(t) is faster than Sort-tree(t) for trees t of about size 30 or larger.

Let us now make a few comments on the comparison of our algorithm with the one in [Bir84]:
i) we have shown, as in the Palindrome Example, that lambda abstraction and tupling strategies are powerful enough to derive a one-pass algorithm, so that circular programs and local recursion are not necessary;
ii) Bird uses two functions, take(k,*l*) and drop(k,*l*), while we use the function cut(k,*l*) (see the equation S5). Their defining relationship is as follows: cut(k,*l*) = <take(k,*l*),drop(k,*l*)>.
A question may arise here: whether or not it would be possible to perform a derivation analogous to the one we have presented above, if we had the following equation S5' [Bir84], instead of S5:
S5'. replace(t1^t2,*l*) = replace(t1,take(k,*l*)) ^ replace(t2,drop(k,*l*)) where k=size(t1).

The answer is positive, and this fact shows again the power of our strategies. The derivation proceeds as follows. By composition strategy the above equation (♦) becomes:

replace(t1^t2,sort(leaves(t1^t2))) = replace(t1,take(size(t1),x)) ^ replace(t2,drop(size(t1),x))
where x=sort(leaves(t1^t2)). (♦♦)

Now we have to look for a folding of the recursive calls of replace. In order to do so, we may use a simple fact (similar to those used in [Bir84, p. 248]): for any list x, take(length(x),x) = x. We then have:
- take(size(t),sort(leaves(t))) = sort(leaves(t)), and therefore:
- if size(t1)+size(t2) = length(x) then drop(size(t1),x) = take(size(t2),drop(size(t1),x)).

Then we can rewrite the equation (♦♦) as follows:
replace(t1^t2,take(size(t1^t2),sort(leaves(t1^t2))))
= replace(t1,take(size(t1),x)) ^ replace(t2,take(size(t2),drop(size(t1),x)))
where x=sort(leaves(t1^t2)).

We are "almost" on the position of folding the recursive calls of replace, but we first need to apply the abstraction strategy.
i) replace(t1,take(size(t1),x)) where x=sort(leaves(t1^t2)) is lambda-abstracted to:

((λx.replace(t1,take(size(t1),x))) sort(leaves(t1^t2))), and

ii) replace(t2,take(size(t2),drop(size(t1),x))) where x=sort(leaves(t1^t2))
is lambda-abstracted twice, and we get:

(λx.((λy.replace(t2,take(size(t2),y))) drop(size(t1),x)) sort(leaves(t1^t2))).

Therefore, since we want to visit the tree t1 only once, by tupling strategy we are prompted to tuple the following three functions together because they all visit the same tree t1:

Z*(t) ≡ < λx.replace(t,take(size(t),x)), λx.drop(size(t),x), sort(leaves(t)) >.

After a few unfolding steps we have:

Z*(tip(n)) = < λx.tip(hd(x)), λx.tl(x), [n] >

Z*(t1^t2) = < λx.(replace(t1,take(size(t1),x)) ^ replace(t2,take(size(t2),drop(size(t1),x)))),
λx.drop(size(t1)+size(t2),x), merge(sort(leaves(t1)), sort(leaves(t2))) >
= < λx.((A1 x) ^ (B1 (A2 x))), λx.(A2 (B2 x)), merge(A3,B3) >
where <A1,A2,A3>=Z*(t1) and <B1,B2,B3>=Z*(t2).

HOSort-tree*(t) = (A1 A3) where <A1,A2,A3>=Z*(t).

The last folding step is based on the fact that:

λx.drop(size(t1)+size(t2),x) = ((λx.drop(size(t1),x)) (λy.drop(size(t2),y))).

As in the Palindrome Example the reader may check that using generalization only (and not lambda abstraction), the derivation process is not successful.

Notice that while Bird need intuition for the invention of the tuple function Z*(t), in our approach that function is derived as a straightforward application of the abstraction and tupling strategies by looking for a "forced folding" [Dar81].

To be more precise Bird uses a function which is not exactly Z*(t) because the third component is leaves(t) instead of sort(leaves(t)). (Indeed Bird uses the two-arguments function leaves(t,*l*) instead of leaves(t) for avoiding the expensive concatenation operation occurring in S3 in favour of a 'cons' operation). That decision derives from the fact that he chooses the function 'sort' as a primitive function, while we choose the function 'merge'. Our choice allows us to perform the sorting of the leaves while the visit of the input tree is in progress.

With reference to [Bir84] let us finally notice that:
i) as in Bird's solution our program in terms of Z(t) (and also the one in terms of Z*(t)) computes some components of the tupled functions which are never used, and
ii) the nested applications (B1 (A2 x)) and (A2 (B2 x)) in the first and second components of Z*(t1^t2) correspond to the double recursion of the function 'repnd'.

As usual, in our approach we do not need to perform any termination analysis, because we have it for free by structural induction of the function definitions.

4. RELATING LAMBDA ABSTRACTION TO OTHER DERIVATION STRATEGIES

1) *Lambda Abstraction and Composition Strategy.*

Often the Composition Strategy (also called Specialization Strategy [Sch81]) is used for eliminating the construction of intermediate data structures which are to be passed from one function to another. A typical example is when we have to compute h(x)≡f(g(x)) and the result of f(y) only depends on some 'limited' portion of the input y. In that case we do not need to construct the entire data structure g(x), and we are able to save memory [Wad85].

However, that improvement is often possible only if we can derive a recursive definition for h(x). For that purpose we need to make a folding step, and it may happen that the expression of h(x) is such that folding is impossible. In that case the strategies one can apply are essentially:

- strategies which modify the structure of the expression of h(x) by 'promoting' constants to variables (generalization strategies) so that the matching may be successful, and
- strategies which make h(x) to equal to the result of applying a lambda expression, that is: h(x) = (λz.e) e', where x occurs free in e or e'. The lambda abstraction λz.e allows the insertion of variables for subexpressions, namely z for e', and it also allows folding steps otherwise

impossible, because one can deal only with the subexpression λz.e instead of the whole expression h(x).

A problem with the Abstraction Strategy is that while it allows for folding, one cannot know in advance the structure of the bound arguments, because they occur as simple variables, and one may not take advantage of their properties for further efficiency improvements. Therefore, the Abstraction Strategy may be considered as opposite to the Composition Strategy where indeed one takes advantage of the properties of the arguments.

The Composition Strategy allows high memory and time perfomances when one can make folding steps and obtain recursive definitions. However, if folding steps are not possible then lambda abstractions steps are to be performed first.

By the Abstraction Strategy we tend to use more memory cells at run time, because we should reserve space for bound variables. But it is possible to save computation time, because data structures are visited less often. For that same reason, in fact, one can release the memory used by the data as soon as it has been visited for the last time.

2) *Lambda Abstraction and Partial Evaluation.*

The relationship between the two techniques can be viewed in the light of the discussion of the previous point. Indeed, the Partial Evaluation approach to program development and program construction includes also the Composition and Specialization Strategies [Sch81].

Partial Evaluation allows us to 'insert' extra information into the functions to be evaluated, so that at compile time we may derive more efficient code. The Lambda Abstraction approach is related to partial evaluation in the sense that it allows us to 'withdraw' information from function definitions, so that they may have enough parameters, and therefore allow (by folding) the derivation of improved program versions. Only at later stages we can 'reinsert' information into the function definitions and that reinsertion will take place when we apply those functions to their actual arguments.

The basic idea is that program manipulation and program derivation, in general, cannot proceed only by specialization of procedures, but it is often the case that in order to derive efficient programs, we need to withdraw the information concerning the structure of the arguments. This is basically what lambda abstraction does for us when it transforms the expression "e[e1]" (that is, "e" where the subexpression "e1" occurs one or more times), into the expression "(λx.e) e1" where "e" is obtained from "e[e1]" by replacing the occurrences of e1 by x.

An example of these ideas is given by the equation (#) of the Palindrome program. In that equation we withdraw from the expression "a=hd(rev(*l*) @ [a]) <u>and</u> eqlist(*l*, tl(rev(*l*) @ [a]))" the information that the initial part of the arguments of hd and tl is indeed the reverse of a list.

At later stages we reinsert the withdrawn information. We do so when that information is relevant and it may play a crucial role for efficiency improvements. This is done by the application of (λx.e) to e1 and by the subsequent substitutions evoked by β-reductions. In particular, in the Palindrome program for a list *l*, we reinserted the information concerning the initial part of the arguments of hd and tl only at the end of the construction of Q(*l*)=<u,v> when computing the application (u v).

If we view the Partial Evaluation as a function Part: Prog×Data → Prog such that: Sem(p,(d1,d2)) = Sem(Part(p,d1),d2) [Esh82], then the Abstraction Strategy may be viewed as a sort of *inverse*: indeed, for that strategy we may think of a function Lambda: Prog → Prog×Data such that: Sem(p)=Sem((λx.p1) d) for some data d occurring in p.
The examples we have given in the previous Sections indicate that there is scope in program development for such 'inverse-partial-evaluation'.

3) *Lambda Abstraction and Higher Order Functions.*

Lambda abstraction may generate functions which return functions as values. Sometimes however, the composition which could follows the abstraction step, eliminates higher order objects. An example of that possibility is given in [PeS87]. In that paper one can see that through function composition, higher order expressions involved in the definition of a one-pass toy compiler, vanish in favour of ground type values.

5. TOWARDS A THEORY OF STRATEGIES

As suggested by various people (see for instance [Ers82]), we may consider the problem of program development in the framework of the following equation:

i) Sem(Specs) = Sem(Prog),

meaning that given a specification Specs we should produce a program Prog with the same semantics.

Actually, we may think that Specs itself is a preliminary version of the desired program which can be executed in some machine. In this case we may want to produce a program which is more efficient than the initial one. Therefore, if we are given a cost function C for executing programs (that is, applying Sem to its argument) we also want:

ii) C(Sem, Prog) $\leq$ C(Sem, Specs).

It would be very good to have a transformation function Tr such that: Prog=Tr(Specs) and the above conditions i) and ii) hold. We cannot hope to find for any given cost function C a universal function Tr, satisfying i) and ii), but we can provide programming tools so that the task of finding Prog from Specs can be simplified, at least in some cases.

Let us now assume that: i) Specs is a program P0, that is, a preliminary executable version of the desired program, and ii) Prog is a program P1, that is, an improved derived version. We also assume that the rules for transforming programs are essentially the fold/unfold rules [BuD77]. Those rules preserve partial correctness only with respect to the semantics function, but we will require that they preserve total correctness as well. (For that purpose it is enough to show the termination of the derived program P1, when necessary). Therefore we have the following commutative diagram:

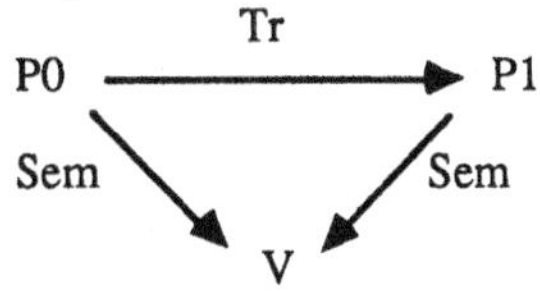

The problem of deriving P1 from P0 amounts to the construction of two program structures: Struct0 and Struct1, and three program transformations: Strategy, fold/unfold, Inverse-Strategy, as specified by the commutative diagram:

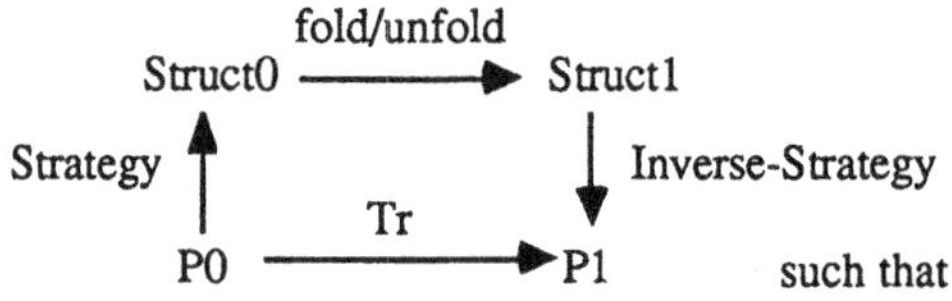

such that Sem(P0)=Sem(P1).

The construction of the above structures is often suggested by some *isomorphisms of data.* This is actually the case for the Tupling Strategy and the Abstraction Strategy.

The Tupling Strategy, in fact, is based on the isomorphism: $(A \to B) \times (A \to C) \cong A \to (B \times C)$. This means that the corresponding diagram is of the form:

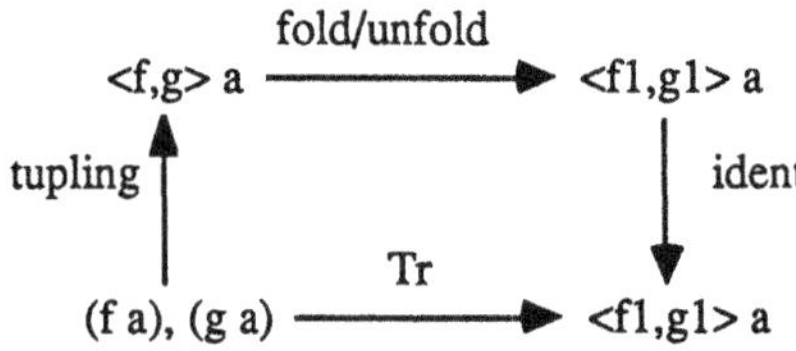

such that Sem((f a),(g a))=Sem(<f1,g1> a),

and time×memory requirements for the evaluation of ((f a), (g a)) may be reduced because the given data 'a' is traversed only once while computing (<f1,g1> a).

The Lambda Abstraction Strategy we have introduced in this paper, is based on the isomorphism: $((A \times B) \to C) \cong (A \to (B \to C))$ and it can be represented by the following diagram:

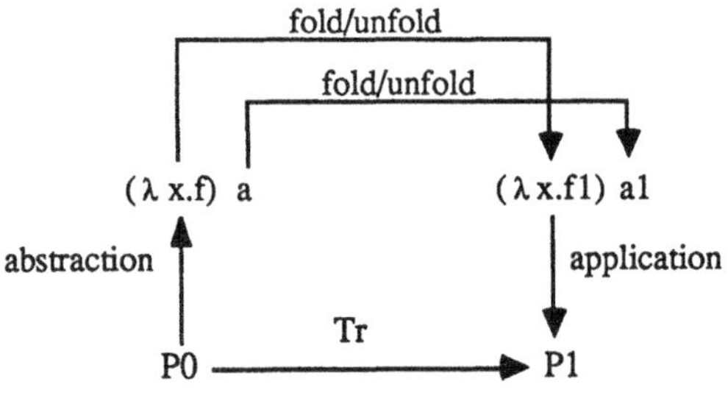

Notice that the strategies "come in pairs", that is, we need to find both an ascending arrow 'Strategy' and a descending arrow 'Inverse-Strategy' for our commutative diagrams. Isomorphisms of data domains give us those pairs in a simple and straightforward way.

Notice also that the two objects P0 and P1 in the lower sides of the diagrams we have presented above, need not be identical, but they must have the same semantics. Therefore, the class of morphisms to be considered for the invention of strategies includes, but it is not restricted to, isomorphisms of domains. Obviously, the application of strategies and rules should also allow better performances, as specified by the above condition ii).

It may also be the case that the transformation from program P0 to program P1 can be done by *language extensions* or *language refinements*. It means that we are given two different semantic functions, say Sem0 and Sem1, and the required commutative diagram is the following:

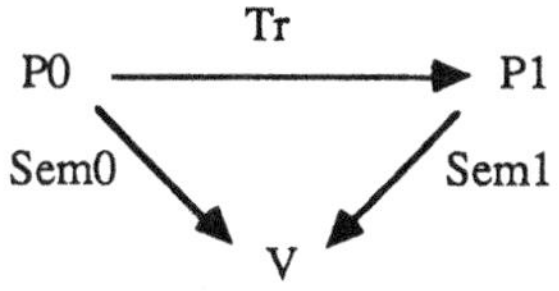

where, as usual, C(Sem1,P1) ≤ C(Sem0,P0). In that case we may get better performances by adopting a more efficient evaluator, namely the one for Sem1 (instead of the one for Sem0). We will not analyze in more detail this issue here.

5. CONCLUSIONS

We have studied the problem of deriving efficient programs which avoid multiple visits of data structures. We have devised a strategy, called Lambda Abstraction Strategy, which achieves the goal and it does not require lazy evaluation and circular programs, as suggested in [Bir84]. We have analyzed the relation of that strategy with respect to other known techniques for program derivation, like the Specialization technique.

We have also proposed a unifying way of considering various strategies for program development, and in particular, we have looked at the *isomorphism of data domains*. That *algebraic* view is a complementary approach to the *deductive* view which have been considered in [ScS85], for instance. In an intuitionistic framework that result does not come as a surprise, but from a methodological point of view it may offer to programmers deeper insights into the program development process.

6. AKNOWLEDGEMENTS

Many thanks to R. Bird who has been for me of great stimulation and encouragement. My gratitude also goes to N. Jones, R. Paige, A. Skowron, D. Swierstra, and the friends of the IFIP WG. 2.1. The referee's suggestions were very valuable.

This work was supported by the IASI Institute of the National Research Council of Rome (Italy).

7. REFERENCES

[AbV84] Abdali, K.S. and Vytopil, J.: "Generalization Heuristics for Theorems Related to Recursively Defined Functions" Report Buro Voor Systeemontwikkeling. Postbus 8348, Utrecht, Netherlands (1984).

[Aub76] Aubin, R.: "Mechanizing Structural Induction" Ph.D. Thesis, Dept. of Artificial Intelligence, University of Edinburgh (1976).

[Bac78] Backus, J.: "Can Programming be Liberated from the Von Neumann Style?" Comm. A.C.M. 21(8) (1978), pp. 613-641.

[Bir84] Bird, R.S.: "Using Circular Programs to Eliminate Multiple Traversal of Data" Acta Informatica 21 (1984), pp. 239-250.

[Bir86] Bird, R.S.: "An Introduction to the Theory of Lists" Technical Monograph PRG-56, Oxford University Computing Laboratory, Oxford, England (1986).

[BoM75] Boyer, R.S. and Moore, J.S.: "Proving Theorems About LISP Functions" J.A.C.M. 22, 1 (1975), pp. 129-144.

[BuD77] Burstall, R.M. and Darlington, J.: "A Transformation System for Developing Recursive Programs" J.A.C.M. Vol.24, 1 (1977), pp. 44-67.

[ChM79] Chirica, L.M. and Martin, D.F.: "An Order-Algebraic Definition of Knuthian Semantics" Mathematical System Theory 13, 1-27 (1979), pp. 1-27.

[Dar81] Darlington, J.: "An Experimental Program Transformation and Synthesis System" Artificial Intelligence 16, (1981), pp. 1-46.

[Ers82] Ershov, A. P.: "Mixed Computation: Potential Applications and Problems for Study" Theoretical Computer Science Vol.18, (1982), pp. 41-67.

[Fea86] Feather, M.S.: "A Survey and Classification of Some Program Transformation Techniques" Proc. TC2 IFIP Working Conference on Program Specification and Transformation. Bad Tölz, Germany (ed. L. Meertens) (1986).

[JøS86] Jørring, U. and Scherlis, W. L.: "Compilers and Staging Transformations" Thirteenth Annual A.C.M. Symposium on Principles of Programming Languages, St. Petersburgh Beach, Florida, USA (1986), pp. 86-96.

[Myc81] Mycroft, A.: "Abstract Interpretations and Optimising Transformations for Applicative Programs" Ph.D. Thesis, Computer Science Department, University of Edinburgh, Scotland (1981).

[Pet78] Pettorossi, A.: "Improving Memory Utilization in Transforming Recursive Programs" Proc. MFCS 78, Zakopane (Poland), Lecture Notes in Computer Science n.64, Springer Verlag (1978), pp. 416-425.

[Pet84] Pettorossi, A.: "A Powerful Strategy for Deriving Efficient Programs by Transformation" ACM Symposium on Lisp and Functional Programming, Austin, Texas (1984), pp.273-281.

[PeS87] Pettorossi, A. and A. Skowron: "Higher Order Generalization in Program Derivation" Proc. Intern. Joint Conference on Theory and Practice of Software Development. Pisa, Italy. Lecture Notes in Computer Science n. 250, Springer-Verlag (1987), pp. 182-196.

[Sch81] Scherlis, W. L.: "Program Improvement by Internal Specialization" A.C.M. Eighth Symposium on Principles of Programming Languages, (1981), pp. 146-160.

[ScS85] Scherlis, W. L., and Scott, D.: "Semantical Based Programming Tools" Mathematical Foundations of Software Development, TAPSOFT '85, Lecture Notes in Computer Science n. 185, Springer-Verlag, Berlin (1985), pp. 52-59.

[Swi85] Swierstra, D.: "Communication 513 SAU-15". IFIP WG.2.1, Sausalito, California, USA (1985).

[Tak87] Takeichi, M.: "Partial Parametrization Eliminates Multiple Traversals of Data Structures" Acta Informatica 24, (1987), pp.57-77.

[Wad85] Wadler, P.L.: "Listlessness is Better than Laziness" Ph. D. Thesis, Computer Science Department, CMU-CS-85-171, Carnegie Mellon University, Pittsburgh, USA (1985).

Relativized Arthur-Merlin versus Merlin-Arthur Games

Miklos Santha

Université Paris-Sud

LRI

91405 Orsay, France

Abstract

Arthur-Merlin games were introduced recently by Babai in order to capture the intuitive notion of efficient, probabilistic proof-systems. Considered as complexity classes, they are extensions of NP. It turned out, that one exchange of messages between the two players is sufficient to simulate a constant number of interactions. Thus at most two new complexity classes survive at the constant levels of this new hierarchy: AM and MA, depending on who starts the communication. It is known that $MA \subseteq AM$. In this paper we answer an open problem of Babai: we construct an oracle C such that $AM^C - \Sigma_2^{P,C} \neq \emptyset$. Since $MA^C \subseteq \Sigma_2^{P,C}$, it follows that for some oracle C, $MA^C \neq AM^C$. Our proof-technique is a modification of the technique used by Baker and Selman to show that Σ_2^P and Π_2^P can be separated by some oracle. This result can be interpreted as an evidence that with one exchange of messages, the proof-system is stronger when Arthur starts the communication.

1. Introduction

Two different formalization of efficient, probabilistic proof-systems were considered recently. Both are extensions of the well known complexity class NP, if we view it as a proof-system. The NP proof-system consists of two participants: a *prover* who guesses the proof and the polynomial time deterministic *verifier* who checks if the proof is correct.

The new proof-systems permit randomization and more complex interaction between the participants. The verifier receives more power: it becomes a polynomial time probabilistic Turing Machine who can also accept statistical evidence as an argument. Moreover, the length of the interaction can be polynomial in function of the common input. In both cases a new complexity hierarchy arises which would collapse to NP if no randomization were permitted.

In what Goldwasser, Micali and Rackoff [GMR] call an *interactive proof-system,* there is no restriction on the way the verifier can use the outcome of his coin tosses: he can perform a polynomial time computation to determine the next message. The prover who has unlimited computational power chooses the message which is the most likely to convince the verifier. The verifier sends the first message, and at the end, he accepts or rejects. An interactive proof-system *recognizes* a language L, if for every input $x \in L$, the prover can make the verifier accept with probability $\geq 3/4$, and for every $x \in \bar{L}$ this probability is $\leq 1/4$ against every prover. The IP hierarchy is defined as follows: $L \in IP[k]$, if there exists a k-move interactive proof-system which recognizes L.

In [B] Babai defined another proof-system by the combinatorial *Arthur-Merlin games.* Here Arthur is the polynomial time probabilistic verifier and Merlin is the powerful prover. The difference between the two proof-systems is that the moves Arthur can make during the interactions are restricted to coin flipping and sending the outcomes to Merlin. Either Merlin or Arthur can start the game on the common output x, and at the end, after a polynomial time evaluation Arthur accepts or rejects (Merlin wins or loses). A language L is accepted by an Arthur-Merlin game if for every $x \in L$, Merlin wins with probability $\geq 3/4$, and for every $x \in \bar{L}$, the probability that Merlin wins is $\leq 1/4$ even for an optimal Merlin. Thus an Arthur-Merlin game is a special interactive proof-system. Babai defined the Arthur

Merlin hierarchy, where AM[k] is the set of languages recognized by a k-move Arthur-Merlin game, when Arthur starts the game; MA[k] is defined similarily except that Merlin moves first. The complexity class AM[2] is denoted by AM and MA[2] by MA.

The class AM is of particular importance, because Babai showed that the constant levels of the hierarchy for k>2 collapse to AM, i.e. for all k>2, AM[k]=MA[k]=AM. Moreover, he showed that $MA \subseteq AM$, $MA \subseteq \Sigma_2^P$, and $AM \subseteq \Pi_2^P$. These results relativize, thus for all oracle B, $MA^B \subseteq AM^B$.

In a surprising result Goldwasser and Sipser [GS] showed that hiding the verifier coin tosses does not increase the power of the proof-system. More precisely, they proved that for every polynomial p(n), $IP[p(n)] \subseteq AM[p(n)+2]$. Combined with Babai's result, we get that for every constant k>2, IP[k] = AM.

The open problems in [B] include the exact relationship between the classes AM[p(n)] and AM, and between the classes AM and MA. Recently Aiello, Goldwasser and Hastad [AGH] proved that for any unbounded function f(n), there exists an oracle B such that $AM^B[f(n)]$ is not contained in the polynomial hierarchy relativized to B. As a corollary, for this oracle B, $AM^B \neq AM^B[f(n)]$. This result provides evidence that polynomial interaction may yield a proof-system more powerful than AM.

In this paper we consider Babai's other open problem. We will show that there exists an oracle C such that $AM^C - \Sigma_2^{P,C} \neq \emptyset$. As a corollary, for some oracle C, $MA^C \neq AM^C$. This result provides some evidence that MA games are not strong enough to simulate AM games. As usual with oracle constructions, it follows from this result that proof techniques which relativize can not show the equality of the classes AM and MA.

The construction of our oracle is similar to that of Baker and Selman for separating Σ_2^P and Π_2^P. In [BS] they constructed an oracle B such that for some oracle dependent language L^B, $L^B \in \Sigma_2^{P,B} - \Pi_2^{P,B}$. By complementation, this implies that $\overline{L}^B \in \Pi_2^{P,B} - \Sigma_2^{P,C}$. As it is, $\overline{L}^B$ needs not to be in AM^B, but it is possible to construct a modified oracle C such that $AM^C - \Sigma_2^{P,C}$ contains a language L(C), which is a variant of $\overline{L}^B$. It is somewhat surprising that the complemented version of the Baker-Selman proof technique can be modified to give the desired construction. Naturally, the original Baker-Selman oracle could not be modified to yield a language in $MA^C - \Pi_2^{P,C}$, as Babai's results imply that $MA^C - \Pi_2^{P,C} = \emptyset$. Thus one would better expect some new ideas from the start up whose complements do not carry through.

In related works, some evidences were found that co–NP is not contained in AM. Fortnow and Sipser [FS] showed that there is an oracle F such that co–NP^F is not contained in AM^F[Poly]. In [BH] Boppana and Hastad proved that if co–NP is contained in AM, then the polynomial hierarchy collapses to Σ_2^P.

2. The relativized classes

In a relativized AM or MA game, Arthur can make polynomially many calls to some oracle. Merlin has already unlimited computational power, thus he does not need this additional capability. As Arthur's messages are restricted to the results of his coin tosses, he makes the oracle queries at the end of the game in the polynomial time evaluation.

We will use the following notation (see e.g. [Z]): If Q(x) is a relation over a finite set X, then $\exists^+ x Q(x)$ means that Q(x) is true for at least 3/4 of the elements in X.

Definition: Let C be an oracle. A language L is in AM^C if there exists a polynomial time relation R^C relativized to C and a polynomial p(n) such that for all x,

$$x \in L \quad \Rightarrow \quad \exists^+ y\ (\ |y| \le p(|x|)\ )\ \exists z\ (\ |z| \le p(|x|)\ )\ R^C(x,y,z),$$

and

$$x \in \bar{L} \quad \Rightarrow \quad \exists^+ y\ (\ |y| \le p(|x|)\ )\ \forall z\ (\ |z| \le p(|x|)\ )\ \neg R^C(x,y,z).$$

Similarily, a language L is in MA^C if

$$x \in L \quad \Rightarrow \quad \exists y\ (\ |y| \le p(|x|)\ )\ \exists^+ z\ (\ |z| \le p(|x|)\ )\ R^C(x,y,z),$$

and

$$x \in \bar{L} \quad \Rightarrow \quad \forall y\ (|y| \le p(|x|)\ )\ \exists^+ z\ (\ |z| \le p(|x|)\ )\ \neg R^C(x,y,z).$$

Finally, a language L is in $\Sigma_2^{P,C}$ if

$$x \in L \iff \exists y\,(\,|y| \le p(|x|)\,)\,\forall z\,(\,|z| \le p(|x|)\,)\,R^C(x,y,z). \tag{1}$$

We suppose that all the languages are defined over the alphabet $\{0,1\}$. In the proof we will use the following oracle dependent language:

$$L(C) = \{0^n : \exists^+ u\,(|u| = n)\,\exists v\,(|v| = n)\,uv \in C\,\}.$$

The language L(C) in general is not in AM^C. However, if the oracle C satisfies the following property: for all n,

$$\left.\begin{array}{ll}\exists^+ u\,(|u| = n)\,\exists v\,(|v| = n)\,uv \in C & \text{or} \\ \exists^+ u\,(|u| = n)\,\forall v\,(|v| = n)\,uv \in \overline{C}\,, & \end{array}\right\} \tag{2}$$

then L(C) is in AM^C.

3. The construction

Theorem: There exists an oracle C such that $AM^C - \Sigma_2^{P,C} \neq \varnothing$.

Proof: The oracle C will satisfy (2). To ensure that L(C) does not belong to $\Sigma_2^{P,C}$, we will diagonalize over all languages in $\Sigma_2^{P,C}$. The diagonalization is done one by one over every polynomial time relativized relation R^C and polynomial p(n).

Let us suppose that at the previous stages of the diagonalization we have already constructed some finite initial segment D of C, and that we are given a query machine M which computes R^C with oracle C, and a polynomial p(n). Let q(n) be a polynomial such that for all n, the cardinality of words of length $\le p(n)$ is $\le 2^{q(n)}$. Let r(n) be a polynomial such that M^C is bounded in time r(n) on input $(0^n,y,z)$ for every y and z of length $\le p(n)$. We choose an integer n big enough such that all the previous stages remain uneffected by the extension of D with words of length 2n. Moreover, n should be big enough to satisfy some inequalities about q(n) and r(n) to be specified at the end of the proof. We want to extend D with some words of length 2n such that for n, C should satisfy (2) but $x=0^n$ and L=L(C) do not satisfy (1). If we can achieve this, then the diagonalization is successful over the $\Sigma_2^{P,C}$

language defined by R^C and p(n). Let us observe that for all n such that C contains no words of length 2n, condition (2) is satisfied.

Let us assume on the contrary, that this is impossible. Then for every extension C of D with words of length 2n, we have the following relations:

$$\exists^+ u\ \exists v\ uv \in C \quad \Rightarrow \quad \exists y\ \forall z\ R^C(0^n,y,z) \tag{3}$$

$$\exists^+ u\ \forall v\ uv \in \overline{C} \quad \Rightarrow \quad \forall y\ \exists z\ \neg R^C(0^n,y,z)\ . \tag{4}$$

In (3) and (4) u and v are words of length n, y and z are words of length $\leq$ p(n). We will use the same convention in the rest of the proof and omit the restriction on the length of the words.

A set is called after Baker and Selman a sample set, if for all u there exists a unique v such that uv $\in$ S, and S does not contain any other elements. The cardinality of a sample set is 2^n, and there are 2^{n2^n} different sample sets. From (3) it follows that for every sample set S, there exists a y such that $\forall z R^{D\cup S}(0^n,y,z)$. Thus there exists a word y such that the cardinality of the sample sets for which $\forall z R^{D\cup S}(0^n,y,z)$ is true, is $\geq 2^{n2^n-q(n)}$. Let $\overline{y}$ be such a word, and let us define

$$T_0 = \{\ S : S \text{ is a sample set}\ ,\ \forall z\ R^{D\cup S}(0^n,\overline{y},z)\ \}\ . \tag{5}$$

For i=0,1,...2^{n-2} we will define sets T_i and Z_i with the following properties:

(i) $|T_i| \geq 2^{n2^n - i\log r(n) - q(n)}$,

(ii) $|Z_i| = i$,

(iii) $Z_i \subseteq \bigcap\{\ S : S \in T_i\}$,

(iv) $T_i \subseteq T_0$.

For i=0 we have already T_0; Z_0 can be chosen the empty set. Let us suppose that T_i and Z_i are already defined. For every S $\in$ T_i, by (iv) and (5)

$$\forall z\ R^{D\cup S}(0^n,\overline{y},z)\ .$$

On the other hand, since $|Z_i| \leq 2^{n-2}$, (4) implies that

$$\exists z\ \neg R^{D\cup Z_i}(0^n,\overline{y},z)\ .$$

Let $\overline{z}$ be such a z. It follows that for all S $\in$ T_i, there exists a word w $\in$ S - Z_i such that $M^{D\cup Z_i}$ queries w on $(0^n,\overline{y},\overline{z})$. The running time of M is bounded by r(n), thus $M^{D\cup Z_i}$ can query at most r(n) different words on $(0^n,\overline{y},\overline{z})$. Thus there exists a word $\overline{w}$ such that

$$|\{ S \in T_i : \overline{w} \in S - Z_i \}| \geq |T_i| / r(n) \ .$$

We define $T_{i+1} = \{ S \in T_i : \overline{w} \in S - Z_i \}$, and $Z_{i+1} = Z_i \cup \{\overline{w}\}$. Now (i) is satisfied, because

$$|T_{i+1}| \geq |T_i| / r(n) \geq 2^{n2^n - i\log r(n) - q(n) - \log r(n)} \ .$$

Conditions (ii), (iii) and (iv) are satisfied by definition. We can observe a contradiction, when $i=2^{n-2}$. From (i) it follows that

$$|T_{2^{n-2}}| \geq 2^{n2^n - 2^{n-2}\log r(n) - q(n)} \ .$$

On the other hand,

$$T_{2^{n-2}} \subseteq \{ S : S \text{ is a sample set }, \ Z_{2^{n-2}} \subseteq S \} ,$$

where $|Z_{2^{n-2}}| = 2^{n-2}$. Thus

$$|T_{2^{n-2}}| \leq 2^{n(2^n - 2^{n-2})} < 2^{n2^n - 2^{n-2}\log r(n) - q(n)} ,$$

if we choose for example n such that $q(n) < 2^{n-2}$ and $r(n) < 2^{n-1}$. Q.E.D.

Let us remark that the additional constraint in our construction compared to the complemented version of the Baker-Selman oracle imposes an upper bound on the indices for which we are able to define the sets Z_i and T_i. If $i \geq 2^{n-2}$, then the size of Z_i becomes $\geq 2^{n-2}$, thus we can not use (4) any more. The important observation is, that if we stop the construction when $i=2^{n-2}$, we already have a contradiction between the lower bound and the upper bound on the size of T_i. Thus we don't have to reach i=n, where the original construction stopped.

Corollary: There exists an oracle C such that $AM^C \neq MA^C$.

References

[AGH] Aiello W., Goldwasser S. and Hastad J., "On the Power of Interaction", Proc. 27th FOCS, 1986, pp. 368-379.

[B] Babai L., "Trading Group Theory for Randomness", Proc. 17th STOC, 1985, pp. 421-429.

[BH] Boppana R. and Hastad J., "Does co-NP Have Short Interactive Proofs", submitted to Information Processing Letters.

[BS] Baker T. and Selman A., "A Second Step Toward the Polynomial Hierarchy", TCS 8, 1979 pp. 177-187.

[FS] Fortnow L. and Sipser M., reported in [GS].

[GMR] Goldwasser S., Micali S. and Rackoff C., "The Knowledge Complexity of Interactive Proofs", Proc. 17th STOC, 1985, pp. 291-305.

[GS] Goldwasser S. and Sipser M., "Private Coins versus Public Coins in Interactive Proof Systems", Proc. 18th STOC, 1986, pp. 59-68.

[Z] Zachos S., "Probabilistic Quantifiers, Adversaries and Complexity Classes: An Overview" in Structure in Complexity Theory, ed. Selman A., Springer-Verlag, 1986, pp.383-400.

Probabilistic Quantifiers vs. Distrustful Adversaries

Stathis Zachos, Brooklyn College of CUNY, New York*
Martin Furer, University of Zurich**

1. Summary

Recently combinatorial games and cryptographic protocols (alias interactive proof systems) have been used in order to define complexity classes for classification of concrete problems. (See, for example, [P 83],[BS 84], [B 85], [GMR 85] and [GHY 85]). The terminology used in such games and interactive proof systems (i.p.s.) is often anthropomorphic, involving adversaries. The players involved (respectively the verifier and the prover in an i.p.s.) alternate in making moves (respectively in sending messages to each other). The main difference between games and i.p.s.'s is the following: In a game, both players have complete knowledge of the history of the game. An i.p.s. relies heavily on the fact that the prover does not have complete knowledge of the verifier's actions. If we make polynomial restrictions on the length of communications, computations, games and the complexity of evaluation of wins or losses (Alice in "Polyland"), we get hierarchies of complexity classes which lie within **PSPACE**. Let us additionally specify that the combinatorial games are played between two unequal players: one (Merlin) able to choose an optimal strategy, the other (Arthur) being indifferent to the final outcome. Babai [B 85] defined such Arthur-Merlin games and then complexity classes **AM[k]** as follows:

$L \in \mathbf{AM}\,[\mathbf{k}]$ **iff** there exists a k-move Arthur-Merlin game such that for every x :

$$x \in L \longrightarrow Pr\,(Merlin\ \ wins\,) > \frac{3}{4}$$

$$\text{and} \quad x \notin L \longrightarrow Pr\,(Merlin\ \ wins\,) < \frac{1}{4.}$$

Similarly Goldwasser, Micali and Rackoff define a hierarchy of interactive proofs where L $\in$ **IP[k]** **iff** there exists a k-communication protocol such that for every x :
$x \in L$ --> the prover can convince the verifier with overwhelming probability that $x \in L$, and
$x \notin L$ --> with overwhelming probability the prover cannot convince the verifier that $x \in L$.
It turns out that these two seemingly different models for describing complexity classes coincide (for bounded number of moves, respectively communications) [see GS 85].

We give here another characterization of complexity classes defined by such games (respectively i.p.s.'s), which has a more classical complexity theoretical flavor. We use polynomially bounded quantifiers $'\exists'$ and $'\forall'$ together with a probabilistic quantifier $'\exists^{+}'$ (which means roughly "for most") to describe these classes. Thus for example **NP** $= (\exists/\forall)$; $\Sigma_2^P =$

* This research was partially supported by a PSC-CUNY grant. ** New address: Dept. of C.S. Pennsylvania State University.

$(\exists\forall/\forall\exists)$; **R** $= (\exists^+/\forall)$ and **BPP** $= (\exists^+/\exists^+)$. A precise definition of the notation (**Q** /**Q**$^{\circ}$) will be given later. Quantifier interchange properties have been studied extensively in [ZH 83, ZH 84, HZ 84, Z 86]. They turn out to be very useful tools for investigating inclusions among complexity classes and hierarchies that collapse. For example it is easy to show that both of the following hierarchies collapse at the second level:

$$(\exists^+/\forall) \subseteq (\exists^+\forall/\forall\exists^+) \subseteq (\exists^+\forall\exists^+/\forall\exists^+\forall) \subseteq (\exists^+\forall\exists^+\forall/\forall\exists^+\forall\exists^+) \subseteq \cdots$$

$$(\exists^+/\forall) \subseteq (\exists^+\forall/\forall\exists) \subseteq (\exists^+\forall\exists^+/\forall\exists\forall) \subseteq (\exists^+\forall\exists^+\forall/\forall\exists\forall\exists) \subseteq \cdots$$

Furthermore, we have $(\exists^+\forall/\forall\exists^+) =$ **BPP** $= (\forall\exists^+/\exists^+\forall)$ and $(\exists\forall/\forall\exists^+) \subseteq (\forall\exists/\exists^+\forall)$.

We show here for Babai's classes that **MA** $= (\exists\forall/\forall\exists^+)$ and **AM** $= (\forall\exists/\exists^+\forall)$. Thus we obtain Babai's results **MA** $\subseteq$ **AM** and the collapse of the Arthur-Merlin hierarchy **AM[k]** as easy corollaries of combinatorial swapping properties of such quantifiers.

We also prove that $\mathbf{NP}^{\mathbf{BPP}} \subseteq \mathbf{MA}$ and $\mathbf{NP}^{\mathbf{BPP}} \subseteq \mathbf{ZPP}^{\mathbf{NP}}$ and $\mathbf{AM} \subseteq \mathbf{co\text{-}R}^{\mathbf{NP}} \subseteq \mathbf{BPP}^{\mathbf{NP}}$ We also answer a question of Babai and Szemeredi by separating **co-NP** and **AM** with an oracle. Furthermore if **co** –**NP** $\subseteq$ **AM** then the polynomial hierarchy collapses.

The Arthur-Merlin games were introduced in order to classify the complexity of matrix group problems [BS 84]. We show here that these problems lie in $\mathbf{D}^{\mathbf{P}}$ (see [PY 82] : $\mathbf{D}^{\mathbf{P}} = \{L : \exists L_1 \in \mathbf{NP}, \exists L_2 \in \mathbf{co\text{-}NP}\ L = L_1 \cap L_2\}$), and raise some open questions concerning similar problems.

2. Computational Model and Notations

Our fundamental machine model is a polynomially time bounded Turing machine M. For simplicity we may view the set of possible computation paths of M on input x (of length |x|) as a complete binary tree of height p(|x|) for some polynomial p. Acceptance of a word $x \in \{0,1\}^*$ by M is defined in terms of the probabilities Pr Acc_M (x) and Pr Rej_M (x) that a path leads to acceptance or rejection of x. For example, $L \subseteq \{0,1\}^*$ is in **NP** **iff** for some such M and all $x \in \{0,1\}^*$,

$$x \in L \longrightarrow Pr\ Acc_M(x) > 0, \textbf{ and } \quad x \notin L \longrightarrow Pr\ Rej_M(x) = 1,$$

and L is in **BPP** **iff** for some such M, some $\epsilon > 0$, and all $x \in \{0,1\}^*$,

$$x \in L \longrightarrow Pr\ Acc_M(x) > \frac{1}{2} + \epsilon, \textbf{ and } \quad x \notin L \longrightarrow Pr\ Rej_M(x) > \frac{1}{2} + \epsilon.$$

The machine M may be provided with an oracle $T \subseteq \{0,1\}^*$ which gives responses to queries concerning membership in T. Classes $\mathbf{NP}^T$, $\mathbf{BPP}^T$, etc. are defined in the obvious way, and for any such machine model **A** and any class of languages **B**, we set

$$\mathbf{A}^{\mathbf{B}} = \cup \{\mathbf{A}^T : T \in \mathbf{B}\}.$$

We think of $\mathbf{A}^{\mathbf{B}}$ as the class of languages accepted by a machine of type **A** with an oracle from **B** (although the behavior of a particular machine heavily depends on its oracle).

Definitions of the probabilistic complexity classes **R, ZPP** and **BPP** can be found in [G 77,Z 82]. We use here uniform characterizations in terms of the ordinary length-bounded quantifiers $\exists y.\ |y| = k$ and $\forall y.\ |y| = k$ together with the quantifier '$\exists^+ y.\ |y| = k$' , where for a fixed real ϵ, $0 < \epsilon < \frac{1}{2}$, $\exists^+ y\ \ |y| = k\ .\ P(x,y)$ means that at least $(\frac{1}{1}+\epsilon).2^k$ of the 2^k strings y of length k, satisfy *P(x,y)*. We suppress the bound k (which is usually p(|x|)) in the notation and write simply: $\forall y\ P(x,y)$, $\exists^+ y\ P(x,y)$, etc..

L is in **R iff** for some polynomial-time predicate P and all $x \in \{0,1\}^*$,

$$x \in L \longrightarrow \exists^+ y\ P(x,y) \textbf{ and } x \notin L \longrightarrow \forall y\ \neg P(x,y).$$

We abbreviate this by writing **R** $= (\exists^+/\forall)$. Similarly, we write **NP** $= (\exists/\forall)$, **BPP** $= (\exists^+/\exists^+)$, $\Sigma_2^P = (\exists\forall/\forall\exists)$, etc. Note also that **co** $-(\mathbf{Q}/\mathbf{Q}^\circ) = (\mathbf{Q}^\circ/\mathbf{Q})$ and that **ZPP** $=$ **R** $\cap$ **co** $-$**R** and $\Delta =$ **NP** $\cap$ **co** $-$**NP** .

We call $(\mathbf{Q},\mathbf{Q}^\circ)$ a **sensible** pair iff **Q** and $\mathbf{Q}^\circ$ are finite sequences of quantifiers ($\exists$, $\forall$, $\exists^+$ *or* $\mathfrak{R}$: see later) of the same length for which

$$\mathbf{Q}^\circ\ \mathbf{y}\ \neg P(x,\mathbf{y}) \longrightarrow \neg\ \mathbf{Q}\ \mathbf{y}\ P(x,\mathbf{y})$$

where of course **y** is a corresponding sequence of variables and P is any predicate. Thus if $(\mathbf{Q},\mathbf{Q}^\circ)$ is a sensible pair and **B** is a complexity class, then $(\mathbf{Q}/\mathbf{Q}^\circ)^{\mathbf{B}}$ denotes the class of all languages L, such that for some predicate $P^{\mathbf{B}}$, and for all x:

$$x \in L \longrightarrow \mathbf{Q}\ \mathbf{y}\ P^{\mathbf{B}}(x,\mathbf{y}), \textbf{ and}$$

$$x \notin L \longrightarrow \mathbf{Q}^\circ\ \mathbf{y}\ \neg P^{\mathbf{B}}(x,\mathbf{y}) \textbf{ and}$$

$P^{\mathbf{B}}$ can be computed deterministically in polynomial time using an oracle from **B**.

It is not difficult to check that the precise choice of the parameter ϵ in the definition of the quantifier '$\exists^+$' does not affect the extent of any of the language classes. Indeed, the quantity $\frac{1}{2} + \epsilon$ (the **threshold**) may be replaced by $1 - 2^{-q(|x|)}$ in that definition. This phenomenon, known as **robustness**, has been studied in some detail in [Z 82, HZ 84]. We use it here informally to allow ourselves some freedom in the use of the symbol '$\exists^+$'; in different contexts different thresholds may be required or implied.

We are also going to use the symbol $\mathfrak{R}$ for a quantifier with a threshold $\frac{1}{2}$. For example, "$\mathfrak{R}$y" means " fifty percent of the y's ". We will call $\exists^+$ the **overwhelming majority** and $\mathfrak{R}$ the **random** quantifier, and both **probabilistic** quantifiers. By employing robustness techniques, namely repetitions of the same algorithm several times, we can easily show that:

$$(\mathfrak{R}/\forall) = (\exists^+/\forall) = \mathbf{R}\ ;\ (\mathfrak{R}/\exists^+) = (\exists^+/\exists^+) = \mathbf{BPP}\ ;\ etc\ .$$

Quantifier characterizations are closely connected with the possibility of **restricting the number of oracle queries** a machine makes along any computation path. We write $\mathbf{A}^{\mathbf{B}[k]}$ when at most k queries are allowed and $\mathbf{A}^{\mathbf{B}[k]-}$ if in addition along all accepting paths only negative answers are given by the oracle. For example, the simplest proof that

$\mathbf{NP}^{\mathbf{NP}} = (\exists\forall/\forall\exists)$ proceeds by showing that $\mathbf{NP}^{\mathbf{NP}} = \mathbf{NP}^{\mathbf{NP}\,[1]-}$. Here are some other useful (unique query) equalities: $\mathbf{NP}^{\mathbf{R}} = \mathbf{NP}^{\mathbf{R}\,[1]-}$; $\mathbf{R}^{\mathbf{R}} = \mathbf{R}^{\mathbf{R}\,[1]-}$; $\mathbf{R}^{\mathbf{NP}\,[1]-} = \mathbf{BPP}^{\mathbf{NP}\,[1]-}$; $\mathbf{NP}^{\mathbf{BPP}} = \mathbf{NP}^{\mathbf{BPP}\,[1]}$

3. Quantifier Classes

Our basic combinatorial lemma is a quantifier swapping property from [ZH 84, HZ 84].

Swapping Lemma: $\forall y\ \exists^+ z\ P(x,y,z) \rightarrow \exists^+\mathbf{C}\ \forall y\ \exists z \in C\ P(x,y,z)$

Implicit in the notation are fixed polynomials f and g such that the variables y and z range over strings of length f(|x|), C ranges over sets of size at most g(|x|) of strings of length f(|x|), and **C** is an encoding of C as a string of length f(|x|)*g(|x|). Note that $\exists z \in C\ P(x,y,z)$ is a polynomial-size disjunction, hence also a polynomial-time predicate if $P(x,y,z)$ is.
Proof Idea: The intuitive way to view this lemma is in terms of 0-1 matrices. Thus, the hypothesis says that every row contains mainly 1's. The conclusion is that for most sets C of columns, every row has a 1 in at least one of the columns in C.
[Somewhat more technically, one shows

$$Pr(\exists y\ \forall z \in C\ \neg P(x,y,z)) \leq \sum_y Pr(\forall z \in C\ \neg P(x,y,z)) \leq \sum_y \prod_{z \in C} (\tfrac{1}{2}) \leq \tfrac{1}{4} \qquad q.e.d.$$

Using this and other similar combinatorial lemmas the following theorem was proved in [ZH 84].

The BPP-Theorem: $\mathbf{BPP} = (\exists^+/\exists^+) = (\exists^+\forall/\forall\exists^+) = (\forall\exists^+/\exists^+\forall)$.

Again using the Swapping Lemma the following inclusion can be proved (cf. [ZH 83], [HZ 84]).

Theorem 1: $(\exists\forall/\forall\exists^+) \subseteq (\forall\exists/\exists^+\forall)$.
Proof: Let $L \in (\exists\forall/\forall\exists^+)$. Then:

$$\begin{aligned} x \notin L &\rightarrow \forall y\ \exists^+ z\ \neg P(x,y,z) \\ &\rightarrow \exists^+\mathbf{C}\ \forall y\ \exists z \in C\ \neg P(x,y,z)\ \ (\textit{by the Swapping Lemma}) \\ &\rightarrow \exists\mathbf{C}\ \forall y\ \exists z \in C\ \neg P(x,y,z) \\ &\rightarrow \forall y\, \exists z\, \neg P(x,y,z) \\ &\rightarrow x \notin L. \end{aligned}$$

Thus all implications are equivalences and the second and third lines imply :
$L \in (\forall\exists/\exists^+\forall)$. **q.e.d.**

We will see in the next section that these two classes correspond exactly to **MA** and **AM** of Babai's Arthur-Merlin games.

Remark: The Swapping Lemma, the BPP-Theorem and Theorem 1 can be extended to any quantified or unquantified formula. It is not difficult to show that polynomial size disjunctions and conjunctions can be interchanged with polynomially bounded quantifiers; in this process of course the predicate P undergoes some polynomial modification, e.g.

$$\exists y \; P(x,y,z_1) \; OR \; \exists y \; P(x,y,z_2) \longrightarrow \exists <y_1,y_2> [P(x,y_1,z_1) \; OR \; P(x,y_2,z_2)] \longrightarrow \exists y \; P' \; (x,y,z)$$

Thus the BPP-Theorem generalizes to:

$(\mathbf{Q}_1 \exists^+ \mathbf{Q}_2 / \mathbf{Q}_3 \exists^+ \mathbf{Q}_4) = (\mathbf{Q}_1 \exists^+ \forall \mathbf{Q}_2 / \mathbf{Q}_3 \forall \exists^+ \mathbf{Q}_4) = (\mathbf{Q}_1 \forall \exists^+ \mathbf{Q}_2 / \mathbf{Q}_3 \exists^+ \forall \mathbf{Q}_4)$.
Theorem 1 also generalizes to: $(\mathbf{Q}_1 \exists \forall \mathbf{Q}_2 / \mathbf{Q}_3 \forall \exists^+ \mathbf{Q}_4) \subseteq (\mathbf{Q}_1 \forall \exists \mathbf{Q}_2 / \mathbf{Q}_3 \exists^+ \forall \mathbf{Q}_4)$.
Using these results it has been shown [ZH 84,HZ 84] that the following hierarchies collapse at the second level:

$$(\exists^+/\forall) \subseteq (\exists^+\forall/\forall\exists^+) \subseteq (\exists^+\forall\exists^+/\forall\exists^+\forall) \subseteq (\exists^+\forall\exists^+\forall/\forall\exists^+\forall\exists^+) \subseteq \cdots$$

$$\text{and} \quad (\exists^+/\forall) \subseteq (\exists^+\forall/\forall\exists) \subseteq (\exists^+\forall\exists^+/\forall\exists\forall) \subseteq (\exists^+\forall\exists^+\forall/\forall\exists\forall\exists) \subseteq \cdots$$

This last hierarchy corresponds level by level to Babai's game hierarchy which also collapses at the second level.

4. Arthur-Merlin Games

"King Arthur recognizes the supernatural intellectual abilities of Merlin but doesn't trust him. How should Merlin convince the intelligent but impatient King that a string x belongs to a given language L?" [B 85].

Babai considers games whose rules depend in a polynomially computable way on an input string x. Arthur is an indifferent player who tosses a sequence of coins and Merlin is a powerful player capable of optimizing his winning chances at every move. The two players alternate moves, the history of the game is always known to both, and after t(|x|) moves a deterministic polynomial-time Turing machine reads the history and decides who wins. We assume that for every input x either Pr(M wins) > 3/4 or Pr(M wins) < 1/4. We write **AM(k)** to denote a k-move game where Arthur moves first. Thus **AM(5)** = **AMAMA** denotes an Arthur-Merlin game of 5 moves, Arthur moving first. As noted in [B 85], **M** = **NP** and **A** = **BPP**. Furthermore **AM** [**k**] $\cup$ **MA** [**k**] $\subseteq$ **AM** [**k** +1] $\cap$ **MA** [**k** +1]. Interpreting Arthur-Merlin games in terms of quantifiers yields:
Lemma: (*i*)**MA** $=(\exists\exists^+/\forall\exists^+)$ and **AM** $= (\exists^+\exists/\exists^+\forall)$.
(*ii*)Similarly for **AM**[**k**] and **MA**[**k**], e.g. **AMA** $= (\exists^+\exists\exists^+/\exists^+\forall\exists^+)$.
Proof Idea: (i) is relatively easy: the first equality, for example, translates the condition *'for most sequences of two moves (first Merlin then Arthur) Merlin wins '* to the condition *'Merlin has a move so that for most moves of Arthur Merlin wins '*, etc.
(ii) Less obvious is the fact that these descriptions generalize to **AM**[**k**] and **MA**[**k**]. To convince oneself about this fact we need the following two ideas:

(1) A **modest bias** can be turned into an **overwhelming** one by playing the same game several times in parallel. This is an obvious **robustness** technique that can be used with all complexity classes which involve the $\exists^+$ quantifier [see Z 82, ZH 84, HZ 84]; and

(2) $\exists^+ <y,z> P(x,y,z) \longmapsto \exists^+ y \exists^+ z P(x,y,z)$ which generalizes to any bounded quantifier sequence (where thresholds for $\exists^+$ must be suitably chosen).

An **AMA** game has the following property: for most sequences of moves $<y,t,z>$, in which Arthur moves first, then Merlin, then Arthur, Merlin wins or for most such sequences Merlin loses. Using (1) and (2) there is another Arthur-Merlin game defining the same language L, so that: for most moves y of Arthur there is a move t of Merlin, so that for most next moves z of Arthur Merlin wins or for most moves y of Arthur, and for all moves t of Merlin and for most next moves z of Arthur Merlin loses, i.e. **AMA** $= (\exists^+\exists\exists^+/\exists^+\forall\exists^+)$, and so forth for other game classes. **q.e.d.**

Thus now we can consider games to have the additional property that if Merlin wins then he has an optimal move for most moves of Arthur in every stage. The following theorem further simplifies the description:

Theorem 2: (*i*)**MA** $=(\exists\forall/\forall\exists^+)$
(*ii*)**AM** $=(\forall\exists/\exists^+\forall)$
(*iii*)Similarly for every **AM[k]** class.
Proof: (i) **MA** $= (\exists\exists^+/\forall\exists^+) = (\exists\exists^+\forall/\forall\forall\exists^+)$ (by the **BPP**-Theorem)
$\subseteq (\exists\exists\forall/\forall\forall\exists^+) = (\exists\forall/\forall\exists^+)$ (by quantifier contraction),
but also: $(\exists\forall/\forall\exists^+) \subseteq (\exists\exists^+/\forall\exists^+) =$ **MA**.
(ii) **AM** $= (\exists^+\exists/\exists^+\forall)=(\forall\exists^+\exists/\exists^+\forall\forall) \subseteq (\forall\exists\exists/\exists^+\forall\forall) = (\forall\exists/\exists^+\forall)$,
but also: $(\forall\exists/\exists^+\forall) \subseteq (\exists^+\exists/\exists^+\forall) =$ **AM**.
(iii) Analogously,
AMA $= (\exists^+\exists\exists^+/\exists^+\forall\exists^+) = (\forall\exists^+\exists\exists^+\forall/\exists^+\forall\forall\forall\exists^+) = (\forall\exists\forall/\exists^+\forall\exists^+)$, and so on for **AM[k]**. **q.e.d.**

Once we have the quantifier characterization, Babai's results become straightforward corollaries that we can obtain by algebraic manipulation.

Corollary [see also B 85]: (*i*)**MA** $\subseteq$ **AM**. and (*ii*) The game hierarchy collapses, i.e.: **AM** $=$ **AM[k]** $=$ **MA[k+1]** for all $k \geq 2$.
Proof: (i) Follows from Theorems 1 and 2. (ii) Follows from Theorem 2 and the methods of [HZ 84](see Remark of section 3). Thus, for example, **MAM** $\subseteq$ **AM**, because,

$$(\exists\exists^+\exists/\forall\exists^+\forall) \subseteq (\exists\exists^+\forall\exists/\forall\forall\exists^+\forall) \; (by\ the\ BPP\text{-}theorem)$$

$$\subseteq (\exists\forall\exists/\forall\exists^+\forall) \; (by\ quantifier\ contraction)$$

$$\subseteq (\forall\exists\exists/\exists^+\forall\forall) \; (by\ Theorem\ 1)$$

$$\subseteq (\forall\exists/\exists^+\forall) \; (by\ quantifier\ contraction)$$

q.e.d

Let **AM[P]** $=$ **MA[P]** $= \cup\{$**AM** $[n^k]: k > 0\}$. Note that robustness for $\exists^+$ and the swapping properties of section 3 have only been shown in case of a bounded number of quantifier alternations. It is not known whether **AM[P]** $=$ **AM**. We have **NP** $\cup$ **BPP** $\subseteq$ **MA** $\subseteq$ **AM** $\subseteq$ **AM [P]** $\subseteq$ **PSPACE** . On the other hand, showing that any of the above inclusions is a proper one would solve the long-standing open problem **NP** $=$ **? PSPACE.**

5. Relationships among Complexity Classes

With the above quantifier representation it is fairly obvious that **MA** $\subseteq \Sigma_2^P \cap \Pi_2^P$ and **AM** $\subseteq \Pi_2^P$ [cf B 85]. (For definitions of Σ_2^P, etc., see [S 76]). In this section, we consider some further inclusions which we establish by quantifier manipulation methods.

Let $\mathbf{A}^{\mathbf{B}[k]}$ denote the class of languages accepted by a machine of type **A** that queries an oracle $\mathbf{Y} \in \mathbf{B}$ k times. $\mathbf{A}^{\mathbf{B}[1]-}$ denotes the class of languages accepted by a machine of type **A** that queries an oracle $\mathbf{Y} \in \mathbf{B}$ only once, with the restriction that on all accepting paths the unique answer from the oracle is negative. Then $\mathbf{NP}^{\mathbf{R}} = \mathbf{NP}^{\mathbf{R}[1]-}$ and $\mathbf{NP}^{\mathbf{BPP}} = \mathbf{NP}^{\mathbf{BPP}[1]-}$ [see HZ 84]. On the other hand $\mathbf{BPP}^{\mathbf{NP}} =? \ \mathbf{BPP}^{\mathbf{NP}[1]-}$ is an open question.

Theorem 3:(*i*) $\mathbf{NP}^{\mathbf{BPP}} \subseteq \mathbf{R}^{\mathbf{NP}}$

(*ii*) $\mathbf{NP}^{\mathbf{BPP}} \subseteq \mathbf{R}^{\mathbf{NP}[2]}$

(*iii*) $\mathbf{NP}^{\mathbf{BPP}} \subseteq \mathbf{MA}$

(*iv*) $\mathbf{co}\text{-}\mathbf{R}^{\mathbf{NP}[1]-} = \mathbf{co}\text{-}\mathbf{BPP}^{\mathbf{NP}[1]-} = \mathbf{AM} \subseteq \mathbf{co}\text{-}\mathbf{R}^{\mathbf{NP}} \subseteq \mathbf{BPP}^{\mathbf{NP}}$

(*v*) $\mathbf{NP}^{\mathbf{R}} \subseteq \mathbf{R}^{\mathbf{NP}}$ (*cf* [*ZH* 83],[*ZH* 84])

(*vi*) $\mathbf{NP}^{\mathbf{BPP}} \subseteq \mathbf{ZPP}^{\mathbf{NP}[2]}$

(*vii*) $\mathbf{MA}^{\mathbf{BPP}} = \mathbf{MA}$ and $\mathbf{AM}^{\mathbf{BPP}} = \mathbf{AM}$

(*viii*) $\mathbf{AM}^{\Delta} = \mathbf{AM}$

Proof: (i - iv) see [Za 86].
(v) Trivially $\mathbf{NP}^{\mathbf{R}} \subseteq \mathbf{NP}^{\mathbf{BPP}}$ and by (i), $\mathbf{NP}^{\mathbf{BPP}} \subseteq \mathbf{R}^{\mathbf{NP}}$.
(vi) Furthermore :$\mathbf{NP}^{\mathbf{BPP}} \subseteq \mathbf{MA} \subseteq \mathbf{AM} \subseteq \mathbf{co}\text{-}\mathbf{R}^{\mathbf{NP}[1]-}$.
(vii) Let $L \in \mathbf{MA}^{\mathbf{BPP}}$. This means

$$x \in L \rightarrow \exists u \ \exists^+ v \ \ P^{\mathbf{BPP}}(x, u, v), \text{and}$$

$$x \notin L \rightarrow \forall u \ \exists^+ v \ \neg P^{\mathbf{BPP}}(x, u, v).$$

Then, by the identity $\mathbf{P}^{\mathbf{BPP}} = \mathbf{BPP}$ and quantifier contraction, for some polynomial-time predicate P' :

$$x \in L \rightarrow \exists u \ \exists^+ y \ \ P' \ (x, u, y), \text{and}$$

$$x \notin L \rightarrow \forall u \ \exists^+ y \ \neg P' \ (x, u, y).$$

Hence $L \in \mathbf{MA}$. Similarly, $\mathbf{AM}^{\mathbf{BPP}} \subseteq \mathbf{AMA}$, and recall $\mathbf{AMA} \subseteq \mathbf{AM}$.
(viii) Analogous to $\mathbf{NP}^{\Delta} = \mathbf{NP}$ q.ed.

The following are also noteworthy:
$\mathbf{BPP} = \mathbf{P}^{\mathbf{BPP}} = \{L : L \in \mathbf{P}^{\mathbf{B}}$, for almost all oracles B$\}$. [Z 82, BG 81]
$\mathbf{AM} \subseteq \{L : L \in \mathbf{NP}^{\mathbf{B}}$, for almost all oracles B$\}$ (Not $=$, as is claimed in [B 85]).

The next theorem answers a question that was raised by Babai and Szemeredi (see [BS 84]:14.4), namely whether there is an oracle **B** such that **co** $-$**NP** $^{\mathbf{B}}$ is separated from **AM** $^{\mathbf{B}}$ providing some evidence that **co-NP** is not contained in **AM**.

Theorem 4: There exists an oracle **B** such that **co** $-$**NP** $^{\mathbf{B}} \not\subseteq$ **AM** $^{\mathbf{B}}$.

The construction is too long and technical to be included here; it will be included in the final paper; the proof is very similar to that of theorem 5.6 in [HZ 84]. Later Fortnow and Sipser [FS] showed that there exists an oracle **B** such that **co** $-$**NP** $^{\mathbf{B}} \not\subseteq$ **AM** [**P**]$^{\mathbf{B}}$.
Remark: Note that an absolute separation (without an oracle) would separate **co-NP** from **NP**. Therefore, only a separation by an oracle is likely, as provided by the theorem.

The following theorem provides further evidence that **co** $-$**NP** $\not\subseteq$ **AM** (see [BHZ 87], [Sc 86]).

Theorem 5: If **co** $-$**NP** $\subseteq$ **AM** then (a) **PH** collapses at the second level, and (b) **PH** $=$ **AM** .
Proof: Assumption: $(\forall/\exists) \subseteq (\forall\exists/\exists^+\forall)$. Then

$$\Sigma_2^P=(\exists\forall/\forall\exists) \subseteq (\exists\forall\exists/\forall\exists^+\forall) \subseteq (\forall\exists\exists/\exists^+\forall\forall)=(\forall\exists/\exists^+\forall)=\mathbf{AM} \subseteq (\forall\exists/\exists\forall)=\Pi_2^P$$

q.e.d.

The following diagram (Figure 1) depicts inclusions among classes discussed here:

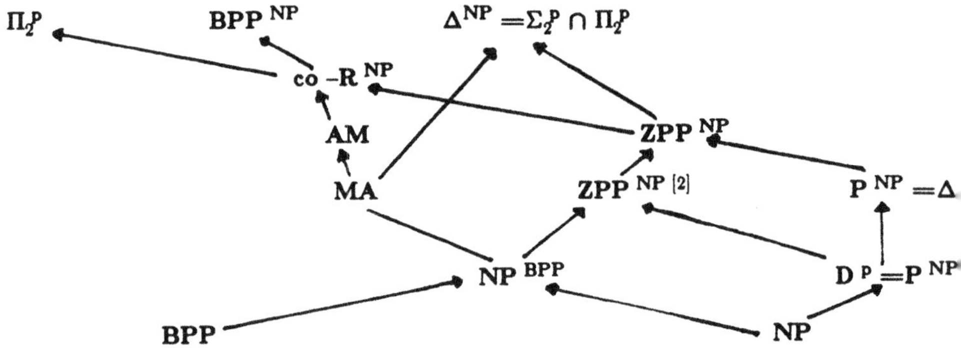

Figure 1

Open problems:

co $-$**NP** $\subseteq$ **AM** [**P**] ?
AM $\subseteq$ **ZPP** $^{\mathbf{NP}}$?
AM [**P**] $\subseteq$ **BPP** $^{\Sigma_2^P}$?

6. Matrix Group Problems

The Arthur-Merlin games have been introduced in [B 85] and [BS 84] in order to classify the order and membership problems for matrix groups over finite fields. Let G denote subgroups of GL(d,q) given by sets of generators. GL(d,q) can be identified with the set of regular d by d matrices over the finite field GF(q) with q elements (q being a power of a prime). Group elements $g \in GL(d,q)$ come suitably encoded by words of length proportional to $d^2 log(q)$. The main problems considered in [B 85], [BS 84] are:

Membership = $\{(g,G) : g \in G\}$,

Exact order = $\{(N,G) : |G| = N\}$, and

Divisor of order = $\{(N,G)$: the integer N divides $|G|\}$.

All these problems are solvable in polynomial time for permutation groups([Si 78], [FHL 80]), but they seem to be harder for matrix groups. Instead of working with matrix groups one could also use black-box groups [B 85] defined as follows:

(1) The elements of the group are encoded by strings of uniform length.

(2) Group operations are performed by an oracle.

The "short presentation conjecture" [BE 82] claims that a short presentation in terms of generators and relations can be found for every finite simple group. Using this short presentation conjecture [BS 84] have shown that :

Exact order $\in$ **NP** $\cap$ **co** –**NP** , and

Membership $\in$ **NP** $\cap$ **co** –**NP** .

Without using this conjecture, it has been shown ([B 85], [BS 84]) that these problems are in **AM** $\cap$ **co** –**AM** . On the other hand *Membership* and *Divisor of order* are in **NP** [BS 84].

Using these results, we now show that *Exact order* is in the class $\mathbf{D^P}$, where [PY 82]:

$\mathbf{D^P} = \{L : L = L_1 \cap L_2$ for *some* $L_1 \in \mathbf{NP}$ and $L_2 \in \mathbf{co\text{-}NP}\}$.

Theorem 6: Exact order is in $\mathbf{D^P}$.

Proof: In order to prove that $|G| = N$, it is sufficient to show that N is a divisor of $|G|$ and that all divisors N' of $|G|$ divide N. Thus we can choose:

$L_1 =$ *Divisor of order*, and

$L_2(N) = \{(N',G) : (N',G) \notin$ *Divisor of order or* $N' \mid N\}$.

Clearly:

$L_1 \in \mathbf{NP}$. $L_2(N) \in \mathbf{co\text{-}NP}$.

For the problem $(N',G) \in ?L_2(N)$, the group G is given by generators. Therefore the length of the input *(N',G)* is $\Omega(d^2 log(q))$. On the other hand $|G| \leq q^{d^2}$. Thus all divisors of $|G|$ have length at most a polynomial in the length of the input. Therefore L_2 is in **co-NP**, where $L_2 = \{(N,G) : \forall N' \leq p(d^2 log(q))\ (N',G) \in L_2(N)\}$. Furthermore $L_1 \cap L_2$ is precisely *Exact order* as desired. **q.e.d.**

This Theorem is interesting because it suggests some open problems. Clearly, $\mathbf{D}^{\mathbf{P}} \subseteq \Delta_2^P = \mathbf{P}^{\mathbf{NP}} \subseteq \mathbf{ZPP}^{\mathbf{NP}}$, but what is the relation of **AM** to these classes? (See Figure 1.) As **AM** is not known to be contained in $\mathbf{D}^{\mathbf{P}}$, it might not be the "right" class for the *Exact order* problem. In fact, because of the [BE 82]-conjecture, this problem is potentially in $\Delta = \mathbf{NP} \cap \mathbf{co}-\mathbf{NP}$ [B 85, BS 84]. But this seems hard to prove. It might be easier to replace L_2 in the Theorem by a language in **co-R**, which would follow from the following *Conjectures:*

(1) The problem of recognizing a Sylow subgroup of a group G is in **NP**.

(2) If a prime p divides |G|, then the order of a random short product g of (some special) generators of G is likely to be a multiple of p.

These conjectures would imply that: *Exact order* $= L_1 \cap L_2$ for some $L_1 \in \mathbf{NP}$ and $L_2 \in \mathbf{co}-\mathbf{R}$, and therefore, *Exact order* would be element of $\mathbf{NP}^{\mathbf{R}} \subseteq \mathbf{NP}^{\mathbf{BPP}} \subseteq \mathbf{MA} \subseteq \mathbf{AM}$.

7. Conclusions

The main contribution of this paper is bridging the gap between different fields. It seems that people working in structural complexity have a completely different terminology and techniques, than people working in cryptography or even those that investigate the complexity of specific problems by means of combinatorial games. By showing that adversary terminology can be formalized using alternations of ordinary and probabilistic quantifiers, we reduce complicated combinatorial arguments to a few principles for swapping quantifiers. Specifically it is shown that Babai's game hierarchy:

$$\mathbf{AM} \subseteq \mathbf{AMA} \subseteq \mathbf{AMAM} \subseteq \ldots$$

is exactly:

$$(\forall\exists/\exists^+\forall) \subseteq (\forall\exists\forall/\exists^+\forall\exists^+) \subseteq (\forall\exists\forall\exists/\exists^+\forall\exists^+\forall) \subseteq \cdots$$

and therefore it is easily seen that the game hierarchy collapses at the second level (like several other variations of this hierarchy). The main tools used for such collapsing results are quantifier swapping properties which are also useful for showing:

$$\mathbf{BPP} = (\exists^+\forall/\forall\exists^+) = (\forall\exists^+/\exists^+\forall) \text{ and}$$

$$\mathbf{MA} = (\exists\forall/\forall\exists^+) \subseteq (\forall\exists/\exists^+\forall) = \mathbf{AM}.$$

We have also placed the game classes MA and AM in their appropriate position in a chart of complexity classes that are defined in a more classical way, namely by use of oracles. Thus we have shown that:

$\mathbf{NP}^{\mathbf{BPP}} \subseteq \mathbf{MA}$; $\mathbf{NP}^{\mathbf{BPP}} \subseteq \mathbf{ZPP}^{\mathbf{NP}}$; and $\mathbf{AM} \subseteq \mathbf{co}-\mathbf{R}^{\mathbf{NP}} \subseteq \mathbf{BPP}^{\mathbf{NP}}$

We have investigated oracle properties of these classes ($\mathbf{MA}^{\mathbf{BPP}} = \mathbf{MA}$; $\mathbf{AM}^{\Delta} = \mathbf{AM}$; $\mathbf{AM}^{\mathbf{BPP}} = \mathbf{AM}$;) and we have separated **co-NP** from **AM** (consequently also from **MA**) by an oracle to give evidence that $\mathbf{co}-\mathbf{NP} \not\subseteq \mathbf{AM}$, which was a problem posed by Babai and Szemeredi. In the last section, we discussed matrix group problem, showing that the "order of a matrix group (over a finite field)" problem lies in the complexity class $\mathbf{D}^{\mathbf{P}}$ and raising some questions about group problems (e.g. about Sylow groups) as well as about structural complexity issues (e.g. relation between $\mathbf{D}^{\mathbf{P}}$ and **AM**).

Acknowledgement : We would like to thank S. Cosmadakis, P. Hinman, R. Ramanujan and M. Yung for helpful discussions.

Remark: Most of these results were obtained in 1984. Many papers have already referenced this work as manuscript[1985]. Some of the results of this paper appeared in an overview [Z 86].

8. References

[B 85]
BABAI, L., Trading Group Theory for Randomness, 17th STOC, (1985), 421-429.

[BE 82]
BABAI, L.,and ERDOS, P., Representation of Group Elements as as short Products, in : Theory and Practice of Combinatorics (A. Rosa et al. eds.), Annals of Discr. Math. 12, (1982), 27-30.

[BG 81]
BENNETT, C.H., and GILL, J., Relative to a Random Oracle A, $\mathbf{P}^A \neq \mathbf{NP}^A \neq \mathbf{co-NP}^A$, SIAM J. Comput 10, (1981), 96-113.

[BHZ 86]
BOPPANA, R.B., HASTAD, J., and ZACHOS, S., Does **co-NP** have Short Interactive Proofs?, (1986), IPL 25, (1987), 127-132.

[BS 84]
BABAI, L.., and SZEMEREDI, E., On the Complexity of Matrix Group Problems I, FOCS 25, (1984), 229-240.

[FHL 80]
FURST, M.L., HOPCROFT, J., and LUKS, E.M., Polynomial-time Algorithms for Permutation Groups, 21st FOCS, (1980), 36-41.

[FS]
FORTNOW, L., and SIPSER, M., Private Communication.

[G 77]
GILL, J., Computational Complexity of Probabilistic Turing Machines, SIAM J. of Computing 6, (1977), 675-695.

[GHY 85]
GALIL, Z., HABER, S., and YUNG, M., A Private Interactive Test of a Boolean Predicate and Minimum - Knowledge Public - Key Cryptosystems, 26th FOCS, (1985), 360-371.

[GMR 85]
GOLDWASSER, S., MICALI, S., and RACKOFF, C., The Knowledge Complexity of Interactive Proof Systems, 17th STOC, (1985), 291-304.

[GS 85]
GOLDWASSER, S., and SIPSER, M., Private Coins versus Public Coins in Interactive Proof Systems, 18th STOC, (1986), 59-68.

[HZ 84]
HINMAN, P. and ZACHOS, S., Probabilistic Machines, Oracles and Quantifiers, Proceedings of the Oberwolfach Recursion-theoretic Week, Lecture Notes in Mathematics 1141, Springer- Verlag, (1984), 159-192.

[P 83]
PAPADIMITRIOU, C.H., Games against Nature, 24th FOCS, (1983), 446-450.

[PY 82]
PAPADIMITRIOU, C.H., and YANNAKAKIS, M., The Complexity of Facets (and some facets of complexity), 14th STOC, (1982), 255-260.

[S 76]
STOCKMEYER, L.J., The Polynomial-Time Hierarchy, TCS 3, (1976), 1-22.

[Sc 86]
SCHOENING, U., Graph Isomorphism is in the Low Hierarchy, (1986), submitted for publication.

[Si 78]
SIMS, C.C., Some Group Theoretic Algorithms, Lect. Notes in Math. 697, Springer-Verlag,

(1978), 108-124.

[SS 77]
SOLOVAY, R., and STRASSEN, V., A fast Monte-Carlo test for primality, SIAM J. of Computing 6, (1977) 84-85.

[W 76]
WRATHALL, C., Complete Sets and the Polynomial-Time Hierarchy, TCS 3, (1976), 23-33.

[Z 82]
ZACHOS, S., Robustness of Probabilistic Computational Complexity Classes under Definional Perturbations, Information and Control, (1982), 54, 143-154.

[ZH 83]
ZACHOS, S., and HELLER, H., On BPP, TM-252, LCS, MIT, (1983).

[ZH 84]
ZACHOS, S., and HELLER, H., A Decisive Characterization of BPP, Information and Control, (1986), 69, 125-135.

[Z 86]
ZACHOS, S., Probabilistic Quantifiers, Adversaries, and Complexity Classes: An Overview, Proceedings of Structure in Complexity Theory Conference, Lecture Notes in Computer Science, 223, (1986), 383-400.

[Za 86]
ZACHOS, S., Probabilistic Oracles are less Powerfull than Nondeterministic Oracles, submitted for publication, (1986).

ON CERTAIN BANDWIDTH RESTRICTED VERSIONS OF THE SATISFIABILITY PROBLEM OF PROPOSITIONAL CNF FORMULAS

V. Arvind[1] and S. Biswas
Department of Computer Science and Engineering
Indian Institute of Technology, Kanpur 208016, India

1. Introduction

In this paper we consider the complexity of certain restricted versions of the satisfiability problem of propositional formulas in conjunctive normal form. We define the corresponding languages in terms of kernel constructibility, where log-bandwidth violation is allowed in the corresponding kernels, but the constructing relations obey the bandwidth restriction (appropriate definitions follow). Thus, these languages can be seen as ones which allow limited amount of log-bandwidth violation in so far as such violation may occur only at the kernel level. While one of the languages is readily seen to be in P, the rest are shown NP-complete. This is of interest as it is known [4] that the satisfiability problem is in P when no log-bandwidth violation is allowed. The languages considered here also illustrate how it is possible to define many restricted versions of an NP-complete language when it is viewed as a kernel constructible language. Another aspect this paper illustrates is the efficacy of Börger's approach [6] for reducing Turing machine acceptance problems to decision problems of logics. Without this approach proofs of Lemma 5 and Theorem 6 would have certainly been far more difficult.

2. Basic definitions and the languages considered

The observation that many languages in NP including all natural NP-complete languages are self-reducible motivates the definition of kernel constructible languages. (As an example of self-reducibility: a graph G is Hamiltonian iff at least one of the graphs obtained from G by removing one of its edges is also Hamiltonian unless G itself is just a Hamiltonian cycle).

A language $L \subseteq \Sigma^*$ is said to be kernel constructible if there exists $K \subseteq L$ and a binary relation R on Σ^* such that

---

[1]Present address: Department of Computer Science and Engineering, Indian Institute of Technology, Madras 600036, India.

(i) K and the graph of R are both in PTIME.

(ii) If $x \in L$ and $x\ R\ y$ then $y \in L$.

(iii) For every y in L-K there is an x in K and some n, such that $x\ R\ x_1$, $x_1\ R\ x_2, \ldots, x_{n-1}\ R\ x_n$, where $x_n = y$ and, n and the lengths $|x|$, $|x_1|, \ldots, |x_{n-1}|$ are all bounded by a fixed (for L) polynomial in $|y|$.

(This definition is a modified version of the one given in [5]).

In the above definition K is called a kernel of L and R a constructing relation. The pair (K, R) is called a construction for L. Often (as is the case in the rest of this paper except in Note 1 below) R is length increasing from left to right, i.e., $x\ R\ y$ implies $|x| < |y|$. In such cases it is natural to fix the polynomial in $|y|$ (in the definition) as $|y|$ itself, then the pair (K, R) uniquely defines a language denoted as L(K, R).

Note 1:

The notion of kernel constructibility is weaker than that of d-self-reducibility [1,2,3] which also attempts to formalize the notion of self-reducibility that is so commonly seen in NP. Kernel constructibility is weaker because of the following: to compare the two notions it will be natural to say x is a proper sub-object of y (in the terminology of d-self-reducibility) if $x\ R\ y$, where R is a constructing relation. Then, kernel constructibility will allow an object to have even infinitely many proper sub-objects; note that, for an x in a kernel constructible language, (iii) in the above definition asserts that there is a decreasing chain of length bounded by a polynomial in $|x|$ with the maximum element x, this chain, however, need not be maximal. In the case of d-self-reducibility, however, the length of every decreasing chain is bounded by a polynomial in the size of its maximum element.

Note 2:

By a formula we shall always mean in this paper a propositional formula in conjunctive normal form with ordered clauses. Let SAT be the set of all satisfiable formulas. A variable or its negation is called a literal.

Kernel constructibility of SAT:

Let the kernel K be defined as the following set of formulas:

$K = \{F \mid F$ is satisfiable and F is a conjunction of literals$\}$.

Define the following binary relation R on formulas: For two formulas F_1 and F_2, the relation F_1 R F_2 holds iff F_2 is obtained from F_1 by disjuncting some literal to some clause in F_1. That is, if F_1 = $\{C_1 \wedge C_2 \wedge \dots \wedge C_m\}$ then there is a j such that $1 \leq j \leq m$ and F_2 = $\{C_1 \wedge \dots \wedge C_{j-1} \wedge C_j' \wedge C_{j+1} \wedge \dots \wedge C_m\}$ where C_j' is the disjunction of literals $l_{j_1}, \dots, l_{j_n}$, y with C_j being the disjunction of $l_{j_1}, \dots, l_{j_n}$ only. Here, y is some literal.

We say that F_2 is obtained from F_1 by <u>literal-adding</u> (y to the jth clause).

It can be easily seen that L(K, R) is precisely SAT.

<u>Constructionally restricting SAT: Languages L_1, L_2 and L_3</u>

Various restrictions of SAT can be obtained by considering different PTIME subsets of SAT as kernels and by restricting literal-adding in different ways. A natural restriction on literal-adding is the <u>log-bandwidth constraint</u>: literal-adding of the literal y to the jth clause of a formula F = $\{C_1 \wedge \dots \wedge C_m\}$ is allowed provided there exists no k, $|j-k| > c.\log_2 m$, such that the kth clause of F contains an occurrence of the variable from which y is built. (c is some a priori fixed constant). We define three restrictions of SAT.

1) $L_1 = L(K_1, R_1)$ where K_1 is the same as K of the construction given earlier for SAT. As for R_1, for two formulas F_1 and F_2, F_1 R_1 F_2 holds iff F_2 is obtained from F_1 by log-bandwidth constrained literal-adding.
2) $L_2 = L(K_2, R_2)$, where the kernel K_2 is defined as:
   K_2 = {F | F satisfiable and any clause in F has at most two literals}.
   The relation R_2 is the same as R_1 above.
3) $L_3 = L(K_3, R_3)$, where K_3 is the set of all satisfiable Horn formulas, i.e., formulas where each clause contains at most one positive literal. As for R_3, for formulas F_1 and F_2, F_1 R_3 F_2 holds provided F_2 is obtained from F_1 by log-bandwidth constrained literal-adding, where the <u>added literal is positive</u> (that is, it is a non-negated variable).

<u>Note 3</u>:

We have defined above what we mean by log-bandwidth constrained literal adding. In [4], the concept of <u>log-bandwidth constrained formulas</u> is defined: a formula $C_1 \wedge C_2 \wedge \dots \wedge C_m$ is said to be log-bandwidth constrained provided there exist <u>no</u> i, j, $|i-j| > c.\log_2 m$, such that C_i and C_j share a variable in common, c being some fixed constant.

Note 4:

Each of these languages, L_1, L_2 and L_3 is clearly a proper subset of SAT. Further, in each there is no bandwidth constraint in the kernel, but the literal-adding obeys the log-bandwidth constraint. Therefore, in the entire formula, only those literals which occur in the kernel part can violate the log-bandwidth constraint. Thus, these languages can be seen as ones which allow log-bandwidth violation in a limited manner.

3. Complexity of L_1, L_2 and L_3

Proposition 1: The language L_1 is in P.

Proof: For a formula F in L_1, every occurrence of a literal that violates the log-bandwidth constraint must be in every kernel formula from which F can be constructed; further, since a kernel formula consists of one literal clauses, F will be satisfiable when all these log-bandwidth violating literals are given the truth value true. But then the resultant simplified formula F' obeys the log-bandwidth constraint, hence its satisfiability can be checked in PTIME [4].

Theorem 2: The language L_2 is NP-complete.

To prove this, we first note that L_2 is in NP (as all kernel constructible languages are). To show its NP-completeness, we define another language L_4, prove that $L_4 \leq^p_m L_2$ (Lemma 3), then we show that L_4 is NP-complete (Lemmas 4 and 5).

Definition: $L_4 = \{F \mid F$ is a satisfiable formula in conjunctive normal form where each clause has at most one literal which violates the log-bandwidth constraint$\}$.

Lemma 3: $L_4 \leq^p_m L_2$.

Proof: Following f is a polynomial-time reduction. If the given formula $F = C_1 \wedge C_2 \ldots \wedge C_m$ has a clause with two or more literals violating the log-bandwidth constraint, then $f(F) = x \wedge \sim x$, because such an F cannot, by definition, be in L_4. Otherwise, $f(F) = F$. This is correct as, $L_4 \subseteq L_2$. To see this, if F is in L_4 then it has a satisfying interpretation, say I. Let I set true the literal x_i in C_i

of F. Let y_i denote the literal in C_i which violates the log-bandwidth constraint if C_i has such a literal (only one such literal is possible, by definition) <u>and</u> this literal is different from x_i, otherwise let y_i be the constant 'false'. Then the formula $\bigwedge_{1 \le i \le m} (x_i \vee y_i)$ is in K_2 and clearly F can be obtained from this formula by log-bandwidth constrained literal adding. Therefore, F is in L_2. ■

Next, our task is to prove that L_4 is NP-complete. We achieve this in two parts — the immediately following lemma shows that a certain NP-complete language is accepted by a somewhat specialized sort of NDTM, then we prove in Lemma 5 that the accepting computations of such machines can be captured by elements of L_4.

The independent set problem which is known to be NP-complete [7] is defined for our purpose as follows:

INDSET = {(n,k,G) | G is an undirected graph with n vertices and has an independent set of size k, i.e., there are k vertices no two of which are joined by an edge }.

The coding of (n,k,G) we use will be explained below.

<u>Lemma 4</u>: INDSET can be accepted by an NDTM M with the following properties:

(i) M uses three tapes, one read-only input tape, one guess tape and a work tape. Once the guess is written on it, the guess tape is used in a read-only manner.

(ii) For an input instance with a graph of n vertices, the space used on the guess tape is n and on the work tape $O(\log_2 n)$.

(iii) Given an input instance, for <u>each time instant</u> t, one can compute in polynomial time what the position of <u>each head</u> will be for the computation of M on that input instance. In fact, the three head positions depend solely on n, the number of vertices in the input graph.

<u>Proof</u>: The input to M is in the following form: n # k # edge-list bit-array; the first two components each occupying $\lceil \log_2 n \rceil$ space, the last component $\binom{n}{2}$ bits. With the n vertices assumed to be numbered from 1 through n, and denoting an edge between vertices i and j as the tuple (min(i,j), max(i,j)), consider the lexicographic ordering of all possible edges, namely (1,2), (1,3), ..., (1,n), (2,3), ..., (2,n), ..., (n-1,n). If the jth edge in this ordering is present in the input graph then the jth bit of the edge-list bit-array is one else it is zero.

If the vertex j is included in the independent set guessed, then the jth bit of the guess tape is one else it is zero.

The work tape consists of nine buffers, $B_1, B_2, \ldots, B_9$, separated by distinctive separators. The first six buffers of $\lceil \log_2 n \rceil$ bits each, whereas the last three, each stores a one bit flag. Thus, the size of the work tape is bounded by $c.\log_2 n$, for some constant c.

n	k	C	v	v_1	v_2	a	b	d
B_1	B_2	B_3	B_4	B_5	B_6	B_7	B_8	B_9

Fig. 1 Organization of the work tape.

Let us name the contents of the work tape buffers as shown in Fig. 1. M first reads in n and k from the input into the first two buffers of the work tape, then M counts the number of 1's in the guess tape into the counter C, then checks contents of the second and the third buffers are equal, i.e. k = C. Next, M enters into the phase that verifies that the guessed set of vertices is indeed an independent set. This is done essentially by considering each possible edge (i,j), traversing the guess tape fully to ensure that both i and j do not belong to the guessed set when the edge (i,j) is there in the graph. During the iteration, v_1 has the value i, v_2 the value j and v the current head position on the guess tape.

The algorithm, in detail, is as follows.

<u>begin</u>

initialize the buffers to contain only zeros;
{in particular d = 0 now}
copy the first two components of the input tape,
i.e., n and k into the first two buffers of the work tape;
count the number of 1's in the guess tape into the third
block of work tape;
<u>if</u> the second and third work tape blocks contents unequal
<u>then</u> {guess set cardinality not equal k}
d := 1 ;
{at this point the input tape head is scanning the first
entry of the edge-list bit-array}
{initialization for the phase to verify that the guessed
set is indeed independent}
v_1 := 1; v_2 := 1;

```
repeat  {iteration for each possible edge}
        {at this point input head is scanning the entry for the
        possible edge (v1, v2)};
        position guess head at the left end;
        v := 1; a := 0; b := 0;
        repeat  {iteration for each entry on guess tape}
                {at this point the guess head is scanning the
                entry for the vertex v}
                if (v1 = v) and guess head scanning 1 and input
                head scanning 1
                then a := 1;
                if (v2 = v) and guess head scanning 1 and input
                head scanning 1
                then b := 1;
                move guess tape head one square to right;
                v := v + 1
        until guess tape head has reached the right end marker;
        if (a = 1) and (b = 1)
        then {the edge (v1, v2) is present in the graph and both these
             vertices are in the guessed independent set}
             d := 1;
        {now updating v1, v2}
        if v2 = n {the value n is available in the first work tape
                  buffer}
        then
        begin
        v1 := v1 + 1; v2 := v1 + 1
        end
        else  v2 := v2 + 1;
        move input tape head by one square to right
until  input tape exhausted;
        {at this point d = 1 implies either the guessed set cardinality
        not equal to k or there is an edge (v1, v2) in the graph with
        both v1 and v2 in the guessed set}
        if d = 0  then  accept
end.
```

It is clear, from the algorithm, that M accepts INDSET. This completes the proofs of (i) and (ii) of our Lemma.

As for (iii), the very point of the above algorithm for M to follow was to ensure that this condition can be satisfied by suitable coding. During the entire computation, the input head makes just one left to right complete sweep. The guess tape head, it can be seen from the above algorithm, makes a number (in fact, $\binom{n}{2} + 1$) of left to right and back complete sweeps. As for the work tape head, M can be coded in such a way that this head too does its work through complete sweeps, the number of sweeps depending solely on n. For example, consider the work needed to make C have the count of the number of 1's on the guess tape. This can be implemented, by making the guess tape head make a left to right sweep, and for each of its positions, the work tape head makes one complete sweep and in the process adds the symbol currently being scanned by the guess head to the buffer containing C. Frequently, M needs to compare the contents of two work tape buffers of size $\log_2 n$ (e.g. checking if $v_1 = v$). This can be implemented by requiring the work tape head to make $\log_2 n + 1$ complete sweeps, with auxiliary symbols replacing the kth symbol in each buffer, $1 \leq k \leq \log_2 n$, in the first $\log_2 n$ sweeps and the last sweep turning the auxiliary symbols back into the original ones. Finally, let us consider the if-then-else statement in the algorithm that updates v_1 and v_2. Both in the 'then' part as well as in the 'else' part a buffer is incremented by 1; this can be implemented by one sweep. Next, in the 'then' part v_1 needs to be copied into v_2 and then v_2 incremented by 1; in the 'else' part, however, similar operations are not needed. But, to make the head movements identical in the two parts, in the 'else' part too redundant head movements are made identical to the 'then' part without, of course, making any final changes on the tape.

Thus, we see that, the coding of M can be done satisfying the condition (iii) of the Lemma. ■

Lemma 5: The acceptance problem of M (defined in the previous Lemma) is polynomially many-to-one reducible to the decision problem of L_4.

Proof: Given an input (n,k,G) for M, we shall construct a formula F such that $F \in L_4$ iff (n,k,G) is accepted by M. This construction of F shall be carried out in time polynomial in n and this would prove L_4 to be NP-complete.

We code the computation of the machine M on an input instance using the approach of Börger [6]. Essentially, this encoding does away with some assertions that are logically unnecessary. E.g., it is unnecessary to assert that the machine is in a unique state at every time-instant or to assert that every tape-head scans at most one symbol at every time-instant. The usual practice is to include these assertions into the sentence F so that if F is satisfiable it has a unique model, i.e., the categorical model [6]. Here, following the idea in [6] we give an encoding which only has to ensure the following:

(i) The initial conditions are correctly specified.

(ii) The description of the quintuples of M, so that there will exist a model of F coding the correct transitions. Further, it is asserted that if at a cell some symbol is there at time t, the same symbol remains there at time (t+1) as well, unless the head was scanning this cell at time t.

(iii) To capture acceptance, a part of the formula asserts that finally the machine is in no state which is an unaccepting state. In this somewhat round-about way, it is ensured that F admits only models corresponding to accepting computations.

The formula F is a conjunction of assertions for (i), (ii) and (iii) so that F is satisfiable iff M accepts the input.

The propositional variables that F uses are given below with their intended meanings:

$C[i,j,t]$ is true if the ith work tape cell has the jth symbol in it at time t, $S[a,t]$ is true if M is in the ath state at time t, $0 \leq i \leq c.\log_2 n$, and $1 \leq t \leq p(n)$ (where $p(n)$ is the running time of M and $c.\log_2 n$ is the work tape size). $Q[i]$ for $1 \leq i \leq n$ are variables corresponding to the n guess-tape cells; $Q[i]$ is true if the ith guess-tape cell is 1, else $Q[i]$ is false.

Now we describe the different components of F which capture the computation of M.

<u>Coding of the appropriate quintuples</u>

At any time t, the positions of the three heads are known (Lemma 4). Further we also know exactly what is the symbol being scanned, for any given t, by the input head and by the guess-tape head for a given guess, contents of the corresponding tapes do not change during the course of the computation. Using this information we define $E_{a,b,t}$ which codes the appropriate quintuples applicable at time t.

Below $H_2(t)$ and $H_3(t)$ denote the position of the guess-tape head and that of the work tape head respectively at time t. Note that for a given t, the values of $H_2(t)$ and $H_3(t)$ are known in advance, and these values are used below.

$$E_{a,b,t} = ((C[H_3(t),a,t] \wedge S[b,t] \wedge Q[H_2(t)])$$
$$\rightarrow (C[H_3(t), a', t+1] \wedge S[b', t+1])) \wedge$$

$$((C[H_3(t),\ a,\ t] \wedge S[b,t] \wedge \sim Q[H_2(t)])$$

$$\longrightarrow\ (C[H_3(t),\ a'',\ t+1] \wedge S[b'',\ t+1]))$$

where a is a work tape symbol, b is a state, and $1 \leq t \leq p(n)$, a', b' etc. are explained below. $E_{a,b,t}$ essentially describes a move by the machine M when the work tape symbol scanned is a and the state is b at time t. The two clauses give the two possible moves depending on the guess-tape cell $H_2(t)$, i.e., whether $Q[H_2(t)]$ is true or false. (Thus, if $Q[H_2(t)]$ is true, then from the appropriate machine quintuple we have that the symbol written in the work tape is a' and the machine goes to state b'. Similarly, for the case when $Q[H_2(t)]$ is false). We note that neither the input head position nor the symbol it is scanning figure in $E_{a,b,t}$ because by computing in polynomial time the head position, as the input-tape is a read only tape, we know exactly which symbol the input head is scanning at time t, and this knowledge is used to choose the appropriate quintuples in defining $E_{a,b,t}$.

<u>Only the work tape cell under the head can change</u>

$D_{k,d,t} = (C[k,d,t] \longrightarrow C[k,d,t+1])$ for $k \neq H_3(t)$,

$1 \leq k \leq c.\log_2 n$, $1 \leq t \leq p(n)$ and for all work tape symbols d.

This component asserts that contents of no work tape cell other than $H_3(t)$ can change at any time t.

<u>Initial work tape contents</u>

$$\text{Init} = C[1,0,0] \wedge \ldots \wedge C[c.\log_2 n,0,0] \wedge S[1,0]$$

Initially work tape contents is all zeros. This component simply asserts that. We need such an initializing component only for the work tape because only work tape contents can change. Also we specify the initial state.

<u>Final state description</u>

$$\text{Final} = \prod_{q \neq q_f} \sim S[q,p(n)]$$

where we assume that q_f is the <u>only</u> accepting state of M.

$$\text{Let} \quad ED = \prod_{t} \prod_{\substack{k \neq H_3(t) \\ a,b,d}} E_{a,b,t} \wedge D_{k,d,t}$$

Now, let $F = \text{Init} \wedge \text{ED} \wedge \text{Final}$.

The proof that F is satisfiable iff M accepts the input instance in question, can be constructed following Börger [6]. This particular layout of F has been chosen to ensure that the required bandwidth constraints are satisfied. Let

$$ED_t = \prod_{\substack{k \neq H_3(t) \\ a,b,d}} E_{a,b,t} \wedge D_{k,d,t} .$$

We observe that the length of ED_t is bounded by $c'\log_2 n$, for some constant c' and, apart from Q[i]'s, variables in ED_t will not occur in ED_j when $j < t-1$ or $j > t+1$. Thus, it is clear that the only literals that violate the bandwidth of $c_o \cdot \log_2 n$ (where c_o is a constant) are Q[i] and ~Q[i] for $1 \leq i \leq n$. But from our definition of components these occur only in the $E_{a,b,t}$'s and at most one such literal is present in any clause. Therefore F is satisfiable iff F is in L_4 and so F is in L_4 iff (n,k,G) is in INDSET. Hence L_4 is NP-complete. ∎

Next, we shall prove that L_3 is NP-complete through the simulation of a different NDTM model where we again use Borger's approach.

<u>Theorem 6</u>: The language L_3 is NP-complete.

<u>Proof</u>: It is easy to see that L_3 is in NP. For given a sentence S in L_3 we can guess the satisfiable kernel Horn formula from which S is constructed and verify that this Horn sentence is satisfiable and that S can be constructed from it using the relation R_3 in polynomial time.

To prove the NP-completeness of L_3 we shall need a somewhat non-standard NDTM model that captures NP. Its description is as follows:

The machine, call it M, has two tapes.

(a) The first is an input-cum-work tape. For a given input x of length n, the main tape has p(n) cells marked off where x is in the leftmost part of the marked off region (where the running time of M is p(n)).

(b) The second is a guess-tape on which a guessed binary string of length p(n) is written down by the guessing module. The guess-tape head starts at the left-most cell and moves only to the right one step at a time and finishes at the right-most cell after p(n) steps.

After a guessed string w has been written on the guess-tape by a guessing module, M functions as a DTM M' running in polynomial time p(n) which accepts or rejects the pair $< w, x >$. In fact, we have $L(M) = \{x \mid (\exists w)(< w, x > \in L(M') \text{ and } |w| = p(|x|))\}$. Clearly every language in NP can be expressed like this [7]. Hence our NDTM model is powerful enough to capture NP. Given such a machine M and input x, we shall construct a sentence F such that F is in L_3 iff M accepts x.

Simulation of the machine M

We again shall use Börger [6] in the encoding of a computation of M. First we give the variables used in F and their intended meanings:

> G[i,1] is true if the ith guess-tape cell contains 1.
> G[i,0] is true if the ith guess-tape cell contains 0.
> C[i,j,t] is true if the ith work tape cell has the symbol j at time t. S[k,t] is true if M is in the kth state at time t. H[i,t] is true if the work tape head is on the ith cell at time t, where $1 \le i,t \le p(n)$ and j,k both have some constant range. We also have auxiliary variables D[i,0] and D[i,1], $1 \le i \le p(n)$, to make sure that the variables G[i,0] or G[i,1] do not violate bandwidth.

We now describe the various components of the sentence F.

Guess-tape contents

The contents of the guess-tape are encoded in the sentence B below:

$$B = \prod_{1 \le i \le p(n)} (G[i,1] \vee G[i,0]) \wedge (\sim G[i,1] \vee \sim G[i,0])$$
$$(\sim G[i,1] \vee D[i,1]) \wedge (\sim G[i,0] \vee D[i,0])$$

We note from the clauses of B that D[i,1] is true if G[i,1] is true and D[i,0] is true if G[i,0] is true.

Initial configuration description

$$\text{Init} = S[1,0] \wedge H[1,0] \wedge \prod_{i=1}^{n} C[i,b_i,0] \wedge \prod_{i=n+1}^{p(n)} C[i,0,0]$$

where $x = b_1 b_2 \ldots b_n$ is the input string and we assume the initial state to be 1.

Encoding of appropriate quintuples

$$E_{i,j,k,t} = ((C[i,j,t] \wedge H[i,t] \wedge S[k,t] \wedge D[t,1])$$
$$\longrightarrow (C[i,j',t+1] \wedge S[k',t+1] \wedge H[i',t+1])) \wedge$$

$$((C[i,j,t] \wedge H[i,t] \wedge S[k,t] \wedge D[t,0])$$

$$\rightarrow (C[i,j'',t+1] \wedge S[k'',t+1] \wedge H[i'',t+1]))$$

The two parts of $E_{i,j,k,t}$ together describe the machine move at time t, if the machine at time t scans in state k the ith cell which has the symbol j. The two parts are true according as $D[t,1]$ is true or respectively $D[t,0]$. Here $1 \leq i,t \leq p(n)$ and both j and k have constant range.

Define

$$E_1 = \prod_{\substack{1 \leq i,t \leq p(n) \\ j,k}} E_{i,j,k,t} .$$

Only cell under H can change

$$E_2 = \prod_{i \neq i_1} ((H[i,t] \wedge C[i_1,j,t]) \rightarrow C[i_1,j,t+1])$$

The meaning for each clause in E_2 is quite clear.

Final state condition

$$\text{Final} = \prod_{q \neq q_f} \sim S[q,p(n)]$$ where q_f is the only accepting state for M. As in the case of the previous theorem, the sentence Final forces M to enter q_f at $t = p(n)$ and no other state than q_f.

Let $F = B \wedge \text{Init} \wedge E_1 \wedge E_2 \wedge \text{Final}$.

Clearly, every $E_{i,j,k,t}$ can be easily put as a conjunction of Horn clauses. Therefore it is immaterial as to which literal in $E_{i,j,k,t}$ violates bandwidth as the kernel consists of satisfiable Horn formulas. Therefore E_1 is a conjunction of Horn clauses. Similarly E_2, Init and Final are all Horn formulas. So it follows that Init $\wedge E_1 \wedge E_2 \wedge$ Final is a Horn formula. Further, in B if a clause contains a log-bandwidth violating literal (which has to be either $D[i,1]$ or $D[i,0]$ for some i) that clause is either $(\sim G[i,1] \vee D[i,1])$ or $(\sim G[i,0] \vee D[i,0])$. But all such clauses are horn clauses and therefore can be considered to be part of the Horn formula in K_3 from which F is constructed. The only non-Horn clauses are of the form $(G[i,1] \vee G[i,0])$ for $1 \leq i \leq p(n)$. But here both literals satisfy log-bandwidth. Therefore, the kernel satisfiable Horn formula $\emptyset$ can be **selected appropriately and the original** formula F can be constructed from $\emptyset$ using the constrained literal adding. Thus F is satisfiable iff F is i

L_3. Since F encodes the computation of M on x, it follows that L_3 is NP-complete.

References

1. Meyer, A.R. and Paterson, M.S., With What Frequency are Apparently Intractable Problems Difficult? Technical Report, MIT/LCS/TM-126, 1979.

2. Schnorr, C.P., On Self-transformable Combinatorial Problems, Math. Programming Study, Vol. 14, pp. 225-243, 1981.

3. Selman, A.L., Natural Self-reducible Sets, manuscript, July 1986.

4. Monien, B. and Sudborough, I.H., Bandwidth Constrained NP-Complete Problems, Proc. 13-th Annual ACM STOC, pp. 207-217, 1981.

5. Arvind, V. and Biswas, S., Kernel Constructible Languages, Proceedings of the Third FSTTCS Conference, 1983.

6. Börger, E., Spektralproblems and Completeness of Logical Decision Problems, Proc. of Symposium "Rekursive Kombinatorik", Vol. 171, Lecture Notes in Computer Science, Springer-Verlag, pp. 333-353, 1983.

7. Garey, M.R. and Johnson, D.S., Computers and Intractability: A Guide to the Theory of NP-Completeness, H. Freeman, 1979.

A LOOK-AHEAD INTERPRETER FOR SEQUENTIAL PROLOG AND ITS IMPLEMENTATION

Ashok Kumar and V.M.Malhotra
Department of Computer Science and Engineering,
Indian Institute of Technology Kanpur.
KANPUR 208 016
INDIA.

KEYWORDS: Interpreter, Prolog, Look-ahead.

Intelligent backtracking [1] has been suggested for reducing the number of calls that a Prolog interpreter makes during its execution. Two main drawbacks of intelligent backtracking are :-

- It does not prevent the first unsucessful execution of a path.
- It needs to carry too much information to make a good guess about the resume point.

In this paper, we introduce an alternate mechanism for reducing the number of calls. The technique is based on look-ahead. We believe, given the generate and test paradigm in Prolog, the look-ahead gives a larger reduction in the number of calls made during an execution and requires less additional information compared to an intelligent backtracking. Table 1 compares the number of calls made by a conventional interpreter with those of the proposed. For this purpose, each successful unification of a subgoal to head of a clause is counted as a call.

TABLE 1: NUMBER OF CALLS MADE BY PROLOG PROGRAMS

PROGRAM	GOAL	INTERPRETER	
		Proposed	Conventional
Queens	solve(4,X)	108	281
Sort*	sort([c,b,a,d],X)	88	269
Sort*	sort([d,c,b,a,e],X)	240	1382

* program Sort is given in Appendix as Example 1.

1. A CONVENTIONAL PROLOG INTERPRETER

We use the terminology similar to that of Clocksin and Mellish [2]. Disregarding efficiency and space considerations, Algorithm 1 gives a conventional Prolog interpreter algorithm [2,7,9]. Clauses for a

Algorithm 1 : A Prolog Interpreter

```
type
  goal_type = record
                next_call_clause : ↑ clause_type;
                goal_structure   : structure
              end;
  clause_type = record
                  head : structure;
                  body : set_of_goals
                end;

function select_goal(S : set_of_goals) : ↑goal_type;
  begin
      return pointer to the most recently created goal from
         set S. Return the  leftmost among  them, if  more
         than one satisfy the condition.
  end;

function satisfy(S : set_of_goals):boolean; /* call by value */
  var
        G : ↑goal_type;
        C : clause_type;
  begin
        if (S = {})
        then
             return true;  /* DONE */
             /* return false for all solutions */
        G := select_goal(S);
        C := make_variables_unique(G↑.next_call_clause↑);
        mgu := unify(C.head, G↑.goal_structure);
        if (mgu exists)
        then
             if (satisfy(substitute(mgu,S  C.body-{G↑})))
             then
                  return true;
         /* else call  failed  */
        G↑.next_call_clause := next(G↑.next_call_clause);
        if (G↑.next_call_clause = nil)
        then
             return false
        else
             return satisfy(S)
  end;
```

goal predicate are tried in the order of their occurrence. When a goal is included in the set of waiting goals, its next_call_clause is initialized to point to the first clause for the goal predicate.

The efficiency considerations, however, require that the stack be maintained explicitly. A trail stack is normally used to undo the effects of the most general unifying (mgu) substitution on a backtrack. In the algorithm, we use an implicit stack because it helps in the presentation of the look-ahead interpreter for Prolog.

2. DEFINITIONS

To understand the cause of inefficiency due to backtracking, consider the following Prolog program :

```
1.  p(X,Y):- q(X),r(Y),s(X).
2.  q(a).
3.  q(b).
4.  r(b).
5.  s(b).
```

Let the user given goal be ?-p(X,b). After the goal q(X) is unified to the clause head q(a), X is bound to a. This binding causes the goal s(X) to fail and backtracking is started. As a result, we end up satisfying the goal r(Y) with head r(b) twice.

In general, the leftmost occurrnce of a variable has a special significance. The leftmost occurrence of a variable usually gets bound to some value and this value is used by all other occurrences of the variable.

We can detect a failure much earlier if we ensure that an assignment to the leftmost occurrence of a variable is consistent with the other (subsequent) uses of the variable. The definitions given below help in presenting an algorithm which accomplishes this efficiently.

ASSIGNMENT: A variable in the goal is considered to have undergone an assignment during a unification if it unifies with a structure (constants are structures defined by functors of arity 0), or if it unifies with another variable in the goal. Specifically, the unification of a variable in the goal to a variable in the head of a clause is not an assignment to the variable. In other words, variable in a goal is considered to have been assigned when some constraint on it's value is imposed. For example, on unification of the goal ?-g(A,B,C,D). with the clause g(a,X,X,Z). the variable A,B and C undergo assignments.

LEFTMOST VARIABLE AND GOAL: For a variable V, we define, a goal G as leftmost for V, if the goal G is the leftmost goal containing V in the body of the clause that introduced V. All occurrences of the variable V in its leftmost goal are leftmost, if V does not occur in the head of the clause. The occurrences of the variable V are potentially leftmost if V occurs in the head.

All occurrences of the variables in the initial (user given) goal are leftmost. A potentially leftmost occurrence of a variable V becomes leftmost, if all occurrences of the variable in the head of the clause are in the terms that unify with the leftmost variables of the goal.

Example 1 in appendix gives a Prolog program and also points out leftmost variables in its clauses. As another example consider the following :-

```
g(X,Y):- r(Y),s(X,Z).

?-g(A,B).
```

Assume that the variable A is leftmost and B is not leftmost in the goal g(A,B). X and Y in the body of the clause are potentially leftmost while Z is leftmost. After the unification X becomes leftmost while Y does not.

MATURE GOAL: A goal G is said to be mature with respect to a clause C if its unification to the head of the clause C does not cause an assignment to any non leftmost variable in G. A mature goal is non expository if it does not cause any assignment to any variable in the goal on unification. Otherwise it is called expository. For example, let L and R be leftmost and non leftmost variables of a goal g(L,R), respectively. The goal is mature (expository) with respect to a clause with head g(X,X) as a most general unifier (mgu) for the case is: L:=R, X:=R (L:=R means replace occurrences of L by R).

WAITING GOAL: A goal that is not mature is said to be a waiting goal. Let a non leftmost variable V in the goal be assigned a term t on unification of the goal with the head of the clause. The goal is said to be waiting on the assignment V := t. A goal may wait on several assignments at a time.

Several other examples of the terms defined in this section can be found in the Appendix.

3. A NEW GOAL SELECTION ALGORITHM

The motivation for the definitions introduced in the section 2 is to introduce a new goal selection function in Algorithm 1. The function prefers a 'test' over 'generation' of a new object. It is assumed that an object is usually generated by an assignment to a leftmost variable. We believe that an early selection of the tests will improve efficiency because of earlier failures of the hopeless cases.

```
function new_select_goal(S : set_of_goals) : ↑goal_type;
  begin
     if (there is a non-expository mature goal in
         S with respect to its next_call_clause)
     then
          return a pointer to a non-expository mature goal in S;
     if (there is an expository mature goal in S
         with respect to its next_call_clause)
     then
          return a pointer to an expository mature goal in S;
     return select_goal(S) /* conventional */
  end;
```

The function new_select_goal first selects the mature non-expository goals to detect any potential failure of it's child goals. A non-expository goal is preferred over an expository goal as it does not lead to assignments. Thus it helps in detecting failures after only a small number of assignments have been made.

We explain the algorithm using the example program given in section 2. Execution trace of the program is given below.

	Goal	Clause head	Remarks
1.	p(X,b)	p(X1,Y1)	mgu: X1:=X,Y1:=b. q(X1) is mature expository as X1 is leftmost variable here and head of the next clause for q is q(a). r(Y1) is mature non-expository as Y1 has unified with b. s(X1) is waiting on an assignment to X1. X1 is not leftmost variable here.
2.	r(b)	r(b)	-
3.	q(X1)	q(a)	mgu: X1:=a. Causes the waiting goal s(X1) to fail and backtrack is initiated.
4.	q(X1)	q(b)	mgu: X1:=b.
5.	s(b)	s(b)	- Done.

A sort program and it's execution trace for a given goal is given in the appendix.

The correctness with respect to the declarative semantics of Prolog follows from the fact that all goals are satisfied. The order of their satisfaction is not important. The proposed algorithm may, however, generate results in an order different from that produced by a conventional interpreter. Rarely is the order important. If required, the desired order on the results can be imposed by introducing dummy variables.

4. AN IMPLEMENTATION OF THE PROPOSED ALGORITHM

The proposed algorithm for a look-ahead interpretation of Prolog programs has been implemented [6]. The novel component of the implementation is a mechanism for identifying mature goals.

A goal is represented by a record having following fields:

- NEXT_GOAL Pointer: Threads the goals in the conventional call order.
- NEXT_CALL_CLAUSE Pointer: On a failure of an attempt to unify the goal with the head of its NEXT_CALL_CLAUSE, as well as, on a backtrack this pointer is updated to point to the next clause for the goal predicate.
- WAIT_COUNT: It indicates the number of assignments on which this goal is waiting. The count is adjusted whenever an assignment is made to one of the variables on which the goal is waiting. An assignment may :
  - decrease the wait count by 1, or
  - cause the unification of the goal to the head of NEXT_CALL_CLAUSE to fail, or
  - cause the goal to start waiting on one or more new assignments. The wait count may actually go up as a result. For example, goal(X) waiting on the assignment X:=[a|b] will have its WAIT_COUNT increased after the assignment X:=[A|B].

  These changes are affected by the procedure preunification (see Algorithm 2).
- GOAL_STATUS: Mature, Waiting, or Proved. After a successful call the goal is marked Proved.
- NEXT_MATURE_GOAL Pointer:
- GOAL_STRUCTURE: The structure representing the goal.
- LEFTMOST_VARIABLES: A list of the leftmost variables of the goal. All references to a variable are implemented by pointing to its leftmost occurrence.

For each leftmost variable we maintain a list identifying the goals waiting on an assingment to the variable. A node in the list of goals waiting on an assignment to the variable has the following fields:

- WAITING_GOAL Pointer: Identifies the waiting goal.

Algorithm 2: Preunify to identify mature goals.

```
procedure match(c,t);
  begin
    if c is a variable in the clause head structure
    then
         c := t
    else
         if not (c = t)
         then
              if c is a leftmost variable of the goal
              then
                   c := t
              else
                   if t is a leftmost variable in the goal
                   then
                        t := c
                   else
                     begin
                        if c is a variable in the goal
                        then
                             the goal waits on assignment c := t;
                        if t is a variable in the goal
                        then
                             the goal waits on assignment t := c;
                        if t and c are both structures
                        then
                             if not(t.functor = c.functor)
                             then
                                   FAIL
                             else
                                  for each pair of arguments (c',t')
                                                 of t.functor in (c,t)
                                  do
                                      match(c',t')
                     end
  end;

function preunification;
  begin
        let goal G was waiting on assignment V := c and
          the variable V undergoes an assignment V := t;
        reduce the WAIT_COUNT of G by 1;
        match(c,t)
  end;
```

- WAIT_STRUCTURE Pointer: The structure whose assignment to the variable the goal is waiting for.
- NEXT_CALL_CLAUSE Pointer: It is set to the value of the corresponding field in the goal record when the node is inserted in the wait list. The goal, if it fails, will have its NEXT_CALL_CLAUSE pointer altered. The node is ignored if the two values differ.
- NEXT_NODE Pointer: Points to the next node in the list.

A goal may occur in the lists of waiting goals of several variables. If assignments to one (or more) variable causes the waiting goal to fail, an attempt is made to unify the goal with the head of the next clause. It is, however, expensive to remove the goal from all lists of waiting goals in which it may be present.

NEXT_CALL_CLAUSE field in a node of lists of waitng goals is used to ignore the redundant elements of the lists. The record representing the goal also contains this field. It points to the clause that is currently being tried for the goal. An element in a list of waiting goals is, therefore, redundant if the two fields are not same.

Unification of a goal to the head of its NEXT_CALL_CLAUSE during a call may cause assignments to some of the variables in the goal. The list of waiting goals for each of these variables is scanned and the term assigned to the variable is preunified with the WAIT_STRUCTURE of the each waiting goal. The goal matures if after a successful preunification its WAIT_COUNT is zero. The assignments made during a preunification are not accessible to the other goals and structures. For this purpose a leftmost variable is represented using the following fields:

- STATUS: Undefined, Hidden_definition, or Defined. Assignments in the function match are hidden definitions. The variables are reset to the Undefined state if preunification fails.
- LEFTMOST_GOAL: Identifies the leftmost goal for the variable.
- WAIT_LIST: Pointer to the first node in the list of goals waiting on an assignment to the variable.
- VALUE Pointer:

5. BACKTRACKING AND RUN-TIME STACK

For reasons of time and space efficiency, one needs to maintain an explicit stack to track the effects of unifications made by various calls. As a call is made, we push an activation record into the stack. Major components of the activation records are: Trail pointers, a pointer to the previous activation record, and a pointer to the goal record. The records for the goals in the body of the called clause are created on top of this activation record. As a goal record is created, we also create a new structure for the head of its initial NEXT_CALL_CLAUSE (see make_variables_unique in Algorithm 1). The procedure match is called with the head structure and the GOAL_STRUCTURE as arguments to place the goal in appropriate wait lists. This procedure is also repeated when a new NEXT_CALL_CLAUSE is selected for the goal.

Similarly, the stack may also be used for the lists of waiting goals. However, the proposed interpreter needs an additional trail stack to save address-value pairs. These pairs are used to restore values after a backtrack. Fortunately, a carefully designed Prolog interpreter does not make an excessive demand on trail stack space, particularly, if some of the simpler steps are repeated after a backtrack.

6. DISCUSSIONS

This section owes its existance to the refrees' comments pointing out the related works [3,4,8] in the context of Prolog and concurrent Logic Programming.

Heck and Avenhaus [4] have devised a criterion for identifying a Prolog program that produces only one 'answer'. The search ends when the answer has been found. GHC [8] uses rules similar to those used in this paper to avoid certain kinds of bindings before the commitment. The work is mainly motivated by the need to restrict the number of environments in the context of parallel executions. Naish [3] has used a wait declaration to delay calls under certain circumstances. He also gives an algorithm to automatically generate the wait declarations to avoid infinite paths in the search trees.

The main purpose of control mechanisms in Prolog is to restrict the search tree size. Naish [3] discusses a variety of heuristics used for this purpose. Interestingly, the proposed mechanism is amalgamation of several of these strategies. For example, it follows the paradigm of lazy evaluation -- assignments are avoided as long as possible. Early failure of the goals is achieved because immediately on an assignment to a variable all goals waiting on it are activated. These waiting goals are exactly the set that would be affected directly by the assignment. Eager consumer syndrome is also evident. Mature goals are consumers and are expanded first. The mechanism can also be used to avoid left recursion and to achieve coroutining by selecting the mature goals in order of their attaining maturity (within their respective class -- expository or otherwise). This scheme will also allow the advantages of breadth first search while retaining the 'depth-first' semantic of the language.

To compare the overheads in the proposed method to that of a standard Prolog interpreter one must note that the preunification algorithm is very similar to a unification algorithm in a standard interpreter. Further, suitable data-structures can be devised to use the bindings made during preunification for making a call. Thus, the major tradeoff is in terms of calls saved versus the number of subgoals that were created and then had to be scrapped. Overall, the balence seems to be in favour of the proposed method in cases involving highly non-deterministic programs.

The number of calls made during the exexution of a program can be further reduced by using an intelligent backtracking algorithm in conjunction with the proposed interpreter.

REFERENCES:

1. Bruynooghe, M. and L. M. Pereira, Deductive Revision by Intelligent Backtracking, in Implementation of Prolog, J. Campbell (ed.), Ellis Horwood Limited, Chichester, 1984.

2. Clocksin, W.F. and C.S.Mellish, Programming in Prolog, (2nd edition), Springer-Verlag, New York, 1984.

3. Naish, L., Negation and Control in Prolog, LNCS 238, Springer-Verlag, Berlin, 1986.

4. Heck, N. and J. Avenhaus, On Logic Programs with Data-Driven Computations, EUROCAL '85, Conf. Proc. in LNCS 204 (ed. B.F.Caviness), Springer-Verlag, Berlin, 1985.

5. Kahn, K.M. and M. Carlsson, The Compilation of Prolog Programs Without Use of a Prolog Compiler, FGCS '84, Proc. of the Intr. Conf. on Fifth Generation Computer Systems, Nov. 6-9,1984, OHMSHA Ltd., Tokyo, 1984.

6. Kumar, Ashok, A Look-ahead Interpreter for Prolog, M.Tech. thesis, Department of Computer Science and Engineering, Indian Institute of Technology Kanpur, 1987.

7. Llyod, J.W., Foundations of Logic Programming, Springer-Verlag, Berlin 1984.

8. Ueda, K., Guarded Horn Clauses, Logic Programming '85, LNCS 221 (ed. E. Wade), Springer-Verlag, Berlin, 1985.

9. Warren, D.H.D., Implementing Prolog -- Compiling Logic Programs 1 and 2, DAI Res. Reps. 39 and 40, Univ. of Edinburgh, 1977.

APPENDIX

Example 1: A Prolog Sort Program.

```
       Program                          Potentially      Leftmost
                                     Leftmost Variables Variables
 sort (X,Y) :-
            perm (X,Y),                 X,Y
            ok (Y).

 perm ([],[]).

 perm ([X|Y],[H|T]) :-
            apnd (U,[H|V],[X|Y]),       H,X,Y             U,V
            apnd (U,V,W),                                 W
            perm (W,T).                 T

 apnd ([],X,X).

 apnd ([X|Y],Z,[X|W]) :-
            apnd (Y,Z,W).               Y,Z,W

 ok ([X]).

 ok ([X,Y|Z]) :-
            more (X,Y),                 X,Y
            ok ([Y|Z]).                 Z

more(a,b).
```

Example 2: Annotated execution trace of sort ([b,a],Y).

Xn denotes the standardized form of the variable X generated in step n.

```
Step    Goal                             Remarks

1. sort([b,a],Y)                         Clause head: sort(X1,Y1)
                                         mgu: X1:=[b,a], Y1:=Y.
                                         New goals: perm(X1,Y1),ok(Y1).
                                         perm(X1,Y1) is mature exp.
                                         ok (Y1) waits on Y1.

2. perm([b,a],Y)                         Clause head: perm([X2|Y2],[H2|T2])
                                         mgu: X2:=b,Y2:=[a], Y:=[H2|T2].
                                         New goals introduced are:
                                         apnd(U2,[H2|V2],[b,a]), apnd(U2,V2,W2)
                                         and perm(W2,T2).
                                         apnd(U2,[H2|V2],[b,a]) is mature exp.
                                         apnd(U2,V2,W2) waits on U2 and V2.
                                         perm(W2,T2) waits on W2.
```

```
3. apnd(U2,[H2|V2] ,[b,a])       Clause head: apnd([],X3,X3)
                                 mgu: U2:=[],H2:=b,V2:=[a], X3:=[b,a].
                                 apnd(U2,V2,W2) becomes mature exp.
                                 due to assignments to U2 and V2.

4. apnd([],[a],W2)               Clause head: apnd([],X4,X4)
                                 mgu: X4:=W2:=[a].
                                 perm([a],T2) becomes mature
                                 exp. due to assignment to W2.

5. perm([a],T2)                  Clause head: perm([X5|Y5],[H5|T5])
                                 mgu: X5:=a,Y5:=[],T2:=[H5|T5].
                                 Goals introduced: apnd(U5,[H5|T5],[a]),
                                 apnd(U5,V5,W5) and perm(W5,T5).
                                 apnd(U5,[H5|T5],[a]) is mature exp.
                                 apnd(U5,V5,W5) is waiting on U5 and V5.
                                 perm(W5,T5) is waiting on W5.
                                 Y is now [b,H5|T5] and so goal ok(Y)
                                 (See step 1) becomes mature non-exp.

6. ok([b,H5|T5])                 Clause head: ok([X6,Y6|Z6])
                                 This goal fails beacuse the goal
                                 more(b,H5) fails. Backtrack is started.
                                 There is no alternative clause for
                                 goals satisfied on steps 4 and 5.

3. apnd(U2,[H2|V2],[b,a])        Clause head: apnd([X3|Y3],Z3,[X3|W3])
                                 mgu: X3:=b,Z3:=[H2|V2],U2:=[b|Y3],
                                                  W3:=[a].
                                 New goal apnd(Y3,[H2|V2],[a]) is
                                 mature exp.

4. apnd(Y3,[H2|V2],[a])          Clause head: apnd([],X4,X4)
                                 mgu:Y3:=[],H2:=a,V2:=[],X:=[a].
                                 apnd(U2,V2,W2) becomes mature exp.
                                 due to assignments to U2 and V2.

5. apnd([b],[],W2)               Clause head: apnd([X5|Y5],Z5,[X5|W5])
                                 mgu: X5:=b,Y5:=[],W2:=[b|W5],Z5:=[].
                                 New goal apnd([],[],W5) is mature exp.
                                 perm(W2,T2) becomes mature
                                 exp. due to assignment to W2.

6. apnd([],[],W5)                Clause head: apnd([],X6,X6)
                                 mgu: X6:=[],W5:=[].

7. perm([b],T2)                  Clause head: perm([X7|Y7],[H7|T7])
                                 mgu: T2:=[H7|T7],X7:=b,Y7:=[].
                                 New goals are: apnd(U7,[H7|V7],[b]),
                                 apnd(U7,V7,W7),perm(W7,T7).
                                 apnd(U7,[H7|V7],[b]) is mature exp.
                                 apnd(U7,V7,W7) waits on U7 and V7.
                                 perm(W7,T7) waits on W7.
                                 The goal ok([a|T2]) (See step 1
                                 and 4.) becomes mature non-exp.
                                 due to assignment to T2.

8. ok([a,H7|T7])                 Clause head: ok([X8,Y8|Z8])
                                 mgu: X8:=a,Y8:=H7,Z8:=T7.
                                 more(a,H7) waits on H7.
                                 ok([H7|T7]) waits on H7 and T7.
```

9. apnd(U7,[H7|V7],[b])	Clause head: apnd([],X9,X9) mgu: U7:=[],H7:=b,V7:=[], X9:=[b]. more(a,H7) becomes mature non-exp due to assignment to H7. apnd(U7,V7,W7) becomes mature exp.
10. more(a,b)	Clause head: more(a,b)
11. apnd([],[],W7)	Clause head: apnd([],X11,X11) mgu: X11:=W7:=[].
12. perm([],T7)	Clause head: perm([],[]) mgu: T7:=[]. ok([a|T7]) becomes mature non-exp.
13. ok([b])	Clause head: ok([X13]) mgu: X13:=b. Done.

EXTENSION OF WEAKEST PRECONDITION FORMALISM TO A LOW LEVEL LANGUAGE

A.Sanyal, S.Biswas and V.M.Malhotra
Department of Computer Science and Engineering,
I.I.T Kanpur, Kanpur 208016 (U.P.), India

1. Introduction

One approach to compiler correctness can be through the use of weakest precondition (abbreviated as wp) [1]; one has to show that for every high level language program, the compiler generates a low level code which preserves the intended predicate transformations. One technical difficulty such an approach will have to overcome is to extend the notion of weakest precondition to jump instructions, which are certain to abound in any low level code. Our paper addresses this problem.

A previous approach [2] defines the weakest precondition for goto statements by using a generalized concept of a state by adding an additional component called control point to its usual notion. However, we show that such a generalization of the notion of state is unnecessary.

In this paper we introduce a new method for finding the weakest precondition of a program with gotos for a specified postcondition. The method uses the usual concept of state and results in a set of simultaneous equations relating the postcondition with the weakest preconditions at different labels of the program. Furthermore, we prove that under a reasonable model of execution, the least fixpoint solution of the set of equations is the same as the weakest precondition.

In Section 2 we give the syntax of a simple language which we use to illustrate our method. In section 3 we describe the procedure to set up the equations for any given program and postcondition. In Section 4 we present a model for program execution. Section 5 contains the main results which relate wp to the least fixpoint solution of the set of equations. We conclude with an example in the appendix, which illustrates the methodology.

2. Syntax of an example language

A simple, but fairly representative low level language is defined below:

<program> ::= <statement>

<statement> ::= <labelled statement> |
<composite statement> |
<if statement> |
<assignment statement> |
<null statement> |
<goto statement>

<labelled statement> ::= <label> : <statement>

<composite statement> ::= <statement> ; <statement>

<if statement> ::=if <condition> then <statement> else
<statement> fi

<assignment statement> ::= <variable> := <expression>

<goto statement> ::= goto <label>

<null statement> ::= ϵ

The syntactic entities <label>, <variable>, <expression> and <condition> have the usual meanings and we do not explicate them any further.

Besides the syntactic structure defined above a program must also satisfy the following conditions:

(i) if goto L is a statement in the program, then L occurs as a label of some statement in the program, and

(ii) a label is defined atmost once in the program.

An important distinction between a statement and a program is that, unlike a program, a statement may have a goto statement whose target label is not defined within its body.

We use the metavariable Pr to denote a program, S to denote a statement, B to denote a condition, Y to denote a variable and E to denote an expression. Subscripts will be used if necessary.

3. Setting up the equations

Given a program and a postcondition, our method to derive the weakest precondition is as follows. Firstly, we associate a predicate variable, representing the weakest precondition, with each label occurring in the program. The weakest precondition at a label represents the set of all states t such that if execution is begun in t at the control point denoted by the label, then, within a finite time the program terminates in a state satisfying the specified postcondition.

Secondly, we set up simultaneous equations which relate these predicate variables. The least fixpoint solution of these equations defines the weakest precondition at the control points associated with these labels.

In this section we describe the procedure for setting up the simultaneous equations.

3.1. Special control points for statements

For any statement, the two control points, at the beginning and end of the statement, are of special interest. The weakest precondition that we are interested in, is associated with the control point at the beginning of the statement. Likewise, the stipulated postcondition is to be satisfied at the control point corresponding to the end of the statement.

We therefore introduce two special labels, START and EXIT, to refer to the control points at the beginning and the end of the statement. These special labels exist only for the overall composite statement under consideration, and not for its components. Accordingly the procedure for setting up the equations eliminate the START and EXIT labels from the equations of the component statements, as it generates the equations for the composite statement.

3.2. <u>Notations</u>

(i) P — denotes a predicate variable. In particular, for each label L we have a predicate variable, denoted by P_L.

(ii) $\underline{P}$ — denotes a vector of predicate variables.

(iii) p, R — denote predicates. R denotes the postcondition for which the weakest precondition is to be derived.

(iv) $\underline{p}$ — denotes a vector of predicates.

(v) T — denotes a functional which takes predicates as arguments and returns a predicate as result.

If e denotes an expression involving predicate variables then

(vi) $\underline{P}|^{P}_{e}$ — denotes a vector which is the same as $\underline{P}$ except for the predicate variable P which has been replaced by e.

(vii) L — denotes a label.

(viii) D — denotes a label or a goto statement.

(ix) $\mathcal{L}_S$ — denotes the set of all labels that are defined in S.

(x) $\mathcal{D}_S$ — denotes the set of all labels and goto statements occurring in S.

(xi) Lext — denotes a label extracting function.
Lext(D) = if D is a label then D else if D is a goto statement goto L then L.

(xii)	t	denotes a state.
(xiii)	Q	denotes the set of all states.
(xiv)	E(t)	denotes the result of evaluating E in the state t.
(xv)	t ∈ p	denotes the fact that t satisfies the predicate p.
(xvi)	$[t]_v^Y$	denotes a state which is the same as t with the possible exception of Y whose value is v.
(xvii)	π_i	denotes the projection operator. If $\underline{a}$ is a vector then $\pi_i(\underline{a}) = a_i$.
(xviii)	lab($\underline{P}$)	denotes the set of all labels L such that P_L occurs in $\underline{P}$.

3.3. Setting up the equations

We now describe the procedure to set up the equations for a statement S and a given postcondition R, by case analysis on the structure of S. Let P_L denote the predicate variable for the label L occuring in S.

case (i) S is ∈

The equations are

(a) $P_{START} = P_{EXIT}$, and

(b) $P_{EXIT} = R$.

case (ii) S is goto L

The execution of the statement goto L will transfer the control to label L without any change of state. Since the weakest precondition at L is denoted by P_L, we have the equations

(a) $P_{START} = P_L$, and

(b) $P_{EXIT} = R$.

case (iii) S is Y:=E

The equations are

(a) $P_{START} = P_{EXIT}\Big|^{Y}_{E}$

where $P\Big|^{Y}_{E}$ is the predicate obtained by substituting E for all occurrences of the variable Y, in a formal expression for the predicate denoted by P, and

(b) $P_{EXIT} = R$.

Let START1 (START2) and EXIT1 (EXIT2) be the labels denoting control points at the beginning and the end of the statement S1 (S2). Assume that equations have already been set up for the statements S1 and S2 with the given postcondition. Let the equation corresponding to a label L in S1 or S2 be denoted as $P_L = T_L\ (\underline{P}_L)$.

<u>case (iv)</u> S is if B then S1 else S2 fi

The equations for S are as follows:

$$\text{(a)}\quad P_{START} = B \wedge T_{START1}\ \Big(\underline{P}_{START1}\Big|^{P_{EXIT1}}_{P_{EXIT}}\Big) \vee \sim B \wedge T_{START2}\ \Big(\underline{P}_{START2}\Big|^{P_{EXIT2}}_{P_{EXIT}}\Big).$$

(b) For every equation $P_L = T_L\ (\underline{P}_L)$ for the statement S1 where $L \neq$ START1 and $L \neq$ EXIT1, include for S the equation

$$P_L = T_L\ \Big(\underline{P}_L\Big|^{P_{EXIT1}}_{P_{EXIT}}\Big).$$

(c) For every equation $P_L = T_L\ (\underline{P}_L)$ for the statement S2 where $L \neq$ START2 and $L \neq$ EXIT2, include for S the equation

$$P_L = T_L\ \Big(\underline{P}_L\Big|^{P_{EXIT2}}_{P_{EXIT}}\Big).$$

(d) $P_{EXIT} = R$.

<u>case (v)</u> S is S1;S2

The equations for S are

$$\text{(a)}\quad P_{START} = T_{START1}\Big(\underline{P}_{START1}\Big|^{P_{EXIT1}}_{T_{START2}\left(\underline{P}_{START2}\Big|^{P_{EXIT2}}_{P_{EXIT}}\right)}\Big).$$

(b) For each equation $P_L = T_L\ (\underline{P}_L)$ for the statement S1, where $L \neq$ START1 and $L \neq$ EXIT1, include for S the equation

$$P_L = T_L(\underline{P}_L \Big|^{P_{EXIT1}}_{T_{START2}(\underline{P}_{START2} |^{P_{EXIT2}}_{P_{EXIT}})}).$$

(c) For each equation $P_L = T_L\ (\underline{P}_L)$ for the statement S2, where $L \neq$ START2 and $L \neq$ EXIT2, include for S the equation

$$P_L = T_L\ (\underline{P}_L \Big|^{P_{EXIT2}}_{P_{EXIT}}).$$

(d) $P_{EXIT} = R.$

__case (vi)__ S is L:S1

The equations for S are as follows :

(a) $P_{START} = P_L.$

(b) $P_L = T_{START1}\ (\underline{P}_{START1} \Big|^{P_{EXIT1}}_{P_{EXIT}}).$

(c) For every equation $P_{L1} = T_{L1}\ (\underline{P}_{L1})$ for the statement S1 where $L1 \neq$ START1 and $L1 \neq$ EXIT1, include for S the equation

$$P_{L1} = T_{L1}\ (\underline{P}_{L1} \Big|^{P_{EXIT1}}_{P_{EXIT}}).$$

(d) $P_{EXIT} = R.$

For an example which illustrates the procedure to set up the equations, see Appendix.

3.4. __Least fixpoint solution for equations__

Since the system of equations generated for a statement are, in general, recursive, the existence of a solution will depend on the nature of the functionals T. The functionals take tuples of predicates as arguments and produce predicates as the result.

A partial order $\sqsubseteq$ can be imposed on the domain of predicates Z as

For $R1, R2 \in Z$ $R1 \sqsubseteq R2$ iff $R1 \Rightarrow R2$.

Under this partial ordering Z is a complete lattice. This partial order can be naturally extended to tuples of predicates. Furthermore, it can be shown by induction on the structure of T that the functionals T are continuous. So the least fixpoint solution of the set of equations exists. We now describe the least fixpoint solution of the set of equations.

Let $P_L = T_L(\underline{P}_L)$ be an equation from our set of equations. Then
$P_L^{\emptyset} = F$, and

$P_L^{n+1} = T_L(\underline{P}_L^n)$ where $\underline{P}_L^n$ is a vector of predicates formed by replacing each predicate variable P_{L1} in $\underline{P}_L$ by P_{L1}^n.

The least fixpoint solution of P_L, denoted by P_L^{lfp} is then
$P_L^{lfp} = \bigvee_{n \geqslant \emptyset} P_L^n$.

4. A model for execution

4.1. Transitions

To show that the least fixpoint solution of the system of equations in Section 3.3 indeed captures the notion of weakest precondition, we need to define a model of execution. Since the predicate variables are associated with labels, it would be natural to model executions as a series of transitions from a label to the next label accompanied by changes in state.

The problem with this approach is that it may not always be possible to derive the transitions in a statement from the transitions in its component statements. As an example consider the statement S which is S1;S2. Assume that S1 contains a statement goto L whose target label L is defined in S2. It is easy to see that the transition which includes the jump from goto L to L cannot be derived solely from the transitions in S1 and S2.

So we model an execution as a series of transitions from *labels to labels or goto statements*. To this end, we first define a function $Succ_S$ to capture executions involving single transitions. From this we define a series of functions $Succ_S^n$, n = 1,2... , which capture executions involving n transitions.

We now define the functions $Succ_S$ and $Succ_S^n$.

4.2. Executions involving a single transition

The partial function $Succ_S : \mathcal{L}_S \times Q \rightarrow \mathcal{D}_S \times Q$ has the following interpretation:

Let $Succ_S(\langle L,t\rangle) = \langle D,t1\rangle$. Then, if execution of S is started at L in a state t, then within a finite time the control reaches another label or goto statement D in the state t1. The function $Succ_S$ is defined inductively as follows:

case (i) S is ϵ

For all states t,

(i) $Succ_S(\langle START,t\rangle)=\langle EXIT,t\rangle$, and

(ii) $Succ_S(\langle EXIT,t\rangle)=$undefined.

case (ii) S is Y:=E

For all states t,

(i) $Succ_S(\langle START,t\rangle)=\langle EXIT,[t]^{Y}_{E(t)}\rangle$, and

(ii) $Succ_S(\langle EXIT,t\rangle)=$undefined.

case (iii) S is goto L

For all states t,

(i) $Succ_S(\langle START,t\rangle)=\langle \text{goto } L,\ t\rangle$, and

(ii) $Succ_S(\langle EXIT,t\rangle)=$undefined.

Assume that we have defined the functions $Succ_{S1}$ and $Succ_{S2}$ for the statements S1 and S2 respectively.

case (iv) S is if B then S1 else S2 fi

For all states t

(i) $Succ_S(\langle START,t\rangle)$ = if $t\epsilon$ B

then if $\pi_1(Succ_{S1}(\langle START1,t\rangle))\neq EXIT1$

then $Succ_{S1}(\langle START1,t\rangle)$

else $\langle EXIT,\pi_2(Succ_{S1}(\langle START1,t\rangle))\rangle$

else if $\pi_1(Succ_{S2}(\langle START2,t\rangle))\neq EXIT2$

then $Succ_{S2}(\langle START2,t\rangle)$

else $\langle EXIT,\pi_2(Succ_{S2}(\langle START2,t\rangle))\rangle$

(ii) if $L \neq START,EXIT$ and L is a label in $S1$,then

$Succ_S(\langle L,t\rangle)$=if $\pi_1(Succ_{S1}(\langle L,t\rangle))\neq EXIT1$

then $Succ_{S1}(\langle L,t\rangle)$

else $\langle EXIT,\pi_2(Succ_{S1}(\langle L,t\rangle))\rangle$

(iii) if $L \neq START,EXIT$ and L is a label in $S2$, then

$Succ_S(\langle L,t\rangle)$=if $\pi_1(Succ_{S2}(\langle L,t\rangle))\neq EXIT2$

then $Succ_{S2}(\langle L,t\rangle)$

else $\langle EXIT,\pi_2(Succ_{S2}(\langle L,t\rangle)\rangle$

(iv) $Succ_S(\langle EXIT,t\rangle)$=undefined.

<u>case</u> <u>(v)</u> S is S1;S2

For all states t

(i) $Succ_S(\langle START,t\rangle)$ =

if $\pi_1(Succ_{S1}(\langle START1,t\rangle)) \neq EXIT1$

then $Succ_{S1}(\langle START1,t\rangle)$

else if $\pi_1(Succ_{S2}(\langle START2,\pi_2(Succ_{S1}(\langle START1,t\rangle))\rangle))\neq EXIT2$

then $Succ_{S2}(\langle START2,\pi_2(Succ_{S1}(\langle START1,t\rangle))\rangle)$

else $\langle EXIT,\pi_2(Succ_{S2}(\langle START2,\pi_2(Succ_{S1}(\langle START1,t\rangle))\rangle))\rangle$

(ii)if $L \neq START,EXIT$ and L is a label in $S1$,then

$Succ_S(\langle L,t\rangle)$ =

if $\pi_1(Succ_{S1}(\langle L,t\rangle)) \neq EXIT1$

then $Succ_{S1}(\langle L,t\rangle)$

else if $\pi_1(Succ_{S2}(\langle START2,\pi_2(Succ_{S1}(\langle L,t\rangle))\rangle))\neq EXIT2$

then $Succ_{S2}(\langle START2,\pi_2(Succ_{S1}(\langle L,t\rangle))\rangle)$

else $\langle EXIT ,\pi_2(Succ_{S2}(\langle START2,\pi_2(Succ_{S1}(\langle L,t\rangle))\rangle))\rangle$

(iii) if $L \neq START,EXIT$ and L is a label in $S2$, then

$Succ_S(\langle L,t\rangle)$=if $\pi_1(Succ_{S2}(\langle L,t\rangle))\neq EXIT2$

then $Succ_{S2}(\langle L,t\rangle)$

else $\langle EXIT,\pi_2(Succ_{S2}(\langle L,t\rangle)\rangle$

(iv) $Succ_S(\langle EXIT,t\rangle)$=undefined.

case (vi) S is L:S1

For all states t

(i) $Succ_S(<START,t>) = <L,t>$

(ii) if L1 $\neq$ START,EXIT and L1 is a label in S1 ,then

$Succ_S(<L1,t>)=$if $\pi_1(Succ_{S1}(<L1,t>))\neq EXIT1$

then $Succ_{S1}(<L1,t>)$

else $<EXIT,\pi_2(Succ_{S1}(<L1,t>))>$

(iii) $Succ_S(<L,t>)=$if $\pi_1(Succ_{S1}(<START1,t>))\neq EXIT1$

then $Succ_{S1}(<START1,t>)$

else $<EXIT,\pi_2(Succ_{S1}(<START1,t>))>$

(iv) $Succ_S(<EXIT,t>)=$undefined.

4.3. Executions involving multiple transitions

The series of partial functions $Succ_S^n : \mathcal{L}_S \times Q \to \mathcal{D}_S \times Q$ is defined as follows:

For any label L and state t,

$Succ_S^{\emptyset}(<L,t>)=<L,t>$,

$Succ_S^1(<L,t>)=Succ_S(<L,t>)$, and for $n > 1$,

$Succ_S^n(<L,t>)=$if $Succ_S(<L,t>)$ is undefined then undefined else

$$Succ_S^{n-1}(< Lext(\pi_1(Succ_S(<L,t>))),\pi_2(Succ_S(<L,t>))>).$$

Lemma 4.1: If execution of a statement S is started at the label L1 in state t1, then, within a finite time the control reaches the label L2 in state t2 iff

$$\exists n : Succ_S^n(< L1, t1>) = < L2,t2>.$$

The proof is by induction on n. A special note may be taken of the role of the label extracting operator Lext. If the first transition of the execution ends in a label, then the $Succ_S^{n-1}$ function is directly applied to the label to obtain the destination after n-1 transitions. Else, if it is a goto statement, then the label extracting operator Lext is used to obtain the target label of the goto statement and the $Succ_S^{n-1}$function applied to it.

Corrollary 4.2 : The weakest precondition for a program Pr and a postcondition R , denoted by wp(Pr,R) can be defined as:

$$(\forall t1)(t1 \in wp(Pr,R) \iff (\exists n)(\exists t2 \in R)(Succ_S^n(<START,t1>) = <EXIT,t2>)).$$

5. Relating wp to the least fixpoint solution

The main result of the paper relates the weakest precondition at the beginning of the program to the least fixpoint solution of the system of equations set up in Section 3. The result is given in the following theorem:

Theorem 5.1

Let p_{START}^{lfp} be the value of P_{START} in the least fixpoint solution of the system of equations set up for the program Pr. Then

$$wp(Pr,R) = p_{START}^{lfp}$$

The proof follows from the definition of p_{START}^{lfp}, wp(Pr,R), and the following theorem.

Theorem 5.2

Let $P_{L1} = T_{L1}(\underline{P}_{L1})$ be an equation from the system of equations set up for a program Pr with postcondition R. Then

$$(\forall t1)(t1 \in p_{L1}^{n+1} \iff (\exists t2 \in R)(\exists k \leqslant n)(Succ_{Pr}^k(<L1,t1>) = <EXIT,t2>)).$$

In other words p_{L1}^{n+1} is the weakest condition such that if execution is started at L1 in a state satisfying p_{L1}, then in n or less transitions the control reaches EXIT in a state satisfying R.

The proof is by induction on n , and uses the following results.

Lemma 5.3

Let L1 be an arbitrary label in a statement S and $P_{L1} = T_{L1}(\underline{P}_{L1})$ be the equation corresponding to L1. If there exists a label or a gotostatement D and states t1 and t2 such that $Succ_S(<L1,t1>)$ =

<D,t2>, then Lext(D) $\in$ lab($\underline{P}_{L1}$) .

The proof is by structural induction on S.

Theorem 5.4

Let $P_{L1} = T_{L1}$ ($\underline{P}_{L1}$) be an arbitrary equation from the set of equations set up for the statement S, such that L1 is different from EXIT. Let $\underline{p}_{L1}$ be a vector obtained by substituting each predicate variable P_{L2} in $\underline{P}_{L1}$ by some predicate p_{L2}. Furthermore, let p be equal to T_{L1} ($\underline{p}_{L1}$). Then

$$(\forall t1)(\ t1 \in p \Leftrightarrow (\exists\ L2 \in lab(\underline{P}_{L1}))(\exists\ t2 \in p_{L2})\ (\ Succ_S(\langle L1,t1\rangle) = \langle L2,t2\rangle \text{ or } Succ_S(\langle L1,t1\rangle) = \langle goto\ L2,t2\rangle)).$$

In other words , p is the weakest condition such that if execution is started at L1 in a state satisfying p, then, in a single transition the control reaches another label L2 or a goto statement goto L2, where L2 $\in$ lab($\underline{P}_{L1}$), and satisfies the corresponding predicate p_{L2}.

6 Concluding remarks

The method is being used to prove the correctness of a small compiler. The compiler is specified as a function called comp. Since the representations of variables and values in a high level program and its translation differ significantly, we need to introduce a function called map to map the predicates specifying states in the source program to corresponding predicates in the object program. The compiler correctness problem can now be stated as the problem of proving for all programs Pr the following equality:

map(wp(Pr,R)) = wp(comp(Pr),map(R))

The details can be found in [4].

References

1. Dijkstra,E.W. : A Discipline of Programming. New Jersey: Prentice-Hall (1976).

2. He,J. : General Predicate Transformer and the Semantics of a Programming Language with Go To Statement. Acta Informatica 20, 35-57 (1983).

3. Stoy,J.E. :Denotational Semantics :The Scott-Strachey Approach to Programming Language Theory. MIT Press (1977).

4. Sanyal,A. :Correctness of Compiling Process Based on Predicate Transformer Semantics. Ph.D Dissertation , Department of Computer Science and Engineering, IIT Kanpur . Under preparation (1987).

Appendix

(i) We illustrate the methodology using a small example. Consider the statement S defined as

```
        L: if x<5 then x:=x+1 ;
                       goto L
                  else x:=x+2
           fi
```

Let the postcondition be x>10. Following the procedure described in the paper, the equations generated for the constituents of S will be:

S1 : x:=x+1	$P_{START1} = P_{EXIT1}\vert^{x}_{x+1}$
	$P_{EXIT1} = x>10$
S2 : goto L	$P_{START2} = P_L$
	$P_{EXIT2} = x>10$
S3 : S1;S2	$P_{START3} = P_L\vert^{x}_{x+1}$
	$P_{EXIT3} = x>10$
S4 : x:=x+2	$P_{START4} = P_{EXIT4}\vert^{x}_{x+2}$
	$P_{EXIT4} = x>10$

S5 : if x<5 then S3 else s4 $P_{START5} = x<5 \wedge P_L|^x_{x+1}$

$\vee\ x \geq 5 \wedge P_{EXIT5}|^x_{x+2}$

$P_{EXIT5} = x>10$

Finally, for the statement S, which is L:S5, the equations will be:

$$P_{START} = P_L$$
$$P_L = x<5 \wedge P_L|^x_{x+1} \vee x \geq 5 \wedge P_{EXIT}|^x_{x+2}, \text{ and}$$
$$P_{EXIT} = x>10.$$

(ii) As can be verified easily, the following are valid single transitions for the statement S:

$Succ_S(\langle L,x=4\rangle) = \langle goto\ L,x=5\rangle$

$Succ_S(\langle L,x=5\rangle) = \langle EXIT,x=7\rangle$

Therefore, we have

$$
\begin{aligned}
Succ^0_S(\langle L,x=4\rangle) &= \langle L,x=4\rangle,\\
Succ^1_S(\langle L,x=4\rangle) &= Succ_S(\langle L,x=4\rangle)\\
&= \langle goto\ L,x=5\rangle,\\
Succ^2_S(\langle L,x=4\rangle) &= Succ^1_S(\langle Lext(goto\ L),x=5\rangle)\\
&= Succ_S(\langle L,x=5\rangle)\\
&= \langle EXIT,x=7\rangle, \text{ and}\\
Succ^3_S(\langle L,x=4\rangle) &= Succ^2_S(\langle Lext(goto\ L),x=5\rangle)\\
&= Succ^1_S(\langle EXIT,x=7\rangle)\\
&= \text{undefined}.
\end{aligned}
$$

RETROSPECTION ON THE PQCC COMPILER STRUCTURE

K.V. Nori Sanjeev Kumar M. Pavan Kumar
Tata Research Development and Design Centre,
1, Mangaldas Road,
PUNE-411 001 INDIA.

ABSTRACT

The Production Quality Compiler Compiler (PQCC) project was perhaps the most comprehensive effort in automated generation of high quality compilers. Unlike other compiler compiler projects, its focus was not limited to formalisable aspects of compilation. Consequently, much that was done in this large effort was empirical, and guided by heuristics employed by experienced compiler designers. Describing this empirical experience has been painful, primarily because of the inability to transcend detail, and due to the difficulty in abstracting principles which underlie the success of that experiment. In large measure, this is the reason for paucity of published material about this project, though considerable internal project documentation exists. This paper describes two separate experiments in compiler construction: the first was heavily influenced by the PQCC effort, though it was carried out at a reduced scale because of local handicaps; the second was a formalisation of some aspects of retargetable instruction selection. The simplifications in the first effort, and the formalisation in the second one, together point to a comparatively tractable synthesis of compiler structure which approximates that embodied in PQCC. This paper contributes to establishing the soundness of the empirical compiler structure in PQCC by presenting rational approximations to it.

1. INTRODUCTION

The Production-Quality-Compiler Compiler (PQCC) project [1] was perhaps the most comprehensive effort in automated construction of production-quality-compilers, viz., compilers comparable to hand coded compilers in standard systems software provided by manufacturers. Unlike other contemporary compiler-compiler projects [2, 3, 4], its focus was not limited to formalisable aspects of compilation. In the late seventies, at a time when little was known on retargetability of code generation, the PQCC venture was particularly bold: it attempted to automatically generate BLISS-11 style code generators, a highly successful compiler which was in extensive use for several years.

Code generation in the BLISS-11 compiler [5] was based on many empirical observations about the coding habits of good systems programmers working in assembly languages. The chief aim in the design of this handcrafted compiler was to generate code comparable to, if not better than, equivalent assembly language programs hand coded by experienced systems programmers - a goal that was well met. The PQCC effort started with this code generator, and attempted to abstract from it a retargetable model of code generation. Much that was done in this effort was empirical, and guided by heuristics used by experienced compiler designers. This was extensively documented [6, 7, 8, 9, 10]. Some of the work led to doctoral dissertations [11, 12, 13], but very little published work [1, 14, 15, 16], compared to the effort which went into demonstrating that such compiler-compilers were feasible.

In large measure, the difficulty was the detail which was interwoven across the model of code generation, and the inability to transcend it so as to articulate principles embodied by the phases. It is conceivable that many of the individual phases, which focus on specific algorithms for aspects of code generation, can be expressed in publishable form, (and there are over 50 phases in the PQCC retargetable code generation model), but it is not easy to perceive how these details add up.

A reasonable understanding of the PQCC effort was the starting point for a local attempt to construct a C compiler [17] which would generate code for an old machine, currently in extensive use for a fail-soft real-time application. The vintage of the architecture, and the size of the applications it was used for, provided very little elbow room for penalty in using a compiled high level language. The non-availability of the PQCC arsenal was a handicap with regard to the development time required to construct the compiler. In retrospection, this aspect was beneficial, for it forced us to simplify the model of code generation used by PQCC. As our goal was to develop a compiler, rather than a compiler-compiler, and as we were hardly as experienced as the PQCC designers, we were forced to work with simple compiler construction tools, and those aspects of PQCC which could be readily absorbed by the team.

Independent of our efforts, but formally articulating the principle which we had empirically adopted, a retargetable code generator was designed [18, 19].

The above two efforts are the basis for retrospection on the code generation scheme of the PQCC generated compilers. The hope is that this retrospection aids in making approximations of the PQCC model tractable.

The next section describes the salient features of the PQCC experiment. Section 3 provides a look at the structure of the C compiler developed by us. Section 4 discusses a retargetable model for code selection. Retrospection and extrapolation of these works in relation to that of PQCC is presented in Section 5. Section 6 is an epilogue on directions for further work.

2. THE PQCC EXPERIMENT

The PQCC experiment [1] was born out of the success of the BLISS-11 compiler [5]. In this section, a brief overview of the salient features of the BLISS-11 compiler, and its influence on the PQCC details, are presented.

2.1 The BLISS-11 Compiler

BLISS is a machine-oriented, high level "expression" language , in that every construct has a value. BLISS-11 is the PDP-11 oriented variant. The design of the BLISS-11 language, and its compiler, was predicated upon the desire to establish that the use of high level languages does not impose any penalty with respect to use of (scarce, at that time) machine resources. To achieve this goal, the compiler attempted to generate high quality code by resorting to optimising program transformations, transformations to shape the program in the mould of PDP-11, and using a host of empirical observations about good coding practices employed by experienced systems programmers.

The book on the BLISS-11 compiler [5] is a detailed account of the empirical ideas which went into the engineering of a high quality code generator. There is a wealth of techniques and implementation detail in it. The only principles discussed in it concern high-level data flow analysis: BLISS-11 is a highly disciplined language with regard to the structuring of control flow. Some aspects of this analysis are carried out at the level of the language, rather than at the level of the intermediate representation. This has been rarely achieved in much of the formal research in global data flow analysis which followed.

One undisputed feature of the BLISS-11 compiler was the quality of code it generated. It is difficult to assess the relative importance of the different techniques used, but they all added up effectively. The front-end of the compiler was BLISS-11 oriented; it performed the functions of parsing, semantic analysis, global data flow analysis and associated program transformations. The resultant intermediate representation was an operator tree for the entire program, in which common sub-expressions were identified. A stack for dynamic elaboration of programs, and procedure-call with allied parameter-passing conventions were found in this representation.

The **back-end** was PDP-11 oriented. The only presupposition in translation was the run-time stack and parameter-passing conventions. All further aspects of translation were delayed till the shape of the program was assessed through the demands on target machine resources:

i) how to use the rich set of **addressing modes** ?
ii) how to use **complex opcodes** which combined many complement operations on operands along with the main function ?
iii) how to use the **'special case'** instructions?
iv) in what order should sub expressions be evaluated, thereby **identifying** the **temporaries** in expression evaluation ?

v) when should machine resources, such as **registers** and **stack locations**, be allocated to represent the local **variables** and the **temporaries** ?

vi) what **redundancies**, and opportunities for **compaction** (use of shorter instruction sequences) should the peephole optimiser cater for ?

One of the principal challenges of PQCC was to make this complex decision making process retargetable.

2.2 A Paradigm for High Quality Code Generation

In order to abstract away the influence of BLISS-11 and PDP-11 from the BLISS-11 compiler, generic phases had to be discovered within it. The purpose of each group of phases, and its position in the compilation process had to be defined clearly. Figure 1 provides the first step in segmenting the problem.

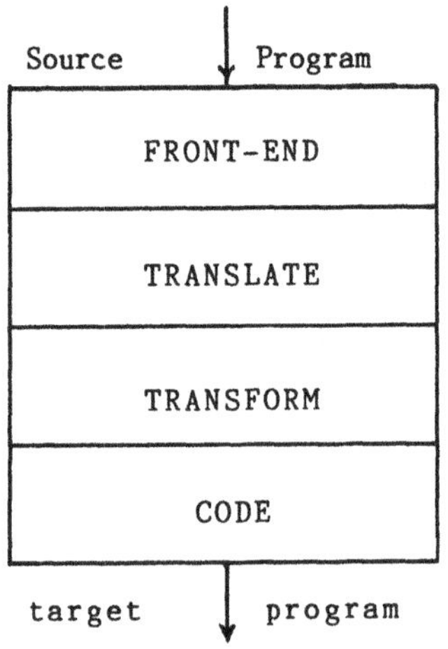

Figure 1: Generic Structure of optimising compiler

The **Front End** is concerned with syntax, semantic analysis and the construction of the source-language-relative Internal Representation (IR) of programs. All translation issues between source language entities and target machine entities (effecting semantic mappings) are taken up next. Optimising **transformations** of the **IR** are performed next. Finally, efficient **coding** of the resultant IR is undertaken.

The first point of note is the earliest known conscious **distinction** between **translation** and **coding**. Translation effects semantics-preserving mappings between source language entities and target machine primitives. Coding results in effective deployment of target machine resources in expressing the translated IR (which only contains target machine cognizable entities) as a program in the target language.

Several translation issues, concerning the use of a stack, the details of parameter passing, and procedure call mechanism, were implicit in the front end of the BLISS-11 compiler. They were moved out into a separate phase group, which was systematically filled out thereafter. They covered issues in the layout of data structures, accesses to components, explication of implicit aspects of source languages, etc..

In the BLISS-11 compiler, high level data flow analysis was performed because of the strict absence of gotos which disrupt implicit control flow. This is not feasible for most languages. Hence, the optimisation phase is moved out of the front-end of the BLISS-11 compiler, and introduced after the translation phases, as low-level flow-graph representations are now discernable in the IR.

The coding phases worry about

i) making effective use of memory to represent the current state of a program;
ii) making good use of scarce register resources; and
iii) using instructions well.

These three aspects are interdependent on each other. A model which attempts to fuse these activities in a sequence of phases is shown in Figure 2.

2.2.1 Shaping the IR with Respect to the Target Machine

Shaping the program, so that it is suitable for coding in the target language consists of several different algebraic restructuring activities [9]

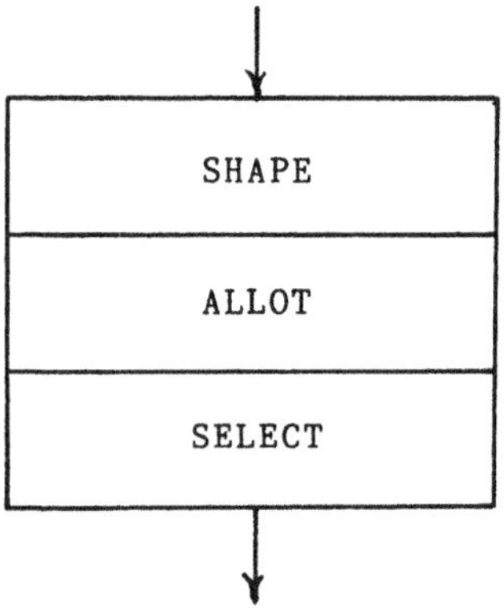

Figure 2: Phases in High Quality Code Generation.

a) factoring-based on distributivity properties, such that the adjacency of certain operators is encouraged, because the opcodes in the instruction sets exhibit them.
b) using associativity properties, such that the demands for resources is reduced, be it storage (multi-general-register architectures) or time (multiple-function-unit architectures)
c) based on commutativity properties, such that the lifetimes of temporary resources, needed for the computation, are reduced.

Further analysis is performed to make sure that the above restructuring is limited to those parts of computations which correspond to opcodes in the target machine instructions: the computation is segmented with respect to operands and operations - as seen in the instruction set of the target machine; and the above restructuring is performed only with respect to the operator component. This segmentation requires a bottom-up scan of the IR representing the computation, so as to discover all possibilities of using the addressing modes in the instruction set.

Another specialized analysis reduces the demand for temporaries by using source program declared variables for this purpose: something akin to definition-use analysis, undertaken in global data flow analysis, is used; the gap between the last use of a variable, and its next definition, all within a basic-block, is exploited.

All of the above analysis and restructuring leads to the determination of the sequence of "instruction-sized" assignment commands, and their respective destinations. The effect is to reduce demands for temporary resources and to prepare for good use of the instruction set. Points (i) to (iv) discussed in Section 2.1 of the BLISS-11 compiler, are addressed by the above aspects of shaping the IR in view of the target machines instruction set. It is as if a trial code selection has been performed so as to look for opportunities which might otherwise be missed. An assumption during this group of phases is that unbounded resources are available in the target language.

2.2.2 Allotting Resources to Meet Demands

The lifetimes of all resources needed are determined. Demands for resources whose lifetimes overlap are said to conflict, for they compete with each other and cannot share a resource. The preceding group of phases, which shaped the IR with respect to the target language, would have left information in the IR about the prepared resource which ought to be allocated. Using the conflict graph, and preference information, another trial pass of code selection is performed with a view of packing the (unbounded) demands for resources into the available resources (if possible, into the prepared ones)[12].

Since actual code selection is deferred, the work done in both these phase groups, of shaping the IR and allotting resources, are based on approximations of the target language. Another view is that they focus on the relevant aspects of the target machine language, pertinent to the phase group, at the expense of others.

2.2.3 Code Selection

The assumptions at the start of the code selection phases are that expressions have been reduced to sequences of assignments/commands and that registers have been allocated (locally for each basic block in the IR). If the approximations used in the preceding phases were adequate, the code selection process would not result in any changes in the sequencing assignment commands nor require any additional temporary registers [10].

The code selection activity is performed by an IR traversal in the reverse-order of the determined sequence of assignments, i.e., target language instructions are selected in the reverse order of their execution. At each visit to the IR, a "Maximal Munch" code selection is performed [15].

Code selection is an ambiguous activity for many sequences of instructions can be selected to represent a single assignment in the IR. "Maximal Munch" effects a choice amongst these alternatives by attempting to locally select the densest code in a "greedy" manner. It uses several metrics to assess the alternatives, all of which quantitatively represent the heuristics which guide experienced assembly language programmers.

2.3 The Structure of the PQCC System

Research in discovering a generic structure of a compiler with a production-quality code generator was but the first step in the PQCC project. The next step was to build a compiler-compiler capable of generating such compilers.

To realise this objective, further refinements to the compiler structure described in the preceding section were necessary. A compiler consists of algorithms of its phases, which are executed at compile-time. Also, it maintains data concerning the program it processes, which is known only at compile-time. Both of the above aspects have to be made generic with respect to the source language and target machine. It is fair to say that most compiler-compilers only attempt to relativize the compilation algorithms by using parser generators, attribute-grammar processors, etc., for handling source language dependencies. In the case of retargetable code generators, a variation of the UNCOL approach [20], that of using a standard, perhaps low-level intermediate, internal representation, is resorted to: register-transfer languages [21], operator trees [2], and hypothetical machines [22, 23] have all been used for this purpose. Except for the latter method, it is not clear whether the representations used have been centrally defined, formally, or otherwise. Once a standard IR was chosen, retargetability was engineering through devising appropriate algorithms, with target machine descriptions being provided as data with respect to the chosen IR.

The PQCC solution structure making generic the compilation algorithms is depicted in Figure 3. A Front End Generator [24] was used to automatically construct compiler front-ends. A representation transformation generator was realised through a rule-based tree-pattern match and replacement system [25]. A generator for automatically constructing global-data flow analysis phases, and the attendant transformation phases, was designed [26]. A generator which would feed required target machine information to different phases in high-quality code generation was implemented [7].

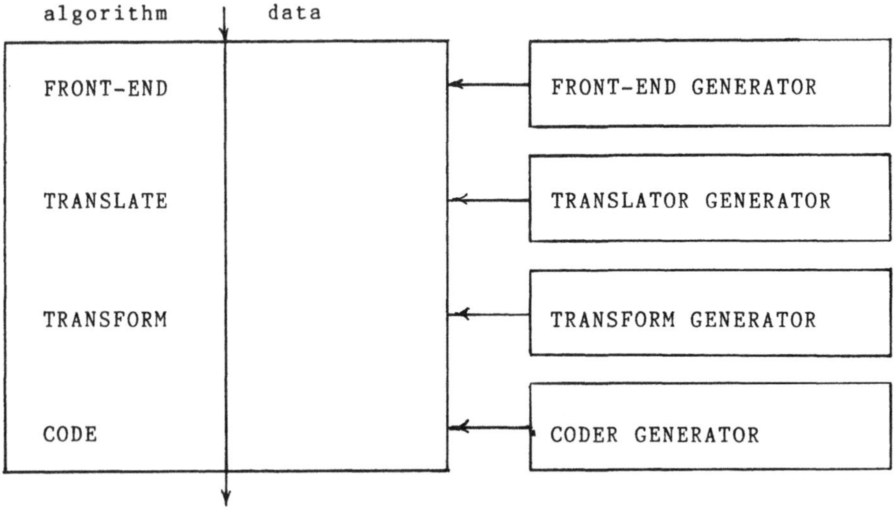

Figure 3: PQCC System Structure

Unlike many compiler-compilers, PQCC was wide-scoped, and attempted the automatic generation of many phases. All these phases are threaded together by the (many) internal representations of programs which flow through them, and are massaged while in transit. A tool was built to handle the interfaces between these phases [13]. The IR used in PQCC was based on operator trees, as in the BLISS-11 compiler [8]. Successive phases massaged these trees in the IR to induce new operators (as in the Translation phases), or restructured them (as in the Shaping phases), or simply decorated them with attributes, such as the register to be used, whether the tree was a common sub-expression, etc.. The purpose of the above interface tool was to smoothen the effect of these massages in passing the information across phases. The use of this tool is depicted in Figure 4.

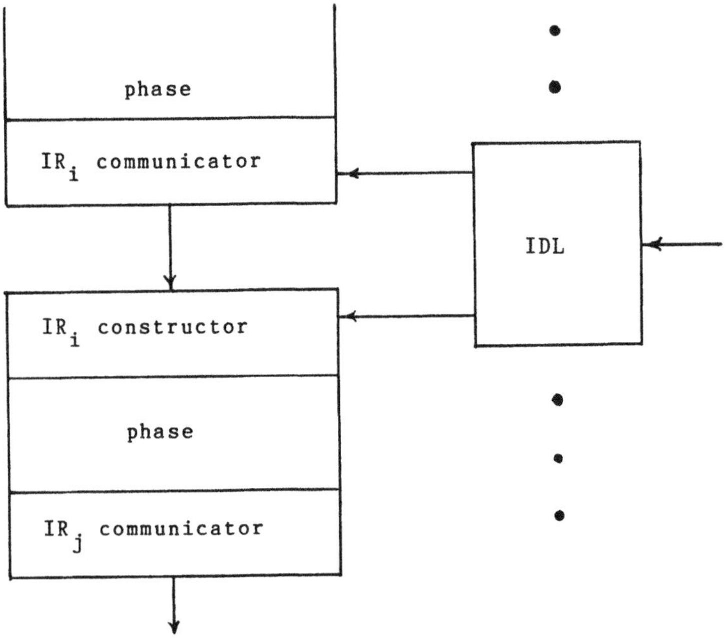

Figure 4: Phase Interface in PQCC System

The scope of the compiler-compiler, viz., the spectrum of source languages and target machine pairs for which compilers would be automatically constructed from specifications, was never consciously defined. It depended implicitly on the capability of the generative tools used. It was generally remarked that Ada and its many simpler von Neumann programming language cousins, and VAX-11 like machines were representative of the richest parts of this spectrum. A subconscious reason for this remark, and an implicit, unarticulated principle used in the design of PQCC was that if the most difficult extant source language and target machine could be handled by the prototype, then all other points in the spectrum of inputs would turn out to be simplifications of this general solution.

An indirect result of the above decision was that a single series of Internal Representations were used by all compilers generated by PQCC. This series was capable of describing the richness of Ada and VAX-11 during the different phases of compilation. All the compilation algorithms in the different phases were generic in source language and target machine characteristics with respect to the series of IRs.

2.4 Closing Remarks on the PQCC Experiment

This section has been quite elaborate. It presents work done elsewhere, which has already been documented, though perhaps over several reports and publications. In part, the motivation for this description is that this paper is self contained. More importantly, this presentation is biased with respect to the sections which follow, concerning our local experiences. In turn, these experiences are the basis for retrospection on the structure of PQCC generated compilers. The detail of this section would allow succeeding sections to be directed, and comparatively brief.

3. THE C CROSS-COMPILER EXPERIMENT

The problem we were faced with was to design a cross compiler for C, generating code for a target machine with a relatively old architecture (early 60's). This machine was used in fail-soft real-time applications. A lot of high performance code was available in assembly language, whose maintenance was becoming increasingly painful. Even more painful was the larger effort in reconfiguring this software to adapt it to new situations. Hence, the need to use C, a higher-level language, which could be effective in exploiting low-level facilities of the machine.

The headroom available, between the size of the currently coded applications, and the gross limits imposed by the architecture was less than 20%. Hence, the compiler had to generate high quality code, so as to induce minimal penalty due to the use of a high level language and its compiler. The only known compilers which addressed such a performance constraint were the BLISS-11 compiler, and its derivative generated by PQCC. The role model was cut out for us. A serious handicap in this effort was the non-availability of the PQCC arsenal (and, for that matter, the problems of porting it out of the DEC-20/VAX-11 environment in which it was constructed). A compiler-compiler was not our goal. Be that as it may, using such tools would give us room for experimentation, and change in our approach even when we were reasonably deep in the project. As the size of the PQCC experiment was forbidding, a conscious decision was to use as many extant, standard, compiler writing tools as possible. The local investment in tool building was limited to those aspects of PQCC which could not be approximated by any available tool.

The development environment for the cross compiler was Unix, as was the execution environment. Yacc [27] and Lex [28] were heavily used. A tool for constructing and displaying abstract syntax was built for handling all IR related problems [29]; it was based on research in language-oriented-editors [30]. Another tool was built for effecting tree transformations [31]. Its need was influenced by a similar tool in PQCC [25]. In contrast to the methods used by that tool, the tree-pattern-matching parts of tree transformations was based on research in identifying redexes [32] in models of computation based on equations [33].

Figure 1 also depicts the structure of the C cross compiler. Two pertinent observations are necessary, for they were the motivating factors throughout the experiment.

Firstly, the normal methods used in effecting global data flow analysis and consequent optimisations throw away most of the information about program structure due to the level of the IR. As a result, the analysis has to recover some of this lost information in an expensive way. We were keen to perform high-level data flow analysis wherever possible. Hence, the nature of the IR [36] is rather different from that used in PQCC. While the above attitude seems to complicate matters, the actual motivation was quite the opposite. One of the requirements was the compile-time performance of the cross-compiler. Our attempt was to have a non-iterative specification of the data flow analysis computations. The idea was to formulate the saturated data flow properties as given by simple formulae over sets. Hence, the logic for computing saturated data flow properties would be shifted from compile-time to language-definition time (equivalently, compiler construction time). This was based on similar formulation in [34], and is presented in [35].

And secondly, the algorithms used in the different phases of PQCC were complex because of the generality of Ada and complexity of VAX. It was decided that these algorithms should be simplified sufficiently so as to only tackle the problem posed by the C Cross Compiler.

It is this second observation which provides the focus for the ensuing retrospection, and is dealt with in the remainder of this section.

3.1 Segmentation of a Compiler

A difficulty with literature on compilers is that the focus is on some particular phase under discussion. Its specification is seemingly precise, in that the nature of its inputs, and the attendant assumptions, and the nature of the output alongwith assertions are given. However, there is little precision in the manner in which the big picture is pieced together. Works on compiler correctness are few, for the problem is immense in scope, as well as deep in content, due the the domains it deals with, and due to the computations it embodies. Most works focus on some aspects of correctness, but a methodology is missing.

A perspective on a methodology of asserting the correctness of compilers is inherent in the way a compiler is segmented, the reasons for distinguishing activities in compiler-construction time from those at compile-time, and the design logic for relegating some activities to link-time, load-time, and run-time. Such a view aids in sharpening the phases of the compiler as segmented in Figure 1.

3.1.1 Front-End Phases

The front-end phases are very nearly standard, and are the ones which have seen maximal formalisation. They accept a source program, check it for syntax, screen all static semantic issues, resolve all ambiguities due to overloading by performing necessary type inference, type coercion, and operator identification, and produce an unambiguous, semantically clean IR [36] suitable for high-level data flow analysis.

The IR is hierarchic, reflecting the structure of the source language compositions used in the source program, with implicit one-in one-out flow. Explicit control flow primitives, such as labels and corresponding gotos, breaks continues, and returns, when used in programs, violate the one-in one-out property. Consequently, the IR is restructured to retain this property, and maximally retain implicit control flow compositions [33]. Continuation-free semantics can be specified for such representations of control flow, using standard, recursively specified, denotational semantic equations. The effect is to localise the need for iterative methods of data flow analysis to those regions of the programs resultant from use of explicit control flow primitives.

One uniform principle is applied to the specification of the IR during its successive manipulations by the succeeding phases. Attributes, evaluated to guide any of the compilation activities, will be local to a phase. All the results of manipulation will be directly reflected in the structure of the IR. The basic intent is that the abstract syntax is sharp enough for the semantics to be syntax-directed in a straightforward manner, i.e., directly derived from the structure and content of the IR, rather than computations which extract the requisite property on which hinges semantics. As a result, there should be only a single thread connecting one phase and its successor: just abstract syntax; there are no attributes in it to reflect further understanding of the processing in preceding phases.

3.1.2 Translation Phases

All source level data types and associated operators are converted to machine-level representations of data and machine-level functions. Similarly, all implicit aspects of source language are made explicit; actual parameter expressions are converted to assignments, as are the expressions related to bounds in control of iterative structures. Where sequencing is unspecified in the source language, such as in the evaluation of procedure parameters, conventions are set up. Control flow representation is the only aspect that is left alone, and is the only direct remnant of the source program.

The resultant IR is such that an on-the-fly code generator can traverse this IR and produce code. Intervening phases which massage the IR must leave this property invariant.

The phase group consists of tree transformations, and is constructed from specifications using the locally devised tree transformer generator [31].

3.1.3 Transform Phases

The transform phases perform global data flow analysis, and effect optimising transformations [35]. These phases can be dropped altogether. They effect common sub-expression elimination, fold constant expressions, remove tail recursion, perform motion of invariant code out of loops, and effect strength reduction. The results of the transformation are explicit in the IR. There are no attributes passed to the next group of phases.

3.1.4 Coding Phases

The coding phases accept an IR and emit sequences of instructions in the target language. The attempt in these coding phases is to approximate the phases depicted in Figure 2. The last of the coding phases, that of instruction selection, by itself would adequately perform the task of coding. The preceding two phases, viz., **shape** and **allot**, only improve the quality of code generated. These phases are discussed in the next section.

3.2 High Quality Code Generation

The target machine we were dealing with is a single accumalator, and 7 Index Register machine. The accumalator is 4 words long. Many opcodes in the instruction set are polymorphic in the length of data, the limit being 16 bytes.

Given this paucity of general registers, and complexity of varying length operands, only a few of which could be identified with source language primitive types, it was indeed necessary to examine the utility of the variety of activities undertaken in the **shape** and **allot** phase groups in PQCC generated compilers. One decision was immediate: an on-the-fly register allocation scheme would be a close approximation of the more complex scheme followed by allot. Hence, we had to worry about the shape and code phases only. These are discussed in the reverse order below.

3.2.1 Code Selection

The "Maximal Munch" code selection scheme, and the tables that drive it, are quite complex [10]. The generative tools to automatically construct these tables were not considered as appropriate investments of our time. Instead, it was felt that this code selection scheme should be replaced by that of Graham and Glanville [2], which was based on parsing technology. The only problem we faced was that their version of the required parser generator was unavailable to us. Hence, we decided to simplify further and use YACC for this purpose.

In order to effectively use YACC, we had to overcome the problems of "blocking" associated with the Graham-Glanville approach. This was got around by manually partitioning the instruction set into basic instructions, and derivable ones. Experiments with this idea gave us a grammar which did not lead to blocking [2], but only generated sequences of basic instructions.

A variation of multiple keyword search in bibliographic applications [37] led to a code compactor. The generated sequence of basic instructions were piped through the compactor to generate complex instructions, wherever applicable.

This division of labour was found adequate for handling complex addressing modes, as well as complex opcodes. However, in practice, it was sensitive to the actual order in which basic instructions were generated. In turn, this depended on the traversal of the IR performed in place of a traditional lexical analyser, which preceded the parser. "Maximal Munch" was approximated successfully by this model. Also, compile-time transformations induced by the "maximal munch" algorithms to convert IR suitable for a three address machine to a sequence of operations on a two address machine, and so on, were avoided.

Register allocation was tackled on-the-fly. Spilling of accumalator was handled by using index registers wherever possible.

On the whole, the code selection phase was designed to produce locally good code, modulo the traversal order of the IR.

3.2.2 Shape

Aside from some algebraic transformations which would shape IR in a canonical form with respect to its traversal in the code selection phase, the only minimisation attempted here was to reduce the temporaries needed by a simple use of Sethi-Ullman ordering [38]. Again this decision was based on the paucity of general registers, and that use of complex instructions was already catered for in the code generation scheme expressed above.

3.3 Closing Remarks on the C Cross Compiler Experiment

Compilers induce explicit costs with respect to language features. The choice of good representations with respect to these induced costs is left to the programmer. The tests conducted during the acceptance of the compiler showed a penalty of 1.3 to 1.8 with respect to hand coded versions of the compiler. This was considered as acceptable.

Some of the drawbacks of the compiler were the inability to utilise some bit oriented instructions, and the inability to utilise varying length operands effectively.

On the whole, with respect to the effort which went into the building of the compiler, the results were a satisfactory approximation of the PQCC generated compilers. No doubt we were lucky in getting away with so many simplifications because of the rudimentary nature of the target machine architecture, but this experience also showed that PQCC could be an overkill, and its generated compilers would incur much wasted effort at compile-time due to the generality of its algorithms and representations.

4. AN EXPERIMENT IN RETARGETABLE CODE GENERATION

Independently of the above work, research in retargetable code generation was done elsewhere [18, 19]. The remarkable coincidence was that the approach to building a locally-high-quality code selection process was identical to ours, but their techniques were formal.

Given a target machine description in a form similar to that devised by Graham-Glanville [2], this description would be algorithmically partitioned into a Basis set and a Simulation set. Parsing was used to implement both the code selector which generated sequences of instructions in the Basis set, and the compactor which found opportunities to use instructions in the Simulation set. The parser generator used was YACC. On-the-fly register allocation was performed during code selection in the Basis-set.

A retargetable code generator produced by the above scheme guarantees that locally optimal code will be produced, modulo the traversal order of the IR. Furthermore, it guarantees to maximise the use of the instruction set of the target machine, with respect to the translation induced by an earlier phase. This latter guarantee, which could not be asserted for the code selector in the C Cross Compiler, is directly dependent on the fact that the partitioning and compacting phases are complementary, and that these relations are automatically established by the algorithmic approach to the problem.

Target machine languages are riddled with ambiguities. Several sequences of Basis instruction set reduce to the same instruction in the Simulation set. The method of partitioning and compaction devised above discovers only a few of these ambiguous situations for each instruction in the Simulation set, amongst each of which a default preference is imposed by the techniques. Clearly, if such a code selection phase should contribute to high quality code generation, it needs preceding phases which will ensure that compaction is realised, by shaping the IR accordingly.

5. RETROSPECTION

The BLISS-11 and PQCC experiments are large monoliths: those experiences had to be accepted as a whole, i.e., parts of them did not rub off on other compiler development efforts. There are no reported approximations to the quality of code they generated. In this regard, the local experiments in building compilers with high quality code generation was both chastening, for it brought us to face with the breadth and depth of the PQCC effort, as well as rewarding, because we were finally able to cull out some simplifications.

In point of fact, as this paper is being written after the entire experience with local experiments, it must be stated that some of the driving principles in our experiments were subconscious, and some started as hunches. They have been presented as principles followed during the experiments, only to make this retrospection seem smoother.

With respect to the BLISS-11 compiler, the PQCC effort did sharply bring out the distinctions between translation and coding during code generation. Translation phases are the mainstay for asserting semantic equivalence between source and target programs. Translation is decided upon at compiler construction time, and is either derived at compiler-compiler time, as attempted by Cattell [11], or specified as inputs to the tools of a compiler-compiler, as in PQCC.

The coding phases, on the other hand, are concerned with segmenting the translated IR into target machine instructions, and threading them into a sequence so as to form a linear representation needed by the target machine languages. All research in retargetable code generation has focussed on this code selection aspect of code generation.

Our experiments have attempted to delve into the reasons for quality in the PQCC code selection phases. Several approximations are possible, as discussed below.

5.1 Approximate Models to PQCC Code Selection

Figure 5 presents a lattice relating the ideal phases of the C cross compiler experiment. Any path from the front-end phase to the select phase represents a possible compiler. Different paths induce different levels of quality of code. In fact, some of these possibilities were of much value in planning the development of the compiler, as well as in testing the different phases, though, as the development team members will testify, a clearer appreciation of this lattice would have saved us many headaches.

Can we extend the above freedom of composition of phases to PQCC?

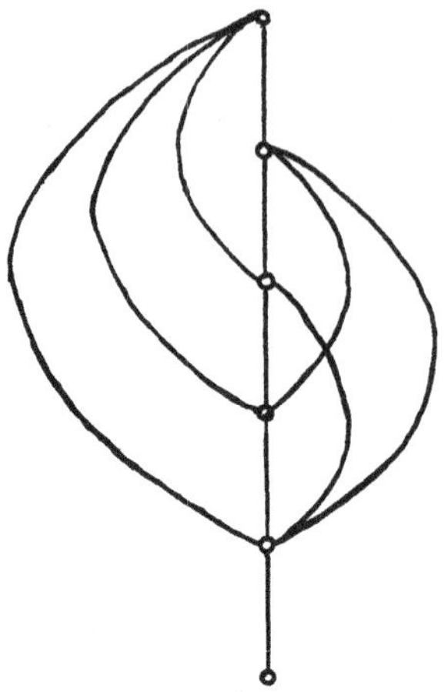

Figure 5: A family of compilers

5.2 Linkages Across Phases

To effectively realise such a family of approximations to high-quality code generation, the linkages between the different phases - which incrementally contribute to the overall quality - must be well specified.

The Front-End phases produce a source-relative IR. The algorithms of these phases must be parameterised both with respect to the source language, and the IR to be used by the rest of the translation process. In PQCC, the IR defaulted to one capable of describing Ada programs. In practice, abstract syntax cannot be directly derived from concrete syntax, (eg, gotos are not commands), neither can it be generalised to an envelope, without detriment to the sharpness of semantic characterisation. The present state-of-the-art programming languages, and the models for defining semantics, are not well meshed, and require that the abstract syntax of source languages be an explicit parameter to the Front-End phase algorithms. The nature of this parameter is one of an abstract data type.

The algorithms of the translation phases have three parameters: the abstract data types defining the source IR and the target IR, and a description of a mapping from source IR to target IR which preserves semantic invariance. The only entities which are left unbound with respect to the target machine are resources which can be allocated on-the-fly, such as registers, memory locations, or functional units (as in the case of machines with multiple functional units). The assumption here is that the IR can be traversed in many ways to effect code selection. Different orders of traversal produce different qualities of code, but all of them use an on-the-fly resource allocation scheme. The observation here is that the register-allocation strategy in PQCC can be replaced by a strategy for deciding on IR traversal order alongwith an on-the-fly register allocation scheme. So long as the latter allows for some resources to be bound, and will allocate only in case of need, the intervening phases between translation and code selection can effect changes to the IR without resorting to attributes. Consequently, a single abstract data type will be adequate for describing the target-machine relative IR throughout the optimising transformations and coding phases. This abstract data type should be an input parameter to a compiler-compiler.

5.3 Shaping the IR

Shaping the IR and allocation of general resources were the weaker parts of our experiments. In this section, and the next one, we extrapolate our experience with regard to these two issues.

As discussed early in section 2.2.1, the transformations which shape the IR, to be suitable for code selection for a target machine, are all based on algebraic properties of operators. In PQCC, these transformations are assessed relative to some costs in the target machine. This information is separately provided for in the model of the target machine [7]. In fact, the construction of a target machine description requires an understanding of the reasons for the different components of this description, to be used by different phases; this may not be the bald truth, but tuning the performance of a generated compiler will require some heuristics to adjust the weights/costs associated with the description. It is in this regard that some simplification is desirable.

The Graham-Glanville [2] style description of a machine is relatively easy to set up, and is the basis for the selection and compaction model of code selection presented here. The computation of weights associated with instructions, so as to order them for the partitioning process is automatic, and is based on a simple syntactic inspection of the trees which define instructions. It would be useful to avoid any further modelling of the target machine, and to use this model repeatedly, to realise different decisions concerning shaping of the IR and allocation of resources.

A first approximation to shaping is:

1) induce left associativity in expressions for machines with general registers, and balance trees of expressions with associative operators for machines with multiple functional units. Note that this is already done in PQCC, the choices being made at compiler construction time.
2) switch operands based on Sethi-Ullman numbering [38] only, introducing reverse operators wherever necessary.
3) use distributivity properties to always transform trees to increase the chances of compaction to complex opcodes.
4) perform code selection using a pre-order linearisation of the IR (Node; Left subtree; Right subtree: NLR-traversal in PQCC terminology) and record the code selected at every node;
5) perform a NRL traversal as a basis for code selection and record the information.
6) compare the code selected by 4 and 5, to record the preferred order of traversal.

The above proposal uses algebra, and an available machine description, to approximate corresponding phases of PQCC. Steps 1 and 2 generally work in the right direction, that of reducing demands for temporaries. Step 3 may contribute to marginal loss of quality in those cases where the transformation turns out to be ill advised with respect to the target machine. Steps 4, 5 and 6 are replacements for PQCC phases which assess the IR with respect to operand access modes, and other target machine dependant features, ascertaining the order of traversal suitable for code selection. Note that instead of an approximate trial-run at code selection, a full scale code selection is performed. The costs, however, are linear with respect to IR.

5.4 Resource Allocation

A basic difference between the register allocation scheme of PQCC and others is that the PQCC scheme undertakes an implicit semantic categorisation for register usage: is it a short term target destination in an assignment sequence for coding an expression, or is it a need which enhances good use of addressing modes, or is it for storing common sub-expressions, etc.. All this analysis is done at the level of a basic block. On the other hand, most other schemes work at a global level, for an entire flow graph. They do not, however, attempt to minimise anything other than the lifetime of temporaries [39].

A problem with the shape and allot phases of PQCC is that they use approximate models of the target language to drive their decision making. Hence, some late opportunities of allocation/spilling can occur in the code selection phase. As register allocation is undertaken on a basic-block basis, the probability of having spare registers is reasonable, and hence spilling is avoided most of the time.

The scheme for shape proposed in the previous section uses an exact model of the target machine, the same one as used in the code selection phase. Given the traversal order of the IR, decided by shape, using the same code-selection phase, the precise usage of registers in the final code for the IR can be known. Based on this knowledge, and the results of data flow analysis like reaching definitions/available expressions, a better use of free registers for the entire flow graph can be effected. Furthermore, the packing of other temporaries into registers which are still free, can be effected. As a result, the performance of the BLISS-11 compiler, which used registers even to store local variables in a block, can be realised.

5.5 Integration of Phases

Compiler-compilers are presented with a classical problem: programming-in-the-small vs. programming-in-the-large.

Automated generation of compilers becomes feasible only when the compiler components (phases) become precise enough to specify. These phases embody a single logical activity in compilation. Compiler-compilers are predicated upon the ability to devise data-driven algorithms for these phases, such that the data can completely capture the individual differences between generated compiler phases, and such that the data can be obtained by processing the specifications. The specification of these phases, the design of data-driven algorithms, and devising tools to process specifications to result in needed data, are all problems of programming-in-the-small. They are all narrowly focussed, and address individual problems. These activities are relatively easy to port from one system to another, as they are strictly within the realm of programming languages used for the different aspects of the problem.

Integrating these phases so as to construct passes of a compiler is a prgoramming-in-the-large problem. The availability of coroutines and abstract data types in the compiler implementation language, and overlays or processes which share data structures in the operating environment of the compiler, would contribute to the simplicity with which such large compositions can be devised. Such facilities are not common in most implementation languages, nor are they found easily in operating systems. As a result, the implemented compiler-structure is not easily ported across systems.

6. CONCLUSIONS

Based on local experiments, we have demonstrated that the quality of code generated by PQCC style compilers can be approximated. Further, these experiments show that the extent of approximation can be flexibly realised by devising phases such that a family of approximations are possible. This requires the segmentation of phases to be clear enough to allow several compositions to be made: all phases beyond the translation phase, and except for the ultimate code selection phase, have the same data type characterising both their respective inputs as well as corresponding outputs. Further, the "Maximal-Munch" strategy of PQCC has been approximated by the select-compact paradigm in these experiments.

Extrapolating from these experiments, a suggestion has been put forward for having a single description of the target machine, and a single devise, viz., the selection-compaction paradigm, for tackling all target machine specific analyses so as to shape the IR and allot resources in pursuance of quality in code selection.

Experimentation with separating the heuristics in target machine description from their influence in the data-driven algorithms, in the manner suggested here, is a worthwhile direction for further research. Another direction worth pursuing is to seek explicit relationship between a methodology for compiler correctness, the structure of a compiler, and the structure of a compiler-compiler.

ACKNOWLEDGEMENTS

Many facets of our work have their roots in Bill Wulf's casual remarks about PQCC, and of the gaps between the original intentions of PQCC, and its final realisation. Without those insights, none of this work would have been possible. We are also fortunate that we were forced on this path by the demanding constraints of the compilation problem posed to us.

REFERENCES

1. Leverett, B.W., R.G.G. Cattell, S.O. Hobbs, J.M. Newcomer, A.H. Reiner, B.R. Schatz, and W.A. Wulf, "An Overview of the Production Quality Compiler Compiler project," Computer 13:8(1980), 38-49.
2. Glanville, R.S., and S.L. Graham, "A New Method for Compiler Code Generation," 5th ACM symposium on POPL, 1978, 231-240.
3. Allen, F.E., J.L. Carter, J. Fabri, J. Ferrante, W.H. Harrison, P.G. Loewner, and L.H. Trevillyan, "The Experimental Compiling System," IBM Journal Research and Development 24:6(1980), 695-715.
4. Giegrerich, R., "Introduction to the Compiler Generating System MUG2," Technical Report, TUM-INFO-7913, Technische Universitat Munchen, 1979.
5. Wulf, W.A., R.K. Johnson, C.B. Weinstock, S.O. Hobbs, and C.M. Geschke, "The Design of an Optimizing Compiler," American Elsevier, New York, 1975.
6. Wulf, W.A., M. Barbacci, B. Brosgol, R.G.G. Cattell, R. Conradi, S.O. Hobbs, P. Knueven, B.W. Leverett, J.M. Newcomer, A.H. Reiner, B.R. Schatz, D. Stryker, and F. Turini, "Specifications for the Phases of the PQCC," Internal document PQCC project, Computer Science Department, Carnegie-Mellon University 1980.
7. Newcomer, J.M., "PQCC Intermediate Machine Description Language," Internal document PQCC project, Computer Science Department, Carnegie-Mellon University 1981.
8. Brosgol, B., J.M. Newcomer, D.A. Lamb, D. Levine, M.S. Van Duesen, and W.A. Wulf, "TCOL-Ada," Computer Science Technical Report CMU-CS-80-105, Carnegie-Mellon University, 1980.
9. Wulf, W.A., and K.V. Nori, "Delayed Binding in PQCC Generated Compilers," Computer Science Technical Report CMU-CS-82-138, Carnegie-Mellon University, 1982.
10. Wulf, W.A., and K.V. Nori, "Code Selection in PQCC Generated Compilers," Internal document PQCC project, Computer Science Department, Carnegie-Mellon University, 1983.
11. Cattell, R.G.G., "Formalization and Automatic Derivation of Code Generators," PhD Dissertation, Computer Science Department, Carnegie-Mellon University, 1978.
12. Leverett, B.W., "Register Allocation in Optimizing Compilers," PhD Dissertation, Computer Science Department, Carnegie-Mellon University, 1981.
13. Lamb, D.A., "IDL - Interface Description Language," PhD Disseartation, Computer Science Department, Carnegie-Mellon University, 1983.
14. Wulf, W.A., "PQCC: A Machine-Relative Compiler Technology," IEEE 4th International COMPSAC conference, 1980, 24-36.
15. Cattell, R.G.G., "Automatic Derivation of Code Generators from Machine Descriptions," ACM TOPLAS 2:2(1980), 173-190.
16. Goos, G., W.A. Wulf, A. Evans Jr., and K.J. Butler, "DIANA An Intermediate Language for Ada," LNCS vol. 161, Springer-Verlag, 1983.
17. "C Cross Compiler Design Document," vol. I, II and III, Project document, Tata Research Development and Design Centre, Pune, 1985.
18. Kumar, S., and V.M. Malhotra, "Automatic Retargetable Code Generation: A New Technique," FST & TCS6 conference, LNCS vol. 241, Springer Verlag, 1986, 57-80.
19. Kumar, S., "Automatic Retargetable Code Generation," PhD Dissertation, Computer Science Department, Indian Institute of Technology, Kanpur, 1986.
20. Steel, T.B., Jr. "A First Version of UNCOL," Proc. Winter Joint Computer Conference, 1961, 371-378.
21. Davidson, J.W., and C.W. Fraser, "Code Selection Through Object Code Optimization," ACM TOPLAS 6:4(1984), 505-526.

22. Tanenbaum, A.S., H. van Staveren, E.G. Keizer, and J.W. Stevenson, "A Practical Tool Kit for making Portable Compilers," CACM 26:9(1983), 654-660.
23. Tanenbaum, A.S., H. van Staveren, and J.W. Stevenson, "Using Peephole Optimization on Intermediate Code," ACM TOPLAS 4:1(1982), 21:36.
24. Nestor, J.R., and M. Beard, "Front End Generator User's Guide," Internal document PQCC project, Computer Science Department, Carnegie-Mellon University, 1981.
25. Wulf, W.A., "BONSAI A Tree Transformer Generator," Internal document PQCC project, Computer Science Department, Carnegie-Mellon University, 1981.
26. Stryker, D., "FLANGE: A Flow Analysis Generator User's Manual," Internal document PQCC project, Computer Science Department, Carnegie-Mellon University.
27. Johnson, S.C., "Yacc - yet another compiler compiler," Computing Science Technical Report 32, AT & T Bell Laboratories, 1975.
28. Lesk, M.E., "Lex - a lexical analyzer generator," Computing Science Technical Report 39, AT & T Bell Laboratories, 1975.
29. Deodhar, R., and S.M. Jorapur, "Treegen - Abstract Syntax Tree Builder," Internal document, Tata Research Development and Design Centre, Pune, 1984.
30. Medina-Mora, R. "Syntax Directed Editing: Towards Integrated Programming Environment," PhD Dissertation, Computer Science Department, Carnegie-Mellon University, 1982.
31. Jorapur, S.M., "TTGEN - Tree Transformer Generator," Internal document, Tata Research Development and Design Centre, Pune, 1985.
32. Hoffman, C.M., and M.J. O'Donnell, "Pattern Matching in Trees," Journal ACM 29:1(1982), 68-95.
33. O'Donnell, M.J., "Computing in Systems Described by Equations," LNCS vol. 58, Springer-Verlag, 1977.
34. Jajoo, B.H., "A Programming System Based on Program Structure," PhD Dissertation, Computer Science Department, Indian Institute of Technology, Kanpur, 1980.
35. Joshi, S.M., and K.V. Nori, "Equational Formulation of Data Flow Analysis," Internal document, Tata Research Development and Design Centre, Pune, 1987.
36. Joshi, R.R., and K.V. Nori, "An Intermediate Representation of Programs with Continuation Free Semantics," Internal document, Tata Research Development and Design Centre, Pune, 1987.
37. Aho, A.V., and M.J. Corasick, "Efficient String Matching: an aid to Bibliographic Search," CACM 18:6(1975), 333-340.
38. Sethi, R., and J.D. Ullman, "The Generation of Optimal Code for Arithmetic Expressions," Journal ACM 17:4(1970), 715-728.
39. Chaitin, G.J., "Register Allocation and Spilling via Graph Coloring," SIGPLAN symposium on Compiler Construction, 1982, 98-105.

Some Recent Applications of Knowledge[1]

Rohit Parikh
Department of Computer Science, Brooklyn College of CUNY
Department of Computer Science, CUNY Graduate Center
and
Mathematics Department, CUNY Graduate Center[2]

Traditionally, the study of knowledge has been a province of Philosophy, studied under the branch of that subject called *epistemology*. However, in recent years, the community interested in knowledge has broadened considerably, and now includes people working in AI, distributed computing, cryptography, and outside computer science, people in Mathematical Economics. There has also been a shift in interest from studying the knowledge of a single individual to that of a group of individuals, not only what they know about the world, but also what they know about each other's knowledge. It turns out that there are interesting combinatorial questions that arise in the case of several individuals which do not arise with one, and sometimes even with two. In this paper we will give a general overview of recent work in this area, and also present some new ideas. We shall tend to emphasise work done by ourselves and by our colleagues P. Krasucki and R. Ramanujam, but we will also describe related work done by others when it falls in the domain of this overview. Being an overview, it will necessarily be the case that the topics will cover a wide range of ground and the transitions will sometimes seem sudden. We hope the reader will excuse this fact.

When we speak of knowledge, we are really speaking of two different notions, *external* knowledge, or information, which is the notion commonly studied and is mathematically more tractable, and *explicit* knowledge, which is what we commonly mean by knowledge, which is a more subtle notion, and which has presented some difficulty in studying. We illustrate by an example.

Suppose that you know that x is 2. You could then infer that x is the smallest prime. However, you may not have made that inference. Still, you *could be convinced* by an argument that x is the smallest prime, an argument that does not tell you any new facts. Thus you have the information that x is the smallest prime, or you have external knowledge of that fact. However, you do not have explicit knowledge of this fact unless you have made the inference.

---

[1] To appear in *FST and TCS 7*, Pune India, December 1987

[2] 33 West 42nd St., New York, NY, 10036. Research supported by NSF grant DCR 85-04825

To take a more interesting example, suppose you know the cyphertext x of a certain message m, and you also know how to compute the encryption funtion E. Then you have external knowledge of the cleartext m, since you can be convinced that m is the cleartext by computng $E(m)$ and verifying that it equals x. However, if public key cryptography is to be of any use, you'd better not have explicit knowledge of the cleartext. Thus having a good theory, of explicit as opposed to external knowledge, is crucial to formalising informal knowledge arguments that occur in cryptography.

To start with the easier notion. External knowledge is explained best in terms of the notions of *evidence* and *possible world* (or situation). We do not have complete information about the world we live in but only see some aspects of it. For example, if we are in Pune, then we can see the sky and can conclude that the weather is clear. On the other hand, we cannot see the weather in New York City, even though it is also an aspect of the world, and hence we do not have evidence about it. Thus we have (at least) two possible states of the world, one in which it is clear in both Pune and New York, and another one in which it is clear in Pune and snowing in New York. These two states are equivalent to us, in that they supply the same evidence to us, though they may not be equivalent to someone in New York City.

To be a bit more formal, if we have n individuals, (knowers) and some propositions $P_1, \ldots, P_m$, then we can construct a knowledge language by closing under truth functions and the rule that says that if A is a formula of our language, then so is $K_i(A)$ where i is any number between 1 and n, and $K_i(A)$ says that i knows that A is true. We give semantics to this language by having a number of possible worlds at each of which, the propositions P_i are stipulated to be true or false, and all the truth functions are computed at each world in the usual way. Thus if w is such a world, then $A \vee B$ is true at w iff either A or B is true at w. To handle the operators K_i we have some equivalence relations between the worlds, one for each i, $1 \leq i \leq n$. Here worlds w and w' are equivalent to knower i iff they supply the same evidence to him/her, and we can now say that $K_i(A)$ is true at world w, iff A is true at every world w' which is i-equivalent to w.

It is easy to see that the logic obtained in this way obeys laws similar to that of the modal logic S5. These laws include the following axiom schemes
(i) $K_i(A) \rightarrow A$
(ii) $K_i(A) \rightarrow K_i(K_i(A))$
(iii) $\neg K_i(A) \rightarrow K_i(\neg K_i(A))$
(iv) $K_i(A \rightarrow B) \rightarrow (K_i(A) \rightarrow K_i(B))$
In addition we have tautologies, the rule of modes ponens, and the rule of generalisation which allows us to conclude $K_i(A)$ if we have proved A. (This last

rule applies only if A has been proved as a *logical* truth without any nonlogical axioms). It is shown in [Pal] that this axiomatisation is complete and that logical validity is in PSPACE. See [HV] for a general survey of other systems for knowledge including the notion of time.

For a concrete example of such a situation, consider a number of processes involved in a distributed computation. Then the various knowers are the sites, and at each moment of time, an event may or may not take place at any particular site. The *global history* of the system is the sequence of events taking place at all the sites, whereas the *local history* at site i is just the sequence of events that take place at site i. The possible worlds are the global histories which are possible behaviors of the entire system, and two global histories are equivalent to site i iff they generate the same local history at site i. This gives a very natural interpretation of our logic and it can be shown that problems like safety or liveness have corresponding knowledge interpretations, see [PR]. See also [CM2] and [HF] for very similar models which appeared a little after, but independently of [PR]. The paper by Moses and Tuttle [MT], shows how common knowledge (described below) can be used to develop optimal fault tolerant protocols for co-ordinating simultaneous actions in synchronous systems.

Levels of Knowledge: If A is some formula, then $K_i(A)$ says that i knows A and $K_jK_i(A)$ says that j knows that i knows A. If this is indeed the case, then it follows that both i and j know A, but the converse is not necesssarily true[3]. Similarly, the formula $K_iK_jK_i(A)$ implies all of the preceding, but is not implied by them. These formulae which express some people's knowledge of other people's knowledge express *levels* of knowledge which can arise in interesting ways. Thus if I inform you of some fact by letter, then you know this fact but I do not know that you know it since I do not know that you have received my letter. If you acknowledge my letter, then when I receive your letter, then I know that you know the fact, but you do not know that I know that you know. I.e. $K_iK_y(F)$ holds, but not $K_yK_iK_y(F)$ where y stands for you, i for me, and F for the fact. On the other hand, as Halpern and Moses have pointed out [HM], if I inform you by telephone, then F becomes common knowledge. I.e. I know; you know; I know that you know, etc. etc. The term common knowledge in this technical sense was introduced by the philosopher David Lewis who pointed out that in cases where two parties are cooperating on some task, common knowledge of certain facts is needed. Thus if I have a red light and you have a green light, then I know that you should go ahead and I should stop. Moreover, you should know that I know this, etc. See [CM1], [HM] and [PR] for examples of

[3]If j knows that i knows A, then i does know A, since j can only know what is true. Also j knows that what i knows must be true, so j must also know A. On the other hand, if i and j are separately informed of A, then they need not know of each other's knowledge.

this situation.

Suppose F = *I have discovered a proof of Fermat's theorem.* A, B, C are three individuals. I would like them all to know that F is true. I would also like A to know that B knows. I want B to know that C knows, and I would like C to know that A knows. On the other hand, I do not want B to know that A knows, I do not want A to know that C knows and I do not want C to know that B knows. Are these requirements inconsistent? And if they are consistent, how do I achieve them? To answer these questions, we need an abstract setting for such questions in general.

Consider a fact F and a community { 1...,n} of individuals. If we let Σ be the alphabet $\{K_1, \ldots, K_n\}$, then each formula about the knowledge of F can be expressed in the form xF where x is a string in Σ^*. Given a world or situation w, we can consider the set L of strings x such that xF is true. Now it is easy to see that F is common knowledge iff L is Σ^*, F is merely true iff L consists solely of the empty string and F is false iff L is empty. Thus levels of knowledge of F in this community can be associated with languages, and the higher the level, the larger the language. Now L must have certain properties. If a string xay is in L, then so is the string $xaay$ in view of the axiom $K_i(A) \rightarrow K_iK_i(A)$ and similarly, the fact that $K_i(A)$ implies A leads to the fact that if x is in L, and y is embeddable in x, then y is in L.

It is shown in [Pa2] that these are the *only* requirements on L. I.e. every nonempty L consistent with these rquirements can be obtained for a true but unknown F. In particular the desired situation with Fermat's theorem can be obtained with six meetings with A, B, C, two at a time. All the languages that correspond to levels of knowledge are regular subsets of Σ^*.

Non-monotonicity: The following sort of question occurs in the PSAT, a test taken in the US by high school students aspiring to college.

"Let x be the distance from the origin to the point $(a,3)$. Let y be the distance from the origin to the point $(4,b)$. Which of the following alternatives is correct? (A) $x < y$ (B) $y < x$ (C) $x = y$ (D) the information given is insufficient to determine the answer."

It is clear that in this case the correct answer is D. However, the answer has a curious property. If, say A were the correct answer, then we might expect to prove it in some simple mathematical system. similarly for B and C. However, the fact that D is the correct answer cannot be proved in any such system. For if P is the proof of D from the given facts, P would also be a proof from the given facts plus the formulas $a = 1$ and $b = 2$. However, this cannot be, because now the correct answer is no longer D, but A. Thus the fact that D is correct can only be proved in a *non-monotonic* logic, where additional information can destroy old theorems. The point is that the usual systems are unable to formalise the implicit assumption that "the given information is all you know about x and y" which is needed to see that D is the correct answer and whose meaning changes when additional information is obtained.

In [Pa1] we discuss a non-monotonic rule proposed by McCarthy to handle the situation. This rule says that the default is ignorance. In other words, if we can consistently have both $K_i(A)$ and $\neg K_i(A)$, then we must infer the latter. Thus we must assert that we do not know the relationship between x and y unless the opposite conclusion is forced on us from other things that we know.

Unfortunately, there are problems with McCarthy's rule. Consider the formula $K_i(P) \vee K_i(Q)$. Both $\neg K_i(P)$ and $\neg K_i(Q)$ are consistent with it, and hence must be derived from it by McCarthy's rule. But this also gives us their *conjunction* which is inconsistent with the given formula.

The solution is to say that this formula is non-monotonically inconsistent. In [Pa1], a model theoretic notion of non-monotonic consistency and a notion of normal proof are defined. Basically the idea is this: among the various finite models of a formula A there is a partial ordering. Generally, a larger model corresponds to less knowledge because it allows for more possible worlds. The formula is *non-monotonically consistent* if it has a largest model with a certain fixed height. A *normal proof* is essentially one that allows use of McCarthy's rule to a formula A iff all *subformulae* of A have already been proved or disproved. It is proved then that for a non-monotonically consistent A, A implies B non-monotonically iff B has a normal proof from A. This is theorem 8(i) of [Pa1]. *Caution:* parts (ii) and (iii) of theorem 8 have a subtle error, pointed out by Joe Halpern, and hence even though we can still assert that non-monotonic consistency is decidable, we do not know if it is is in PSPACE as asserted in [Pa1]..

External versus actual knowledge: To see that the notion of knowledge that we have discussed so far is not adequate, we consider some examples.

1) Two children have played in mud and have got their foreheads dirty. (The puzzle also works with more than two children.) The father comes on the scene and says, "one of you has a dirty forehead". He then asks the first child, "do you know if your forehead dirty?". The child says, "I don't know". He then asks the second child the same question. At this point, in the *standard* version of the puzzle, the second child says, "my forehead is dirty". And its reasoning is as follows: "If my forehead were clean, then the child before me would have known that *it* must be the dirty child intended by the father. Hence it would have said that its forehead was dirty. However, it said 'I don't know'. So my forehead must be dirty."

Now consider what happens if the children are not perfect reasoners. In the first case, the second child might not come up with the argument above. In the second place, even if the second child is quite smart, it still might have doubts about the reasoning ability of the *first* child. It may be that the second child has a clean forehead, and the first child just did not make the right inference. Thus the dirty children puzzle, though it is quite 'cute', does not represent what happens realistically.

To give an argument even more striking, suppose two mathematicians are asked if Fermat's theorem is true. The first one answers, "I don't know". Would the second one be justified in saying. "If Fermat's theorem is false, then there is a counterexample. The first mathematician knows arithmetic. Hence he would know that Fermat's theorem is false. But he said, 'I don't know'. Hence Fermat's theorem must be true." Clearly not. It is true that if Fermat's theorem is false, then in theory this fact can be discovered by calculation. However, it is not reasonable to assume that the first mathematician *has* carried out all calculations, that he *could* carry out.

The problem with the notion of external knowledge is that a true mathematical assertion is true in all possible situations. But for someone not to have external knowledge of A, A must be false in some situation which is possible for that person. If A is a true mathematical assertion, then such a situation cannot exist and so we always have external knowledge of every true mathematical assertion.

Thus external knowledge, while it accounts for how knowledge increases through increase in *evidence*, fails to represent the increase in knowledge that arises from *reasoning* and *calculation*. We illustrate by a further example which will also be a key to the solution of this problem.

Here is a dialogue between a questioner q and a respondent r:

```
q: Do you  know the factorisation  of 143?
r: Not off hand.
q: Is 11 a prime?
r: (After thinking  a little) Yes.
q: Is 13 a prime?
r: Yes,
q: How much is 11 times 13?
r: Let us see; 11 times 10 is  110. 11 times 3 is 33.
   110 plus 33 is 143.  Oh, I see.
q: Can you factorise 143 now?
r: Of course, it is 11 times 13.
```

There is nothing mysterious about this dialogue. However, note that q only asked questions. How then could he increase r's knowledge?

To deal with this problem we consider the question of *computing* knowledge, a question which involves resource bound considerations. In general, the goal is to compute external knowledge, but it may be incomputable or intractable and what one may succeed in computing will generally be *less* than external knowledge.

Let us turn to a discussion of the role of resource bounds which, we claim, are implicit in every query about knowledge.

Suppose I ask someone, "Do you know what time it is?" He is likely to look at his watch and say "four PM", or whatever his watch shows. At this point it would be silly for me to say, "If you didn't know what time it was, since you had to look at your watch, why didn't you say so?" Presumably he took my inquiry, not really to be an inquiry about his state of knowledge, but about the time. What happens is that he is carrying out an algorithm which terminates with his knowing the value of the time. If I now ask the same question of a person not wearing a watch, she is likely to say, "I don't know". If, however, I say, "Do you know what time it is? I have a plane to catch at six". Then she may suggest calling the special number for time, or remember someone around who is wearing a watch. Thus the algorithm is carried further if the likely benefit from the answer exceeds the cost of carrying out the algorithm. Note also, that unlike a computer, when a person is asked the same question twice, and the question was answered successfully the first time, then the second query is answered quite fast. This clearly points to some database that has been updated in the meanwhile.

Definition: A *knowledge algorithm* consists of a database together with a procedure that takes as input a question (say the truth value of some formula) and some resource bound, and operates on the question and the database upto some point determined by the value of the resource bound. Then either an answer is obtained or the bound is exceeded. In the first case, the answer is given and the database may be updated, even if the answer depended logically on evidence already at hand. In the second case the answer "I don't know" is given[4]. The database may also be updated as a result of information received from the outside.

The algorithm is *sound* if it only gives correct "yes" and "no" answers. It is *complete* if it gives one of these answers whenever there is external knowledge of the correct answer and the bound b is large enough.

---

[4]This answer really should be distinguished from the same answer given when one knows that one lacks external knowledge.

We illustrate this by describing a possible knowledge algorithm for factorisation. The database in this case consists of a finite sequence of primes, not necessarily in increasing order. A query consists of a pair n, b where n is the number to be factorised and b is a resource bound. The algorithm uses some test for primality, perhaps a probabilistic one. On receiving the query, the number is first tested for divisibility by a number in the database. If the answer is positive, say n is divisible by p, then p is set aside as a factor and n is replaced by n/p. If no prime in the database divides n, then n is tested for primality. If n turns out to be a prime, then the factorisation of n is trivial and *n is added to the database.* If n is not a prime and is not divisible by any prime in the database, then some dreary routine for factorisation is started. If, at any time during this process, the bound b is exceeded then the answer "I don't know" is given.

The dialogue between q and r above illustrates the use of a database. At first the person asked only has the possibility of trying all possible factors up to the square root of 143 and does not want to bother. (If money were offered, then this would increase the value of an answer and increase the value of b.) However, the rest of the dialogue puts 11 and 13 in the database, and the same question is now easily answered. Similarly, in public key cryptosystems, the private key is part of the database so that two people with different databases will be in different positions regarding the decoding of some message. It is also clear that if one party knows a fast algorithm for factorisation and the other party does not even know that there is one, then their situation is quite unsymmetric, a fact that the S5 logic cannot represent.

Under special circumstances, external knowledge or the lack of it may be decidable relatively cheaply. If a person knows this, then he might respond to a query by carrying out the computation till it terminates in a "yes", "no", or a stable "I don't know".

We have so far talked only about how inquiries about knowledge may be answered. But what then is *knowledge*? Given that a person has a knowledge algorithm, we may perhaps like to say that A is *knowable* to him if his algorithm is, sound and given input A it will terminate for some large b and give a "yes" answer. A person might then be called a perfect reasoner if his knowledge algorithm is sound and complete.

Of course all this makes the problem of knowing about other people's knowledge quite subtle. If I know that you have external knowledge of A, I cannot conclude that you bave knowledge of A. For you might not have made the inference. If I know that you do not have external knowledge of A, then of course I can conclude that you also do not have actual knowledge of A. But you may fail to have knowledge of A also for other reasons. I must have some information about the knowledge algorithm that you are using, and the amount of time you have invested in checking for A. This is a highly unsatisfactory situation. But it does correspond with how things are.

In the following section we point out an interesting connection between knowledge and the problem of identity and use it to solve a knowledge paradox that goes back to the 14th century french philosopher Jean Buridan. We begin, however with a quote from Plato.

Knowledge and Identity: In *Meno*, one of Plato's dialogues, takes place a famous conversation between Socrates and a young slave (hereafter called "the boy") belonging to Menon. In this conversation, Socrates undertakes to elicit geometrical facts from the boy, purely by means of questions. Socrates first gets the boy to agree that a square A whose side is two units, has an area of four units. Socrates then asks the boy to construct a square whose size is double that of A, and after a couple of false starts it becomes evident to the boy that a square B whose side is the diagonal of the square A, would have area exactly 8 units, i.e. twice that of A. At this point Socrates turns back to Menon, and I quote some of the ensuing conversation:

```
S: And no one having taught him, only asked questions, yet
   he will know, having got the knowledge out of himself?
M: Yes.
S: But to get the knowledge out of yourself is to remember,
   isn't it?
M: Certainly it is.
S: Well then: This knowledge which he now has - he either
   got it sometime, or he had it always?
M: Yes.
S: Then if he had it always, he was also always one who knew;
   but if he got it sometime, he could not have got it in his
   present life.
```

And later still,

```
S: Then if the truth of things is always in our soul, the soul
   must be immortal.
```

Plato is not here interested in assertions depending on contingent facts, but in mathematical and philosophical ones, so that the question of knowledge obtained from (contingent) evidence does not arise. However, putting this issue aside, there is a dualistic notion here of a soul residing in the body and keeping its identity even through death. It is clear also that the problem of logical omniscience that we discussed in the previous section is connected with Plato's view of the self.

A very different point of view towards the self is taken by the buddhist work *Milindapanho* which relates a (possibly apocryphal) dialogue between the Greek king Menander (125-95 BC) and the buddhist monk Nagasena, with the latter taking the position that there is no continuous self that endures through life, but merely a series of complex phenomena, what one might call self-stages, with a cause-effect relation to each other. We give two quotes from the dialogue between these two.

How is your Reverence known? What is your name, Reverend sir?

As 'Nagasena' great king, am I known; 'Nagasena', great king, is what my fellow-religious are accustomed to call me. However, although mothers and fathers give such names as 'Nagasena' or 'Surasena' or 'Virasena' or 'Sihasena', yet great king, this 'Nagasena' is only a conventional epithet, designation, appellation, style - a mere name. For no individual is thereby assumed to exist.

And later,

Precisely so, great king, there is an uninterrupted succession of mental and physical states. One state ceases to be, and another comes to exist. The succession is such that there is, as it were, none that precedes, none that follows. Thus it is neither the same person nor yet a different person which goes to the final summation of consciousness.

A somewhat similar, sceptical point of view towards the self is taken by the Scottish philosopher David Hume:

There are some philosophers, who imagine we are every moment intimately conscious of what we call our SELF; ... For my part, when I enter most intimately into what I call myself, I always stumble on some particular perception or other, of heat or cold, light or shade, love or hatred, pain or pleasure. I never can catch myself at any time without a perception, and never can observe any thing but the perception.

But why should *we* be interested in the philosophical notion of self if our primary interest is in a viable theory and logic of knowledge? The answer is that the currently used logics of knowledge in Computer Science go back to Hintikka [H], whose own notion is closely related to the argument given in Meno. (See [H], page 38, footnote 11). Thus we need to decide if we really want to accept the notion of self on which *Meno* is so dependent, and attribute it not only to human beings, but even to Turing machines and other devices.

The other, related issue is this: even for persons, some properties, like race, sex, "is son of y", etc. hold through life, if ever. If x is the son of y at some stage of his life, then he is that at all stages of his life. On the other hand, some other properties like "is bald", "is a teenager", "is angry", may hold at some moments and not at others. Yet others, like "panics easily" are really dispositional properties, and need a decription of the panic-inducing stimuli to be explained fully. Thus we need to ask, if properties like "knows A" are properties of the first, second or third kind. If we accept Plato's stance, then "knows A" for mathematical A, becomes identical with "A is true", and this does not really accord with our experience, nor do we wish to assert that all knowledge ie merely remembering. Rather, we want a theory of what mathematical learning can consist in.

We will now illustrate the issues involved by solving a paradox about belief that is due originally to the French logician Buridan and has recently been discussed by Tyler Burge [B].

(*) Socrates does not believe the starred sentance in this paper.

Socrates' first reaction on seeing this sentence is to say to himself "I don't believe that". Then he realises that that in fact is what the sentence says. He says, "Oh, I see it is true". However, now, on reading it again, he sees that it is false, and then again that it is true, etc. Clearly, there can be no stable way to answer the question, "Does Socrates believe the sentence?".

However, the situation changes if we stop thinking of Socrates as an unchanging entity, and the sentence as expressing a fixed proposition about that entity. Rather we see that what we have is a series of *different* individuals, $Socrates_i$, where for odd i, the sentence expresses a true proposition about $Socrates_i$ and is not believed by $Socrates_i$, but is believed by $Soctrates_{i+1}$, whereas for i even, it expresses a false proposition about $Socrates_i$, and is believed by $Socrates_i$ but not by $Socrates_{i+1}$. Each step of thinking about the sentence turns $Socrates_i$ into $Socrates_{i+1}$ who has a different opinion about it. The paradox vanishes.

It is clear from our discussion that dealing with actual knowledge as opposed to external knowledge is a function both of the evidence and one's state of mind, or in the case of a computer, its internal state. Thus a theory of knowledge that is realistic will need lot more information than just the evidence.

References

[B] Tyler Burge, "Buridan and Epistemic Paradox", *Philosophical Studies* 34 (1978) pp. 21-35.

[B2] Jean Buridan, *Sophisms on Meaning and Truth,* Meredith publishing company, New York, 1966.

[CM1] H. Clark and C. Marshall, "Definite Reference and Mutual Knowledge" in *Elements of Discourse Understanding* Ed. Joshi, Webber and Sag, Cambridge U. Press, 1981.

[CM2] K. M. Chandy and J. Misra, "How Processes Learn", *Proceedings of the 4th PODC* (1985), 204-214. Also *Distributed Computing* 1 (1986) pp. 40-52.

[H] J. Hintikka, *Knowledge and Belief,* Cornell U. Press, 1962.

[H2] *Reasoning about Knowledge*, Ed. J. Halpern, Morgan Kaufman, 1986.

[H3] J. Halpern, "Reasoning about Knowledge: an Overview", in [H2] above, 1-17.

[HF] J. Halpern and R. Fagin, "A Formal Model of Knowledge, Communication and Action" in *Fourth Annual ACM Symposium on Principles of Distributed Computing*, pp. 224-236.

[HM] J. Halpern and Y. Moses, "Knowledge and Common Knowledge in a distributed Environment", *ACM-PODC 1984*, pp. 50-61.

[Hu] David Hume *A Treatise of Human Nature*, first published 1739-40, Penguin edition 1969, Book I, part IV, section VI.

[HV] J. Halpern and M. Vardi "The Complexity of Reasoning about Knowledge and Time" *Proceedings of the 18th ACM-STOC* (1986) pp. 304-315.

[Le] David Lewis, *Convention*, Harvard U. Press, 1969.

[Me] *The great Dialogues of Plato*, translated by W. H. D. Rouse, Mentor Books, 1956.

[Mi] "Questions of Milinda" (*Milindapanho*) in *The World of the Buddha* Ed. Lucien Stryk, Doubleday 1968.

[MT] Y. Moses and M. Tuttle, "Programming simultaneous actions using common knowledge" *27th IEEE-FOCS* (1986) pp. 208-221.

[Pa1] R. Parikh, "Logics of Knowledge, Games and Dynamic Logic", in *FST/TCS 4*, Springer LNCS no. 181, pp. 202-222.

[Pa2] R. Parikh, "Levels of Knowledge in Distributed Computing" in IEEE *Symposium on Logic in Computer Science*, Boston 1986, pp. 314-321. (Note that one of the theorems in this paper is joint with P. Krasucki)

[Pa3] R. Parikh, "Knowledge and the Problem of Logical Omniscience", to appear in *ACM-SIGART International Symposium on the Mathodology of Intelligent Systems*, Charlotte, NC, 1987.

[PR] R. Parikh and R. Ramanujam, "Distributed Processing and the Logic of Knowledge", in *Logics of Programs '85* Springer LNCS no.193, pp. 256-268.

INDEX OF AUTHORS

Vol. 245: H.F. de Groote, Lectures on the Complexity of Bilinear Problems. V, 135 pages. 1987.

Vol. 246: Graph-Theoretic Concepts in Computer Science. Proceedings, 1986. Edited by G. Tinhofer and G. Schmidt. VII, 307 pages. 1987.

Vol. 247: STACS 87. Proceedings, 1987. Edited by F.J. Brandenburg, G. Vidal-Naquet and M. Wirsing. X, 484 pages. 1987.

Vol. 248: Networking in Open Systems. Proceedings, 1986. Edited by G. Müller and R.P. Blanc. VI, 441 pages. 1987.

Vol. 249: TAPSOFT '87. Volume 1. Proceedings, 1987. Edited by H. Ehrig, R. Kowalski, G. Levi and U. Montanari. XIV, 289 pages. 1987.

Vol. 250: TAPSOFT '87. Volume 2. Proceedings, 1987. Edited by H. Ehrig, R. Kowalski, G. Levi and U. Montanari. XIV, 336 pages. 1987.

Vol. 251: V. Akman, Unobstructed Shortest Paths in Polyhedral Environments. VII, 103 pages. 1987.

Vol. 252: VDM '87. VDM – A Formal Method at Work. Proceedings, 1987. Edited by D. Bjørner, C.B. Jones, M. Mac an Airchinnigh and E.J. Neuhold. IX, 422 pages. 1987.

Vol. 253: J.D. Becker, I. Eisele (Eds.), WOPPLOT 86. Parallel Processing: Logic, Organization, and Technology. Proceedings, 1986. V, 226 pages. 1987.

Vol. 254: Petri Nets: Central Models and Their Properties. Advances in Petri Nets 1986, Part I. Proceedings, 1986. Edited by W. Brauer, W. Reisig and G. Rozenberg. X, 480 pages. 1987.

Vol. 255: Petri Nets: Applications and Relationships to Other Models of Concurrency. Advances in Petri Nets 1986, Part II. Proceedings, 1986. Edited by W. Brauer, W. Reisig and G. Rozenberg. X, 516 pages. 1987.

Vol. 256: Rewriting Techniques and Applications. Proceedings, 1987. Edited by P. Lescanne. VI, 285 pages. 1987.

Vol. 257: Database Machine Performance: Modeling Methodologies and Evaluation Strategies. Edited by F. Cesarini and S. Salza. X, 250 pages. 1987.

Vol. 258: PARLE, Parallel Architectures and Languages Europe. Volume I. Proceedings, 1987. Edited by J.W. de Bakker, A.J. Nijman and P.C. Treleaven. XII, 480 pages. 1987.

Vol. 259: PARLE, Parallel Architectures and Languages Europe. Volume II. Proceedings, 1987. Edited by J.W. de Bakker, A.J. Nijman and P.C. Treleaven. XII, 464 pages. 1987.

Vol. 260: D.C. Luckham, F.W. von Henke, B. Krieg-Brückner, O. Owe, ANNA, A Language for Annotating Ada Programs. V, 143 pages. 1987.

Vol. 261: J. Ch. Freytag, Translating Relational Queries into Iterative Programs. XI, 131 pages. 1987.

Vol. 262: A. Burns, A.M. Lister, A.J. Wellings, A Review of Ada Tasking. VIII, 141 pages. 1987.

Vol. 263: A.M. Odlyzko (Ed.), Advances in Cryptology – CRYPTO '86. Proceedings. XI, 489 pages. 1987.

Vol. 264: E. Wada (Ed.), Logic Programming '86. Proceedings, 1986. VI, 179 pages. 1987.

Vol. 265: K.P. Jantke (Ed.), Analogical and Inductive Inference. Proceedings, 1986. VI, 227 pages. 1987.

Vol. 266: G. Rozenberg (Ed.), Advances in Petri Nets 1987. VI, 451 pages. 1987.

Vol. 267: Th. Ottmann (Ed.), Automata, Languages and Programming. Proceedings, 1987. X, 565 pages. 1987.

Vol. 268: P.M. Pardalos, J.B. Rosen, Constrained Global Optimization: Algorithms and Applications. VII, 143 pages. 1987.

Vol. 269: A. Albrecht, H. Jung, K. Mehlhorn (Eds.), Parallel Algorithms and Architectures. Proceedings, 1987. Approx. 205 pages. 1987.

Vol. 270: E. Börger (Ed.), Computation Theory and Logic. IX, 442 pages. 1987.

Vol. 271: D. Snyers, A. Thayse, From Logic Design to Logic Programming. IV, 125 pages. 1987.

Vol. 272: P. Treleaven, M. Vanneschi (Eds.), Future Parallel Computers. Proceedings, 1986. V, 492 pages. 1987.

Vol. 273: J.S. Royer, A Connotational Theory of Program Structure. V, 186 pages. 1987.

Vol. 274: G. Kahn (Ed.), Functional Programming Languages and Computer Architecture. Proceedings. VI, 470 pages. 1987.

Vol. 275: A.N. Habermann, U. Montanari (Eds.), System Development and Ada. Proceedings, 1986. V, 305 pages. 1987.

Vol. 276: J. Bézivin, J.-M. Hullot, P. Cointe, H. Lieberman (Eds.), ECOOP '87. European Conference on Object-Oriented Programming. Proceedings. VI, 273 pages. 1987.

Vol. 277: B. Benninghofen, S. Kemmerich, M.M. Richter, Systems of Reductions. X, 265 pages. 1987.

Vol. 279: J.H. Fasel, R.M. Keller (Eds.), Graph Reduction. Proceedings, 1986. XVI, 450 pages. 1987.

Vol. 280: M. Venturini Zilli (Ed.), Mathematical Models for the Semantics of Parallelism. Proceedings, 1986. V, 231 pages. 1987.

Vol. 281: A. Kelemenová, J. Kelemen (Eds.), Trends, Techniques, and Problems in Theoretical Computer Science. Proceedings, 1986. VI, 213 pages. 1987.

Vol. 282: P. Gorny, M.J. Tauber (Eds.), Visualization in Programming. Proceedings, 1986. VII, 210 pages. 1987.

Vol. 283: D.H. Pitt, A. Poigné, D.E. Rydeheard (Eds.), Category Theory and Computer Science. Proceedings, 1987. V, 300 pages. 1987.

Vol. 284: A. Kündig, R.E. Bührer, J. Dähler (Eds.), Embedded Systems. Proceedings, 1986. V, 207 pages. 1987.

Vol. 285: C. Delgado Kloos, Semantics of Digital Circuits. IX, 124 pages. 1987.

Vol. 286: B. Bouchon, R.R. Yager (Eds.), Uncertainty in Knowledge-Based Systems. Proceedings, 1986. VII, 405 pages. 1987.

Vol. 287: K.V. Nori (Ed.), Foundations of Software Technology and Theoretical Computer Science. Proceedings, 1987. IX, 540 pages. 1987.